INTERNATIONAL
PRIVATE EQUITY

INTERNATIONAL PRIVATE EQUITY

Eli Talmor and Florin Vasvari

A John Wiley and Sons, Ltd, Publication

ISBN 978-0-470-97170-3 (hardback)
ISBN 978-1-119-97388-1 (ebook)
ISBN 978-1-119-97389-8 (ebook)
ISBN 978-1-119-97798-8 (ebook)

A catalogue record for this book is available from the British Library

Project management by OPS Ltd, Gt Yarmouth, Norfolk
Typeset in 10/12pt New Caledonia
Printed in Great Britain by TJ International Ltd., Padstow, Cornwall

Contents

Preface

We are ever amazed at the wide range of issues that are covered in private equity. Nearly all business aspects are at the heart of the matter—valuation, accounting and control, strategy, operations, financial structuring, asset allocation, management, entrepreneurship, regulation, and government policy. It is squarely at the crossroads of academia and practice where there is no mercy for just being conceptual or lacking timeliness. This creates challenges—yet great fun—in understanding the subject; in particular, in trying to break down what makes it so effective, fascinating, and perhaps addictive.

The motivation for our book is to provide a comprehensive overview of the main topics in private equity that are relevant to students in graduate programs, investors, other professionals seeking to understand the many facets of private equity, and private equity practitioners wanting a more complete analysis of this asset class.

The book has grown out of our teaching the "Private equity and venture capital" elective course at London Business School. Over the years the focus of the course has broadened internationally and by subject matter, which is reflected both in the text chapters and the case studies. Working closely with the professional private equity community in London proved particularly valuable in generating first-rate material and direct contributions through chapter co-authorships. Much of that was achieved through the Coller Institute of Private Equity and its Advisory Board. Added value came from our students who provided insights both in the classroom and outside it.

Dwight Poler, Head of Bain Capital in Europe, has been a co-instructor of our private equity course and a great supporter. Dwight's contribution to the book and to private equity education at London Business School has been immeasurable.

Our thanks go to the private equity partners and corporate executives who agreed to graciously share their time and provide case material such as transaction data and detailed internal memoranda which subjected their firms to our close examination process. We are particularly grateful to Yoram Amiga (SunPower), Ted Berk (Bain Capital), Philippe Costeletos (TPG), Chris Freund (Mekong Capital), Anne Glover (Amadeus), Mounir Guen (MVision), Francesco Santinon (Aberdeen), and the partners at Denham Capital, Investindustrial, Realza Capital, and Swicorp. Our academic colleague Josh Lerner (Harvard Business School) also contributed in case sourcing. In writing the case studies we heavily relied on students who shouldered the burden of gathering data on the arduous projects: Jo Coles, Benjamin Dimson, Michael Geary, Edward Gera, Richard Harvey, Enrique Ho-Fernández, Oriol Juncosa, Ashish Kumar, Norman Lee, Geoff Leffek, Charmian Long, Alberto Pons, Vishal Radhakrishnan, Vijay Sachidanand, Tamara Sakovska, Thibaud Simphal, Andrew Strachan, Richard Turner, Matthias Vandepitte, Lode Van Laere, Adolfo Vinatea, and Ananth Vyas Bhimavarapu.

The text chapters are divided into three main parts which cover fund-level topics, deal-level topics, and early-stage investing. They discuss a wide variety of subjects and that involved teaming up with leading practitioners on each topic: Jim Strang (Jardine Capital), Anthony Cecil (KPMG), Kay Nemoto and John Maloney (Alix Partners), Brenlen Jinkens (Cogent Partners), and Thomas Meyer (EVCA). For some chapters we collaborated with other academics: Oliver Gottschalg (HEC Paris), Christoph Kaserer

(Technical University Munich), and Henry Lahr (University of Cambridge). On other topics we benefited from working with current and past students: Mike Glossop, Sonia Katyal, Anya Kleymenova, Bjoern Koertner, William Lamain, Fardeen Nariman, and Rebecca Zimmerman. Natalie Brawn (Bowmark Capital) provided valuable comments on earlier drafts of chapters.

The Coller Institute of Private Equity provided support in administration and references to industry knowledge. Our colleagues there were a constant source of good advice: Francesca Cornelli who actually proposed the idea of writing the book, Hans Holmen, and Ann Iveson.

The project was most effectively directed by the Wiley team. Jenny McCall cheerfully led the process from its inception, Gemma Valler and Amy Webster were a pleasure to work with and Neil Shuttlewood handled the editorial process professionally and very efficiently. We owe them all a great deal of thanks.

Last but not least, our families coped with us with patience and understanding through the laboring process. The book is dedicated to them.

Abbreviations

ABS	Asset-Backed Security	CPA	Certified Public Accountant
ACA	Angel Capital Association	CVC	Corporate Venture Capital
ADB	Asian Development Bank	DCF	Discounted Cash Flow
ADIA	Abu Dhabi Investment Authority	DD	Due Diligence
AICPA	American Institute of Certified Public Accountants	DFI	Development Finance Institution
		DSCR	Debt Service Coverage Ratio
AIFM	Alternative Investment Fund Manager	DVPI	Distributed Value to Paid-In ratio
AIM	Alternative Investment Market	EBAN	European Business Angel Network
ARPU	Average Revenue Per User	EBIT	Earnings Before Interest and Taxes
ASB	Accounting Standards Board	EBITA	Earnings Before Interest, Taxes, and Amortization
ASCRI	Asociación Española de Entidades de Capital Riesgo (Spanish Venture Capital Association)	EBITDA	Earnings Before Interest, Taxes, Depreciation, and Amortization
ASEAN	Association of Southeast Asian Nations	ECB	European Central Bank
ATN	Access Technology Now	ECF	Enterprise Capital Fund
BBAA	British Business Angels Association	EGFP	Early Growth Funding Program
BCC	Blank Check Company	EIB	European Investment Bank
BDC	Business Development Company	EIS	Enterprise Investment Scheme
BEE	Black Economic Empowerment	EMPEA	Emerging Markets Private Equity Association
BIMBO	Buy-In Management Buy-Out	EPC	Engineering Procurement and Construction
BIS	Business Innovation and Skills	ERISA	Employee Retirement Income Security Act
BRIC	Brazil, Russia, India, and China	ESOP	Employee Stock Ownership Plan
BVCA	British Private Equity and Venture Capital Association	ETF	Exchange-Traded Funds
		EURIBOR	Euro Interbank Offered Rate
CAGR	Compound Annual Growth Rate	EV	Enterprise Value
CalPERS	California Public Employees' Retirement System	EVCA	European Private Equity and Venture Capital Association
CAPM	Capital Asset Pricing Model	FCF	Free Cash Flow
CalSTRS	California State Teachers' Retirement System	FFT	Fund for Technological Fund
		FMCG	Fast-Moving Consumer Goods
CDIF	China Direct Investment Fund	FPCR	Fonds de Promotion pour le Capital Risque
CDO	Collateralized Debt Obligation	FPP	Full Potential Program
CEE	Central and Eastern Europe	FRSSE	Financial Reporting Standards for Smaller Entities
CfE UK	Capital for Enterprise UK		
CFO	Collateralized Fund Obligation	FSA	Financial Services Authority
CIC	China Investment Corporation	G&A	General and Administrative
CIP	Carried Interest Partner	G7	Group of Seven
CIS	Commonwealth of Independent States	GAAP	Generally Accepted Accounting Principles
CLO	Collateralized Loan Obligation	GCC	Gulf Cooperation Council
CNMV	Comisión Nacional del Mercado de Valores	GDP	Gross Domestic Product
COC	Cash-On-Cash return	GLPEI	Global Listed Private Equity Index
COGS	Cost of Goods Sold		

GP	General Partner	OFEX	Off Exchange
GPS	General Partner's Share	OTECF	Oxford Technology Enterprise Capital Fund
HCMC	Ho Chi Minh City		
HNWI	High-Net-Worth Individual	P/E	Price to Earnings
HoSE	Ho Chi Minh City Stock Exchange	PBT	Profit Before Tax
HPSU	High-Potential StartUp	PDI	Personal Disposable Income
HR	Human Resources	PE	Private Equity
IASB	International Accounting Standards Board	PIK	Payment In Kind
ICB	Industry Classification Benchmark	PIPE	Private Investments in Public Equity
ICFC	Industrial and Commercial Finance Corporation	PME	Public Market Equivalent
		PPE	Property Plant and Equipment
ICP	International Consumer Products	PPM	Private Placement Memorandum
IF	Internally Flawless	PPS	Priority Profit Share
IFRS	International Financial Accounting Standards	PSERS	Public School Employees' Retirement System
ILPA	Institutional Limited Partners Association	RIC	Regulated Investment Company
ILPEI	International Listed Private Equity Index	RMB	Renminbi
IP	Intellectual Property	RVCF	Regional Venture Capital Fund
IPEV	International Private Equity and Venture	RVPI	Residual Value to Paid-In ratio
IPO	Initial Public Offering	SA	Sociedad Anónima
IRR	Internal Rate of Return	SAMA	Saudi Arabian Monetary Agency
ISCR	Interest Service Coverage Ratio	SBIC	Small Business Investment Company
JSE	Johannesburg Securities Exchange	SBLG	Small Business Loan Guarantee
KPI	Key Performance Indicator	SBS	Small Business Service
LBO	Leveraged Buyout	SEC	Securities and Exchange Commission
LCC	Low-Cost Country	SG&A	Selling, General and Administrative
LIBOR	London Interbank Offered Rate	SGECR	Sociedad Gestora de Entidades de Capital Riesgo
LP	Limited Partner		
LPA	Limited Partnership Agreement	SME	Small and Medium-sized Enterprise
LPE	Listed Private Equity	SOE	State-Owned Enterprise
LPEI	Listed Private Equity Index	SPA	Stock Purchase Agreement
LSIF	Labor-Sponsored Investment Fund	SPAC	Special Purpose Acquisition Company
LSVCC	Labor-Sponsored Venture Capital Corporation	SPV	Special Purpose Vehicle
		STAC	Structured Trust Acquisition Company
M&A	Mergers and Acquisitions	SUIR	Société Unipersonnelle d'Investissements à Risque
MBI	Management Buy-In		
MBO	Management Buy-Out	SWF	Sovereign Wealth Fund
MENA	Middle East and North Africa	TCGA	Taxation of Chargeable Gains Act 1992
MFO	Manufacturing Footprint Optimization	TMT	Telecommunications, Media, and Technology
MIRR	Modified Internal Rate of Return		
MMP	Minimum Monthly Payment	TVPI	Total Value to Paid-In ratio
MPDF	Mekong Private Sector Development Facility	UNAIDS	Joint United Nations Program on HIV/AIDS
MSCI	Morgan Stanley Capital International	VAF	Vietnam Azalea Fund
NAV	Net Asset Value	VAR	Value Added Reseller
NOL	Net Operating Loss	VaR	Value-at-Risk
NPV	Net Present Value	VC	Venture Capital
NVCA	National Venture Capital Association	VCT	Venture Capital Trust
NWC	Net Working Capital	WHO	World Health Organization
OECD	Organization for Economic Co-operation and Development	WTO	World Trade Organization

About the authors

Eli Talmor is a professor at London Business School and founding Chairman of its Coller Institute of Private Equity. He was previously a professor of finance at the University of California (UCLA and Irvine), Tel Aviv University, and the Wharton School (University of Pennsylvania). Professor Talmor is a seasoned private equity practitioner and has been a director of European and American corporations. He served on the advisory board of the African Venture Capital Association and the Board of Governors of London Business School. He has frequently been invited to deliver keynote speeches to business executives worldwide and interviews to the international media on timely private equity matters. In recent years he has been asked by the U.K. Parliament to provide leading testimony at its high-profile hearings on private equity and to advise the U.K. Prime Minister's office. Professor Talmor holds a Ph.D. from the University of North Carolina at Chapel Hill and a B.Sc. from the Technion Israel Institute of Technology.

Florin Vasvari is an Assistant Professor of Accounting at London Business School and a fellow of the Coller Institute for Private Equity. He co-teaches the Private Equity and Venture Capital elective at London Business School with Professor Talmor, and consults with several organizations. Professor Vasvari is actively pursuing research on private equity topics and debt markets. He has published several articles in top-tier academic journals such as the *Journal of Accounting Research* and *Review of Accounting Studies* and has been invited to present his research at top business schools such as Chicago GSB, Columbia Business School, Wharton School, MIT Sloan School of Management, Harvard Business School, INSEAD, and others. He is on the editorial board of *Contemporary Accounting Research* and the advisory board of the Center for Accounting Research and Education. Professor Vasvari holds a Ph.D. from the University of Toronto, Rotman School of Management and an M.A. from the University of Toronto, Department of Economics.

To Zippy, Dahlia, Yael, and Lauren
To Albert and Mirela

PART 1

Overview and fund-level analysis

1

Introduction and overview

1.1 INTRODUCTION

In recent years the profile of the private equity industry has increased dramatically. While the industry has been actively investing in companies across a wide range of industries for several decades, the combination of astute buying by private equity funds focused on buyouts in the early part of the last decade and the extremely liquid credit markets of 2004–2007 fueled some impressive exits. Similarly, private equity funds focused on venture investments had very successful exits in the late 1990s. These exits helped to substantially increase the profile of the industry.

Over the last 20 years or so private equity has grown to become a sizable asset class at its peak, responsible for up to a quarter of global M&A activity and as much as half of the leveraged loan issues in the capital markets. At the top of the last cycle, private equity funds found themselves able to acquire very public assets and seemed to be able to deliver extraordinary returns, both for their investors and for their managers. This "institutionalization" of private equity saw its profile rise substantially with a number of commentators focusing on this "new" industry.

Towards the end of this decade the industry, like every other, had to weather the financial crisis. During the crisis a number of new private equity investments fell dramatically, despite the historically high level of capital commitments made to private equity funds. The prevailing economic uncertainty combined with a very significant reduction in the amount of leverage available to dealmakers combined to severely restrict new-deal activity. The global financial crisis and associated recession also led to a sharp slowdown in fundraising.

Despite the considerable challenges, the economic environment produced a surprisingly small number of private equity–backed business failures. Many portfolio companies benefited from the active, hands-on involvement of their private equity owners. As a result, private equity portfolio companies managed to weather the economic downturn through a combination of revenue protection, production efficiencies, cost cutting, and careful working capital management. Also, lower commodity prices, lenders willing to restructure the debt, and new opportunities to refinance the debt due to a strong high-yield bond market have helped to mitigate financial pressures.

Indeed today it may be that the private equity industry has become a victim of its own success. The exceptional performance of the early part of the last decade certainly

This chapter has been co-authored with Jim Strang (Jardine Capital).

attracted ever more capital into the industry and some of it has been deployed to acquire large and visible companies. Thus, for the first time, private equity has been brought into the public arena and, now that it is there, it is likely to remain. In the future it seems clear that the industry will have to communicate more effectively with the various stakeholders and will be subject to increasing levels of external scrutiny and regulation. The calls to regulate the industry have increased, mainly due to the perception that the industry has contributed to the severity of the credit crisis. Such initiatives as the Alternative Investment Fund Manager (AIFM) regulations may prove to be the beginning of an increasingly onerous regulatory process.

However, despite the challenges that the industry faces (not least of which, the difficult economic environment that seems likely to persist in the medium term in most of the Western world), many within the industry retain their high hopes for the future.

Background

Private equity is the name given to that part of the asset management industry where investments are made into securities which are usually not quoted in the public markets. Private equity investments are normally made through special purpose fund structures of finite life which are established to follow specific investment strategies. These funds provide capital to a wide array of companies, ranging from business startups to very large and mature companies. One of the reasons the private equity industry exists is that, in many cases, companies have needs for capital which, for various reasons, cannot be met from the public markets. Investors that provide capital to private equity funds invest in an asset class that entails relatively high risk and high illiquidity in what remains a largely unregulated market.

At its highest level, the private equity industry can be subdivided into *buyout* and *venture capital* funds. Both buyout funds and venture capital funds share similar organizational structures in terms of their management fee structure and longevity. However, they are quite different when it comes to their investment strategy. Buyout funds usually focus on established and mature companies rather than young businesses and use debt as well as equity financing. They also tend to be larger in size than the venture funds. Venture funds focus on startups, young and high-growth companies, and do not use debt capital when providing financing. In both cases the general partners (or managers of the funds) normally play an active role in the lives of the portfolio companies that they invest in, often taking seats on the management board of portfolio companies and monitoring the delivery of an agreed strategic plan. Typically, a successful investment would see the execution of this strategic plan and the eventual exit of the private equity owner after between 3 and 7 years.

Private equity funds differ significantly from other investment funds found in the public markets in that the typical concentration of ownership allows the investor a far higher degree of control. In essence, private equity fund managers seek to influence the companies they invest in and, in the case of buyouts, choose an optimum capital structure. Prior to investing they conduct extensive due diligence and have significant access to the views of management of these companies. It could easily be argued that private equity funds operate with much better information and stronger controls over portfolio companies than, for example, mutual funds holding quoted equities.

Worldwide, private equity funds manage approximately USD2.5tn of assets and committed capital of which the vast majority is in buyout funds (CityUK, 2010). Some of the largest investors in the asset class are pension funds (who in turn supply the capital to the various special purpose vehicles that actually make the underlying investments).

Leveraged buyout transactions have grown significantly over the last two decades. In 1991, new buyout transactions were USD10bn and by the beginning of 2006 they had reached USD500bn. This annualized total was equivalent to 5% of the capitalization of the U.S. stock market (Acharya et al., 2007). This growth was fueled by a virtuous circle of supportive economic environment, favorable credit terms, and continuing demand from investors for steadily larger private equity funds.

Origins of private equity

The history of private equity as an asset class goes back to before the Second World War with the beginning of angel investing in the 1930s and 1940s. Wealthy families, such as the Vanderbilts, Rockefellers, and Bessemers provided capital to private companies as angel investors. One of the first venture capital firms, J.H. Whitney & Company, was founded in 1946.

The early seeds of the venture capital industry can be traced to 1946 with the founding of two venture capital firms: American Research & Development Corporation (ARDC) and J.H. Whitney & Company (Wilson, 1985). General Georges F. Doriot, an influential teacher and innovator at Harvard University is known for his role in the formation of ARDC which raised outside capital solely for investment in companies. In its 25-year history, ARDC helped fund more than a hundred companies and earned annualized returns for its investors of 15.8% (Fenn et al., 1995; Kocis et al., 2009). ARDC is credited with the first major venture capital success story when its 1957 investment of USD70,000 in Digital Equipment Corporation increased in value to over USD355mn after the company's initial public offering in 1968.

In 1958 early venture capital got a boost from the U.S. government when small business investment companies (SBICs) were licensed. This license gave these finance companies the ability to leverage federal funds to lend to growing companies. SBICs became very popular in 1960s. During this period, the development of limited liability partnerships for venture capital investments took place. In this arrangement corporations put up the capital, with a few percentage points from this capital paid every year for the management fees for the fund. The remaining capital was then invested by the general partner in private companies.

However, the big boost for venture capital in the U.S. came in the 1970s. The first boost was the reduction of capital gains tax. Despite inroads made by SBICs and the reduction in capital gains tax, total venture capital fundraising in the U.S. was still less than USD1bn a year throughout the 1970s. The second boost was from the U.S. Congress in 1974, when it enacted the Employee Retirement Income Security Act (ERISA), a set of pension reforms designed to help U.S. pension managers into more balanced custodianship. This act was clarified in 1979 to explicitly permit pension funds to invest in assets like private equity funds. Consequently, in the late 1970s and early 1980s a few pension funds added a small amount of venture capital to their portfolio and a few university endowments joined in (Metrick, 2007).

The first of today's big private equity firms, Warburg Pincus, was formed only in the late 1960s, and had to raise money from investors one deal at a time. Another large private equity firm today, Thomas Lee Partners, was founded in 1974 and was among the earliest independent firms that focused on the acquisition of companies with leverage financing. KKR was another early firm and managed to successfully raise the first institutional fund of investor commitments in 1978. By the late 1980s private equity had grown big enough to be noticed by the general public, but it made hostile headlines with a wave of debt-financed "leveraged buyouts" (LBOs) of big, well-known firms. In the late 1980s, funds often borrowed massively to pay for buyouts, many of which were seen as hostile by the management of the intended targets. When KKR bought America's Safeway supermarket chain in 1986, it borrowed 97% of the USD4.8bn the deal cost (Bishop, 2004).

1.2   CYCLICALITY OF THE PRIVATE EQUITY INDUSTRY

Private equity activity appears to experience recurring boom and bust cycles that are related to past returns and to the level of interest rates relative to earnings. Since it emerged as a major asset class in the 1980s, private equity has experienced three major expansions followed by sharp downturns.

In the 1980s, the private equity industry capitalized on the sale of many poorly run public companies and corporate divestitures available at low cost and largely financed with junk bonds. That expansion ended abruptly when the main provider of financing, the high-yield bond market, collapsed.[1] The collapse was followed by a recession (1990–1992) due to a crisis triggered by savings-and-loan institutions in the U.S. The bond market recovered very slowly after this episode, so activity in the private equity industry was very slow for almost 5 years.

In the 1990s, debt financing played a less prominent role. First, the Telecommunications Act of 1996, a major overhaul of United States telecommunications law, fostered competition and fueled private equity investments in the sector. Second, the private equity industry was driven by the accelerated economic expansion. This period saw the emergence of more institutionalized private equity firms and a maturing of the investor base. In particular, venture capital firms benefited from a huge surge of interest in the new internet and computer technologies that were being developed in the late 1990s. These firms started raising bigger pools of capital to finance larger deals at higher valuations. This boom ended, however, when the dotcom technology bubble burst in March 2000. Over the next 2 years, many venture firms were forced to write off significantly their fund investments. Meanwhile, the leveraged buyout market also declined dramatically. A lot of buyout funds invested heavily in the telecommunications sector which suffered after the dotcom bust.

The private equity industry recovered relatively quickly. By 2003 deal activity had exceeded the peak before the recession that started in 2001. Over the past decade, private equity rode a credit bubble inflated by low interest rates to record deal values. In 2005, 2006, and the first half of 2007 new buyout records were set. The buyout boom was not limited to the U.S. but also spread in Europe and the Asia–Pacific region. The boom has been driven primarily by the availability of syndicated bank debt. Leveraged lending grew larger and more complex than ever before, and investor demand for structured finance vehicles such as collateralized loan obligations (CLOs) powered the market for leveraged loans to new heights. In CLOs the bundled pools of loans were sold to investors in various risk tranches. Searching for different returns from different markets, hedge funds found fertile ground in the syndicated loan market, especially second-lien and mezzanine debt and payment-in-kind securities. This last

---

1. One investment bank, Drexel Burnham Lambert, was largely responsible for the boom in highly leveraged private equity transactions during the 1980s due to its dominance in the issuance of high-yield debt. The bank was sued by the Securities and Exchange Commission for insider trading and fraud in 1988. The bank filed for bankruptcy protection in early 1990 after dismantling its high-yield debt department.

boom came to an abrupt end with the mortgage-led debt crisis that froze credit markets in 2008 and triggered a global recession.

The burst of the credit bubble in 2008–2009

The economic slowdown triggered by the credit crisis had a significant impact on completed private equity deals. Buyouts' share of total investments fell for the second year running in 2009, a direct result of the abrupt economic slowdown, huge uncertainty, and virtual evaporation of the debt markets. Despite an increase in the share of total investments, venture capital deals were also down. The stress and dislocation in the system caused by this abrupt shock to the system has more recently led to a significant pickup in activity in the "secondary" market for private equity interests as investors strive to reconfigure their balance sheets for the new reality.

The global credit crisis that started in 2008 had a significant effect on the number, size, and type of PE deals concluded ever since. The crisis manifested itself in many ways:

- *Debt became scarce and expensive*. The most immediate impact of the crisis was a significant tightening of private equity funds' access to leverage. By the middle of 2009 the loans extended to buyout transactions virtually disappeared, falling to a small fraction compared with the previous years. Equally dramatic was the impact on the cost of debt financing. The spread on syndicated term loans and revolving credit had more than doubled from 2005 levels. This decline in leveraged financing dampened the buyout activity to its lowest level since 2001, when the industry was just a fraction of its current size. The drop was most dramatic in the buyout industry's traditionally strong North American and European markets. Even deals in the fast-growing Asia–Pacific markets decreased although not as much. While leveraged loan issuance for buyouts had a significant drop, high-yield debt issuance saw significant increases in 2010. Most of this went into refinancing existing portfolio company debt as the high-yield bond market filled the financing gap left by the decline in bank lending.

- *Buyouts started using less debt*. With debt-financing scarce, the buyout deals struck in 2008 and 2009 were structured with modest amounts of leverage, well below peak levels. Therefore, buyout deals needed far bigger infusions of equity. In U.S., the average equity contribution reached 52% of the total purchase price on average in 2009, the highest level since at least 1997, while in Europe the average equity contribution increased to 56% in 2009 (Bain & Co., 2010).

- *The size of buyouts decreased*. The credit crisis marked an end to the blockbuster transactions that dominated headlines between 2005 and 2007. Buyout deals valued at USD10bn or more accounted for nearly one quarter of the total value of buyout transactions at the peak in 2007, but in 2009 there was no deal that large. In parallel with the shift to smaller deals was a rotation in the types of investments private equity funds were making. The trend that saw many private equity funds convert public companies into private businesses reversed as the proportion of public-to-private deals declined to its lowest level in more than 5 years.

- *Buyout firms readjusted their focus*. Buyout funds started to focus their investments on carveouts and sales of non-core assets by cash-strapped parent companies and increased their international presence in emerging markets. They also started to invest with strategic buyers through minority stake investments and provide capital to finance add-on acquisitions for their portfolio companies. Finally, buyout funds started to invest in debt and distressed debt investments trading below par value. Some of these debt securities enabled private equity funds to acquire ownership stakes via debt conversions.

• *Fundraising decreased significantly.* Fundraising came almost to a halt in 2009, when new funds raised worldwide raised less than 40% of what the industry brought in during 2008. Funds focused on buyouts saw the biggest declines. In addition, new funds took longer to close. One reason for some investors' lack of interest in making new commitments to the asset class was that for those investors whom private equity formed part of a balanced asset portfolio they found their de facto allocation to private equity rose sharply as the value of public asset investments fell (the so-called "denominator" effect). A cash flow imbalance between capital calls and distributions further contributed to the squeeze.

1.3 STATISTICS ON THE PRIVATE EQUITY INDUSTRY

Putting the effect of the recent crisis aside, the private equity market has been growing rapidly in terms of funds raised. However, international fundraising patterns differ markedly. Only 10% of U.S. private equity funds are raised from foreign investors while European and Asian funds are much more international since more than half of their funds come from foreign investors. International funds largely come from the U.S. market. In mature markets, such as the U.K. and Continental Europe, U.S.-based investors are the largest providers of capital (EVCA, 2008). Also, the development of private equity funds in India and China is to a large extent caused by flows from U.S.-based institutions (e.g., Deloitte, 2005).

Private equity investments are now found on most continents and international flows of capital are increasing rapidly. For example, 34% of the amount raised by European venture capital and private equity firms in the period 2003 to 2007 is dedicated to non-domestic investments (e.g., EVCA, 2008). During the same period, U.S. private equity firms accounted for 32% of all international buyout investments. The Asia–Pacific market has developed as a third important private equity market with strongly developed markets in Japan, Australia, Singapore, Hong Kong, South Korea, and Taiwan, and emerging markets in China and India.

An important reason for the increased interest in the private equity market since the 1980s has been the fact that the private equity asset class on average has generated consistently higher returns than most public equity markets and bond markets. Evidence provided by private equity industry trade associations indicates that private equity funds outperform public equity indices, although the variation between the top-performing buyout and venture funds and the others is very wide. However, academic evidence attempts to adjust for the inherent risk associated with private equity invest-ments as well as fees charged by private equity managers and finds that, on average, private equity funds do not outperform the public indices (Kaplan and Schoar, 2005; Phalippou and Gottschalg, 2009). Nevertheless, this academic work still finds that the top-performing funds (the top quartile of the funds) have significant and persistent outperformance.

Preqin, an independent data provider, offers one of the most comprehensive and detailed sources of private equity performance data covering both buyout and venture funds. Their statistics are based on data from a number of different sources, including from GPs themselves. This dataset covers over 5,000 private equity funds of all types

EXHIBIT 1.1

PERFORMANCE OF VENTURE FUNDS AS OF DECEMBER 31, 2009, WORLDWIDE (PREQIN MEDIAN BENCHMARKS)

Vintage	No. funds	Median fund			Median quartiles			IRR quartiles			IRR	
		Called (%) DPI	Dist (%) RVPI	Value (%)	Q1	Median	Q3	Q1	Median	Q3	Max	Min
2008	34	21.8	0.0	84.4	1.08	0.89	0.75	n/m	n/m	n/m	n/m	n/m
2007	50	43.7	0.0	92.8	1.05	0.94	0.79	2.4	−3.5	−16	182	−38.3
2006	52	65.6	0.2	83.9	1.02	0.88	0.78	0.4	−7.3	−12.7	52.0	−51.8
2005	44	80.1	10.8	77.6	1.19	0.95	0.78	7.2	−2.3	−7.3	32.9	−93.5
2004	22	91.4	17.4	75.5	1.11	0.95	0.74	4.2	−2.9	−9.7	55.4	−22.0
2003	19	90.0	21.1	65.0	1.50	1.01	0.83	14.0	0.1	−5.5	35.1	−17.2
2002	35	94.5	41.2	62.9	1.31	1.03	0.79	7.3	0.2	−7.4	23.0	−47.2
2001	59	99.8	46.0	50.1	1.35	0.95	0.70	7.5	−1.8	−8.0	28.6	−100.0
2000	69	97.0	52.2	41.2	1.29	1.00	0.65	5.3	0.0	−6.9	28.8	−22.7
1999	48	100.0	47.5	21.1	1.32	0.73	0.51	7.2	−6.7	−14.4	28.7	−40.6
1998	31	100.0	131.9	4.1	1.63	1.39	0.62	22.0	8.4	−10.2	514.3	−46.1
1997	38	100.0	207.5	0.0	4.18	2.26	1.20	80.5	32.8	3.7	267.8	−35.0
1996	18	100.0	199.9	0.0	3.27	2.00	1.46	61.1	17.8	8.5	133.3	−33.3
1995	22	100.0	213.2	0.0	5.45	2.13	1.12	89.7	22.6	3.4	447.4	−19.9
1994	20	100.0	190.2	0.0	4.99	1.90	1.37	47.9	25.5	7.0	73.2	−22.0
1993	27	100.0	247.5	0.0	3.53	2.48	1.59	40.8	31.7	8.0	87.4	−14.8
1992	26	100.0	187.9	0.0	3.32	1.88	1.39	34.1	18.6	4.4	110.4	−20.1
1991	15	100.0	247.0	0.0	3.61	2.47	1.56	39.7	25.3	10.6	346.4	1.2
1990	20	100.0	183.0	0.0	2.52	1.83	1.11	24.9	16.0	3.9	74.4	−35.9

Source: Preqin (2009a).

and a geographic focus that represents about 70% of all private equity capital committed worldwide (Preqin, 2009). As private equity investments are generally medium and long-term investments, 1-year returns are inappropriate as a realistic measure of private equity performance due to the volatility in returns. As a result, most data providers that measure the performance of private equity funds rely on multiples on investments and internal rates of return (IRR). We discuss these measures in detail in Chapter 3.

Exhibit 1.1 presents the performance of 649 venture funds with vintages starting in 1990 until 2008. The sample covers all regions of the world. For early vintages, the performance is higher both in terms of multiples and IRRs provided to investors due to the fact that the funds have liquidated or are close to liquidation. The median fully liquidated venture fund (i.e., funds with vintages prior to 1998) returned a multiple

EXHIBIT 1.2

NET IRR PERFORMANCE OF VENTURE FUNDS AS OF 31 DECEMBER 2009, WORLDWIDE

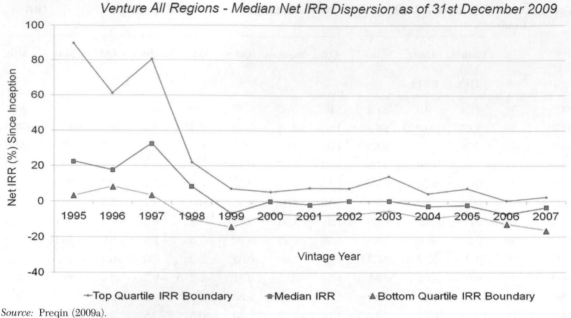

Source: Preqin (2009a).

varying from 1.83 times the money committed to the fund to 2.48 times the money committed (for the same group of funds the IRRs vary between 16% and 32.8%). Net IRRs are computed after removing the management fees, expenses, and the carried interest received by the fund managers. The median venture fund raised at the peak of the dotcom bubble (in 1999) generated losses to its investors (multiple is 0.73; IRR is −6.70). It is worth noting the large variation in performance. The top-quartile fund delivers, on average, across all vintages returns that are twice as large than the bottom-quartile fund.

A plot of the net IRR performance of the median fund (Exhibit 1.2) shows a significant gap between the top-quartile and bottom-quartile venture fund. It also indicates a sharp drop in the performance of venture funds in general starting with the 1999 vintage.

Exhibit 1.3 presents the performance of 676 buyout funds with vintages starting in 1990 and ending in 2008. Again, the sample covers all regions in the world. As in the case of venture funds, the performance of buyout funds is higher in early vintages (i.e., the funds were liquidated or close to liquidation). The median buyout fund close to liquidation (i.e., funds with vintages prior to 1998) returned a multiple varying from 1.57 times the money committed to the fund to 2.23 times the money committed (for the same group of funds the IRRs vary between 10.6% and 23.8%). Net IRRs are computed after removing the management fees, expenses, and the carried interest received by the fund managers. The top-quartile buyout fund delivers significantly higher returns than the bottom-quartile buyout fund indicating great variation in the performance of the funds.

EXHIBIT 1.3

PERFORMANCE OF BUYOUT FUNDS AS OF DECEMBER 31, 2009, WORLDWIDE (PREQIN MEDIAN BENCHMARKS)

Vintage	No. funds	Median fund			Median quartiles			IRR quartiles			IRR	
		Called (%) DPI	Dist (%) RVPI	Value (%)	Q1	Median	Q3	Q1	Median	Q3	Max	Min
2008	53	23.6	0.1	86.9	1.04	0.93	0.76	n/m	n/m	n/m	n/m	n/m
2007	72	43.0	0.4	89.2	1.05	0.92	0.79	4.6	−5.7	−14.2	24.3	−52.4
2006	53	67.3	2.4	82.8	1.05	0.89	0.78	3.6	−5.6	−12.8	28.9	−76.7
2005	64	87.2	24.4	87.9	1.36	1.18	1.01	14.6	7.1	0.4	76.9	−26.7
2004	33	91.1	32.7	82.6	1.76	1.23	1.04	25.3	7.2	1.5	90.4	−14.2
2003	22	93.1	65.6	84.5	2.49	1.60	1.31	46.9	18.5	11.3	92.9	−7.8
2002	31	93.9	85.5	53.3	1.98	1.59	1.38	30.3	16.9	11.0	72.0	−3.5
2001	29	97.0	160.8	38.7	2.77	2.16	1.51	40.3	29.0	13.8	95.7	9.5
2000	59	97.0	136.3	47.8	2.24	1.72	1.42	24.7	17.3	11.0	34.8	−9.5
1999	36	97.3	134.3	14.4	2.03	1.56	1.22	19.4	11.3	5.4	40.3	−25.1
1998	46	99.8	142.7	6.7	1.87	1.48	1.08	15.9	8.6	0.3	31.3	−45.4
1997	35	100.0	149.5	1.2	2.15	1.61	1.25	20.6	11.8	4.2	84.5	−13.9
1996	21	99.6	179.9	0.6	2.36	1.82	1.13	25.6	12.8	1.4	147.4	−8.9
1995	23	100.0	151.7	0.0	2.29	1.57	1.19	34.5	10.6	2.7	59.9	−15.5
1994	30	100.0	205.8	0.0	2.47	2.06	1.52	37.4	21.6	13.9	92.2	−1.2
1993	18	100.0	200.7	0.0	3.12	2.03	1.51	25.3	18.0	9.0	58.0	0.8
1992	19	100.0	195.5	0.0	2.54	1.96	1.19	36.9	21.2	4.7	58.1	−49.9
1991	9	100.0	219.2	0.0	3.19	2.19	2.01	30.3	23.8	19.8	54.7	−0.5
1990	23	100.0	222.6	0.0	3.21	2.23	1.54	27.0	16.8	7.0	70.0	2.4

Source: Source: Preqin (2009b).

The time series performance pattern of the median buyout fund is different from that of the median venture fund. The performance (net IRR) peaked for the 2003 top-quartile vintage and then started to drop for the funds raised after. This is also the year where the gap between the top-quartile and bottom-quartile performance is the largest.

Exhibits 1.4 and 1.5 present disaggregated information on buyout fund performance for the two largest markets: North America and Europe. The data on North American funds spans a longer period with vintages as early as 1980.

In Exhibit 1.7 we present a ranking of the largest private equity firms and their location based on the capital raised over the 5-year period prior to the end of 2009 (the ranking has been compiled by *Private Equity International*). Goldman Sachs Principal Investment Area is the largest private equity firm in the world. The private equity division of Goldman Sachs has managed to raise USD54.5bn for private equity direct

EXHIBIT 1.4

PERFORMANCE OF NORTH AMERICAN BUYOUT FUNDS AS OF DECEMBER 31, 2009 (PREQIN MEDIAN BENCHMARKS)

Vintage	No. funds	Median fund			Median quartiles			IRR quartiles			IRR	
		Called (%) DPI	Dist (%) RVPI	Value (%)	Q1	Median	Q3	Q1	Median	Q3	Max	Min
2008	32	23.8	0.2	93.4	1.07	0.95	0.85	n/m	n/m	n/m	n/m	n/m
2007	45	40.1	0.9	90.3	1.05	0.95	0.83	3.7	−5.4	−11.2	22.2	−40
2006	31	64.8	2.8	82.9	1.02	0.88	0.78	0.9	−5.9	−11.9	28.9	−76.7
2005	38	85.5	14.7	94.7	1.23	1.12	1.01	10.1	4.7	0.6	41.0	−20.6
2004	21	91.1	30.6	93.4	1.62	1.22	1.04	20.0	6.9	1.5	60.9	−7.5
2003	15	90.3	61.6	84.2	2.25	1.57	1.30	40.6	14.8	8.0	92.9	1.0
2002	18	95.5	73.4	61.1	1.65	1.51	1.28	22.2	12.0	8.6	35.9	−3.5
2001	16	96.7	167.2	39.3	2.53	2.04	1.47	39.7	28.1	13.6	95.7	9.5
2000	38	96.7	105.0	53.3	2.09	1.65	1.39	22.1	14.7	9.7	34.8	−0.8
1999	23	98.5	118.2	20.6	1.82	1.49	0.93	15.0	9.2	−1.2	29.6	−25.1
1998	33	99.8	126.2	9.3	1.72	1.43	0.96	15.3	7.3	−2.3	26.9	−20.7
1997	23	100.0	149.5	1.7	2.15	1.59	1.08	15.0	11.8	1.9	33.6	−13.9
1996	15	98.7	130.8	1.1	2.28	1.31	1.02	23.4	6.4	0.6	147.4	−8.9
1995	16	100.0	147.8	0.0	2.30	1.51	1.21	29.8	10.1	4.0	59.9	−8.6
1994	22	99.5	200.7	0.0	2.24	2.01	1.52	32.6	18.8	13.9	92.2	−1.2
1993	15	100.0	230.0	0.0	3.27	2.30	1.71	28.1	19.8	11.4	58.0	2.7
1992	13	100.0	156.2	0.0	2.39	1.56	0.86	41.4	21.2	−6.1	58.1	−49.9
1991	6	100.0	246.5	0.0	n/m	2.47	n/m	n/m	22.1	n/m	54.7	−0.5
1990	13	100.0	247.1	0.0	3.62	2.47	1.82	31.7	15.3	8.8	54.2	2.9

Source: Preqin (2009b).

investment over the past 5 years, including the USD20.3bn GS Capital Partners VI raised in 2007. The top 10 list is dominated by American private equity firms (8 out of 10). The largest private equity firms outside North America are CVC Partners with USD34.2bn raised and Apax Partners with USD21.7bn raised, both based in London.

The largest non-American or European firm comes at the bottom of this league table: Abraaj Capital, based in Dubai, raised USD6.5bn. The largest firm headquartered in Asia is Beijing-based CDH Investments, with USD4.1bn in capital raised over the past 5 years (not in the top 50).

The top 300 private equity firms in the 2010 ranking by *Private Equity International* have raised a total of USD1.315tn over the past 5 years, a decrease from the USD1.337tn raised by the largest 300 firms over a similar timespan ending in April 2009.

EXHIBIT 1.5

PERFORMANCE OF EUROPEAN BUYOUT FUNDS AS OF DECEMBER 31, 2009 (PREQIN MEDIAN BENCHMARKS)

Vintage	No. funds	Median fund			Median quartiles			IRR quartiles			IRR	
		Called (%) DPI	Dist (%) RVPI	Value (%)	Q1	Median	Q3	Q1	Median	Q3	Max	Min
2008	12	21.3	0	72.5	1.00	0.77	0.49	n/m	n/m	n/m	n/m	n/m
2007	19	48.5	0.0	84.0	1.11	0.85	0.69	9.6	−10.3	−20.3	24.3	−52.4
2006	17	67.1	4.1	80.9	1.09	0.86	0.72	4.5	−6.3	−15.2	11.7	−32.1
2005	18	87.7	44.0	79.7	1.61	1.25	0.94	26.5	10.2	−2.9	76.9	−26.7
2004	10	89.1	82.0	69.8	1.94	1.62	1.13	65.7	22.0	5.5	90.4	−13.0
2003	6	97.1	120.1	75.6	2.49	2.16	1.46	47.1	26.9	19.3	48.7	−7.8
2002	13	91.8	157.1	49.0	2.52	1.83	1.51	42.9	29.0	13.2	72.0	11.0
2001	10	99.5	218.9	26.9	3.23	2.39	1.55	44.2	32.0	13.7	52.6	10.0
2000	18	97.9	164.7	23.1	2.49	2.31	1.43	26.7	23.0	17.3	33.2	−5.5
1999	10	93.5	154.3	7.1	2.19	1.82	1.52	24.4	16.8	9.3	40.3	6.0
1998	10	90.4	166.6	7.2	2.32	1.76	1.48	18.1	15.0	8.0	31.3	−3.2
1997	11	98.9	166.8	0.0	2.49	1.67	1.47	24.0	17.9	7.6	84.5	0.1
1996	5	99.6	220.7	0.0	3.28	2.21	1.77	45.4	23.2	19.6	63.0	17.2
1995	5	98.7	185.6	0.0	2.73	1.87	0.84	45.4	22.0	−6.9	55.4	−15.5
1994	8	100.0	250.6	0.0	3.13	2.51	1.55	55.5	41.8	18.5	56.1	10.1
1993	4	100.0	119.9	7.0	n/m	1.27	n/m	n/m	9.0	n/m	16.9	0.8
1992	5	100.0	206.1	0.0	2.83	2.06	1.84	34.3	22.4	13.5	40.0	11.0
1991	3	100.0	210.2	0.0	n/m	n/m	n/m	n/m	n/m	n/m	25.3	25.0
1990	8	99.9	165.1	0.0	2.99	1.65	1.43	26.0	21.1	15.4	70.0	7.0

Source: Preqin (2009b).

1.4 RECENT REGULATORY ACTIVITY

Until now, private equity firms were exempt from many of the oversight treatments that other types of investments face such as daily and quarterly reporting requirements and registration with financial regulators. However, private equity firms are coming to terms with more regulatory oversight. Certain proposals, such as registration and some increased reporting requirements, are not likely to have a major impact on larger private equity firms but will definitely affect the smaller ones.

New financial regulation will place additional requirements and restrictions on private equity funds. Although there is considerable uncertainty around the detail of any long-term regulatory changes two pieces of recent legislation will have a significant impact on the activities of private equity firms. In the U.S., lawmakers

EXHIBIT 1.6

NET IRR PERFORMANCE OF BUYOUT FUNDS AS OF DECEMBER 31, 2009, WORLDWIDE (PREQIN MEDIAN BENCHMARKS

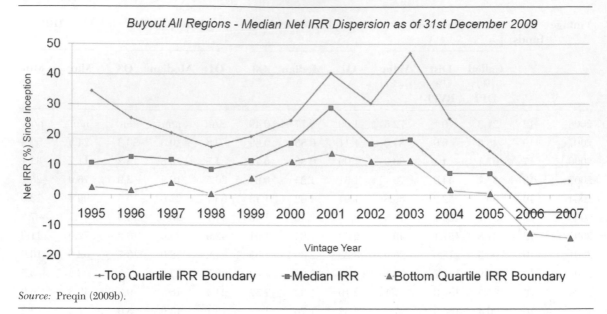

Buyout All Regions - Median Net IRR Dispersion as of 31st December 2009

→ Top Quartile IRR Boundary   ■ Median IRR   ▲ Bottom Quartile IRR Boundary

Source: Preqin (2009b).

passed a financial reform bill in July 2010 (i.e., The Dodd–Frank Wall Street Reform and Consumer Protection Act 2010) which will require private equity funds with more than USD150mn in assets to register with the Securities and Exchange Commission. In Europe, the Directive on Alternative Investment Fund Managers (AIFM), adopted in November 2010, will bring a number of changes including increased disclosure and governance requirements, capital requirements, and limits on leverage. This directive is expected to significantly increase compliance costs and to make it more difficult for managers based outside the European Union (EU) to market their funds in the EU.

The pace of regulation of private equity entities in other parts of the world is much slower as governments are still focused on cutting risks that were responsible for the collapse of the global financial system. Tax pressures on the private equity industry are likely to rise around the world as governments seek to increase tax revenues in order to reduce large deficits. In both the U.S. and U.K. there are discussions about proposals to tax carried interest as ordinary income. Whether these will materialize into final legislation remains to be seen.

AIFM Directive

The AIFM Directive is a response to the recent financial crisis and aims to establish uniform requirements governing fund managers in order to moderate risks in the financial system. The Directive will generally apply to fund managers managing all types of hedge, private equity, and real estate funds (these are typical alternative investment funds). The Directive applies to fund managers that are (i) based in the EU, (ii) are not based in the EU but manage EU funds, and (iii) are not based in the EU but market funds within the EU. Fund managers with total assets under management up to €100mn and fund managers with unleveraged total assets under management of up to €500mn with no redemption rights do not have to comply with many of the requirements.

The Directive allows non-EU fund managers the same rights of access as EU fund managers to the European Union markets via a "passport" system at the cost of a regulatory burden. The new regulations will be introduced over time with most rules becoming effective in early 2013. The passport system for non-EU fund managers will not be implemented until 2015 or later. It is important to note that the Directive focuses on the fund managers and does not regulate the funds themselves.

Some of the provisions of the Directive that affect private equity firms include

- Small fund managers (whether EU based or not) of portfolios with total assets of under (i) €100mn or (ii) €500mn where the funds are not leveraged and investors are locked in for at least 5 years, only need to register with their home regulator and provide sufficient information as to their investment strategies and exposures to enable the regulator to monitor systemic risk.

- Fund managers need to publish annual reports of non-listed companies controlled by their funds (with control being defined as 50% of the voting rights of the company) within 6 months of the end of the fiscal year. These reports need to contain a fair review of the company's business and also its likely future development.

- Fund managers need to provide notification requirements on reaching, exceeding, or falling below the thresholds of 10%, 20%, 30%, 50%, and 75% of the voting rights of non-listed companies.

- Fund managers need to have initial capital of at least €125,000. If the assets under management of a fund manager exceed €250mn, the fund manager must provide an additional amount of own funds equal to 0.02% of the amount by which the value of the assets under management exceed €250mn, up to a maximum amount with the initial capital of €10mn.

- Fund managers have to set a maximum level of leverage used within each fund managed. While most funds already do this, the maximum level of leverage needs to be clarified (e.g., how are short-term facilities that are typically used by managers to bridge the capital calls on the fund investors classified?). Managers will also have to report regularly to their home regulator on the leverage position within their funds.

- New restrictions on senior personnel remuneration will be introduced although much of the detail is still to follow. The transparency provisions of the Directive require the fund's annual report to identify the amount of carried interest paid to each member of the relevant carry scheme.

- Fund managers must separate the functions of risk management from the operating units. Fund managers must also have a documented and updated due diligence process and ensure that the risks associated with each investment can be properly measured and monitored by the use of appropriate stress-testing procedures. Stress tests are also required regularly to assess and monitor the liquidity risks of the fund.

- Fund managers must put in place procedures for independent valuation of fund assets at least annually. If the manager chooses not to appoint an external valuer,

EXHIBIT 1.7

RANK OF EUROPEAN BUYOUT FUNDS AS OF DECEMBER 31, 2009

Rank	Name of firm	Headquarters	Capital raised over last 5 years (USD million)
1	Goldman Sachs Principal Investment Area	New York	54,584.0
2	The Carlyle Group	Washington DC	48,175.5
3	Kohlberg Kravis Roberts	New York	47,031.0
4	TPG	Fort Worth (Texas)	45,052.0
5	Apollo Global Mgmt	New York	34,710.0
6	CVC Capital Partners	London	34,175.4
7	The Blackstone Group	New York	31,139.4
8	Bain Capital	Boston	29,239.6
9	Warburg Pincus	New York	23,000.0
10	Apax Partners	London	21,728.1
11	First Reserve Corporation	Greenwich (Connecticut)	19,063.5
12	Advent International	Boston	18,179.8
13	Hellman & Friedman	San Francisco	17,300.0
14	Cerberus Capital Management	New York	14,900.0
15	General Atlantic	Greenwich (Connecticut)	14,700.0
16	Permira	London	12,963.3
17	Providence Equity Partners	Providence (Rhode Island)	12,100.0
18	Clayton Dubilier & Rice	New York	11,704.0
19	Terra Firma Capital Partners	London	11,645.0
20	Bridgepoint	London	11,203.0
21	Teachers' Private Capital	Toronto	10,890.5
22	Charterhouse Capital Partners	London	10,762.4
23	Fortress Investment Group	New York	10,700.0
24	Madison Dearborn Partners	Chicago	10,600.0
25	Oaktree Capital Management	Los Angeles	10,559.9
26	TA Associates	Boston	10,547.5
27	Citi Alternative Investments	New York	10,197.0
28	Thomas H. Lee Partners	Boston	10,100.0
29	Riverstone Holdings	New York	9,800.0
30	Cinven	London	9,606.8
31	AXA Private Equity	Paris	9,535.1
32	JC Flowers & Co.	New York	9,300.0
33	Silver Lake	Menlo Park	9,300.0
34	BC Partners	London	8,897.3
35	3i	London	8,340.9
36	Nordic Capital	Stockholm	8,340.9

Rank	Name of firm	Headquarters	Capital raised over last 5 years (USD million)
37	HarbourVest Partners	Boston	7,953.8
38	PAI Partners	Paris	7,929.2
39	Lindsay Goldberg	New York	7,800.0
40	NGP Energy Capital Management	Dallas	7,519.0
41	Lone Star Funds	Dallas	7,500.0
42	AlpInvest Partners	Amsterdam	7,399.2
43	EQT Partners	Stockholm	7,372.4
44	Welsh Carson Anderson & Stowe	New York	7,309.0
45	Onex Partners	Toronto	7,278.2
46	Marfin	Athens	6,955.2
47	WL Ross & Co.	New York	6,900.0
48	Oak Hill Capital Partners	Stamford (Connecticut)	6,606.5
49	Sun Capital Partners	Boca Raton (Florida)	6,500.0
50	Abraaj Capital	Dubai	6,458.8

the valuation task must be functionally independent from portfolio management to avoid conflicts of interest. The manager's home regulator may require procedures and/or valuations to be verified by an external valuer or an auditor.

The Dodd–Frank Act

This Act contains several provisions that impact private equity firms, including new registration requirements for private equity funds. Most fund managers with more than USD150mn in assets under management will be required to register with the Securities and Exchange Commission (SEC) and be subject to SEC regulatory oversight (venture capital funds will be exempt, with a definition of such funds to be provided by the SEC within a year of enactment). Fund managers that are required to register will need to establish a formal compliance policy and a framework that identifies conflicts of interest, hires a chief compliance officer, and reports to the SEC.

The Act provides an exemption from the registration requirements of foreign fund managers who (i) have no place of business in the U.S.; (ii) have, in total, fewer than 15 clients and investors in the U.S. in the private funds managed; (iii) have less than USD25mn of U.S.-based assets under management (or a higher amount that the SEC may specify). Exemptions from the registration requirement are also available for (i) venture capital fund managers, (ii) small business investment company advisers, (iii) family offices, and (iv) managers of private funds with under USD150mn of assets under management in the U.S.

The Act also requires registered private equity fund managers to take steps to safeguard client assets in their custody. Unlike the European Directive, the Act does not require a depositary to be appointed but it may still lead to increased operational costs and additional interference from independent accountants which it must appoint to verify the custody of client assets.

Another provision affecting private equity firms is the *Volckerr Rule*. Limitations are now imposed on proprietary trading and investments in hedge funds and private equity funds by banking entities. Going forward investment levels in hedge funds and private equity funds of no more than 3% of their Tier 1 capital are permitted. An additional provision limits ownership to 3% of the equity of any single private equity fund. The bill also restricts bank employees' investments in bank-managed private equity funds only to those employees who are actively involved in the managing of the fund. The Volckerr Rule is likely to reduce significantly the investor base for private equity funds as banks achieve compliance. Banks have a 2-year transition period to bring their activities into compliance with the Volckerr Rule after July 2010, although the Act contemplates few further exemptions to the transition period.

The Directive and the Act only contain a framework for the new regulatory regimes in Europe and the U.S. and there remains in practice much detail to be discussed. Once the additional details and rules are published it will be possible for the private equity industry to determine the depth of the impact of these regulatory enactments.

What is certain, however, is that the private equity industry will be subject to greater regulation, supervision, and oversight. Although private equity firms will incur greater compliance costs, the private equity industry will need to embrace these new regulations.

1.5 THE OUTLOOK OF THE PRIVATE EQUITY INDUSTRY

Increased focus on operational improvements

Simplistically, the strong returns generated in the asset class have increased competitive intensity in nearly all country markets where private equity funds operate. Moreover, as the accumulated experience in the industry rises, funds have to strive ever more to recreate the returns of the past. Gone are the days when assets could be acquired at modest prices and returns generated from executing relatively simple value creation plans. In the highly competitive world in which most funds operate the imperatives are more around deep industrial insight, flawless execution, and talent and experience in crafting and delivering more complex value creation strategies. This phenomenon, first seen amongst the largest funds, is slowly filtering down to smaller and smaller funds.

More attention is being paid to increasing the value of portfolio companies in the absence of leverage. For both financial reasons (i.e., decreased costs) and competitive reasons, there seems to be growing interest in having research conducted in-house. This will place increased importance on due diligence and understanding the competitive trends and contexts in which portfolio companies are operating. More attention will be paid to debt structures, quality of earnings, risk management, IT structure, marketing and competitive intelligence, and operational efficiency.

As a result, the emphasis will continue to shift away from "megafunds" toward those funds that specialize. In this environment, private equity firms with specialized niches, good market upturn, and, importantly, good market downturn strategies become attractive and viable.

Move towards other activities

The U.S. government's financial reform package forces investment banks to spin out their private equity businesses and limit riskier business activities. This reform package opens the door for private equity firms to get into the very same business lines that are seen as problematic for investment banks today. Sprawling private equity firms like Blackstone, Carlyle, and KKR, which built up significant lending and advisory businesses over the past few years, are likely to benefit. The large private equity firms are likely to start investing in credit, arranging financing for leveraged buyouts, and providing mezzanine and rescue financing to other businesses. These are the types of activities that will be shunned by investment banks due to the new regulations.

Emerging markets will become more important

Emerging markets seem set to form an increasing part of the global private equity landscape. Despite subdued and challenging deal activity in emerging markets, great opportunities exist in these markets. Private equity investments in developing countries are mainly based on growth—not leverage—so one could argue that they are less risky than widely believed. Most emerging markets present infrastructure opportunities as their economies need to develop their infrastructures to support growth. Emerging markets are likely to lead the worldwide economic recovery and will see their share of private equity transactions increase over the next decade. The prospect of earning better returns will likely outweigh any concerns arising from political, legal, and structural market uncertainties. Emerging markets such as Brazil, China and India will continue to garner private equity firms' interest.

1.6 REFERENCES

ACHARYA, V., FRANKS, J., AND SERVAES, H. (2007) "Private equity: Boom and bust?," *Journal of Applied Corporate Finance*, **19**(4), 1–10.

BAIN & CO. (2010) *Global Private Equity Report.*

BISHOP, M. (2004) "The new kings of capitalism," *The Economist*, November 25.

CITYUK (2010) *Private Equity 2010, www.thecityuk.com*

DELOITTE (2005) *Venture Capital Goes Global: Key Findings from the 2005 Global Venture Capital Survey.*

EVCA (2008) *Pan-European Private Equity & Venture Capital Activity Report.*

FENN, G.W., LIANG, N., AND PROWSE, S. (1995) "The economics of private equity market," *Federal Reserve Bulletin*, **168**, 1–69.

KAPLAN, S.N., AND SCHOAR, A. (2005) "Private equity performance: Returns, persistence, and capital flows," *Journal of Finance*, **60**, 1791–1823.

KOCIS, J.M., BACHMAN, J.C. IV, LONG, A.M. III, AND NICKELS, C.J. (2009) *Inside Private Equity: The Professional Investor's Handbook*, John Wiley & Sons Ltd.

METRICK, A. (2007) *Venture Capital and the Finance of Innovation*, John Wiley & Sons Ltd.

PHALIPPOU, L., AND GOTTSCHALG, O. (2009) "The performance of private equity funds," *Review of Financial Studies*, **22**(4), 1747–1776.

PREQIN (2009a) *Preqin Private Equity Benchmarks: Venture Benchmark Report.*

PREQIN (2009b) *Preqin Private Equity Benchmarks: Buyout Benchmark Report.*

WILSON, J. (1985) *The New Ventures: Inside the High Stakes World of Venture Capital,* Addison Wesley Longman.

2

Private equity fund economics

2.1 OVERVIEW

Private equity plays an increasingly important role in the financing of a wide range of businesses. Over the past 20 years, private equity has been one of the fastest growing markets for corporate finance. Private equity funds under management totaled about USD2.5tn at the end of 2009, more than double the amount in 2003 which stood at slightly less than USD1tn (CityUK, 2010).

By its very nature this market is private, not subject to the same disclosure requirements and regulation as the public markets and is characterized by poor levels of publicly available information. Thus, it is extremely challenging for the outsider to understand and form a view on the workings of the industry.

The stated purpose of a private equity fund is normally to make equity investments in an unlisted company (or more typically, a number of companies). However, private equity finance can be applied to other parts of a company's capital structure (e.g., mezzanine or junior debt) and into companies at different stages of their development (turnarounds, startups, or buyouts), in different geographies (one county or pan-regional) and with different control rights (i.e., minority investments or majority ones).

The substantial majority of private equity investments is made through funds whose legal structure is that of a limited partnership. These funds are created (raised) for the specific purpose of making private equity investments. Such partnerships have a separate legal identity and are established by investment managers to follow a clearly prescribed investment mandate.

Most of the capital invested in private equity comes from institutional investors. These are typically pension funds, financial institutions, or, increasingly, sovereign wealth funds. These investors either make their investments into the asset class directly or via a specialist private equity investment manager (a so-called "fund of funds"). Investment in the asset class made by individual investors is typically limited to high-net-worth individuals. Retail investors can typically invest in the asset class only through one of the many listed private equity funds.

As regards a typical limited partnership fund, investors are asked to make a "commitment" of a certain amount of capital to the partnership which, as well as having a clear investment mandate, will also have a certain target size. For instance, investors might decide to make a "commitment" of £10m to a fund targeting £500m of total

This chapter has been co-authored with Jim Strang (Jardine Capital).

EXHIBIT 2.1

STRUCTURE OF A PRIVATE EQUITY INVESTMENT VEHICLE

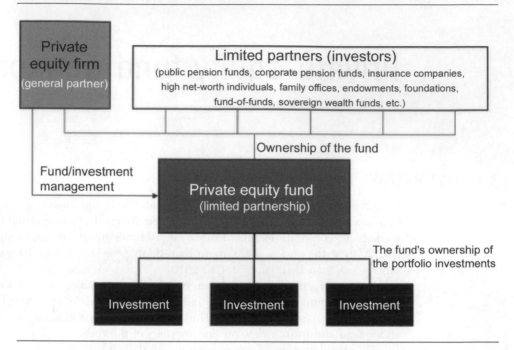

---

commitments with a mandate to make control buyout investments of private companies based in the U.K. By making a "commitment" the investor becomes a limited partner (LP) in the fund and effectively makes a legally binding promise to deliver it's pro rata share of the aggregate fund commitments as and when they are asked for by the investment manager. The private equity investment manager will act as the general partner (GP) of the fund and take responsibility for all of the investment-related matters within the partnership. We present the basic structure of the private equity investment vehicle in the Exhibit 2.1.

Private equity funds differ depending on the source of their capital or their investment specialization. Based on their capital source (LPs) and the ownership of the management company (GP), private equity funds can be classified into:

- *Independent private equity funds*—those in which third-party LPs are the main source of capital and where the management company is substantially owned by the GP. An independent fund is the most common type of private equity fund.

- *Captive private equity funds*—those in which a parent organization or sponsor (e.g., a bank or an insurance company) provides all the capital for investment. In such cases the management company of the fund is normally a wholly owned subsidiary of the parent.

- *Semi-captive private equity funds*—those which fall part way between being wholly captive and fully independent. Typically, such funds receive a significant proportion of their capital from their parent organization but also seek to raise independent capital from unrelated third parties. In such circumstances the management company may or may not be wholly owned by the parent. Semi-captive funds can be subsidiaries of a financial institution or an industrial company that operate as an independent company (certain corporate funds fall into this category).

Based on their investment specialization, private equity funds can be broadly classified further into (1) buyout, (2) venture capital, (3) mezzanine, and (4) distressed investment funds. We discuss these types in detail below.

2.2   PRIVATE EQUITY FIRMS OR GENERAL PARTNERS (GPs)

Main role

The main role of the private equity firm is to provide investment advice to the private equity fund created in joint partnership with the investors. The firm, which acts as a general partner of the fund, also executes the investment decisions, oversees the fund's investments, and receives fees for these services. We discuss these fees in Section 2.4.3.

The typical private equity firm is organized as a partnership or limited liability corporation. Bain Capital, Blackstone, Carlyle, Kleiner Perkins, KKR (formerly known as Kohlberg, Kravis & Roberts), Texas Pacific Group (TPG), are some of the most prominent private equity firms. In the late 1980s, these organizations were described as lean, decentralized, and with relatively few investment professionals and employees (Jensen, 1989).[1] Today, the largest private equity firms are substantial businesses, although they are still small relative to the firms in which they invest. All but the very largest private equity firms tend to have fewer than 200 private equity investment professionals. These pofessionals have a wide variety of skills and experience. Senior team members in private equity funds typically have various backgrounds with invest-ment partners coming from the worlds of industry, finance, accounting, and strategy consulting. Generally, investors view an element of diversity in the makeup of the investment team as a positive.

Investment teams come together for the purpose of raising funds, making investments, and, ultimately, returning profits to investors. To raise funds successfully teams have to present a cogent and deliverable investment strategy, appropriate invest-ment credentials, and, fundamentally, evidence of prior success in executing a similar investment strategy.

Incentive alignment

To make a fund an attractive investment proposition not only must the fundamental investment strategy appear attractive but the LPs must believe in proper alignment of interest between the LP and the GP. The alignment is achieved in several ways: (1) reputation; (2) equity interest; (3) incentive scheme; (4) direct control mechanisms.

---

1. In Jensen's survey of seven large leveraged buyout partnerships, found an average of 13 investment professionals who tended to come from an investment-banking background.

1. *Reputation*. The GPs must establish a favorable track record to raise new funds.[2] In the private equity market, reputation plays a key role because the market consists of a few actors that repeatedly interact with each other. In fact, reputation is regarded as a key value by many private equity firms. The following quote is taken from the values statement of one GP: "The firm's assets are our people, our investor franchise and reputation. If any of these are ever diminished, the last is the most difficult to restore." Reputation and a consistent record of delivering against stated objectives is thus a critical factor for any fund. Furthermore, from an LP's perspective the fact that performance amongst top private equity managers is persistent (unlike in the public markets) places added emphasis on this.

2. *Equity interest*. The GPs typically make a substantial commitment to the fund that contributes to the alignment of interest with the investors. The significant participation of the general partner ensures that they have so-called "skin in the game". In addition to their commitment (which may be as much as 10% of total commitments), GPs may also operate a co-investment scheme. In each case, for optimal alignment, LPs prefer that any commitment and investment is made in real cash and not from the recycling of management fees.

3. *Incentive scheme*. GPs operate under a pay-for-performance scheme in which most of their expected compensation is a share of the profits earned on investments, so-called "carried interest". Furthermore, the management fees are specified in the partnership agreement; thus, the amount of investment capital that can be consumed in the form of manager salaries and other perquisites is capped. These expenses are transparent making it easier for investors to compare expenses across different partnerships.

4. *Direct control mechanisms*. Investors stipulate direct control mechanisms in the partnership agreements and participate in advisory boards. Partnership agreements often specify covenants that place restrictions on a fund's investments and on other activities of the GPs. For example, partnership agreements can give investors direct control consisting mainly of restrictions on allowable investments and other partnership covenants, which the advisory board can waive by majority vote. Restrictions on investments are particularly important because a considerable portion of the GPs' compensation is in the form of an option-like claim on the fund's assets which can lead to excessive risk taking. To address this problem, partnership covenants usually set limits on the percentage of the fund's capital that may be invested in a single firm (usually that is set at 15%). Covenants may also preclude investments in publicly traded and foreign securities, derivatives, other private equity funds, and private equity investments that deviate significantly from the partnership's primary focus. LPs also demand covenants that restrict the use of debt at the fund level and in most cases require that cash from the liquidation of portfolio assets be distributed to investors immediately instead of being reinvested. LPs may further their own interests by using various other protective mechanisms that relate to performance incentives for GPs.

---

2. Private equity firms typically raise a new private equity fund at about the same time the investment phase for an existing fund has been completed. Thus, GPs are raising new funds approximately every 3 to 5 years and at any one time they may be managing several funds, each in a different phase of its life.

Ultimately, GPs signal investment quality to institutional investors by the extent to which they remain consistent with their investment mandates or styles and have flexibility to price-discriminate by changing the balance between management and performance fees.[3]

GPs' experience

The management team of private equity firms are expected to bring to the businesses they invest in their experience and success. They need to demonstrate that they are able to turn the business plan into reality. They should be experienced in complementary areas, such as management strategy, finance, and marketing and their roles should be well specified. In the case of technology companies, there will be a combination of technological and business skills that will be relevant.

GPs' experience is key given that the typical manager may receive hundreds of investment proposals each year. Of these proposals, only a very small percentage are chosen for fund investment. Their success depends upon GPs' ability to select these proposals efficiently. Efficient selection is properly regarded as more art than science and depends on the acumen of the general partners acquired through experience operating businesses as well as experience in the private equity field. That said, having a rigorous and efficient process for screening opportunities as they arise is very much to the benefit of the GP.

Investment proposals are first screened to eliminate those that are unpromising or that fail to meet the fund's investment criteria. Private equity firms typically specialize by type of investment and by industry and location of the investment although very large private equity funds take a generalist investment approach. Specialization reduces the number of investment opportunities considered and reflects the degree of specific knowledge required to make successful investment decisions.

There are some major differences between venture capital firms and buyout firms—the two main sectors of the private equity industry. Using a sample of 238 funds raised between 1993 and 2006, Metrick and Yasuda (2010) find that buyout GPs earn lower revenue per managed dollar than do venture capital GPs. However, buyout GPs build on their prior experience by increasing the size of their funds faster than venture capital GPs do. This leads to significantly higher revenue per partner and per professional in later buyout funds, despite the fact that these funds have lower revenue per dollar suggesting that the experience gained in the buyout business is more scalable than that in the venture capital business.

Both types of private equity are inherently labor-intensive, skill-based businesses. The crucial difference between buyout GPs and venture GPs derives from the fact that a buyout manager's expertise can add value to extremely large companies, whereas a venture manager's expertise can add value to only small companies. Venture capital GPs focus on small firms, with typical valuations in the tens of millions. Their skills are critical in helping firms in their developmental infancy and are not applicable to more mature firms that are 10 times larger and already in possession of core management skills.

---

3. See, for example, academic evidence provided by Gompers and Lerner (1996, 1999), Litvak (2004), and Cumming et al. (2009).

2.3 INVESTORS IN PRIVATE EQUITY FUNDS OR LIMITED PARTNERS (LPs)

Main investors

Investors in private equity funds are entities or persons that provide the equity capital to the fund. They provide a pool of capital which is governed by strict legal rules (established in the LP agreement or LPA) and task the private equity manager (the GP) with executing the prescribed investment strategy of the fund and delivering attractive risk-adjusted returns. The LPs are effectively passive investors with no influence on the investment matters of the fund once it is established. However, it is normal for funds to establish an advisory board. This board is typically formed by the larger and more experienced LPs in the fund. The advisory board normally meets twice per year and its role is to provide guidance and support in matters relating to the running of the partnership and to deal with any potential conflict of interest issues that arise. LPs who are not members of the advisory board rely on the annual meeting of the fund and the quarterly reporting provided by the manager as the formal means by which they are informed of the progress of their investments.

There are several types of investors in private equity funds:

1. Endowments, foundations, and other not-for-profit organizations (colleges and universities, medical institutions, professional and research organizations, religious and cultural institutions).
2. Public and private pension funds.
3. Family offices.
4. Funds of funds (funds that invest solely in other private equity funds).
5. Government funds.
6. Financial institutions (banks, insurance companies, etc.).
7. Corporations.
8. Sovereign wealth funds.
9. Wealthy individuals.

The principal sources of capital for private equity funds are institutional investors (e.g., pension funds, endowments, foundations, and funds-of-funds), accounting for a large portion of total investment in private equity funds, but also sovereign government funds, government entities, and wealthy individuals, often through family offices or investment vehicles. Institutional investors comprise 71% of private equity capital in the U.S. and 36% in Europe (Fleming, 2010). Pension funds represent the majority of capital in the U.S. The *Private Equity Analyst* (2008) lists the top 25 investors in private equity and the very large public pension funds (e.g., CalPERS—California Public Employees' Retirement System, CalSTRS—California State Teachers' Retirement System, PSERS—Public School Employees' Retirement System, and the Washington State Investment Board) occupy the top four slots (Kaplan and Strömberg, 2009). In Europe, financial institutions are the largest group (almost twice the proportion in the U.S.). Also, funds-of-funds are three times as important a source of finance in Europe than in the U.S. (Fleming, 2010).

Why invest in private equity?

Most LPs invest in private equity for strictly financial reasons. Some of the financial benefits that are expected from private equity investments are:

- Attractive risk-adjusted returns (from the best performing funds)
- Lower correlation to the returns of other asset classes
- Benefits of active ownership
- Diversification away from the public markets.

By investing through a fund partnership rather than directly in the firms in which these funds buy stakes, the investors also gain access to highly skilled investment professionals (i.e., GPs) with demonstrated abilities. Investors delegate to these professionals the responsibilities of selecting, structuring, managing, and eventually liquidating the private equity investments.

Co-investments

In recent years a number of institutional investors (e.g., pension funds, endowments, or sovereign wealth funds) have begun to invest directly in the underlying investments made by private equity funds. So doing not only lowers the aggregate fee burden to the LP but also allows for an element of investment timing (as the capital is immediately committed and drawn). These direct investments are implemented by co-investing alongside private equity partnerships managed by private equity firms with whom these investors have close relations and in most cases have invested. Effectively, the co-investing LP becomes a small minority investor in the transaction led by the GP in whose fund a major commitment has been made.

These co-investment opportunities are usually offered by GPs to those significant and experienced investors that have contributed a significant amount of capital to the fund and may occur when the private equity fund cannot invest the full amount due to concentration or diversification restrictions. Besides providing savings in terms of lower fees and, thus, potentially enhancing the returns, co-investments allow the investor to gain experience in structuring, monitoring, and exiting private equity transactions.[4]

2.4 PRIVATE EQUITY FUNDS OR LIMITED PARTNERSHIPS

Legally, private equity funds are normally organized as limited partnerships in which the GPs manage the fund and the LPs provide most of the capital. U.S. private equity funds are usually structured as partnerships registered in Delaware although some are registered in the Cayman Islands or Bermuda. The U.K.-based and European-based funds are usually registered in Jersey or Guernsey which are offshore jurisdictions within the U.K.

The private equity funds are established as a "blind pool" of capital. Consequently, once LPs commit their investment to the fund only the GPs have discretion on how to invest the money and when to invest it or return it. Most private equity funds are "closed-ended" funds of a finite life. In a "closed-end" fund, investors cannot withdraw

---

4. Investors that co-invest in the fund do not pay carried interest but might be charged a share of the management fee.

their funds until the fund is terminated. This contrasts with mutual funds (e.g., where investors can withdraw their funds anytime).

Private equity funds have several important characteristics that distinguish them from other alternative investment funds such as hedge funds:

1. *Life of the fund*. Each private equity fund or partnership has a contractually fixed lifetime, generally 10 years, with provisions to extend the partnership, usually in 1-year or 2-year increments, up to a maximum of 4 years.

2. *Committed capital*. Upon launch, only a fraction of the investors' committed capital will be payable. The balance is drawn down when investments are identified by the GP. As a result, the capital calls are irregular. This drawdown feature minimizes the holding period of the investor's capital.

3. *Investment characteristics*. The fund's investments are mainly in private (i.e., unlisted) companies which are highly illiquid.

4. *Investment cycle*. During the first 3 to 5 years (normally 5 years from the date of the final closing of the fund), the partnership's capital is invested into companies. Thereafter, the investments are managed and gradually liquidated. As the investments are liquidated, distributions are made to the limited partners in the form of cash or securities. When all investments are fully divested, the limited partnership can be terminated or "wound up".

Because of the limited life of a private equity fund, the GPs must regularly raise new funds. The legal rules concerning the raising of subsequent funds are usually contained within the limited partnership agreement (LPA). Typically GPs cannot embark on the raising of successor vehicles until 75% of the committed capital of the current fund has been called or the investment period of the current fund has ended. The fundraising process is time consuming and costly, especially if a fundraising adviser (placing agent) is used to facilitate the process. Typically, GPs turn to their existing investors in the first instance and look to them to provide the necessary commitments for a "first closing" of the fund. On aggregate, the fundraising process can take anything from several months to as many as 18 months.

2.4.1 Types of private equity funds

Private equity firms began to specialize in various segments and niches in the mid-1980s. Private equity firms are typically segmented by the types of companies or instruments that they invest in. Common labels for categorizations of private equity funds are buyout, venture capital, mezzanine, and distressed investment funds.

Buyout (or leverage buyout) funds

Buyout is the strategy of making investments in which a company or a unit of a company is acquired from its existing shareholders typically with the use of significant financial leverage. In buyouts, the investors usually invest significant equity stakes in target companies and then borrow the rest of the acquisition consideration from banks (leveraged loans), public markets (non-investment grade or junk bonds), and mezzanine investors. The amount of equity as a percentage of the total consideration varies considerably depending on the specific circumstances and the appetite of the other finance providers. Typically, the equity percentage is around 30% of the total consideration in the transaction. However, the figure can vary from less than 5% to, currently, in excess of 50%. The target companies that are being bought out are typically mature business of scale and, thus, can generate operating cash flows that can support the leverage structure. Chapter 12 on buyout transactions and valuation issues presents an in-depth description of these funds, their investments, and the ways buyout investments generate value.

Although temporary almost by definition, since the private equity sponsor has a fiduciary responsibility to exit the investment in a relatively short period, buyout transactions nonetheless account for an increasingly large fraction of corporate finance. Buyouts are the largest category of private equity, with total funds under management about three times as great as for venture capital (Axelson et al., 2009).

Buyout funds pursue a variety of strategies, but a key feature is that they normally seek to take majority control of their portfolio companies. In 2006 and 2007, a record amount of capital was committed to private equity buyout funds, both in nominal terms and as a fraction of the overall stock market. Buyout commitments and transactions rivaled, if not overtook, the activity of the first wave in the late 1980s that reached its peak with the USD25bn buyout of RJR Nabisco in 1988. However, post the financial crisis of 2008 new fundraising by buyout funds has declined very substantially (Kaplan and Stromberg, 2009).

Despite the publicity generated by buyouts of very large companies such as RJR Nabisco in the U.S.A. and Boots plc in the U.K., most buyout firms are involved in the purchase of "middle-market" companies of enterprise values up to €500mn. Such companies often respond well to the tools and approach that buyout firms adopt.

Venture capital funds

Venture capital is a broad subcategory of private equity that refers to investments typically made in companies in the very early stages of their development. Venture capital is also typically associated with investments and innovative companies that have potential for high growth. Venture capital frequently focuses on new technologies, such as clean-tech. These young companies have significant information asymmetries due to the fact that they have a very short history and their value lies mainly in hard-to-value intangible assets.

Unlike buyout investing, venture capital funds normally take a minority stake in their portfolio companies. Moreover, venture capitalists usually invest in syndicate with other venture capital investors. Although the venture capital funds take minority stakes, they receive significant rights that protect their investment such as veto rights on major decisions or board seats. These funds invest in different stages, each stage representing a different milestone in a company's evolution. We describe these funds and their investments in detail in Chapter 17.

Venture capital funds typically aim for capital gains as a result of their investments since the startup and high-growth companies they have in their portfolio do not usually have the financial ability to pay dividends or interest on debt. Venture capital funds not only supply the necessary capital but also significant knowledge to the firms they invest in by providing financial, administrative, and strategic advice or by facilitating network opportunities.

Mezzanine funds

Mezzanine funds first arose in the mid-1980s when investors began to use subordinated debt with some equity participation (in the form of warrants) to provide another layer of debt financing for highly leveraged buyout (LBO) transactions. Most private equity firms with "mezzanine" in their title are involved in this type of investing.[5]

The subordinated debt in which mezzanine funds invest is often structured with partly accruing interest, meaning that only a portion of the interest charge has to be paid in cash on a periodic basis with the remainder being rolled up and payable at maturity (this type is also called "pay-in-kind debt"). Equity participation in the form of warrants (i.e., "equity kickers") provides additional returns on the upside which compensate for the higher risk taken with subordinated debt.

Distressed investment funds

Distressed investing is involved in special situations—mainly financially troubled companies. Because many distressed investments are buyouts, this category intersects with the previous one. The distressed category encompasses two broad substrategies including:

- "Distressed-to-control" or "loan-to-own" strategies where the fund acquires debt securities in the hope of emerging from a corporate restructuring in control of the company's equity.

- "Special situations" or "turnaround" strategies where the fund provides debt and equity investments (i.e., "rescue financing") to companies undergoing operational or financial challenges.

2.4.2   Life of a private equity fund

Most private equity funds are organized as limited partnerships, with private equity firms serving as general partners of the funds, and large institutional investors and wealthy individuals providing the bulk of the capital as limited partners. These limited partnerships typically have a life of 10 years with extension clauses that allow this life to be extended, normally subject to investor consent. Typically, these funds raise equity at the time they are formed, and raise additional capital when investments are made. This additional capital usually takes the form of debt when the investment is collateralizable (such as in buyout investments) or equity from syndication partners when it is not (such as in venture investments).

The life of a typical private equity fund is divided into three main periods:

(1) The fundraising period

This is the period during which the investors pledge capital to the fund. Pledges of capital to the private equity fund are known as committed capital. It can take up to 18 months or more for the investment manager (prospective GP) to raise a new fund. The actual timing depends on the stage in the business cycle, the nature of the investment strategy being proposed, and the credentials of the investment manager (e.g., whether the fund is a "first time" fund or forms part of a well-established fund series). Normally, funds will have a series of "closings" as increasingly more limited

---

5. The term mezzanine has an alternative meaning within the private equity industry. It is also referred to as a form of late-stage venture capital investment in companies that are close to an initial public offering. This type of funding (also termed "growth capital") can be provided by other financial intermediaries, including hedge funds, banks, insurance companies, or specialty finance firms. This financing is typically in the form of subordinated debt with some additional equity participation in the form of options.

partners have their commitments accepted into the partnership. At the final closing the last of the LPs will be admitted and the fund will be closed for new capital. Committed capital does not need to be paid to the fund all at once but rather when investments are made.

(2) The investment period

During the investment period the GP is tasked with sourcing, evaluating, and executing investments consistent with the investment strategy of the fund. This period normally lasts between 3 and 5 years from the year of the final closing (*vintage year*). Over this period GPs make investments in various companies (*portfolio companies*). Typically, funds with the same vintage year are frequently compared with each other to assess their relative success.

When a GP identifies an investment opportunity, it "calls" money from its LPs up to the amount committed (undiscounted), and it can do so at any point in time until the investment period of the fund ends. Such capital "calls" are referred to as *drawdowns* or *takedowns*. The investors share in the risk and benefits of the performance of companies in which the fund invests, but have no active involvement in the management of these companies or the partnership once their capital is committed.

At the end of the investment period the GP cannot draw down further capital to fund further primary investments (new deals). The end of this period normally also sees a change in the management fee structure payable to the GP. During the life of the fund the GP's role is to maximize the value of the investments already made. This may include some additional acquisitions to create value within certain portfolio companies.

(3) The harvesting period

This is the period during which the GPs exit the investments of the fund and distribute the proceeds net of fees to investors. The GPs use the following 5 years after the investment for improvements in the performance of these companies. The expected holding period for an individual portfolio company is normally well below 10 years, and most commonly in the range of 3 to 7 years before the GP exits, by means of an initial public offering, sale to another private equity firm, or to a strategic buyer.

The GP distributes the proceeds to its LPs either in kind (i.e., shares) or in cash when investments are liquidated. The timing of these exits and, thus, the cash flows to investors is typically unknown ex ante. Extensions to the life of the fund might be necessary to ensure successful exits. The distribution is based on the "waterfall" provisions in the fund partnership agreement. These provisions indicate how the distributed funds will flow to the investors:

- First, the investors will receive back the capital invested in the fund
- Second, investors might be paid a preferential return on that capital (usually 8%)
- Third, after proceeds in excess of the drawn capital plus the preferential return have been distributed, the general partner can begin earning carried interest, in the first instance via a "catchup" mechanism.

2.4.3 Fees

GPs are compensated for managing the partnerships that they establish through an ongoing fees and a share of the profits from the investments that the fund makes (termed "carried interest"). There are several sources of revenue for the private equity firms that manage the funds: (1) management fees, (2) carried interest, (3) monitoring and transaction fees.

(1) Management fees

The bulk of the fixed revenue earned by the GPs comes from management fees, calculated as a percentage of the fund's size. These fees are usually paid quarterly and can be determined using four different methods: fixed fee for the whole life of the fund; decreasing schedule of fees; constant rate but with changing basis (changing from committed capital to invested capital); and, finally, using both decreasing rate and changing from committed to invested capital.

Over the lifetime of the fund some of the committed capital is used for these fees while the remainder is used to make investments in portfolio companies. The former part is the *lifetime fees* while the latter is *investment capital*. The portion of the investment capital that has already been employed in portfolio companies is known as *invested capital*.

Typically, while the fund is in its investment period the management fee amounts to between 1% and 2% of the total committed capital of the fund. This fee is used to pay for the day-to-day expenses of managing the fund. This includes the full costs of maintaining the investment team and generally conducting investment business. Among smaller funds (of less than £1bn) the typical fee is 2%. Significantly larger funds normally operate with lower fee percentages to reflect the aggregate scale of the fund. LPs are reluctant to accept fee levels which would see significant value accrue to the managers of the fund in the absence of investment performance. It is normal for funds to have a "step-down" in their management fee at the end of the investment period. Typically the fee basis moves from 1 to 2% of the committed capital to 1 to 2% of the cost of the investments that have been made by the fund. Management fees typically end after 10 years, although the fund can be extended thereafter.

In circumstances when a private equity fund makes poor investments and carried interest (see explanation below) is very small, GPs may become dependent on the management fees especially for large funds that generate significant fee income. Rather than risk exiting poorly performing investments that receive reasonable offers, the incentives might be to delay such realisations and wait for the life of the fund to wind down in order to keep the more lucrative fee revenue.

Basic example. Assume that a private equity firm raises a private equity fund with USD2bn of capital commitments from limited partners which is being fully invested or paid in fees. At a 2% management fee, the private equity firm would receive USD40mn per year for the 5-year investment period. The fund invests the difference between the USD2bn and the cumulative management fees (over the life of the fund) into companies. The management fees decline over the following 5 years as the fund liquidates its investments.

(2) Carried interest ("carry")

All GPs earn variable (performance-based) revenue from carried interest. The GP's carried interest reflects the share of the aggregate profits that the GP can claim from a successful investment. Most normally carried interest is calculated and paid on the entire fund of LP interests as this allows for better alignment of interest between the LP and the GP. However, in certain circumstances, carried interest can be generated on a deal-by-deal basis. This is a relatively rare structure in Europe; however, it is considerably more prevalent in the U.S.A.[6]

The precise mechanism by which carried interest is generated and paid is complex and details vary from one situation to another. However, the basic premise is straightforward. Normally, funds charge a fixed carry of 20% of the profits of the fund (i.e., *carry level*).[7] This means 20% of the gross capital gain generated by the fund is distributed to the GP (and then subsequently allocated among carry-holding individuals pro rata to their respective interests). The remaining 80% of the gross proceeds are distributed to the LP pro rata to their individual investments in the partnership. A carry of 20% is very much market standard; however, some groups have successfully negotiated a higher figure or indeed a "ratchet" mechanism where increasingly higher percentages of carry are paid for exceptional investment performance.

To protect the interests of LPs most carry schemes employ a "hurdle" return (i.e., *hurdle rate or preferred return*).[8] Typically, this is set at 8% and means that carry only becomes payable after the cost of investments has been returned plus the hurdle return on the capital cost of these investments which grows at 8% compounded per annum. Under these terms, LPs would receive every dollar of exit proceeds until they had received back their entire committed capital plus the hurdle rate, and then the GPs would receive 20 cents of every dollar after that. Another approach is for the GP to "catch up" with the LPs after the preferred return is paid. In other words, the GPs receive more than 20 cents of every dollar, after the payment of the preferred return, for a period (i.e., *catch-up period*) until they receive the full 20% of the gross profits that were initially distributed to LPs. The presence of a hurdle rate in the partnership agreement achieves a few objectives:

- It discourages the GPs from taking excessive risks
- It motivates the GP to exit the investments early
- It ensures that the LPs obtain a minimum return that is potentially superior to public market investments (although no risk adjustment is considered)
- It eliminates GPs that are not able to deliver a successful investment strategy.

Basic example: Continuing the example above, assume that the fund's investments turned out to be quite successful and the fund managed to realize USD6bn from its investments, a profit of USD4bn. The LPs would receive back their capital committed plus a preferred rate of return of 8%, as the fund started to exit successful investments. Once the LPs receive their full preferred returns, the GPs would be entitled to a carried interest or profit share of USD800mn (or 20% of the USD4bn profit).

6. The "fund as a whole" approach in the U.K. and Europe means that all capital contributions of investors are returned before the GP begins to receive any carry. Under the U.S. "deal-by-deal" approach the general partner receives carry upon each realized investment to the extent that the investors' capital necessary to acquire that investment has been paid first. The U.S. approach basically accelerates the receipt of carry by GPs. Clawback provisions, however, require the GPs to return the excess carry received if subsequent exits generate losses.

7. In their recent study of private equity funds Metrick and Yasuda (2010) find that in their dataset the overwhelming majority of fundsincluding all 144 BO fundsuse 20% as their carry level. The clustering of the carry level around 20% is consistent with the prior literature; for example, Gompers and Lerner (1999) report that 81% of their sample VC funds use a carry level between 20% and 21%.

8. In many cases, the limited partnership agreements of venture funds do not specify a hurdle rate.

(3) Monitoring and transaction (deal) fees

In addition to management and carry fees, GPs sometimes charge deal and monitoring fees that are paid by the portfolio companies.[9] The precise nature of these fees, how they are charged, and how the economic benefit is shared between interested parties is a contentious area and seems set to come under increasing scrutiny in the future. However, while these are in themselves substantial they are modest in comparison with the carried interest that can be earned on a fund. These fees are commonly split 50–50 between GPs and LPs although there is a lot of variation.

Typically buyout funds charge a transaction fee to the company which is purchased that is between 1% and 2% of transaction value. These transaction fees are another way for buyout funds to earn revenue. From the perspective of an LP, all that matters is that some fraction of the committed capital is not going directly to purchase a company, so the GP must somehow find a way to create enough value to replace that loss.

Monitoring fees are yet another way for private equity funds to earn a revenue stream. LPs make this an indirect way to pay the GPs for their services. From the perspective of the LPs, it should not matter whether these payments come directly through management fees or indirectly through monitoring fees, as long as the GP can create sufficient value to justify them. As with transaction fees, it is difficult to get hard evidence on the size and frequency of these fees. Annual monitoring fees typically vary between 1% and 5% of EBITDA, with smaller companies at the high end of this range and larger companies at the low end. Since these fees vary with firm performance, they are a component of variable revenue to the GPs.

2.4.4 Fund example

Travis Capital is seeking to raise a fund of £250m to make investments in the U.K. You are interested to model the vehicle to understand the pattern of cash drawdowns and distributions. You also want to understand the pattern of gross and net returns to investors.

To do this you need to ask several questions regarding the fund's activities. In this example we make a series of assumptions about all the key elements and combine them to show the resulting outputs. Clearly, a number of different scenarios can be modeled resulting in many differed outputs.

1. *How much of the total commitments of the fund will be "drawn" and how much invested?* Travis raises a fund of £250m of commitments. We assume that 80% of this total is actually invested (leaving the balance for management fees plus a buffer). Furthermore, we assume startup costs borne by the fund of 0.3%.

2. *What fees will the fund charge both in managing the vehicle and in performance fees?* Management fees are set at 2% of commitments for the investment period (set at 5 years). The management fee then sets down to 2% of the cost of invested assets for the remaining life of the fund. No deal fees are charged. We further assume a performance fee of 20% of gains above a hurdle rate.

3. *What "hurdle" mechanisms are in place regarding the flows of capital?* The hurdle rate is 8%, payable subject to a payment waterfall.

---

9. In some cases these fees might be offset against the management fees. The amount of offset ranges between 50% and 100% depending on the negotiated partnership agreement and the ability of the investors to negotiate.

4. *How many investments will the fund make? How large will each investment be?* In terms of the underlying investments we assume the fund makes 15 investments of £13.3mn (80% × £250mn/15).

5. *What will the patterns of these investments be over time?* For simplicity, we assume that all 15 investments are spaced evenly throughout the 5-year investment period of the fund.

6. *What returns will these investments generate? When will these returns be realized?* We assume each investment generates a return of 2.5× the cost of the capital invested, that 100% of the gain is received on the exit of the deal and that value within each investment builds over the period up to the exit date according to the pattern below:

> Year 1—25% of total value
> Year 2—45% of total value
> Year 3—60% of total value
> Year 4—80% of total value
> Year 5—100% of total value/exit.

Results

After running this scenario we compute that the fund will draw down £233.5mn of the £250mn of commitments. Thus, the undrawn commitments are £16.5mn. Of the drawn commitments, £200mn were invested into deals that yielded gross proceeds of £500mn (a gross IRR of 20% and a multiple of 2.1×), the rest of £33.5mn or 2.6% of total commitments were paid on management fees. Additionally, this fund generated carried interest of £53.3mn. LPs will receive total distributions of £413.2mn after all fees (a net IRR of 15% and a multiple of 1.77×).

We present two plots in Exhibits 2.2 and 2.3: one for the cumulative drawdawns and distributions and another for the cumulative cash flows received by the investors

---

EXHIBIT 2.2

PATTERN OF DRAWDOWNS AND DISTRIBUTIONS

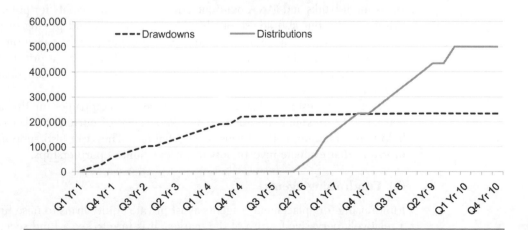

EXHIBIT 2.3

CASH FLOW BALANCE FOR LIMITED PARTERNS

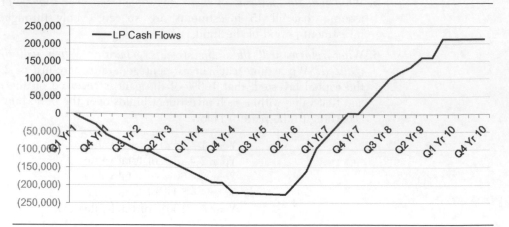

---

throughout the life of the fund. The limited partners break even on their investment during the third quarter of Year 7 of the fund.

2.5 ADVISORS AND AGENTS

With a growing level of sophistication of the private equity market, various groups of intermediaries have developed, aiming to support and assist market participants. Their formation has helped to raise the efficiency and transparency of the market. These are the agents and advisers who facilitate the search by private companies for equity capital, place private equity capital, raise funds for private equity partnerships, and evaluate partnerships for potential investors. These intermediaries overall reduce the costs associated with information problems that arise in private equity investing.

The types of agents and advisers for main market participants are discussed below.

(a) Investment banks

Investment banks and M&A boutique advisory firms are agents for potential issuers of private equity but also advise on the structure, timing, and pricing of private equity issues and assist in negotiations. First, they provide search, valuation, and advisory services by identifying firms that are potential candidates for a private equity investment, accumulating information and data about these firms, and distributing it to potential investors.

Second, investment banks offer assistance to companies in the assessment of contractual terms and conditions. Their knowledge of current market conditions can help with obtaining better terms in negotiations. They can also support institutional investors that evaluate investments in various limited partnerships.

(b) Fundraising agents

Fundraising (or "placement") agents assist private equity firms to raise funds. They are a relatively pervasive feature of the market. It is rare to see a fund successfully raised without the involvement of a placement agent in some form. The possible exception to the rule would be the GPs who have successfully raised several funds, have deep and long-lasting relationships with investors and substantial dedicated in-house investor relations teams. GPs that are attempting to raise very large sums in excess of USD1bn, that have no track record, and that specialize in investments which are less known to institutional investors, frequently approach agents for help. These agents add credibility and recognition to the fund being raised and accelerate the fundraising process. Their role is also to educate investors and expand the potential investor universe by addressing relevant queries during the fund due diligence process.

Even a limited partnership that has experienced and well-respected GPs may prefer to take advantage of an agent's contacts and expertise in raising money from large pension funds rather than undertake the fundraising themselves, given the complex decision-making structures involving trustees and investment committees at large institutional investors. Some partnerships may also use agents for fundraising simply to avoid diverting the GPs' time from investment activities, as on average partnership funds can take 18 months or longer to raise.

These agents charge fees between 0.5% and 2% of funds raised, given the specialized nature of the task of raising money from public and corporate pension funds and also the still small number of agents that compete in this market.

(c) Other advisors

These advisors cover a large array of services to the private equity fund, from legal aspects to accounting and communication issues. Most GPs still retain the services of outside advisors, regardless of how much in-house resources they may already have put in place.

The role of the legal advisors is to advise on legal aspects of private equity transactions or even the structuring of the private equity fund. For instance, they deal with the legal issues of the acquisition agreement with the vendor in a buyout transaction, with the investment documentation of a venture-financing deal, the portfolio company's arrangements with its bankers, the general partners' positions as directors or employees of the portfolio company, etc.

The accountants act as financial advisors to the general partners and the management of the portfolio companies. They can carry out feasibility studies at an early stage of an investment opportunity. They also advise in detail on management business plans and on negotiations with the owners of the companies in which the fund invests.

Other advisors include personal tax advisors to the general partners or the management of the portfolio company as well as pension advisors. Sometimes, portfolio companies need the advice of insurance brokers in order to obtain cover for insurable risks.

2.6 REFERENCES

AXELSON, U., STRÖMBERG, P.J., JENKINSON, T., AND WEISBACH, M.S. (2009) "Leverage and pricing in buyouts: An empirical analysis," EFA 2009 Bergen Meetings Paper.

CITYUK (2010) *Private Equity 2010, www.thecityuk.com*

CUMMING, D., FLEMING, G., AND SCHWIENBACHER, A. (2007) "The structure of venture capital funds," *Handbook of Research on Venture Capital*, Edward Elgar Publishing.

FLEMING, G. (2010) "Institutional investment in private equity: Motivations, strategies, and performance," in D. Cumming (Ed.), *Private Equity: Fund Types, Risks and Returns, and Regulation*, John Wiley & Sons Ltd.

JENSEN, M. (1989) "Eclipse of the public corporation," *Harvard Business Review*, **67**, 60–70.

GOMPERS, P.A., AND LERNER, J. (1996) "The use of covenants: An empirical analysis of venture partnership agreements," *Journal of Law and Economics*, **39**(2), 463–498.

GOMPERS, P.A., AND LERNER, J. (1999) "An analysis of compensation in the US venture capital partnership," *Journal of Financial Economics*, **55**(3).

KAPLAN, S.N., AND STROMBERG, P. (2009) "Leveraged buyouts and private equity," *Journal of Economic Perspectives*, **23**(1): 121–146.

LITVAK, K. (2004) "Venture capital limited partnership agreements: Understanding compensation arrangements," working paper, University of Texas Law and Economics Research.

METRICK, A., AND YASUDA, A. (2010) "The economics of private equity funds," *Review of Financial Studies*, **23**(6), 2303–2341.

3

Performance measurement in private equity

3.1 OVERVIEW

A major reason for the explosive growth of the private equity market since 1980 has been the expectation by institutional investors of financial returns substantially higher than those of other investment alternatives. However, the measurement of private equity funds' performance has been historically a relatively difficult task as private equity funds have no obligation to publicly disclose detailed information about their investments in privately held companies and the returns on these investments. Application of the Freedom of Information Act in the U.S. and the publication of the David Walker Guidelines for Disclosure and Transparency in Private Equity in the U.K. has made certain private equity fund performance data more readily available to a large set of investors.

Nevertheless, computational issues still remain due to several factors. First, private equity investments are substantially more risky and illiquid than other assets. These characteristics make comparisons between the performance of the private equity funds and alternative investment benchmarks a difficult challenge. Second, the ability of some investors to gain access to the asset class may be limited. Third, there is a lack of widely accepted benchmarks for the private equity asset class. This prevents investors from fully understanding the risk, return, and correlation characteristics of private equity investment returns and thus the extent of the allocation to private equity in a diversified portfolio.

An investment in a private equity fund reflects an investment in a stream of cash flows provided by the underlying portfolio companies. This seems to be similar to an investment in a bond that pays coupons but in fact there are significant differences between the two. Bonds typically have a cash outflow at the beginning and cash inflows whose timing and magnitude can be predicted with relative accuracy given the terms of the bond contract. However, in the case of a private equity fund, the timing and magnitude of the series of cash flows is highly uncertain. The GPs can draw down the money over a period of up to 5 years from the fund's inception and might not draw down the entire committed amount. Similarly, the GPs distribute the proceeds from the fund's investments back to the investors as they are realized but the timing and the

This chapter has been co-authored with Oliver Gottschalg (HEC Paris).

39

amounts of these realizations cannot be predicted in advance because many times they are dependent on market conditions. Further, the largest cash inflows tend to occur towards the end of the fund's 10-year life (this is particularly the case with venture funds, whose average investment holding period is usually longer than that of buyout funds).

As a result, measuring the performance of an investment in a private equity fund is not obvious. The most widely used measure of performance is the internal rate of return (IRR). Calculation of the IRR takes into consideration the timing of cash contributions and distributions to and from the fund partnership and the length of time an investment in the fund has been held. Another widely accepted measure of performance is the investment multiple. This measures the proceeds received from a fund plus the valuation of any remaining investments divided by the capital contributed by the investors to the fund.

3.2   MEASURES OF PRIVATE EQUITY FUND PERFORMANCE

During the holding period, private equity funds' investments in companies are typically fair-valued based on various valuation methods.[1] In subsequent years, the sale of portfolio companies or public offerings of their shares generates cash and/or stock distributions to investors. Thus, over time, increasing proportions of a fund's performance reflect actual cash distributions received by investors, rather than valuation estimates of portfolio companies.

Despite the fact that private equity funds have an agreed fixed life of 10 years, the funds will often show a residual asset value for a considerable time beyond these 10 years before they are finally wound up. This amount represents investments that have not been realized yet and where the underlying investee companies still have value.

In order to calculate the rate of return of a private equity fund, the final and definitive valuation of the residual assets in the fund's portfolio and the exact timing and magnitude of the cash distributions to investors are needed. By definition, this implies that the rate of return can be measured without error only when the fund is at the end of its life. That is the time when information about cash distributed to investors is fully available and when the residual investments left in the portfolio should be insignificant.

As stated above, the private equity industry typically computes two sets of measures to determine the performance of a private equity fund: multiples and internal rates of return (IRRs). These are computed during the fund's life based on portfolio company valuation estimates. We first discuss below the multiple measure which is relatively straightforward and then we switch our attention to IRR.

3.2.1   Multiples

Return multiples are probably the most popular way to assess the performance of a private equity fund investment. They are computed by dividing the value of the returns

---

1. Under recent accounting rules (SFAS 157 in U.S. GAAP and IAS 39 in International GAAP), fair value is defined as the amount at which the portfolio company could be bought or sold in a current transaction between willing parties, or transferred to an equivalent party, other than in a liquidation sale. The increasing use of fair value accounting in the financial reporting of private equity funds came about because investors have come to the conclusion that fair value meets their informational needs better than other measurement bases such as the historical cost or amortized cost, among others.

from the private equity fund by the amount of money invested in the private equity fund. These ratios of "proceeds over investment" are simple to calculate and easy to interpret: if the fund triples the investor's money, the fund return multiple is 3. Funds typically report three multiples: distributed value to paid-in ratio, residual value to paid-in ratio, and total value to paid-in ratio. Paid-in capital is the portion of the committed capital that has been drawn down for investments, fees, or fund expenses.

Distributed value to paid-in ratio (DVPI)

The DVPI (also called *realized multiple*) measures the ratio of distributions to the limited partners compared with the amount of capital contributed by the limited partners to the fund:

$$\text{DVPI} = \frac{\sum_{t=1}^{t<T} \text{CF}_i^{\text{PAST,RECEIVED}}}{\sum_{t=1}^{t<T} \text{CF}_i^{\text{PAST,PAID IN}}}$$

where $\text{CF}^{\text{PAST,RECEIVED}}$ are net cash flows distributed by the fund as a result of past investments (including the return of uninvested funds and stock distributions as well); and $\text{CF}^{\text{PAST,PAID IN}}$ are cash flows paid into the fund (e.g., capital invested, fees paid).

This multiple is usually relevant for measuring the performance of the fund towards the end of its life. DVPI shows the net performance of the investment relative to all money that has been used either to compensate the management of the fund (fees and carry) or to invest in portfolio companies. DVPI is not a good measure of fund performance when the fund is at a stage where the capital committed has not been fully invested (i.e., at the beginning of the fund's life).

Residual value to paid-in ratio (RVPI)

The RVPI (also called *unrealized multiple*) measures the net asset value of the private equity fund (i.e., unrealized gains) compared with the amount of capital contributed by the limited partners to the fund:

$$\text{RVPI} = \frac{\text{NAV}_T}{\sum_{t=1}^{t<T} \text{CF}_t^{\text{PAST,PAID IN}}}$$

where NAV is the net asset value (i.e., the fair value of the PE fund's holdings at the date of TVPI computation T); and $\text{CF}^{\text{PAST,PAID IN}}$ are cash flows transferred to the fund (e.g., capital invested, fees paid).

This ratio is most useful early in the life of a fund before there have been many distributions since it reflects the extent of portfolio companies' revaluation. RVPI shows the current value of all remaining investments (portfolio companies) within the fund relative to the total amount paid in to date by the investors. This measure is highly dependent on the quality of the valuation estimates provided by the fund and may show a misleadingly low return if the fund is accounting for its investments very conservatively.

Total value to paid-in ratio (TVPI)

TVPI is the ratio of the current value of remaining investments within a fund plus the total value of all distributions to date to the total amount of capital paid into the fund to date. In other words, it is the sum of DVPI and RVPI:

$$\text{TVPI} = \frac{\sum_{t=1}^{t<T} \text{CF}_i^{\text{PAST,RECEIVED}} + \text{NAV}_T}{\sum_{t=1}^{t<T} \text{CF}_i^{\text{PAST,PAID IN}}}$$

where $\text{CF}^{\text{PAST,RECEIVED}}$ are net cash flows distributed by the fund as a result of past investments (including the return of uninvested funds and stock distributions as well); $\text{CF}^{\text{PAST,PAID IN}}$ are cash flows transferred to the fund (i.e., capital invested and fees paid); and NAV is the net asset value (i.e., fair value of the PE fund's holdings at the date of TVPI's computation T).

TVPI is perhaps the best available measure of performance before the end of a fund's life. Residual asset values should be subject to conservative accounting valuations and should ideally represent the lower limit of capital that will be distributed at a later stage. The ratio of the sum of past distributions and residual value to paid-in capital therefore should represent the minimum multiple that investors can expect from private equity investments.

Drawbacks

The main drawback of multiple measures is that they do not take into account the length of time for which the money has been invested in the fund. In other words, a return multiple of 3 does not capture the difference between an investment that took 10 years to triple investors' money and an investment that achieved the same return in only 2 years. In the former case, the investor might have been better off with a basic investment such as a savings account or a government bond, whereas the performance of the second investment is clearly very good and cannot be matched by a "safe" alternative. In addition to the fact that multiples disregard the time value of money, they also do not inform the investor about the underlying risk involved or whether early realizations have been reinvested.

There is, however, a solution to these problems that allows the funds to maintain simplicity by reporting multiples and at the same time accurately inform investors about the return performance. The prospectuses of the funds should report the multiples together with additional information such as:

- The *duration* of the investment. Obtaining a multiple of 3 over a shorter period is significantly better than obtaining a multiple of 3 over a longer period.

- The *extent of leverage* used to achieve the multiple (in the case of buyout funds). Obtaining a multiple of 3 by borrowing one euro for each euro invested is significantly better than obtaining a multiple of 3 with two euros borrowed for each euro invested.

- The *amount of capital reinvested*. Some GPs recycle their early realizations rather than distribute them to LPs, thus creating a higher multiple than GPs that do not recycle the capital.

3.2.2 Internal rates of return

The internal rate of return (IRR) is defined mathematically as the *discount rate* which, when applied to discount a series of cash outflows followed by cash inflows, returns a net present value (NPV) of zero. The most intuitive way of understanding the meaning of the IRR is to think of it as the equivalent constant interest rate during the life of the fund at which a given series of capital drawdowns must be invested in order for the private equity investor to earn a given series of cash distributions as income. Typically, IRRs are computed net of management fees and carried interest to reflect the net return to the investor.

The IRR reflects the effects of the timing of cash flows in the private equity fund's portfolio. Thus, private equity returns are calculated and stated not as annual returns of any particular year, but as *compound returns* from a certain year (the year of formation of the fund, the vintage year) to a specified year. The performance figures for the private industry as a whole, or any part of it, are based on funds that are grouped together because they were raised in the same year. Their returns thus become that *vintage year return*.

A time-weighted rate of return measure, like the one typically used in public markets, does not capture the critical effects of cash flow management within the control of the GP and, thus, is not comparable with the IRR measure used for private equity returns. The time-weighted rate of return eliminates the effects of interim cash flows by revaluing the portfolio at each cash flow date while IRR gives weight to interim cash flows based on their amounts and timing. This is why IRR is sometimes called the *money-weighted rate of return*.

Interim vs. final IRRs

The IRR is computed during the life of the fund, even in situations when the fund is not close to liquidation. This IRR measure is called an *interim IRR*. This IRR is the discount rate that equates the present value of all capital drawdowns with the sum of the present value of all cash distributions accruing from it and the present value of the unrealized residual portfolio (i.e., unliquidated holdings):

$$\sum_{t=1}^{t \leq T} \frac{\mathrm{CF}_t^{\mathrm{PAST,RECEIVED}}}{(1 + \mathrm{IRR}_{\mathrm{interim}})^t} + \frac{\mathrm{NAV}_T}{(1 + \mathrm{IRR}_{\mathrm{interim}})^T} = 0$$

where $\mathrm{CF}^{\mathrm{PAST,RECEIVED}}$ are net cash flows distributed by the fund as a result of past investments (including the return of uninvested funds and stock distributions); and NAV is the net asset value (i.e., value of the PE fund's holdings at the date of the computation T).

When the fund is liquidated, we can then compute the *final IRR* which is the discount rate that equates the present value of all capital drawdowns to the present value of all cash distributions during the life of the fund. After a fund is liquidated there is nothing left in the portfolio (i.e., NAV in the formula above is zero or insignificant).

In general, interim IRRs fluctuate around the final IRR towards the end of the fund's life. While we can get a good picture of the performance of an individual private equity fund after a few years, certainty can only be obtained much later when the fund is liquidated. Most of the evidence on performance presented by the industry or by researchers relies on interim IRRs since many funds in their samples are not liquidated.

Drawbacks

There are several important drawbacks of IRR measures that investors should be aware of when reading private equity funds' placement memorandums:

- The IRR formula is complex depending on the timing and variances in the cash flow amounts. Without a computer or financial calculator, IRR can only be computed by trial and error.

- IRR calculations are highly sensitive to the timing of the cash flows. Two similar private equity fund investments over a 10-year period can produce very different IRRs although the multiples on investment can be the same. The private equity fund that distributes cash earlier will report a higher IRR. Because of the sensitivity of IRR to the distribution of cash flows, GPs have incentives to drive up the IRRs by running just-in-time cash management.[2] As a result, they draw funds from investors on a deal-by-deal basis and, despite the 10-year life of the fund, the period of time during which the invested capital is returned can be as short as 2 years.[3]

- IRRs implicitly make the assumption that after one portfolio investment is over and cash is distributed to investors, another equally profitable opportunity to place money just received by investors can be found. This so-called reinvestment hypothesis is questionable, especially in the private equity sector. There is no guarantee that a private equity investor can identify similarly profitable investment opportunities at little notice. Consequently, the effective rate of return received by investors differs from IRR. They are equal only if investors can reinvest intermediary distributions at the IRR rate and borrow at the IRR rate to finance intermediary payments, which is impossible in practice.[4] Therefore, investors prefer a short investment with a high IRR only if the proceeds can be reinvested at attractive returns. If this is not the case, a longer investment with a lower IRR may actually be preferable.

- Interim IRRs are measured based on investments that are not fully realized, as captured by the fund's net asset value.[5] The value of these investments is computed using valuation methods applied by the fund itself which may or may not follow valuation standards set by the industry. Aggressive revaluations of ongoing investments could exaggerate the performance or, alternatively, valuations may not be updated.

- Another shortcoming of the IRR is due to its mathematical computation. In some cases in which the private equity fund generates a certain mix of positive and negative cash flows over time, the iterative algorithm which computes the IRR

2. The incentives to report high IRRs are due to the fact that GPs usually raise money for new funds based on their past performance as measured by IRR.

3. Limited partnership agreements often allow the reinvestment of capital coming from investments that are shorter than 12–18 months. Such a provision provides an incentive to exit the first few investments early because it offers GPs a chance to reinvest funds. The reinvestment increases the assets under management thus generating potentially higher fees and carried interest.

4. When IRR is high the spread between IRR and the effective rate of return is positive and large, and when IRR is low the spread between IRR and the effective rate of return is negative and large (Phalippou, 2009).

5. This criticism applies also to multiple measures based on the net asset value.

may not converge or may generate multiple IRRs that make the NPV of these cash flows equal to zero (i.e., the solution is not unique).

- The IRR assumes that all cash flows are invested at the same discount rate. In the real world these rates will fluctuate, particularly with longer term investments.

Modified IRRs

Investors can overcome the IRR problem with the reinvestment assumption by using a modified IRR (MIRR). To compute a modified IRR, it is assumed that the capital committed to a private equity fund is put in a "savings" account that earns the hurdle rate (which is usually 8% per year). The capital called by the fund is taken out of this account and the capital distributed goes back to this account. When the fund is liquidated, the MIRR is computed by taking the amount on the account at liquidation and dividing it by the capital paid in, everything raised to the power of 1 divided by the duration. This basically boils down to calculating NPV but gives a per annum number.

The range of returns obtained for a fund is much more narrow when a measure like the MIRR is used because it better reflects the actual effective rate of return. Despite the advantages of using the MIRR, many practitioners resist using it because it requires that a cost of capital and reinvestment rate be identified.

The J-curve effect

As already explained, it is very important to note that a definitive evaluation of an individual private equity fund can only be made when a fund is liquidated. During the early years of a fund, the value of the (interim) IRRs tends to be zero or negative. This is due to several factors:

- The management fee and startup costs of a limited fund partnership are usually financed out of the first drawdowns. This means that part of the sums drawn down during the first year do not create net book value for the limited partnership.

- Conservative valuation guidelines suggested by industry bodies suggest that investments are valued at acquisition cost at the very beginning. Upward adjustments are only made when the portfolio company has substantially increased in value. If the early investments do not perform well they are immediately written off. Since these losses usually impact earlier on the fund performance than successful realizations, interim valuations of young funds tend to be lower.

- The portfolio valuations may take a few years to reflect the efforts of the GPs. Over time, as progress is made, the valuations will increase above the acquisition cost.

In the final years of the fund, the higher valuations of the businesses are confirmed by the partial or complete sale of companies, resulting in cash distributions to the investors which offset their initial investment. As a result, interim IRRs turn positive. This pattern generates the so-called J-curve, which we reproduce in Exhibit 3.1.

The J-curve is generated by looking at the cumulative interim IRR. The first observation plotted represents the interim IRR of the fund for the first year of its life, the second represents the interim IRR of the fund for the first 2 years of its life, the third the interim IRR for the first 3 years, and so on. Interim returns are typically negative in the early years (the "investment phase"), breakeven in middle years (the "maturity phase"), and positive in later years (the "harvesting phase").

EXHIBIT 3.1

THE J-CURVE OF A PRIVATE EQUITY FUND

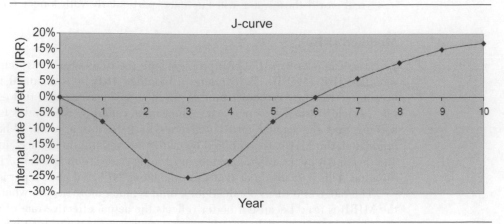

The plot in Exhibit 3.1 is not saying that the fund returned −25% in Year 3. It is saying that if we map all the cash flows from the beginning of the fund to the end of Year 3 an IRR of −25% can be calculated. Similarly, it is not saying that the fund's performance for Year 6 was flat. It is saying that from the beginning of the fund to the end of Year 6 positive cash flows exactly match negative cash flows, so that the IRR of the first 6 years is zero.

The J-curve here does not represent the J-curve of any particular fund in real life, but is a broad generalization of what is expected. The only difference will be the shape of the curve. For example, buyout funds tend to pay back their capital more quickly than venture funds. Yet, even this generalization is enough to show that it is meaningless to look at the performance of a private equity fund in its early years.

Computation of IRRs for a set of private equity funds

In order to assess the performance of an individual private equity fund, IRRs are calculated as above. However, there are several ways of measuring the returns of a group of private equity funds. One alternative is to calculate an average IRR across all funds in the group. This method, however, may be problematic since it attaches equal weight to all funds irrespective of their size. The solution is to calculate a capital-weighted IRR in order to reflect these size differences.

The approach above does not take into account the different time periods that the money has been under management. For this reason, another alternative can be used. Monthly cash flows from all funds in the group can be pooled and, then, the IRR is calculated based on the net cash flows of this "mega" fund. This method is referred to as *pooled IRR* and is used for most private equity performance measurement exercises.

Computation of the aggregate IRR of a group of funds is usually appropriate only when the funds in the group have similar investment strategies and the same vintage year. In many situations, private equity firms that raise money report the performance of all their past funds by pooling them arbitrarily. The arbitrary grouping of funds to compute a pooled IRR can bias performance dramatically, especially when firms have had some highly performing investments in their early days. By grouping all funds together, the reinvestment assumption of the internal rate of return will kick in—that future payouts can be reinvested and earn the same return as past payouts—and will hide bad recent investments.[6]

3.2.3   Alternative performance measures

Another measure which can be used to assess the performance of private equity funds is the net present value (NPV). This measure is difficult to implement in practice. First, it requires an assumption about the cost of capital whose magnitude varies from one private equity investor to another. It is clearly not straightforward for a fund to choose its discount rate given the different types of investors it may have. Some, however, argue that the hurdle rate of the fund can be used as a constant discount rate. In addition, it makes the performance comparable across many funds since most have a similar hurdle rate of about 8%. Second, NPV is scale dependent thus making cross-sectional comparisons impossible.

3.3   BENCHMARKING PRIVATE EQUITY PERFORMANCE

3.3.1   How to pick a benchmark?

Private equity performance can only be assessed by comparing the return of the private equity fund with something else (e.g., past returns, peer returns, or public equity benchmarks). Benchmarks need to have some qualities to be valid. Applying the framework of Bailey et al. (1990) to private equity markets, the ideal benchmarks should be:

- *Unambiguous*. The investor should have certainty about the names and weights of all securities in the benchmark portfolio
- *Investable*. The investor should be able to invest in the benchmark by adopting a totally passive approach
- *Measurable*. The investor should be able to calculate returns to the benchmark reasonably frequently
- *Appropriate*. The benchmark chosen should be consistent with the style of the private equity firm whose performance is being assessed
- *Accepted*. All investors in the private equity market must be able to have current knowledge of the benchmark
- *Specified in advance*. Benchmark computation should be constructed prior to the start of an evaluation period.

Given the criteria above, investors have a difficult time to find appropriate benchmarks when attempting to measure and monitor the performance of private equity funds. Generally, they use two sets of benchmarks which are not perfect:

1. *Peer group*. Investors may use an average (or median or first-quartile) return of a group of private equity funds. This peer group generally includes private equity funds with similar investment focuses, raised in the same geographical location and during the same vintage year as the private equity fund assessed.

2. *Public market equivalent*. Investors may compare private equity returns with

---

6. Phalippou (2009) finds that about 50% of private equity buyout firms pool all their investments when reporting results.

some index of public equities. We discuss the procedure to construct such a benchmark in detail in Section 3.3.2.

Benchmarking the performance of private equity funds is particularly important when investors decide to invest in a new fund. Typically, an investor relies on analyzing the historical performance of the funds managed in the past by the GP raising the new fund. This past performance is compared with some established peer group indexes published by data providers and/or national industry associations. A judgment is then made depending on whether or how often the GP's prior funds fall within the first or second best performance quartiles according to these benchmark statistics. Such a comparison is of value, as it allows assessment of the performance of the GP's prior funds relative to the population of all funds of the same stage and geographic focus that were raised in the same vintage years.

With respect to the second benchmark, the standard approach used in most industry statistics is to compare the long-term IRR of private equity investments with the annualized long-term passive ("buy-and-hold") returns from public market indexes. However this approach ignores important aspects, such as the irregularly timed cash flows of private equity fund investments and the differences in operating and leverage risk between private equity fund investments and "the market" as captured by these indexes. These issues confound attempts to compute standard time-weighted returns typical of publicly traded assets for comparison. The IRR, a cash flow–weighted return rate, which is widely used for ranking competing funds, cannot be directly compared with time-weighted public benchmarks. More importantly, since IRR does not measure the opportunity cost of capital, it ignores the benchmarking objective. Given these difficulties, we provide a more detailed discussion of methodologies that use public market benchmarks in the following section.

3.3.2   Public market equivalent

The basic idea behind the comparison of private equity fund investments with public market investments is fairly straightforward. We simply answer the question: "How much (less) performance would a *similar* investment in the public markets have generated?" Things become tricky, however, when it comes to the exact definition of "similar" investments. The investments of the "mimicking" public market portfolio need to match the private equity investments in terms of:

a. The timing of their cash flows (investments and distributions).

b. The systematic risk pattern of private equity, which is much more challenging.

Cash flow timing

One pragmatic approach to the construction of a mimicking portfolio is to calculate the returns to a broad public market index, such as the S&P 500 or the MSCI Europe, assuming that the pattern of stock purchases and sales matches the timing of the PE cash flows. This method underlies, for example, the "public market equivalent" calculations provided by Thomson Venture Economics and has also been used in a number of academic studies (e.g., Kaplan and Schoar, 2005). It explicitly assumes, however, that the risk pattern of private equity investments is identical to that of the chosen public market index. However, companies who receive venture capital financing are typically much smaller and younger and those who receive buyout funding typically have much higher financial leverage than the average company in a broad stock market index. Both these aspects influence the risk pattern substantially.

Risk adjustments

One possibility to correct for the differences in risk between private equity investments and public market investments is the matching of operating betas and financial leverage between the two.[7] The exact determination of the risk-adjusted mimicking portfolio requires for each transaction of the private equity fund:

    i. Identification of a peer group of publicly traded companies with the same operating risk.

    ii. Calculation of the equity betas for each of these "public peers".

    iii. Unlevering these beta factors to derive their operating or unlevered betas.

    iv. Determination of a market-weighted average of these operating betas for every peer group.

    v. Relevering of these betas on the level of the PE investment's transactions at closing and exit. The unlevering and relevering procedures also require specification of the risk, which is borne by the lenders, the risk of tax shields the equity investor can benefit from, as well as an applicable corporate tax rate.

An equal amount of equity for every private investment transaction of the fund is invested in a representative market portfolio and is levered up with borrowed funds to the same beta factor as the private equity investments at closing. The risk of the public market transaction is then adjusted every year tracking the risk of the private equity investment in the fund. Therefore, every position is liquidated annually, interest is paid, debt is redeemed, and the residual equity is levered up again with borrowed funds (respectively, funds are lent) to the prevailing beta risk of the private equity investment. This procedure is repeated until the exit date. A detailed description of the corresponding methodology can be found in Groh and Gottschalg (2009).

Alternative approach

We suggest another approach to provide a more accurate account of the relative performance of private equity fund investments and to gain further insights into the different components of private equity returns. This approach avoids the use of betas which can be unreliable due to data limitations. It spans four distinct stages:[8]

Stage 1. Compute the IRR of the private equity fund based on the net of fees cash inflows and outflows. The residual values of unrealized investments (i.e., the net asset values or NAVs) can be considered as accurately reflecting the net present value of these investments and, thus, they can be treated as a final cash inflow in the IRR calculation. Alternatively, these residual values can be set to zero (this is the most conservative approach). The IRR measure of the fund's net cash flows will be compared with the return on the public benchmark.

---

7. This has been demonstrated in a number of recent academic studies. For example, Ljungqvist and Richardson (2003) and Phalippou and Zollo (2005) consider operating betas in their analysis of private equity investments, while Groh and Gottschalg (2009) benchmark the fully risk-adjusted performance of U.S. buyouts by correcting for differences in operating risk *and* financial leverage.

8. This approach is based on the methodology we have implemented for our BVCA report (Gottschalg et al., 2010).

Stage 2. Replicate the approach used in standard industry statistics and calculate the compounded annualized passive ("buy-and-hold") returns from a public market index over the period from the first cash flow to the last cash flow of the fund. The IRR that results from this computation is the return that could be obtained by an investor that makes investments in the amount of the capital committed to the private equity fund at the day of the fund's first cash flow and liquidates this position at the day of the fund's final NAV.

Stage 3. Consider the particular timing of the cash flows and the operating risk of the private equity funds to compute an industry-matched (unleveraged) public market equivalent (PME) return. Similar to the approach taken by Kaplan and Schoar (2005) and Phalippou and Gottschalg (2009), the observed annual net cash flows from private equity can be imposed on a public market index by purchasing shares to represent negative net cash flows and selling shares to represent positive net cash flows. Since the aim is to capture the operating risk of the underlying investments, the investment is not in the overall market index but in industry indexes that reflect the industry mix of the private equity fund. This industry mix should change from one year to another to track any industry changes that occur at the fund level.

To calculate the industry-matched (unleveraged) public market equivalent (PME) return, the portfolio holdings in sector indexes are constructed according to the industry mix at the fund level. The final value of the public equity market portfolio created is calculated based on the market value of the portfolio on the last day of the fund (i.e., the day on which the net asset value of the fund is available). This value can be thought of as being the additional final cash flow representing the liquidation value of the final public equity market portfolio. The IRR of the industry-matched (unleveraged) public market equivalent is calculated by using both the mimicking annual net cash flows and the final cash flow:

- If the final value of the industry-matched (unleveraged) PME portfolio is positive, it implies that the public market has produced a greater return than the private equity whose cash flows were superimposed on the public market index.
- If the final value of the industry-matched (unleveraged) PME portfolio is negative, it implies that the public market has produced a smaller return than private equity.

The IRR that results from this computation is the return that could be obtained by an investor that makes investments in the industry-matched bundles of public securities and exits these securities by mimicking exactly the timing of the private equity investments and exits.

Stage 4 (for buyout funds). Estimate the performance of the buyout fund had it not been levered up, but had the typical degree of leverage of publicly traded firms at the time. This enables differentiation between the portions of buyout returns attributable to fundamental performance, on the one hand, and the effect of higher leverage, on the other. The difference between the average level of leverage of the portfolio of the buyout fund and the level of leverage of industry-matched public market investments should be assessed in each year. An investment vehicle that replicates the level of leverage of industry-matched public market investments for the buyout fund can be constructed. Finally, the IRR of the cash flows that investors in such a vehicle would have achieved is computed.

This four-step approach allows decomposing the buyout funds' returns into four elements: (a) the portion driven by returns on the broad stock market (the IRR of the vehicle at Stage 2), (b) the portion driven by the performance differential between the broad stock market and returns of the industry sectors in which the fund invests after taking into account the timing of these investments (difference between the IRR computed at Stage 3 and the IRR computed at Stage 2), (c) the effect of buyout-typical leverage on the buyout funds' returns (difference between the IRR at Stage 1 and the IRR of the vehicle at Stage 4), and (d) the residual intrinsic value generation of the buyout fund (i.e., the private equity alpha—difference between the IRR at Stage 4 and the IRR at Stage 3).

3.4 ACADEMIC FINDINGS ON THE PERFORMANCE OF PRIVATE EQUITY FUNDS

The academic literature on private equity returns vs. public equity returns is mixed. Most statistics provided by industry associations as well as some academic papers report superior returns for private equity investments depending on the assumptions made.

Ljungqvist and Richardson (2003), for example, evaluate 73 mature private equity funds of one large U.S.-based investor over 1981 to 2001 and find that private equity investments of closed funds outperformed the S&P 500 by more than 5%. They also find that the main factor behind the large excess returns was the early timing of the investments. Kaplan and Schoar (2005) study the returns to private equity and venture capital funds and report that the performance of the 746 funds in their sample was above that of the S&P 500. However, they find that private equity fund investors earn slightly less than the S&P 500 index net of fees. They also find that experienced funds and U.S.-based funds offer significantly higher performance.

Similarly, a very recent study by Gottschalg et al. (2010) in collaboration with the British Venture Capital Association and Pantheon, a large London-based fund of funds, concludes that U.K.-based buyout funds' private equity continues to outperform investment strategies based on public market equivalents. Their report finds that the IRR for their sample buyout funds stands at 19.61% outperforming the public market benchmark equivalent by about 4.5%.

The paper by Phalippou and Gottschalg (2008) finds that private equity funds underperform the S&P 500 by 3% to 6% per year net of fees. They show that few adjustments contribute to the discrepancy relative to other studies. First, they show that the estimated performance of private equity funds depends critically on the valuation of non-exited investments at the end of the sample period. For instance, Kaplan and Schoar use funds' self-reported values of such non-exited investments and find that the value-weighted performance of PE funds exceeds S&P 500 return by about 5% per year. However, Phalippou and Gottschalg (2009) argue that it is more reasonable to write off non-exited investments after a certain period of time.

Second, the prior academic studies that investigate the performance of private equity funds might be subject to selection biases. Some of these studies use funds that are larger, more U.S. focused, and more experienced. These characteristics are all found to be positively related to performance. They also obtain the data from large LPs (e.g., Gottschalg et al., 2010). However, it has been shown that funds in which large LPs invest tend to perform better. The results in Lerner et al. (2007) indicate that performance can vary dramatically across different types of LPs.

Third, these prior papers do not capture the significant variance in the funds' returns. Lerner et al. (2007) document a wide dispersion of returns among private equity funds. In this case, reporting the aggregate performance of IRRs can be misleading. As described in more detail in Phalippou and Gottschalg (2009), aggregating IRRs from multiple funds overstates the historic performance. They find that both the "size-weighted average IRRs" and "pooled IRRs" overstate performance, relative to the more accurate method of weighting each fund IRR by the product of the present value of its investments and its duration.[9] The magnitude of this overstatement is about 3% per annum.

Regardless of the study, there is enough evidence to show that, historically, private equity fund managers have created substantial value: their average gross of fees performance usually exceeds public market indexes significantly. However, the fee structure of private equity funds is such that the average private equity fund manager may collect significantly more fees than whatever value is created. Thus, the investor in the average private equity fund is left with returns that are below those of a broad public market index fund. The evidence also indicates that returns to private equity have at times substantially exceeded those in the public market. To a certain extent, returns have been driven by capital availability: for both venture and buyout funds, returns have been greatest during periods when relatively small amounts of capital were available. Conversely, there is evidence that periods of large capital availability depress future returns.

3.5 WHY THE PERFORMANCE ASSESSMENT OF PRIVATE EQUITY REMAINS DIFFICULT

The question of how private equity as an asset class performed compared with investments in the public markets has received much attention from practitioners and academics alike. Data limitations and the long investment cycle in PE make it difficult to provide a definitive answer to this question.

Challenge I: Finding an unbiased sample of the entire PE universe

To assess whether returns of PE investments are on average better than comparable stock market investments we have first of all to compose a dataset on the returns of the entire universe of PE investments—or at least a representative (unbiased) sample thereof. This first step constitutes a major challenge already in an industry that calls itself private and that is famous for its lack of transparency. Professional database service providers such as Thomson Venture Economics have over many years been able to compose what can be considered the most comprehensive commercially available database on PE investments and PE fund returns. Still, it is fair to assume that even this enormous database does not capture every single PE investment ever made. Missing data become a problem as we cannot exclude the possibility that the missing deals perform substantially better or worse than those included in the database, which would make a performance assessment based only on the deals in the database inaccurate.

---

9. Phalippou and Gottschalg (2009) report that the correlation between fund performance and duration is very high and negative. Funds with longer duration do perform worse, hence the average IRR is upwardly biased.

Phalippou and Gottschalg (2009) show that to some extent such a bias is present in the Thomson Venture Economics PE Fund performance database. At least for the early vintages, the funds included in the performance database seem to be less successful in terms of their exit success rate (percent exited through IPO or M&A) than the larger universe of funds. This suggests that even the large sample of funds in the performance database may be upwardly biased by about 2% per annum. Several academic studies draw on much smaller samples, sometimes with an obvious bias introduced in the way the data were collected. While statistical methods to correct for these biases are able to make such data suitable for the analyses performed in the respective papers, these biases still limit the generalizability of any performance assessments (e.g., Ljungqvist and Richardson, 2003; Cochrane, 2005; Groh and Gottschalg, 2009).

Challenge II: Avoiding noisy valuations of residual values

Whenever private equity funds still have unrealized investments on their books, any performance measurement becomes unreliable. Absent market valuations for the corresponding companies makes it difficult to determine their fair valuation at a given point in time at a sufficient level of precision. Potentially, these investments are developing nicely and will soon lead to realizations at a value far beyond the residual value recorded on the books. Maybe the residual value, which is fair-valued, is quite accurate as a proxy for the NPV of future returns. But, it is also possible that the residual values belong to living dead investments that will never return a dollar to investors and should have been written off some time ago.

It is easy to see that the greater the percentage of residual values, the less precise the performance measurement for the corresponding sample of funds. One way out of this dilemma is to look at funds with no or minimal residual values only. However, such a selection filter exchanges one evil for another, as fully realized funds tend to be relatively better performers than same age funds that still have many deals on the books. Consequently, one can increase precision, but sample bias also increases.

A practical way to deal with this challenge is to look at a sample of entire vintage years' sufficiently mature funds, in the sense that these were raised so long ago that non-exited investments should be few and in any case unlikely to lead to substantial cash distributions. A detailed analysis of the residual value dynamics of mature funds performed in Phalippou and Gottschalg (2009) strongly suggests that these correspond for the most part to "living dead" investments and should consequently be written off. In any case, the residual value challenge limits the analysis to funds raised a long time ago and limits our ability to gain insights into more recent PE performance.

Challenge III: Considering different risk patterns of PE and stock investments

It is intuitive to see that PE investments have very different risk characteristics compared with stock market investments. They differ in key determinants of investment risk, such as the average size and age of the company (especially relevant in the VC segment) and in the degree of financial leverage (especially relevant in the buyout segment). If the risk of investing in a portfolio of pre-IPO startups or mature but highly leveraged businesses is substantially different from that of an investment in, say, the S&P 500, it is clear that the returns of the two options cannot simply be compared. Instead, a careful adjustment for the risk pattern of all private equity investments has to be made.

In sum, we need data on the entire universe of private equity investments, or at least a sufficiently large and unbiased subsample thereof. This data should cover a time period up to as recently as possible, while non-exited investments should be absent from the data or their residual values should be unambiguously determined. Finally, we do not only need cash flow data for these investments, but also relevant information to determine their risk pattern (i.e., at least the companies' age, size, sector of activity, and the evolution of the capital structure over the time of the investment). Today, such a "first best" performance assessment is unavailable, as data limitation in the notoriously secretive PE industry makes it impossible to gather the necessary data.

3.6 CONCLUSIONS

The most important challenge going forward is to refine our understanding of what works and what does not work in private equity. Only then can we make sure that the enormous potential of the private equity model to generate great returns and to benefit the companies that are acquired is being fully realized. Giving up the illusion of genuinely high private equity returns across the board may actually be the first step in the process.

The constant repetition of the (empirically unwarranted) claim that private equity offers great returns per se is in fact dangerous for the industry. It attracts additional capital at times when fund sizes and deal sizes are at a record high. Most importantly, it also attracts capital from less experienced and less sophisticated investors who may end up backing the wrong GPs, based on the belief that even a random fund selection process would lead to supposedly attractive average returns. In fact, these average returns are not necessarily attractive and, more problematic for the industry as a whole, as long as less skilled GPs continue to get funded average future returns are less likely to increase than they otherwise would be.

3.7 REFERENCES

BAILEY, J., RICHARDS, T., AND TIERNEY, D. (1990) "Benchmark portfolios and the manager/plan sponsor relationship," in F. Fabozzi and D. Fabozzi (Eds.), *Current Topics in Investment Management*, Harper & Row, pp. 71–85.

COCHRANE, J. (2005) "The risk and return of venture capital," *Journal of Financial Economics*, **75**, 3–52.

GOTTSCHALG, O., TALMOR, E., AND VASVARI, F. (2010) "Private equity fund level return attribution: Evidence from U.K. based buyout funds, working paper," London Business School.

GROH, A.P., AND GOTTSCHALG, O. (2009) "The opportunity cost of capital of U.S. buyouts," working paper.

KAPLAN, S.N., AND A. SCHOAR (2005) "Private equity performance: Returns, persistence, and capital flows," *Journal of Finance*, **60**, 1791–1823.

LERNER, J., SCHOAR, A., AND WAN WONGSUNWAI (2007) "Smart institutions, foolish choices: The limited partner performance puzzle," *Journal of Finance*, **62**(2), 731–764.

LJUNGQVIST, A., AND RICHARDSON, M. (2003) "The cash flow, return and risk characteristics of private equity," NBER Working Paper 9454.

PHALIPPOU, L. (2009) "Beware of venturing into private equity," *Journal of Economic Perspectives*, **23**(1), 147–166.

PHALIPPOU, L., AND GOTTSCHALG, O. (2009) "The performance of private equity funds," *Review of Financial Studies*, **22**(4), 1747–1776.

PHALIPPOU, L., AND ZOLLO, M. (2005) "Performance of private equity funds: Another puzzle?" working paper, University of Amsterdam.

56

4

Private equity investing in emerging markets

4.1 INTRODUCTION

4.1.1 Overview

Emerging economies represent over 80% of the world's population and landmass, yet their financial markets are currently much smaller relative to GDP than those in mature markets. The total value of all emerging market financial assets is equal to just 165% of GDP, well below the 403% financial depth of developed economies (Roxburgh and Lund, 2009). While the share of emerging economies in the global capital market has grown fast, this has been from a relatively small base. Emerging economic regions, which do not yet have well-developed markets for finance, continue to have a considerable need for capital to finance infrastructure and communication investments. Consequently, private equity (PE) investors are increasingly being attracted by this need for financing, especially from non-quoted corporations.

A discussion of the PE landscape in emerging economies is inherently difficult due to the very large variation in their characteristics. As a result, any sweeping generalizations that we make on the causes and consequences of the PE investment activity in these countries are disputable. Nevertheless, we make an attempt to provide a basic framework that describes what we think are the most important issues associated with PE investing in emerging markets.

Emerging markets appeal to PE investors for many reasons. Strong economic growth, improving macroeconomic conditions, better physical and legal infrastructures, increased receptivity of governments to foreign investors, and the prospects of earning high returns encourage PE investors to allocate more capital to these markets. In addition, geographically dispersed investments potentially reduce the risk of capital supply–demand imbalances, with their adverse consequences for PE investment returns. Recently, however, emerging markets started to become increasingly integrated with developed markets, both in absorbing foreign PE capital and as global suppliers of PE capital. Such developments have potentially negative implications for the future performance of the PE asset class and the volatility of its returns.

This chapter has been co-authored with Sonia Katyal.

Emerging countries are a heterogeneous group and PE investors must take into account important differences across these countries. The pace of political change and the size of economic gains have not been uniform. Some countries managed to achieve macroeconomic stabilization while others are still working on it. Also, development of market institutions, such as legal infrastructures that provide the basis for effective corporate governance, has been slower and difficult to achieve in many emerging economies. The lack of well-defined property rights and strong legal frameworks in some countries provide additional hurdles. However, domestic policies are becoming more market oriented and governments are opening their countries to foreign markets and joining regional trading associations. Most importantly, emerging economies have enormous growth potential.

Although emerging economies need a significant influx of PE investment to enhance growth, competitiveness, and entrepreneurial activities, investment biases and risk perceptions limit the PE investment supply which is still small compared with that in developed economies:[1]

1. The investment process, from limited partners (LPs) to the end-recipient corporations, is *geographically biased*. When general partners (GPs) in developed markets are searching for deal opportunities, they tend to focus on a particular region, or even just on a single country. Usually these regions are not very far from the GP's home country.

2. Institutional investors' approach to *international capital allocation* is not efficient. In their search for diversification, LPs commit capital to funds that sometimes overinvest in some geographical locations and underinvest in others. This investment pattern is reflected in emerging economies, where some regions are the dominant recipients of PE funds and interest from investors. For example, in 2009, emerging Asian markets captured 63% of investments by value, and 70% of emerging market PE transactions by number (EMPEA, 2010a). China accounted for the largest share and India for the second largest.

3. Many institutional investors view the *potential risks* associated with investments in emerging markets as being too high. While these markets might provide significant financial returns, there is concern among some investors that the returns fail to compensate enough for the inherent investment risks. Such investors demand risk premiums to compensate even for procedural uncertainties associated with making, managing, and collecting investments in emerging markets. Information on local rules and enforcement is often asymmetrically known and sometimes there is inconsistent application of written laws. Relative to industrial countries, emerging countries typically have weaker legal, institutional, and regulatory safeguards to give investors confidence that their rights will be enforced.

4.1.2 What are emerging countries?

It is important to define what we mean by "emerging countries" because economic indicators alone are not always sufficient. An *emerging country* can be defined as a country that satisfies two criteria: (1) it is in a transitional stage, typically moving from a closed to an open economy and having embarked on a reform path, and (2) it faces a rapid pace of economic development, undertaking significant efforts to improve its

---

1. It is worth noting that more than two thirds of the LPs surveyed recently plan to increase their exposure to emerging countries in the future (EMPEA/Coller Capital, 2010).

past, DFIs encouraged investors to support identical PE fund structures and investment approaches even though sometimes the regulatory and legal frameworks in emerging countries did not provide adequate investor protection. Fund managers used similar processes for identifying, analyzing, and valuing target companies as well as for structuring deals, despite large differences in accounting standards, corporate governance practices, and exit possibilities across different emerging countries. Nowadays, PE funds have become less foreign and more local and DFIs have started to assist governments to strengthen regulatory environments.

In recent years, SME financing has been a priority in development policy. DFIs invest directly via intermediaries, through PE funds and through other types of financial institutions, which then provide access to finance for SMEs in all types of sectors. DFIs also invest indirectly in financial institutions that are expected to support SME financing.

4.2.3 Outlook and prospects

Economic forecasts suggest that the emerging markets will continue to grow for the foreseeable future, supporting *growth-based* PE investments. While the PE industry is fundamentally about value creation through improving companies, the emerging markets have been dominated by PE growth capital.

Recent studies by leading industry associations such as EMPEA have highlighted some key trends relating to LP interest in emerging markets. LPs have started to view emerging market PE opportunities as attractive, both in their own right and relative to PE opportunities in developed markets. The emerging market share of new PE commitments is therefore expected to continue to grow. In terms of performance, most LPs now expect emerging market PE funds to outperform the PE industry as a whole.

Geographically, most studies rank China, India, and Central and Eastern Europe as the most attractive, followed by South East Asia, Latin America, the CIS, and MENA. Africa is ranked lowest. A recent survey found that, over 2011 and 2012, the greatest expected expansion in commitments from existing investors will be in Asia: 44% of investors plan increased exposure in China, 28% in India, and 26% in other Asian emerging PE markets (EMPEA/Coller Capital, 2010). However, things are changing rapidly and it is difficult to predict which regions will provide the best investment opportunities in the future.

4.3 DRIVERS FOR PE INVESTMENTS IN EMERGING ECONOMIES

Successful PE investments require interesting businesses in which to invest, combined with access to equity stakes with influence over those businesses. Both the breadth and the quality of emerging market PE opportunities have improved markedly over the last few years. An adequate flow of good opportunities can support the setup of local investment teams that can significantly improve the quality of PE transactions. Deal origination and structuring, and advice to the investee companies, can be done more effectively in close proximity and in real time by PE professionals embedded in the local market.

Favorable growth drivers (which we discuss below) have partly sustained the increase in PE activity, but three main macrotrends have amplified both the number of good PE investment opportunities, and the PE funds' ability to acquire control in emerging countries:

- *Economic liberalization policies* and the *movement to market-based economies* since the 1990s have increased entrepreneurial and new business activity and, thereby, have increased the potential for PE investments.

- The *opening up of economies* has increased both the business opportunities to expand and the competitive pressure, leading to more business owners seeking private capital.

- The close identification of family status and wealth with direct ownership of a company has reduced. This in turn has generated *less reluctance to engage in third-party equity financing*. The last decade has seen a gradual shift in the appetite for PE capital, even by family-owned businesses.

Emerging markets have been attractive to risk capital investors, and increasingly so in recent years, mainly for the higher growth rates and consequently the higher expected financial returns. However, expected growth is not the only thing that matters to investors in the PE asset class. Many criteria affect PE funding. We list below the main macrofactors that likely affect the flow of PE investments to and across these economies:

- *Expected growth rates* and *market size*—most PE investors look at the size and growth rates of their domestic markets when investing in emerging economies. The growth rates seen in developing economies are often higher than in mature developed economies—sometimes more than double. This is a significant driver for investing in businesses positioned to cater for these markets. Market size is also a critical determinant for most PE investors. Much attention has therefore been focused on the so-called BRIC countries of Brazil, Russia, India, and China, whose combined population constitutes more than 40% of the world's inhabitants. This huge population implies a large—and fast-growing—consumer pool, which should provide economies of scale as well as high and continuous growth rates for businesses that exploit this potential.

- *Political stability*—PE investing patterns show that democracy is important, but political stability is even more so. China and India, for example, receive by far the largest volume of PE investments. They are polar opposites on the political spectrum, but both have excellent track records of stable government and peaceful transitions of power. By contrast, emerging regions that are inherently politically unstable receive a lower level of interest from PE investors.

- *Legal environment, investor protection, and corporate governance*—company and investment protection laws have undergone revision, and codes of corporate governance practice have been introduced in many emerging markets, in part supported by assistance from multilateral development banks. Transparency and disclosure have also improved and international accounting standards (IFRS) are increasingly adopted. The legal environment as well as accounting and corporate governance practices have a natural impact on the success of any external investor. In particular, large PE investors have a wide choice of investment options, hence they are naturally drawn to environments that are better structured and supportive for foreign investors. Funds that operate in common law countries may find it easier to enforce their rights in commercial contracts.[3] On the one hand, better laws facilitate deal screening and origination but also investors' board representations and the use of desired types of securities. The choice of securities in emerging market PE deals is driven by the legal and economic circumstances of the nation and of the investing PE fund (Lerner and Schoar, 2004). On the other hand, weak property rights and investor protection are likely to limit PE investors' ability to run efficiently the businesses in which they invest. Further, rigid labor market policies might make a PE market less attractive. Institutional investors might hesitate to invest in countries with exaggerated labor market protection and immobility.

- *Receptivity to private investments*—sometimes certain industries are off limits to foreign investors but, on the whole, most emerging countries are clearly receptive to private investments in all industries. Since PE is a relatively long-term asset class and needs a favorable environment for new businesses to succeed, regulatory policies and entry barriers often have a significant impact on PE investment flows. The sectors that are high growth and are accompanied by favorable policies for investment naturally attract more PE investment.

- *Stage of development of the capital markets*—there is a strong relation between PE activity and the development of public local stock markets. The ability to exit PE investments via listings on local stock exchanges is the strongest driving force for PE investing. As a result, PE capital flourishes in countries with deep and liquid stock markets (Gompers and Lerner, 2000). There is a growing list of highly profitable exits by selling to strategic and financial investors, which suggests that experienced PE firms are adapting successfully, but this element of risk will continue to differentiate emerging markets from developed markets. Finally, the availability of debt financing, a key source of capital, is an important determinant of the success of PE investments that focus on capital-intensive businesses.

- *Maturity of the local PE market*—the maturity of the local PE is reflected by the number of players and supporting institutions, such as law firms, investment banks, M&A boutiques, auditors, consultants, and other advisors. If investors have confidence in the efficiency of the local PE market and the PE market has an established track record, they will continue to invest in follow-on funds. Annual PE fundraising volume depends on the previous year's market liquidity (Balboa and Marti, 2007). In addition, there is a positive relationship between the size of the economy and the level of PE activity. If an economy is too small, it falls outside the scope of internationally acting institutional investors, the main source of PE funds.

- *Availability of skilled human capital*—countries with a relatively deep pool of skilled human capital are more attractive than those with low-wage labour alone. Many emerging countries have well-regarded systems of higher education in technical disciplines, and therefore rank highly on the list of PE investments. If university systems are severely deficient, it makes it difficult to recruit

3. Judges develop common law through the decisions of courts and similar tribunals, rather than through legislative statutes or the actions of states' executive branches. That is, common law is based on precedent. Common law systems are usually found in emerging countries that trace their legal heritage to England as former colonies, such as Malaysia, Pakistan, India, and South Africa. Most Latin American countries as well as Russia and China, have legal systems based on the civil code, which relies on state-initiated legislation.

competent local managerial and technical personnel. This, in turn, acts to deter PE investors, who tend to prefer economies with a more efficient and developed pools of human capital.

Which of these factors is the most important? There is no clear agreement on this. Groh and Liechtenstein (2009) survey the relevance of some of these issues to institutional investors when allocating PE capital to emerging markets. They find that investors perceived protection of property rights and corporate governance as very important for international PE allocation decisions. These were followed by the assessment of the management quality of local GPs and entrepreneurs according to Western management standards, by expected deal flow, and by the amount of bribery and corruption. Institutional investors in PE are not particularly swayed by government programs to stimulate local risk capital markets. They rely on the quality of the GPs they invest in. The GPs in turn rely on the managers of the corporations they back. If investors' claims are poorly protected, or if they doubt the quality of their investees, or integrity in a host country, then they are likely to refrain from investing.

For these reasons PE investors favor India, Central Eastern Europe, China, and now increasingly Latin America. They are less attracted by South East Asia, the Commonwealth of Independent States, and Africa. We discuss investment risks in the following section.

4.4 RISKS OF INVESTING IN EMERGING ECONOMIES

Although institutional investors are attracted by the expected growth and entrepreneurial opportunities in emerging economies, they need to be aware of the potential risks. Emerging markets can indeed provide a significant financial return on PE investments, but much of this is driven by inherent risks. PE investors are expected to weigh up the risk–return tradeoff before they commit funds to the various emerging markets.

PE investors face risks in emerging markets both at a country and at an individual company level. At the country level, these risks tend to reflect political risks, economic volatility, and regulatory risks, while for individual companies they often relate to gaps in corporate governance, management quality, and information disclosure. We start with a discussion of the main risks at the country level (macrolevel risks) and then continue with a discussion of risks at the company level (microlevel risks).

4.4.1 Macrolevel risks

While the long-term growth potential of the emerging markets remains significant, the path of growth is likely to be volatile. Moreover, emerging markets comprise a very heterogeneous group of countries: some will show steady long-term improvements and some will languish behind. At the same time, high economic growth in emerging markets exerts pressures on the prices of food and mineral resources which have contributed to mounting inflation in emerging markets. Rising inflation levels coupled with a recessionary environment can create short and medium-term uncertainty for PE investors whose investment horizon is usually medium term.

Political risks

Until the 1990s, PE investment in emerging markets was difficult, because of multiple restrictions on foreign direct investments. Most PE investments were provided by state-backed development finance institutions. From 1990 onwards, a series of reforms in emerging countries, which resulted from significant political changes, have made access easier for private providers of risk capital. After years of instability, the political risks in most emerging countries have been diminishing very fast. However, PE investors still need to be alert to political conflicts, which can generate wars, or riots, or just unpredictable changes in regulations. These have direct negative effects on PE investments. They are also associated with macroeconomic instability, which can quickly erode companies' attractiveness because of inflation, a poorly functioning financial system, high unemployment rates, or negative growth rates. One of the top priorities for PE investors should be an effective political analysis and a continuous monitoring of the political landscape in emerging countries.

Political risks not only indirectly affect an emerging market investment through their impact on the macroeconomic environment, they can also have direct effects. Some governments may protect local industries that create jobs and ignore international laws for political gains. What seems right for the local emergent economy may trump foreign investors' rights in courts, so they have to protect themselves at the front end by buying stakes in companies with other defenses. Lawsuits are an option, but may be expensive and ineffective, especially if the legal system is different. Therefore, PE investors from developed countries often emphasize good relations with the local government. This can speed up permit approvals and other government processes significantly and, sometimes, can provide a competitive advantage.

Currency risks

Most emerging countries' currencies fluctuate significantly, although some are tied directly to the U.S. dollar (China's yuan is a notable example). The PE investor should try to form a 3-to-5-year view of local currency depreciation relative to the currency in which the PE fund has been raised in the country of domicile. It is difficult to make currency forecasts, but they can be extremely informative when investing, because devaluations can easily "eat" the returns in, say, USD or EUR at the time of exit. Forecasts can be obtained from large financial institutions or commissioned from specialist advisors.

One way to deal with this particular risk is to allocate PE funds across different emerging markets, in the hope that such diversification will limit the potential losses due to currency movements. An alternative is to hedge investments denominated in foreign currency by using derivatives that are traded in currency markets.

Regulatory risk

Successful investing in emerging markets requires PE investors to master complex regulatory environments for competitive advantage. The legal and regulatory environment in many emerging countries is constantly changing (e.g., allowing certain businesses or activities and then disabling them). In addition, complex regulations and licencing requirements can vary across national, provincial, and city levels. These changes can be driven in part by economics but also by politics. Although sudden regulatory changes can be costly to PE investors, they can also provide good opportunities (e.g., licencing requirements can be leveraged as a barrier to competitive entry). Turning regulations to advantage should be a key skill of many PE investors in these markets. They need to have an inside track on regulatory changes that allows them to anticipate coming opportunities as well as pull out of disfavored sectors.

The problems of implementing legal frameworks and enforcement are accentuated in emerging markets, because local business owners tend to be adept at navigating the legal system. This puts outside PE investors at a disadvantage, particularly when they need to resort to the law to resolve contractual disputes. The best way to mitigate this problem is to partner with carefully selected local agents and intermediaries as a common modus operandi at some or all stages of the deal execution.

PE investors should also try to fund firms that are concentrated in one region and seek to build relationships with local authorities in order to be able to understand and manage the local regulatory regime that their funded firms face. Understanding and controlling the risk from regulatory institutions can become difficult and very costly if the PE firm's investments are geographically diverse.

Finally, PE investors can create innovative financial and legal structures that are a mix of local and Western structures. Offshore Western financial and legal structures, such as in the Cayman Islands or British Virgin Islands, provide a legal oasis where emerging market PE investors can still meet the objectives of investment protection and access to liquidity while adhering to local laws. The investor's limited partnership may be a permissible U.S. or U.K. entity but its portfolio company may be incorporated somewhere else. Simplistically, incorporating in efficient jurisdictions with strong legal frameworks permits instruments such as both preferred and common stock, employee stock options, and the ability to list on stock exchanges in developed markets, thus solving the lack of access to local capital markets.

4.4.2 Microlevel risks

Particularly in emerging markets where there is weak protection of investors' rights and the enforcement is poor, investors must be alert to the quality of the management in charge of the portfolio company and the corporate governance. When the broader macroeconomic environment is stable or positive, many corporate level risk factors may not come to the surface. However, in more challenging environments, the management and governance quality as well as the accuracy of the information reported by the company are likely to be key factors that differentiate successful PE investments.

Management risks

Managerial risk is one of the main drivers of poor investment performance, and it needs to be thoroughly assessed by the PE investor. Ineffective management, lack of focus, or failure to implement strategies properly can easily transform a good PE deal into a loss-making investment. Other managerial issues, such as corruption or lack of integrity, may also play a role.

Emerging countries may have many talented entrepreneurs and managers, but there is a perceived lack of professional managerial skills, particularly in sectors that require specialized knowledge. Good and experienced new managers are usually a scarce resource. Management turnover rates in some fast-growing emerging markets are high and the pool of world-class talent can be shallow, particularly for CFOs. However, there is talk of a reverse braindrain, especially due to the recent financial crisis and the improvement of professional education in these countries. Many educated professionals who worked abroad bring their experience back home. This phenomenon positively impacts the quality of the management teams put in place by the PE funds.

PE investors must always be mindful of their relationship with key managers in emerging markets. Replacing management, while possible, may become much more complicated in emerging markets as the loyalty of employees and possibly of customers is to key managers—not to the company as such. Replacing these managers may trigger replacing an entire management team.

Management risk can be minimized by using a selective recruiting process with detailed reference checks. The PE investor also needs to be aware of the changing environment and to provide competitive and timely incentives for very talented managers, in order to discourage them from leaving. Rapidly improving economic conditions and the limited pool of candidates combine to increase the competition for managerial talent. Aligning managerial, employee, and shareholder interests may require innovative approaches since employee stock options, a key instrument to incentivize employees in developed markets, may be simply unavailable as a financial instrument in emerging markets.

Corporate governance risks

In terms of corporate governance, the PE investor should put in place effective management information systems that can provide timely feedback on managerial performance and protect the invested capital. Installing and maintaining financial controls becomes critical as the company's capital must be viewed as separate from the local entrepreneur's personal finances. Hence, PE investors should install tight restrictions such as forbidding the purchase of speculative assets and unnecessary expenditures. In addition, good financial controls and receivables management can reduce the investment capital required to run the company.

PE investors should require board seats for the firms they fund. However, they need to be aware that the power and information provided to board members is sometimes less than in developed markets. Information can often be withheld from the board, and the influence of outside directors may be weak. In addition, the market for corporate control might be virtually non-existent. In part, this reflects the fact that in the regulatory environment of many emerging countries a board of directors is not required for a firm. Thus, it is more important to remain close to their invested firms to obtain the desired information and ensure its accuracy than to depend on a board seat for it.

Another way to minimize corporate governance risks is to use two classes of stock to guarantee that the investment has a preferential return—especially in cases of liquidation. The most commonly used instrument that guarantees this return is preferred stock, which is the class of stock that PE investors should hold. All other shareholders should receive common shares which may not have these special preferential rights. However, some emerging countries might not allow preferred shares (e.g., the most notable example is China). Other protection instruments are antidilution clauses or penalties for non-performance.

Information risk

PE investors always have to make investment decisions based on incomplete information that is controlled by management. This information asymmetry tends to be far more serious in emerging economies. Regulations in emerging markets do not require the same level of public information to be provided to the government or other regulatory bodies as in developed countries. Further, owners of private companies in these countries are used to retaining complete control of information and of its visibility. In addition, some countries have accounting and legal rules that leave considerable room for interpretation.

Valuation is more art than science in the best of circumstances, but this is particularly true in emerging markets. Forecasting future company performance is complicated by the dearth of reliable data on markets, competitors, and product pricing, and by the volatility that characterizes developing economies. It can also be hard to value a business at the time of acquisition or exit, because of thin domestic equity markets, which provide minimal guidance on comparable company values. Since the ability to accurately obtain full information on a firm is so constrained, due diligence in emerging markets commonly focuses on the entrepreneur's background and his or her contracts.

Very often PE investors face local managers who are not educated on international business and reporting standards. This could mean that a portfolio company could have one accounting book filled out according to international GAAP and one book completed according to local standards. And they do not have the same numbers. Even three sets of financial accounts are not uncommon, which makes processing the information and pricing a business appropriately a daunting challenge. Therefore, it is important that PE investors take the time to educate the owners and managers of local companies when investing.

In addition, to mitigate the information risks, PE investors should ask firms to produce financial reports in a form that is interpretable and can be verified. This usually requires that an international accounting firm is hired to help with the financials and audit of the firm.

Intellectual property risks

An important aspect relating to PE investments in emerging markets is the management of intellectual property rights. Protecting intellectual property can involve a change in thinking for most emerging market entrepreneurs. Many of them think of intellectual property quite differently from their foreign counterparts. In particular, they might not consider copying a crime. Different risks about intellectual property rights can arise. For instance, an entrepreneur or employee might want to split off another, independent enterprise even though it may be based on the intellectual property of the entity in which a PE fund invests. Also, some employees might come to the organization and use the proprietary intellectual property of their former employers. In yet another example, competitors may counterfeit a venture's products creating economic and reputation risks, especially as the costs of advertising escalates and the venture is approaching an exit.

To mitigate these risks PE investors have to instill the very concept of intellectual property and an understanding of the company's intellectual property rights in both the entrepreneur and the employees of the company.

4.5 MARKET STRUCTURE AND INVESTMENT CHARACTERISTICS

4.5.1 The role of local knowledge

PE investors going into emerging markets need to commit to these markets for the long term. If they cannot, then they are likely to have a difficult time competing with local PE firms and foreign groups who have gone local. Given the current crowded nature of the PE market, PE money has become more of a commodity than ever, so investment managers need to distinguish themselves. They need to build up a reputation for success and trust and the only way to achieve this is by spending time in emerging markets. This will also allow them to cultivate strong relationships with local partners who can help navigate and source deals and to collect local knowledge that puts them in a better position to assess the best deals.

The home offices of PE firms are not always able to bridge the culture and knowledge gap to understand why a certain emerging market branch is pushing certain deals. In fact, successful PE firms, who have local offices or have partnered with local PE firms, usually keep the final decision-making authority with the local fund managers. If the investment decisions are vetted at home, then many relationships may not work. If the ideas of the local representatives are constantly disregarded, they can become frustrated and leave. Such outcomes can be problematic given that good local representatives may be irreplaceable. Their knowledge and relationships may not be easily duplicated.

Therefore, a key feature of PE investing in emerging economies is that, even if most funding comes from investors based in the developed economies, the development of local knowledge is critical. The solution is not only to hire local partners, but also to come to the emerging market to learn and build trust with these local partners.

4.5.2   Deal dynamics in emerging markets

Screening and selection

PE funds in emerging markets are typically proactive in deal selection. Rather than wait for business proposals to land on their desks, or for investment bankers to make a pitch on behalf of a client, PE professionals typically approach companies they find attractive. This also avoids getting involved in a bidding auction.

Most funds still approach emerging markets with a generalist strategy, focusing on a basket of the most promising sectors, based on the size of transactions they seek. Funds with a single-sector focus, such as infrastructure, natural resources, or financial services, were slightly less prominent in 2009 than in 2008 or 2007. Each PE fund's strategy is tailored to the investment environment in each emerging market (e.g., funds recently focused more on consumer opportunities in China, agribusiness in Brazil, or telecommunications and financial services in Sub-Saharan Africa).

As a result of recent trends in deregulation and openness, most PE deals in emerging markets comprise companies targeting growth: two thirds (67%) of transactions fell into this category in 2009 (EMPEA Insight, 2010a).

Structuring and monitoring

Typically, once a firm has passed its initial screening, PE investors proceed with due diligence, which includes confirmation of the nature and status of the firm's product, production capability, market demand, and status of key relationships with other organizations. In emerging markets this process is complicated given the limited availability of accurate information. Local bureaucrats and business owners have significant control over information crucial to understanding the market and the regulatory environment providing a serious disadvantage to outside PE investors.

In addition, business owners in emerging markets may be reluctant in dealing with foreign PE investors. Building up a comfort level that would enable these individuals to judge the PE funds, and the PE funds to judge them is crucial, and takes some time. Learning about the founder, his colleagues, and even family is important in the due diligence process.

Once an investment is made, PE funds typically monitor their investments through memberships on boards of directors or via reporting mechanisms they set in place. They can also seek to protect themselves from abuses by having extensive minority protection clauses in the investment agreements. It is, however, difficult to anticipate all the potential problems, and the enforcement of the agreements is often problematic due to underdeveloped regulatory institutions like the court system and the commercial code.

PE investors' main goal is profit maximization. However, when monitoring their investment, they might need to recognize that the local entrepreneur or the local government departments with influence over the firm might have different goals. For instance, maximization of employment and/or production might be more important for these parties. Without careful oversight, firms can end up with extra employees and overproduction of goods that will result in unsalable inventory.

Investments in emerging markets are typically structured with the following common characteristics (see Schoar and Lerner, 2004 for a more extensive discussion):

- Minority positions are quite common and have proved not "too" risky. They have performed well in all forms of exit, indicating that the risks associated with minority positions can be managed effectively.

- Unlike developed markets, where the use of convertible preferred securities is common, in emerging markets more than one half of the transactions involve common stock while a significant subset employ instruments that are essentially debt. When preferred securities are not used, PE funds are more likely to obtain a majority of the firm's equity and to make the size of their equity stakes contingent on the performance of the company.

- Antidilution provisions which are common in developed markets are encountered far less frequently in emerging markets.

- Larger financings and transaction values are seen in emerging markets with a common law tradition. Also, transactions in these countries are generally associated with more contractual protections.

Exit strategies

PE investors in emerging markets should assess exit strategies rigorously before deciding on an investment. Despite the uncertainties of an event that will not occur for 3 or 5 years hence, it is important to ensure that the company's management understands and commits to the strategy.

The goal is to ultimately exit investments in emerging markets before the PE partnership is terminated. Exits through IPOs are very common. However, they may be problematic, even for successful investments. There are several reasons that contribute to this outcome:

- A host of laws on securities markets, disclosure, and accounting standards that should facilitate such IPOs are not yet in place in many emerging markets.

- The selection of which firms may list on the local stock exchange might be principally a state decision (especially in China).

- Local exchanges are very small and illiquid.

Consequently, many PE funds do not consider listing their investments locally but instead choose foreign exchanges. They also prefer to look for strategic buyers. This is typically the only major exit strategy readily available in many emerging markets.

Some PE investors in emerging markets are willing to experiment with new, more creative approaches to exit. For example, one Latin American fund has launched a mezzanine fund that offers debt financing with many of the same characteristics as equity, but provides investors with greater assurance of a steady income stream. Another has begun to recapitalize some successful portfolio companies, which allows the fund to realize capital gains while waiting for an opportune time to exit.

4.6 COMPARATIVE LANDSCAPE OF EMERGING MARKETS

Emerging markets have heterogeneous characteristics and can differ widely in many respects, but they have some common features that seem to attract PE investors across all these economies such as high growth rates and improving legal environments. Geographically, the main emerging regions are competing with each other to attract funding from institutional investors.

We shall now look at some of the highlights of a few key emerging market areas. China, India, and Brazil remain the most attractive emerging markets for GP investment. We start with a discussion of these three markets and then continue with short discussions about Central Eastern European (CEE), Sub-Saharan Africa, and Middle East and North Africa (MENA) markets.

4.6.1 China

China is the only emerging market that compares in size with the U.S. and European PE markets. Within Asia it is on track to displace the more developed PE markets such as Japan and Australia for both volume and investor attention. Investors continue to be extremely optimistic about China.

Investments in China held steady at USD9bn in 2008, down only slightly from USD9.5bn in 2007, making China home to the greatest amount of PE investment dollars across the emerging markets to date. The main reason for the small dip in investments is China's stimulus plan which has flooded the market with inexpensive debt, making PE less attractive to companies seeking financing.

PE funds were unknown in China until the late 1990s. They initially were popular with Chinese companies short of capital and knowhow. Before 1992, the principal vehicles for private equity entry were China Direct Investment Funds (CDIFs). These funds were typically listed on the Dublin, London, or Hong Kong stock exchanges in order to attract money from institutional investors.[4] Today, most PE investment funds raised are not listed as investment funds on stock exchanges. Rather, they are organized as limited partnerships in a manner similar to U.S. PE funds or are units of large international financial institutions. Most funds first create an offshore corporation for the joint venture with the local Chinese firm.

China has traditionally been a difficult place for deals. It is still difficult to execute large, foreign-sponsored investment in strategically sensitive domestic sectors such as

---

4. Stock exchanges recognized these funds as investment companies and, thus, restricted their investments. For example, the London Stock Exchange (the most common listing for CDIFs) required that such funds invest only as a minority investor, taking less than 49% of stock of the target investee firm. Typical additional listing regulations required CDIFs not to play a significant role in management of the firm or place more than 20% of the fund in any one investment.

media and defense, and some sectors remain off limits to foreign investors altogether. The challenging regulatory environment in China, which includes unclear rules and regulations for foreign investors regarding procedures and taxation, has meant that, historically, the location of the PE investment process has been offshore.

However, the landscape is changing. The Chinese regulatory authorities seem committed to establishing a framework that recognizes and promotes PE as a distinct asset class. For instance, various local and provincial government initiatives that have been launched across the country introduce incentives for foreign firms to establish wholly foreign-owned or foreign-invested fund managers based in China, and the national government has signaled its intention to allow foreign firms to establish local currency–denominated funds via onshore vehicles.

Social capital in the form of "guanxi" is essential as a source of relevant information and as a basis for influencing business behavior in every part of a PE deal in China: from sourcing and developing, to its management and exit (Deloitte, 2005). Guanxi is a network of social and business relations that enable preferential favors based upon trust or mutual benefit. While in America or Europe, business can easily be conducted among strangers based on the trust placed in institutional and legal recourse, this is not the case in China. Guanxi can overcome the inefficiency of information markets and the trust gap among business people in China during the due diligence process. Since there is much less reliance on contracts and institutions and far greater emphasis on personal relationships, this mutual due diligence can be a significant and critical stage of deal making in China.

China is poised to continue to lead the emerging markets as the foremost destination for both fundraising and investment. Going forward, the expected shift in focus to onshore firms and capital will be crucial for the PE industry in China. Foreign fund managers may have longer track records, but domestic players have a large role to play in the industry's development, because they are not restricted to particular sectors, are subject to far fewer approvals, and have a distinct advantage in their ability to take advantage of local relationships and knowledge. In fact, funds denominated in *renminbi* (RMB) constitute an increasing share of the capital being raised by both local and foreign players.[5] These funds were born under China's amended Partnership Law passed in 2007 and accounted for almost half of all capital raised in the first half of 2009.

4.6.2 India

India's PE industry has been developing rapidly over the last 5 years. The Indian economy has grown at an average annual rate of more than 8% over the last 5 years, and other macroeconomic factors and policies have complemented this growth. As a result, India has emerged as an attractive PE investment destination. Rivaling China, India saw USD7.7bn in funds raised and USD7.5bn in capital deployed in 2008 as PE investors were enticed by its growing status as an economic powerhouse, its strong entrepreneurial spirit, and its highly skilled, English-speaking workforce. In addition, another driving factor is India's size as the world's largest democracy with the second highest population in the world and a huge pool of intellectual talent and varied skills.

Since its economy opened up in the early 1990s, India has encouraged the growth

---

5. RMB-denominated funds can be domestic or foreign-invested funds. Domestic funds are raised from Chinese investors and governed by laws relating to domestic commerce. Foreign-invested funds are either fully or partially owned by foreign investors. Hence, they are subject to laws governing foreign investments in China.

of this asset class, taking steps towards relaxing restrictions on PE investments to encourage greater capital flows into the country, including allowing government-owned banks to invest in PE directly. In sharp contrast to the time when PE funds were invested in India from an overseas base such as Singapore, many PE firms have now established their presence in the country. But significant barriers to investment remain. The primary deterrent to entry is India's complex regulatory framework.

Small family-owned and family-managed businesses in India account for a high proportion of the investment opportunities pursued by PE funds. Typically, deal sizes are smaller in India than in other major emerging economies, but this is mainly due to the robust VC industry in the country. However, several recent investments, mostly at late stage in industries such as telecommunications and financial services, have seen deal sizes unprecedented in the Indian PE arena.[6]

Most of these PE funds investing in India are sector agnostic, but specialized funds are becoming more common. Infrastructure and technology are the leading industries attracting sector-specific PE funds in India. Real estate and infrastructure have gained prominence over the last 5 years as magnets for PE investments, driven by the gap in India's infrastructure needs, and by the government's drive to launch large-scale projects to meet the economy's growing needs. However, dedicated vehicles targeting the agribusiness and clean technology sectors are also beginning to emerge. Some of India's most recent entrants are focusing on niche sectors such as healthcare and education.

Large Indian corporations (e.g., Tata Group, Aditya Birla Group, Mahindra & Mahindra, or Reliance Industries) and financial institutions started to see PE as a critical part of their growth strategy. These companies have either recently begun PE operations or intend to raise third-party capital in order to do so. They have the advantage that they can operate under a unique platform, with a local presence and significant capital resources.

As India continues to build its PE industry, critical drivers for success will be the growth of domestic sources of capital and the relaxation of investment restrictions for foreign investors. Despite its internal challenges, India offers long-term economic growth and a large and growing middle class focused on domestic consumption. The country's strong fundamentals will continue to make India an attractive destination for PE investors.

4.6.3 Brazil

Brazil's appeal as an investment destination rests on stable government policies and a rapidly growing middle class, which has grown from 38% of the population in 2003 to 49% in 2010 (EMPEA, 2010a). Brazil is intensifying its investments in infrastructure through government-backed initiatives and private investment. PE investors are playing an increasing role in financing the growth and development of Brazil's infrastructure.

Brazil continues to tap its massive natural resources, both biofuels and hydro-carbon, to meet its rapidly growing energy demands. The country has made major investments in the renewable energy sector over the last four decades, helping to make the country the world's most cost-efficient producer of ethanol fuel. PE firms continue to play a pivotal role in financing the growth of the ethanol fuel industry and are also targeting other renewable energy sectors.

---

6. Nearly 70% of PE–VC investment deals in India are valued below USD20mn. This is similar to PE investments in the U.K., where 77% of deals are below GBP10mn. Also, only 5% of deals in India have been above USD100mn in size (EMPEA Insight, 2009).

Brazil leads Latin American fundraising efforts.[7] Although the number of active fund managers continues to increase, PE investment as a percentage of Brazil's GDP remains low (typically less than 0.5%), compared with the penetration rate in the U.S., which typically is between 1% and 2%. In this environment, competition for deals is still minimal, and auctions are rare, but PE firms do face competition in the demand for capital from the soaring public markets. The participation of pension funds has unlocked a massive source of domestic capital for local fund managers, but some PE firms continue to target foreign LPs, citing the lack of an established LP culture among domestic institutions as a deterrent.

PE firms that raise capital abroad to invest in Brazil typically establish their funds offshore as limited partnerships although a growing number of funds are being established in Brazil. Still, more than two thirds of capital is raised by offshore funds, as international investors are the main source of capital raised and are more familiar with offshore jurisdictions.

4.6.4 Central and Eastern Europe (CEE)[8]

The CEE countries offer institutional investors a wide range of opportunities. Expectations for economic growth for the coming decades are promising, and the legal system is favorable to investments given the membership of many of countries in the European Union. The accession to European Union (EU) membership resulted in stability and a reduced country risk. CEE countries have good long-term growth potential. Most recently witnessed booming economies, high GDP growth rates, rising income levels, and profitable companies; however, the credit crisis has significantly negatively affected these economies.

The supply of risk capital is relatively poor in relation to the opportunities in this region and compared with other countries.[9] Although raised and invested PE funds have been gradually increasing over the years, the lack of liquidity and access to debt remains a concern, as it impacts exit opportunities. The insufficient size and liquidity of the CEE capital markets is another obstacle.

While a significant source of deal flow in the 1990s, privatization has since diminished in importance in the CEE countries. A majority of the investments are made in the infrastructure, financial services, and real estate sectors. PE investors are also responding to a surging middle class across the CEE markets by channeling investments into consumer goods, retail, communications, and healthcare sectors.

Trade sales continue to play a central role in CEE. According to a report issued by EVCA in 2008, 41% of the total number and 60% of the total value of CEE PE-backed exits in 2007 were trade sales. Strengthening capital markets have made IPOs an increasingly attractive exit path, with the capital markets in Poland being the largest.

4.6.5 Sub-Saharan Africa

From a meager annual average GDP growth rate of approximately 2% throughout the 1980s and 1990s, growth in Sub-Saharan Africa peaked at 6.5% in 2007, according to

---

7. As of December 2009 approximately USD39bn of funds were available for PE investments in Brazil, a large increase from the USD5bn available in 2000 (Furtado, 2010).

8. CEE comprises the countries of Bulgaria, Croatia, the Czech Republic, Estonia, Hungary, Latvia, Lithuania, Poland, Romania, Slovakia, and Slovenia.

9. The ratio of private equity investments measured as a percent of GDP of the CEE region was 0.21% in 2008, much lower than the ratio in the European Union (0.40%) (Bernoth et al., 2010).

the World Bank. The World Bank estimates that GDP growth in Sub-Saharan Africa will average 5.1% in 2011, significantly trumping the anticipated average of 2.3% for OECD countries.

The region's growing macroeconomic stability has been complemented and enhanced by political reforms. Another significant factor contributing to the region's rebound has been the strong and rising global demand for the continent's vast resources, particularly from other emerging markets. Sub-Saharan Africa is home to 90% of the world's platinum and chromium, 67% of phosphates, and over 40% of gold (EMPEA Insight, 2010c). China is the biggest single driver of growth on the continent, and increasingly a huge indirect competitor to PE firms in Sub-Saharan Africa.

As a result, capital flows to Sub-Saharan Africa have been growing at a rapid pace. Significant developments are currently taking place, in particular expanding the scale of investment opportunities (particularly beyond South Africa) and an improving exit environment. At the behest of local governments, and with some donor encouragement, Africa has increased the number of its domestic stock exchanges from five in the late 1980s to 15 today. Despite this modest headway, Africa's "frontier markets", outside South Africa, still receive a small fraction of investments. Overall, Sub-Saharan Africa still lags the PE volumes in China or India.

Investors continue to command a high risk premium for Africa which remains a complicated place to do business. The EMPEA/Coller Capital *Emerging Markets Private Equity Survey* (EMPEA/Coller Capital, 2010) asked institutional investors what they considered to be the primary factors deterring them from beginning to invest in Africa, inclusive of North Africa. A "shortage of experienced GPs" ranked first as the greatest barrier to first-time PE investment in the region (60% of LPs), followed closely by political risk (58%), and a weak exit environment (34%). Anecdotally, many investors also cite fragmented markets, lack of infrastructure, and health concerns, including persistently high rates of HIV infections, as key factors limiting their willingness to invest in the region. There are also concerns about whether international investors receive the same terms as local investors or, in some countries, whether a government concession might be withdrawn on a change of government. In many African countries, rules are not transparent around certain sectors such as mining and energy.

In addition to the concerns above, the currency risk presents another hurdle for PE investors. The South African rand tends to be quite volatile, as can be the Nigerian naira, which devalued by 15% amidst a banking crisis in early 2009. Investor interest in Zimbabwe spiked in the same year, when the new unity government gave up on trying to tame runaway inflation and switched to the U.S. dollar and South African rand. Some PE investors say it is too costly to hedge their investments in Sub-Saharan Africa, and some factor in large devaluations for worst case currency scenarios.

Nevertheless, Africa has made significant progress in developing its domestic capital markets. Information on African markets is improving, regulatory and financial sector reforms have been implemented, and countries are beginning to adopt modern technologies such as automated trading and central depository systems. South Africa has successfully risen to the ranks of the leading emerging market destinations.

4.6.6 Middle East and North Africa (MENA)

The PE industry has expanded rapidly in MENA, particularly in the Gulf Cooperation Council (GCC) states over recent years. Buoyed by petrodollar-fueled economic growth since 2001, local wealth has exploded, and GCC-based investors have increasingly looked at investment opportunities at home. In addition to a unified language, the

GCC economies benefit from a unified economic agreement. The GCC common market, launched in January 2008, removed numerous barriers to cross-country investment. Further, GCC has one of the fastest growing populations in the world. As a result, most MENA-focused funds put GCC markets at the core of their strategies and international PE investors starting new operations in the MENA region often enter via the GCC.

Government expenditures across MENA, in areas such as infrastructure and healthcare, reached approximately USD550bn (EMPEA Insight, 2010b). In response, several sector-focused funds have formed; and, with one of the fastest growing travel industries in the world, MENA has also become the focus of several hospitality funds. The pace of PE investment has slowed recently in MENA economies, with total known investments valued at USD2.2bn in 2009 compared with USD3.4bn in 2008. With USD19.2bn raised between 2005 and 2009, and only USD11.4bn invested during the same time period, the MENA region is home to large amounts of money committed but not invested yet (EMPEA Insight, 2010b).

MENA fund managers have traditionally targeted local investors as sources of capital. The region's sovereign wealth funds, family offices, and high-net-worth individuals have, to date, formed the core of MENA's PE investors.

According to a recent survey of MENA, there is long-term confidence in the MENA market: 78% of surveyed firms anticipate increased investment in the near term (Deloitte, 2009). Most investments to date have represented minority stakes in family-owned enterprises, but control/buyout opportunities are likely to emerge, as many local firms face the pressures of operating in difficult economic times, as well as transitioning to third and subsequent generations of family control.

4.7 SUMMARY

The long-term appeal of the emerging markets to PE investors is undisputed. There is little doubt that these economies will become increasingly integrated into the global capital markets, and attract an increasing share of PE capital commitments, but in the short to medium term investors still face important challenges. Depending on how individual PE fund managers deal with these challenges, we would expect a greater dispersion of PE returns than in more mature markets. In addition, fundraising and investing in emerging markets, relative to developed markets, are likely to remain more cyclical. A gradual upward trend of PE capital inflows will likely make these cycles less pronounced over time.

4.8 REFERENCES

BALBOA, M., AND MARTI, J. (2007) "Factors that determine the reputation of private equity managers in developing markets," *Journal of Business Venturing*, **22**(4), July, 453–480.

BERNOTH, K., COLAVECCHIO, R., AND SASS, M. (2010) "Drivers of private equity investment in CEE and Western European countries," working paper, DIW Berlin, German Institute for Economic Research.

DELOITTE (2005) *Seven Disciplines for Venturing in China*, Research Study, Deloitte Research.

DELOITTE (2009) *Shaping Up for 2010: MENA Private Equity Confidence Survey*, Deloitte Corporate Finance.

EMPEA (2010a) *Fundraising and Investment Review*, Emerging Markets Private Equity Association, April 2010 report.

EMPEA (2010b) *Quarterly Review*, **VI**(1), Emerging Markets Private Equity Association.

EMPEA/COLLER CAPITAL (2010) *Emerging Markets Private Equity Survey*.

EMPEA INSIGHT (2008) *CEE/CIS: An Overview of Trends in Select Sectors and Markets*, Emerging Markets Private Equity Association, July 2008 report.

EMPEA INSIGHT (2009) *India: An Overview of Trends in Select Sectors and Markets*, Emerging Markets Private Equity Association, July/August 2009 report.

EMPEA INSIGHT (2010a) *Brazil: An Overview of Trends in Select Sectors and Markets*, Emerging Markets Private Equity Association, May 2010 report.

EMPEA INSIGHT (2010b) *MENA: An Overview of Trends in Select Sectors and Markets*, Emerging Markets Private Equity Association, March 2010 report.

EMPEA INSIGHT (2010c) *Special Edition: Private Equity in Sub-Saharan Africa*, Emerging Markets Private Equity Association, November 2010 report.

FURTADO, C. (2010) "Overview of the Brazilian private equity and venture capital industry," *ABVCAP Conference, Rio De Janeiro*.

GOMPERS, P., AND LERNER, J. (2000) "Money chasing deals? The impact of fund inflows on private equity valuation," *Journal of Financial Economics*, **55**(2), February, 281–325.

GROH A., AND VON LIECHTENSTEIN, H. (2009) *International Allocation Determinants of Institutional Investments in Venture Capital and Private Equity Limited Partnerships*, Financial Management Association (FMA), Reno, NV.

LERNER, J., AND SCHOAR, A. (2004) "The illiquidity puzzle: Evidence from private equity partnerships," *Journal of Financial Economics*, **72**(2), 3–40.

PERRYMAN, F. (2010) *Sovereign Wealth Funds Assets Grow to USD 3.51trn*, Private Equity Wire, Hedgemedia.

RAJAN, T., AND DESHMUKH, A. (2009) "On top of the world; still miles to soar: An analysis of venture capital and private equity investments and exits during 2004–08," working paper, Indian Institute of Technology.

ROXBURGH, C., AND LUND, S. (2009) "Look to emerging economies," *Forbes.com*

SCHOAR, A., AND LERNER, J. (2004) "Transaction structures in the developing world: Evidence from private equity," MIT Sloan Working Paper No. 4468-04.

SEIU (2008) *Sovereign Wealth Funds and Private Equity: Increased Access, Decreased Transparency*, Service Employees International Union.

5

Fund due diligence

5.1 WHAT IS FUND DUE DILIGENCE?

Fund due diligence is a process that investors in the private equity asset class undertake to investigate and evaluate the investment premise of specific private equity funds. The main objective is to arrive at better investment decisions by following a rigorous stepwise investigation of specific investment opportunities.

The due diligence process can take several weeks to complete. It usually consists of a thorough analysis of the investment opportunity across several dimensions. Diligence normally focuses on five broad areas:

- The attractiveness of the investment strategy that the fund will follow
- The organization of the management company that will invest the fund
- The specific skills and attributes of the team that will make the investments
- The prior investment performance of this team
- The legal terms and conditions associated with the fund.

Diligence activities are both quantitative and qualitative: they involve data analysis as well as extensive qualitative research.

The evaluation of private equity funds is a challenging process, for two reasons. First, the fact that they are typically structured as private partnerships means that publicly available information is very limited. Unlike registered investment companies such as mutual funds, private equity funds are generally not forced to pass information on their investments and activities into the public domain. This makes it difficult to compare different funds and general benchmarks. Second, general partners (GPs) are normally reluctant to provide commercially confidential information that would confer an advantage if it fell into the hands of a competitor.

GPs therefore provide potential investors with a suite of information that they hope will form a significant body of knowledge to aid the diligence process. They often do this in conjunction with their appointed advisers, so-called *placing agents*. This information is valuable, but it is insufficient to complete a rigorous diligence process. Private equity investors or limited partners (LPs) need to structure their own quantitative and qualitative diligence processes so that they can move from plain analysis to insightful conclusions.

This chapter has been co-authored with Jim Strang (Jardine Capital).

Unlike the investment decisions that investors in the public markets are asked to make, investment in a private equity partnership does not allow investors to form a view on the assets they are being asked to invest in. The investment that an LP is asked to make is actually a *commitment* to a series of future investments that the GP will make over the investment period of the fund in question (typically 5 years). LPs are asked to form a view on the fund's strategy and on the management team's ability to deliver lucrative investments in the future. In this respect the evaluation methods used to assess investments in public equity markets are not really relevant to private equity assets.

Due diligence of private equity funds has evolved significantly over recent years as this class of assets has become a larger part of institutional investors' asset allocations. Also, the growing relevance of industry bodies such as ILPA (Institutional Limited Partners Association) has helped to drive the thinking on diligence processes to a wider and wider audience. But diligence practices still exhibit a wide degree of variability, depending on the skills and experience of the LPs making the investment decision.

Some institutional investors rely heavily on advisors in performing due diligence or even in recommending the appropriate levels of asset allocation and investments in specific private equity funds. Why do they depend on such intermediaries? There are several reasons:

- Private equity fund level information may not be easily accessible to them. Their staff and board members (particularly those at smaller investors) are unable to perform extensive due diligence on their own, because they lack the necessary expertise to analyze data or review the economic and legal aspects.

- These investors' budgets are small or have shrunk significantly after the recent crisis, and this means they cannot hire sufficient investment professionals.

The context of the investment decision being contemplated also plays its role. LPs view investing in large multinational private equity firms with serial successful funds to draw on as a very different proposition from investing in newly established funds (so-called *first-time* funds) or funds targeting investments in emerging markets.

5.2 LP INVESTMENT PROCESS

Before we discuss the due diligence process in detail, it is important to first present an overview of the overall LP investment process.

LPs typically engage in four activities when planning and making investments:

1. Strategic asset allocation.
2. Portfolio construction.
3. Individual fund selection.
4. Fund monitoring.

We discuss each of these below. Due diligence, which we look at in detail in Section 5.3, is part of individual fund selection (Activity 3).

5.2.1 Strategic asset allocation

The first step in the investment process requires the investor to form a clear view on the role the private equity program will play in their broader asset allocation. Clearly, this is a straightforward analysis for investors whose sole activity is to invest in private equity, but for many institutional investors this process is far from straightforward, as the private equity program is likely to form only a small part (say up to 5%) of a global asset allocation.

To develop a point of view on the high-level allocation to the asset class, clear thinking is needed on how the expected risks and returns from the asset class will impact on a broader portfolio construction. At this stage investors need to consider not only the impact of private equity–style risks and returns on the overall portfolio, but also cash flow planning and liquidity management for what is an inherently long-term and illiquid investment.

Once LPs have determined the aggregate allocation to the asset class in terms of the amount of capital required, the proportion of the total investment program, and the investment time horizon, they then need to consider how to allocate their capital across the private equity asset class.

LPs need to decide how they will allocate capital to the various private equity asset classes and to specific geographies. This process also has to reflect the amount of capital LPs are seeking to invest, because some strategies, such as investing very substantial capital in small and emerging private equity markets, would not be deliverable.

It can be extremely challenging to form a view on the asset class and geographical allocation, because the number of options available to investors increases with each passing year. For instance, the number of secondary funds (funds investing in previously established vehicles) coming to market has recently increased significantly. The number of funds targeting either investment in distressed assets or investment in debt instruments (as opposed to equity) also complicates the picture. Further, the growth in the industry that has allowed multijurisdictional funds[1] to develop (especially in Europe) has added yet more complexity.

LPs need to navigate themselves through this complex picture in some structured manner. One way to achieve this is to evaluate different asset classes and geographical market opportunities according to a specific framework. One possible such framework involves forming a view on opportunities across six different dimensions:

1. The strengths of the underlying macroeconomic environment.

2. The structural drivers for private equity returns.

3. The relative valuation metrics for private equity assets.

4. The cultural drivers for private equity (in specific geographies, where applicable).

5. The standards of governance that are in force (once again, in specific geographies).

6. Foreign exchange risks.

This is a challenging analysis, but its final product is an asset allocation decision that can be acted on. It articulates the proportions of capital that the LP wants to see allocated to the various asset classes.

Underlying macroeconomic environment

Private equity is an inherently cyclical business. In forming a view of this asset class's attractiveness, an obvious starting point is to consider the current and likely future economic environment in which investments will be made. The general economic environment can be analyzed from various perspectives to develop a view on how

---

1. Multijurisdictional private equity funds invest in several countries.

EXHIBIT 5.1

MACROECONOMIC FRAMEWORK

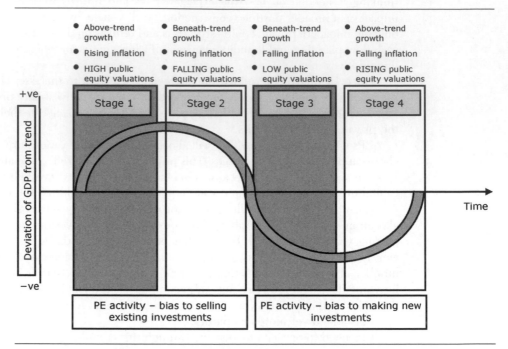

conducive it will be to successful private equity investment. Legitimate indicators are, for example, metrics such as GDP per capita (and, importantly, recent changes to GDP growth), the state of the labor markets, and the current and prospective inflation, interest, and exchange rates. The analysis should also consider the impact of any structural imbalances present within the economy, such as excessive levels of personal indebtedness (at the time of writing, these factors are particularly significant). The economic analysis should be structured in a way that allows it to be used both across asset classes and over time.

It is important to develop a point of view on the current position in the economic cycle, because the various asset classes will have differing degrees of attractiveness. For example, primary investments into buyout funds tend to be countercyclical in terms of investment timing. All things being equal, the best time for new investment is in a period of declining economic growth, and the best time for diverting is in a period of economic expansion. This is illustrated in Exhibit 5.1.

Structural drivers for private equity returns

As well as the state of the economic environment, the strength of the structural drivers of the asset class is also key to determining market attractiveness. A good starting point for this analysis is to understand the penetration of private equity in any given country market. A useful metric is annual private equity investment as a percentage of GDP, because it is freely available for many markets and over several years.

Other useful metrics are the breadth and depth of the M&A market in a specific geography and the share of total activity accounted for by private equity transactions. Again, these data points are generally available.

Another fundamental driver of any given market is its industrial structure and, specifically, the number of corporate entities of different sizes within the economy. For example, the German economy is renowned for the number of small and medium-sized private companies that operate in the so-called *Mittelstand*. A logical further step in this analysis is to review the trajectory over time of both the volume and value of private equity transactions completed in specific markets.

Valuation metrics

A key driver of value creation in any transaction is the difference between the multiple that is paid for an asset and the multiple it is sold for. So, any analysis of a local market needs to take into account the typical acquisition multiples paid for businesses. This analysis needs to be interpreted with care, because structural differences across markets can affect average entry multiples. For example, multiples have historically been lower in Germany than in the Nordic markets—a result driven partly by the typical transactions completed in these markets. The analysis can also be complicated by the nature of the GPs operating in a local market. For instance, in the U.K., where many of the larger pan-European GPs are based, the statistics can be affected by the very large transactions that these groups complete, which are generally completed at higher multiples than those exhibited by small transactions. Any review of transaction multiples can also usefully include an analysis of the typical debt structure and debt multiples in use across different markets, because the availability (or lack) of credit can have a major impact. This information can be readily obtained from credit rating agencies such as Standard & Poor's, who collate statistics for the syndicated loan markets.

In forming a view of the valuation metrics of private equity in a market, a further key variable is the amount of current committed but uninvested capital. As private equity funds are typically raised with a 5-year investment period, arithmetically there should always be an element of "overhang" in terms of such capital. A more fruitful analysis is to consider this in terms of how many years' worth of transactions it currently reflects and how this metric changes over time. For instance, in the aftermath of the financial crisis of 2008, the amount of committed but uninvested capital was at historically very high levels.

Finally, no analysis would be complete without reviewing the historical valuations metrics in the private equity market, and comparing them with their public equity market benchmarks.

Cultural drivers

Private equity has developed considerably in recent years, but despite the recent global growth of this asset class, all markets are still not created equal in terms of the cultural understanding of private equity. Here the key issue is the level of cultural acceptance and understanding of the role of private equity as a mechanism for securing a change in corporate control. This process is essentially subjective. In developing a point of view on the cultural acceptance and understanding of private equity, factors that can be analyzed include the level of governmental support for free market practices, the entrepreneurial culture within the country, and the types of agency relationships between shareholders and managers at play in the economy. To form a robust view here it is essential to bring local market experience to bear, either through accumulated experience within the market or through the use of extended networks.

Standards of governance

Yet another important stage in the process of strategic asset allocation is forming a view on the quality of corporate governance. This focuses on understanding the particular systems for corporate control operating in each specific country. In particular, it involves evaluating the legal and accounting frameworks in operation and understanding the political agenda of the incumbent government and their likely impact on economic development, corporate growth, and fiscal policy. One way to develop an understanding of the conditions that prevail in a specific market is to engage with one of the many legal firms of global scale.

Foreign exchange risks

Finally, the LP needs to consider carefully two main related foreign exchange risks. The first arises from the potential mismatch between the currency of the LP's investment funds and the currency of denomination of the private equity fund. Making commitments to funds denominated in other currencies generates foreign exchange risks when the funds are called and the currency spot rates move significantly against the LP. In extreme cases of highly volatile currencies this can even trigger the LP's insolvency.

The second risk arises from the potential currency mismatch between the private equity fund's commitments and the currency of denomination of the underlying company investments. This type of foreign currency risk does not affect the LP directly, but it *will* affect the performance of the private equity fund making the investments.

It is important that the LP understands the main factors driving the performance of the private equity funds that they are investing in and, specifically, if it is due to favorable or unfavorable movements of the currencies of the underlying portfolio companies. If a particular portfolio company has a large share in the private equity fund's investment pool and its value is denominated in another currency, the foreign currency risk can have a major impact on the overall fund performance. To make an informed decision on this factor, LPs need to understand the hedging of foreign exchange risks that may, or may not, take place at the multiple levels involved.

The strategic asset allocation process allows an LP to develop a strong view on the attractiveness of each geography and asset class for private equity investing, both in absolute and—critically—in relative terms, both to other private equity markets and to other asset classes. As a result of completing this process, an LP can articulate the anticipated risk and return tradeoff for each private equity market and go on to design a coherent asset allocation that is consistent with its investment objectives.

5.2.2 Portfolio construction

Following the strategic asset allocation, the next stage in the investment process is portfolio construction. Here the LP develops a high-level map of the prospective portfolio to articulate a recommended GP diversification strategy within the context of the broader strategic asset allocation. In addition to the strategic framework, the GP diversification strategy is also driven by the projected timeframe of the investment activity and by the list of attractive and addressable GPs likely to be open for investment in the various markets and asset classes throughout the investment period.

EXHIBIT 5.2

EXAMPLE: FUND INVESTMENT PROGRAM PORTFOLIO MAP

Programme Size	300,000,000
Base Currency	GBP
Invest. Currency	EURO
Rate	1.25
EURO Value	375,000,000
Fund share	80%
Co-Invest share	20%
Fund Programme	300,000,000
Co-Investment Programme	75,000,000
Target number of funds	25
Investments / Sub Fund (Vintage)	5
Target number of co-invests	10
Average Fund Commitment	12,000,000
Average Co-Invest Bite Size	7,500,000

Asset Allocation	Total Commit	Commit / GP	GPs	Share
UK	45,000,000	15,000,000	3	15%
France	45,000,000	15,000,000	3	15%
Germany	90,000,000	22,500,000	4	30%
Italy	15,000,000	7,500,000	2	5%
Spain	15,000,000	7,500,000	2	5%
Nordic	45,000,000	15,000,000	3	15%
CEE	15,000,000	7,500,000	2	5%
Benelux	15,000,000	5,000,000	3	5%
New Groups / Other	15,000,000	5,000,000	3	5%
Total	300,000,000		25	100%

Example Fund Investment Programme

Fund Investments 300,000,000					Co-Investments 75,000,000	
Vintage 2010	Vintage 2011	Vintage 2012	Vintage 2013	Vintage 2014	Programme 2008 - 2012	
Nordic1	Nordic 2	Nordic 3	France 2	Benelux 3	Deal 1 7,500,000	Deal 6 7,500,000
Spain 1	Germany 1	TBD	Germany 3	Spain 2	Deal 2 7,500,000	Deal 7 7,500,000
CEE 1	Italy 2	UK 2	France 3	CEE 2	Deal 3 7,500,000	Deal 8 7,500,000
UK 1	Benelux 1	France 1	Germany 4	Italy 2	Deal 4 7,500,000	Deal 9 7,500,000
Italy 1	TBD	Germany 2	Benelux 2	UK 3	Deal 5 7,500,000	Deal 10 7,500,000
SF target 60,000,000	SF target 60,000,000	SF target 60,000,000	SF target 60,000,000	SF target 60,000,000	Overall Programme	
Invested 0	Invested 0	Invested 0	Invested 0	Invested 0	Invested 0	
Remaining 60,000,000	Remaining 60,000,000	Remaining 60,000,000	Remaining 60,000,000	Remaining 60,000,000	Remaining	75,000,000
					GBP (Inv)	0
					GBP (Re)	60,000,000

Overall programme				Invested	Remaining
Invested	0	Remaining	300,000,000	0	375,000,000
GBP	0	GBP	240,000,000	0	300,000,000

So far we have focused on the LP's role as an investor in private equity vehicles managed by third-party managers. However, more recently many LPs have expanded their investment activity to include direct co-investment. This sees LPs invest directly in specific transactions that are normally (but not exclusively) sourced by funds in which the LP has invested. LPs can thus "time" their investments, as each co-investment relates to an actual transaction as opposed to a commitment; gain broader access to the operations of the GP concerned; and, usually, lower the overall fee burden for their clients (as co-investments are typically completed at lower fee levels). Therefore, in the portfolio construction phase, the LP may wish to set aside some of the capital to be allocated to a direct co-investment program.

A typical high-level portfolio map of individual private equity fund investments is shown in Exhibit 5.2.

5.2.3 Individual fund selection

Today LPs face a huge universe of private equity funds operating in different geographies and following different strategies. With a few thousand funds in operation worldwide, LPs need to adopt a robust process for analyzing prospective investment opportunities. This process starts with the development of a comprehensive universe of potential investments. It can be a time-consuming task to establish all the "qualified" groups that fall within the mandate of the investment program, but this has been made easier by the increased number of private equity data providers (e.g., Thompson Venture Economics, Preqin) and the many local market trade associations that now operate.

The central premise of the process is to start with the broadest possible universe of potential investments in each geographic area and asset class and to work from this broad list to a set of fund investment opportunities. Having ensured that any attractive fund investment identified is suitable, both technically and legally, the next step is to

---

EXHIBIT 5.3

FUND INVESTMENT PROCESS OVERVIEW

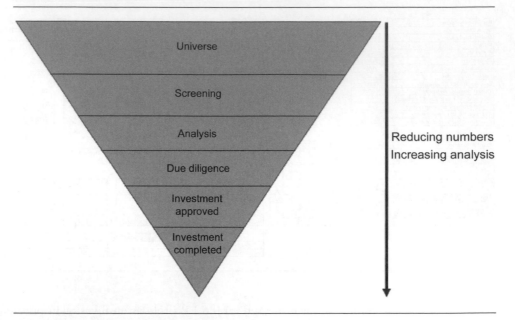

---

progress—as rapidly and efficiently as possible—to a list of actual investments. Exhibit 5.3 shows a high-level representation of this process.

LPs also need to develop a perspective on the addressability of specific investment opportunities. Depending on the circumstances, it may be very difficult for new investors to gain access to investment funds that are highly attractive, but may largely be unavailable. Traditionally, some of the most renowned U.S. venture capital groups have fallen into this category.

Therefore, as LPs go through the fund investment process, they need to be mindful as to whether they will be able to execute all the investments they would seek to (or more commonly to commit the amount of capital they would wish to). This fund selection process is shown in Exhibit 5.4.

LPs use several different decision forums to progress opportunities through the investment process, and a decision whether to continue is needed at each stage of the process. At the end of the process (after the due diligence phase) the outcome will be whether the opportunity is approved for investment or not. Only if the opportunity is approved will it be considered for the portfolio, bearing in mind the overall portfolio construction (which has already been set). In the early stages, the investment team usually meets informally to manage opportunities through the process, but at the analysis and due diligence stages go/no-go decisions are likely to be made by the fund manager's formally appointed investment committee.

Investment sourcing

Once LPs have developed a detailed understanding of the different GPs operating in the market, they must then ensure that they log the maximum number of new invest-

EXHIBIT 5.4

FUND SELECTION PROCESS

	Investment sourcing	Investment screening	Investment analysis	Investment due diligence
Objective	• Maximize investment opportunity set	• Eliminate non-investment grade opportunities	• Filter out highest potential investment opportunities	• Identify opportunities approved for investment
Actions	• Identify widest possible set of investment opportunities	• Develop high-level understanding of manager group and fund strategy	• Validate strategic attractiveness of fund and investment capability of manager	• Complete detailed validation of investment opportunity
Timing	• Ongoing	• 2–3 hours	• 2–3 days	• 30 days
Responsibility	• All members of the investment team	• One member of investment team	• One member of investment team	• Two members of investment team

ment opportunities. The aim is to identify as many opportunities as possible that have the potential to produce attractive, risk-adjusted returns at the very highest level of the evaluation process. As LPs identify individual opportunities, they form a preliminary view of their quality; if an opportunity qualifies, they pass it through to the next step of the process.

New fund opportunities are identified through various sources. For LPs to be best positioned, they require strong local market knowledge, which they have gained either through accumulated investment experience or through a local network of advisors. However, they are also often introduced to opportunities through fund-placing agents, who match investment opportunities to appropriate well-funded investors.

Investment screening

At the investment-screening stage, LPs complete some preliminary analysis to understand the nature of the opportunity. High-level screening often involves desk analysis, and the application of existing knowledge; actual face-to-face time with staff from the GP concerned is usually fairly limited. At this stage the LP seeks to identify any "deal breaking" characteristics of the opportunity and to develop a high-level hypothesis on the opportunity. Deal breakers may be issues specific to the opportunity or may relate to the LP's internal issues, such as portfolio concentration limits. The key output from this stage is a short report or presentation that articulates the opportunity at a high level and presents a recommendation and rationale for the next steps (i.e., whether to proceed with the opportunity or to pass). An example is shown in Exhibit 5.5.

Investment analysis

Opportunities that move into the analysis stage see significantly higher levels of diligence performed, and considerably more engagement with the team members of the GP. In this stage the LP spends time developing a full understanding of the fund's

---

EXHIBIT 5.5

SUMMARY

German group XYZ LLP is seeking to raise its first independent fund after spinning out from Bank ABC. This team, who have invested together for several years, is seeking to raise a fund of €130mn (hard cap €150mn). The fund is expected to have a first closing around April 2012.

Criteria	Preliminary ranking
• Strategy and process	• 4.0
• Organization	• 3.75
• Team	• 4.0
• Track record	• 4.5

Recommendation: This certainly appears a very interesting fund opportunity. The fund offers many of the attributes of a successful investment—a clear strategy targeting a relatively uncompetitive market, an independent organization, a strong and cohesive senior team who have worked together extensively, and a long track record of investment success (52% of realized deals (11/21) returning over 5× the investment cost). Key questions for diligence involve fully validating the team's investment credentials and gaining clarity over the role and relationship the team enjoyed with its prior parent organization. First-time fund risks also require to be considered. Further analysis is recommended.

---

investment premise and, validating it, develops a working hypothesis of the ability of the GP and its team to deliver. Analysis is now both quantitative and qualitative, and inevitably involves spending considerable time with the GP's team members. If it is decided that the opportunity merits full diligence, the LP should develop a full diligence hypothesis that articulates all the outstanding issues that need an answer. The LP should identify not only what those elements are, but also how they should be addressed.

Investment due diligence

This is the final stage of the diligence process. Its goal is to reach a final decision on whether to approve the opportunity under review for investment (although there may be some iterative steps). This stage sees the LP execute the diligence activities identified in the diligence hypothesis that was established and agreed in the analysis. Final diligence is a time-consuming and detailed process. It involves extensive qualitative and quantitative analysis, and may also involve the use of external consultants to deal with specific topics. Section 5.3 discusses the due diligence process in detail.

5.2.4 Fund monitoring

Once LPs have invested in a fund, they play a passive role in it. Many funds establish an advisory committee to enable the GP to engage with LPs, but the responsibility for investment decision making lies solely with the GP. The monitoring of GPs' investing, managing, and exit activities should therefore form a fundamental part of the LPs' investment process. Informal monitoring should be continuous, but formal monitoring usually takes place at specified periods (e.g., quarterly or semi-annually). As part of the LP agreement (LPA) the GP will provide a broad range of detailed information on the investment, including financials at both the fund and portfolio company levels. Generally, GPs are helpful in acceding to the information requests of their LPs and are increasingly bound by the stipulations of the various reporting standards (e.g., the International Private Equity Valuation, IPEV).

In addition to monitoring the financial progress of the fund and its constituent investments, the LP must also monitor developments within the GP management company, as these can have a material impact on investment performance. Thus, the LP monitors both the health of the fund and its investments and the status of the GP employed to manage the fund.

The aim of monitoring should be to ensure that the GPs follow the private equity fund's investment strategy and that the underlying level of performance meets or exceeds the LP's expectations. Any deviations from acceptable levels of performance or unacceptable developments within GP groups should be raised as action points.

5.3 FUND DUE DILIGENCE IN DETAIL

The previous section discussed the different stages of the multifaceted diligence process and outlined the process and steps within it. The central principle of the process is to form an efficient and effective means to process large numbers of opportunities and to develop rigorous data-driven answers. This section will develop the diligence process further, focusing on the specific elements that need to be addressed at each step.

Due diligence activities should be designed to deliver meaningful insights that lead to better investment decisions. To achieve this, LPs need to have not only a fully developed point of view on the specific opportunity being investigated (an investment hypothesis), but also a clear picture of the pros and cons of the other investment opportunities in the "peer" universe of competing investments.

We can best think of due diligence on a specific fund as a 2×2 matrix (see Exhibit 5.6). LPs will want to test two broad areas: the commercial aspects of the investment opportunity and its legal (and taxation) aspects. In so doing LPs will conduct diligence on certain items as a matter of course (i.e., steps that they would follow for every fund that they conduct diligence on) while also tailoring specific items to the working investment hypothesis for the particular opportunity in question.

Most LPs have developed a checklist of questions that they need answers to in any diligence process (an example checklist is included in Appendix 5.A). The idea is to maintain a list of questions that are universal constants in any diligence process (e.g., have any of the team members of the general partner been convicted of a crime?). The aim of these standard questions is to convey information. It is highly unlikely that these questions (or their answers) will convey a great deal of insight or improve the quality of a decision, but they may reveal certain deal-breaking pieces of information.

Funds that are attempting to raise capital often provide a due diligence questionnaire (DDQ) designed to cover many of the standard information-gathering questions that form part of the LP's diligence process. These DDQs can help get LPs through much of their standard diligence questioning, but they are unlikely to cover all the questions.

EXHIBIT 5.6

DUE DILIGENCE AS A 2 × 2 MATRIX

General diligence items	Opportunity-specific items
Legal issues	
• Is the fund structure acceptable from the investors' perspective?	• Is the keyman clause appropriate?
• Etc.	• Etc.
• Etc.	• Etc
Commercial issues	
• Is the full investment track record of the proposed team accurately disclosed?	• What is the proposed sharing of carried interest within the investment team?
• Etc.	• Etc.
• Etc.	• Etc.

As the diligence process progresses, LPs will dedicate increasing amounts of time and resource to it and will spend much of the time in face-to-face diligence sessions with the GP. To make best use of the time and resources of the LP and the GP, the most effective way to manage these sessions is to use a *hypothesis* to drive the diligence process.

This means that the LP develops a hypothesis for the investment that articulates what they need to believe to be true, for them to want to make the investment. The most effective way to develop such a hypothesis is to form a *logic tree*. An example of this is shown in Exhibit 5.7.

5.3.1 Approaches

The LP's task is to cover the points along the critical path, seeking answers along the way. The various questions can be addressed in various ways.

Internal quantitative analysis

There are two key areas of focus here: an analysis of the GP's financials and an analysis of the track record that the GP is presenting to support the fundraising process. LPs will want to know in detail the financial flows into the GP's management company. The main rationale for this is the need to form a view on alignment of interests. LPs aim for full and proper alignment with the GP, insofar as the prime objective is to deliver significant capital gains. If substantial profits are generated from the day-to-day business of running the management company, then this affects the desired alignment. So, LPs will analyze the GP's accounts to form a view on appropriate alignment.

Most of the LP's analytical work will center on the track record that the GP presents to support the fundraising process. LPs will examine the track record across three dimensions:

EXHIBIT 5.7

DUE DILIGENCE HYPOTHESIS: WE SHOULD MAKE A COMMITMENT TO ABC LLP

Strategy/Process	Organization	Team	Track record
1. The strategy of investing in control buyouts with EVs principally <€80mn in the German market is attractive • the specific strategy of this fund appears attractive in light of our point of view on the underlying market opportunity in the German market 2. The competitive environment that this fund will operate in is not expected to deteriorate over the investment period • no new entrants/GPs dropping down 3. Any step-up in deal size for this fund will not detract from its overall attractiveness 4. ABC has strong, maintainable, and attractive deal flow as a function of the longevity of the team in the local market	1. The new management company is likely to be a stable organization with no underlying tensions between the senior partners • decision making is inclusive 2. The organization is sufficiently large and has the necessary capacity to deliver on the investment strategy 3. The distribution of carried interest is sufficient to incentivize and retain the investment team 4. There are no legacy issues involving the separation of the team from its previous parent • the separation arrangements are finalized • we are satisfied with any issues pertaining to the history of the organization in prior ownership	1. The team of ABC has sufficient strength in depth to execute the prescribed investment strategy • the core partner group has a deep and varied network of contacts within the target set of potential investments 2. The spread of the GP's franchise is sufficiently strong to survive the departure of any one senior partner	1. The track record of the GP is accurately portrayed and attributed • ABC's role on each deal is accurately portrayed • valuation policies are consistent with IPEV best practice • the track record is wholly inclusive of all deals done 2. The most significant overall driver of performance has been EBITDA growth within the portfolio companies 3. The GP has been able to source transactions at multiples that compare favorably with those paid by other competing GPs 4. There is evidence of value creation within the portfolio of unrealized investments coming from a number of different sources (e.g., multiple arbitrage, EBITDA growth)

1. *In absolute terms*—what realized and unrealized returns has the GP generated?
2. *In relative terms*—how do these returns compare with other funds that the LP regards as peers?
3. *In detail*—what has driven the returns that the GP has generated previously?

An obvious area of focus for LPs is the GP's aggregate performance, in both absolute and relative terms. The mechanics for this process are covered in Chapter 3, which deals with the performance measurement of private equity funds. Interrogating performance data in an insightful way is not a trivial task.

In detailed analyses, the main area of focus will be disaggregation of realized returns from exited transactions. In any transaction, value can be created in three ways: improving profitability, reducing the leverage between acquisition and exit, and multiple arbitrage (i.e., selling the business for a larger multiple of profits than it was acquired for). Ideally, the GP benefits from all three of these, but in the LP's eyes the first—growing the profits of the underlying business—is the hardest to achieve (and therefore the most valuable).

Private equity is a long-term investment and, thus, LPs will normally find that a significant number of the portfolio companies managed by the GP are unrealized. These companies are still within the portfolio and under the management of the GP. The challenge for LPs is to form a view on the performance of these companies and, critically, their valuation. Valuation of unrealized investments is a complicated business, because the valuation methods applied are notoriously sensitive to a small number of assumptions, such as selecting the appropriate multiple for valuing the company. The latest set of valuation guidelines (IPEV) go some way to solving this problem, but forming a view on current valuations and future prospects for unrealized portfolio companies remains a real challenge.

Internal qualitative analysis

LPs will inevitably spend a lot of time in qualitative diligence. This mostly involves interviews with GP team members, portfolio company management teams, and other third parties with a relevant point of view. These interviews can be very important in terms of the insight they generate. LPs need to consider three elements when undertaking qualitative interviews: What to ask, who to ask, and how to ask?

In terms of *what to ask*, LPs can look to the logic tree and the investment hypothesis to develop a relevant list of questions. In terms of *who to ask*, LPs often need to be creative in their thinking. GPs normally furnish a list of referees, in addition to making their own teams available for interview, but these interviews may not provide the most insightful answers. LPs need to make use of their own personal networks to source interviews that can deliver more insight.

Finally, and critically, LPs need to give careful consideration to *how to ask*: how they actually structure and conduct the interviews. Few LPs are skilled interviewers, able to structure and conduct interviews to optimum effect. For interviews to be effective the right people need to be in the room and the right questions need to be asked in the right way. For instance, should the interview be one to one, one to few, one to many, or some other? What questions should be asked, in which order, and should they be open ended or closed? LPs may seek help from external consultants to address these concerns.

External support

No matter how skilled or competent the LP is, at some point external advisers are likely to be involved in the diligence process. The most obvious way in which this happens is through the involvement of legal advisers. They are normally involved to assist in negotiating the LPA (LP agreement)—the key document that covers the legal terms of the fund and the relationship between the investor and the fund manager.

LPs may also call on the services of other business advisers, depending on the circumstances. Normally, the investment hypothesis and diligence logic tree will show whether there are any diligence elements that cannot be addressed though normal means. For instance, the LP may need to do a detailed background check on a GP that operates in a distant country. This is likely to fall outside the LP's core network and, so, a third party will need to be involved to do the work.

The diligence process is like a funnel. As an opportunity passes through each successive stage in the process, fewer and fewer issues are investigated, but in greater and greater detail.

5.3.2 Investment due diligence

Typically, each fund opportunity should be evaluated across three broad dimensions:

1. The strategy of the fund.

2. The investment process of the fund.

3. The assessment of the GP.

As already mentioned, the approach to analyzing fund opportunities is to form a working hypothesis on the attractiveness of each opportunity and, then, to test this hypothesis fully in the detailed stages of the due diligence process.

Exhibit 5.8 shows a high-level overview of the objectives in analyzing each of the different elements.

The strategy of the fund

LPs spend much time investigating the investment strategy of the fund under consideration. They then consider this in conjunction with the work already completed during the portfolio construction process. When LPs are evaluating the fund's strategy, they consider both the attractiveness of the broader geographic and asset class strategy that the fund will adopt and the GP's approach to value creation.

LPs should evaluate in detail the consistency with which the fund's broader strategy has been adopted in the past. If the GP has let its strategy "drift", this detracts from the comfort that LPs can attach to prior performance as a leading indicator of future performance.

EXHIBIT 5.8

OVERVIEW OF THE OBJECTIVES

	Fund strategy/Investment process	GP assessment
Objective	• Understand the strategy of the fund • Develop a point of view on the attractiveness of this strategy in the specific geographic area and asset class • Determine the strength of the investment process • Critically assess the ability of the process to deliver against the strategy	• Understand the organizational structure of the GP • Develop a point of view on the strength and likely longevity of the organizational structure • Develop a point of view on the appropriateness of the organizational structure of the strategy being followed • Understand the strengths and weaknesses of the investment team • Develop a perspective on the likely stability of the team and its ability to deliver against the chosen strategy given the organizational structure • Develop a point of view on the quality of the risk-adjusted returns generated in the past and the likely return profile expected in future funds

5.3.3   The investment process of the fund

The approach to value creation that the GP adopts can vary widely, from a purely "financial" model to one based on significant "hands-on" involvement in the day-to-day operations of investee companies. Different approaches to value creation are more or less attractive in terms of their potential to generate returns, depending on the market conditions prevailing in the geographic market or asset class.

The view formed on the operating model employed, as defined in the fund's strategy, is used in conjunction with the overview of the general attractiveness of the asset class and geography to frame the parameters within which the GP's investment process can be evaluated (see Exhibit 5.9).

By examining the fund's strategy and investment process, LPs should obtain answers to some important questions:

- How does the fund's specific strategy play against the LP's macroview for the geography/asset class?
- Given the maturity of the market/asset class, what is the relative importance of the different elements of the investment process?
- What are the strengths of the process and its ability to deliver high levels of investment return in the context of the market environment?

Exhibit 5.10 illustrates the thinking behind the differences in importance of the constituent elements of the investment process, dependent on the market environment.

Here the light-coloured boxes represent one possible hypothesis on the more important aspects of value creation. This example shows an understanding of the contributions made by different elements of the GP's investment process to generating high levels of return in different market scenarios.

Sourcing

In evaluating the strength of the GP's deal-sourcing capability, there are some key metrics that need to be properly understood:

- The volume of deal opportunities seen each year by the GP, both in absolute terms and, where applicable, as a percentage of the total deal flow in the segment
- The relevance of the deal flow as it relates to the fund's investment objectives

---

EXHIBIT 5.9

FUND INVESTMENT PROCESS

Sourcing	Investment evaluation	Execution	Value creation	Exit
• Sourcing executable investment opportunities	• Evaluating the attractiveness and potential returns from specific opportunities	• Successfully completing transactions including negotiating with sellers and structuring debt/management packages	• Constructing and delivering against a cogent plan for value creation	• Successfully exiting the investment and returning capital to LPs

EXHIBIT 5.10

THINKING BEHIND THE DIFFERENCES

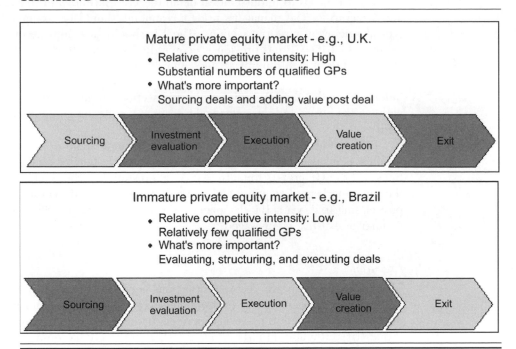

Mature private equity market - e.g., U.K.
- Relative competitive intensity: High
  Substantial numbers of qualified GPs
- What's more important?
  Sourcing deals and adding value post deal

Sourcing > Investment evaluation > Execution > Value creation > Exit

Immature private equity market - e.g., Brazil
- Relative competitive intensity: Low
  Relatively few qualified GPs
- What's more important?
  Evaluating, structuring, and executing deals

Sourcing > Investment evaluation > Execution > Value creation > Exit

- Sources of deal flow by type (e.g., proprietary vs. intermediated)
- Key sourcing initiatives in place
- The current deal pipeline (i.e., potential investment opportunities set).

Investment evaluation

In assessing the GP's investment process, the LP needs to understand the team's ability to evaluate specific deal opportunities. In practice, the LP could evaluate whether the GP:

- Understands the industry's dynamics and the business's position within it
- Develops an executable business plan
- Creates a transaction structure that introduces appropriate leverage and management incentive, consistent with the strategy contained in the business plan
- Develops an "edge" in the transaction that gives it an advantage in the competitive bidding processes.

LPs should evaluate both the effectiveness of the GP's internal resources, and the effectiveness with which the GP engages with external parties (such as due diligence providers and part-time operating partners).

The LP needs to understand whether the GP operates a sector-based investment model and, if so, how long this model has been in place. Managers who follow sector-based strategies generally have a deeper understanding of the specific areas that they focus on and, so, are better positioned to make sound judgments on the attractiveness of investment opportunities in these sectors.

The LP needs to understand in detail the GP's attitudes to transaction valuation and structuring. The manager's prior investments should be examined to reveal the typical pricing of past transactions. The LP should take into account the types of business that the GP has previously acquired (insofar as growth transactions typically change hands at high multiples), and compare the prices paid with historical averages for the market subsector in which the GP operates. The LP should analyze the levels of indebtedness that the GP loads onto its transactions to understand how this compares with market norms and the individual investment strategies adopted in varying circumstances.

LPs should also invest heavily in seeking to understand how the GP designs the business plans that its investments follow. This analysis focuses on the types of transactions that the GP prefers to make (e.g., a rollup strategy, where multiple small firms in the same market are acquired and merged), the way the GP will seek to deliver value post closing (e.g., via a 100-day plan), the way ongoing value will be created, and the manner of exit that is envisaged.

Execution

The manager's ability to execute transactions needs to be tested. Here the LP takes a view on the manager's ability to negotiate successfully with counterparties to the sale process. Accumulated transaction experience within the GP is an appropriate metric for this analysis. It is also important to learn whether the GP has employed any functional experts (e.g., a debt-structuring expert) to help in the execution process. The LP should gain further comfort on the execution ability through extensive referencing with intermediaries used by the GP.

Value creation

A critical part of the overall evaluation process is to assess the GP's ability to add value to portfolio companies. There are few relevant questions:

1. What kinds of strategy does the GP have experience of implementing? The scope of the kinds of value creation strategy the GP has implemented in the past is important. For example, is the GP a specialist in executing "roll-ups" within a market, or is it a specialist in executing international expansion? The LP will try to understand the full scope of the strategic options that the manager may seek to adopt in different circumstances and the manager's relevant credentials with respect to each.

2. What model does the GP implement to deliver against the chosen strategy? This question should provide an answer about the way the GP engages with the investee company. The GP may be a relatively "hands-off" investor, choosing instead to enfranchise a strong management team to deliver against a previously agreed business plan, with the GP monitoring the investment via standardized reporting; or the GP may be extremely "hands-on", implanting members of its own investment team in portfolio companies to assist in delivering the plan. This approach may see the appointment of part-time "operating partners" to the board.

3. What is the GP's record of success? The LP needs to examine thoroughly the levels of success—in terms of value creation enjoyed by each investment. This value should be disaggregated into the three drivers of overall value creation: EBITDA generation, debt reduction, and transaction multiple arbitrage. The LP should also identify any differences in value creation according to transaction size, sector invested, and generic strategies employed.

4. What actions has the GP taken in instances where the transaction has underperformed? In developing an understanding of the GP's ability to add value, it is important to look at the record of turning around "difficult" investment situations where the original investment hypothesis has failed, for whatever reason. How quickly did the GP react to the failure of the original plan? What was the strategic redirection? What ultimate success was achieved?

5. Exit. The LP should understand the quantum of exits the GP has achieved, both in volume and in terms of the value created. The LP should also assess the GP's breadth of experience with regard to achieving exit through different means (e.g., IPO, trade sale, and secondary purchase).

Assessment of the GP

The GP's organization

The GP's organization can be evaluated from three perspectives:

1. Is the GP's ownership structure best organized to maximize likely returns to investors? The LP should evaluate the GP's ownership structure to understand whether the alignment of interests between the GP and investors is optimal. As part of this process the incentive structures in place should be evaluated.

2. Is the GP likely to be stable? Evaluating the likely stability of the GP involves understanding the GP's ownership structure in detail, including which members of the GP hold significant proportions of the equity in the GP management company. As part of this evaluation, the LP should understand the succession plans in place at the GP.

3. Is the day-to-day running of the management company effective? The way the management company is run provides an indication of the organization's effectiveness. The LP could evaluate the internal processes and committees used to run the company and the way resourcing is managed. It is also relevant to understand the organizational hierarchy and how this contributes to effective decision making.

GP's investment team

The LP should spend considerable time in one-on-one sessions with individual team members and with groups of team members (to assess interpersonal dynamics). The team could be analyzed separately by seniority groups (i.e., senior leadership, middle-level members with experience and execution skills, and junior employees).

The first purpose of the investment team analysis is to understand the team's basic background. Elements considered could include the team's physical size, the ages of team members, their educational backgrounds, professional experience, the level of applicable private equity experience, team leavers/staff turnover, and remuneration/ incentive structures.

A second aim is to investigate the intrateam dynamics, to understand how effectively the various investment teams work together. This will also provide information on the coaching and mentoring activities within the team and the career path for team members at different levels within the GP.

GP's track record

Managers who can demonstrate how they have created value in the past, beyond just benefiting from favorable market developments, and who are able to make a compelling case for future value creation, should be high on an LP's list of potential investments. Before investing in a private equity fund, an LP should have sufficient evidence that the manager stands out compared with his or her peer group.

Analysis of the track record is an absolute imperative in the due diligence process—and presumably the most important—due diligence criterion. It starts with a detailed portfolio analysis of all past investments made by the fund manager to quantify the return generated by each investment—the total amount of gain created, with the associated IRR and loss rate. Historical information on past fund performance is essential. The fund-by-fund track record should provide information about the drivers of return for each fund.

Is performance driven by a particular team member, by a particular size of transaction, by a particular strategy, or by deals completed in a particular sector? Interactions with the fund manager can clarify his or her impact on the value contribution of past and future investments. A key part of this analysis is understanding the key drivers of return, deal by deal. This involves allocating the total return between EBITDA growth, debt paydown, and transaction multiple arbitrage. The LP should evaluate both realized and unrealized transactions, paying particular attention to the valuation approach used to evaluate unrealized deals, and adjusting as necessary.

Once the individual track record of the manager has been analyzed, the results should be compared with the track records of other GPs operating in the same market space (thus deep industry knowledge is key). This peer group benchmarking allows fund offerings with a good risk–return potential to be identified.

The performance data from prior funds managed by the GP should be measured as of the beginning of the vintage year of the focal fund, as this snapshot would have been relevant for focal fund due diligence purposes. The final performance of these funds when they reach their liquidation age may differ from this snapshot. If performance data from several prior funds are used, their performance should be aggregated by weighting funds by their size and duration. This is the closest possible approximation of the overall performance of the GP.

Various performance measures can be used. For example:

- IRR of the latest mature fund
- Incremental IRR of the latest mature fund computed as fund IRR minus weighted-average IRR of same vintage weighted-average IRR of all prior peer funds
- Performance quartile ("4" = top quartile) relative to the same vintage and similar stage peers of the latest mature fund
- Weighted-average performance quartile ("4" = top quartile) relative to the same vintage and similar stage peers of all prior funds.

5.3.4 Legal due diligence

The key points of the fund's legal structure are typically disclosed in the *term sheet* that is made available to LPs at the start of the diligence process. Thus, LPs are normally aware of any deal-breaking legal stipulations very early in the process and can thus act accordingly. We provide an extensive legal due diligence checklist in Appendix 5.B.

A term sheet typically covers the following items:

- Investment objective
- Strategic focus
- Manager
- Minimum commitment
- Drawdown procedure
- Investment period of fund
- Actions on subsequent closings
- Treatment of fees and abort costs
- Operating expenses
- Escrow provision
- Re-investment policy
- Advisory committee
- Removal of GP
- Keyman provisions
- Transfer provision
- Tax considerations.
- Size of partnership
- Legal structure
- Currency
- Commitment by named executives
- Actions on default
- Term of fund
- GP's share (management fees)
- Establishment costs
- Carried interest
- Distribution policy
- Fund reporting
- Exclusivity
- Named executive
- Borrowing
- Indemnification

As nearly all funds have their own lawyers advising them on the legal aspects of fund creation, *market standard* terms are generally well known. Thus, the usual picture is for new funds to conform broadly to this standard. If a GP seeks to raise a fund with a clear deal-breaking legal structure (e.g., demanding deal-by-deal carried interest), the legal adviser is likely to counsel strongly against this in Europe. Thus, most funds are launched with a set of terms that are broadly in line with what is regarded as market standard. Every fund has its own nuances as regards the broad terms; and, generally, GPs' willingness to "stretch" terms depends on how they view the strength of their own franchise and to some extent on the conditions prevailing in the fundraising market. For instance, a major fund with a long and successful track record of raising money in a buoyant fundraising market will feel more able to stretch terms at the margin than a first-time fund.

Typically, LPs conduct more detailed legal due diligence towards the end of their own diligence process. At this stage of the process LPs are seeking comfort around the detailed terms of the LPA and, very possibly, are negotiating a *side letter* to this document relevant to their particular circumstances. In these negotiations, the LP's ability to make material changes to the document depends on the strength and scale of the LP and, critically, on where the fund is in the fundraising process. A large and powerful LP looking to make a commitment to a fund in the first closing of the fundraising process has far more power to make changes to the LPA to its favor than a small investor looking to invest at the end of the process. However, investors that do invest at the end of the fundraising process often benefit from what is termed the *most favored nation* clause. This allows LPs to benefit from a range of amendments to the LPA negotiated by earlier investors.

Legal advisers report in two broad areas: the fund's specific legal terms and its suitability for the investor from a tax perspective.

Regarding the specific terms, the legal adviser will report on the key terms of the LPA and will give a point of view on each. Some of the key elements for consideration are:

- *Investment strategy*—how specifically defined it is
- *Fund length*—investment periods, harvesting periods, and extensions
- *Management fees*—levels, periods, and stepdowns
- *Carried interest structures*—percentages and mechanisms
- *Wind-up clauses*
- *Keyman clauses.*

The investor can then form a view on these key terms and negotiate whichever points are important. Any amendments may be incorporated in a revised LPA or they may be included in a *side letter* that is specific to the investor concerned.

As regards taxation, the structures that are being used by the fund and the LP must be compatible from a tax perspective. Normally, the structures can be designed so that the investment gains are tax transparent, but some jurisdictions (e.g., Japan) have their own national tax complications and LPs need to be assured that the tax structuring of their investment is suitable.

5.4 SUMMARY

Private equity fund due diligence needs a lot of hard work. Its aim is to produce a clear assessment of investment segments and geographies that, based on the fundamental drivers, look attractive for investment. For bottom-up evaluation of fund managers, a proper due diligence process must be established, with clear milestones. This process must be supported by tools that allow structured assessment of a fund offering and ensure that different funds are comparable. When professionals are working in a large team, it is essential that they work within the same framework and that evaluations by different people lead to comparable results. Finally, it must be emphasized that, although there may seem to be many promising investment opportunities, the essential element of due diligence is identifying the risk behind each opportunity.

APPENDIX 5.A

DUE DILIGENCE QUESTIONNAIRE

5.A.1 Strategy

Sector/Geography

- What sectors/geographies will the fund focus on?
- What is the strategy within each sector/geography?
- What are the current trends in each sector/geography, and how do these trends relate to the fund's strategy?

Market environment

- Who are the peers/competitors? What is the fund's comparative advantage?
- How does the fund's strategy/target market compare with that of the peers/competitors?
- How does the current environment impact on the fund's strategy?

5.A.2 Investment process of the fund

Sourcing

- What is the GP's ability to generate deal flow?
- What are the deal-sourcing channels?
- How relevant is the deal flow to the fund's strategy?
- Does the GP have initiatives in place to improve the deal flow?
- How many deals are expected to be completed per year?

Investment evaluation

- What is the GP's ability to evaluate specific opportunities?
- Does the GP have knowledge to structure transactions appropriately?
- How does the GP design the business plans for each investment? Does the fund's strategy differ from the prior strategies of the GP?

Execution

- What is the GP's ability to negotiate with counterparties?
- What is the GP's execution experience?
- Is the GP receiving good references from parties she/he has interacted with?

Value creation

- What kinds of strategy does the GP have experience of implementing?
- What model does the GP implement to deliver against the chosen strategy?
- What is the GP's record of success?

- Is the GP's success driven by EBITDA generation or by debt reduction and multiple arbitrage?
- What actions has the GP taken in instances where the transaction has underperformed?
- What is the GP's approach to deal structuring and risk controls (relating to deal risk, sector risk, country risk, currency risk, etc.)?
- What is the GP's approach to the supervision of investments?
- Exit. What is the GP's ability to exit transactions?

5.A.3 Assessment of the GP

Organization of the GP

- Is the GP's ownership structure best organized to maximize likely returns to investors?
- How are incentives provided to staff?
- How was the carry split among the GP's staff in previous funds? How about the current fund?
- Is the GP likely to be stable?
- Does the GP have plans to hire additional staff?
- Is the management company run effectively on a day-to-day basis?

GP's investment team

- What is the background of each team member? What is their professional experience?
- What is the performance of each member when working with other members?
- How much capital will each principal commit to the fund? Will this commitment be in the form of cash/other?
- What other business interests do the key team members have?

GP's track record

- Request a summary of the GP's prior investment performance by deal and by fund. This information should include:
  1. Detailed cash flow information for each deal previously completed by the firm/team. In addition, provide management fee and carried interest cash flows.
  2. Realized and unrealized gains/losses for each deal to date.
  3. Gross and net IRR for each deal.
  4. Multiple earned on capital invested in each deal.
- What is the role played by the GP team members in identifying, monitoring, and exiting the investments?
- Which particular team members are associated with better performance?
- What are the core drivers of the returns, deal by deal?
- What is the GP's approach to valuation of portfolio holdings?

APPENDIX 5.B

LEGAL DUE DILIGENCE CHECKLIST

5.B.1   Documents

1. Limited partnership agreement (plus side letters to all LPs, etc.).

2. Subscription materials.

3. Management/advisory agreements.

4. Co-investment agreement(s) with parallel vehicles, if any.

5. Legal opinions.

6. Private placement memorandum.

5.B.2   Form and structure of investment vehicle

1. Legal form of investment vehicle. Governing law.

2. Limitations on the size of the fund. What is the target size? Is there a minimum (critical mass) requirement? Is there a commitment to a maximum size?

3. Limitations on marketing period. Date of closing. Is there a limitation on the period between the first and final closing dates? Provisions to extend marketing period? Do additional LPs pay for their proportionate share of the cost of existing investments, incurred expenses plus interest?

4. Formation of parallel vehicles. Co-investment agreements between parallel vehicles (pro rata, etc.). Are favorable economic terms on offer to subsets of investors ("friends and family", entrepreneurs' side funds, etc.)?

5.B.3   Duration and termination

1. Initial duration of fund's life. Provisions for extension. Approvals required to extend (e.g., at GP's discretion, with reference to or consent of advisory committee, majority, or supermajority vote of LPs). Limitations, if any, on activity during period of extension.

2. Duration of investment period. Under what conditions can funds be invested after the investment period has ended (e.g., existing obligations, follow-on investments, fees, and expenses)? Is the manager permitted to re-invest capital (i.e., proceeds of all or part realizations)? If so, under what conditions, for what time period, and on what terms (e.g., right to re-invest investment proceeds up to acquisition cost with a time limit of 2 years after distribution)?

3. Are there any means of exiting the fund prior to the expiration of its term?

4. Transfer provisions. Level of GP control over transfers and acceptance of substitutes (absolute discretion, etc.). Is there reference to the types of associated entity (e.g., subsidiaries, beneficiaries) to which transfers will be permitted?

5.B.4   Commercial terms

1. What is the GP's capital commitment, and/or that of affiliates? Is it absolute or variable?

2. Management fee (or priority profit share, etc.) How is the GP to be compensated? Is the compensation to be paid to the GP a fund level expense, or will the investors bear such amounts directly, and in addition to their capital commitments? What calculation base is used to compute the fee (e.g., committed vs. invested capital), and is there a changeover point between alternative methods (e.g., expiration of investment period), or a "greater/lesser of . . ." provision? Is the management fee calculated with reference to the fair market value of assets held? If so, is there provision for an independent check on valuations? Is short-term income offset against the management fee? Is there a right of waiver, with a complementary right to a priority distribution? How often is the management fee payable: quarterly/semi-annually?

3. Other sources of fee income: List each fee and the terms (e.g., transaction fee, investment banking fee, directors' fees and options, monitoring fees, and all other income). Fee offsets: Is a proportion of any or all such fees offset against the management fee?

4. Are fees and expenses charged to portfolio companies by the GP? Are the LP's fees reduced by fees charged to portfolio companies?

5. Establishment/organizational costs. Are these chargeable to the fund LPs? Are they capped? How are placement agents compensated?

6. Ongoing costs. Treatment of fees/costs incurred, such as consultants' fees, auditors' fees, travel expenses, broken deal costs. Are these offset against transaction fee income (as opposed to being charged to the fund LPs)? Treatment and level of other expenses: accounting, legal, printing, and AGM costs, etc. Who bears abort costs?

7. Other sources of income and potential conflicts. Will the GP or its affiliates receive management, advisory, or other fees from the partnership or other parties in transactions with the fund?

8. Carried interest, or other forms of incentive payments. Is the carried interest calculated on a fund as a whole, or on an investment-by-investment basis? Is there a preferred return? Operation of "waterfall" provisions (GP "catch-up", etc.). Clawback provisions: Will the GP be required to return amounts received in payment of its carried interest if the fund incurs subsequent losses? If so, is the amount to be repaid gross or net of tax? Do all the managers guarantee the clawback, and is there a "vehicle" over which the LPs would have a claim (e.g., escrow account, in which case what are the terms for early payment from the escrow account)? Is the guarantee joint and several, so that on the death of one manager the liability does not cease? If the fair market value of investments held (or securities/other assets in kind distributed) used in determining the GP"s carried interest entitlement? If so, what valuation method is applied, and is there an independent check? Are any other forms of incentive arrangements in place (such as employee co-investment schemes)? Are there provisions for tax distributions to all partners, and do these have priority over other distributions?

9. Are there any safeguards or independent checks over the amounts paid to the GP (e.g., audit review, advisory committee oversight, requirements of notice to the investors, specific annual or other period reports of all compensation to the general partner and its affiliates)?

10. What is the notice period for calls on contributions? What is the period for which cash may be held by the GP if a proposed investment is not made? Is there a requirement to invest in short-term AAA investments?

11. What is the timing of distributions after disposal of a portfolio company?

5.B.5 Investment policy and restrictions

1. What is the stated investment purpose?

2. Restrictions (where appropriate) on investments relating to:
   - Concentration of the fund's capital invested in a single portfolio company (e.g., 15–25%)
   - Geography, or regional concentration
   - Sector, or concentration by sector
   - Public company investment
   - Hostile transactions
   - Investment in other funds or pooled schemes (except for funds of funds)
   - Specific industries
   - Ethical issues.

3. Provisions concerning cross-fund investment.

4. Distributions. Can the fund distribute securities or other assets in kind as well as in cash? If so, must these be freely marketable?

5. Limitations on fund indebtedness.

5.B.6 Reporting and communications

1. Reporting:
   - Is there a requirement to produce audited accounts? Is there a provision to ensure that reputable auditors will be used, and that the accounting principles are acceptable? Is there a maximum period between the end of the accounting period and the production of accounts? Are items of information to be included defined (e.g., a list of the fund's investments and the value thereof, capital accounts for individual LPs, balance sheet and income statements, explanation of any revaluation of securities listed therein)?
   - Is there also a requirement to produce more frequent (e.g., quarterly or semi-annual) reports? What will the reports contain? Is there a maximum period between the end of the period and the production of this report?
   - Will reports and valuations conform to applicable guidelines from local associations (e.g., BVCA, EVCA)?

2. Meetings. What types of meeting are planned to inform limited partners? How frequently will they be held?

3. Advisory committee (or similar). Will such a body be constituted, and what will its composition be? Who has rights of appointment and removal? What will the scope of its activity be (e.g., review of valuations, resolution of conflicts of interest such as cross-fund investments,)? How will its authority be limited (e.g., consultative vs. right of review vs. required approval)? Do any members have weighted votes depending on the size of commitments? Indemnification of LP representatives and LP appointers. Rights of other (non-member) LPs to attend or have access to proceedings (minutes, etc.). Frequency of meetings.

5.B.7 Other investor protections

1. Provisions pertaining to the departure of the GP:

   - Does the agreement permit the GP (or principals of the GP) to withdraw from the fund?
   - Provisions for removal of GP, or otherwise suspending or terminating the fund, for cause and without cause "for fault" and "no fault divorce" provisions. What is the period of notice to be given to the GP? Voting arrangements in such cases, and requirements for majority and/or supermajority votes. What are the terms of the financial settlement with the departing GP? Are appropriate parties excluded from sensitive votes, such as to remove the GP (e.g., related parties, sponsors)?
   - Indemnification: is protection provided (including the exclusions) to the GP/ manager reasonable?
   - Keyman provisions. Are the right people included, and is the trigger point sufficiently sensitive? Is there a suspension period if the keyman provisions are effective, and are there reinstatement provisions?

2. LP protections, and potential conflicts between LPs' interests:

   - Do the documents contain provisions addressing potential conflicts of interest between the fund and the GP?
   - Do the documents contain provisions limiting the formation of future funds until after a specified portion of the investors' commitments have been invested?
   - Are there restrictions on investments in affiliates of the GP, and in portfolio companies of prior associated funds?
   - How will investors who default in making their capital contributions be treated? Expulsion? How will the capital account balances of defaulting partners be allocated?
   - Counsel to the general partner(s) should render an opinion concerning the limited liability of the limited partners. In making and managing investments, the GP and manager should take due care to ensure that limited liability is preserved.
   - Are side letters or other undertakings being given to any LPs? Is there a "most favored nation" clause?
   - IIow is demand for co-investment among LPs satisfied?

3. Taxation, regulation, and related matters:

   - Does the fund structure permit participation by an LP of the type and domicile?
   - Do the documents contain covenants by the GP (e.g., "best efforts" or similar language) to ensure that tax-exempt LPs will not be subject to tax on unrelated business taxable income?
   - Do the documents contain covenants by the GP (e.g., "best efforts" or similar language) to protect against the creation of tax reporting obligations or tax liabilities to non-domiciled investors arising from effectively connected income trade or business income?

4. General LP protections:

   - LPs' liability for liabilities, debts, etc. of the partnership to be limited to their stated capital commitment with an exception for recycling (see above).

- Amendments to the LPA: What is the proportion of LPs required to bind all LPs? No amendment to be made to increase financial obligations of LPs, or which affects their limited liability.
- LPs not to participate in management or control (subject to any safe harbor laws of jurisdiction of partnership's incorporation).
- Are there excuse provisions to enable LPs not to contribute if legal/constitutional/regulatory prohibitions apply?
- Confidentiality obligations by LPs and the GP relating to information concerning portfolio companies, the GP, and LPs. Are there acceptable carve-outs?
- Time and attention and non-competition restrictions by keymen.
- Warranties by the fund to LPs about its incorporation, powers, and authorities, etc.
- Warranties by LPs to the fund.
- Is there an obligation to effect indemnity insurance cover?
- Calls: What is the minimum period of written notice? Payments to be in cash (and not in kind).
- Are there monetary limits on total calls per annum?

6

Private equity fund accounting

6.1 WHAT IS HAPPENING IN PRIVATE EQUITY ACCOUNTING?

Private equity as an industry and as an asset class has "grown up" significantly over the last 20 years. This maturing of the industry has pushed private equity and venture capital from a quiet and veiled corner of the room, where it was regarded as a poor relation to the wider asset management family, to center stage. This transformation has brought with it many strains and stresses from public accountability through all areas of governance to reporting.

In essence the private equity and venture capital ("private equity") business model is relatively simple. It is to invest pooled funds in assets that are typically not liquid to generate returns for the investors.

This chapter focuses on the accounting issues encountered in the U.K. private equity environment. Due to the many different detailed business models which fall under this simple business idea, it would be impossible to cover all the potential eventualities which may arise in a business designated as private equity. This chapter focuses on accounting common in the U.K., principally from the point of view of the most commonly used fund structure presented in Exhibit 6.1.

This chapter sets out the principles of and rationale behind accounting from the perspective of U.K. GAAP and IFRS. On occasion references are made to principles under U.S. GAAP. This chapter is not intended to provide any form of guidance in relation to U.S. GAAP and any references to it are for interest purposes only, particularly when anticipating the future for all accounting standards.

Care must be taken when applying these broad brush principles in practice to any individual situation as relatively small changes in facts can markedly change the consideration of the accounting.

6.1.1 Fund structure

Any fund is structured with two fundamental principles in mind. First, that the fund needs to be able to efficiently acquire, manage, and dispose of investments and, second, that the investor in the fund is not disadvantaged from a tax perspective when compared

This chapter has been written by Anthony Cecil (partner at KPMG LLP and member of the International Private Equity and Venture Capital Valuation Guidelines Board, IPEV). Anthony has assisted in the writing of this book in a personal capacity and his views should not be taken to be those of KPMG or IPEV.

EXHIBIT 6.1

MOST COMMONLY USED FUND STRUCTURE

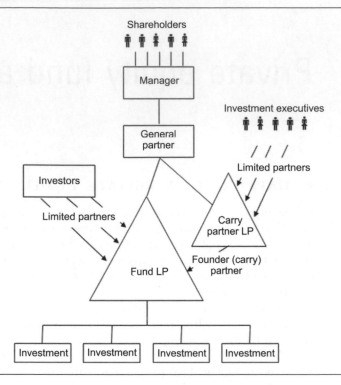

---

with investing directly in the underlying asset. This basic structure is then added to, usually to optimize the after tax returns to the individual managers.

Whilst the principles are relatively simple, the complexities of tax laws and the different applicable tax jurisdictions can result in enormously complicated structures. This chapter is based on a simple limited partnership structure set out in Exhibit 6.1. The principles discussed in this chapter are equally applicable to much more complicated structures but, for ease of explanation, this structure is assumed.

6.1.2   Why different GAAPs are used

There are two reasons that any entity prepares accounts for its investors, either because it is required to do so under statute or it has agreed that it would. In the U.K. commonly used GAAPs include:

- U.K. GAAP
- EU-adopted IFRS ("IFRS")
- U.S. GAAP
- "Other".

There has been a clear intention for many years for U.K. GAAP and IFRS to merge into a single set of standards. Many of the recent standards issued by the Accounting

Standards Board (ASB) in the U.K. are designed to be clones as far as possible of their IFRS counterparts issued by the IASB. Sooner or later U.K. GAAP and IFRS will be deemed to be sufficiently identical for U.K. GAAP to no longer be relevant. In October 2010 the ASB published a *Financial Reporting Exposure Draft* on the future of financial reporting in the U.K. and the Republic of Ireland. This proposes a three-tier system: listed groups and publicly accountable companies will follow IFRS; medium-sized entities will report under the IFRS for SMEs; and the smallest companies will continue to follow the U.K. GAAP FRSSE.[1]

It has long been suggested that IFRS and U.S. GAAP would merge and the current publicly stated convergent date is December 2011. There have been significant steps towards convergence; however, there are obstacles remaining. There are still many differences between the principle-based IFRS and the more rule-driven U.S. GAAP (not least in the length, with U.S. GAAP being 15,000 pages long against IFRS at 5,000); however, with the recent issuance of the minutes of their joint meetings on consolidation, there is a clear intention to address the major issues quickly.

Which of the above GAAPs an entity uses will depend on its legal structure, the way it undertakes business, and any agreements with its investors. The common private equity vehicles in the U.K. are:

- Venture capital trusts ("VCTs")
- Investment trusts
- "Qualifying" limited partnerships
- "Non-qualifying" limited partnerships
- Offshore limited partnerships.

Venture capital trusts

VCTs are vehicles that were established by the U.K. government with a view to encourage individuals to invest in venture capital by providing tax incentives to the investors. To qualify as a VCT there are many rules and regulations that must be followed, one of which is that the entity must be listed on the U.K. stock exchange. This means that the vehicles used are public limited companies. This automatically pushes the VCT into a rigid legislative framework, filing its accounts which have been prepared under U.K. GAAP or IFRS. In the U.K., listed companies are required to prepare their consolidated accounts in accordance with IFRS. As many VCTs do not take controlling stakes in their underlying investments, they can prepare accounts under U.K. GAAP or IFRS. Those that take control stakes are required to prepare consolidated accounts under IFRS. (The issues around consolidation are discussed in Section 6.2.1.)

Investment trusts

Similar to VCTs, this is a listed corporate vehicle and, so, is under a U.K. GAAP or IFRS reporting regime. Investment trusts are generally larger than VCTs and more likely to have invested in control positions. Those with control positions in underlying businesses are required to prepare consolidated accounts and report under IFRS. Those with no control positions may report alternately under U.K. GAAP.

---

1. The FRSSE is a standard that may be applied by companies that qualify as small under the Companies Act in the U.K. and other entities that would have qualified as "small" had they been incorporated.

"Qualifying" limited partnerships

From a reporting perspective, these are treated as if they are private limited companies. This means that they are required to prepare and file accounts under either U.K. GAAP or IFRS. Any limited partnership is governed by its limited partnership agreement (LPA). This sets out the contract agreed between the partners as to how the limited partnership will be managed and operated.

For many years, the interpretation by the lawyers of the legislation defining qualifying partnerships has meant that the limited partnership used in a typical private equity structure was determined not to be a qualifying partnership.

The Department for Business Innovation and Skills (BIS) under pressure from the EU has drafted an amendment and clarification to that definition which would result in the majority of limited partnerships being defined as "qualifying" and brought into the statutory reporting and filing regime. The implementation of this amendment, and the extent to which any non-standard structures are included within the definition, remains open. The amendment is expected to apply to accounting periods beginning on or after April 6, 2011.

"Non-qualifying" limited partnerships

A non-qualifying limited partnership has no statutory filing requirement. Accordingly, the only reason that accounts are prepared is because the LPA mentions that they will be. If the LPA states that "the accounts will give a true and fair view", that statement would immediately push the reporting to be under U.K. GAAP or IFRS. A "true and fair view" is a defined term under the Companies Act and the only way to comply with the LPA requirement is full Companies Act accounting and disclosures.

Many LPAs state that "the accounts will be prepared on the basis of the policies agreed between the Manager and the Auditor". This allows the manager (within reason) to select those accounting policies which he or she believes are appropriate for the fund, and to ignore those elements of GAAP, either policy or disclosure, which the manager considers unnecessary. These are the policies described as "Other". A non-qualifying limited partnership can of course adopt any of the recognized GAAPs (U.K., U.S., or IFRS) should it so choose.

In practice this usually means that the fund will follow, rather than comply with, U.K. GAAP with certain exceptions, notably consolidation and the accrual of income. The issues arising from a requirement to consolidate are discussed further in Section 6.2.1. If the accounting policies state that the fund will not consolidate control positions, then these issues fall away at the fund level. U.K. GAAP would require that income on instruments that are loans is accrued evenly over the period, even when interest is only expected to be paid at the point of realization of the loan. A common policy adopted is that the fund will recognize income in relation to a particular investment when that investment is realized.

Whilst the accounting framework of "Other" simplifies certain aspects of reporting, it does not remove the requirement for the fund to prepare taxation returns under either U.K. GAAP or IFRS accounting policies.

In addition to any statutory reporting requirements, additional reporting may be required by the terms of the LPA. Due to the drafting in New York State of the regulatory requirements of insurance companies, U.S. investors in a limited partnership will be subject to an additional capital requirement if they do not receive U.S. GAAP accounts for the limited partnership. As a result, it is common for LPAs with U.S.

investors to include a requirement to additionally report under U.S. GAAP to the investors.

Offshore limited partnerships

An offshore limited partnership will be governed by the local statutory and regulatory environment. The private equity market has tended to utilize those offshore centers that provide them with the appropriate tax regime, coupled with limited statutory reporting. As a result, any of the GAAPs referred to above may be encountered in offshore structures, depending on jurisdiction.

6.2 CURRENT MAJOR ISSUES AND COMPLEXITIES

In discussing accounting issues, implications, and proposed courses of action to change the accounting, the principles that may be followed are set out in this section. For many of these issues, the preparer of the accounts must use his or her judgment as to how to apply these principles. In any situation it is crucial to assess the individual case on the basis of the available facts and not merely assume that these broad brush principles may be applied automatically in all similar situations without that detailed consideration.

The first rule of accounting for any limited partnership is to read the limited partnership agreement (LPA) to completely understand the contractual relationships between the partners.

6.2.1 Consolidation issues

The case against consolidation

Accounting standards have generally been formulated to fit the majority of business models encountered in a corporate environment. For a shareholder in a conglomerate, it is highly relevant to them to understand the overall financial operations of the group as a whole and the group's financial position. This consolidated information gives the reader of the accounts a basis upon to make relevant judgments as to the performance and expected future cash flows that they might derive from that business.

This is one clear area where the business model of private equity is not suited to the developed accounting standards. Private equity entities will commonly take control positions in underlying businesses to give them the ability to manage the new investment in the manner that they see fit.

In a conglomerate, the investor can judge the management team and look for their investment return from all the entities that are controlled within the group. In a conglomerate the dividends to the investors are paid from profits generated by the group and, indeed, the earnings of the group and expected dividend stream are important metrics in establishing a price for the shares.

In private equity, this information on the consolidated operations is largely irrelevant to an investor. Their investment returns are generated from the ultimate realization of the underlying entities. The financial position of the fund is not assessed by an investor adding together all the individual underlying asset and liability classes. The performance of the fund is not judged by adding together the turnover, costs, and profits or losses of a collection of disparate businesses. The investor assesses the fund by considering the value of the underlying businesses, and it is this assessment which allows the investor to estimate his or her anticipated investment returns from future realizations. Accounting standards generally agree with this assertion, so long as the fund only holds a small equity position. Accounting standards require that, once you own sufficient equity to control a business, that the accounts should reflect a consolidation of all the businesses so controlled.

For a private equity investor, the value of the investments in the fund, treated in the same way regardless of the size of the equity holding, is highly relevant information— a summation of assets and liabilities is not.

This focus towards value also reflects the way that private equity managers run their businesses. They are closely involved with the strategic direction of the company and board decisions, focusing on deriving value for their investors. Whichever GAAP is used, there are commonly applied processes, practices, and judgments that remove the requirement to prepare consolidated accounts, but each situation must be considered on its own merits and facts.

Consolidation within the fund

As noted above, consolidated accounts do not provide relevant information to the investors. As a result, fund reporting focuses on being able to provide information on the basis of fair value rather than consolidation. To understand how this is achieved in most situations, we need to consider the accounting standards and other pieces of legislation that drive the requirement to consolidate.

Reporting under IFRS

Under IFRS, IAS 27 ("Consolidated and separate financial statements") requires that an entity consolidates the entities it controls. "Control" is defined as "the power to govern the financial and operating policies of an entity so as to obtain benefits from its activities." In a situation where a single entity owns more than 50% of the equity in an underlying investment, it is difficult to argue that these control conditions are not met. This is one of the major reasons why the private equity community avoids IFRS whenever possible.

If, by careful fund structuring, no single entity "controls" the underlying investment, there is no requirement at fund level to consolidate. So, for a fund proposed to be structured as a limited partnership, if a number of parallel limited partnerships, bound together by a co-investment agreement and ensuring that no single partnership is larger than all the others put together, jointly acquire a controlling interest, then no individual limited partnership can be deemed to control the investment.

The option of splitting the fund vehicle into subscale elements may not be possible in certain situations, such as a standalone investment trust. When an investment trust directly owns a controlling stake in an underlying business, it is likely that the trust will be required to consolidate the results of all its underlying controlled investments. In this situation, the best option may be to accept that consolidated accounts are required and to provide relevant valuation information to the investors alongside the consolidated accounts. Single-entity accounts which include all investments at valuation may be prepared and published together with the consolidated accounts.

In addition IFRS 8 ("Operating segments") may support the provision of valuation information. Generalizing, IFRS 8 requires that information be reported on the same basis that senior management use to make resource allocation decisions. In that a private equity fund's acquisition and disposal decisions are made on the basis of investment valuation, the valuation of investments might be expected to be the basis of any IFRS 8 disclosures.

Reporting under U.K. GAAP

U.K. GAAP (FRS 2, "Accounting for subsidiary undertakings") has the same definition of control as IAS 27. There is, however, an important distinction. U.K. companies reporting under U.K. GAAP report in accordance with the Companies Act 2006. The requirement for an entity to consolidate those other entities it controls is embodied in that Act, not merely in the accounting standards.

Also embodied in the Companies Act is the concept of a "true and fair override". If those responsible for the accounts of an entity believe that the accounts would not give a true and fair view by following a particular accounting standard, then the override may be invoked and the accounts can be prepared on the alternate basis, disclosing the impact of the departure (where available). It is common for fund accounts to be prepared on the basis of all investments being reported at fair value, invoking the true and fair override. It is usually not possible for the preparers to disclose the impact of the departure, as these amounts are unknown.

It is worth noting that this route is not permitted when reporting in an IFRS environment. Under IFRS, an equivalent of the true and fair override is technically available, but hard to achieve in practice. This is partly because IFRS has no facility for non-consolidation for held-for-sale assets and, second, because IFRS is a global GAAP. At a global level the prevailing view of accountants applying IFRS is far less inclined to see consolidation as not true and fair.

A qualifying partnership is exempt from preparing consolidated accounts if the partnership is dealt with on a consolidated basis in the group accounts of its parent. In the context of a limited partnership with a single general partner (GP) and that GP or its parent prepares consolidated accounts, the limited partnership is permitted to take this exemption. This exemption removes the requirement to prepare consolidated accounts, but moves the issue higher up the control structure. Consolidation within these higher entities is discussed in the section below.

Reporting under U.S. GAAP

U.S. GAAP has anticipated these issues arising from consolidated accounts. For a private equity entity once it has determined that it is an "investment company" (as defined), it may follow the AICPA's Investment Company Accounting Rules. In essence, these remove the requirement to consolidate and all investments may be included in the balance sheet at fair value.

It is worth noting that with the convergence program, the IASB would appear to be considering a similar principle for IFRS.

Consolidation within the manager or GP

In a typical structure (as set out in Exhibit 6.1), the limited partnership is a subsidiary of the GP, which is in turn a subsidiary of the manager. This would suggest that the manager is the ultimate controller of the limited partnership and, potentially, any controlled underlying portfolio companies. Typically, the manager has a small or even zero interest in the fund with the economic benefit going to the investors and the carried interest partners. In the extreme situation, where that interest is negligible, the manager's accounts would consolidate the results and financial position of the GP, all the limited partnership and portfolio subsidiaries, with all profits and net assets arising from fund activities being included as a minority interest. Deciphering, from a set of accounts that were prepared on this basis, the results of the financial operations arising from management activities and the financial position of the manager would be very difficult.

Reporting under IFRS

In the structure shown in Exhibit 6.1, the GP is the only entity entitled to manage the operations of the limited partnership, but the question arises as to whether the GP "controls" the limited partnership as defined in IAS 27. The fact that the GP has the ability to govern the financial and operating policies is not open to debate. Questions arise as to whether these policies are controlled "for benefit" or whether there are other restrictions over its ability to govern.

In this context "benefit" may be interpreted as meaning ownership benefits. The question then arises as to whether the GP is managing the limited partnership to derive ownership benefits or remuneration from management activities. For the purposes of interpreting the standard, these functions are considered separately.

In the event that the GP's interest in the limited partnership is negligible and is only remunerated (in line with market rates) for management services, the inflows received are clearly from its management activities and not from "controlling the policies for benefit". In this situation, it may be reasonably held that the GP does not "control" the limited partnership.

It is common for GPs (or managers) to be required by the limited partners (LPs) to invest in the limited partnership. In this situation, the GP is acting in a dual role, partly as manager, partly owner. When considering whether the GP, acting in a dual role, is deriving benefit from its ownership or management activities, we need to ascertain for which activity the "benefits" are being received over the expected life of the fund. This question is further complicated where carried interest is also received by the manager, GP, employees, or partners. It is typically argued that carried interest is a benefit of management (regardless of how it is structured for taxation purposes) since it is only available to the management team, does not carry the full downside risk if performance is negative overall, and is linked to the profits generated from the management activity.

The whole question of "for benefit" is highly judgmental and each situation must be carefully considered on its own facts. If it is decided that the manager receives significant benefit from ownership interests, then it might be expected that the limited partnership is consolidated by the manager as the owner of the GP. Conversely, if the majority of the inflows are anticipated from management activities, then it might be reasonably held that the GP, whilst controlling the limited partnership, does not do so for ownership benefits.

The limited partnership agreement (LPA) will establish the rights and responsibilities of the individual partners. Limited partners are excluded from the management of the limited partnership, since involvement in the management imperils their limited liability protection. The LPs can, however, retain rights of removal and appointment over the GP, without damaging this status.

If LPs reserve the right to remove the GP and appoint a successor (commonly referred to as "kick-out rights"), then it may be held that the powers of the GP are restricted. Whether these kick-out rights are sufficient to maintain that the GP does not have control ("substantive kick-out rights") is a matter of judgment. Typically, to be substantive it must be reasonable that these rights may be exercised. This consideration would include the number or percentage of the LPs who would need to vote for removal, whether specific grounds were required to initiate the process, the overall cost to the LPs by following this course of action, and anything else that might provide a barrier to the rights being exercised.

Where the LPA is structured to ensure that substantive kick-out rights exist, particularly in situations where there is a single LP with a significant interest, the right to eject the GP (and thereby control the limited partnership) may have inadvertently been placed in the hands of a single investor. Should this be the case, the requirement to consolidate the limited partnership has merely moved from the GP to one of the LPs.

Reporting under U.K. GAAP

Much of the U.K. GAAP analysis is similar to that for IFRS, but there are subtle distinctions. As noted in the section above, the requirement to consolidate is enshrined in the Companies Act. FRS 2 then provides guidance as to how you should undertake the consolidation.

In the section above (considering this issue in an IFRS environment), the requirement to consolidate is only present where the control (i.e., governing the policies for "benefit") test is met. Although FRS 2 has the same definition of control as IAS 27, the analysis—which concludes that there is no benefit to the controller—is less relevant under U.K. GAAP, since the Companies Act has determined that consolidation is required.

Preparing consolidated accounts at the level of the manager allows the exemption from consolidation to be taken by the limited partnership. Rather than prepare fully consolidated accounts with a significant minority interest, we may prepare consolidated accounts that consolidate the underlying subsidiaries on a proportionate basis ("proportional consolidation"). This requires an invoking of a true and fair override of the method of consolidation required by the Act. Under proportional consolidation the accounts of the parent include, on a line-by-line basis, its share of the underlying entity's results and financial position. Where the interest in the limited partnership is zero, there will be no differences between the entity-only accounts and the consolidated accounts. This way the results arising from the activities of the manager group can be clearly reported.

Where the effective interest of the manager in the limited partnership is small but not negligible, judgment is required. The question arises as to whether the exclusion of accounting entries representing the manager's small share of each accounting item is materially incorrect, or not. Typically, the manager's consolidated accounts would show no differences to the entity standalone accounts, so long as the interest is only a few percent.

The analysis under IFRS of restrictions over control equally applies under U.K. GAAP and, in the event that substantive kick-out rights exist, the manager would not be required to consolidate the limited partnership. In this event, however, the available exemption from consolidation through being included in the consolidated accounts of a parent would not be available to the limited partnership.

6.2.2 Priority profit share

In a limited partnership structure, the GP is commonly entitled to receive a priority share of profits in consideration for managing the limited partnership and for having unlimited liability. This may be referred to as management fee, priority profit share (PPS), or GP's share (GPS). Frequently, this share is around 2% of the committed capital or net cost of investments made.

The LPA is structured such that the GP is entitled to this amount of any profits arising, before any profits are allocated to the LPs. To ensure that the GP has sufficient resources to meet its costs of management, in the event that there are insufficient profits to cover the PPS, an interest-free loan is made by the limited partnership to the GP. This loan is not repayable, it may only be settled by the future allocation of profits.

In the accounts of the fund (U.K. GAAP and IFRS)

From these facts, it is clear that the GP receives an annual amount for taking on its role as GP, which is never repaid. In substance, this is akin to a management fee and it should be recognized in a similar manner in the accounts of the limited partnership.

Commonly, this will be shown as a deduction from profits (or losses) in the income statement. In early years the fund is unlikely to generate profits, and it is important that the PPS is recognized in full in the income statement and allocated fully in the partners' accounts.

The rationale for this treatment is that:

- The substance of the transaction is an expense payment rather than a loan
- The loan cannot be recognized in the balance sheet as an asset since it does not meet the definition of an asset
- Even if it were recognized as an asset, it should be considered as impaired, since it is not repayable.

In the accounts of the manager (U.K. GAAP and IFRS)

The treatment under the accounting standards and the U.K. taxation rules differ widely for the receipt of PPS for the manager. In the accounts, the receipt is recognized as turnover on the basis that it is in relation to an annual contract and is not repayable.

It is worth noting that, for taxation purposes, the tax nature of the receipt follows the strict legal form rather than the accounting form and, so, only falls to U.K. tax as taxable profits are generated by the limited partnership and allocated to the manager.

6.2.3 Carried interest

The carried interest partner (CIP) (also sometimes known as the founder partner or special LP) is an investor in the limited partnership. Its purpose is to be a vehicle that aligns the interests of the investors and the managers, rewarding those managers with a share of realized profits in a tax-efficient manner. Carried interest schemes typically operate on the basis of realized profits—and not portfolio valuations as for some schemes common in other alternative asset classes.

The CIP will typically have an investment in the limited partnership capital, but no loan commitment. This capital commitment entitles it to a percentage (10% to 25%, but most commonly 20%) of the realized profits generated by the fund. A target rate of return (the "hurdle rate") may be set for the fund. Hurdle rates vary depending on the type of fund, anticipated market returns in that geography, and the overall carry arrangements. Typically, these are between 5% and 12%.

The timing and share of the profits to which the CIP is entitled are set out in the LPA. In considering the accounting treatment of any carry scheme, the exact terms of the agreement must be considered in detail. To discuss the principles of the accounting, this section focuses on three different types of schemes:

1. Deal by deal with no hurdle or clawback (one end of the range).
2. Deal by deal with a whole fund calculation and clawback.
3. Whole fund with hurdle (the other end of the range).

What do these descriptions mean in terms of the commercial reality in the carry schemes? "Deal by deal with no hurdle or clawback" means that the CIP shares in the profits realized on each deal as it arises, does not need to return a target rate of return to the investors prior to sharing in the profits, and does not share in any realized losses. This type is scheme is rarely seen in Europe any more, since it is generally viewed as being too generous to the CIP at the expense of the investors.

"Whole fund with hurdle" means that the CIP only shares in realized profits after the investors have received all their original investment, plus a target rate of return. This is probably the most common basis agreed in the current market as it ensures that the CIP only benefits from its investment after the managers have fulfilled the fund objectives. This typically results in carry only being paid to the CIP 6 to 10 years after the fund was raised.

"Deal by deal with a whole fund calculation and clawback" is essentially the same commercial term as "whole fund with hurdle", but the scheme allows payments to be made and subject to reclaim by the fund. Payments may be made to the CIP when profits are realized, so long as the fund remains on course to achieve its objectives and that the amounts can be recovered from the CIP in the event that this proves to be false. The obvious advantage to the CIP of this scheme is that payments may be received earlier in the lifecycle of the fund. Commercially, it is the same as a whole fund scheme allowing for payments on account.

Between the extremes there is an infinite number of quirks and variations that may be introduced through the LPA negotiations. Whatever the quirks and variations, the accounting issues arising should all fall within the same principles as the three schemes set out in this section.

In the accounts of the fund (IFRS)

In considering the treatment of carried interest in the accounts, it is important to appreciate the distinction between profits being allocated and distributions being made. Once the fund has been raised, there are two critical trigger points in the lifecycle of a fund which significantly change the expectations of carry being paid.

The first trigger (Trigger Point A) is when the fair value of the fund's investments exceeds a value whereby, if all the investments were sold at that value, carry would be due to the CIP. The second (Trigger Point B) is when the conditions are met such that carry is actually due to the CIP.

In considering the accounting for carry in the common limited partnership structure, it is crucial to appreciate that carry can never be an expense of the limited partnership. The carried interest mechanism is merely an allocation of profits between the various partners in the limited partnership.

Typically, in a fund investments are classified as "fair value through profit and loss". Whilst "available for sale" may appear to be an accurate description of the fund business model, private equity frequently uses complex capital structures and special terms on realization. If the assets are designated as available for sale, detailed consideration and possible separation of any embedded derivatives are required.

The terms of the carried interest arrangement are commonly that the CIP's entitlement to receive carry is only at the point of realization.

For any type of scheme, typically fair value movements during the asset-holding period are taken to the LPs' accounts. To simplify the reading of the accounts, many preparers of limited partnership accounts will credit all fair value movements to a separate "fair value" reserve.

Whichever treatment is adopted, after Trigger Point A is passed, a useful disclosure to make is a simple statement that discloses the amount that would be allocated to the CIP in the event that the investments were sold at their carrying value. The different types of scheme determine when profits are allocated to the CIP and distributions made to them.

With a deal-by-deal scheme, since the CIP is entitled to a share of the profits at the point of realization, a share of each realized profit together with a transfer of historic fair value movements is allocated to the CIP. On realization, cash is distributed to the partners in accordance with the LPA. The cash will reduce the balance outstanding on the LPs' loan accounts and the income accounts of both the LPs and the CIP.

Under a "whole fund with hurdle scheme", proceeds from realization and other realized profits are distributed to the LPs as repayments of their loan capital and any profits allocated. All profits are allocated to the LPs (or the fair value reserve) until Trigger Point B, when the CIP is due to receive its share (commonly 20%) of all future distributions from the fund. This is reflected in the accounts by transferring an amount equal to the CIP's share of all remaining net assets from the LPs' accounts to the CIP. Future profits are allocated in the profit-sharing ratio and cash distributions follow the terms of the LPA.

The terms of the LPA will determine when Trigger Point B is achieved. This may be when the LPs have received back in cash from the fund their loan capital together with the hurdle. If a fund draws more loan capital down from the investors after Trigger Point B (sometimes permitted under the terms of the LPA to provide additional funding to existing investments), the CIP is not entitled to any profits until that further loan and hurdle thereon is repaid. During this period after the trigger being met and undone and before Trigger Point B is re-achieved, the accounting is less clearcut and subject to judgment. It may be held that the subsequent drawdown of loan is of such a size that Trigger Point B will not be reached again, in which case the allocation to the CIP should be reversed. More commonly, it is anticipated that Trigger Point B will be achieved again in a reasonable period of time and allocations to the CIP are merely ceased until that date.

As might be imagined, "deal by deal with a whole fund calculation and clawback" is an amalgam of these accounting treatments. The terms of these types of agreements vary hugely, but a typical commercial agreement would be that the CIP partners may share in the profits arising on realizations, so long as the valuation of the investments in aggregate exceeds the amount of loans and hurdle outstanding. Any amount distributed is paid into an escrow account, under the control of the CIP, which is available to be clawed back by the limited partnership in the event that the fund does not ultimately meet its objectives (clawback). The CIP may withdraw funds from the escrow account subject to a separate set of rules and conditions.

In these situations, calculating Trigger Point B can be a complex calculation depending on the LPA terms. Once it is passed, the CIP may participate in the next realization, so long as it continues to be passed at that time. On realization of an investment, the appropriate share of the profit is allocated to the CIP and an amount is distributed to the escrow account. At this time, although the fund expects to achieve its objectives, this ultimate outcome remains uncertain. Accordingly, it is unlikely that there will be an allocation of unrealized profits to the CIP from the LPs within the partners' accounts.

So long as the fund continues on track, it is unlikely that the accounts of the limited partnership will reflect any balance held in the escrow account. Typically the fund is excluded from the LP accounts as the CIP, subject to the escrow rules, has control over the funds. If the performance of the fund declines, the amounts distributed to the CIP may be accessed by the limited partnership to distribute to the LPs. The amount required to restore the LPs' position might then be recognized as a receivable amount in the limited partnership accounts. Whether the full amount of the receivable should be treated as recoverable will depend on the individual circumstances. If the balance resides in the escrow account, recovery is reasonably certain. Once amounts have been distributed to individual managers who participate through the CIP, recovery is likely to be more difficult.

In the accounts of the fund (U.K. GAAP)

U.K. GAAP still retains a choice of alternate accounting policies for investments. The accounting policy of reporting investments at the "lower of cost or net realizable value" remains valid. It is, however, rarely used since the value of investments is critical to a proper understanding of the affairs of the fund.

FRS 26 ("Financial instruments measurement") results in accounting treatments similar to reporting under IFRS. FRS 26 is optional for most entities at the present time and is rarely adopted by private equity funds due to the additional standards that are required to be adopted and the extensive disclosures.

As a result, the majority of private equity funds will adopt an accounting convention of "historical cost as amended for the revaluation of fixed asset investments." This allows the preparer of the accounts to include investments at valuation, without significant additional disclosure. Typically, the fair value movement will be shown underneath the profit and loss account, the balance of which is taken to a revaluation reserve or allocated to the LPs' accounts. Alternately, the fair value movement is included in a separate statement of total recognized gains and losses.

The accounting principles for recognizing profit allocations and distributions to the CIP under the different schemes are common to those followed under IFRS.

In the accounts of the CIP (IFRS)

In preparing the accounts of the CIP, the main considerations are the recognition of income and the treatment of the investment in the fund.

Carried interest vehicles are commonly limited partnerships, as this can preserve the tax nature of receipts from the fund. These have historically been non-qualifying limited partnerships and may be managed by the GP, the LPs being the individuals involved in the management of the fund. Since the potential recipients of the accounts are themselves closely involved in the management of the fund, they often will believe that they are sufficiently aware of the results and financial position not to need audited financial statements and, accordingly, the reporting requirements of the CIP are minimal. It would be extremely unusual for the managers to prescribe a requirement for IFRS accounts through the LPA.

Carried interest should be recognized by the CIP when it is probable that future economic benefit will flow to the CIP. Under the terms of a typical LPA, these conditions are both met at the point of realization of an underlying asset in the fund. The contractual receipt of realized gains is relatively straightforward. The complications arise in the interaction between the carrying value of the CIP's investment in the fund, the realization of gains, and any clawback provisions.

Although it may be suggested that the CIP's interest in the fund is a derivative of sorts, this investment by the CIP in the fund is best regarded as an extremely highly geared investment. Under IAS 39, the investment in the fund is recognized at fair value. Fair value of unquoted private equity assets is discussed in more detail in Chapter 10. In considering the fair value of the CIP's investment in the fund, there is usually no market for that interest and the preparer has to estimate the fair value based on what a hypothetical third party might pay for that interest.

At the establishment of the limited partnership that will become the fund, following the commitments of LPs, the only asset of the limited partnership is the capital introduced. If there are no further assets or agreements, the cost of the capital introduced is likely to be the most reliable indicator of value on the date when it is introduced. Thereafter, the fair value estimate is subject to significant judgments and opinions.

One cannot set out established rules for estimating the value of the CIP's interest in the fund. Ultimately, the fair value will be based on the expected timing and quantum of returns generated from that investment. The following points in the life of the fund might reasonably be expected to change an individual's views of the likelihood or quantum of those returns:

- The LPs making commitments to the limited partnership and the fund closing
- The fund being fully invested
- Trigger Point A when carried interest would be paid if the investments were sold at their carrying value
- Trigger Point B when the CIP is entitled to a share of future realizations
- Actual receipts of carried interest
- Liquidation of the fund.

In the accounts of the CIP (U.K. GAAP)

If the LPA stipulates U.K. GAAP and the manager has adopted FRS 26, then the accounting treatment would be the same as for IFRS above. More usually, FRS 26 is not adopted and the accounting policy for investments is that they are held at the lower of cost and market value. This removes the requirement for the accounts' preparer to estimate the fair value of the CIP's interest in the fund. Income from realizations is recognized as it is earned, commonly on realization of the underlying investment assets.

In the accounts of the manager

The CIP may be consolidated into the accounts of the manager under either GAAP. The consideration of whether consolidation is appropriate is similar to that for consolidation of the fund (i.e., is the manager "controlling the CIP for benefit"?). If the carried interest receipts are entirely directed to the individual managers as LPs on the basis of their original personal investment with no carried interest being paid to the manager, it is likely that the CIP will not meet the requirements for consolidation. If the manager receives a significant element of the carried interest in its own right or is able to direct the payments amongst the individuals after the CIP's establishment, then it is likely that the manager would be held to be "controlling for benefit" and the CIP consolidated.

In practice, the situation is generally less clear than these extremes. The preparer of the accounts needs to consider all the terms by which the individuals invest including vesting rights and the provisions regarding an individual's rights to the investment on leaving the organization. The more terms that exist putting rights into the hands of the manager over the individuals, then the more likely it is that the CIP should be regarded as a vehicle of the manager and consolidated. If the CIP is consolidated, then the receipts by the CIP would be income in the manager's consolidated accounts and the payments to the carry recipients treated as minority interests. When the manager does not consolidate the CIP or the fund, there will be no entries in the primary statements relating to the receipts and subsequent payments.

The payment of carried interest through these vehicles is, however, generally held to be a payment from a subsidiary to senior members of management. The existence and the total amount paid or allocated should be disclosed under U.K. GAAP and IFRS in the accounts as a related party transaction.

6.2.4   Partners' capital

In a typical limited partnership, there are two types of "capital". All the partners make a capital contribution with the LPs additionally providing loan capital. The ratios of the capital contribution are commonly the same as the carried interest participation by the CIP, so for a 20% carry scheme the ratio for the CIP to the LPs will be 1 : 4. The GP will normally only make a nominal contribution to the capital, unless required to make a contribution as a co-investment alongside the LPs. The loan capital provided by the LPs is a significant multiple (up to 100,000 times) their capital contribution. The bulk of the "capital" for investment is provided in the form of subordinated loans, since this allows for the simplest legal processes in terms of drawdown and distribution.

The first question is whether the capital contribution may be regarded as equity or whether, being of a finite life and due to be repaid at the end of that life, this should be regarded as a liability.

Under IAS 32 and FRS 25

The principal feature of this capital contribution is that it entitles the holder to participate in the profits and net assets of the entity on a winding up. The winding-up date is largely predetermined by the LPA. The only feature that would suggest that this is a liability is that it will ultimately be repaid. A reading of the standards can reasonably conclude that, where an equity instrument is redeemable at the end of the expected life of the vehicle, this factor alone would be insufficient to make the instrument a liability. Accordingly, the capital contribution is generally regarded as equity capital.

In a private equity limited partnership, the "loan capital" or "commitment" from the LPs has the following characteristics:

- It is drawn down on demand by the GP
- It is redeemable when the GP deems it appropriate
- It is not subject to any repayment schedule
- It bears no rate of interest
- It is unsecured

- It is only repayable to the extent that funds are available to make the repayment
- To the extent that it has not been redeemed at the conclusion of the limited partnership, it will be written off
- It ranks below any external creditors.

To many, this would appear to have few characteristics or risks associated with a loan and be more akin to an equity risk. However, although subordinated, these "loans" do not entitle the holder to participate in the residual net assets of the entity and the capital contribution of the partners ranks lower than these loans. Hence, these loans should properly be shown as a liability of the limited partnership.

As the allocation of profits and losses are predetermined by the LPA, amounts allocated to the partners are similarly shown as liabilities of the partnership. This results in a balance sheet adding down to a small figure, being the capital contribution of the partners. In order to assist the LPs in interpreting the accounts, all the amounts due to and from the partners are usually included at the foot of the balance sheet.

6.2.5   Responsibility shift

The fund accounts are a critical element of the reporting that a fund makes to its investors. It is likely to be an annual part of a range of regular investor reports covering portfolio companies and fund progress.

Investor reporting has advanced significantly as the private equity market has matured and continues to develop further each year. Much of the current drive behind the enhancement in investor reporting has been driven by changes in accounting by the investors. Prior to 1999, most investors would report their private equity interests in their own accounts at (impaired) cost. Accordingly, investor reports were treated as a reassuring signpost that the fund was heading in the right direction, but little use was made of the accounting data in the reports.

Now, the majority of investors will be required to include their private equity interests in their own accounts at fair value. This has resulted in an important shift in responsibilities from the GP to the LPs. If a LP is to use the valuation of the fund reported to it by the GP, it must satisfy itself that the valuation is free from material error. In effect, the GP's reported number becomes the LP's number the moment that the LP includes it in its accounts. An LP needs to have processes in place to allow it appropriately to assess and challenge the limited partnership accounts.

6.3   INTERPRETING FUND ACCOUNTS

The fund accounts can provide the investor with a large amount of information, but for this case study we shall focus on a number of questions that are fundamental to the LP's understanding of the accounts. These questions are:

- What GAAP is used?
- How much did the LP put in?
- How much more might the LP be called upon to invest?
- How much has the LP received back?
- What is this costing the LP?

- How much will the LP get back and when?
- What value should the LP put in his/her accounts?

Appendix 6.A to this chapter contains the financial statements of Zebra Fund LP for the year ended December 31, 2009. Zebra Fund is an English limited partnership, established by an LPA dated June 4, 2004 as restated and amended on May 12, 2007. The fund commitments at final close amounted to USD130mn.

We consider the questions above for the LP entitled *Employees Fund* in the subsections below.

Which GAAP is used?

Confirming the GAAP used and the basis of preparation is the first step in interpreting the accounts. The GAAP provides the broader background within which the accounts are prepared.

Note 2 "Accounting policies" includes the reference to the accounting convention as: "These financial statements have been prepared in accordance with the applicable accounting standards and in accordance with the historical cost accounting convention as modified by the revaluation of investments." There is no clear reference to which GAAP these have been prepared under.

Throughout Note 2 there are references to financial reporting standards. These are U.K. GAAP terms, but there is no reference to U.K. GAAP. This would indicate that the accounts are prepared under the GAAP referred to in Section 6.1.2 as "Other" and, whilst it has adopted many U.K. GAAP standards, the basis of preparation is not fully in compliance with U.K. GAAP.

This is confirmed by the report of the auditors which gives as the opinion, "In our opinion the financial statements for the year ended 31 December 2009 have been properly prepared in accordance with the accounting policies set out in note 2 to the financial statements and in accordance with the LPA."

The key identifiers in this report are the absence of the term "a true and fair view" and no reference to a particular GAAP in the audit report. It is the report of the auditor which confirms the GAAP used. This means that all that the reader of the accounts can assume in relation to the accounting policies adopted will be set out in the notes to the accounts.

How much did the LP put in?

This should be a question to which the LP already knows the answer, and Zebra Fund's financial statements provide a confirmation or reconciliation to that amount. Note 9 "Total Partners' Funds" gives details of the transactions between the fund and the LPs. The size and format of partners' notes varies widely. If a fund has a large number of LPs, disclosing in the notes the movement for the year on each partner's account, together with the cumulative movements since inception, will lead to a note of many pages in length. This example is typical in format whereby the movement in the year is shown for the LPs as a whole and the cumulative movement by individual partner. The final table in Note 9 shows that the Employees Fund has provided cumulative loan drawdowns of USD14.65mn.

Lack of symmetry

There are a number of factors—which stand out when considering this note—that should alert the reader that this fund has an unusual allocation structure. In a typical limited partnership all transactions with the LPs take place symmetrically across all LPs. If an LP provides 20% of the total LPs' commitment, the LP would expect 20% of the drawdowns, distributions, and income allocations. Maintaining symmetry is preferable from an administrative point of view, but is not always possible. This asymmetry complicates any interpretation of the accounts.

Clearly the Zebra Fund is asymmetric as we have loans drawn down from the investors and income allocations which are not in proportion to their individual commitments. The fund has made distributions to only two of the LPs and the CIP, whilst the other LPs have received nothing.

There are several ways that asymmetry may be introduced into the limited partnership. Certain investors may be excused from investments in certain jurisdictions or industries. In the situation of Zebra Fund LP, there is a long period from commencement (June 4, 2004) to final closing (May 12, 2007). The fund is established within the single limited partnership as two separate pockets in which individual investors (including the CIP) have invested, depending on when they joined the limited partnership. The fund was originally set up with a commitment of USD60.00mn. Drawdowns were made from the first two investors (Employees Fund and Pension Fund) of USD22.00mn in the ratio of their commitments 20:40. These investments were realized prior to the other partners being admitted, generating gains of USD55.00mn. These realizations triggered an allocation to the CIP under the terms of the original LPA since all loans that had been drawn down at that date, together with the hurdle, had been repaid. This information was all included in prior period accounts.

When additional partners were admitted at the final closing and the Pension Fund increased its commitment, for accounting and carry purposes two pockets were effectively created, being these original investments and all subsequent investments.

Whilst it is clear that in the early period the partners had asymmetric allocations and returns, the important factor going forward is the knowledge that all LPs now participate in existing investments in accordance with their capital contributions. This piece of crucial information is not set out in the accounts, but it would already be known to the LPs.

How much more might the LP be called upon to invest?

To date USD14.65mn has been drawn down in loans. This would also suggest that there is a further USD5.35mn that may be drawn down (being the Employees Fund share of the LPs' combined capital contribution multiplied by the overall fund size, less drawdowns to date). That is the obvious calculation, but without checking the LPA, it is not possible to conclusively state that it is correct. Many LPAs allow for additional amounts to be drawn in excess of the agreed commitment, if required to fund GPs' share or to redraw amounts that related to investments that were realized within a relatively short timeframe and distributed back to the LPs. The accounts only show the outstanding commitment by derivation. If there was an amount that could be recalled by the GP in excess of the amount calculated, this would probably be disclosed.

How much has the LP received back?

Again this should be a known number by the Employees Fund. Note 9 clearly shows that the Employees Fund has received back USD21.11mn since the inception of the Zebra Fund.

What is this costing the LP?

There are several elements to the question of what this management service costs, principally the management fee and the carried interest.

Note 2 sets out in full the basis of calculation of the management fee. For the year ended December 31, 2009, this amounts to 2% of the total commitments, plus expenses incurred by the manager in investigating deals that did not proceed ("abort costs") and deducting any fees received by the manager from the portfolio ("monitoring, directors', or transaction fees").

In 2009, the total commitment amounted to USD130.00mn, so simple mathematics suggests a management fee of USD2.60mn, against USD2.23mn in the Profit and Loss Account. The difference being the net amount by which fees charged into the portfolio companies exceeded abort costs on transactions. The gross amount of abort costs and fees are not disclosed in these accounts.

What the management service is costing the Employees Fund will depend on its view of costs. The manager receives 2% of the aggregated commitments, plus any abort costs incurred. A proportion of this is being charged directly to the portfolio companies, the balance is received by them from the Zebra Fund. Whether the fees that are charged to the portfolio companies should be regarded by the LPs as a cost to them is clearly a matter of debate.

The CIP has been allocated USD8.35mn of gains realized in a prior period. So, for the Employees Fund, we can either consider our annual costs to be:

- USD0.40mn (being the Employees Fund's share of USD2.60mn)
- An amount in excess of USD0.40mn to reflect abort costs and fees
- USD0.34mn (being the Employees Fund's share of USD2.23mn)
- USD0.87mn.

USD0.87mn is calculated as the sum of the Employees Fund's share of the management fee since inception of the Zebra Fund (USD2.00mn) and the share of the carried interest allocation (USD2.78mn), divided by the period since inception of over $5\frac{1}{2}$ years.

Whilst this gives a more comprehensive figure of the cost by including the carried interest previously allocated, this is not necessarily the only or indeed the "right" answer. This calculation includes the annual charge to the fund for management fee, excluding costs borne by the portfolio companies and including carried interest paid to the CIP on a cash basis.

It would not be sensible to compare the annual returns received against the calculated annual cost. A comprehensive assessment of costs can only be reasonably calculated when the fund is approaching the end of its life and the performance of the fund as a whole on the basis of an annual rate of return can be calculated.

How much will the LP get back and when?

This is one of the questions that no set of accounts can answer. What the accounts can answer is: "What is the amount that is disclosed as being due to the LP at the year-end?" Note 9 to the accounts shows that the amount allocated to the Employees Fund at December 31, 2009 is USD7.45mn.

In the Partners' Accounts note, the Unrealized Fair Value reserve is held as a single balance and is not allocated to the individual partners (loss USD40.80mn). In the event that the fund was wound up and this loss realized, the Employees Fund would suffer its share of the loss. Again, with the asymmetric allocations, the accounts do not show precisely what the Employees Fund's share of that loss would be. When allocating the fair value reserve, it is likely that an allocation might be made to the CIP. Note 9 discloses the fact that there is no amount of the unrealized fair value reserve due to the CIP. As noted above, the Employees Fund's allocation is 2/13ths of the total, so the share is a loss of USD6.28mn.

Overall, these accounts show that the balance due to the Employees Fund at December 31, 2009 is USD1.17mn. There may be an additional amount potentially available though a clawback of the prior year payments made to the CIP, but again this is not disclosed in these accounts.

What value should the LP put in his/her accounts?

The techniques used in estimating the fair value of private equity investments and the International Private Equity and Venture Capital Valuation Guidelines (IPEV Guidelines) are discussed in detail in Chapter 10.

The Employees Fund accounts are being prepared under a GAAP that requires that investments are reported at fair value. The Board of the Employees Fund is required to prepare accounts that are free from material misstatement and error. The fair value of the interest in Zebra Fund LP, included in the accounts of the Employees Fund, is solely the responsibility of that Board. It is likely to use information from the accounts of Zebra Fund LP, but the fact that it is extracted from these underlying accounts does not reduce the Board's responsibilities. Accordingly, the Board needs to establish processes to enable it to ascertain that the information it is using is free from material error.

The fund accounts disclose that the Employees Fund's share of the net assets at December 31, 2009 is USD1.17mn.

Fair value is defined in different words depending on which GAAP and standard is being followed, although the concept remains constant. Fair value is the price at which a transaction would take place at the reporting date. In considering the fair value of an interest in a fund, the expected cash flows arising from a realization of the assets at the reporting date would appear to be a good starting point. When estimating the fair value of the interest in the fund, the valuer should consider whether adjustments should be made to his or her share of the net assets. For the purposes of this section, let us assume that the processes over the underlying investment valuations have indicated that the fair values of the underlying investments are "right" at the reporting date.

The valuer should then consider from the point of view of a prospective purchaser what factors he or she might take into account when entering into a transaction. Any matter that might affect the views of an external acquirer should be included in the consideration. These might include changes that have arisen in the period since the accounts of Zebra Fund were prepared, either internally with acquisitions and disposals; an issue arising in an underlying investment which would impact valuation; or, externally, such as the market dislocation that impacted almost all investment valuations in October 2008. There may be terms in the LPA that might impact the attributable share of net assets. As noted in the sections above, allocations of profit to the CIP are generally made when contractually due. An adjustment may be required to reflect potential future allocations to the CIP.

The strongest evidence supporting fair value is that from a transaction that actually takes place in the market. There are situations when interests in funds are sold. Whilst a price determined by a secondary transaction can provide good evidence of fair value, these prices need to be treated with caution. Generally, secondary prices are negotiated based on factors and assumptions pertinent to the individual parties and considerably wider than simply a view of underlying assets at fair value. If the Employees Fund has decided to sell its interest, then any secondary prices would be of primary importance. In most situations secondary prices provide a useful reference point, but of limited value without a clear understanding of the pricing assumptions and motivations of the parties.

So, the original question cannot be answered in the absence of additional information; however, the consideration of value should commence with the attributable share of net assets of USD1.17mn.

APPENDIX 6.A

ZEBRA FUND LP FINANCIAL STATEMENTS FOR THE YEAR ENDED DECEMBER 31, 2009

6.A.1   Contents

6.A.2   The manager, the general partner, and advisors

Manager:	Zebra LLP
General Partner:	Zebra GP Limited
Advisors:	Licus LLP
Bankers:	Warthogs Plc
Auditors to the Partnership:	Auditors LLP

6.A.3   Report of the manager, Zebra LLP

We are pleased to present the financial statements of Zebra Fund LP (the Partnership) for the year ended December 31, 2009.

Zebra Fund LP is an English limited partnership, established by a limited partnership agreement dated June 4, 2004 as restated and amended on May 12, 2007. The limited partnership agreement states that the limited partnership shall continue until the expiration of 10 years from the initial closing date, namely June 4, 2014. The limited partnership may be extended for a further 2 years in order to permit the orderly liquidation of investments, pursuant to limited partner consent.

The primary purpose of the partnership is to make investments in medium-sized European and North American businesses, which will typically be medium to long term in nature with the principal objective of generating capital growth.

The following closings occurred bringing the total commitments to USD130,000,000. Drawdowns to date are USD87,402,930 representing 67.23% of the committed capital to date. Distributions of USD71,682,933 have been made to date (including USD8,346,979 to the Carried Interest Partner escrow account). The general partner of the partnership is Zebra GP Limited.

During the year, the partnership made the following investments:

- USD0.90mn in the Book Club LP, primarily operating in South East England.

The financial statements of the partnership are set out together with detailed notes on pp. 135 to 146.

Statement of manager's responsibilities

The limited partnership agreement requires the manager to prepare financial statements for each financial period in accordance with the accounting policies set out in Note 2. In preparing those financial statements, the manager is required to:

- Select suitable accounting policies and then apply them consistently
- Make judgments and estimates that are reasonable and prudent
- State whether applicable accounting standards have been followed, subject to any material departures disclosed and explained in the financial statements
- Prepare the financial statements on a going concern basis unless it is inappropriate to presume that the partnership will continue in business.

The manager is responsible for maintaining proper accounting records which disclose with reasonable accuracy the financial position at any time of the partnership. The manager has general responsibility for taking such steps as are reasonably open to it to safeguard the assets of the partnership and, hence, for taking reasonable steps for the prevention and detection of fraud and other irregularities.

Disclosure of information to auditors

The manager confirms that, so far as it is aware, there is no relevant audit information of which the partnership auditors are unaware, and the manager has taken all the steps that ought to have been taken as manager to make itself aware of any relevant audit information and to establish that the partnership's auditors are aware of this information.

For and on behalf of Zebra LLP
February 28, 2010

6.A.4   Report of the independent auditors to the partners of Zebra Fund LP

We have audited the financial statements of Zebra Fund LP for the year ended December 31, 2009 which comprise the profit and loss account, the balance sheet, the cash flow statement, the statement of total recognized gains and losses and the related notes. These financial statements have been prepared under the accounting policies set out therein.

This report is made solely to the partners, as a body, in accordance with the terms of our engagement. Our audit work has been undertaken so that we might state to the partners those matters we have been engaged to state to them in this report and for no other purpose. To the fullest extent permitted by law, we do not accept or assume responsibility to anyone other than the partners, as a body, for our audit work, for this report, or for the opinions we have formed.

Respective responsibilities of partners and auditors

As described in the statement of manager's responsibilities on p. 133, the manager is responsible for the preparation of the financial statements in accordance with the limited partnership agreement dated June 4, 2004 as amended and restated on May 12, 2007 (the LPA).

Our responsibility under the terms of our engagement letter dated December 18, 2008 is to audit the financial statements having regard to International Standards on Auditing (U.K. and Ireland).

We report to you our opinion as to whether the financial statements have been properly prepared in accordance with the accounting policies set out in Note 2 to the financial statements and in accordance with the LPA.

We also report to you if, in our opinion, the manager's report is not consistent with the financial statements, if the partnership has not kept proper accounting records, if we have not received all the information and explanations we require for our audit, or if information specified by the LPA regarding other transactions is not disclosed.

Basis of audit opinion

We conducted our audit having regard to International Standards on Auditing (U.K. and Ireland) issued by the Auditing Practices Board. An audit includes examination, on a test basis, of evidence relevant to the amounts and disclosures in the financial statements. It also includes an assessment of the significant estimates and judgments made by the partners in the preparation of the financial statements, and of whether the accounting policies are appropriate to the partnership's circumstances, consistently applied, and adequately disclosed.

We planned and performed our audit so as to obtain all the information and explanations which we considered necessary in order to provide us with sufficient evidence to give reasonable assurance that the financial statements are free from material misstatement, whether caused by fraud or other irregularity or error. In forming our opinion we also evaluated the overall adequacy of the presentation of information in the financial statements.

Opinion

In our opinion the financial statements for the year ended December 31, 2009 have been properly prepared in accordance with the accounting policies set out in Note 2 to the financial statements and in accordance with the LPA.

Anthony Cecil
for and on behalf of Auditors LLP
Chartered Accountants

6.A.5 Profit and loss account

	Notes	Year ended 31 December 2009 USD	Year ended 31 December 2008 USD
Income			
Interest income	2, 5	2,054,265	715,596
Bank interest		—	29,230
Other income		—	—
		2,054,265	**744,826**
Expenditure			
General partner's priority share of profits	2	(2,231,779)	(2,320,501)
Interest on bridge loan		(7,855)	(228,326)
Other expenditure		(138,530)	(132,338)
Provision for interest accrued	7	(2,054,265)	(717,345)
		(4,432,429)	**(3,398,510)**
Net loss for the year before realized gains		**(2,378,164)**	**(2,653,684)**
Realized gain on sale of investments		39,159	—
Net loss for the year after realized gains		**(2,339,005)**	**(2,653,684)**

Statement of total recognized gains and losses

	Notes	Year ended 31 December 2009 USD	Year ended 31 December 2008 USD
Net loss for the year		(2,339,005)	(2,653,684)
Movement in unrealized fair value reserve	4	(17,416,055)	(23,382,267)
Total recognized loss for the year		**(19,755,060)**	**(26,035,951)**

The notes on pp. 138 to 146 form part of these financial statements.

6.A.6   Balance sheet

	Notes	As at 31 December 2009 USD	As at 31 December 2008 USD
Fixed assets			
Investments	4	17,367,490	33,860,573
Current assets			
Cash at bank		871,045	1,193,780
Debtors	6	292,283	113,220
Current liabilities			
Creditors: Amounts falling due within one year	8	(234,298)	(116,397)
Net current assets		**929,030**	**1,190,603**
Total assets less current liabilities		**18,296,520**	**35,051,176**
Financed by			
Capital contribution account	9	1,625	1,625
Loan account	9	24,065,676	21,065,272
Income account	9	35,029,388	37,368,393
Net unrealized fair value reserve	9	(40,800,169)	(23,384,114)
Total partners' funds		**18,296,520**	**35,051,176**

These financial statements were approved by the manager on February 28, 2010. The notes on pp. 138 to 146 form part of these financial statements.

For and on behalf of Zebra LLP
February 28, 2010

6.A.7 Cash flow statement

	Notes	Year ended 31 December 2009 USD	Year ended 31 December 2008 USD
Operating activities			
Net loss for the year		(2,378,164)	(2,653,684)
Bank interest received		—	(29,230)
Interest on bridge loan		7,855	228,326
(Increase)/Decrease in debtors	6	(179,063)	826,351
Increase /(Decrease) in creditors	8	117,901	(1,205,245)
Net cash outflow from operating activities		**(2,431,471)**	**(2,833,482)**
Returns on investments and servicing of finance			
Bank interest received		—	29,230
Interest on bridge loan		(7,855)	(228,326)
Net cash outflow from returns on investments and servicing of finance		**(7,855)**	**(199,096)**
Capital expenditure and financial investment			
Purchase of investments	4	(923,071)	(22,923,227)
Disposal of investments	4	39,258	—
Net cash outflow from investing activities		**(883,813)**	**(22,923,227)**
Financing activities			
Loans drawn down from limited partners	9	3,000,404	26,359,906
Distribution to limited partners	9	—	—
Distribution to carried interest partner escrow	9	—	(8,346,979)
Net cash inflow from financing activities		**3,000,404**	**18,012,927**
Decrease in cash during the year		**(322,735)**	**(7,942,878)**
Reconciliation of net cash flow to movement in net cash			
Net cash at the beginning of the year		1,193,780	9,136,658
Cash at bank at the end of the year		871,045	1,193,780
Movement in cash during the year		**(322,735)**	**(7,942,878)**

The notes on pp. 138 to 146 form part of these financial statements.

6.A.8 Notes to the financial statements

1. The partnership

Establishment of the partnership

Zebra Fund LP (the partnership) is a United Kingdom limited partnership, established by a limited partnership agreement dated June 4, 2004 as restated and amended on May 12, 2007:

- The carried interest partner is Zebra Executive LP
- The general partner of the partnership is Zebra GP Ltd.

The manager of the partnership is Zebra LLP, and is responsible for the management, operation, and administration of the affairs of the partnership in accordance with the limited partnership agreement.

Business of the partnership

The primary purpose of the partnership is to carry on the business of making investments with the principal objective of achieving a high rate of return from income and capital gains.

Duration of the partnership

The limited partnership agreement states that the partnership shall continue until the 10th anniversary of the initial closing date, namely June 4, 2014. The partnership may be extended by up to 2 years in order to permit the orderly liquidation of investments, pursuant to consent of the limited partner.

2. Accounting policies

The following accounting policies have been applied consistently in dealing with items which are considered to be material in relation to the financial statements.

Accounting convention

These financial statements have been prepared in accordance with the applicable accounting standards and in accordance with the historical cost accounting convention as modified by the revaluation of investments.

The manager has a reasonable expectation that the partnership has adequate resources to continue in operational existence for the foreseeable future, including recourse to loan commitments. Accordingly, the manager continues to adopt the going concern basis in preparing the financial statements.

Income

Bank interest and loan interest income are accounted for on an accruals basis. If there is doubt over the recoverability of dividends or interest income, a provision will be made. Dividend income is recognized when the right to receive payment is established.

General partner share

The general partner, Zebra GP Ltd., is entitled to receive a priority profit share. Until the earliest of the end of the investment period or the stepdown date, this is calculated as 2% per annum of total commitments. Thereafter, this is 2% per annum of the aggregate acquisition cost of investments which have not been realized. The stepdown date will occur on May 12, 2010 and 3 years after the final closing of Zebra Fund LP. The general partner's share is increased by an amount equal to the aggregate abort costs incurred by the manager, general partner, or any of their associates (including any irrecoverable VAT or similar tax thereon) in the immediately preceding accounting period to the extent such abort costs have not already been recovered by the manager, general partner, or associate either from the partnership or third parties.

The share will be reduced in accordance with the LPA where the aggregate of fees earned and retained by the general partner, manager, or any of their associates in connection with the management of the fund's portfolio exceeds the retained fees level.

Such share ranks as a first charge on capital gains of the partnerships in any accounting period. Where the gains of the fund exceed the amount to be allocated to the general partner, the general partner may elect which items of capital gain form part of the share taken.

If there are insufficient capital gains in any one accounting period, the general partner may take an interest-free loan in respect of the balance of the general partner's share entitlement. Drawings are taken annually in advance through 2006, and sem–annually thereafter. In no circumstances shall such interest-free loans be repaid by the general partner other than by set-off of allocations of capital gains. As the general partner is entitled to draw the amount even if profits are not made, and such drawings are not repayable in the event that there are no profits, Financial Reporting Standard 5 "Reporting the substance of transactions" has been adopted and the priority profit share for the relevant period is accounted for as an expense of the limited partnerships.

Transaction and funding costs

All ancillary costs associated with the making of investments are recognized on an accruals basis and expensed in the relevant accounting period.

Foreign exchange

Monetary transactions denominated in foreign currencies are recorded at actual exchange rates prevailing at the date of the transaction. Assets and liabilities in currencies other than U.S. dollars are translated into U.S. dollars at the rates of exchange prevailing at the balance sheet date. Exchange differences are taken to the profit and loss account or the statement of total recognized gains and losses, as appropriate.

Distributions

All capital and income receipts shall be distributed among the partners based on allocations made in accordance with the limited partnership agreement. Any other income of the partnership shall be distributed to the investors pro rata to their commitments.

The carried interest partner is not entitled to payment in respect of any carried interest until the limited partners have received an amount equal to the aggregate commitments previously drawn down by the partnership, plus an amount representing an annualized internal rate of return of 8%, calculated in accordance with the provisions of the limited partnership agreement.

Taxation

Taxation has not been recorded in these financial statements as any tax liabilities that may arise, on income or capital, are borne by the individual partners comprising the limited partnership. Accordingly, no provision for taxation is made in these financial statements. Capital losses are allocated to the partners in accordance with the LPA.

Investments

Investments are included in the balance sheet at fair value. Fair values have been determined in accordance with the International Private Equity and Venture Capital Valuation Guidelines. These guidelines require the valuer to make judgments as to the most appropriate valuation method to be used.

Each investment is reviewed individually with regard to the stage, nature, and circumstances of the investment and the most appropriate valuation method selected. The valuation results are then reviewed and an amendment to the carrying value of investments is made as considered appropriate.

- *Quoted investments*—quoted investments for which an active market exists are valued at the closing bid price at the balance sheet date.
- *Unquoted direct investments*—unquoted direct investments are valued using certain valuation techniques. The techniques that may be used include:
  - Startups that have yet to generate positive cash flows are valued by reference to whether they have reached certain predetermined milestones. When this results in the investment being held at cost then a revaluation adjustment is made for the fluctuation in foreign exchange between the disbursement and balance sheet dates.
  - Investments in which there has been a recent funding round involving significant financing from external investors are valued at the price of the recent funding.
  - Investments in an established business which is generating sustainable profits and positive cash flows (or where these may be anticipated with reasonable certainty) are valued using earnings multiples.
  - Investments in a business the value of which is derived mainly from its underlying net assets rather than its earnings are valued on the basis of net asset valuation.
  - Investments in a business which is not generating sustainable profits or positive cash flows and for which there has not been any recent independent funding but cash flows of the underlying business can be estimated with some certainty are valued by calculating the discounted cash flow of the investment.
- *Gains and losses*
  - Realized gains and losses are reported in the profit and loss account as the difference between proceeds received from sale of investments and the carrying value of such investments at the last balance sheet date.
  - Net unrealized fair value adjustments are recognized in the statement of total recognised gains and losses. An adjustment is made to the unrealized fair value reserve on the realization of any investments to transfer any amounts previously recognized in the fair value reserve to the income account.

Consolidation

The partnership has investments which may be regarded as subsidiaries or associated undertakings under Financial Reporting Standards No. 2 and No. 9, respectively, which would require these to be consolidated using the equity method of accounting. As the nature of the partnership's business is to achieve long-term capital growth by the provision of risk capital and that the general partner and the partnership are consolidated into the ultimate parent undertaking of the general partner, Zebra LLP, these investments have not been consolidated into the financial statements of the partnership.

3. Contribution of capital

The following closings occurred bringing the total commitments to USD130,000,000. Investors have subscribed to the partnership in commitments of which 0.001% represents capital contributions and 99.999% represents a loan commitment. Total commitments as at May 12, 2007 (the date of final closing) were USD130,000,000 of which USD1,300 represented capital and the balance represented loan. The carried interest partner has subscribed to the partnership an amount of capital of USD325 representing 20% of the total subscribed capital.

4. Fixed assets—investments

Name of investee company	Date of original acquisition	Cost at Jan. 1 2009 USD	Additions during the year USD	Disposal during the year USD	Cost at Dec. 31 2009 USD	Interest accrued USD	Opening unrealized fair value USD	Closing unrealized fair value USD	Manager's valuation USD	% of equity in investee
Unquoted										
Danish Pastries Plc[1]	Aug-04	99	—	(99)	—	—	(99)	—	—	—
Pueblo Clothing Plc[2]	Mar-06	8,134,500	—	—	8,134,500	—	(4,465,590)	(4,913,856)	3,220,644	37.8%
Bad Decision Group[3]	Jul-07	26,000,000	—	—	26,000,000	—	(18,918,425)	(26,000,000)	—	46.8%
The Book Club (U.K.) Ltd.[4]	Oct-07	383,775	923,071	—	1,306,846	—	—	—	1,306,846	4.6%
Chariot Skates Plc[5]	Aug-08	22,726,313	—	—	22,726,313	—	—	(9,886,313)	12,840,000	87.4%
Total investments		**57,244,687**	**923,071**	**(99)**	**58,167,659**	**—**	**(23,384,114)**	**(40,800,169)**	**17,367,490**	

Notes: 1. The investment in Danish Pastries Plc was held through Pasties Ltd., a subsidiary of the partnership. Pasties Ltd. is incorporated in Jersey.

2. The investment in Pueblo Clothing Plc is held through Rags Holdings (Luxembourg) Ltd.

3. Bad Decision Group is held by Oops Holdings (Cayman) Ltd.

4. The Book Club (U.K.) Ltd. is held by Bookworm (Jersey) Ltd.

5. Chariot Skates Plc is held by Speedy (Luxembourg) Ltd. Notes to the Financial Statements

5. Interest income

Interest income is presented net of provisions below:

	Year ended 31 December 2009 USD	Year ended 31 December 2008 USD
Interest accrued during the year	2,054,265	715,596
Provision for interest accrued	(2,054,265)	(717,345)
Net interest income for the year	—	**(1,748)**

6. Debtors

	Year ended 31 December 2009 USD	Year ended 31 December 2008 USD
Loan interest receivable	2,771,610	717,345
Provision for interest accrued	(2,771,610)	(717,345)
Receivable from manager	0	49,180
Other debtors	292,283	64,040
	292,283	**113,220**

7. Specific provisions

The following specific provisions are held against interest accrued where the interest relates to an investment valued below cost.

	Year ended 31 December 2009 USD	Year ended 31 December 2008 USD
Balance as at January 1	717,345	—
Amount recognized in the year	2,054,265	717,345
Balance as at December 31	**2,771,610**	**717,345**

8. Creditors: Amounts falling due within 1 year

	Year ended 31 December 2009 USD	Year ended 31 December 2008 USD
Amounts payable to manager	19,922	64,827
Bridge facility	149,739	—
Other creditors including accruals	64,637	51,570
	234,298	**116,397**

9. Total partners' funds

Capital contribution account

	Limited partners	Carried interest partner	Total
	USD	USD	USD
As at January 1, 2009	1,300	325	1,625
Contributions during the year	—	—	—
As at December 31, 2009	1,300	325	1,625

Drawdowns and distributions

	Limited partners	Carried interest partner	Total
	USD	USD	USD
Balance as at January 1, 2009	21,065,272	(8,346,979)	12,718,293
Drawdowns during the year	3,000,404	—	3,000,404
Distributions during the year	—	—	—
Balance as at December 31, 2009	24,065,676	(8,346,979)	15,718,697

Income account

	General partner	Limited partners	Carried interest partner	Total
	USD	USD	USD	USD
Net Income as at January 1, 2009	—	37,368,393	—	37,368,393
Net income during the year	1,000	(2,339,005)	—	(2,338,005)
Distributions during the year[1]	(1,000)	—	—	(1,000)
As at December 31, 2009	—	35,029,388	—	35,029,388

Notes: 1. The net income which has been allocated to the carried interest partner is as a result of the partnership having reached its hurdle based on the carried interest calculation, pursuant to Clause 6.2.2 of the LPA. As the drawdowns from limited partners continue until May 12, 2010 or when the fund is fully invested, if earlier, this amount is held in an escrow account by the manager. In the event that the fund does not return the minimum amount to the limited partners, this balance in escrow may be clawed back. If the hurdle continues to be achieved at May 12, 2010 or when the fund is fully invested, if earlier, it will be distributed to the carried interest partner. In the event that all investments are realized at their carrying value, nothing (previous year USD2.8mn) would be payable to the carried interest partner.

Unrealized fair value reserve

	2009 USD	2008 USD
As at January 1	(23,384,114)	(1,847)
Movement in unrealized fair value reserve on account of other investments	(17,416,055)	(23,382,267)
As at December 31	**(40,800,169)**	**(23,384,114)**

Total partners' funds

	General partner USD	Limited partners USD	Carried interest partner USD	Total USD
Allocated partners' funds as at December 31, 2009	—	59,096,364	325	59,096,689
Net unrealized fair value reserve				(40,800,169)
Total partners' funds as at December 31, 2009				**18,296,520**

	General partner USD	Limited partners USD	Carried interest partner USD	Total USD
Allocated partners' funds as at December 31, 2008	—	58,434,965	325	58,435,290
Unrealised fair value reserve				(23,384,114)
Total partners' funds as at December 31, 2008				**35,051,176**

Partners' accounts

	Capital contribution account USD	Loans drawn down USD	Total[1] distribu- tions USD	Income account USD	Total partners' accounts USD
Limited partners					
Pension Fund	900	60,320,500	(42,223,969)	23,034,496	41,131,927
Employees Fund	200	14,649,944	(21,111,985)	13,908,346	**7,446,505**
Retirement Fund	100	6,215,593	-	(956,727)	**5,258,966**
Zebra Fund of Funds LP	100	6,215,593	-	(956,727)	**5,258,966**
	1,300	**87,401,630**	**(63,335,954)**	**35,029,388**	**59,096,364**
Carried interest partner					
Zebra Executive LP	325	—	(8,346,979)	8,346,979	325
General partner					
Zebra GP Ltd.	—	—	—	—	—
	1,625	**87,401,630**	**(71,682,933)**	**43,376,367**	**59,096,689**
Unrealized fair value reserve					(40,800,169)
Partners Funds					**18,296,520**

Notes: 1. Realized gains have been distributed to the partners other than excused partners as per the provisions of the limited partnership agreement.

10. Reconciliation of movements on partners' funds

	2009 USD	2008 USD
As at January 1	35,051,176	43,074,200
Net loss for the year after the general partner's share	(2,378,164)	(2,653,684)
Drawdowns from limited partners	3,000,404	26,359,906
Distributions to limited partners	—	—
Distribution to carried interest partner escrow	—	(8,346,979)
Realized gain for the year	39,159	—
Movement in unrealized fair value reserve	(17,416,055)	(23,382,267)
As at December 31	**18,296,520**	**35,051,176**

11. Related party transactions

During the year, a number of recharges for deal costs, abort fees, and other such expenses were made between the fund and the manager in accordance with the LPA; these transactions and balances due at the end of the year have been disclosed elsewhere within the notes to the financial statements.

The limited partnership agreement states that Zebra GP Ltd. shall act as general partner of the partnership and is entitled to priority profit share payments of USD2,321,379 as described in Note 2. Zebra GP Ltd. is a wholly owned subsidiary of Zebra LLP.

Zebra Executive LP is a carried interest partner and is entitled to participate in profits as described in Notes 2 and 9 of the financial statements.

12. Ultimate controlling party

The immediate controlling party of the limited partnership is Zebra GP Ltd., a wholly owned subsidiary of Zebra LLP (the ultimate controlling party), a limited liability partnership incorporated in Great Britain and registered in England and Wales.

7

Gatekeepers

7.1 INTRODUCTION

Gatekeepers are professional advisors operating in the private equity market on behalf of their clients. They exist because most institutional investors do not have sufficient exposure to the private equity asset class to justify building and/or retaining the in-house expertise. Gatekeepers first emerged in the 1970s in the United States, when they developed close relationships particularly with public pension plans that were operating under strict rules which often made the use of investment consultants obligatory (see Borel, 2002). They focus on helping clients develop allocation strategies across asset classes, private equity portfolio construction, fund due diligence, and fund selection. Institutional investors such as insurance companies, pension funds, banks, family offices, endowments, foundations, and high-net-worth individuals often even use several gatekeepers in parallel.

The so-called *fund of funds* is probably the most common type of vehicle in this context and will therefore be covered in more detail in this chapter.[1] A fund of funds pools a group of investors and uses the capital to assemble a diversified portfolio of private equity funds. There are many degrees of engagement by advisors. What is common though is that their role is solely as intermediary where the ultimate fund commitment, directly or indirectly, is by their clients. Gatekeepers help their clients to assemble portfolios of funds. Thus, institutional investors, as "limited partners" (LPs), enter into a relationship with the private equity firms that raise these funds.

7.2 MAIN TYPES OF PROFESSIONAL ADVISORS

Institutional investors often do not see alternative assets as their core competence and often only allocate a small proportion of the funds into it. As such they typically do not see a legitimacy to retain a complete team of private equity investment professionals with experience in all the relevant areas, such as accounting, due diligence, legal

---

1. Especially, small institutions, endowments, or high-net-worth individuals and families are often unable to bring up sufficient capital for "serious" investing in this illiquid asset class. Figures mentioned in this chapter should be seen as indicative, in continuous flux, with ups and downs according to changing market conditions.

This chapter has been written by Thomas Meyer, Director of EVCA's Limited Partner Platform.

services, executive recruitment, fund administration, distribution management,[2] or software application development and support. Such services are offered by various parties, but it is difficult to assess and to compare all of them, as literally no single provider operates like another. For some service providers private equity is core business, whereas for others (e.g., law firms) it is just part of a larger range of activities.

Consultants and account managers (see Exhibit 7.1) are types of gatekeepers that offer non-discretionary services where investment decisions require the client's consent who thus keeps control over the investment process.

Another type of gatekeeper, the fund of funds, tends to operate on a fully discretionary basis where it is given the authority to make investment decisions without first notifying its clients. The gatekeeper's role can range from a complement by concentrating on areas not covered by in-house staff to a wholesale outsourcing of the entire activity. Even if investors want to build up such capabilities they will—at least initially—lack the skill and resources to do everything internally and, thus, have to resort to external help. It is mainly gatekeepers that are relevant to this discussion but the picture would be incomplete without mentioning placement agents (see Exhibit 7.2).

7.2.1 Consultants

Consultants focus on the needs of institutional investors and offer a wide range of services: analyzing the objectives of investors, program design and planning, asset allocation review, portfolio design, manager identification, due diligence, cash flow forecasting, risk management, portfolio monitoring, performance evaluation, performance reporting and attribution analysis, controlling and reporting of investments, etc. Other important services are advisory board representations and providing private equity–related education for in-house staff. Consultants are also hired for special projects. There are clearly overlaps with other private equity service providers, such as law firms or due diligence firms.

Consultants help with research and assist in the assessment of investment proposals, but they leave the final investment decision to their clients. Not all investment proposals need to be originated by the consultants. Clients often request an evaluation of an investments proposal or a request to conduct confirmatory due diligence on funds sourced by the client directly (see Exhibit 7.3).

7.2.2 Account managers

Over time, many of the original consultants have moved closer to asset management by offering their clients a range of discretionary investment products, often in addition to providing non-discretionary investment services. Account managers as gatekeepers are increasingly assuming complete responsibility for negotiating the partnership terms and conditions and managing allocations. Usually, large clients prefer to retain a final say in major allocation decisions through a formal approval process. Such non-discretionary account managers, like consultants, charge fees for specific services, such as deal sourcing, due diligence, or monitoring.

Whereas consultants or account managers offer similar benefits compared with funds of funds, they provide more flexibility and control for the clients in combination with a competitive fee structure. However, their clients often lack the resources to

---

2. To handle distributions in kind for an orderly sale of securities distributed by private equity partnerships.

EXHIBIT 7.1

COMPARISON OF INTERNAL STAFF VS. GATEKEEPER

Internal staff	Gatekeeper	
	Consultant/Account manager	Fund of funds
Pros • Institutional investors can build up and retain experience • Synergies with an institution's other activities possible • Can be small investment sizes	*Pros* • Can provide "tailor-made" solution to match the institution's needs • Well-suited for gaining knowledge and experience	*Pros* • Institutions can commit smaller investment sizes and still achieve diversification (scaling upwards) • Allows collapsing many tedious fund level approvals into an umbrella approval (scaling downwards) • Full outsourcing provides solution for technical and regulatory complexity
Cons • The burden of research, due diligence, ongoing monitoring, reporting, and administration is high: diseconomies related to the limited scale of the investment activity • Hiring and retaining experienced private equity professionals requires incentives that often do not match the institution's culture • Limited geographical reach for sourcing deals • Effective monitoring of geographically diversified portfolios is difficult • Lack of cultural fit with organization	*Cons* • Requires the institution's active participation if program is non-discretionary • Fund of funds or large discretionary accounts managed by the gatekeeper can create conflicts of interest • Requires, on balance, a larger investment size	*Cons* • Little or no ability to influence the investment program • Minimal learning experience for the institutional investor • Highly driven by fundraising cycles with huge inflows during booms can lead to underperformance

Source: Classification according to Fenton (2001).

evaluate proposals themselves and, therefore, cannot react quickly enough to the investment recommendations. As a consequence, it can be more practical to delegate fuller responsibility to a fund of funds that retains strategic and discretionary authority over the investor's assets.[3]

7.2.3 Placement agents

There is clearly a significant overlap between a non-discretionary gatekeeper and a placement agent. Both have a middle-man status to gather and analyze information for

3. In fact, the line is blurred as funds of funds also offer separate account services, as will be discussed later in Section 7.4.

EXHIBIT 7.2

APPROACHES TO INTERMEDIATION

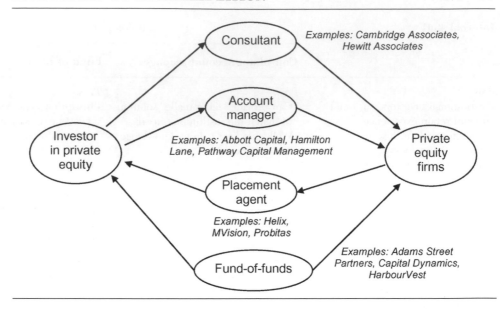

EXHIBIT 7.3

A SNAPSHOT: CAMBRIDGE ASSOCIATES

Cambridge Associates is considered one of the world's leading consultants in alternative assets. Founded in 1973 and headquartered in Boston, Massachusetts it has over 900 employees of which 100 are professionals dedicated to research, portfolio construction, and monitoring in private equity. The firm has seven offices: four in the U.S., London, Singapore, and Sidney. As of August 2010, total assets under advisory are estimated at $80bn of which $17bn is dedicated to private equity. Unlike most other gatekeepers, Cambridge Associates does not manage assets directly, but is retained by institutional investors to conduct intensive research and to provide unbiased advice. Further services include advice on competitive fund terms, fund due diligence, tracking fund performance, design of investment policy and asset allocation, manager structure, administration and audit support, and ongoing governance.

From its consultancy services, Cambridge Associates has accumulated an extensive proprietary database over the years which it uses to leverage its services. These data are well regarded in the industry for their reliability and objectivity. In particular, performance results are compiled into two widely used benchmark statistical indexes on U.S. venture capital and private equity, both being widely considered to be the industry standards.

As part of its private equity advisory activities, Cambridge Associates advises on both real estate and infrastructure vehicles. For the latter it only covers core economic sectors at all project stages (greenfield, brownfield, and secondary stage) and does not advise on public private partnerships (PPPs).

It is estimated that about 150 clients have direct private equity allocation ranging in size from $75mn up to $1bn. The firm has a long history of serving university endowments and other charitable foundations. In addition, its client base consists of corporate pension schemes, sovereign wealth funds, and others globally spread.

general and LP constituents. Placement agents are retained by the general partners (GPs) to place a new fund. They specialize in identifying those institutional investors for which the strategy of the new fund fits most closely. While gatekeepers are representing the LPs' interest, formally speaking placement agents are appointed by the GP which pays them a fee for this service.

Placement agents must maintain a balance between the needs of both investors and fund managers. Developing an enduring relationship and influencing an investor to become a LP in a fund requires persistent transparency, integrity, and fair treatment.

Placement agents bring an industry network of established and new relationships that most fund managers and investors do not have. In addition, placement agents are increasingly sought for *thought leadership and insight*, rather than just contacts (see Snow, 2006). Consequently, institutional investors find value in cooperating with them as it helps them to access high-quality emerging teams and get into new markets. To do this, the placement agent has to understand the institutional investor's objectives and strategy and has to be proactive in conducting thorough due diligence to justify an investment case—not just to introduce it.

7.3 IN-HOUSE OR OUTSOURCING?

Private equity investments can either be managed in-house or the management can be outsourced to a specialist intermediary. Due to the difficulties and constraints related to setting up the necessary infrastructure, the outsourcing route is often the only viable and even attractive option.

7.3.1 How much to outsource?

Investors can use a gatekeeper who is able to provide all services as a "one-stop shop". Alternatively, they may consider combining various leading service providers in a "best-of-breed" approach. Both approaches have pros and cons:

- A wholesale outsourcing to one party (e.g., a fund of funds) allows capital to be put to work in private equity quickly, particularly if a host of integrated services is offered as a one-stop shop. There are disadvantages as well: it is unlikely that one gatekeeper can offer all the services in an equally strong fashion. In other words, a one-stop shop tends to be a suboptimal solution. Moreover, for institutional investors aiming to become autonomous in managing their program, it is difficult to "un-bundle" the services from one gatekeeper as they learn, because switching between services and providers is costly.

- Alternatively, investors can purchase private equity services from different providers in order to obtain the best service of its kind in each area. But such a "best of breed" strategy is also problematic: tradeoffs include the costs of defining, procuring, and integrating several third parties and the need for managing and coordinating their contributions; they may well offset the benefits.

In reality neither a pure one-stop shop nor a pure best-of-breed approach is feasible. Due to the diverse range of services needed, multiple advisory services are often retained in parallel.

7.3.2 Development of the investment program

Even when opting for an in-house solution, building a successful private equity program takes a concentrated effort over several years and should be undertaken in phases, involving different types of gatekeeper (see, e.g., LGT Partners, 2001).

- In the first "startup" phase from Year 1 to Year 3 the objective is to get properly started in private equity. This requires understanding how this market is organized, its issues and pitfalls, and the risk and return profile of private equity portfolios. For newcomers to the asset class an allocation to funds of funds offers the opportunity to instantly access the necessary skillset as an efficient way of jump-starting their private equity investment program and over time to learn the due diligence and selection processes and how to develop and implement a sound investment strategy.

- In the second "development" phase—usually between Year 3 and Year 5—institutions often focus on building up a dedicated private equity team, with the capability to source fund proposals, to conduct due diligence, to structure and negotiate fund agreements, and to monitor the funds after signature of the limited partnership agreement. During this phase it is advisable to use an account manager in parallel.

Over time, more of the program will be brought in-house as internal staff gain experience and their confidence grows:

- The objective of the third "expansion" phase following Year 5 of the program is to strengthen the private equity team's skills and to give it a global reach. Secondary transaction and co-investment capabilities become essential for investment success, but require additional skills and experience in valuing funds, assessing investments, and generating exits. Processes and procedures need to be well defined for this purpose. Gatekeepers—mainly consultants—are still used selectively. Finally, institutional investors have to increasingly reflect on proper incentive structures to retain and motivate the now experienced and knowledgeable in-house private equity team.

Exhibit 7.4 describes a learning curve where, due to the initial lack of experience, institutions first have no other option than to go through a fund of funds, then become LPs in funds, and with increasing sophistication build their own portfolio of companies, either through co-investing or through independent sourcing of deals. Funds of funds are viewed as a first step into private equity, which, by avoiding the costs of learning and by providing access to funds, may be worth the additional layer of fees. Having said this, there are also cases where larger investors simply do not wish to build up an in-house team for a dedicated private equity investment program and do not move beyond a fund of funds.

7.4 OUTSOURCING TO A FUND OF FUNDS

Exhibit 7.5 describes the investment process through a fund of funds. Gatekeepers operating as funds of funds manage pools of capital from multiple investors on a fully discretionary basis. Fees are charged for bundled services, institutional investors join a pool of other investors and turn over the complete responsibility for building and monitoring the private equity investments to a gatekeeper. For gatekeepers, the

---

EXHIBIT 7.4

LEARNING CURVE

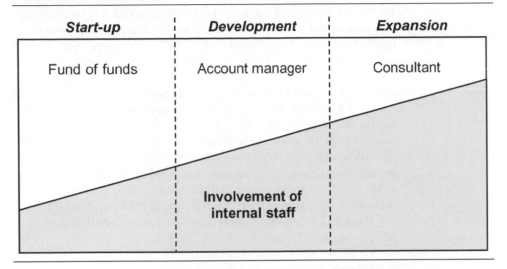

EXHIBIT 7.5

INVESTMENT PROCESS THROUGH A FUND OF FUNDS

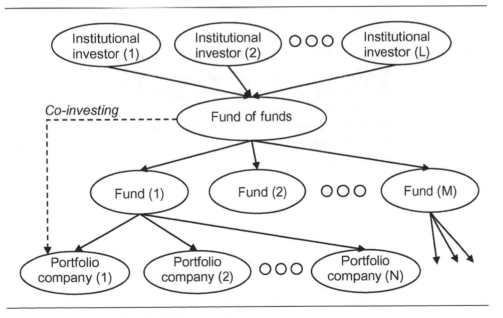

---

fund-of-funds structure is attractive because fees—usually fixed and to be paid annually—are typically higher, thus guaranteeing revenues over several years, as opposed to a consultant's retainer that can be terminated on short notice. For comparison: if we convert the usual consultant's retainer into a management fee based on the amount of assets advised on, the standard rate would be just around five basis points. Without an income stream stemming from fund-of-funds management fees it is hard to pay competitive wages and grow the business.

Funds of funds and comparable structures date back to the late 1970s and early 1980s, but they mainly grew in the 1990s. One factor contributing in the U.S.A. to the tremendous growth of this industry was a change in SEC regulation. Prior to 1996, funds were essentially limited to fewer than 100 accredited investors, while after the change of regulation funds were allowed to raise capital from up to 499 qualified[4] investors. Also, the extraordinary success of U.S. venture capital during these years and a growing number of high-net-worth individuals created demand for such vehicles.

In 1999, funds of funds comprised approximately 20% of all the private equity capital raised in the U.S.A. and by 2003 about 160 firms in Europe and the U.S.A. managed one or more funds of funds (see Jo, 2002 and Reyes, 2004, correspondingly). According to Preqin there were over 700 funds of funds managed by over 300 different private equity firms from around the world in 2010. EVCA counted more than 150 funds of funds active in Europe. Funds of funds accounted for about 18% of total committed capital to private equity funds in 2009, up from 14% in 2008.

Exhibit 7.6 lists the largest funds of funds globally based on their allocation to private equity.

Outsourcing to funds of funds can take various forms. Exhibit 7.7 lays out the three main approaches: separate accounts, commingled accounts, and pooled private equity vehicles.

Even for more experienced investors in private equity hiring a fund-of-funds manager can make sense (e.g., to pursue niche strategies in which they lack expertise or as a way to scale up their allocation).[5] Some funds of funds specialize in certain private equity sectors or geographies while others follow a more generalist approach.

7.4.1 Separate accounts

A separate account is a vehicle operating on behalf of a single institutional investor, for a fixed duration and with a structure established jointly with the fund-of-fund manager to meet specific legal, tax, strategic, and other portfolio management needs. Such requirements can relate to the exclusion of investments in certain markets where the investor has an overconcentration or stronger allocation to other sectors. The agreement is only between the two parties and generally includes confidentiality provisions. From the investor's point of view separate accounts are by far the most flexible approach but require some additional effort not only to identify the fund-of-fund manager to work

---

4. Investors have to be "qualified purchasers" as defined in Section 3c(7) of the Investment Company Act of 1940 (generally includes individuals owning as least USD5mn in unleveraged investments). They must also be "accredited investors" under the Securities Act of 1933: this category generally includes entities with total assets in excess of USD5mn, individuals whose net worth exceeds USD1mn, individual income in excess of USD200,000, or joint income with the prospect's spouse in excess of USD300,000.

5. According to Steiner-Dicks (2005), more than one third of investors use funds of funds to get initial exposure to private equity but still nearly half of them continue using this approach for managing a specific component of a large portfolio. Non-financial corporations (which include corporate pension funds) were found to use funds of funds less. One possible explanation is that the non-pensions among them are corporate ventures who prefer direct investments of strategic interests. Lai (2006) reported that educational institutions (universities) use more funds of funds and found this surprising as endowments tend to be performance oriented. He saw this as evidence that funds of funds deliver value to some types of investors.

EXHIBIT 7.6

LARGEST PRIVATE EQUITY FUND OF FUNDS' MANAGERS[1]

Firm	Location	Current Allocation to private equity (USD billion)
AlpInvest	The Netherlands	56.6
Goldman Sachs PE	U.S.	32.0
HarbourVest Partners	U.S.	30.0
Credit Suisse	U.S.	25.0
Pantheon Ventures	U.S.	24.0
AXA PE	France	23.0
Pathway Capital	U.S.	23.0
Adams Street	U.S.	22.0
Partners Group	Switzerland	21.2
Capital Dynamics	Switzerland	21.2
JP Morgan Asset Management PE	U.S.	18.6
PineBridge Investments	U.S.	18.4
Altius Associates	U.S.	17.5

Source: Preqin, August 2010.

Note: 1. Based on allocation to private equity.

EXHIBIT 7.7

APPROACHES OF OUTSOURCING TO A FUND OF FUNDS

Separate accounts	Commingled accounts	Pooled vehicles
• Single investor • Design and implementation of investment strategy according to investor's specific requirements • Tailor-made solution • Small size	• Two or more investors • Strong influence of investor on design and implementation of investment strategy • Common objectives and constraints • Medium size	• Many investors • Investment strategy developed, marketed, and implemented by fund-of-funds manager • From investors' perspective little flexibility regarding investment strategy • Large size

with but also to find a suitable structure. Nevertheless, investors tend to prefer separate accounts to other funds-of-funds' structures.

First, it gives investors more flexibility for switching managers. Even if there is often still a penalty of some sort, it is far easier than getting out of a structure with several pooled investors. Second, fees on separate accounts are said to be lower (25 bp and 50 bp) than those on pure funds of funds. This is mainly caused by the strong pricing power commanded by large investors, although we could also argue the other way around: because of the low fees the separate account route is only open to investors who want significant capital to be managed. For fund-of-fund managers, however, this approach by its nature is inefficient compared with scale investment efforts for a large number of investor clients. The minimum size of a separate account would be around USD50mn to commit over a 2-to-3-year period, although the typical size of a separate account rests between USD100mn and USD200mn, otherwise a fund-of-fund manager would not be able to cover the costs for his or her service, notably so if a dedicated investment team is taking care of it.

The low-cost argument could also be elusive: on the contrary, a separate account service provider may even require much higher fees to justify the more stylized effort (see Bushrod, 2004). In any case, capital under management can only be limited for separate accounts, as such a program is likely to be quite specialized and the pool of available top-quality opportunities will by definition tend to be very shallow. Scale is a critical success factor in asset management and, therefore, fund-of-fund managers will find it challenging to implement a truly tailored separate account. Moreover, investors should be careful that the manager only takes on the number of clients and amount of capital that can be supported by predictable allocations to quality investments within a strategy during the investment period.

The line between separate accounts and non-discretionary mandates is difficult to draw. On the one hand, the manager running a separate account retains responsibility for everything from renegotiation of fees, dealing with offshore structure issues, to administration (i.e., performing capital calls or returning distributions). On the other hand, investors can have significant influence over the investment strategy and its execution (e.g., by exercising the right to veto over fund selections suggested by the manager) or by adjusting the investment strategy during the investment period (e.g., to address changing needs, such as the shifting of focus in the remainder of their asset mix or to fine-tune liquidity management).

7.4.2 Commingled accounts

Often two or more institutions have common objectives, such as a focus on a geographical region, or on venture capital, or on socially responsible investments and, therefore, share the same asset allocations in a commingled account. This allows them more discretion than they would receive from a straightforward pooled vehicle, as will be discussed below.

Moreover, commingled accounts are attractive for fund-of-fund managers because this allows them to diversify their investor base and grow the assets under management. What is more, the discounts available to large investors are not usually available on commingled accounts as, with an increasing number of investors, the negotiating power shifts to the fund-of-fund manager. For commingled accounts, typically around 1% is charged as fees and, when combined with more assets under management, the overall profitability of such vehicles grows.

From an investor's point of view, however, this works against the hoped-for high returns of the account managed on his behalf. Generally, in alternative assets there is a noted decline in performance once assets under management have grown beyond a certain size. The same holds for fund-of-fund managers: as more capital is taken on, there is a necessary focus on increasingly larger funds to accommodate these allocations.

7.4.3 Pooled vehicles

With growing assets to be managed, there comes a point where separate and commingled accounts become inefficient compared with a traditional large fund of funds into which investors pool their capital.

Limited partnerships

Funds of funds set up as pooled vehicles typically mirror the private equity fund structure and are set up as limited partnerships, with the GPs managing the day-to-day operations. After committing to such a fund of funds there is little opportunity for investors to have an impact beyond side agreements such as optouts. Small-sized to mid-sized investors, in particular, have limited influence; usually, the strategy cannot be changed during the investment period, because it was the basis upon which the fund of funds went out to raise capital. The investment strategy can therefore be inflexible and unable to adapt to adverse changes in the economic environment. Arguably, funds of funds are also more exposed to the cyclicality of the private equity market, where many institutional investors are likely to commit at its peak. Most funds of funds demand a minimum investment of several million euros, which can be an issue for some investors that need an exposure to private equity. Moreover, investors need to be committed for 12 years or more. To exit such a vehicle, the investor must either sell its partnership interest at a discount on the secondary market or default by ceasing to honor new capital calls and, thus, become subject to penalties.

Listed funds of funds

Listed private equity funds of funds offer liquidity and a quick buildup of a diversified portfolio of private equity funds. Typically, they are set up specifically to attract smaller investors such as high-net-worth individuals wanting to get access to the private equity asset class without going through the setup of a dedicated program and without being exposed to the illiquidity of unquoted investments.

Publicly quoted private equity funds of funds are based on familiar investment trust-like structures, whereas fund-of-fund investors exercise tight control over usage of funding in the usual limited partnership structure (i.e., strict segregation of management fees from capital calls). In listed vehicles, interests are less well aligned and shareholder control over the usage of the capital is reduced. Listed vehicles are seen as less relevant for institutional investors but, nevertheless, could be a meaningful way of entering the asset class as they increase flexibility in tactical asset allocations and allow fast exposure to private equity fund investments, while maintaining some degree of liquidity.

Such vehicles to a large degree display the same characteristics as public stocks where liquidity depends on issuance size and public awareness. Like second-line stocks, share prices of most fund of funds are traded at a discount which can make it difficult, if not impossible, to get out without incurring losses. In fact, the discount for less liquid listed funds is even more noticeable than for their public stock counterpart. This is because of the reported net asset value (NAV) which provides a formal discount (or very rarely a premium) compared with a more objective asset-based valuation.

EXHIBIT 7.8

KEY FEATURES OF LISTED PRIVATE EQUITY FUNDS OF FUNDS AND LIMITED PARTNERSHIPS

Listed private equity fund of funds[1]	Structured as limited partnership
• Usually evergreen (indefinite life) and irredeemable	• Generally fixed life of 12 to 15 years
• Usually fixed size, but can raise additional capital (both debt and equity) or return capital	• Fixed size
• No minimum size	• High minimum size of investment
• Limited shareholder control over the usage of the capital is reduced and less well-aligned interests	• Fees perceived to be high but investors exercise tight control over usage of funding (i.e., strict segregation of management fees from capital calls)
• Traded on stock exchange and offered to the public	• Transactions among investors restricted, require consent of fund-of-fund manager and cannot be offered to the public
• Shares can be sold on stock exchange but thin markets can lead to significant discounts	• Can be difficult to sell, transactions negotiated, time pressure leads to significant discounts
• No specific terms and conditions or co-investment opportunities for individual investors	• Specific terms and conditions or co-investment opportunities can be negotiated
• Produce reports and accounts, but full disclosure often limited by commercial sensitivities; potential insider issues	• Detailed information available to investors that can go beyond what listed private equity can make available; no insider issues
• Relatively weak shareholder influence	• Investors can sometimes participate on advisory boards and can change managers
• Realization proceeds usually reinvested; cash drag pending reinvestment motivates risky overcommitment strategies	• Realization proceeds are returned to investors; the structure is self-liquidating

Note: 1. Based on JPMorgan Cazenove, *Limited European Listed Private Equity Bulletin*, referred to in *http://www.lpeq.com/pdfs/LPEQ_Preqin_LPE_Report.pdf*, last accessed December 12, 2010.

Exhibit 7.8 compares the key features of listed private equity funds of funds with those structured as limited partnerships. Exhibit 7.9 lists the largest publicly listed funds of funds.

7.5 FUND-OF-FUNDS ECONOMICS

Funds of funds typically charge management fees between 50 bp and 150 bp based on the committed capital. This can vary between 50 bp and 100 bp because institutional investors often pay less than high-net-worth individuals, who are charged between 100 bp and 125 bp. Generally, there will be discounts for larger commitments. There is a performance component in the fee schedule in the form of carried interest (usually, a percentage of the profit between 0% and 20%, with 5% being standard), normally in combination with a hurdle rate between 5% and 15%—so that fund-of-fund managers only profit once a minimum level of performance has been achieved.

EXHIBIT 7.9

LARGEST PUBLICLY LISTED PRIVATE EQUITY FUND OF FUNDS

Name	Exchange	Year listed	Market capitalization ($ million)	Main segments
Conversus Capital	Euronext Amsterdam	2007	1,901	Buyout
SVG Capital	London Stock Exchange	1996	1,674	Buyout
AP Alternative Assets	Euronext Amsterdam	2006	1,387	Buyout
Pantheon International Participations	London Stock Exchange	1987	1,174	Balanced
Absolute Private Equity AG	Swiss Stock Exchange	2001	929	Buyout
HarbourVest Global Private Equity	London Stock Exchange	2007	769	Buyout
Princess Private Equity Holding	Frankfurt Stock Exchange	2006	743	Buyout
NB Private Equity Partners	Euronext Amsterdam/ London Stock Exchange	2007	557	Buyout
Castle Private Equity AG	Swiss Stock Exchange	1997	555	Buyout
Graphite Enterprise Trust	London Stock Exchange	1981	506	Buyout
J.P. Morgan Private Equity	London Stock Exchange	2005	499	Buyout
Standard Life European Private Equity	London Stock Exchange	2001	488	Buyout

Source: LPX Group, *http://www.lpx-group.com/lpx/listed-private-equity.html* as at June 30, 2010; average €/$ exchange rate of June 2010 published by the ECB.

Funds of funds have a 10-to-15-year term, matching the investment horizon of the targeted funds, which are normally identified during a 3-to-4-year investment period. Management fees begin to decrease after the investment period is over (see Otterlei and Barrington, 2003; AltAssets, 2003).[6] To align interests, the fund-of-fund managers should contribute 1–2% of the resources and, thus, also manage their own money. Investors have no control over the management of the partnership. Despite the performance component, established fund-of-fund economics is largely driven by the management fee. For such stronger players in the fund-of-fund market, growing assets under management are the primary means to increase their own profitability and firm value.

Even for large and experienced investors in private equity, funds of funds can complement their investment strategy by giving them an allocation to niches such as

6. Of course, as in all areas of private equity, there is also continuous experimenting with structures. See, for example, AltAssets (November 4, 2003), "ViaNova launches new European fund of funds with novel fee structure," describing the strategy to launch a new €500mn European fund of funds in a crowded market in the hope that its new fee structure will differentiate it from the competition. To respond to investors' concerns about the double layer of management fees for funds of funds, ViaNova did not charge any establishment costs, annual management fee, or carried interest. Instead, ViaNova simply took a 2% interest in the fund and required an initial one-off fee equal to 2% of the investor's commitments.

emerging markets. Funds of funds manage the following activities, which tend to complement each other:

- *Primary investments in newly formed limited partnerships*—because of the "blind pool" nature of such investments, assessment of the fund management team's skills is most acute.

- *Selectively, direct co-investments alongside the GPs*—this activity requires direct investment experience and skills.

- *Secondary investments in existing funds*—while this is generally a niche activity for most industry players, in recent years specialists like Coller Capital have emerged that focus on such opportunities. As for co-investments, being able to assess and extract the value of the companies already in portfolio and quick execution are key success factors.

The management fees may be seen as costly, but funds of funds add value in several respects (e.g., by giving investors instant diversification and scaling of their financial resources). They are a solution to the sorting problem between "good" and "bad" private equity investments, provide a number of value-added services (e.g., risk management), and address the information gap for investors not familiar with the asset class through their expertise in due diligence and monitoring. Finally, they provide the proper incentives for investment professionals, exercise a credible threat against fund managers' potential misbehavior, and help to improve the terms and conditions of limited partnership agreements.

7.5.1 Costs

It is often argued that the fund-of-fund industry offers poor value to investors. The additional layer of management fees charged by funds of funds is often said to be too high and to outweigh their efficiency gains. Jo (2002) argues they would have to perform between 0.7% and 3.4% better to compensate for these "fees on fees".[7] For financial institutions willing to take a long-term commitment to this asset class, there arises the question whether the fund of funds is not a "wasteful" business model and whether the setup of an in-house private equity investment program could avoid controversial double fees. However, this argument is to be challenged because, due to economies of scale, investors may pay less than in the case of setting up an in-house program. Comparing fund-of-funds returns with the underlying returns from private equity funds misses a number of points.

In fact, the annual costs of an in-house team can be significant compared with a typical fund of funds. Due to diseconomies of scale the yearly costs of an internal team are estimated to be more than three times higher than the annual fees charged by a fund of funds (see Pease, 2000; Smith, 2000; Otterlei and Barrington, 2003; Sormani, 2005a; Mathonet and Meyer, 2007).[8] Even with a 5% carried interest the fees charged by the

---

7. Jo (2002) analyzed 48 U.S.-based funds of funds launched between 1992 and 1999 (13 asset managers, 15 banks, and 20 independent funds). For asset managers the author found an average carried interest of 3.8% (only 5 of the 13 asset managers charged carried interest) and an average management fee of 0.85%. For investment and commercial banks, management fees were in the range 0.88–1.25%; 12 of the 15 banks charged carried interest (average carry was 6.6%; typical carry was just 5%). At the end of the 1990s annual management fees were in the region of 0.8% and carried interest was 10%; 5 years later the difficult market environment brought that down to 0.7% and carried interest dropped to 5%.

8. Smith (2000) argues that expenses for in-house teams and management fees charged by funds of funds are comparable.

fund-of-fund manager have an insignificant impact on returns to the institutional investor.

Lai (2006) argues that funds of funds do not necessarily deliver superior returns but perform "well enough" for some of their investors. In fact, gatekeepers that offer "advice only" can be expensive as well: commitments to 10 funds will result in success fees for each, whereas funds of funds charge only one fee. For larger institutions, intermediation through funds of funds allows them to focus on their core businesses. This advantage outweighs most cost considerations. To sum up, the "double layer of fees" or the "fees on fees" often appears to be a more "politically charged" argument than based on rational assessment of the situation.

7.5.2 Diversification and scaling

Smaller institutions have difficulties achieving a meaningful level of diversification, while for larger institutions investments in private equity funds may be too cost-intensive, as the size of such investments is too small compared with the significant administration effort. As a consequence of the need to diversify, Lai (2006) identifies the ability to scale upwards or downwards as the strongest attraction of investors to funds of funds. They can mediate the size issues by "scaling up" through pooling smaller investors or by "scaling down" by making one large commitment to a fund of funds.

Diversification

Funds of funds are seen as "safe havens" for private equity investors. This is especially so in new technologies, new teams, or emerging markets, as funds of funds allow for reasonable downside protection through diversification. Not surprisingly, various studies have shown that, because of their diversification, funds of funds perform similarly to individual funds but with less pronounced extremes. However, according to Lai (2006), reducing risks through diversification does not appear to be the main motivation for investors to use funds of funds.

Upward scaling

Funds of funds generally have lower commitment minimums than those required by private equity funds. Through this upward scaling, smaller institutional investors could theoretically achieve diversification over a wider set of funds and get to a minimum efficient scale. Lai (2006) suggests that the upward scaling story has validity in one area: funds of funds appear to help smaller investors to reduce their costs by outsourcing. He found that most small institutional investors invest only in small funds of funds. He speculated that this was probably for the same reason that they do not invest in larger funds for diversification. An alternative explanation is that institutions pursuing private equity investments seek exposure to niche investments and other unique attributes which smaller investors in large funds of funds would be unable to do.

Downward scaling

Sophisticated investors recognize the need to invest in smaller funds to gain exposure to less efficient private equity sectors because of their potential for greater returns and to defensively expand relationships with the "star" fund managers of tomorrow. Larger institutions can use funds of funds to scale downwards to invest larger amounts without being forced to consider many small investment proposals. This improves efficiency as many tedious fund level approvals can be collapsed into an umbrella approval for a fund of funds given discretionary authority. This is reminiscent of the economic argument that ownership of assets and residual rights should optimally be in the hands of the party that has a comparative advantage in capabilities (in this case, in moving fast). Outsourcing allows investors to be more efficient as they do not have to build capacity during the sparse investment points and capital calls, only to have the capacity underutilized at other times.

7.5.3 Access to top teams

The top private equity funds are hard to find, hard to evaluate, hard to monitor, have high minimums for commitments, and—depending on the overall market situation—are often closed to new LPs. Securing access to top-performing funds traditionally has been the fund-of-fund industry's major value proposition. Investors expect funds of funds to have access to successful "invitation only" funds or the capacity to identify future stars among the young and less known ones.

For private equity firms, raising funds is a significant burden and, therefore, funds of funds are convenient LPs because they have already pooled various investors. Furthermore, funds of funds have a consistent style of investment and are committed to the asset class, which make them a convenient and reliable source of capital. A smaller customer base means that less time needs to be spent on fundraising and managing LP relationships. From a private equity firm's point of view, funds of funds could be viewed as an outsourced sales and customer relationship department. Unlike for other institutions, such as pension funds or banks that may have a change of investment strategy imposed on them from higher echelons, for a fund of funds private equity is the only business. They are ever present and speak the "language" of the industry. As industry specialists, funds of funds can help fund managers in certain transactions either through their network or as providers of additional funding.

From the viewpoint of fund managers, all of this makes funds of funds desirable LPs. Therefore, funds of funds can improve the terms and conditions of limited partnership agreements and exercise a credible threat against fund managers' potential misbehavior.

7.5.4 Value-added services

Over time, investors become more experienced in the private equity asset class and more comfortable doing things in-house. Consequently, funds of funds continuously lose clients and need to offer more value-added services (e.g., monitoring, research, risk management or handling special situations).

Monitoring

Monitoring is an obligation of LPs in the context of a private equity fund's corporate governance to approve procedures, processes, waivers and amendments to limited partnership agreements, and, especially, to review valuations for reasonableness.

This requires considerable effort and is based on regular communication with all parties involved, attending board and annual meetings, contributing to advisory boards, and visiting or calling portfolio companies informally for updates. Monitoring comprises, for example, tracking planned vs. implemented strategy; analysis of fund financial, investment, valuation, and divestment information; analysis of relevant market trends, individual investment, and portfolio risk; performance measurement, benchmarking, assuring continuing legal and tax compliance, etc.

An adequate monitoring system reduces the likelihood of any potential non-compliance of private equity funds with the terms of the limited partnership agreement. Monitoring funds for likely distributions is also relevant for liquidity planning. Through quarterly conference calls, information is gathered for cash flow projections, or issues regarding expected drawdowns, projected uses, whether the full amount will be drawn, whether the fund size should be reduced, and so on. Monitoring is not only related to the specific fund investments, it also needs to consider the composition of their portfolio of funds and correcting severe imbalances through active portfolio management.

Research

As private equity is more and more becoming an international asset class, investors are faced with the "tyrannies of time and distance". To be successful, a globally oriented research process needs to be built up to identify regions, search for and evaluate local GPs, and structure contracts with the right incentives and investor protection clauses according to national legislations and regulations. More than the average institutional investors, funds of funds have the specific knowledge and the staff with international expertise to design and build a geographically diversified portfolio.

Risk management

Risk management and associated tasks like liquidity management, compliance with regulation, and due diligence pose significant challenges. The successful management of the liquidity of a portfolio of private equity funds needs to take interdependencies among the overall investment strategy, the management of the undrawn capital, the available resources, and timing aspects into account. Therefore, achieving a high overall return for the investments is a complex task that requires not only quantitative modeling and financial engineering skills, but also a high degree of judgment and management discipline. This demands a full-time team with adequate resources, access to research databases and models, and skills and experience in due diligence, negotiation, and contract structuring.

Handling special situations

Not all investments go as planned, and regularly LPs are faced with special situations like failing funds or so-called "tail-ends" (i.e., non-exited portfolio companies either managed by GPs who do not have a strong incentive to care much about the fate of these investments or directly held by the LPs after the fund management team disintegrated).

There are a number of ways of handling such situations—sells on secondary markets, restructuring funds, creating side-funds, or bringing in new managers and giving them new incentives to do their best for the remaining portfolio companies. Again, a fund of funds can take away the burden of dealing with these tedious problems.

7.5.5 Active portfolio management

Sophisticated investors in private equity funds create value by actively managing through purchases and sales on the secondary markets, securitizations, or co-investments. Such transactions, however, require more technical skills and experience than the typical institutional investor has.

Secondary transactions

Occasionally, secondary transactions are suggested to accelerate the buildup of portfolios with an acceptable vintage year spread. As the competition for secondary investment opportunities is as cyclical as the private equity market as a whole, this may not always be a feasible option, but given that investors sell their private equity holdings for a variety of reasons, the secondary market has begun to shake off its association with distressed sellers seeking liquidity at nearly any price.

Secondary transactions are becoming more and more complex. They require detailed due diligence, including complicated valuations. Furthermore, compared with primary transactions, they require large amounts of cash in hand. For these reasons, they have traditionally been restricted to secondary specialists and comparably experienced funds of funds.

Securitizations

When secondary discounts are too high, reducing exposure via securitization is an alternative to asset sales at low valuations.[9] Additionally, through securitization of the portfolio of funds, further liquidity can be injected into investments. This financial technology can be an important portfolio management tool.

While there has been growing interest in CFOs over recent years—at least, until the economic crisis from 2008 onwards—securitization backed by private equity investments remains a niche market and can only be conducted by experienced fund-of-funds players such as Partners Group and Capital Dynamics.[10]

Co-investments

Co-investing is the syndication of a financing round between a private equity fund and one or more of its LPs. Theoretically, this brings complementary capabilities together where funds that lack the financial resources team up with LPs that usually lack knowledge of technologies and sectors and do not have an industry-specific network.

Co-investments—like secondary transactions—can lead to a reduction of the J-curve effect and improve capital deployment and returns. For their risk and reward profile they slot in between a direct investment and a normal partnership. Co-investments are more risky than investing in a private equity partnership. Their downside is comparable with those of direct investments—while in a fund's portfolio a failed investment often does not have a high adverse impact and is handled by the fund's

---

9. Securitization is the mechanism by which financial assets (e.g., loans, bonds, credit card receivables, derivatives, and investments in hedge funds or private equity funds) are packaged together in a pool which is sold to a special purpose vehicle (SPV). The SPV refinances itself by issuing debt instruments (such as an ABS), with various risk profiles, sold to investors with different appetites for risk. Securitization of private equity investments is classified as collateralized debt obligations (CDOs) or, more specifically, as private equity collateralized fund obligations (CFOs). Therefore, private equity CFOs simply represent an application and an adaptation of traditional technologies of securitization to portfolios of private equity investments.

10. Partners Group closed the first private equity securitization transaction in 1999: its Princess Private Equity Holding Ltd. (Princess) was used to fund new investments in private equity funds. Princess was set up as a private equity investment company, established to acquire primary funds and funded by a USD700mn zero-coupon convertible bond, with a par value guaranteed at maturity by the re-insurance company Swiss Re. Following Princess, significant transactions put forward to the market have also included transactions originated for portfolio management purposes.

management, failing co-investments carry legal expenses and significant staff time from the LP.

Many LPs indicate interest in co-investments, but few have the staffing and infrastructure to respond and commit to such opportunities in a timely manner. For funds of funds, however, co-investing is becoming much more mainstream and important and can comprise 25% or more of their overall exposure. Recently, leading funds of funds insist on receiving co-investment opportunities at no or reduced management fees, as a condition for investing in a limited partnership.

7.5.6 Incentives

For institutional investors, managing private equity in-house can cause problems, mainly associated with their corporate culture and the inadequacy of their incentives structure. There is a significant learning curve and, without performance-related pay, employees will most likely jump ship as soon as they are competent in the area and understand their opportunities better. The institution will need to start again almost from square one. Moreover, the lack of incentives to take risk and to find value will affect investment decisions.

Salaried employees tend to play safe and invest where others do (i.e., they go for "brands"). Here it is easier to explain underperformance than for a firm that is lesser known but has the potential to generate more value. The reward for spectacular performance is typically promotion into other areas or increased managerial responsibility. This is at odds with the long-term nature of private equity investing and can also have a negative effect on the important networking in this industry. Conversely, if things go wrong it is likely to have a negative impact on the career of the employee involved. Instead of "pulling the plug" there will be a tendency to say it is "too early to tell" and hope that the problem can be avoided or at least will only blow up after the employee has moved on in the profession.

While institutional investors do not lack staff with the intellectual caliber to evaluate investment proposals and to structure transactions, the incentives are not in line with those of the private equity market. For typical conservative and seniority-based institutions like banks, pension funds, or insurance companies, a theoretically unlimited carried interest does not fit into the salary scheme. On the other hand, whether an in-house program can work without investment performance-related incentives is questionable. Outsourcing to a fund of funds is one solution to this problem. Finally, funds of funds have a role as experts to explain to comparatively unsophisticated investors that the fund—despite apparently "horrible losses" in the early years—is still "good" and just in the midst of its J-curve.

7.6 SELECTING A FUND OF FUNDS

Outsourcing leads to a certain loss of control for an institutional investor. It has to be noted that even searching for and selecting a fund of funds is not trivial and often requires qualified advice itself.

7.6.1 Assessment

Funds of funds have discretion over their assets under management, and as they are also set up according to vintage years, like-for-like comparison against comparable vehicles would be possible in theory. However, for funds of funds there are even fewer data than in other areas of private equity for benchmarking. Moreover, for a separate account—even if the manager has discretion—the customized strategy is set by the clients and comparisons would be meaningless. The same, of course, holds even more for non-discretionary accounts or consultants, as the decision-making power is with the client, or the client is a member of the decision-making body, or has veto rights. Here, there is in addition a lack of meaningful performance measures.

Instead, important evaluation criteria are the years of experience, the depth of a fund-of-fund management team, the historical performance of partnerships recommended, or the number and quality of relationships the gatekeeper can offer. Because there are already established relationships with private equity firms, we can argue that a fund of funds is not a really "blind pool" investment. The new portfolio to be built up is likely to largely comprise funds raised by these firms. In fact, funds of funds are marketed on either a "partially blind" or a "fully informed" basis. For a "partially blind pool" some but not all of the intended general partnership groups are identified, while for a "fully informed pool" virtually all the intended partnerships have been identified to the investors.

Particularly relevant are indicators for quality of service such as reputation, references, client base, or repeat customers. Potential investors should also check that the revenue stream earned from the fees for all of the mandates under management just cover the firm's reasonable operating costs, or does this fee stream already provide rich compensation for the fund-of-funds managers?

7.6.2 How many funds of funds?

Another question is about how many funds of funds, which are expected to broadly cover the same vintage years, should be invested in? Lai (2006) identifies two problems for institutional investors: on the one hand, spreading the money to several funds of funds increases the chance of them competing for investing in the same portfolio company. One way of dealing with this problem is to assure that the fund-of-fund investment strategies do not overlap and that they invest in exclusive areas.

On the other hand, putting the money with a single fund of funds subjects the investors to the so-called "holdup problem", where the fund-of-fund manager as the sole party holds significant bargaining power and, especially, when it is difficult to monitor its real effort.

7.6.3 Potential conflicts of interest

Apart from being fund-of-fund vehicles, gatekeepers offer a range of other services and, in general, may be inclined to discriminate and give less priority to smaller or apparently less important clients. Before engaging a gatekeeper, investors should ask for the firm's list of clients and get a clear schedule of the standard and ad hoc services that are provided. Investors should ensure that gatekeepers respect their fiduciary duties, as they often manage several types of funds of funds and accounts alongside direct investment vehicles, secondaries, and co-investment funds, each with a different compensation structure.

There may be instances where a limited allocation to a fund must be divided among several vehicles, which can put a gatekeeper in a difficult position when it comes to prioritizing them. How can a non-discretionary client be certain to get a fair share out of an allocation to a fund when the gatekeeper manages its own fund of funds on a discretionary basis and charges other clients fees for managing a separate account on their behalf?

An adequate mandate management should be in place that resolves allocation conflicts; for example, that a different team is responsible for each mandate and that teams do not interact with each other, except on an informal basis. Such "Chinese walls" are usually seen as sufficient for avoiding conflicts (see Borel, 2002).

Fund-of-fund managers use their "access to top-quartile firms" as their key selling point to investors, but this may result in a conflict of interest where the fund-of-fund manager feels that the long-term relationship with the GPs is more important than the fleeting commitments of his own investors. This can result in leniency regarding new fund terms and conditions, reporting requirements, valuation reviews of underlying portfolio companies, as acting too much in the interest of the fund-of-funds' own investors might jeopardize this relationship. Investors should ask a fund-of-fund manager about his or her policy regarding the investments in a GP's subsequent funds. For example, they should request a complete record of post decisions whether to re-up existing relationships with funds or not and the rationale behind these decisions.

7.7 OUTLOOK

The demise of the fund-of-fund industry has been regularly predicted and every financial crisis adds weight to this prediction. In 2003, some foresaw a shakeout and predicted that around 40% of private equity funds of funds would struggle to survive over the medium term. At that time, a number of industry insiders saw the market as well past its peak (see AltAssets, 2003). Again, 2010 saw a consolidation in the fund-of-fund industry which was seen as "inevitable". However, as Ang et al. (2005) comment, the conclusion that funds of funds provide little value in terms of investment performance would require the "incredulous belief that a large, active industry has been built on the sole advantage of mere convenience at the expense of investment under-performance".[11]

Economies of scale imply the need to cover global private equity markets and the associated increased resource requirements (see Sterescu, 2010). Responding to the question about the minimum amount of capital needed to run a global fund of funds, HarbourVest's George Anson commented: "My guess is €1bn if you want to be able to offer globally diversified longevity and for the clients to feel you're going to be around. You wonder how the small groups will survive" (Sormani, 2005b). Before the financial crisis in 2008, funds of funds grew in step with mega-buyouts and built up this critical mass.

But there are also limits to growth in private equity in any case and, in particular, in venture capital which has been described as "oversupply of ideas for undersupply of money". In addition, to the mega-generalist fund of funds, groups with niche strategies are emerging. Funds of funds in the size range of EUR50mn to EUR100mn and focusing on a specific niche could be sufficient if the strategy is very specialized (see Sormani, 2003).

---

11. The quote relates to funds of hedge funds, but the argument holds for private equity as well.

Despite the many—often unjustified—critical comments, funds of funds are likely to remain a robust and thriving industry. It is not just the financial considerations that matter. There are growing requirements related to responsible investing, good corporate governance (especially in underdeveloped markets), or compliance with regulation such as Solvency II or Basel III. This leads to increased complexity of management and moves investing in private equity beyond what non-specialist organizations can do. Individual investors may switch in and out of the asset class, but funds of funds give private equity funds stable access to funding. Whereas banks, pension funds, or insurance companies typically rein in their investment activities during economic downturns, funds of funds often have significant "dry powder" still to invest which makes this industry an important stabilizer of the private equity market.[12]

7.8 BIBLIOGRAPHY

ACHARAYA, S., AND DIMSON, E. (2007) *Endowment Asset Management: Investment Strategies in Oxford and Cambridge*, Oxford University Press.

ALTASSETS (2003) "The fund of funds market: A global review," AltAssets research paper.

ANG, A., RHODES-KROPF, M., AND ZHAO, R. (2005) "Do funds-of-funds deserve their fees-on-fees?" working paper, Columbia Business School.

BERGMANN, B., CHRISTOPHERS, H., HUSS, M., AND ZIMMERMANN, H. (2010) "Listed private equity," in D.J. Cumming (Ed.), *Companion to Private Equity*, John Wiley & Sons Ltd.

BOREL, P. (2002) "Should advisors manage money?" *Private Equity International*, October.

BRIERLEY, A. (2010) *Listed Private Equity: Back from the Abyss*, report, Collin Steward, May 12.

BRIERLEY, A., AND BARNARD, B. (2005) *Listed Private Equity: Bridging the Gap*, DrKW Investment Trust Research Report, Dresdner Kleinwort Wasserstein.

BUSHROD, L. (2004) "Grappling the fund management problem," *European Venture Capital Journal*, March.

COWLEY, L. (2002) "Swiss fund-of-funds: Leading the way," *European Venture Capital Journal*, April.

FENTON, J. (2001) "Options and opportunities in private equity," presentation, Altius Associates.

GRABENWARTER, U., AND WEIDIG, T. (2005) *Exposed to the J-Curve*, Euromoney Books, London.

HOBOHM, D. (2010) *Investors in Private Equity Funds: Theory, Preferences and Performances*, Gabler, Wiesbaden, Germany.

HOFFMAN, M. (2005) "Separate accounts: An expanding approach for institutional investors," *Financier Worldwide*, April.

---

12. For this reason funds of funds could also be an important policy tool. The 2010 EVCA Venture Capital White Paper (see *http://www.evca.eu/knowledgecenter/PublicationDetail.aspx?id=PBWPCG* (last accessed July 19, 2010) identifies the difficulty to scale appropriately as one of the major obstacles to investing in venture capital and proposes funds of funds as a solution to this problem.

JO, H. (2002) "Perspectives and problems of private equity funds-of-funds," working paper, Santa Clara University.

LABY, A.B. (2006) "Differentiating gatekeepers," *Brooklyn Journal of Corporate, Financial & Commercial Law*, **1**.

LAHR, H., AND HERSCHKE, F.T. (2009) "Organizational forms and risk of listed private equity," *Journal of Private Equity*, Winter.

LAHR, H., AND KASERER, C. (2010) "Net asset value discounts in listed private equity funds," CEFS Working Paper, Technical University, Munich.

LAI, R.K. (2006) "Why funds of funds?" working paper, University of Pennsylvania, available at *http://ssrn.com/abstract=676999*

LGT PARTNERS (2001) *How to Build a Successful Private Equity Programme*, AltAssets, London.

MATHONET, P.-Y., AND MEYER, T. (2007) *J Curve Exposure: Managing a Portfolio of Venture Capital and Private Equity Funds*, John Wiley & Sons Ltd.

MEEK, V. (2004) "New direction for Swiss listed PE funds?" *European Venture Capital Journal*, April.

MEEK, V. (2005) "Placement agents are dead," *European Venture Capital Journal*, November.

OTTERLEI, J., AND BARRINGTON, S. (2003) *Alternative Assets: Private Equity Fund of Funds*, special report, Piper Jaffray Private Capital, Minneapolis, MN.

PEASE, R. (2000) *Private Equity Funds-of-Funds: State of the Market*, research report, Asset Alternatives Inc., Wellesley, MA.

PREQIN (Various reports) *http://www.preqin.com* (last accessed August 2010).

REYES, J. (2004) "Fund-of-funds are here to stay," *European Venture Capital Journal*, February.

RÖSCH, M. (2000) "Investieren in Risikokapital muss nicht überaus riskant sein," *Finanz & Wirtschaft*, July 5.

SMITH, M.D. (2000) "Private equity funds-of-funds: Getting what you pay for," presentation at *Asset Alternatives' Fund-of-Funds Summit 2000*.

SNOW, D. (2006) "Agents of boom," *Private Equity International*, April.

SORMANI, A. (2003) "Fund-of-funds: A bubble burst?" *European Venture Capital Journal*, September.

SORMANI A. (2005a) "Fund-of-funds: Working to stand," *European Venture Capital Journal*, August.

SORMANI, A. (2005b) "Working to stand out from the crowd," *European Venture Capital Journal*, September.

SPENCE, T., AND DUMAS, M. (n.d.) "Eight steps for analysing listed private equity," available at *http://www.lpeq.com/listed-private-equity/8-steps.html* (last accessed August 12, 2010).

STEINER-DICKS, K. (2005) *The Middle Man*, Real Deals, London.

STERESCU, D. (2010) "Hermes and Gartmore deliver consolidation message," *Private Equity Europe*, April.

TRICKS, H. (2005) "Equity funds fight to maintain privacy," *Financial Times*, January 17.

8

Listed private equity

8.1 INTRODUCTION

Private equity vehicles that are quoted on international stock markets are the subject of this chapter. Listed private equity (LPE) are listed vehicles—companies or funds—that offer investors exposure to the private equity asset class. These vehicles pursue a defined private equity strategy (e.g., venture, buyout, mezzanine) and are committed to the private equity investment process in deal screening and selection, structuring transactions, and monitoring and divesting portfolio companies. Underlying investments must be predominantly non-public companies (for more precise classifications of LPE see Bilo, 2002; LPX GmbH, 2008; Partners Group, 2008; RedRocks LPE, 2008; Lahr and Herschke, 2009).

LPE has been around for a long time with the first listings of LPE vehicles dating back to the 1960s.[1] Despite these early occurrences, LPE is a fairly new asset class. Exhibit 8.1 tracks listing and unlisting of funds during the 25-year period 1985–2009. Two peaks in the listing of private equity can be noticed from this figure: a surge during the dotcom era and from 2005 to 2007. In 2000, 53 LPE vehicles listed their stock on exchanges, while the latest peak occurred in 2006 when 50 companies went public. Listing numbers in general seem to follow the business cycle. Listings declined sharply in 2007, alongside the overall economic climate. De-listings reached their peak in 2008 when 23 vehicles dropped out. The relative proportion of de-listings is highest for IPOs in 2000, of which 37% have been de-listed since then. Altogether, 20 of all vehicles have been de-listed over the 25-year period, and an additional 10% of the vehicles lack any trading activity. Recent market consolidation left its mark on the total number of listed vehicles which had dropped significantly since its peak in 2007.

Total market capitalization of global LPE vehicles was USD141bn at the end of 2009, a 60% drop when compared with the overal size of USD350mn in early 2000 (see Exhibit 8.2). In terms of geography, most of the listed vehicles are located in Europe. Of the 512 private equity vehicles that have been in existence over the last 25 years, 210 were listed in the U.K., 67 were located in the U.S., and 41 in Germany. Other sizable markets are Israel (21), Australia (20), Canada (19), and Switzerland (16). The average

---

1. For example, Capital Southwest in 1961.

This chapter was co-authored with Henry Lahr (Centre for Business Research, University of Cambridge) and Christoph Kaserer (Center for Entrepreneurial and Financial Studies, TUM School of Management, Technical University Munich). We thank Hans Holman for valuable comments.

EXHIBIT 8.1

LISTED PRIVATE EQUITY VERHICLES OVER TIME: (A) NUMBER OF LPE VEHICLES; (B) LISTINGS AND DELETIONS OVER TIME

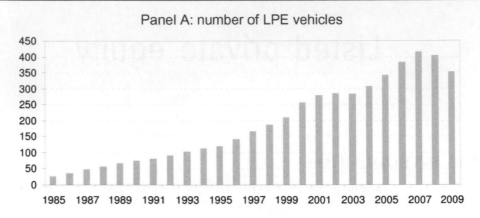

Panel A: number of LPE vehicles

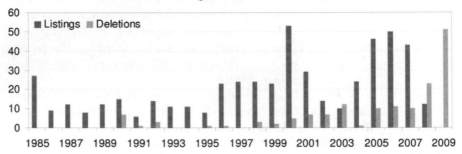

Panel B: Listings and deletions over time

Source: Listings of LPE vehicles prior to and including 1985 show up in 1985. New listings in 2009 are likely not zero, since the last full screening for LPE vehicles has been done for 2008. Deletions are either dates marked as "inactive" by Thomson Datastream or prices recorded by Datastream did not change after that date. If an inactive date is recorded, this is given priority over inactivity, inferred from an absence of price changes. Since stocks have to be inactive for at least 8 weeks, some deletions in 2009 might be erroneous due to illiquidity.

---

market capitalization amounts to USD300mn with a median of USD32mn as of December 31, 2009. As such, many of the vehicles tend to be small and illiquid. In terms of volatility, LPE market cap shows large swings in excess of equity market movements, which is reflected by the large market betas of LPE (as will be discussed in Section 8.5).

8.2   BENEFITS AND DISADVANTAGES OF LISTED PRIVATE EQUITY

LPE vehicles offer several advantages over more common LP/GP unlisted private equity funds. These advantages are mainly associated with investors being able to continuously trade shares on regulated public markets. The benefits and drawbacks can be summarized as follows:[2]

2. Based in part on *http://www.lpeq.com*

EXHIBIT 8.2

MARKET CAPITALIZATION OF LPE VEHICLES

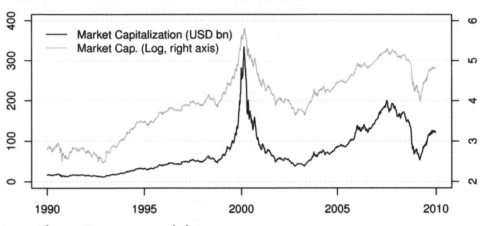

Source: Thomson Datastream, own calculations.

Advantages of listed private equity

- No minimum investment required thereby enables access to retail investors as well as institutions. These investors invest in a portfolio of mainly unlisted companies. In contrast, investing in private equity directly has high minimum commitments.

- Listing provides relative liquidity to an otherwise far less liquid private equity asset class. The typical 10-year time horizon of a fund and the obligation to undertake the unfunded portion of the capital commitment inhibits the size of the secondary market for unlisted private equity positions. In addition, transactions among limited partners are restricted in that they require the consent of the general partner and cannot be legally offered to the public.

- Ability to achieve a wide diversification within the private equity asset class, as each listed fund manager has different investment strategies and criteria.

- Capital gains retained within certain trusts are often not taxed.

- Listed vehicles handle the cash management and administration, which can be complex for limited partnership interests.

- The performance of an investment in a listed private equity vehicle can be easily observed through a quoted price.

Disadvantages of listed private equity

- Potential illiquidity of small closely-held listed private equity vehicles: although technically a holding in a listed private equity company can be bought or sold at any time, there are times when this is difficult to do in practice, especially with large blocks of shares.

- Less control over exposure to private equity investments, since listed funds often invest in instruments other than private portfolio companies.

EXHIBIT 8.3

ORGANIZATIONAL FORMS OF LISTED PRIVATE EQUITY

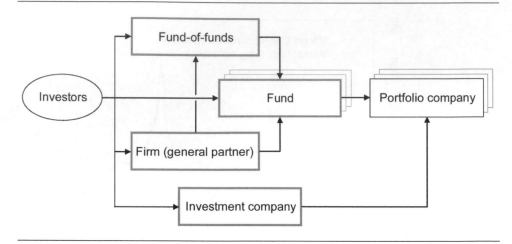

• Leverage and, therefore, underlying exposure can vary considerably. Listed funds may borrow at times whereas, at other times, there may be a great deal of net cash in the portfolio (e.g., as a result of a number of realizations and a lack of immediate investment opportunities). Surplus cash may act as a drag on performance.

• Shares in listed private equity companies usually trade at a discount or premium to their net asset value (NAV). NAV is necessarily an estimate of the value of the underlying assets—albeit according to strict valuation guidelines—and these valuations are conducted infrequently and with a lag. Shares can trade at a discount to NAV for long periods, particularly when stock market sentiment is depressed or subdued.

8.3 ECONOMIC AND ORGANIZATIONAL FORMS

It should be noted that LPE vehicles can have different organizational characteristics reflecting differences in underlying economics. As opposed to traditional PE, where the vast majority of entities are structured as limited partnerships, the LPE universe is quite heterogeneous with respect to the vehicle's legal and underlying economic structure.

Listed private funds fall under four main categories (see Lahr and Herschke, 2009):[3]

— *Funds that invest directly in unlisted companies*

— *Funds that invest in companies (henceforth "firms") that provide investment management for funds* (see Exhibit 8.3)

---

3. In practice there is considerable overlap between the groups. Therefore, classifying listed vehicles into categories requires close inspection of portfolios and legal structures.

— *Listed funds of funds*, which offer indirect exposure but higher degrees of diversification

— *Investment companies*, which invest directly in private companies.

The four groups offer different value generation processes and, consequently, vary in their risk and return profiles. Exhibit 8.4 lists the 20 largest LPE vehicles and indicates for each of them the category in which they fall.

Another way to present these distinctions is by grouping the listed vehicles along two dimensions:

— Internally or externally managed companies

— Single or multiple funds.

A further characteristic is the width of the investment mandates. Often, LPE funds are not restricted to invest in private companies, but are allowed to invest in other assets, such as AIM-quoted companies or third-party funds (see Exhibit 8.5).

EXHIBIT 8.4

THE 20 LARGEST LPE VEHICLES BY MARKET CAPITALIZATION

Vehicle	Market cap as at October 2010 (USD million)	Nation	Organizational form
The Blackstone Group LP	15,150	U.S.	Firm
Investor AB	9,314	Sweden	Investment company
HAL Trust NV	7,973	The Netherlands	Investment company
Partners Group Holding AG	4,887	Switzerland	Firm
3i Group PLC	4,649	U.K.	Firm
Ratos AB	4,254	Sweden	Investment company
Eurazeo SA	4,401	France	Investment company
Wendel SA	3,908	France	Investment company
Onex Corp.	3,472	Canada	Firm
Apollo Investment Corp.	2,141	U.S.	Investment company
American Capital Ltd.	2,378	U.S.	Firm
Intermediate Capital Group PLC	2,046	U.K.	Firm
Prime Infrastructure Holdings Ltd.	1,717	Australia	Fund
3I Infrastructure PLC	1,478	U.K.	Fund
KKR Financial Holdings LLC	1,392	U.S.	Fund
Conversus Capital, LP	1,272	The Netherlands	Fund of funds
Gimv NV	1,280	Belgium	Firm
Jafco Company Ltd.	1,008	Japan	Investment company
Clal Industries & Investments Ltd.	1,174	Israel	Investment company
HSBC Infrastructure Ltd.	932	U.K.	Fund

Source: Thomson Financial, authors' own research.

EXHIBIT 8.5

ORGANIZATIONAL FORM OF A TYPICAL LPE FUND

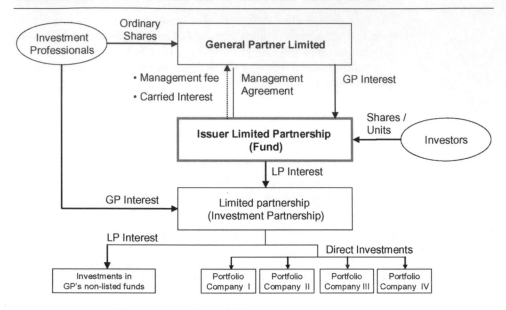

Source: Adapted from AP Alternative Assets LP, *Prospectus*, July 2006, p. 41; KKR Private Equity Investors LP, *Prospectus*, April 2006, p. 48.

8.3.1 Funds

LPE funds are externally managed vehicles that invest directly in private companies similar to traditional PE funds (e.g., Electra Private Equity, KKR Private Equity Investors, and HgCapital Trust). From a legal perspective, funds could either be organized as public limited partnerships or be incorporated (PLC, AG, SA, etc.). These vehicles invest their balance sheet, which consists of funds provided by unit-holders or shareholders with the purpose of earning capital gains from investments in private companies.

Similar to conventional traditional private equity limited partnerships, investment management is provided by a third party (i.e., a management company), which is often a traditional general partner. Managers are paid management fees as well as performance-based fees, which are mostly based on net-asset-value returns, but sometimes depend on the fund's market value. Funds typically invest directly or hold co-investments alongside traditional private equity funds that are managed by the same general partner.

8.3.2 Funds of funds

Funds of funds are externally managed investment vehicles (see Exhibit 8.6). Legally structured as limited liability entities (e.g., PLC, etc.) they pursue investments as limited partners in traditional private equity funds (e.g., Pantheon International Participations and Castle Private Equity). Cash flow is generated from investment activities within the private equity business cycle.

EXHIBIT 8.6

ORGANIZATIONAL FORM OF A TYPICAL LPE FUND OF FUNDS

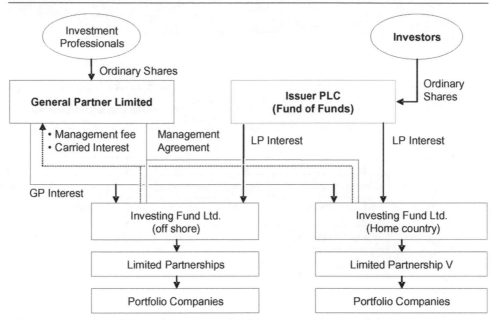

Source: Adapted from shaPE Capital, *Information Memorandum*, October 2001, p. 12; Castle Private Equity AG, *Listing Memorandum*, October 2000, p. 7.

Similarly to their unlisted counterparts, listed funds of funds tend to diversify across a broad spectrum of strategies: financing stages, general partners (PE groups), fund vintage years, and geographical region. Investments are managed by a management company which is typically paid management fees and carried interest. From an investor's perspective, these fees constitute a second fee layer between the investor and underlying portfolio investments. However, funds of funds offer access to due diligence expertise and long-standing relationships with private equity groups. For a further discussion see Chapter 7.

8.3.3   Firms

Listed private equity firms are internally managed vehicles that have a similar role to that of general partners in traditional private equity groups (see Exhibit 8.7). However, they typically take the legal form of a standard listed company (e.g. PLC, AG), although partnership structures exist in some cases. Management is rewarded in much the same way as GPs are motivated in private PE vehicles: through management agreements and performance fees (carried interest).

8.3.4   Investment companies

Investment companies hold a portfolio of direct investments in private companies and are internally managed by professionals. Investment companies come in a wide range of local flavors. Many jurisdictions provide a special legal status to investment companies,

EXHIBIT 8.7

ORGANIZATIONAL FORM OF A TYPICAL LPE FIRM

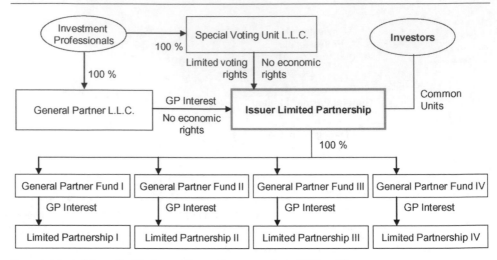

Source: Adapted from the Blackstone Group, *Prospectus*, June 2007, p. 16.

EXHIBIT 8.8

ORGANIZATIONAL FORM OF A TYPICAL LPE INVESTMENT COMPANY

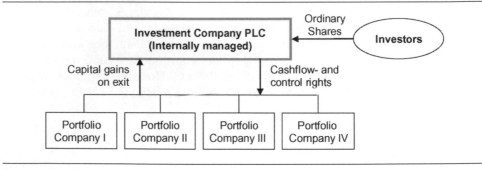

such as business development companies in the U.S. and venture capital trusts in the U.K. (see Exhibit 8.8).

Except for their commitment to the private equity business model, investment companies often lack features that distinguish them from ordinary holding companies. They usually report both a consolidated financial statement alongside a detailed portfolio breakdown, which is similar to the reporting of fair values of portfolio investments by listed funds. Portfolios held by investment companies are comparable with those of listed funds. However, investment companies tend to use considerably more debt financing, in much the same way as any conventional company.

8.4 LEGAL FORMS

The organizational forms described above could be obtained through diverse legal structures. Several legal structures that are well suited for private equity investments have emerged, particularly in the U.K. and the U.S., countries where LPE is concentrated.

8.4.1 Investment trusts

Investment trusts are a special type of U.K. investment companies, which invest in securities and whose shares are quoted on the London Stock Exchange.[4] Their organizational form classifies them as closed-end fund vehicles. These vehicles have to comply with Section 842 of the Income and Corporations Taxes Act 1988, which states that the company's income must be derived wholly or mainly from shares or securities, and no holding in a company other than an investment trust represents more than 15% of the trust's assets. The distribution of capital gains as dividends must be prohibited by the company's memorandum or articles of association, and the trust must not retain more than 15% of the income it derives from shares and securities every year.

The two main advantages of U.K. investment trusts are their exemption from tax on chargeable gains at the company level and the tax deductibility of management charges.[5] The lack of dividend payments can be seen as a disadvantage, in addition to the fact that management charges are subject to value-added tax.

Investment trusts can borrow to purchase additional investments. This ability to take on debt distinguishes them from other collective investment schemes like unit trusts.

8.4.2 Split capital trusts

Investment companies that issue only one class of shares are commonly known as "conventional" investment companies. Split capital trusts (splits) were introduced in the U.K. in 1965 and originally had a limited life with a fixed windup date and two classes of shares: income shares and capital shares.[6] The different classes of share are designed to meet different investors' needs, as they entitle investors to income generated from the investments (income shares) or the capital value of the company at windup (capital shares). Over time, several more share types have developed, such as zero-dividend preference shares. At least one share class within a split capital trust is likely to have a limited life (usually between 5 and 10 years) with a fixed windup date. The different share class priorities and entitlements lead to varying risk levels between these classes. Other kinds of collective investment vehicles cannot offer different share classes within one fund.

8.4.3 Venture capital trusts (VCTs)

Venture capital trusts (VCTs) are a type of company very similar to investment trust companies. They were introduced in the U.K. in 1995 and invest in small potentially

---

4. See *http://www.aitc.co.uk/Guide-to-investment-companies/What-are-investment-companies/How-they-work/* (last accessed March 17, 2010).
5. See s100(1) Taxation of Chargeable Gains Act 1992 (TCGA).
6. See *http://www.theaic.co.uk/Documents/Factsheets/AICSplitsFactsheet.pdf* (last accessed March 17, 2010).

high-growth private companies and new shares of companies that are traded on the Alternative Investment Market (AIM) and PLUS Market.[7]

VCTs offer investors income and capital gains tax reliefs, which include income tax relief on the initial investment when subscribing to new VCT share issues, tax-free dividends, and tax-free capital gains. To qualify for income tax relief on subscription, investors must hold VCTs for a minimum of 5 years. These rules governing the tax benefits of VCTs have, however, changed several times over the past years. VCTs have to adhere to several restrictions with respect to the types of companies they can invest in. At least 70% of their investments must be in shares in private U.K. companies which must have pre-money valuations of less than GBP7mn although, prior to April 2006, this limit was GBP15mn. The maximum amount any VCT can invest in a single company in any tax year is GBP1mn. Because of tax benefits and due to their special statutory governance mechanisms, VCTs are sometimes believed to underperform the market on a share price basis (see Cumming, 2003).

8.4.4 Business development companies (BDCs)

Business development companies (BDCs) are publicly traded closed-end companies that are regulated under the U.S. Investment Company Act of 1940, Section 54 (Election to be regulated as business development company) and seek to invest in small and mid-sized private companies. They are required by law to provide support and significant managerial assistance to their portfolio companies. To qualify as a BDC, companies must elect to be registered in compliance with the Investment Company Act. A major difference between BDCs and traditional PE funds is that BDCs allow smaller non-accredited investors to invest in startup companies.

The Investment Company Act imposes certain restrictions on the operations of a BDC. They must hold at least 70% of their total assets in shares of private companies or securities for which there is no ready market, cash equivalents, U.S. government securities, or high-quality debt securities maturing in 1 year or less from the time of investment. Most BDCs have regulated investment company (RIC) status, which requires them to distribute at least 90% of their taxable income to shareholders every year. No more than 5% of their assets can be from a single issuer, and 10% is the upper limit BDCs are allowed to own of the outstanding voting securities of any one issuer. BDCs cannot invest more than 25% of their assets in businesses that they control or businesses that are in similar or related trades or businesses.

8.4.5 Special purpose acquisition companies (SPACs)

A special purpose acquisition company (SPAC) is a shell company (or blank check company) registered with the U.S. Securities and Exchange Commission (SEC) which is formed to raise capital for a yet unidentified business that will be acquired in the future.[8] Similar to internally managed investment companies, SPACs provide investors with potential access to acquisitions of private companies. They have become a popular new investment vehicle, raising more than USD20bn since 2003 and comprising 20% of

---

7. See *http://www.theaic.co.uk/Documents/Factsheets/AICVCTFactsheet.pdf* (last accessed March 17, 2010). Similar structures under Canadian Law are labor-sponsored investment funds (LSIFs) and labor-sponsored venture capital corporations (LSVCCs), which are organized as mutual funds and therefore excluded (see Cumming and MacIntosh, 2007).

8. See Hale (2007) for this definition, Davidoff (2008) for a legal description of SPACs, and Berger (2008) for an economic discussion of three case studies.

total funds raised in U.S. IPOs in 2007 (see Lewellen, 2009; Jenkinson and Sousa, 2009). Moreover, there have been recent listings of SPAC shares in Europe issued as units consisting of common stock and one or two separate warrants that typically can be exercised only if the SPAC completes an acquisition. The warrants, which are normally callable by the firm at any time during the exercise period, may trade separately from the common stock 90 days after the IPO.

After price manipulations in blank check companies (BCCs), the SEC adopted Rule 419, which imposes several restrictions on BCCs, prohibiting trading of the BCC's securities by requiring them to be held in an escrow or trust account until consummation of an acquisition (see Sjostrom, 2008).[9] SPACs avoid the application of Rule 419 by not issuing penny stock. However, SPACs voluntarily incorporate a number of Rule 419–type provisions in their IPO terms. For example, SPAC charters usually require an acquisition within 18 to 24 months after the effective date of the offering. Until that date, 90% of the IPO proceeds must be held in an escrow or trust account. The initial target must have a fair market value of at least 80% of the SPAC's net assets excluding deferred underwriters' discounts and commissions. If management does not find a target within a specified period, the SPAC is liquidated and the firm's net assets are returned to shareholders.

SPACs resemble a risk-free asset in the early stages of their lifecycle, yet many become single-transaction buyout funds if successful. They trade on stock exchanges and invest in private companies and, therefore, may be considered LPE. In order to qualify as LPE, companies must commit to the private equity business model, which includes buying and selling portfolio companies. The selling part is clearly up to the investor. After an acquisition has been consummated, SPACs are very similar to normal holding companies from an economic point of view. SPACs should therefore be excluded from most analyses of LPE on these grounds, as do most LPE indexes.

8.4.6 Structured trust acquisition company (STACs)

Structured trust acquisition companies (STACs) are tax-structured corporate entities that initiate offerings to acquire private companies (see Davidoff, 2008). Similar to traditional private equity fund group structures, investors buy shares in an entity whose sole property is shares in a holding company that invests in private portfolio companies. A management company provides investment services to the holding company. In contrast to SPACs, a STAC identifies its target before going public. Furthermore, STACs enable long-term control-stake ownership of operating companies, and no shareholder approval is necessary for business combinations. They must consolidate financial statements of majority-owned businesses and are subject to "pass-through" taxation instead of entity level taxation of income and capital gains received from portfolio companies. Two STACs have listed their stock so far: Macquarie Infrastructure Company Trust and Compass Diversified Trust, each raising more than USD700mn, which was immediately used to acquire previously earmarked private companies (see Krus et al., 2006).

8.5 ESTIMATED RISK PROFILE OF LISTED PRIVATE EQUITY

As discussed in previous chapters, measuring risk, return, and market correlation are difficult for traditional (i.e., unlisted) private equity investments. The LPE segment

---

9. See 17 C.F.R. §230.419(b)(2)(i) & (vi) (2007).

EXHIBIT 8.9

ORGANIZATIONAL FORMS AND RISK (MARKET BETA) OF LPE VEHICLES

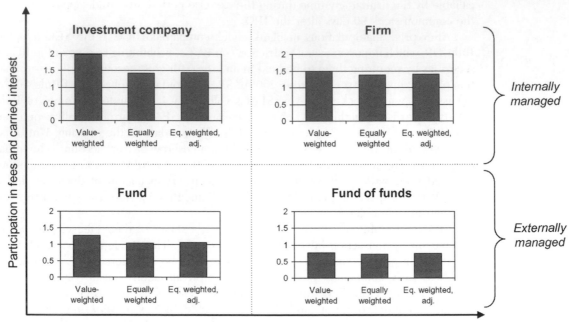

Source: Adapted from Lahr and Herschke (2009). Coefficient estimates are based on CAPM time series regressions of weekly logarithmic LPE index returns on MSCI world returns and currency risk factors. Equal-weighted indexes are unadjusted (middle column) and corrected for bid–ask spreads (right column).

lends itself to studying these patterns in a straightforward way using readily available market prices. Since business models and organizational forms of LPE vehicles bear a strong resemblance to traditional PE funds and firms, statistical results obtained from examining LPE vehicles should shed light regarding the broader asset class as well.

However, LPE vehicles exhibit different exposures to market risk depending on organizational forms. In a study of 274 liquid LPE entities, Lahr and Herschke (2009) find that externally managed LPE vehicles exhibit a substantially lower systematic risk than internally managed entities (see Exhibit 8.9). For value-weighted indexes, the estimated beta for investment companies is 2.0 and for firms 1.5. These figures differ from a beta estimate of 1.3 for funds and a mere 0.8 for funds of funds.[10] In equal-weighted spread-adjusted indexes, these betas are 1.4 for investment companies and firms, but 1.0 and 0.7 for funds and funds of funds, respectively. The different betas for value-weighted and equal-weighted indexes indicate the impact of a few large volatile investment companies on LPE returns. Betas for the entire LPE sample are 1.8 for a value-weighted index and 1.2 for an equal-weighted and spread-adjusted index. Excess returns (alphas) in these CAPM regressions are generally negligible.

10. For all figures, the Dimson (1979) procedure was used to handle infrequent trading.

EXHIBIT 8.10

MEAN 1-YEAR BETA

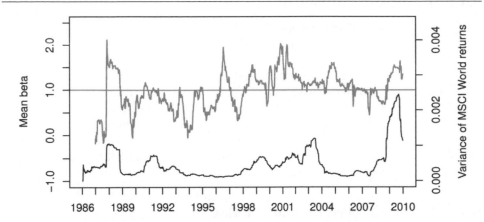

Notes: Betas (top line) are measured on the left scale, return variance (bottom line) on the right scale. Betas and MSCI world return variance are estimated over rolling windows of 52 weeks.

In addition to the large variance of betas across vehicles, Kaserer et al. (2010) find that aggregate market risk of LPE vehicles varies strongly over time and is positively correlated with market return variance as given in Exhibit 8.10. Individual betas are found to be highly unstable and are predictable only up to 2 to 3 years into the future. Beta stationarity over time depends, however, on individual fund risk profile. High-risk and low-risk LPEs portray a stationary beta over time, whereas betas of medium-risk companies vary more.

8.6 LPE INDEXES

Several stock indexes based on varying subsamples of the LPE universe have been developed to measure the performance of this sector. ETFs, certificates, and mutual funds tracking these indexes are offered by financial intermediaries such as ALPS Fund Services, BlackRock Advisors, Deutsche Bank, Invesco, Merrill Lynch, RBS, and UBS.

8.6.1 LPX® listed private equity index family

The first and probably best known provider of LPE indexes is LPX GmbH. Since 2004, a family of indexes have been developed consisting of global indexes varying in scope (LPX Composite, LPX50®, and LPX Major Market®), regional reach (LPX Europe, LPX UK, and LPX America) as well as in investment style (LPX Buyout, LPX Venture, LPX Direct, LPX Indirect, and LPX Mezzanine).[11] A database of over 300 LPE companies listed worldwide provides the basis for the construction of all LPX indexes.[12] In

---

11. See *Guide to the LPX Indices*, February 2009, available at *http://www.lpx-group.com/lpx/fileadmin/images/indices/LPX_Guide_to_the_Equity_Indices.pdf*

12. See Deutsche Bank, 2005, *DB Platinum V Liquid Private Equity Funds*, fund brochure.

order to be eligible for inclusion, a proportion of net assets greater than 50% must be private companies.

8.6.2 Red Rocks LPE indexes

Red Rocks provides LPE indexes similar to those constructed by LPX GmbH. Their index family consists of three indexes with different geographical focus. The Listed Private Equity Index (LPEI) covers the 25–40 largest and most liquid LPE companies that are traded on nationally recognized exchanges in the U.S. To qualify for inclusion, these companies can invest in, lend capital to, or provide services to privately held businesses. The International Listed Private Equity Index (ILPEI) focuses on 30–50 companies traded outside the U.S., whereas the Global Listed Private Equity Index (GLPEI) comprises the 40–60 most liquid LPE vehicles worldwide. Index constituents must have, or publicly intend to reach, a majority of their assets invested in equity, loans, or services to private companies.[13]

8.6.3 S&P Listed Private Equity Index

Standard & Poor's Listed Private Equity Index is constructed from 30 large liquid LPE companies trading on exchanges in North America, Europe, and the Asia–Pacific region, which meet the size, liquidity, exposure, and activity requirements.[14] Index constituents are drawn from Standard & Poor's Capital IQ (CIQ) database and must engage in the private equity business, excluding real estate income and property trusts. Stocks that have an exposure score of 1.0 or 0.5 to PE investments (out of the three assigned values 0, 0.5, and 1.0) are eligible for inclusion.

8.6.4 SG Private Equity Index (Privex)

The Société Générale Private Equity Index includes the 25 most representative stocks of the private equity companies listed on a stock exchange in Western Europe, North America, Singapore, Hong Kong, Japan, South Korea, Australia, and New Zealand. Constituents must be covered by Dow Jones in the Dow Jones World Index and have their largest revenue share in the private equity sector.[15] To be included, companies must be involved in private equity investment activities such as leveraged buyouts, venture capital, or growth capital.

8.6.5 DJ STOXX® Europe Private Equity 20

The Dow Jones STOXX® Europe Private Equity 20 index is constructed to reflect the performance of the 20 largest LPE companies in Europe.[16] Constituents must be classified by the Industry Classification Benchmark (ICB) as either "specialty finance" or "equity investment instruments" and/or must have at least 40% of their investments in private equity assets.

13. See *http://www.redrockscapital.com/lpei_meth.html* (last accessed March 17, 2010).
14. See *http://www.standardandpoors.com/indices/sp-listed-private-equity-index/en/us/? indexId=spsal-lpe-usdw—p-rgl—* (last accessed March 17, 2010).
15. See *http://www.sgindex.com/services/quotes/details.php? family=6* (last accessed March 17, 2010).
16. See *http://www.stoxx.com/indices/index_information.html? symbol=SPEP* (last accessed March 17, 2010).

8.7 REFERENCES

BERG, A. (2005) *What Is the Strategy for Buyout Associations?* Verlag für Wissenschaft und Forschung, Berlin.

BERGER, R. (2008) "SPACS: An alternative way to access the public markets," *Journal of Applied Corporate Finance*, **20**(3), 68–75.

BILO, S. (2002) "Alternative asset class: Publicly traded private equity, performance, liquidity, diversification potential and pricing characteristics," Ph.D. thesis, University of St. Gallen, St. Gallen, Switzerland.

CUMMING, D.J. (2003) "The structure, governance and performance of UK venture capital trusts," *Journal of Corporate Law Studies*, **3**(2), 191–217.

CUMMING AND MACINTOSH (2007) "Mutual funds that invest in private equity? An analysis of labour-sponsored investment funds," *Cambridge Journal of Economics*, **31**(3), 445–487.

DAVIDOFF, S.M. (2008) "Black market capital," *Columbia Business Law Review*, **1**, 172–268.

DIMSON, E. (1979) "Risk measurement when shares are subject to infrequent trading," *Journal of Financial Economics*, **7**, 197–226.

GOMPERS, P.A., AND LERNER, J. (2000) "Money chasing deals? The impact of fund inflows on private equity valuation," *Journal of Financial Economics*, **55**, 281–325.

HALE, L.M. (2007) "SPAC: A financing tool with something for everyone," *Journal of Corporate Accounting & Finance*, **18**(2), 67–74.

JENKINSON, T., AND SOUSA, M. (2009) "Why SPAC investors should listen to the market," paper presented at *AFA 2010 Atlanta Meeting*.

KASERER, C., LAHR, H., LIEBHART, V., AND METTLER, A. (2010) "The time-varying risk of listed private equity," *Journal of Financial Transformation*, **28**, 87–93.

KRUS, C., PANGAS, H., BOEHM, S., AND ZOCHOWSKI, C. (2006) "United States: Taking private equity public," available at *http://www.mondaq.com/article.asp?articleid=41446*

LAHR, H., AND HERSCHKE, F.T. (2009) "Organisational forms and risk in listed private equity," *Journal of Private Equity*, **13**(1), 89–99.

LEWELLEN, S. (2009) "SPACs as an asset class," working paper, available at SSRN: *http://ssrn.com/abstract=1284999*

LPX GMBH (2008) "Listed private equity index," available at *http://www.lpx.ch* (last accessed March 17, 2010).

PARTNERS GROUP (2008) Available at *http://www.partnersgroup.ch* (last accessed December 17, 2009).

REDROCKS LPE (2008) "Listed private equity," available at *http://www.listedprivateequity.com* (last accessed March 17, 2010).

RITTER, J.R. (1984) "The "hot" issue market of 1980," *Journal of Business*, **57**(2), 214–240.

SJOSTROM, W.K. (2008) "The truth about reverse mergers," *Entrepreneurial Business Law Journal*, **2**, 743–759.

9

Secondary fund transactions

9.1 INTRODUCTION

Over the past 10 years, the secondary private equity market has experienced rapid and unprecedented growth. Fueled by the development of the primary market, *private equity secondaries*, or simply *secondaries*, exist to provide liquidity to an intrinsically illiquid asset class. As private equity investors have become increasingly sophisticated and the economic environment has become increasingly volatile, there has been a growing need for investors to revaluate their portfolios over shorter timeframes and adapt to changing circumstances. As a result, the secondary market has flourished, allowing investors far greater flexibility in their investment decisions and encouraging new participants into the private equity arena. Given that this is a relatively immature market, it seems clear that greater complexity and scope lie on the horizon.

Private equity secondaries refer to the buying and selling of pre-existing investor commitments (i.e., limited partnership interests) to buyout, venture capital, and other alternative investment funds. Interests sold not only include the current investments in private equity funds, but also the remaining unfunded commitments into these funds. Typically, a secondary transaction involves the sale of a limited partner (LP) interest in a fund or a portfolio of funds, although some secondary transactions may instead involve the sale of direct investment portfolios in operating companies. Sales of an interest in an individual company from one fund to another or trade sales of a venture or buyout-backed portfolio company to a corporate acquirer are not considered to be secondaries.

Transaction volume in the secondary market has increased from approximately USD1.5bn in 1998 to a record USD20bn in 2008 (Penn and Welsch-Lehmann, 2004; Johnson, 2009). At the end of 2009, Preqin, a London-based data provider, counted over 70 managers with dedicated secondary funds. While 2009 was a difficult fundraising year for private equity funds, secondaries raised aggregate commitments of about USD23bn (Preqin, 2010a). Even traditional institutional investors have started to display interest in secondary transactions. The average age of limited partnership interests sold was more than 7 years in 1998, but transactions over the last few years have included a significant percentage of young funds, averaging less than 3 years (Preqin, 2010a).

This chapter has been co-authored with Brenlen Jinkens (Managing Director, Cogent Partners) and Anya Kleymenova (Ph.D. candidate, London Business School).

This explosive growth of the secondaries market was fueled by several important factors:

- The slowdown in private equity funds' distributions to their investors
- LPs' desire to rebalance their portfolios and manage the relations with general partners (GPs) more actively
- LPs' liquidity requirements
- The changing regulatory framework in different jurisdictions
- Pressure from LPs' shareholders
- Management changes
- The merger and acquisition activities that LPs engage in.

We explore some of these factors in the sections that follow.

9.2   SECONDARY MARKET DEVELOPMENT

Secondary private equity started to emerge after the equity market crash in October 1987 and the world economic crises of the early 1990s. These challenging economic conditions produced an intense need for liquidity among many financial institutions and corporations, which forced some to sell their investments in private equity funds. The interest from these sellers attracted a small number of buyers, thus creating a new market for secondary interests in private equity funds or in companies in which these sellers had invested (e.g., Soulignac, 2004; Meyer and Mathonet, 2005).

During these early days, sellers generally sold assets to generate liquidity. Many also wished to reduce their funding obligations on committed capital, rebalance their private equity portfolios relative to public equity, or divest interests in underperforming private equity funds. Given the illiquidity of private equity investments and the novelty of the market, these transactions were considered as distressed and the prices paid, therefore, reflected a significant discount to the *net asset value* (NAV) of these interests (Gordon and Toomey, 2004).

The number of secondary deals was relatively low until the mid-1990s, after which the market expanded dramatically. Secondary transactions had previously been viewed as an admission of failure, but this stigma slowly faded. Selling assets in the secondary market was no longer an option of last resort for distressed sellers; it had evolved into an attractive portfolio optimization tool for long-term private equity investors. The secondary market started to be perceived as a place where investors could mitigate the *J*-curve effect by investing in more mature funds and, thereby, obtain returns over a shorter horizon. An increasing inflow of capital into private equity after 1995 (with a peak in early 2000) also contributed to the rapid increase in secondary transactions.

If in the late 1990s a small group of specialists had been the main buy-side participants, by the early 2000s numerous specialist firms, funds of funds, and leading institutional investors such as endowments, foundations, and pension funds had started to enter the secondary market. The additional demand from these institutional investors improved pricing, as these new investors had a lower cost of capital than dedicated secondary firms and the traditional fund of funds, with their own fees and carried interest. With these lower underwriting rates, new buyers could significantly outbid specialists in competitive situations. Moreover, these non-traditional secondary buyers

EXHIBIT 9.1

SECONDARY MARKET TRANSACTION VOLUME

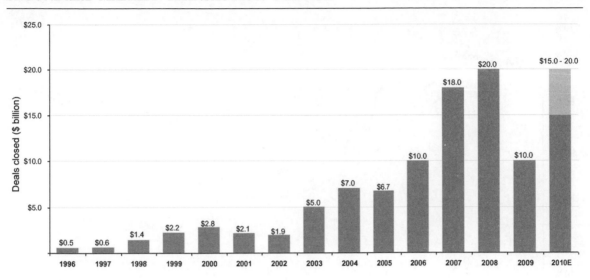

Source: Cogent Partners and *Private Equity Analyst.*

started to participate in transactions that involved not only single limited partnerships but also interests in large portfolios of funds (Konkel, 2004).

In addition to the increasing number of non-traditional buyers, secondary specialist buyers bolstered their continued presence in the market with ever growing pools of capital. As this trend continued, GPs became more accustomed to seeing stakes in their funds trade on secondary markets and no longer viewed such deals with suspicion.

With the growth of competition in the secondary market, what had once been known as a *buyer's market* became more evenly balanced. While transactions in which sellers negotiated directly with buyers continued, the market entered a new phase in which auctions, often administered by qualified sell-side advisory firms, became more prevalent. This contributed to significant increases in the pricing levels of secondary transactions and to a leveling of the playing field between experienced purchasers and sellers who were relative newcomers (Cogent Partners, 2005).

As public equity markets experienced dramatic volatility and deep lows in 2008 and 2009, pricing understandably also fell for private equity positions on the secondary market, which were less liquid, and often more highly levered. According to Cogent Partners, a private equity–focused investment bank and leading secondary intermediary, during the first half of 2009 deals were being struck at an average of below 50% of face value, compared with 85% in the first half of 2008 and a peak of 108% in 2006 (Cogent Partners, 2006, 2008, 2009). In a 2010 report, research group Preqin records that secondary pricing reached its lowest point in March 2009, with bids of 50.7% and 53% of net asset value for interests in buyout and venture funds, respectively (Preqin, 2010a). Indeed, there were even reports of investors having to pay buyers to take stakes off their hands. Exhibit 9.1 shows that, after strong transaction volume growth in the secondary market, volumes were down approximately 50% in 2009

EXHIBIT 9.2

PUBLIC EQUITY VS. SECONDARY MARKET PRICING

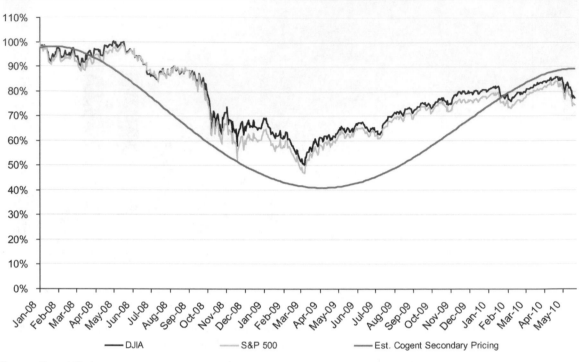

Source: Cogent Partners.

due to increased market uncertainty, substantial risk premiums, the pace of capital calls, and the risk in public markets, which heightened the impact of the "denominator effect" on private equity allocations.[1]

By the end of 2009, as the overall securities markets had rebound, pricing for secondary sales also recovered significantly, rising to 72% of NAV, according to Cogent's statistics covering its own deal flow (Cogent Partners, 2010). Secondary funds, the main buyers of secondary interests, had raised a record USD23bn during 2009 despite there being fewer than 50 sophisticated secondary buyers globally (Preqin, 2010a). Based on various estimates, between 3% and 5% of primary fundraising is likely to continue to be sold on the secondary market, which could create a market worth up to USD60bn in the next few years (Permal Capital, 2009). This growth in both good and bad times highlights the resilience of the market and its firm setting in the industry going forward.

1. The denominator effect arises due to the way large LPs allocate their portfolios across different asset classes. Assume that a large LP allocates 5% of its portfolio to private equity investments while the remaining 90% is allocated to public markets. If a significant decline in public share valuations occurs, the portfolio will experience a severe drop in the public market allocation. As a result, the LP will be overallocated in private equity. This imbalance can be resolved by increasing the denominator (i.e., investing more money in the public markets) or reducing the denominator (i.e., selling a percentage of the private equity holdings).

The financial performance of dedicated secondary funds is one of the best indicators of the profitability of secondary purchases.[2] According to Preqin, median net IRRs for secondary funds from 1999 to 2004 vintages have been mostly in the range of 15% to 25%, which is ahead of the median primary fund (Preqin, 2010b). As the secondary market becomes more mature, the returns are likely to move closer towards the primary private equity markets.

Secondary markets exhibit a certain level of correlation with the primary public markets. This, for example, can be seen from Exhibit 9.2, which shows major public market indexes together with high bids received by Cogent Partners for the secondary transactions they oversaw.

9.3 PARTIES INVOLVED IN SECONDARY TRANSACTIONS

There are at least three, and sometimes four, parties involved in secondary transactions: buyers, sellers, intermediaries, and GPs. Each party is driven by its own motives and goals.

9.3.1 Sellers

Typical sellers in the secondary market are LPs invested in buyout, venture, or other investment strategies, such as natural resources, real estate, or credit. These LPs usually include pension and endowment funds, sovereign wealth funds, banks, hedge funds, insurance companies, foundations, family offices, funds of funds, and other institutional investors. There are also secondary funds that subsequently decide to sell a portfolio of fund interests purchased earlier, perhaps because of a change in strategy caused by fund liquidations.

LPs sell private equity interests for a variety of reasons. Beyond simple access to liquidity, the secondary market has become an important portfolio management tool for investors. Factors that contribute to the decision to sell include:

- Poor actual or expected fund performance
- Re-allocation of capital across asset classes
- Changes in human resources or investment strategy
- Regulatory changes
- M&A activities.

Recently, difficult economic conditions seem to have triggered asset re-allocation decisions that have affected private equity holdings. For example, as the market value of various publicly quoted asset classes fell in 2009, the value of allocations to private assets, including private equity, rose above allocation targets. In some cases this led to sales of private equity commitments in order to re-instate these targets. Reduced distributions from prior investments in private equity have also meant that LPs can no longer rely on recycling distributions to support their commitments to new funds. Thus, investors were forced either to sell fund investments earlier or to surrender these commitments.

---

2. The main secondaries players are Coller Capital, Adams Street Partners, Lexington Partners, HarbourVest, Pantheon Ventures, and Paul Capital.

9.3.2   Buyers

Typically, buyers in the secondary market are interested in acquiring stakes in buyout and venture funds, although there is also some interest across a wide variety of investment strategies. Buyers differ in their approaches: some are completely opportunistic, while others have a dedicated investment strategy.

The universe of potential buyers for secondary transactions has been expanding steadily. These buyers have varying levels of experience and different reputations and objectives. On the one hand, there are dedicated secondary funds and other funds of funds whose main or partial investment objective is to buy private equity interests on the secondary market. On the other hand, there are the so-called *non-traditional* buyers, such as pension funds, endowment funds, hedge funds, insurance companies, sovereign wealth funds, banks, family offices, foundations, and even GPs. Many of these non-traditional investors view secondaries as a significant component of their overall investment strategy. About 40% of investors currently seeking fund opportunities on the secondary market are traditional secondary market buyers, consisting of primary and secondary fund-of-funds managers. Thus, non-traditional investors account for a substantial 60% of investors looking to purchase fund stakes on the secondary market (Preqin, 2010a).

Most institutional investors seeking exposure to the secondary market invest in dedicated secondary funds, which allows them to counteract the *J*-curve effect. By investing in interests of more mature funds, they potentially avoid paying early management fees and portfolio losses. With dedicated secondary funds they can obtain immediate exposure to a diverse range of managers, underlying companies, and vintage years, which also smoothes the *J*-curve effect.

By 2010, public and private pension funds accounted for more than one third of the commitments to secondary funds. Geographically, North America accounted for about 50% of investors with an interest in secondary funds, Europe for about 40%, and Asia and the rest of the world for the remaining 10% (Preqin, 2010a).

Investors in the secondary market can also minimize, or even eliminate, the risk of investing in a *blind pool*. Whereas investors in the primary market make commitments to funds to finance future investments in portfolio companies that are not yet known, investors in the secondary market buy an existing pool of assets. Thus, these transactions offer greater transparency of the underlying investments, which can allow buyers to create downside protection based on the identifiable value.

Exhibit 9.3 illustrates the distinct preferences different types of buyers have and their varying target rates of return.

9.3.3   Intermediaries

In the past, the only option LPs had for managing a secondary sale process was to do so themselves. However, managing a secondary sales process can be a daunting prospect, given the limited resources and expertise of most LPs. Secondary transactions occur infrequently, and the necessary up-to-date knowledge of market conditions and potential buyers is not always available in-house. The secondary sale process is also time consuming. It involves contacting the GPs; collecting, organizing, and distributing information about the fund interests to be sold; identifying and contacting a shortlist of prospective buyers; and, most importantly, understanding how to price a portfolio of fund interests (PEI, 2009).

EXHIBIT 9.3

SEGMENTATION OF BUYER UNIVERSE

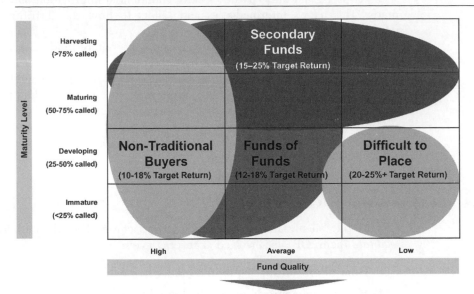

Different types of buyers have distinct asset preferences and varying target rates of return that drive unique transaction opportunities

Source: Cogent Partners.

As a result, several advisory firms have identified the opportunity to offer such services to sellers. Secondary advisory services include valuation and market research. They are used mainly by sellers that want to dispose of large private equity portfolios, and need assistance in the sale process. Since 2005, more than a third of secondary transactions have been completed through intermediaries (Cogent Partners, 2009). Cogent Partners, Campbell Lutyens, and UBS are the main secondary advisors; other advisors are mainly firms that are normally active as placement agents, such as Probitas Partners and Triago. Intermediaries generally charge a transaction fee of between 1% and 2% of the value of the transaction, depending on the services they offer.

These intermediaries play an important role in the structuring of fund interest offerings. Confidentiality remains of critical concern to many GPs and, as a sale process may include the disclosure of fund documents, there are naturally obstacles to executing a transaction. Intermediaries provide a way to alleviate these concerns by standardizing practices and by offering to protect confidential information by demanding execution of non-disclosure agreements with potential secondary buyers before sharing sensitive information. Intermediaries also provide consistency in transaction management, which addresses the market's need for a more formal and systematic mechanism for the exchange of limited partnership interests.

Secondary advisors market fund offerings in order to maximize the possibility of achieving a good price. To maintain a competitive process, marketing of secondary private equity sales can therefore involve calling on many potential buyers, with varying profiles, sizes, and primary lines of business. At the start of the sales process, advisors frequently inform the GP of the interest being sold, which helps to obtain the manager's consent and identify upfront any concerns a GP may have. If a large portfolio of fund interests is up for sale, intermediaries might divide the portfolio into multiple subsets involving multiple buyers. They assign groups of prospective bidders to specific assets, and these parties receive confidential information only on the relevant funds. This allows intermediaries and sellers to limit the distribution of sensitive information.

Buyers seeking to purchase stakes in private equity funds also benefit from the services that intermediaries offer. Advisors can help buyers identify and acquire stakes in funds that fit with their existing portfolios and strategy. They also offer help in negotiations and guidance regarding appropriate pricing. According to a 2010 survey by Preqin, 56% of buyers stated that they would use an intermediary when purchasing stakes on the secondary market. The survey also found that, even when investors approach a GP directly to make a purchase, secondary advisors act as an important point of contact for buyers (Preqin, 2010a).

9.3.4   General partners (GPs)

GPs are the "silent partner" in secondary transactions. They do not initiate deals; they *facilitate* them. GPs get involved at several levels:

- Control of data sharing on the fund(s)
- Review and approval of potential purchasers
- Response to due diligence enquiries during the later stages of the sale process
- Completion of transfer documentation to move ownership of the interest(s) from seller to buyer.

Given the recently increased velocity of secondary sales, most fund managers treat secondary sales in a thoroughly non-emotional, professional manner. Indeed, the most astute GPs treat secondary sales as an investor relations opportunity and work with the seller or the intermediary to find a replacement LP of equal or greater quality.

9.4   SECONDARY TRANSACTIONS

9.4.1   Types of transactions

Traditional secondaries

Traditional secondaries involve the transfer of LP interests in a given private equity fund to a new investor. For an agreed price, this investor assumes ownership of the selling LP's capital account value and any remaining unfunded obligations from the selling LP. Traditional secondaries in any given year typically represent the vast majority of transaction volume: 90% to 95%.

Very occasionally, these transactions are linked to the raising of a new fund by a GP: these types of secondary deals are often referred to as *stapled transactions*. A secondary buyer purchases an interest in an existing fund from a current investor and, simultaneously, makes a commitment to the new fund being raised by the GP. These transactions lost their appeal during the credit crisis as the appetite for investments in the private equity primary market decreased.

Synthetic secondaries

Synthetic secondaries (also called *secondary directs*) involve creating a new partnership to purchase a portfolio of direct investments. They use an incumbent or a new GP, contracted to oversee and ultimately sell the assets in the partnership. In this transaction there is a transfer of ownership of interests held in a portfolio of private companies. The crucial difference from the traditional secondary market is that, in secondary directs, interests transferred are held directly in underlying portfolio companies, whereas in the traditional secondary market the interests are generally in limited partnerships, which themselves hold interests in the underlying portfolio companies. Synthetic secondaries typically represent a much smaller portion of transaction volume: 5% to 10%.

Structured secondaries

Structured secondaries involve creating a new special purpose vehicle that establishes a unique legal framework or structure in order to accomplish a particular seller's goals in closing a transaction. For example, the seller may keep some or all of the fund interests on its balance sheet, but the buyer agrees to fund all future capital calls of the seller's portfolio in exchange for a preferred return secured against future distributions of the seller's portfolio. These types of secondary transaction were explored from mid-2008 and throughout 2009, as many sellers did not want to take a loss through a straight sale of their portfolio at a steep discount, but were instead ready to abandon some of the future upside in exchange for a bridge of the uncalled capital commitments.

Structured secondaries tend to be discussed, and occasionally completed, at either the end or the beginning of a macroeconomic cycle (e.g., during 2002–2003 and 2008–2009). As they do not feature regularly, it is impractical to estimate their overall share of transaction volume.

9.4.2 The secondary transaction process

Some transactions, typically for individual funds or small portfolios (c. USD25mn), continue to be negotiated bilaterally or with only a small number of buyers involved. However, intermediated auctions have become increasingly common. Most of the large transactions and more than 50% of overall secondary transactions, go through an intermediary and a bidding process. The number of buyers per fund in auctions varies, but for multi-hundred-million dollar deals there are usually many buy-side participants (VCFA, 2002; Penn and Welsch-Lehmann, 2004).

If an intermediary is used, it will generally manage all aspects of the sale. Transaction management is typically divided into three distinct phases: transaction origination, structuring and execution (Penn and Welsch-Lehmann, 2004).

Transaction origination

During this first phase, secondary advisors evaluate the investor's situation and motivation and determine the transaction's feasibility. They also provide up-to-date information on current market conditions and pricing guidance for the specific funds or relevant segments of the private equity industry.

Transaction structuring

In the structuring phase, intermediaries determine the most efficient transaction structure in terms of tax, legal, and regulatory considerations, and set specific milestones and targets. Transaction structuring is particularly important when sellers are rebalancing their portfolios. The structure of such a transaction would typically be driven by the seller, and would depend on the seller's objectives and needs. Intermediaries will design a package for sale based on the vintage year, subasset class, geography, or quality of a GP according to the seller's preferences (Penn and Welsch-Lehmann, 2004).

For example, a portfolio manager might want to reduce its overall private equity exposure while optimizing price in a sale. However, the institution might not be as concerned about when it receives sales proceeds. So, a transaction could be structured in such a way that the portfolio manager received deferred payments in order to obtain a higher purchase price.

In a different scenario, a portfolio manager might want to reduce its overall private equity exposure, but maintain its relationships with the GPs. In this case a portfolio manager might offer to sell a *strip* of its entire portfolio (e.g., a 25% interest in a basket of fund interests instead of the whole fund or portfolio) allowing it to maintain relationships and subclass weightings while reducing overall exposure.

In yet another scenario, a portfolio manager might want to sell down its portfolio, but be worried about the headline risk of a subsequent large winner the manager might not be familiar with. The transaction could be structured so that the buyer shared a portion of all proceeds after it had received back twice its invested capital.

As these examples show, there are many ways in which a transaction could be structured to meet individual objectives.

Transaction management and execution

The management and execution of the transaction are as critical as the transaction-structuring phase. Advisors guide the sale process through the creation of the relevant legal agreements, such as purchase and sale agreements and transfer agreements. Advisors often also provide guidance on transfer conditions, consents, and other closing matters (Penn and Welsch-Lehmann, 2004).

Intermediaries typically organize a *managed auction* to ensure best value for the selling client. They reach out to a group of buyers, picked jointly with the seller, typically from a database of active purchasers around the world. The intermediary selects participants before the first round of bidding, and these potential buyers undergo the required due diligence. The intermediary will provide all buyers with the same set of information to make their valuation decisions, such as financial statements, capital account statements, and (in most cases) fund performance guidance.

Although bids provided by buyers are collected in an openly competitive process and all buyers have access to standard information and asset insight from sell-side representation, the range of bids presented for the same portfolio of fund interests can still be wide (Cogent Partners, 2005).

After the first round of bidding, the client and intermediary decide on whom to invite to the second round. The intermediary then informs the parties whether they have been successful, and the bidding proceeds to the second round. It is common for bidders to revise their valuations in the second round, as they are better informed at that stage. The bidding process can take 3 to 6 weeks, depending on whether the auction takes place in one or two rounds (McGrady, 2007).

9.5 THE PRICING OF SECONDARY TRANSACTIONS

In all markets, buyers and sellers must agree on the value of an asset to trigger a transaction. The secondary market for alternative assets is no different. However, the lack of transparency in the secondary market and the inexperience of many sellers of alternative assets mean there is often a notable discrepancy between the valuations of a given asset by buyers and sellers. Sellers are concerned with what the asset is worth *today*, and their view is typically some distillation of the current NAV ascribed by the GP. By contrast, buyers are much more focused on what the asset will be worth in the *future*.

9.5.1 Buyers' valuation of secondary assets

In order to determine the value of an asset and the price they are willing to pay for an asset today, most buyers of secondary assets will conduct a discounted cash flow (DCF) analysis. The DCF uses several factors to arrive at the cash flow stream: expected exit value and exit timing for current portfolio investments, projected future capital calls and the return on future investments made using these capital calls, the legal structure of the fund, and the return the buyer would like to earn on the transaction (the *target return* or *discount rate*).

Current portfolio valuation

With the implementation of FAS 157 and IAS 39, GPs face increased pressure to value their underlying portfolio companies at what they believe they could sell the companies for in the current market. However, a secondary buyer is not concerned with the GP's estimated value of a given company today, as it is unlikely that the manager will be selling the company today. Rather, a buyer is interested in a portfolio company's future value at the time of realization, as a portion of the proceeds from that realization will be payable to the buyer.

What is the appropriate method for determining portfolio companies' exit value? That depends on the type of investment. To determine the value of a privately held buyout company at the time of sale or of any company generating significant revenue or earnings before interest, taxes, depreciation, and amortization (EBITDA), the buyer will probably calculate the expected enterprise value of the company at exit. If the company is generating significant revenue or EBITDA, this should be relatively straightforward. Exhibit 9.4 shows a simple example of pricing for a mini-LBO in a secondary transaction.

To perform this calculation, buyers need basic data on the company, such as EBITDA (or another metric for which enterprise value multiples are available) and the company's debt load, net of excess cash on the balance sheet. The fund's ownership in the company is also a necessary input. In addition, the buyer must estimate the remaining length of time the manager will hold the company; the EBITDA growth rate; the rate of debt paydown; and the future EBITDA multiple.

The number of years until exit can be estimated by looking at the GP's historical holding periods, tempered with a view of the current and future exit environment. The EBITDA growth rate can be based on several things, including the company's own historical growth rate and the analyst consensus industry growth rate, or possibly the company's own projections. Applying the expected growth before exit to the current EBITDA provides the estimate of EBITDA at the time of sale.

EXHIBIT 9.4

EXAMPLE OF A MINI-LBO: ENTERPRISE VALUE CALCULATION

Date of financials	December 31, 2008
EBITDA as of December 31, 2008	USD100,000,000
Growth rate per year	10%
Years to exit	3.00
Expected exit date	December 31, 2011
Calculated EBITDA at exit	*USD133,100,000*
EBITDA multiple	7.5×
Calculated enterprise value at exit	*USD998,250,000*
Net debt as of December 31, 2008	USD500,000,000
Net debt annualized paydown	10%
Calculated net debt at exit	*USD364,500,000*
Equity value at exit	USD633,750,000
% Ownership as of December 31, 2008	50.0%
Fund exit proceeds	*USD316,875,000*
Current cost	USD200,000,000
Current value	USD150,000,000
Implied current equity value to fund	USD125,000,000
Projected multiple to cost	**1.58×**
Projected multiple to value	**2.11×**

Possibly the most unpredictable variable is net debt at exit. Often a company's net debt does not change significantly over time. However, sometimes a company will be expected to have sufficient free cash flow for the net debt to be paid down, to some extent, before exit. Likewise, for companies that have the option of payment in kind, net debt may actually increase before exit. This is best dealt with case by case.

The liquidity crisis has created a bigger issue with debt. Given the number of highly levered companies that have large debt principal payments coming due over the next few years, buyers are also having to project whether that debt can be refinanced and, if so, when. Most of these companies will be unable to simply pay off the principal and may be forced to refinance at more punitive terms than those of the current debt, which will have a significant impact on equity value.

An estimate of the exit EBITDA multiple should begin with an analysis of comparable public companies. The EBITDA multiple at which these companies are currently trading can provide a starting point. This multiple can be adjusted, using the historical trading ranges for the companies, to indicate multiple expansion or contraction. A liquidity discount may need to be applied to this multiple if the company is not a likely IPO candidate.

These steps will provide an estimated exit value for this set of assumptions. However, buyers may perform multiple calculations, perhaps assuming lower or higher growth rates, shorter or longer holding periods, multiple contraction or expansion, and varying levels of net debt, and then assign probabilities to each case. For companies that are highly levered, the buyer may consider a scenario in which the company is unable to refinance or service its debt and is forced into bankruptcy. Buyers are typically conservative in their assumptions, assigning higher weights to the more negative scenarios and, quite possibly, arriving at a lower future exit value than if a seller were to perform the same exercise.

Venture valuation is much more difficult since it is quite a complex assignment to supply a value for a venture-backed company, even for a venture capitalist. Buyers will be much more reliant upon receiving information from the manager and may base their valuations largely on that manager's reputation. As venture investments have a notoriously wide range of potential outcomes, from a writeoff to a Google-sized exit, buyers may attempt to assign probabilities to different outcomes. History suggests that the largest probability weights should be assigned to outcomes that result in a loss.

Venture investments have also suffered as a result of the liquidity crisis and may need to raise more equity capital than previously expected. Buyers must now examine whether a fund has sufficient capital to participate in these future funding rounds for its investments. If it does not, the buyer must assume that the fund's equity stakes in its companies will be significantly diluted, because of the participants' liquidity preferences in future rounds.

The valuation of portfolio companies that are public is also relevant. GPs are required to mark these companies to market. However, a buyer is unlikely to pay market price for public stock that is potentially restricted and over which the buyer has no control. As a result, buyers are likely to apply a significant discount to the current market value of the holding.

Value of unfunded capital

One major component of value that the GP's NAV does not take into account is a fund investor's legal obligation to contribute unfunded capital to the fund in the future. Depending on the buyer's opinion of the fund manager's quality and the buyer's viewpoint on the current investment environment, this can be considered either as a liability, which will subtract from value, or as an asset, which will add to value.

The first step in valuing the unfunded capital is estimating how much of it will be used for investments and how much will be used for fund fees and expenses. The rate at which this investment capital will be called can be estimated by looking at historical data on how much capital funds have called at various points in their lifecycles. This information can be tempered with a current macroeconomic viewpoint to project future capital calls.

The next step is estimating what value these capital calls will generate. A buyer may assume that the estimated capital calls will generate a certain multiple or *internal rate of return* (IRR). This can be based on the GP's quality and historical returns. If the manager is of high quality, then the unfunded capital may add value to the fund, as the buyer will pay for the manager's investment selection skills. However, if the manager is of poor quality, the buyer may assume that it will lose a portion of every dollar it contributes, which will have an obvious drag on the valuation.

In funds whose investment periods have ended, the buyer's expected return on capital called will be much lower, given that the GP will be making only follow-on investments going forward. As these investments typically support portfolio companies only for working capital needs or to preserve a liquidity position, they often generate a much lower return than new investments.

Fund structure

Another factor that the GP's current NAV does not take into account is the fund structure. Estimating the exit value and timing for current portfolio holdings and future capital calls and distributions related to these capital calls provides the buyer with a gross cash flow stream. The buyer will then create a financial model of the fund that takes into account key fund terms, such as management fees, preferred returns, and carry.

The method the GP uses to account for carry may substantially depress secondary market pricing. In some cases the GP may have accrued carried interest but not yet have taken it. If the accrued carried interest has not been deducted from the LP's capital account, then the nominal price of the fund will be much lower (the absolute price will be divided by a larger NAV).

Discounting estimated net cash flows

After the buyer has taken the fund structure into account, the only remaining input required is the buyer's target rate of return or the *discount rate*. This will vary, depending on the type of fund in question and the current state of the market. All other things being equal, a mezzanine fund will have a lower required return than a buyout fund and a buyout fund will have a lower discount rate than a venture fund. Cogent Partners' data indicate that buyers' target rates of return dipped below 15% at the peak of the private equity boom in 2006–2007. Similarly, target returns may have been as high as 30% in late 2008 and early 2009 (Cogent Partners, 2006, 2008, 2009). Cogent Partners believe that the long-term average discount rate is likely to be between 15% and 20%, but this varies depending on the perceived risk in the interest and the market at large.

Buyers will sometimes underwrite to a multiple, rather than to a rate of return. This will typically happen with very mature funds, for which the buyer may use a target multiple to ensure that it receives a sufficient cash-on-cash return from the short duration of the investment.

Other buyer valuation considerations

Other factors to consider that might lead a buyer to pay either a premium or a discount to a fund's modeled value include supply of and demand for a given fund interest, blind pool risk, and a GP's reputation.

Many mega-buyout funds with 2007 or 2008 vintage years have seen investors looking to sell. Given the large amount of supply, buyers are unwilling to bid aggressively, as they can simply wait for the next interest to hit the market. In addition, a buyer may have purchased a large amount of the fund already and have reached a diversification limit. As with any other market, a large number of investors attempting to sell the same interest will cause a decrease in pricing.

The liquidity squeeze of 2008–2009 has also highlighted a difficulty associated with highly unfunded assets. Secondary buyers always prefer the highest possible visibility into a potential purchase. However, sellers have increasingly been attempting to shed funds that may be only 10% funded and have only a handful of investments. There are some secondary buyers that simply will not bid on these assets because of the blind pool risk and the similarity to investing on a primary basis. Those who do bid will typically assign a large risk premium to the unfunded position; in some cases taking on the liability of the unfunded position without paying anything for the current NAV or even asking the seller for payment to take on the liability. In practice, highly unfunded positions will be valued at a large additional discount by potential buyers.

Sometimes a fund may be given additional value over the modeled value. This most often occurs in venture funds, when the fund's manager has a top-tier reputation. Some investors will pay an "access premium" in order to invest with these managers, particularly if they have not invested with the manager before. By purchasing a fund interest on the secondary market, they hope to be invited to invest in the manager's future funds, and the value of the potential future commitments filters into the secondary price for the asset. Such opportunities are rarely on the market, unless a seller wants to exit a position only partially or is exiting the asset class in general.

9.5.2   How sellers view valuation

Sellers typically approach valuation from a very different viewpoint than buyers. Whereas buyers are concerned mainly with the price they should pay to achieve their target returns, sellers are concerned much more with the buyer's valuation relative to the fund's NAV as provided by the manager. This is particularly the case when a buyer is offering to purchase a fund at a discount to the fund's most recently reported NAV, thereby creating a loss on the seller's books. No seller ever looks favorably on a loss, but alternative asset investors might be particularly unwilling to accept losses, because of compensation issues (personal compensation tied to performance) or political concerns (investors that have to report publicly).

Few sellers are equipped to perform a typical buyer-style valuation. Sellers will typically use more aggressive assumptions than buyers. This is partly due to comfort with the assets and partly due to psychology. The seller has probably been in constant contact with the fund manager for the life of the fund and may be more familiar than a buyer with a given portfolio company's prospects, thereby allowing more confidence in an aggressive assumption. The seller may also have made the initial recommendation to make the fund investment and may be anchored to a positive outlook for the investment.

Another major difference in a seller valuation can be the discount rate used. Sellers, like buyers, typically have a target rate of return for a given asset, but a seller's targets are often lower than a buyer's targets, which will cause the seller's valuation to be higher. Even larger discrepancies can be seen when an organization uses its cost of capital, which should always be lower than the target rate of return, or when pension funds use target rates of return that must be quite low for actuarial reasons. However, the reasons for selling would typically increase the required rate of return for the seller. If a sale is planned for liquidity reasons, the target rate of return for the asset is no longer particularly relevant, and the discount rate should be increased in proportion to the size of the liquidity problem. If the seller wants to redeploy the capital from the sale into another asset with a higher expected return, the discount rate should also be increased for the asset being sold, in line with the desired return in redeployment. Seller discount rates can normally be moved in line with buyer targets when the circumstances of the sale are fully taken into account.

Exhibit 9.5 shows bid spreads across multiple buyers building for the same fund interest over time. As can be seen from the chart, during the period of economic

EXHIBIT 9.5

RELATIVE SECONDARY MARKET BID SPREADS OVER TIME

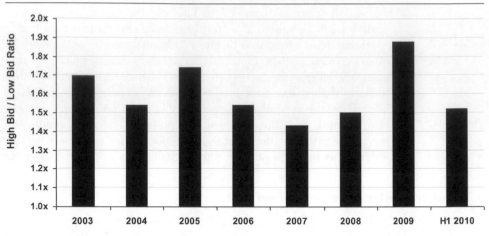

Source: Cogent Partners.

Note: Includes only funds for which multiple bids were received.

uncertainty in 2009 the spreads reached all time highs. The narrowing of the spreads in the first half of 2010 shows a lower degree of disparity in buyers' expectations of macroeconomic trends and specific fund performance.

9.6 CONCLUSION

There has been explosive growth in the secondary market over the past decade, fueled by LPs' needs for liquidity, increased interest from non-traditional investors such as pension and family funds, changes in the regulatory framework, and other structural changes. The recent financial crisis has spurred further growth of secondaries, with investors facing pressure to exit their primary investments early because of liquidity needs and, thus, increasing the supply of funds available for sale in the secondary market. Furthermore, more non-traditional investors have entered the secondary market on the buy-side.

Although publicly traded asset classes have now returned to relative normality, and there is renewed activity in the primary private equity market, the secondary private equity market is expected to continue to grow, as investors continue to rebalance their portfolios and use secondaries to mitigate the effects of the *J*-curve. The growth of the market has also given rise to specialist advisory firms that assist with structuring and managing secondary transactions. Most potential secondary market buyers now consider relying on the services of such intermediaries. Finally, pricing in the secondary market is of great importance to both buyers and sellers, who typically have different motives and considerations when estimating prices for funds. Bidding processes through managed auctions have thus gained prominence, as they optimize the outcome for both buyers and sellers.

9.7 REFERENCES

COGENT PARTNERS (2005) *Secondary Pricing Analysis, FY2005: A Look at Pricing Data and Implications for Achieving Optimal Pricing*, by C. McGrady, Cogent Partners, Dallas, TX, No. 15.

COGENT PARTNERS (2006) *Secondary Pricing Analysis, Mid-Year 2006: Cogent Secondary Pricing Level Eclipses NAV for the First Time*, by C. McGrady, Cogent Partners, Dallas, TX, No. 16.

COGENT PARTNERS (2008) *Mid-Year 2008 Secondary Market Pricing and Outlook: Secondary Pricing Declines with Public Market Drop*, by C. McGrady and B. Heffern, Cogent Partners, Dallas, TX, No. 20.

COGENT PARTNERS (2009) *Secondary Pricing Analysis Interim Update: Cogent Closes Over \$2.5B in Transactions—Less than 20% Purchased by Secondary Funds*, by C. McGrady and B. Heffern, Cogent Partners, Dallas, TX, Summer.

COGENT PARTNERS (2010) *Cogent Partners' Analysis Reveals Secondary Market Pricing of 72.0% of NAV for H2 2009, with Portfolio Bids Returning*, Cogent Partners, Dallas, TX, February.

GORDON, B.A., AND TOOMEY JR., J.M. (2004) "The secondary market: Sellers challenge buyers to be more creative," *The Private Equity Analyst Guide to the Secondary Market*, 2004 edition.

JOHNSON, S. (2009) "Investors facing private equity trap," *Financial Times*, May 10.

KONKEL, T. (2004) "Secondary prices: A rising tide," *The Private Equity Analyst Guide to the Secondary Market*, 2004 edition.

MCGRADY, C. (2007) "2006 secondary pricing analysis and outlook," *Guide to the Secondary Market*, Dow Jones, 2007 edition.

MEYER, T., AND MATHONET, P-Y. (2005) *Beyond the J Curve: Managing a Portfolio of Venture Capital and Private Equity Funds*, Wiley Finance, John Wiley & Sons Ltd.

PEI (2009) *Active Portfolio Management in Private Equity*, by P. Borel, A. Janis, and J. Gull, Private Equity International, available at *www.peimedia.com/secondaries*

PENN, L. AND WELSCH-LEHMANN, A.O. (2004) *The Private Equity Analyst Guide to the Secondary Market*, 2004 edition.

PERMAL CAPITAL (2009) *Private Equity Observations: Golden Age of Secondaries?*, Permal Capital Management, Boston, MA, August.

PREQIN (2010a) *The 2010 Preqin Private Equity Secondaries Review*, Preqin, London.

PREQIN (2010b) *Preqin Secondary Market Monitor Online*, Preqin, London.

SOULIGNAC, C. (2004) *The Private Equity Analyst Guide to the Secondary Market*, 2004 edition.

SOULIGNAC, C. (2007) "Measuring performance as the secondary market evolves," *Guide to the Secondary Market*, Dow Jones, 2007 edition.

VCFA (2002) *Secondary Sales of Private Equity Interests: The Advent of Secondary Private Equity Fund Interest Transactions*, Venture Capital Fund of America, VC Experts, February 2.

PART 2

Deal-level analysis

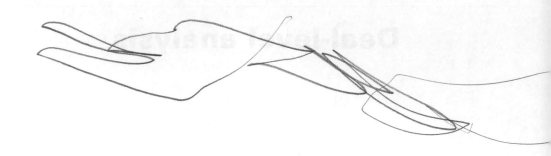

10

Valuation of private equity companies

10.1 INTRODUCTION

Valuation is a process in which the private equity professional estimates the value of a company's assets based on a series of relevant variables that are perceived to affect the long-term performance and success of the company. It is important that investors understand the fundamental factors that drive the underlying value of the companies in which they choose to invest. While valuations are critical for successful private equity investors we need to be aware of several aspects:

- Valuations may be quantitative but they are usually not objective or precise
- Valuations age quickly, they can change significantly as new information becomes available
- Valuations can take significant time and effort but are very informative. They help the valuer better understand the business.

The principles of valuing private companies are similar to those of valuing public companies; however, there are estimation problems that are unique to private companies. For instance, the valuer needs to deal with limited information available in terms of history and depth because private firms do not report their performance publicly and do not need to meet accounting and reporting standards that apply to public entities in many countries. Another significant hurdle when valuing private firms is the difficulty of estimating risk parameters for discount rates. These require stock prices for equity which are not available for private firms. Further, private companies—in particular, startups and emerging companies—face acute uncertainties regarding their future operations making forecasting difficult. In fact, often they have negative cash flows and earnings. Since their profitability is expected to occur at some point in the future, the assessment of their current value can be a challenging task. Private companies also tend to have concentrated ownership, thus reported earnings might reflect discretionary expenses or are affected by tax motivations.

This chapter was co-authored with Anthony Cecil (partner at KPMG LLP and member of the International Private Equity and Venture Capital Valuation Guidelines Board, IPEV). Anthony has assisted in the writing of this book in a personal capacity and his views should not be taken to be those of KPMG or IPEV.

Managers of private equity funds assess the values of private companies at several points in time when they invest in a financing round of the company (venture funds), acquire a company (buyout funds), list the company on an exchange, sell or liquidate the company, or for reporting purposes. Managers of private equity funds are usually required to carry out periodic valuations of their portfolio investments as part of the reporting process to their investors. The International Private Equity and Venture Capital Valuation Guidelines Board (IPEV Guidelines Board) has developed a set of guidelines for this purpose.

10.2 VALUATION GUIDELINES

Private equity fund investments are usually reported to the investors at fair value.[1] Fair value is relatively easy to determine when an active market exists in that asset and recent transaction prices or quotes are publicly available. In private equity, the majority of the investments are unquoted and no clear market is available. As a result, private equity funds are required to estimate what a third party might pay for the asset in their portfolio.

In order to assist private equity valuers, the International Private Equity and Venture Capital Valuations Board issued a set of valuation guidelines (the IPEV Guidelines) in 2009.[2] These guidelines are intended to promote best practice and, thereby, enhance investor confidence in the valuation reports. This section, which should be read in conjunction with the guidelines, explains some of the rationale behind the guidelines and notes some common pitfalls, but does not attempt to reproduce or replace the guidelines.

The crucially important ethos of the IPEV guidelines is that "valuation is an art, not a science". It is therefore impossible to set out prescribed rules that a valuer must follow to estimate what price a third party might consider appropriate for acquiring a particular asset. Valuers have to be allowed and, indeed, encouraged to use their professional judgment in estimating that value.

The IPEV Guidelines provide a framework within which the valuer can exercise that judgment and, importantly, explain the rationale behind his or her valuation judgments to investors. They are based on the concept of "substance over form". It is important that the valuation decisions are based on the expectations of the outcome and not necessarily on the strict legal form.

It is also important to recognize what the IPEV Guidelines are not. They are intended to follow GAAP (IFRS, U.S. and U.K.). If we prepare a valuation in accordance with the IPEV Guidelines, then compliance with these GAAPs is achieved. It is impossible to state that the valuation will always be in compliance with GAAP, as much of the accounting documentation is drafted as detailed rules and, by definition, guidelines are less rigid than rules. The IPEV Guidelines are definitely *not* an accounting standard.

They also focus on estimation of the fair value. They do not include guidance on where the private equity fund might report that value to the investors, nor do they include suggested controls and procedures appropriate to that estimation process.

1. Fair value is defined by the International Accounting Standards as "The price that would be received to sell an asset or paid to transfer a liability in an orderly transaction between market participants at the measurement date."

2. These guidelines are endorsed by some 40 private equity and venture capital associations around the world. They can be obtained from the Board's website: *http://www.privateequityvaluation.com*

10.2.1 Valuation methodologies

In private equity, the underlying portfolio investments are usually held by a relatively small number of shareholders. The value of the underlying business is commonly realized by a transaction which involves the business as a whole. It is less common for individual small stakes in a business to be realized. Accordingly, the IPEV Guidelines start with the value of the firm as a whole to assess the value of a stake in that business.

To assess the value of a stake in a business, the steps set out in the IPEV Guidelines may be crudely summarized as:

- Determine the value of the business as a whole (enterprise value)
- Adjust for any known relevant factors
- Deduct any amounts that rank higher
- Allocate the balance amongst the relevant instruments and investors.

In determining the enterprise value, valuers will attempt to put themselves in the position of an acquirer, considering all relevant information available. Due to the number of implicit or inherent judgments it must be recognized that proceeds on realization may differ significantly from the estimated fair value and it is unlikely that the fair value is exactly "right".

The initial step is to select an appropriate valuation methodology. The methodology selected should be applied consistently over time. The IPEV Guidelines consider six different valuation methodologies as those most commonly used in the private equity market:

1. Price of recent investment.
2. Multiples.
3. Net assets.
4. Discounted cash flows or earnings (of the underlying business).
5. Discounted cash flows (from the investment).
6. Industry valuation benchmarks.

Valuers collate and assess all relevant information available and references their judgment decisions against market data when possible. The philosophy is simply that "if I cannot observe a market price for my or an identical asset, how close an asset's price can I observe and can I demonstrate that adjustments from that price are supported?" This push towards market data will inherently steer the valuer towards market measures and away from the more theoretical processes.

What might the appropriate methodology be over the holding period of an investment? It would be appropriate to value the investment at the price of the recent investment when it is made. This might be uplifted on the basis of milestones passed for the next 18 months, until profits are forecast for the next accounting period, when the valuer might shift to a multiple basis. Finally an agreement is entered into to realize the asset in 6 months and a DCF could be used. This pattern of changes is expected and justifiable.

It is important that, post realization, the valuer compares the proceeds of realization with their valuation or model, identifying and understanding any differences arising and potential impact of those differences on other valuation models.

Price of recent investment

On the day that a transaction takes place, the fair value of the investment is usually the price paid by the market participant. The price of recent investment methodology is simply using the evidence of the actual cost paid by the investor as the best indicator of fair value. Valuers may equally use the evidence of the price paid subsequently by another investor.

Price of recent investment is particularly strong evidence of fair value, since the evidence is entirely market based, although valuers should consider whether there are any pertinent reasons why the price might not be reflective of fair value. Assuming that there are no such reasons, this gives a relatively easy answer on that day.

The difficult question is how long thereafter does that cost remain the best indicator of fair value? The guidelines deliberately do not opine on the appropriate period length. When the guidelines suggested that many people regarded a year as reasonable, this was mistranslated as acceptable in all circumstances. Valuers need to satisfy themselves that nothing has changed in the period from investment to the valuation date that might indicate that fair value is no longer equivalent to the cost. It is important that the factors considered are both internal to the entity and external in the wider market.

Price of recent investment is commonly used on all investments on the day of acquisition and for startup investments or any development entity prior to the generation of revenues, profits, or positive cash flows. For many venture companies or in development, the period between initial investment and profitable trading may be several years. During this period, the only market data available might be subsequent investments made, so any assessment of fair value must be at least based on the price of those investments.

The guidelines expand the concept of price of recent investment to cover this extensive period. The guidelines encourage valuers to consider all aspects of the business, wider than merely financial targets and data. Anything which the management of the company might use as a key performance indicator can be a useful milestone or indicator of progress, change, and potential value in the underlying business. However, any fair value estimate based on milestones after an initial investment is clearly highly subjective. Importantly, this assessment should not always be looking for impairments and downward valuation movements. Achieving milestones against a plan may indicate that the current fair value of the investment exceeds the cost incurred, even though that investment has yet to deliver positive financial returns.

Multiples

This is probably the most common form of market-based valuation methodology. In concept it merely ascertains what prices are achieved for a similar asset and use these data to support the valuer's own opinion of fair value. This methodology involves the application of a multiple of value (based on earnings or other financial measures of performance) to the company being valued.

Purists often criticize multiple-based methodologies as merely being an abbreviation of a discounted cash flow (DCF) calculation. In essence, that is true, they are an abbreviation, but, crucially, they are the market's abbreviation rather than a theoretical exercise.

The guidelines suggest that the valuer should "apply a multiple that is appropriate and reasonable to the maintainable earnings of the company." The words that require significant judgment are "appropriate", "reasonable", and "maintainable".

Net assets

Many businesses will be traded at a value basis on their reported net assets, rather than earnings streams. This methodology is used where the inherent value of the assets may exceed their income-generating abilities. Property and resource companies are usually valued on the basis of the net asset value of their properties and resources. This methodology may also be used as a floor in valuing a poorly performing business. While tangible assets might not be generating profits they have an inherent value.

Discounted cash flows (DCFs) from the underlying business

This is a classic valuation methodology which is both extremely powerful, yet potentially very weak. In a DCF, the valuer projects into the future the expected cash flows from the business and discounts those flows back to the present day at a discount rate reflective of the cost of capital.

The discount rate applied should reflect the cost of capital and the risk associated with the cash flows. Due to the nature of private equity and the expected returns and risks, it is common to see DCF calculations with discount rates from as low as 15% to those as high as 40%. The calculation is quite sensitive to minor changes in the discount rate applied.

Discounted cash flows (DCFs) from the investment

This is similar in concept to the methodology above, but instead of considering all the cash flows from the business, it merely considers the cash flows that relate to the investment instrument itself. This methodology is particularly useful when the cash flows from the investment may be predicted with a high level of certainty, such as a standalone mezzanine loan investment or an investment whose terms have been agreed for a future sale price (e.g., the terms of the imminent flotation of the business have been agreed).

Industry benchmarks

Some companies can be valued based on industry-specific benchmarks such as price per square foot (property), price per bed (residential care homes, hospitals), price per room (hotels), price per customer (asset management), price per subscriber (telecommunications), etc. Valuation based on these benchmarks implicitly assumes that what drives value is market share and that the profitability within the industry does not vary too much.

Clearly, some industry benchmarks are more valid than others but, whatever their validity, it would be unusual to use this methodology in isolation to estimate fair value. Commonly, they are used to provide a check against another methodology to ensure that the fair value estimated is within the range expected in the market.

10.3 IMPLEMENTATION OF THE MAIN VALUATION METHODS: MULTIPLES AND DCF

10.3.1 Valuation steps

In general, the valuation of a private company involves five basic steps:

Step 1. Understand the purpose of the valuation. Many private equity valuations are performed for a specific purpose. When valuing private firms, the motive for the valuation matters and can significantly affect the value obtained. In particular, the value of a private firm will be different if it is being valued for sale to a private trade buyer, for sale to a publicly traded firm, or for an initial public offering. If a private trade buyer is involved then a discount might be appropriate to reflect the additional liquidity risk in holding the share. Liquidity discounts are not necessary for publicly traded buyers or for exchange listings.

Another reason the valuation of the company might be different is the value of control. In valuations whose purpose is to value companies that are being acquired the valuer should incorporate the effect of control. Buyers of poorly managed firms that acquire control can remove the incumbent management and change existing practices and strategies, thus making these firms potentially more valuable. Therefore, the value of the same private company will be higher if a buyer acquires control. If the buyers acquire only a minority stake then the buyers will pay less since they cannot influence the decision process and small stakes require a marketability discount. Buyout transactions usually reflect the value of control when valuing the targets. It is no surprise that buyout funds tend to acquire underperforming companies relative to their industry or the overall market and pay a premium for them relative to their existing market value.

Differences in tax rates across potential buyers of a private firm can also affect the valuation output. The tax rate of a buyer can vary from the corporate tax rate (if the potential buyer is a corporation) to the highest marginal tax rate for individuals (if the potential buyer is a wealthy individual). In a methodology such as discounted cash flows the tax rates affect both the cash flows (through the after-tax operating income) and the cost of capital (through the tax shields provided by leverage). Therefore, the value of a private firm can vary across different buyers.

Step 2. Understand the industry and the company's competitive position. Various valuation frameworks exist for companies in different industries. A deep understanding of the industry will help isolate important economic drivers that affect the value of the company and highlight aspects of the business that present great challenges and opportunities and, thus, justify further scenario analysis.

Porter's (1985) five-forces model is a good place to start in order to understand the attractiveness of a given industry. These forces affect the company's long-term profitability. Industries with low rivalry, high barriers of entry, that create/sell products with few potential substitutes and where both suppliers and buyers have limited power are likely to have good profitability prospects. The five-forces analysis can help with a more informed estimation of the industry's growth rate, an important parameter in some valuation methodologies. Besides industry-wide prospects, the competitive position of the company within an industry as well as its long-term strategy in overcoming any competitive pressures will help the valuer assess whether the company's value should be higher or lower relative to its peers. The competitive position of a company can be highlighted by several measures such as market share, the company's ability to confine costs (i.e., the cost advantage relative to its peers), or to produce and sell unique products (i.e., the differentiation advantage relative to its peers). This analysis provides an indication about the expected short-term and medium-term growth rate of the company relative to the industry average.

Important firm-specific factors affect the company's ability to meet its long-term goals and succeed within its industry segment. Valuers should take into account such factors using as much historical information about the company or industry as possible especially if company level information is limited because it is young. Time trends can reveal management's ability to run the company and adapt to different challenges. They can also reveal the long-term potential of the industry. Information about the industry and the competitive position of the company might be difficult to come by in situations when the industry is relatively young. Also, the valuation of private equity companies makes the information-gathering process even more challenging given that these companies do not have to file public reports about their financial position. Important sources are industry organizations, reports of publicly traded companies, regulatory agencies, or dedicated providers of market information.

Step 3. Select the appropriate valuation method. There are no rules as to which methodology should be used in a particular setting, but it is important that the methodology selected is appropriate for the private company analyzed. The selection will include a consideration of the stage of development of the underlying business, the nature of the transaction (if the valuation's purpose is to help with an investment decision), the industry in which it operates, and the availability of data.

   We have discussed potential methodologies that could be used above. These methodologies measure value either in absolute (discounted cash flows) or relative (price of recent investment, multiples, industry benchmarks) terms.

Step 4. Perform scenario analyses to investigate the sensitivity of the results to critical valuation assumptions. Discounted-cash-flow models estimate the intrinsic value of a private company but have many challenges in applications. Depending on the assumptions made a range of values can be generated. Similarly, multiples or industry benchmark methods are characterized by a wide range of implementation choices—one can choose different multiples or different peer groups.

   As a result, sensitivity analysis is essential. The valuer should try to value the company under different assumptions and implementations and assess how they affect the outcome. Some sensitivity analyses are common such as different assumptions regarding growth rates and risk premiums for DCF models. Other sensitivity analyses depend on the context. If the industry is competitive then the valuer should assess the sensitivity of forecasted cash flows to improvements or declines in market share.

Step 5. Analyze the valuation outputs based on the purpose of the valuation. Depending on the purpose of the valuation, the valuer uses the outputs to provide an investment recommendation or to just report to private equity investors. It is important that the valuation exercise is properly described in the valuation report received by users. This report should clearly identify and provide the key assumptions and inputs used, describe relevant aspects of the macroeconomic environment and industry context, and provide some background information about the company. The report should also contain a discussion about the risk factors that might negatively affect the value of the company.

10.3.2 The multiples (comparables) method

The multiples method is a relative valuation methodology whose objective is to value the private equity company based upon how similar companies trade in public markets. The method relies on three basic steps. In the first step, the valuer attempts to find publicly traded firms that are similar to the private company being valued. This is difficult in many situations since no two firms are identical. Even firms in the same business and with similar size can differ on risk characteristics and growth potential. In the second step, the valuer standardizes the market values of the similar publicly traded companies, usually by converting them into multiples of earnings, book values, or sales.

In the third and final step, the valuer obtains the value of the private company by multiplying its earnings, book value, or sales by the appropriate multiple computed in the second step.

The multiples method is the most used method. Several factors contribute to its popularity:

- It requires far fewer assumptions and it is quicker than the DCF methodology
- It is easy to understand and present to investors
- It reflects the market's view on the value of the company.

While multiples are relatively easy to use and intuitive, implementation issues are very important. The implementation of the multiples method involves several decisions.

How to pick the benchmark publicly traded companies?

Key to selecting an appropriate and reasonable multiple is the choice of benchmark companies. The ideal comparable firm is one that has cash flows, growth potential, and risk characteristics similar to the firm being valued. Therefore, when picking benchmark companies, the conventional practice is to look at firms within the same industry or business. Clearly, these should be as close as possible in nature to the entity being valued, but it is impossible to find completely identical companies. As a result, differences will remain between the firm and comparable firms.

Once a suitable set of comparators is identified, these differences might impact a third party's pricing of the investment; therefore, they need to be identified and quantified. Figuring out how to adjust for differences relative to peer firms is a significant part of relative valuation. This requires a significant exercise of judgment as points of difference are potentially wide-ranging. In addition, identification and quantification cannot be subject to prescribed processes and rigid formulas.

Commonly, a valuer will compare business models by considering many commercial aspects and risks including, for example, geographical spread of the business, brand, reputation, product range, rate of growth, quality of management, currency exposures—the list is potentially unlimited. Comparable firms that are significantly different across dimensions that are deemed to be very important should be eliminated from the set of comparators.

Once a multiple is calculated for each of the remaining comparable firms, typically an average or median is computed. The idea is that remaining differences between the individual firms and the firm valued in terms of growth, risk, or cash flows are averaged out, thus minimizing the measurement error. An alternative is to modify individual peer firm multiples based on the differences observed and, then, use these individual ratios or an aggregate of them to value the firm.

One can also use sector multiples which are often seen as a simple way of averaging the multiple across the entire sector. Justifying points of difference between the entity being valued and the sector as a whole is difficult, though. In addition, these multiples are calculated by adding the market value of the sector and dividing that by the sum of the relevant fundamental variable (e.g., earnings, revenues) across the sector. If the sector contains a large firm with unusually good performance, the sector multiple can be mathematically calculated in excess of most of the underlying multiples, creating a large bias in the valuation.

In developed markets it is relatively easy to find a number of suitable companies to use as comparators. However, in an emerging market, there may be no obvious local domestic comparators. In this situation, valuers need to broaden their search to other geographies. A combination of foreign company multiples and local and foreign stock exchanges over time may be a good start to points-of-difference quantification.

Which multiple to use?

A valuer could potentially measure the value of a private company based on a large set of multiples which can be classified in two types: (1) equity price multiples (computed as ratios of equity values to some measure of fundamental value) and (2) enterprise value multiples (computed by dividing the total value of the company including its debt by measures of fundamental value for the entire company). Depending on the fundamental value used in the denominator we can classify multiples in additional categories:

- *Earnings multiples: price to earnings (P/E) and firm value to EBITDA*. Price-to-earnings multiples are regularly published for quoted companies and, thus, have the advantage of being readily sourced. However, they require adjustments to reflect substantially different levels of gearing commonly seen in portfolio companies acquired via buyouts. This multiple can be estimated using current earnings per share (current P/E), earnings over the last four quarters (trailing P/E), or expected earnings per share in the next year (forward P/E). Firm-value-to-EBITDA multiples are used by many private equity practitioners, as EBITDA is seen as a proxy for cash generation within the business. EBITDA multiples usually need to be calculated from either public information or from recent acquisitions in the market. These multiples are appropriate for valuing private companies with different financial leverage, since EBITDA is a pre-interest earnings number.

- *Revenue multiple*. This multiple is computed as firm total value divided by sales. This is an extension of the earnings multiples, based on the assumption that the companies in a particular industry are all capable of generating similar margins. The advantage of using revenue multiples is that it becomes far easier to compare firms in different sectors with different accounting rules. Sales are less affected by distortions introduced by accounting rules than earnings or accounting book values. This multiple is often used when the private company has negative or zero earnings. It is also appropriate when the private company's business is cyclical and the company is mature. The main drawback is the inability to capture differences in cost structures and profitability.

- *Book value multiples: price-to-book value of equity and firm value to total assets*. The first book multiple is computed as the market price of the company's equity divided by the book value of equity (or net worth). This ratio can vary widely across industries, depending on the growth potential. When valuing a private company's entire value, the valuer should use the second ratio which is estimated as the value of the benchmark publicly traded firm and the book value of all its assets (rather than just the equity). An alternative to the book value of all assets is to use the replacement cost of all assets (this ratio is called Tobin's Q). These multiples are appropriate for private firms that have relatively liquid assets (e.g., property, finance, and insurance) since these assets' book values are likely to be close to market values. They are also used when the private firm is not expected to be a going concern (i.e., it is expected to be liquidated in the future).

When computing multiples it is important that the valuer ensures consistency between the numerator and the denominator. If the numerator is the equity value then the denominator should be an equity measure of performance such as net income or book value of equity. If the numerator is a firm value measure (i.e., the enterprise value, which is the sum of the values of debt and equity, net of cash) then the denominator should also reflect a firm measure (e.g., operating income, EBITDA or book value of all assets).

Similarly, if the multiples are computed for several peer publicly traded firms, the valuer should make sure that the multiples are defined uniformly across different companies. Consider, for instance, the firm value to EBITDA, which is commonly used in private equity investing. The market value of equity used to compute the firm value in the numerator should be based on the stock price at the same point in time for all benchmark firms. Further, the market value of the debt should not only be computed at the same point in time but the measurement should also be consistent (since debt is not traded or traded infrequently valuers typically use the book value of debt—they need to make sure that the debt is accounted similarly for all companies). Finally, EBITDA in the denominator can be from the most recent financial year (current EBITDA), from the last four quarters (trailing EBITDA), or expected earnings in the next financial year (forward EBITDA). The valuer should make sure that the choice of EBITDA number is consistent across all companies chosen as a benchmark.

How to establish the benchmark multiple?

The valuer might compute several types of multiples for a group of peer firms in an effort to answer the question: Which one to pick and how to aggregate the multiples of the peer group? Each multiple computation provides some relevant information for valuing the private company, thus using a single valuation indicator is hard to defend.

In most cases, valuers compute an average multiple by type. If there are outlying observations it is more appropriate to focus on the median peer group multiple or to even compute a harmonic mean (this mean gives more weight to low multiples and less weight to high multiples thus mitigating the impact of large outliers).

What additional adjustments are necessary?

The valuer of a private company should include a discount or premium against a comparator to reflect any differences between the company and the comparator. The most obvious adjustment is the discount that reflects the lower marketability and liquidity of the private company. With publicly traded firms, liquidation risks are low; the transactions costs for publicly listed stocks are usually a small percent of the value. With equity in a private business, liquidation costs as a percent of firm value can be substantial. Consequently, the value of equity in a private business obtained by means of a multiplier needs to be discounted for illiquidity. We discuss the illiquidity adjustment as well as other adjustments in Section 10.3.4.

The valuer should also take into account differences between the business valued and the benchmarks used. There may be additional adjustments required for matters that fall outside the normal business model. This would include any matter that a prospective purchaser might consider relevant. Typically, adjustments arise from:

- Surplus assets to the business
- Contingencies arising from lawsuits

- Impending regulation which might impact the business model
- Financing considerations.

In recent years, the most likely adjustments have arisen from financing considerations where the valuer applies a deduction to the enterprise value to reflect the possibility that banking covenants will be breached during the next year and require renegotiation.

10.3.3 Valuation based on discounted cash flows (DCFs)

Discounted-cash-flow (DCF) valuation (also called net present value) views the intrinsic value of a private firm as the present value of its expected cash flows that will be generated in the future. Typically, the method is implemented by first estimating the value of the firm and then subtracting the face value of non-common stock capital (e.g., debt, stock options, preferred shares, etc.) to arrive at the value of common equity. The values of operating and non-operating assets are estimated separately and, then, are combined to find the firm value.

The methodology can be summarized in a few steps. We discuss private equity–specific issues in the implementation in each of these steps. The first three steps compute the value of the operating assets of the company.

Step 1. Calculate firm cash flows:

$$CF = EBIT * (1 - t) + DEPR - CAPEX - \Delta NWC$$

where

$$
\begin{aligned}
CF &= \text{firm cash flows (which belong to both equity and debtholders)} \\
EBIT &= \text{earnings before interest and taxes} \\
t &= \text{corporate tax rate} \\
DEPR &= \text{depreciation} \\
CAPEX &= \text{capital expenditure} \\
\Delta NWC &= \text{change in net working capital, can be negative.}
\end{aligned}
$$

Capital expenditures are this year's net of depreciation property plant and equipment (PPE) minus last year's net PPE. Net working capital consists of the following balance sheet items: operating cash plus trade receivables plus other receivables plus inventories plus prepaid expenses minus accounts payable minus other current liabilities. Change in working capital is hence this year's working capital minus last year's working capital.

The cash flow formula above computes cash generated by the operations of the firm, after paying taxes on operations only, and after capital expenditures and expenditures for additional working capital. These cash flows represent cash that is available for distribution to the holders of debt and equity in the firm, and/or for investment in additional excess marketable securities.

The valuer should not only develop forecasts for these cash flows for an initial period of 5 to 10 years but also for the cash flows in perpetuity. These forecasts should be constructed based on discussions with the management keeping in mind potential managerial upward biases.

There are few adjustments that need to be made to the cash flow formula above in the case of private firms:

- *EBIT might be negative.* In this case the valuer needs to normalize earnings (i.e., the assumption being that negative earnings are temporary). Earnings are normalized usually based on revenue projections for which margins are estimated.

Valuers should estimate a sustainable margin and the length of the adjustment period over which earnings turn from negative into positive.

• *Salary of the owner/entrepreneur.* Many private firms do not pay salaries to owner-managers or, even if they do, the salary might not reflect the market value of the services provided to the firm. This is because in many countries the tax system does not distinguish between income earned as a salary or income from dividends for private firms making owners indifferent between them. The valuer should treat salaries as operating expenses, otherwise EBIT is overstated. Appropriate salaries should be estimated based upon the role the owners play in the firm and the cost of hiring replacements for them.

• *Intermingling of personal and business expenses.* This often occurs at small private businesses because sometimes there is no separation between ownership and control. This can cause EBIT to be measured with error. The intermingling of business and personal expenses is a particular problem for small private businesses, since owners that have full control of the business may maintain offices at their home, or make business expenses for personal activities or services they receive. The valuer should remove all these personal expenses from EBIT.

• *CAPEX and ΔNWC are difficult to forecast* if the private firm is in a high- growth stage. CAPEX and ΔNWC can be measured as percentages of revenues. The valuer can assume that they grow at the same rate as revenues and that their percentage in revenues will approach the industry average.

• *Effect of taxes.* Public firms are typically valued using the marginal corporate tax rate. However, private firms may face different marginal tax rates since individual tax status and tax rates vary much more widely than corporate tax rates. Also, differences in tax rates across potential buyers of a private firm can be significant. The tax rate affects not only computation of the firm cash flows but also the cost of debt capital.

• *Other accounting adjustments.* Private firms might use inconsistent accounting rules given that they are not expected to have high-quality audited financial statements that follow the same accounting standards as public firms. The valuer should make adjustments such that the EBIT measurement is consistent with generally accepted accounting practices (e.g., recognize provisions based on beliefs of future losses).

Step 2. Calculate the terminal value:

$$TV_T = [CF_T * (1 + g)]/(r - g)$$

where

TV_T = terminal value at time T
CF_T = cash flow at the end of the forecasting horizon
g = growth rate in perpetuity
r = discount rate (weighted average cost of capital) calculated as: $r = (D/V) * r_d * (1 - t) + (E/V) * r_e$; r_d is the cost of debt; r_e is the cost of equity; D is the market value of debt; E is the market value of equity; and $V = D + E$ is the total firm value.

The terminal value captures the business value at the end of the initial forecasting period for the cash flows. It is computed based on the assumption that cash flows in the terminal year (the last year of the forecasting horizon) will continue to grow at a constant rate in perpetuity. Typically, the cash flow and discount rates are in nominal terms and are not adjusted for inflation. Estimation of both the growth and the discount rates is particularly difficult for private firms. We discuss these in detail below.

Growth rate. With private firms, the valuer will not have available sell-side analyst estimates of growth. Also, the historical growth numbers have to be used with caution especially if the private firm is at an early stage in its life. The valuer can estimate the perpetual expected growth rate of cash flows as the product of the re-investment rate $(CAPEX + R\&D - DEPR + \Delta NWC)/EBIT(1 - t)$, and the return on capital, $EBIT(1 - t)$/book value of capital at the beginning of the year. In each future year, this estimated growth rate will be a combination of inflation and real growth.

It is important to note that, with private firms, the going concern assumption has to be made with far more caution. Private firms are younger and untested. The implication is that the terminal value for a private firm will be lower than the terminal value for a publicly traded firm. If there is reason to believe that the private firm will cease to exist at some point in time in the future then the valuer should use a liquidation value for the assets as the terminal value. These liquidation values are usually lower than the value of continuing operations.

Discount rate. The discount rate is the weighted average cost of capital, which is based on three important variables: the cost of equity, the cost of debt, and the debt/equity ratio. It should reflect the risk of achieving the cash flows projected given the purpose of the valuation exercise. For instance, the discount rate will be lower if the company is valued for an initial public offering than for an acquisition or just for reporting (i.e., continuous operation as a private company). Initial public offerings are addressed to a larger group of diversified investors with lower risk premiums. If the company remains private then its access to debt financing is more restricted than the access of a similar public company; thus, its cost of debt will be higher. In general, the information disclosed about a private company is limited introducing greater uncertainty about the quality of the cash flow projections which leads to a higher discount rate than for a public company.

- *Cost of equity.* The cost of equity for publicly traded firms is typically estimated based on the CAPM model (risk-free rate plus beta times the market risk) using historical stock prices. In the case of private equity firms, there is no historical price information and, in addition, the owners of private firms might not be diversified (diversification is a core assumption of CAPM). In a private equity setting there are few approaches to estimate beta (all have their weaknesses due to data issues or quality of the benchmarks used): (i) accounting betas (coefficient of changes in market earnings in a regression of changes in firms earnings on market earnings), (ii) fundamental betas (betas of similar publicly traded firms are related to observable variables such as earnings growth, debt ratios, and variance in earnings. Parameters of this model are then used to estimate the beta for the private firm), (iii) bottom–up betas (the beta for a private firm can be estimated by looking at the average betas for similar publicly traded companies).

  Whatever the method chosen to estimate the beta, the valuer might need to adjust betas if the owner/potential buyer of the private company is undiversified.[3] Alternatively, the valuer should consider other risk premiums specific to private firms such as the small-stock premium or company-specific risk premiums in

3. Damadaran (2009) discusses the adjustment of beta for undiversified buyers/owners of private companies whereby the market beta, measured for a set of peer publicly traded firms, is divided by the correlation between the peer firm's returns and the market returns.

addition to the market risk captured by the CAPM beta. These premiums compensate for the higher risk associated with firm size and the less diversified operations of the firm and/or its owners. The earlier the development stage of the company, the higher the company-specific risk premium.

• *Cost of debt.* For private firms, this is measured by looking at the interest rate on the firm's debt (which is likely to be bank debt). If the private firm never used debt capital then we can use the cost of debt of similar publicly traded firms and add an extra spread to reflect the incremental riskiness of the private firm relative to the public peers. If the private firm is close to an initial public offering then the valuer can assume a cost of debt similar to that of the publicly traded companies in the same industry without any additional adjustments.

• *Debt ratio.* While market values of equity and debt are not available for private firms, we can use the industry average or target debt ratios. If the company is valued for an acquisition then the valuer should use a ratio that reflects the likely capital structure of the target at the time of exit.

Step 3. Calculate the value of operations

$$\text{EV}_{\text{operations}} = [\text{CF}_1/(1+r)] + [\text{CF}_2/(1+r)^2] + [\text{CF}_3/(1+r)^3]$$
$$+ \cdots + [(\text{CF}_T + \text{TV}_T)/(1+r)^T]$$

All variables are defined above.

Step 4. Calculate the enterprise value

$$\text{EV} = \text{EV}_{\text{operations}} + \text{EV}_{\text{non-operations}}$$

The value of the non-operating assets is added to the value of operating assets computed in Step 3. Non-operating assets are defined as those assets that are not necessary for the ongoing operations of the private firm. Some examples include excess cash, marketable financial securities in which the firm invests excess cash, non-performing assets, real estate not used for operating activities, etc.

Step 5. Adjust the enterprise value and compute the value of equity. At this stage, the valuer should adjust the total value of the enterprise for illiquidity and/or control premiums depending on the purpose of the valuation. Finally, the valuer can compute the value of the common equity by removing the value of the debt in the capital structure and that of dilutive claims. We discuss these final adjustments separately in Section 10.3.4.

The power of discount-cash-flow methodology outlined above lies in the fact that it can calculate a value for the private company in *all* situations. However, there are several reasons why the above DCF method might not be appropriate for private equity companies:

• Discount rates are difficult to estimate for many private companies given the scarcity of available publicly traded firms that are similar in terms of risk, growth, and cash flow patterns.

• The method does not deal with changing capital structures that are specific to buyout transactions. The debt ratio used to compute the discount rate is constant throughout the forecasting period.

• Forecast cash flows might not be reliable given the high uncertainties that early-stage young private companies face. In a dynamic business environment, most managers would be reasonably confident in their cash flow projections for the next 12 months, but levels of confidence fall as the period extends into the future. If a significant growth rate is projected and, particularly, when projected from a loss-making position in the early years, most if not all of the value calculated resides in the terminal assumptions. That makes the outcome of the DCF valuation highly sensitive to discount rate and growth assumptions. In addition, basing a valuation entirely on the predictability of cash flows anticipated in the period after the forecasting period lacks credibility.

- The method might not reflect actual market conditions but valuer's assumptions.

We present two additional methods that are variants of the DCF methodology and deal with some of the issues raised above. They are commonly used in private equity transactions.

Adjusted discount cash flow method

This method is typically used to value buyout targets. When a firm's capital structure is changing or it has net operating losses (NOLs) that can be used to offset taxable income, an adjusted DCF method should be used. If a firm has NOLs then its effective tax rate changes over time, as NOLs are carried forward for tax purposes and netted against taxable income. The adjusted method accounts for the effect of the firm's changing tax status by valuing NOLs separately.

Under the adjusted DCF method the valuer computes the present value of the cash flows by ignoring the capital structure. In other words, the discount rate used is the cost of equity as opposed to the weighted average cost of capital, assuming that the company is financed fully with equity ($\text{PV}_{\text{cash flows}}$).

The tax benefits associated with the capital structure are then estimated separately by computing the present value of the tax savings from the tax-deductible interest payments. The interest payments will change over time as debt levels change due to repayments. By convention the discount rate for this calculation is the pre-tax cost of debt:

$$\text{PV}_{\text{interest shield}} = [I_1/(1+r_d)] + [I_2/(1+r_d)^2] + [I_3/(1+r_d)^3] + \cdots + [I_T/(1+r_d)^T]$$

where

I_n = interest-related tax shield in Year n computed as interest expense $*$ tax rate (based on the debt repayment schedule)

r_d = pre-tax cost of debt.

Finally, NOLs available to the company are quantified. They are computed as (EBIT − interest expense) $*$ tax rate every year. Please note that EBIT − interest expense must be negative in order to obtain a tax shield. The discount rate used to value NOLs is often the pre-tax rate on debt. If it is certain that NOLs will result in tax benefits then the risk-free rate can also be used as the discount rate:

$$\text{PV}_{\text{NOL shield}} = [\text{NOL}_1/(1+r_d)] + [\text{NOL}_2/(1+r_d)^2] + [\text{NOL}_3/(1+r_d)^3]$$
$$+ \cdots + [\text{NOL}_T/(1+r_d)^T]$$

where

NOL_n = net operating loss–related tax shield in Year n computed as above

r_d = pre-tax cost of debt.

The enterprise value is the sum of the present value of cash flows ($PV_{\text{cash flows}}$), interest tax shields ($PV_{\text{interest shield}}$), net operating losses tax shields ($PV_{\text{NOL shield}}$), and non-operating assets. Similarly to the DCF method, final adjustments of the enterprise value are necessary (illiquidity, control, etc.) (see Section 10.3.4 for more details).

Venture capital method

This method is commonly applied in the private equity industry when venture capitalists provide financing to young startup firms raising additional equity. The method starts with forecasting the earnings of the private firm in a future year, when the venture capitalist expects an exit either via a public offering or a trade sale. This earnings forecast in conjunction with an earnings multiple, estimated by looking at publicly traded firms in the same business, is used to assess the value of the firm at the time of exit. We can also forecast revenues for the firm in the exit year and apply a revenue multiple to estimate the terminal exit value.

This terminal value is discounted back to the present at a target rate of return, which measures what venture capitalists believe is a justifiable return on their investment, given the risks involved:

$$\text{Firm value} = \text{Exit value}_N / (1 + \text{Target return})^N$$

where

Exit value_N = expected value of the firm at the time of exit
Target return = rate of return expected by the venture capital investor.

This target rate of return is usually set at a much higher level than the traditional cost of equity for the firm. It is a typically a very high discount rate of 40% to 75%. What can justify such a high return? Venture capitalists argue that it provides compensation for the illiquidity of their investment, the risk involved (startup companies are at the beginning of their life and the failure rate is very high), and the valuable services they provide to the company in terms of time and advice. The target return also adjusts for the sometimes overoptimistic exit projections which are provided by the management.

10.3.4 Final adjustments

As discussed above, once the enterprise value has been measured, regardless of the methodology, the valuer needs to make few final adjustments to measure the value of the common equity in the company. These final adjustments depend on specific circumstances such as the type of the transaction for which the company is valued or the capital structure and other characteristics of the company.

Illiquidity discount

Given that private equity companies are not traded in liquid markets, private equity investors demand compensation for the risks of being illiquid. The magnitude of the illiquidity discount is likely to vary depending on the characteristics of the private firm. Few factors can guide the valuer in justifying the magnitude, such as the liquidity of the identifiable assets, the financial health of the company, the size of the firm, or the likelihood that the company can be listed on an exchange at some point in the future. Much of the practice seems to rely on rules of thumb that often set the illiquidity discount at 20% to 30% of estimated value. For reporting purposes, the accounting standards require that any liquidity discounts should be built into the multiple considerations, or discount rates.

When valuing a private equity investment with the purpose of reporting to investors, an important check is comparing the size of any discount applied at the valuation date against the difference between the multiples at the date of acquisition. This will not remain constant over the holding period of the investment, but any significant movements should be explained.

Control premium

There are implications for valuation if a large portion of the private firm being valued is offered for sale. If that portion provides a controlling interest (i.e, the right to pick the firm's management), it should have a substantially higher value than if it does not provide this power. Estimation of the control premium is challenging given measurement issues, but it ranges in practice anywhere from 10% to 50%. If the portion acquired provides a non-controlling small interest then the value of the company should be smaller. For small stakes the valuer should apply marketability discounts.

Contingency-related adjustments

Contingencies represent potential future payments to the seller of a private company or the management if the company achieves a certain level of agreed-on performance or certain events stipulated in the purchase agreement (e.g., obtains regulatory approval for a product, etc.). The introduction of a contingent consideration introduces uncertainty when valuing the company. The valuer needs to estimate the probability that the events will occur, assess the magnitude of the likely future payments, and adjust downward accordingly the value of the company.

Debt-related adjustments

A typical structure for a private equity buyout transaction may result in several layers of financing, which include senior debt provided by a bank, mezzanine debt provided by another financing house, and—ranking below these—debts and/or a combination of debt and equity provided by the private equity fund. All debts that would be redeemed at the point of sale and rank higher than the private equity fund's highest ranking interest are deducted from the enterprise value.

In a simple situation, the amount deducted would be the principal outstanding, including any accrued interest. Where redemption premia apply these would normally be included. The outstanding debt may be reduced by surplus cash in the investee company. Cash that is required as a part of the normal working capital should not reduce the debt. Only the cash that could be used to pay down the debt without impacting the operations should reduce outstanding debt amounts.

There may be situations where the senior debt is traded and a market price, below the outstanding amount, can be observed. In theory, the private company could acquire debt in the market at the lower value and cancel it. This theory does not support the suggestion that the senior debt deduction should take place at market value, rather than the repayable amount in a liquidation scenario. Once the debt has been acquired, then the "profit" on canceling the debt might be recognized in the fair value calculation.

Dilution-related adjustments

The private equity market has developed a wide range of schemes that are intended to either incentivize the management of the investee company or favor one investor over another. Many of these schemes are as tax efficient as possible, thus making them enormously complicated. Typical schemes will include:

- *Ratchets*. Where the holder will receive additional equity if certain targets are achieved. There can also be "reverse ratchets" where the holder increases his/her percentage holding of his/her shares by the buyback at a fixed price of another's equity
- *Options and warrants*. The rights to acquire additional equity under certain conditions
- *Liquidation preferences*. Where the holder will receive a return in preference to other investors
- *Conversion clauses*. The ability to switch into a different instrument.

Whatever the individual terms of these schemes, the valuer needs to reflect the impact on the company valued. It would be unusual for a valuer to resort to complex derivative valuation models to separately value each derivative instrument. The valuer should assess the expected impact and consider what adjustments a prospective purchaser of the instrument might make.

Typically, a valuer will consider the expected outcome at the future realization. If, for example, an option is held by the management team and the option exercise price is below the value that would be attributed to the shares that it represents, the valuer will assume that the dilution will take place and value the remaining share accordingly. When considering the likely outcome, it is important to recognize that the terms, particularly those affecting the management team, may need to be amended to facilitate a sale. The strict legal position may not be the expected outcome.

In the event that the private equity fund holds a significant position in derivative instruments itself, then the valuer should consider using a derivative valuation model.

10.4 PITFALLS TO BE WARY OF WHEN VALUING PRIVATE COMPANIES

Cross-country differences

Valuers of private equity investments should be aware that cross-country differences affect the quality of the valuation outputs. Different countries have different accounting standards. Even if they use international accounting standards the levels of implementation and enforcement are likely to vary. Thus, valuations of fund investments in different countries can be distorted and inconsistent due to variation in the recognition of revenues and expenses. Further, differences in macroeconomic factors such as inflation or exchange rates can be potentially problematic if not accounted for when reporting the net asset value of the fund to investors.

Excessive caution

Many valuation processes are affected by accounting conservatism, which is a fundamental principle. This prudence in reporting and estimation generates under-valuation of investments in some circumstances. This is further emphasized by the reaction of the investors. It appears that the investors would prefer to be surprised by a large uplift on valuation, rather than the smallest loss. In private equity, there is no reward for overvaluing investments.

Volatility

One of the initial complaints against the valuation guidelines we discussed in this chapter is the use of multiples that can make a private equity investment "volatile". In fact, investments are volatile and the use of multiples merely pushes the valuer towards reflecting it. That does not mean that the valuer is required to use the multiple from a comparator exactly for the valuation date. Equally, a multiple that clearly does not reflect the current market environment is unacceptable. A multiple which is reflecting the market over a short period is permissible on the basis that a third party considering acquiring an illiquid asset is unlikely to alter their pricing view of the value on the basis of daily movements in the comparators.

Reasonable assumptions and estimates

Whenever assumptions and estimates are used, these should be supportable in the context of "what might a third party consider?" This might include matters that take place after the reporting date where these provide more evidence as to the conditions existing at the reporting date.

APPENDIX

CASE STUDY

This section considers an example of valuation reports that have been made available to the investors in a PE fund. The purpose is to see whether these may give rise to any adjustments. It is not the intention of the valuation guidelines to push investors towards second-guessing and analyzing in detail all valuations submitted to them. The investor should assess whether there is a risk of material error from the information presented since the report is by its nature a summary of the thought processes and judgment calls made by the valuer.

Whilst this section is in the form of a case study, there are no answers, merely questions. We will all have views on what we think is an acceptable judgment call. Equally, these valuation reports are being assessed by Zebra Private Equity (as the investor) to establish what number is suitable for inclusion in their own accounts. The size of Zebra's fund will determine their level of materiality and the extent to which they need to challenge the valuations.

We reproduce a report on the valuation of two fictitious companies, *Pueblo Clothing SpA* and *Chariot Skates Plc*, at December 31, 2009. Zebra's fund is relatively small, so both companies would be considered material in the assessment.

Questions

1. Having read through the valuation report, would you be happy to conclude that there is unlikely to be a material error?

2. If you are unable to make that conclusion, which areas are of concern and is there additional information that would help?

10.A   PUEBLO CLOTHING SpA

Sector:	Retail
Investment date:	12-Nov-06
Equity holding:	95.9%
Valuation date:	31-Dec-09

Overview

Pueblo is an Italian clothing retailer, specializing in designer and bespoke suits for celebrities and professionals alike. With stores in the fashionable districts of Milan and Rome, we are ideally placed to target our fashion-conscious market. Zebra Private Equity holds 95.9% of the equity, with the founder retaining the remaining shares.

Current performance

Performance of the business has been relatively strong in comparison with our competitors. Sales have fallen slightly in 2009, but we are confident that the worst of the recession is now over in Italy. Current management forecasts indicate a 2010 sales forecast of USD3.2mn, 10% ahead of current year. Additionally, we have managed to maintain our pricing levels outside the normal sales periods. Over the next 2-to-3-year period we will continue to build on our core base of loyal customers.

Summary of performance data (USD million)

Historical				Projected	
Year-end September 30	**2007**	**2008**	**2009**	**2010**	**2011**
Revenue	4.6	3.2	2.9	3.2	3.3
Growth	27.8%	−30.4%	−9.4%	10.3%	3.1%
EBITDA	2.2	1.2	0.9	1.1	1.4
% Margin	47.8%	37.5%	31.0%	34.4%	42.4%
% Growth	22.2%	−45.5%	−25.0%	22.2%	27.3%

Multiples

Data for selected listed companies in the sector

	Market cap (USD million)	EV/EBITDA				
		2009	**2008**	**2007**	**2006**	**2005**
Balls	72	3.4	3.8	6.9	9.9	11.2
Cornics	220	3.2	5.1	10.2	11.2	11.9
Drakes	49	5.9	4.4	9.8	8.4	9.1
Edwins	245	7.1	5.5	12.1	12.1	11
Finos	143	1.9	2.4	9.2	10.3	13.2
		4.3	4.24	9.64	10.38	11.28
Average		8.0				

This average multiple is also supported by recent transactions in the clothing retail space, most notably the acquisition of Cheap Fashion by BrightSpark Private Equity in September 2008 at an EBITDA multiple of 8.5× and the acquisition of NewImage by KXY in August 2008 at a PE multiple of 10.8×. Headroom on covenants is sufficient to meet the June 2010 test.

Valuation

	USD million
Earnings for valuation purposes	1.1
EV/EBITDA multiple	7.7
Gross enterprise value	8.47
Priority debt	(5.10)
Attributable enterprise value	3.37
Equity stake	3.22

We have valued the business using an earnings multiple resulting in a valuation of approximately 40% of the original equity investment. Given the boom-and-bust cycle that we are just now emerging from, we did not feel that depressed multiples of the past 2 years or the inflated multiples of the previous years were the most suitable basis of comparison. Therefore, the investment team concluded that "through-the-cycle multiples" were the most reasonable basis to value our investment in Pueblo. In addition, Edwins is by far the single best comparable for Pueblo, although Pueblo is a much higher quality product. Furthermore, Edwins has had to significantly reduce prices to maintain sales volumes.

The analysis above shows the range of multiples of our closest comparables over the past 5 years. We used the discounted average as a basis for our multiple. We have taken a c. 5% discount for risk reflecting the lower quality of earnings in Pueblo vs. its comparables and the lack of certainty surrounding a number of contracts.

10.A.1 Analysis: What are the big judgments made in the valuation?

Environment

The valuation is prepared in the context of a retail market in recession. The valuer has made certain fundamental assumptions as to how this business environment will impact the company. Are these assumptions reasonable and appropriate?

The fund prepares accounts in USD. Pueblo appears to be entirely Italian based, yet the underlying data are reported in USD. Have movements in the exchange rate emphasized or masked trends? It would be preferable if the valuation was calculated in the base currency of Pueblo, probably EUR, and converted to USD for reporting purposes.

Valuation methodology

Has an appropriate methodology been selected? Pueblo is an established and profitable business, so a multiple-based valuation would appear to be the most appropriate.

Earnings

The earnings used in the calculation should be considered maintainable and those that a prospective purchaser might use. Is it reasonable to base the valuation on the forecast 2010 EBITDA? Is there additional data to support the "management forecasts"? Do the quarter's results from October to December give any additional information?

Multiple

Assessing whether a multiple is appropriate and reasonable requires significant judgment. This judgment should be supported by market data where possible. The questions listed below cannot be answered directly from the valuation report. This does not imply that the answers to all these questions are negative and the absence of information in the report may simply arise from the valuer summarising his or her conclusions, rather than providing a detailed analysis:

- Have we got an appropriate set of comparators? Is an entity that is nearly 30 times as big really "the best" comparator?
- Are there any multiple outliers that should be excluded?

- Have points of difference been considered and adjusted? By using the average, there is an inherent assumption that the investee company is reflective of the average business in the market.

- Would a 5% risk premium be sufficient?

- What was the comparison of the original acquisition multiple to the comparators at the acquisition date? What does the pattern of the multiples show that the market as a whole has been doing?

- Is a 5-year average relevant? Would a prospective purchaser consider acquiring an unlisted company on the basis of historic market sentiment, when they could acquire a quoted company on the basis of current market conditions?

- Are the EBITDA multiples of transactions that occurred in August and September 2008 relevant? In a relatively static environment, a comparable transaction that falls within a reasonably short period (say 18 months, as in this case) of the valuation date should provide good supporting evidence. These transactions took place at the peak of the market in 2008 and, over the subsequent 6 months, the FTSE 100 in London fell by some 30%. The majority of this fall in the index recovered by December 31st, 2009, but this level of volatility will reduce the quality of that support.

What other information might be sought?

There is little information on covenants, merely a statement that the next covenant test will be passed. Clearly, the investee company has experienced difficulties since the November 2006 acquisition date but, without knowing more, any potential impact cannot be assessed.

How are the EBITDA margin and growth rates expected to be achieved? There is a statement at the end of the report which suggests that there might be significant issues arising (lack of certainty surrounding a number of contracts). If that is a significant issue, more explanation might be expected?

Alternate valuation

In the absence of additional information, the investor might conclude that they would have made different assessments. The valuation report suggests that the earnings might be slightly high and a slight discount might be applied to the "unsupported" forecasts. Regardless of additional information that might be provided, the use of a 5-year average multiple is difficult to support. The alternate below uses 4.9 which is an average of the current multiples, excluding Finos, which appears to be an outlier. This is then discounted by 25% to reflect points of difference. This judgmental discount is based on the lack of liquidity, the size of the entities, and the comments around contract uncertainties.

The multiples and earnings used in the valuation below are easier to support on the information made available, but it does not necessarily make this valuation "more right". A prospective purchaser and the valuer might concur that Edwins is the best comparator and that next year's earnings are sufficiently underpinned to be reasonably secure, but that is a matter of judgment.

	USD
Earnings for valuation purposes	1.0
Multiple from comparator	4.9
Multiple after discount (25%)	3.7
Gross enterprise value	3.7
Senior debt	(5.1)
Equity value	0.0

10.B CHARIOT SKATES PLC

Sector:	Retail
Investment date:	12-Jan-08
Equity holding:	87.4%
Valuation date:	31-Dec-09

Overview

Chariot Skates is an exciting innovative new mode of transport. Invented by Australian Mike Moyers in 2006, the skates are patent protected and work by supporting the wearer's foot in a harness, just inches from the ground, allowing them to generate exhilarating speeds by pushing out on the edges of the wheels.

Background

In 2007, Mr. Moyers was struggling to raise additional capital to make some necessary changes to the product. He also lacked experience in getting a product to market. Zebra Private Equity managed to negotiate a USD22.7mn investment for 87.4% of the company in January 2008, which will also hold the rights to all of Mr. Moyers future inventions. Mr. Moyers is a graduate of MIT and has invented a number of successful sports products in the past, including one used in popular in-line boarding.

Investment thesis

- Innovative patent-protected product
- Environmentally friendly mode of transport with zero running costs
- Likely new sport in 2016 Olympic Games
- Benefit from Mr. Moyers future inventions.

Current performance

Sales growth in 2009 has been very strong increasing by over 60% year on year. In addition, market research has been very positive. Currently, production costs exceed selling price, but it is vital that we maintain our pricing level in order to penetrate the market as fast as possible.

The team has expanded to include six new joiners—four in production and two in sales and marketing. The sales and marketing team have been campaigning aggressively and have even secured promotional slots on primetime TV shows such as *Saturday*

Kitchen. Alternative routes to market such as Facebook, Twitter, and Bebo are proving successful in targeting our core market of 15-year-olds through 35-year-olds. The online website receives 200 hits a day and approximately 0.5% to 0.7% of these translate into sales.

Production has been transferred to China and, despite a small number of quality issues initially, this setup is now working well, resulting in cost savings of 55%. The product is currently on sale on a trial basis at a number of Halfords outlets.

Valuation

We have valued Chariot Skates using a discounted-cash-flow basis (see Exhibit 10.1) resulting in a valuation of USD12.84mn (56% of cost). The value of our investment has been negatively impacted by recent safety concerns which meant that this product was not approved for use for children under 12 and, therefore, sales projections have been modified accordingly. However, the overriding ambition remains that Chariot Skates will be the ride of choice for commuters in the long term.

Popularity and, hence, sales are expected to increase significantly in advance of the 2016 Olympics and decrease following this as we reach saturation. There is potential to release various updates and modifications to stimulate sales once the market becomes more mature.

We strongly believe that the current revenue growth rates are relatively modest, particularly in light of the fact that following the approval of Olympic BMX for the 2008 Olympics, sales of BMX bicycles rose by 800%.

Additionally, on the basis that Mr. Moyers is currently pursuing legal action to limit Zebra Private Equity's right to benefit from future inventions, our discounted cash flow has only taken Chariot Skates cash flows into account. (However, we have been advised by lawyers that Mr. Moyers has very limited chance of success.) Overall, we believe that our projections and resulting valuation are very conservative.

10.B.1   Analysis: What are the big judgments made in the valuation?

Environment

For an entity like Chariot Skates, assessing the state of the business environment within which it operates is extremely difficult. The plan is to manufacture and market a unique product. The general state of the retail trade may provide some useful background material, as might more focused analysis on manufacturers and retailers of such items as skateboards, but nothing will be directly applicable.

The investment thesis is based on this single product being hugely successful following its inclusion at the 2016 Olympic Games.

Valuation methodology

The company is currently loss making at the EBITDA level and, in fact, selling its products below manufacturing costs. The price of the recent investment methodology may be an appropriate basis for valuation, considering the investment by the Zebra Fund and subsequent milestones, but the valuation report gives insufficient details as to whether this would be practical. In the absence of positive earnings, an earnings multiple basis is not possible. DCF will always permit a valuation to be calculated.

EXHIBIT 10.1

CHARIOT SKATES' DISCOUNTED CASH FLOW ANALYSIS

(USD million, unless otherwise stated)

Assumptions

Tax rate	30%
Discount rate	28%
Terminal FCF growth rate	2%

Projected financials

Year-end December	2007	2008	2009	2010	2011	2012	2013	2014	2015	2016	2017	2018	2019
Revenue	**5.0**	**8.0**	**13.1**	**13.8**	**15.1**	**18.2**	**23.6**	**40.1**	**76.2**	**213.5**	**256.2**	**281.8**	**295.9**
Growth (%)		*50.0*	*63.8*	*5.0*	*10.0*	*20.0*	*30.0*	*70.0*	*90.0*	*180.0*	*20.0*	*10.0*	*5.0*
EBITDA	**(30.0)**	**(35.0)**	**(10.0)**	**1.7**	**2.0**	**2.4**	**3.1**	**5.7**	**11.0**	**31.6**	**38.9**	**43.1**	**46.0**
Margin (%)	*(600.0)*	*(437.5)*	*(76.3)*	*12.7*	*13.0*	*13.0*	*13.0*	*14.2*	*14.4*	*14.8*	*15.2*	*15.3*	*15.6*
Less D&A	(5.2)	(5.7)	(10.0)	(0.5)	(0.6)	(0.7)	(0.9)	(1.7)	(3.4)	(10.2)	(10.8)	(12.1)	(13.5)
EBIT	**(35.2)**	**(40.7)**	**(20.0)**	**1.2**	**1.4**	**1.6**	**2.1**	**4.0**	**7.6**	**21.3**	**28.2**	**31.0**	**32.5**
Margin (%)	*(704.8)*	*(508.6)*	*(152.7)*	*9.0*	*9.0*	*9.0*	*9.0*	*10.0*	*10.0*	*10.0*	*11.0*	*11.0*	*11.0*
Less taxes	10.6	12.2	6.0	(0.4)	(0.4)	(0.5)	(0.6)	(1.2)	(2.3)	(6.4)	(8.5)	(9.3)	(9.8)
Net income	**(24.7)**	**(28.5)**	**(14.0)**	**0.9**	**1.0**	**1.1**	**1.5**	**2.8**	**5.3**	**14.9**	**19.7**	**21.7**	**22.8**
Plus D&A	5.2	5.7	10.0	0.5	0.6	0.7	0.9	1.7	3.4	10.2	10.8	12.1	13.5
Less CAPEX	(13.8)	(15.6)	(12.2)	(0.8)	(0.7)	(0.7)	(0.7)	(1.2)	(2.3)	(5.3)	(6.4)	(7.0)	(7.4)
As a % of sales	*276.0*	*195.0*	*93.1*	*5.5*	*4.8*	*3.7*	*3.0*	*3.0*	*3.0*	*2.5*	*2.5*	*2.5*	*2.5*
Less NWC	0.5	0.8	1.5	1.4	1.5	1.8	2.4	4.0	7.6	21.3	25.6	28.2	29.6
As a % of sales	*10.0*	*10.0*	*11.5*	*10.0*	*10.0*	*10.0*	*10.0*	*10.0*	*10.0*	*10.0*	*10.0*	*10.0*	*10.0*
Less change in NWC			(0.7)	0.1	(0.1)	(0.3)	(0.5)	(1.7)	(3.6)	(13.7)	(4.3)	(2.6)	(1.4)
Less other	(1.9)	(2.0)	(1.9)	(3.0)	(2.5)	(2.0)	(1.5)	(1.1)	(0.6)	(0.4)	(0.5)	(0.5)	(0.5)
Free cash flow	**(35.2)**	**(40.4)**	**(18.8)**	**(2.3)**	**(1.8)**	**(1.1)**	**(0.4)**	**0.6**	**2.2**	**5.7**	**19.3**	**23.7**	**26.9**
Terminal value													**105.7**
Total	**(35.2)**	**(40.4)**	**(18.8)**	**(2.3)**	**(1.8)**	**(1.1)**	**(0.4)**	**0.6**	**2.2**	**5.7**	**19.3**	**23.7**	**132.6**

Total value to Zebra		**Sensitivity analysis**					**Reasonableness check**	
				Discount rate				
				26%	28%	30%		
NPV	14.6						NPV	14.4
% to Zebra	87.4	Terminal	1%	15.4	12.4	10.0	As a multiple of 09 EBITDA	−1.4×
Less net debt	0	FCF growth	2%	15.9	12.8	10.2	As a multiple of 10 EBITDA	8.3×
Total value to Zebra (€ million)	**12.8**	Rate	3%	16.5	13.1	10.5		

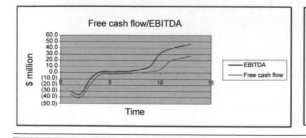

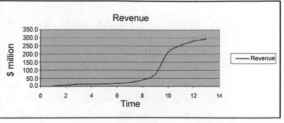

EXHIBIT 10.2

CHARIOT SKATES' TRANSACTION COMPARABLES

(USD million, unless otherwise stated)

Date	Target	Acquirer	Target country	Enterprise value (€ million)	EV/ Sales	EV/ EBITDA	EV/ EBITA
12-Dec-05	Sandcity Ltd.	O'Neill Europe BV	U.K.	0.0	n.a.	n.a.	n.a.
02-Jun-08	Eider	Lafuma	France	5.0	0.23	n.a.	n.a.
06-Dec-07	Overtons	Gander Mountain	U.S.	48.0	0.78	8.75	n.a.
07-Nov-07	Cycle Surgery Ltd.	Snow & Rock Sports Ltd.	U.K.	n.a.	n.a.	n.a.	n.a.
24-Sep-07	Nevisport	Sports Direct Int.	U.K.	n.a.	n.a.	n.a.	n.a.
16-Aug-07	S.I.R. Warehouse Sports Store	Cabelas Inc.	Canada	n.a.	n.a.	n.a.	n.a.
10-Aug-07	Hawshead Retail Ltd.	Regatta Ltd.	U.K.	n.a.	n.a.	n.a.	n.a.
12-Jul-07	Field & Trek Plc	Sports Direct Plc	U.K.	18.0	0.58	n.a.	n.a.
10-Jul-07	Mountain Warehouse Ltd.	Kcaj + management	U.K.	33.0	0.86	6.88	8.57
17-Jul-06	Wiggle Ltd.	Isis Private Equity + management	U.K.	17	1.0	n.a.	n.a.
12-Jun-06	Moresport Ltd.	Ethos Private Equity + management	U.K.	105	n.a.	n.a.	n.a.
11-Jun-06	JJB Sports	Exista and Chris Ronnie	U.K.	n.a.	1.0	10.81	n.a.
23-May-06	Coronel Tapioca	Gala Capital	Spain	n.a.	n.a.	n.a.	n.a.
04-May-06	The Sportsmans Guide Inc.	VLC Corporation	U.S.	168	0.6	8.61	9.27
30-Mar-06	Pacific Trail Brands	Columbia Sportswear Co.	U.S.	17	n.a.	n.a.	n.a.
26-Jan-06	Montrail, Inc.	Columbia Sportswear Co.	U.S.	12	n.a.	n.a.	n.a.
31-Oct-05	Allsports	John David Groupe	U.K.	26	0.1	1.82	3.91
05-Apr-05	Jack Wolfskin	Barclays PE	Germany	93	1.0	4.19	4.56
21-Mar-05	Reef Holdings Corporation	VF Corporation	U.S.	141	2.5	n.a.	n.a.
			Mean		0.87	6.8	6.6
			Median		0.82	7.7	6.6

Cash flows

Historic and projected cash flows show a significant outflow of resources in early years, presumably as a result if investing in research and development and capital equipment. The projections turn to be slightly positive at the EBITDA level from 2010, increasing significantly after 2016.

What information is available to support the projected cash flows? Are the short-term assumptions about improving the manufacturing cost structure in China reasonable?

Sales are increasing rapidly and margins improving in the forecast period, but is this relevant in the longer term? The cash flows that drive the valuation are those from 2017 onwards, with 61% of the calculated value residing in the terminal assumptions.

Can the significant growth between 2014 and 2017 be supported? Might other products be developed to reduce the risk inherent in the assumed rapid growth?

DCF calculations

DCF calculations always appear to give an appearance of "scientific" support to the valuation. The valuation is extremely sensitive to cash flows, particularly the terminal assumptions, together with the discount rate used.

How has the discount rate of 28% been calculated? Is 28% a sensible discount rate considering the risk associated with a single product whose success may be reliant on acceptance at the Olympics? Is the sensitivity analysis helpful? Is the range of changing parameters sufficient?

How can the DCF be linked back to market data?

It is extremely difficult to arrive at a DCF calculation for this type of business because transaction multiples appear to be of value for well-established businesses and, generally, are 2 to 5 years old. That said, the valuation estimated by the DCF calculates a fair value at 1.1× 2009 revenue and 8.3× forecast 2010 EBITDA.

There is no right answer!

10.C REFERENCES

PORTER, M.E. (1985) *Competitive Advantage*, The Free Press, New York.

DAMODARAN, A. (2009) *Private Company Valuation*, http://pages.stern.nyu.edu/~adamodar

DAMODARAN, A. (2002) *Investment Valuation*, Second Edition, John Wiley & Sons Ltd.

11

Deal analysis and
due diligence

11.1 INTRODUCTION

Imagine you are a private equity investment professional. After months of searching in one of your preferred industry sectors, you think you have found a great target for investment. It is likely to cost in the region of £300mn—about the right size for your fund. It is a solid industrial business (turnover £400mn, EBITDA £60mn) with factories in four European countries, a sales operation in the U.S., a series of distribution outlets, and joint ventures in Asia. The widgets the company sells are in a sector you believe will benefit from the current upswing in this industry.

11.1.1 A buyer's perspective

Before you part with £300mn of the fund's capital you will have lots of questions you need to get answers to. How have sales progressed, are revenues growing or shrinking? Has growth been achieved organically or by acquisition? Are the factories safe and efficient? Are there any environmental hazards or risks? Why are there no direct Asian operations? Is the U.S. operation healthy? Is the economic environment and the market sector a safe bet, or is the upswing already turning down? What kind of pension scheme is operating and is it in deficit?

Trying to get satisfactory answers to these and many other critical questions is the task of "deal analysis and due diligence". There are many different ways of doing it; it can involve no, some, or many advisors; it can take from a few weeks to many months; it can be in one, two, or three distinct phases. Whatever the exact pattern, though, the fundamental aim is the same—the potential buyer getting sufficient understanding of issues and risks to get to a position where the buyer is prepared (and his or her banks and backers are prepared) to make an investment.

Due diligence is hugely important for the buyer in this or any purchase situation. If you were purchasing a house you would ensure you had a good survey conducted to see if the foundations are sound, the heating works, and to develop an assessment of what improvements and alterations you might make to the house to enhance its value. Due diligence on a company performs much the same function. It is a process that

This chapter has been written by John Maloney and Kay Nemoto.

ensures not only that the business is sound financially, organizationally, and operationally, but that the buyer has assessed conceivable risks, identified potential areas for improvement (upside), and developed a robust plan for achieving an enhanced value and sale of the asset in the future.

11.1.2 A seller's perspective

Imagine you are head of a family that has spent 25 years building its business. You think it's worth £350mn+, but you also know that you have issues that could reduce that valuation, and you are loyal to your employees. You want to find a "good home" for the business at the right price. How much do you have to divulge? What is a safe process? What if you put the business up for sale and among the bidders are your fiercest competitors—how can you protect your hard-fought unique R&D secrets? What happens if the sale falls through. You would not wish to have given your competitors all the information they need to compete with you. Clearly, as a seller you will want a process where you release as little information as possible at the start (when many hands may get it) and only provide detailed information to a few bidders who have demonstrated their seriousness.

Due dilligence is essential for the buyer, but for the seller it is a process that can be difficult to manage, with risks of overdisclosure of information, but also management distraction from the important day-to-day work of running the business. Resolving this potential minefield is a process that, with many variations, is really quite simple—albeit often expensive and time consuming.

11.2 THE SALE PROCESS

A typical process for sale of a company or a division of a business might run as follows:

1. *Approaches / discussions*—in some cases a sale will be premeditated on the part of a company, in others it comes about as the result of an approach or multiple approaches by interested buyer(s); in some other cases the sale may be forced by banks or administrators. Depending on the origins of the process, discussions can be wide ranging or cursory. In many cases they will stimulate nothing—the seller feels the timing is wrong or the buyer isn't serious. One CEO reports "I get on average two approaches a week to sell this business—even though it's a pain I always listen politely . . . after all you never know what might be on offer."

2. *Developing a prospectus or an information memorandum*—if a company owner decides to think about selling the business. The owner pulls together documentation—often in the form of an "information memorandum" which sets out (usually in a very positive light) the company's history, prospects, and basic financial situation, and outlines the assets for sale (sometimes only a subsidiary may be for sale).

3. *Commissioning a sales process*—in order to maximize the number of potential bidders a seller will often commission an agent to handle the sale process. Good agents will be effective at identifying and marketing the business to a long list of potential bidders. Some businesses choose to handle these themselves, which runs the risk of not getting the best price, but saves on fees.

4. *First-round due diligence*—the company invites bids. This is sometimes referred to as the *long list stage* or *first round*. Often, many parties may express an interest

at this stage and will in return receive a copy of the prospectus or information memorandum. The exact process will often be determined by the number of potential bidders (where this ranges into many tens of bidders a three-stage process may be instituted). If there are a large number of bidders, a non-binding bid is sometimes required—done with very little information and to get to a shortlist of serious bidders to whom greater access will then be offered. A degree of carefully controlled access is usually granted to either the shortlist or longlist—often through a secure data room—and access will be offered to key personnel in the selling company. Usually, but not always, this will be restricted at this stage to the CEO, CFO, and a few board members whose involvement is required. This stage of the process often takes between 2 and 4 weeks (but is highly dependent on the complexity of the potential deal). Through the data room, the company provides a range of financial, commercial, legal, and other relevant documentation for potential sellers to review. Access to facilities is likely to be limited to key sites such as major factories that are critical to an understanding of price and risk.

5. Potential buyers will be invited to offer a "compliant bid" by a set deadline according to a set of rules put forward by the seller (these may specify information required of the buyer such as guarantees, the form of any non-cash offers, etc.). In most cases the bids will be issued by the buyers subject to due diligence and in some cases with specific exclusions or caveats which will require more information. From the bids, a preferred bidder is usually selected for final due diligence and negotiation.

6. *Formal due diligence*—a further period is granted for full and widespread access between the preferred bidder and the seller. Often at this stage, a larger team on both sides will be mobilized to share information and drill down on key areas of uncertainty. Key potential risks and "deal breakers" will be dealt with. Often, the scope of this diligence will have been limited as part of the previous process to only those key issues identified by the buyer as affecting value.

7. *Sale and purchase agreement*—the parties (buyer and seller) in this agreement will agree the terms of the deal—the price, how payment will be made (cash, shares, other assets), the assets being bought, how brands will be handled, and many other details that are intended to both clarify the transaction and protect the buyer and seller from risks.

8. *Financial closure/Ownership transfer*—at an agreed date the transaction will happen, money will change hands, and the new ownership is established. The new owner by this point will want to be fully prepared for ownership, with post-ownership plans in place (sometimes called *100-day plans* or *integration plans* depending on the process). Many otherwise great deals go sour at this point because private equity and other owners, schooled in the ability to make deals, fail to create effective plans and implement them quickly. A good integration plan will establish the groundwork for future company growth, a poorly executed one at best may create a 12-month delay in getting benefits.

9. *Integration*—in the context of "trade sales" where the buyer is another company in the same or related industry, this will mean integration of the purchased business with an acquiring business—often with restructuring of staff, closure of facilities, and many other classic merger opportunities captured as quickly as possible. Where the acquirer is a pure investor or private equity fund, the

integration phase will be about delivering on their investment thesis (more about this later).

11.3   CIRCUMSTANCES INFLUENCE THE DUE DILIGENCE PROCESS

Different sale situations lead to very different processes; here are a few examples:

- *Go private*—a go private is where a private equity firm bids to gain control of a company through its publicly quoted stock. Depending on which stock market and jurisdiction this happens in there may be a variety of detailed rules in place, but typically the fund will need to gather a minimum level of stake (e.g., $x\%$ in the U.K.) to enable the triggering of a formal bid process. The process may be agreed by the management team or it may be contested. Such a process is likely to commence with a "stalk", where the private equity firm will gather public information, develop an investment thesis, and outline valuation. During this process the private equity firm will usually perform "pre–due diligence" work—to develop the investment thesis, establish valuation, and spot any "red flags". As the private equity firm buys up shares it will aim to gather these at the lowest price possible. If the action becomes known in the market the price will usually rocket and make the formal bid harder to achieve, so this early action is particularly sensitive. Once enough shares are owned, a formal bid will be triggered. The management of the company at this point has a duty to provide information and put in place a timeline and process. After this point the process reverts fairly closely to the standard above (albeit with more hoops and rules imposed by the market in which the shares are traded).

- *Family sale ("primary")*—this is in many respects the classic or standard process. However, families can differ widely. Where a business is first generation and the founder is still very much part of the business, it is not untypical for the process to be very much as discussed in the standard process. However, the nature of the deal analysis will need to cover the issue of succession planning in a careful way as many businesses with founders still involved can struggle when the founder steps back. Where a family business has existed for a couple of generations, however, it is not untypical for there to be substantial family politics. This can be an opportunity for the private equity firm to gather support from family members on a step-by-step basis so that a formal bid is never needed, or at least is made exclusive. In both situations it is possible for a deal to be done without a formal auction, and many primary deals are done this way. Most families though are now aware that there may be multiple bidders available and that a best offer is more likely to come from an auction (see Exhibit 11.1).

- *Sale by a private equity firm ("secondary—non-distressed")*—this will generally follow the standard process. However, there is likely to be substantially different investment theses for the different bidders involved and a quite different selection of bidders. Some private equity firms focus exclusively on primary companies— believing they offer more opportunity for efficiency improvements and returns. Other private equity firms prefer the secondary market, looking for well-run growing businesses or businesses in need of restructuring. The different perspectives can lead to different investment theses and approval and, therefore, a different focus in due diligence.

EXHIBIT 11.1

CASE EXAMPLE: FAMILY BUSINESS, OWNER WANTS TO SELL

A typical example of the kind of "primary" investment opportunity that is attractive to private equity and trade buyers is this family-run business. The business was founded in the 1970s by a scientist whose work in blood laboratories led him to identify a range of diagnostic innovations to speed up the processing of blood sampling. The company had expanded from delivery of simple diagnostic tools into specialized lab equipment and services.

A classic "primary-oriented" private equity firm did due diligence for the company. Their interest was in buying assets from private ownership or buyout—rather than from other private equity firms or banks (secondary sales). Their investment goal was to buy well-managed businesses with growth potential in solid industries.

Therefore, the key issues would be: Is the management sound? Are the factories and assets of the company in a good state for use? What potential is there for profit improvement? Is there scope for driving working capital improvements?

The private equity firm engaged several consultants to help: a Big-4 accountancy to look at the company financials to verify the underlying profitability and check the accounts; another consultancy to review the company's market, competitors, and the likelihood of the company's growth predictions being achievable; a consultant to look at the company's operations, manufacturing plants, cost base, and operating effectiveness. In addition they contracted lawyers to review contracts and the legal structure.

For the consultant, the due diligence process in this case started with access to a physical data room where all the accountants, lawyers, and other consultants sat crowded elbow to elbow and read documents like crazy to absorb as much as possible in a limited timespan. In this case the company was very concerned about information leakage, so it refused to allow even photocopies to leave the room. Now, thankfully, physical data rooms are a rare occurrence as most sales use the web to deliver data in a "virtual data room".

- *Distressed restructuring ("secondary—distressed")*—where a business gets into trouble, the private equity firm may find itself "under water" and new capital will be sought. This can come via either further capital from existing equity holders, the banks, or from new equity through a form of auction. A whole range of alternative processes can ensue during such a period.

11.4 DEAL ANALYSIS AND DUE DILIGENCE DURING THE SALE PROCESS

In its broadest sense, deal analysis may have commenced well before a company comes up for sale. The previous stage is the process of looking for and finding candidate assets. During this process many companies will have been reviewed and assessed. However, that assessment will only identify potential opportunities. At the point where a deal becomes real and possible, deal analysis will start in earnest. Deal analysis is the process by which the private equity firm develops a clean view of the value, potential, and possible risks of an asset. It goes on through pre due diligence, due diligence, and

EXHIBIT 11.2

DEAL ANALYSIS AND DILIGENCE PROCESS

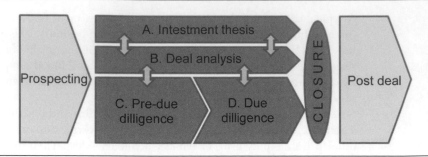

EXHIBIT 11.3

DETAILED COMPONENTS OF DEAL ANALYSIS AND DILIGENCE

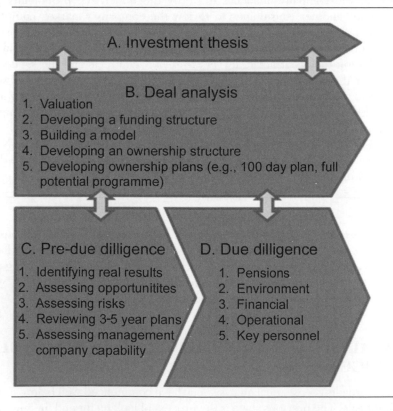

closure of the deal. Deal analysis should be informed throughout by an investment thesis which is, at its simplest, a summary of the reasoning behind buying the business (i.e., how does the private equity fund believe it will make money?) (see Exhibits 11.2 and 11.3).

11.4.1 Investment thesis

This is the driving force of the work undertaken during a deal. It is also, iteratively, one of the key results. Take, for example, two private equity firms. One is looking to buy into growing IT software suppliers to the financial sector. Their fund thesis is finding growth-minded companies at an emerging stage. A second private equity firm is looking to buy and build around a portfolio company it already owns which provides outsourcing to banks.

While the first firm will focus deal analysis and diligence on market growth, management capability, R&D capability, etc. and will very likely hire consultants to assist with both commercial and operational due diligence that focuses on basic capability, the second firm on the other hand will focus on potential overlaps, synergies, and costs and may be much more heavily focused, therefore, on operational due diligence (Exhibit 11.4).

Expressing an investment thesis is often required of a private equity investment professional (whether formally or informally) as part of the internal checks and balances in the private equity firm. Understanding and testing the investment thesis is a critical skill for an investment professional. He should be able to explain in one or two statements to his investment committee or backers why this deal will make money for the fund and fit within the fund's risk profile. In addition, he will need to be very clear about what needs to be investigated and confirmed during deal analysis and diligence, what would represent a red flag to his thesis, and what factors are most important post deal to make the future happen as he would wish it. Exhibit 11.5 shows typical key aspects of the investment thesis.

The investment theses discussed above for the two private equity firms should cover points 1, 2, 3, and 4 in Exhibit 11.5. An investment thesis does not need to be complex, but it does need to be clear and point at key issues to check and at critical judgments that the private equity investment professional is making. This identification

---

EXHIBIT 11.4

ALTERNATIVE EXAMPLES OF INVESTMENT THESIS

EXHIBIT 11.5

ASPECTS OF AN INVESTMENT THESIS

High level thesis

1. Timespan	How long to own the asset?
2. Exit	IPO, trade sale, secondary, MBO?
3. Value creation principle	Revenue growth, margin improvement, overhead reduction, asset selloff, breakup, integration with others
4. Value creation actions	Reduce head office, urgent manufacturing optimization, salesforce training, market entry, etc.

More detailed thesis

5. What must be true to succeed/red flags   For example,
- management quality
- market is growing
- manufacturing plants must be able to consolidate
- etc.

---

of the judgments is viewed by some as a critical factor in the success or failure of investment professionals. With the data available to multiple potential buyers, the investment professional who spots the right way to view the sector or the company and makes good judgments about what can be done with the business has a huge advantage. He will have a better handle on the right price to pay as well as a clear view on what to do with the business if the purchase succeeds.

11.4.2   Deal analysis

Deal analysis is required irrespective of whether a formal due diligence is conducted. It is the means by which an investment professional assesses the potential value of a target, the purchase price he is prepared to recommend his private equity firm will pay, etc.

Deal analysis can be broken down into key elements as follows:

1. Valuation.

2. Developing a funding structure.

3. Building a model.

4. Developing an ownership structure.

5. Developing ownership plans (e.g., 100-day plan, full potential program).

Valuation

Determining an appropriate valuation is critical to the deal. In essence, of course, valuation is what someone is prepared to pay, but the key components will be:

a. The current and future EBITDA. Predicting future revenue and earnings growth in the light of understanding the market and competitive situation.

b. The multiple (i.e., price/earnings ratio) on purchase and on exit.

c. Future cash flow.

d. The value of underlying assets (particularly, if any have value that only the investment professional has understood!).

Point a.   *The key component of valuation is usually EBITDA.* An investment director will want to assess underlying EBITDA and identify whether non-recurring items distort it up or down. The adjusted real or underlying historical EBITDA is usually referred to as pro forma, and often a financial advisor will be asked to identify pro-forma EBITDA for the current year and the previous 2–3 years so that underlying trends can be seen. For example a company may have EBITDA as shown on the left in Exhibit 11.6.

However, stripping out the effects of an acquisition in 2006/07 (£10mn addition of EBITDA), the change of depreciation policies in 2008 (£3mn negative), and the release of £5mn reserves against a complex litigation in 2009 will completely change the picture. The resulting pro-forma EBITDA shows a company with zero organic growth in the past years, calling into question the management or the sector.

The second key aspect of EBITDA is predicted future performance, which comes largely from:

— Growth %

— Margin %

— Overhead %.

The most critical part of the deal analysis will be evaluating what an owner can achieve in these three key factors during ownership (assuming the investment thesis involves

---

EXHIBIT 11.6

THE IMPORTANCE OF GETTING PRO-FORMA HISTORICAL INFORMATION

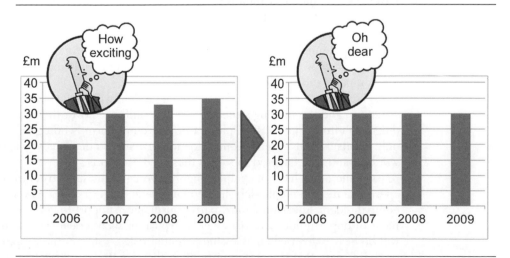

long-term ownership). Companies can grow EBITDA tenfold or more in a 3-year period through addressing one or more of these key factors.

Point b. *Multiple*. This factor is down to market factors but can be heavily influenced by:

— The company's "story"—for example, "we have built an efficient operating platform that could be the springboard for further acquisition and is also poised for organic growth" vs. "tough times ahead". Creating the right story for a company is a key component of a successful exit (see the next subsection, 'Developing a funding structure").

— Timing—multiples for an industry and the market as a whole rise and fall with the economy and "sentiment". Catching a wave can be a key part of an investment thesis (although a potentially risky one).

Point c. *Future cash flow*. The primary cash flow is usually EBITDA (and the proceeds of exit), but improving working capital, reducing capital expenditure, or freeing up cash tied up in assets are all ways in which an investment will be quickly repaid. It is not untypical for a private equity firm having invested £200mn of equity in Year 0 to have pulled out all that £200mn by cash measures within 18 months, leaving any proceeds from eventual exit as "pure profit".

Point d. Some private equity firms invest specifically in situations where the underlying assets— such as buildings, intellectual property—are in some way "impaired", so their true value is hidden. Finding a way to unlock this hidden value can change the valuation radically. In popular parlance, this might be referred to as asset stripping. However, even where disposing of assets is not a key part of the investment thesis, a view on the underlying value of physical and virtual assets is critical to striking the right price.

Developing a funding structure

In this section we are not going to cover funding structures in any detail, but rather review at a high level generic types of funding, the factors involved, and the impact this may have on due diligence and analysis.

In general, any funding structure will consist of equity, debt, and quasi-equity/debt instruments. Debt in the structure creates leverage which, with strongly growing EBITDA or value, can multiply the return to the equity holder. Unfortunately, the reverse is also true, if EBITDA falls or fails to grow, debt service can become an issue leading to the loss of the company and the investment.

The potential risk of loss is uppermost in all investors minds, so the eventual funding structure will be a reflection of the appetite for and assessment of risk in the company and the deal.

Therefore, a key aspect of constructing a deal will be formulation of the funding structure, and the funding structure will have influence over the deal analysis and due diligence effort. Put at its simplest, a private equity firm is doing an all equity deal; it only has its own investment committee to persuade, so deal analysis and due diligence will be minimally targeted to satisfy these requirements.

On the other hand, a complex highly leveraged funding structure will require the "permission" of multiple debt holders, mezzanine players, and, potentially, secondary equity holders. Substantial third-party consultancy support to generate detailed assessment of opportunities and risks will be typical of such a deal. The nature of diligence will be heavily focused on assessing potential risks—often in the form of a "downside" or "base" case that is less optimistic than the "equity" or "stretch" case.

EXHIBIT 11.7

EXAMPLE: COMPANY BOUGHT FOR £200mn, £20mn EBITDA

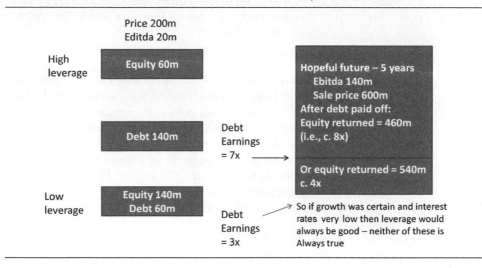

Price 200m
Editda 20m

High leverage — Equity 60m

Debt 140m — Debt Earnings = 7x →

Low leverage — Equity 140m / Debt 60m

Debt Earnings = 3x →

Hopeful future – 5 years
Ebitda 140m
Sale price 600m
After debt paid off:
Equity returned = 460m
(i.e., c. 8x)

Or equity returned = 540m
c. 4x

So if growth was certain and interest rates very low then leverage would always be good – neither of these is Always true

---

Building a model

The example funding structure shown in Exhibit 11.7 is absurdly simplified to just a beginning price/ investment and a sale price/investment. In reality, the private equity firm will need to model cash flows, the balance sheet, and covenants for a substantial period (2-to-5 years) and at monthly or quarterly intervals. The key operating measure used by equity, mezzanine, or debt providers is IRR (internal rate of return). Detailed cash flows are, therefore, modeled to allow this to be calculated.

As a minimum, a model will hold two scenarios—a "base" case and a "stretch" case, one pessimistic and the other optimistic—but often it will go further and allow for multiple scenarios. Because the value of early repayment outweighs later repayment due to cost of capital, the model will be used to develop scenarios for:

— Early debt repayment
— EBITDA enhancement
— Impact of potential risks
— Impact of alternative inflation/economic conditions
— Disposal of assets.

Constructing a model is usually kept within the private equity firm, with input demanded from different advisors as the deal analysis progresses. However, where complex modeling is required an external modeler can sometimes be contracted or one of the key advisors asked to "hold the model".

Developing an ownership structure

A large effort will often go into understanding the target company's ownership structure and designing the post-acquisition ownership structure. The aim of the first part of this is simple: to understand what assets are owned, how they are owned, what restrictions are in place, and what are the tax and legal implications of the structures?

In designing the future structure, the primary aim is usually tax planning, but the investment thesis may point towards other aims such as early breakup, integration with another portfolio company, early sale of shares to additional equity partners, IPO, etc.

Developing ownership plans

The final key part of deal analysis (too often neglected by some private equity firms) is formulation of clear plans to deliver the investment thesis. Such plans, often formalized as either a "100-day plan" or "full potential program" (or both), are especially critical when the investment thesis relies on prompt and concerted operational actions.

While outline plans are not part of due diligence, they are often requested of the consultants supporting due diligence, as an adjunct to due diligence reports. It is also true in leveraged deals where banks will want to be reassured that clear plans are in place to deliver at least the base case or better.

A typical 100-day plan would cover:

- Organizational leadership (e.g., outline of future structure, changes to the management team)
- New structures
- Delivery of key programs (outline plans including resource and time estimates) (e.g., restructuring/cost reduction, cash management, and working capital)
- Quick wins.

A typical full potential program would set out in priority order how to achieve all the key opportunities—operational and strategic—for the business over a 2-to-5-year period. It could cover:

- Manufacturing footprint optimization (such as plans to shift production to Far East manufacturing sites or to insource/outsource components)
- Cost reduction (with targets including SG&A, staff costs, material costs, sourcing, etc.)
- Sales effectiveness (plans to improve salesteam performance through training, better incentives, revised team structures, etc.)
- Organizational structure
- New products/markets (R&D focus, launch of new lines, etc.)

11.4.3 Pre–due diligence

Pre–due diligence is a process of assessment of all aspects of the target company, identification of opportunities and risks, development of plans, and identification of "red flags". This assessment comes at the stage before formal due diligence, when the private equity firm may still be on the longlist or the "long shortlist" (i.e., before exclusivity or formal due diligence access has been granted). It is typical that the degree of information access is partial through a data room—with access only to company top teams and with controlled supervised sight of a few key facilities (e.g., the main factory, R&D center, or warehouse).

Pre–due diligence assessments will typically cover the following:

1. Identifying real results.

2. Assessing opportunities.

3. Assessing risks.

4. Reviewing 3-year to 5-year plans.

5. Assessing management's capability to achieve the business plan.

Real results

Critical to the development of a clear picture of the target company is identification of the real or underlying performance. This was discussed in Section 11.4.2, "Valuation". Here we will discuss in more detail the pre–due diligence assessment to inform this view. The private equity firm may make its own determination of real results, more often it may employ external advisors to review the financial records in detail. The review will typically look at full profit and loss accounts for the previous 2–5 years:

- *Historical revenues*—broken down into sectors, products on geographies to enable understanding of trends
- *Historical EBITDA*
- *Operating margins*—broken down as per revenues where possible
- *SG&A costs*
- *Balance sheet*—with particular focus on items impacting on cash flows
- *Cash flows.*

The external advisor charged with understanding real results will typically demand time with the chief financial officer (CFO) to drill down into results, identify unusual and one-off items, and attempt to construct a view of the underlying results. The report the advisor will write will typically review each of the financial statements in detail, showing what movements are due to normal trading and what may be from one-off actions. The advisor will typically also comment on the trends identified, highlighting both positives and negatives.

Another aspect of this review will be the assessment of available budgets and forecasts. Management will usually have produced a least a budget or forecast for the next year, but often they will release to buyers their 3-to-5-year strategy or business plan. The financial due diligence report will often cover in some detail how budgets have been produced, what level of growth would be implied in the budget vs. the "run rate" of the last quarter's actual, or in other ways assess the quality and level of risk in the budget.

Generally, the private equity firm will want to see that budgets and forecasts are developed robustly and get a view whether they are aspirational (built to create hard-to-reach objectives for middle management) or realistic (built to give certainty to allow financial planning).

Assessing opportunities

The investment thesis will inform the thinking of the private equity firm on how detailed an assessment it makes during pre due diligence, but typically it will investigate:

- Opportunities for growth—product/market
- Opportunities for profit improvement
- Opportunities for cash generation and early payback of investment capital.

Opportunities for cash generation may come from better use of working capital, control of capital expenditures, or disposal of assets—each of these may be investigated.

Opportunities for growth

Opportunities for growth (revenue or "top-line" improvement) are often investigated through a review of the market or markets the target company operates in. Often, a consultancy will be tasked to identify market trends, growth areas, the positioning of the target vs. competitors, and customers. Sometimes, this review stops at general market trends, but frequently it may go further by asking detailed questions of customers or developing a prediction (base and stretch) of top-line growth, with detailed assessment of the issues and actions required to achieve it. Typically, such a growth report will list the growth potential of the market sector and the relative competitiveness of the target company within it, showing potential market risks and opportunities. For a complex business, such a report will look in detail at each of the major market segments the company can or should play within.

Opportunities for profit improvement

Opportunities for profit improvement will typically be formulated through a review of the operating capabilities of the company by a consultancy (or by an operating partner in the private equity firm). Conducting such a review will typically involve visits to key factories or facilities and detailed discussion with the CEO, COO, and other operational staff.

The review will aim to identify short, medium, and long-term opportunities for profit improvement (based on flat reviews or the results of a top-hire review). Opportunities will range from quick wins such as elimination of insurance costs or scrapped sourcing to restructuring of manufacturing facilities, which could take 18 months or more to deliver. Developing a prioritized list of such opportunities will feed into both the model being developed and the base-and-stretch valuation that is used by the private equity firm to decide its bid.

Assessing risks

Analysis of risks breaks down into three broad categories, but will as ever depend on circumstances:

- Market risk
- Operational/Business risk
- Environmental/Legal.

Market risk is a key element of the work of the "top-hire" review conducted by the private equity firm or by independent consultants. The key risk is systematic market risk (e.g., the economic cycle in heavy industrial, construction, or retail businesses). For example, a private equity firm may decide not to pursue a deal after it concluded through market review at the pre–due diligence stage that margins in the industry are falling for all participants that do not fit with its investment philosophy.

Operational/Business risk can sometimes be harder to assess as it requires detailed assessment of the capability of company management, facilities, and staff to sustain profitable operation and growth. A third-party operations consultancy is often used to conduct such a review. The assessment will typically involve review of:

a. *Management capability risks*—is there strength, depth, and a track record to deliver the business plan? Does the management have credible plans in place to deliver short and medium-term targets? Is their sales and marketing set up to deliver ambitious growth plans? Etc.

b. *Facility risks*—do the factories have capacity for growth? Are there safety concerns? Do improving output figures hide safety shortcuts.

c. *Customer/Contractual risks*—what percentage of future revenue is already contracted or ordered? Is the order pipeline robust? What attitude are customers likely to take to a change of ownership? Some customers feel great loyalty to the owner of a business, rather than to the business itself. This is particularly true in services businesses such as recruitment. What risk is there that key salesmen will leave if new owners wish to adjust working conditions or contracts? Such risks can be tested by means of selected customer interviews, for example.

Environmental/Legal risks will typically be explored in more detail during formal due diligence, but at the pre–due diligence stage the target company will typically release information on any environmental audits for key facilities and make declarations on any ongoing/unresolved legal issues such as patent infringements or IP disputes.

A target company the authors reviewed a few years ago was a division of a much larger pharmaceutical firm. The sale included assets associated with a product that was the subject of a class action in the U.S. for an unknown/unproven number of deaths. Clearly the c. £100mn price tag for the business could have been doubted by the legal costs if the link to injury turned out to be true. Unsurprisingly, the client (and others) withdrew from the auctions when it became clear the current parent company was unwilling to exclude this product from the sale. This highlights a key point about the risks review in pre due diligence. The private equity firm wants and usually instructs its advisors to highlight major risks as early as possible in the process (before the private equity firm wastes millions in fees!).

Reviewing 3-year to 5-year plans

In many cases the target company's management will have developed a 2, 3, or 5-year "business plan" or "strategic plan". Where such a plan exists and is provided to bidders a key task in pre due diligence will be to validate the plan and to develop a view on the "delta" or "variance" in this plan that represents the most likely conservative (base) or best (stretch) case. These will be modeled by the private equity firm and comparisons made with the management's plan. Typically, a base case will represent the more conservative assumptions on market growth combined with inclusion of only those profit improvement projects that management have demonstrated to be well founded on resourced projects. The stretch case will include projects that the advisor judges are achievable given the advisor's assessment of the potential upside areas balanced by a viewpoint on the likelihood of all good things happening being unlikely. A degree of judgment is needed here, which is the reason an experienced advisor is essential.

Base and stretch cases produced in this way can be significantly above or below the management's view, and this difference can depend greatly on the investment thesis and plans the private equity firm has (e.g., integration with another business).

The outcome of pre due diligence is a decision by the private equity firm to bid (and how much to bid) or a decision not to bid (and withdraw from the auction). That decision will be made by assessing each of the different inputs discussed above and coming to a view on whether the initial outline investment thesis is borne out by the evidence thus far.

11.4.4 Due diligence

The pre–due diligence stage investigates issues to the best level possible by means of data and access made available by the target to the private equity firm and other bidders. It enables the private equity firm to either make a bid or decide to withdraw without bidding. Assuming the private equity firm wins the bidding or gets through to the exclusivity round, the formal due diligence stage will start. During formal due diligence a range of specific issues can be reviewed with full access. This full access stage can last from 1–2 weeks to 1–2 months. Only in exceptional circumstances would a firm want to spend substantially longer on the process as it is highly distracting to management and staff.

Normally, formal due diligence is set up as follows:

- A specific period of time is allowed
- Only specific and pre-agreed issues are explored (those that can affect price)
- Detailed discussions/negotiations will go on in parallel to finalize the deal.

Typical issues that will be included in this formal due diligence review would be:

1. Pensions.
2. Environment.
3. Financial.
4. Operational.
5. Key personnel.

Pensions review

The exact state of the company's pension plans is often a subject for review at the due diligence stage simply because the potential liabilities can sometimes substantially exceed the scale of current profitability. The new owner could suffer a cash outflow and potential loss if it became apparent that the company pension needed to have its funding increased. Bidders will want to ensure they are aware of any potential risks ahead of time so they can take this into account in the price they pay. These days the key pension risk is underfunding, which may require future cash injections from the company, but other technical risks will be looked at (not discussed in detail here).

Environment review

At the pre–due diligence stage, the environmental review will typically have identified potential risks or issues. With full access to sites of concern, these will now be investigated and risks guaranteed. An environmental review may involve a detailed review of documentation to ensure permissions and regulations have been complied with or, in some circumstances, it may include onsite surveys of biological or chemical controls. The nature of the review will be determined by the types of potential risks identified during pre due diligence.

Financial review

Usually, most financial diligence will have been completed during pre due diligence. However, certain issues may have been raised by the bidder as part of a "qualified" bid. These could include, for example, waiting to see details on the most current trading figures before closing the deal or asking for a copy of all current orders and contracts to ensure that stated revenues/orders are not falsified. Hence, a full open-access review of the books may be part of due diligence, where this is considered necessary. For example, it would be unusual for a company to offer customer-specific information during pre due diligence but in the full access period this may be made available.

Operational review

Typically, most operational assessments will have been performed during pre due diligence but, where access at that stage was very limited or concerns were raised about specific assets or issues, a more detailed operational review may be incorporated in due diligence. For example, a target company the authors reviewed in pre due diligence had major factories in Europe, but a joint venture in China produced over 30% of its products. The European factories were visited and assessed in pre–due diligence, but access to the joint venture was reserved until exclusivity was granted, so a visit to the Chinese facility became part of the due diligence process.

Key personnel review

Occasionally, there will be concern that key personnel may leave the company on a change of ownership. In such circumstances, a retention assessment may be conducted during due diligence to identify key personnel who may need to be incentivized to stay. Incentives may be equity, bonuses, or other measures.

11.5 MOTIVES/PERSPECTIVES OF STAKEHOLDERS

In the discussions above, we focused on processes very much from the point of view of the buyer—the private equity firm. It is useful to consider other stakeholders in the process and discuss their perspective. We will now consider the views, issues, and concerns of:

- The seller
- The management
- The lending banks and other financial backers
- The advisors to the private equity company.

11.5.1 The seller perspective

For obvious reasons in the sale process, sellers are generally interested to maximize their return. As a result, they will run whatever processes they feel will achieve this end with their advisors. If there is likely to be a lot of interest from multiple parties, then it makes sense to spread the net wide. However, return is rarely the only motivation. The seller may often be concerned to retain control over the path the company takes—for reasons of sentiment, continued involvement of family members or a belief that there is more money to be made even after a change of ownership.

To reiterate, sellers will do all in their power to maximize the price of the sale, and for this reason the buyer needs to be wary, hence the underlying need for due diligence. However, a successful private equity firm must also take into account the other interests of the seller and not simply assume that money is everything. It rarely is that simple.

11.5.2 The management perspective

The interest of senior management is rarely fully aligned with either the existing owner or the new owner. They will generally have a financial interest in maximizing the price for the sale. Indeed, they have a duty to the shareholders to act in this way but, on the other hand, if they expect to participate in the business going forward they also have an interest in ensuring it is not saddled with enormous debt and will be wanting to encourage the buyer to give them a strong incentive to stay and perform. In short, they will be looking for the most attractive deal for them, and that is unlikely to be the highest purchase price. In addition, the price paid will in large part depend on the likely future EBITDA flow, yet whatever plan underpins that will be the one that the management will have to try to deliver.

The result is that the management is usually in a state of tension between creating an optimistic future plan to show themselves in a good light and sell the business for the existing owners and downplaying the potential, so they can keep good news and opportunities in their own back pockets.

The bidder and its advisors will try very hard during the sales process to get to know the management, to understand their commitment to the plans in place, whether there are hidden opportunities, or whether there is exaggeration.

11.5.3 The lender perspective

Lenders generally want the highest fees possible with the lowest risk. The bidder will want to present as much evidence as possible that risks are low, so that it can borrow more at the lowest possible price. Lenders are well aware of this and, therefore, are very likely to insist on reading not just what the private equity firm has to say on risk, but they will want to explore the views of the management (as set out in the information memorandum) and views of the advisors. This puts advisors in a powerful but perilous position.

Lenders will demand more information and reassurance the higher the perceived risk. What generates risk for a lender is economic uncertainty, political risk, market risk, operational risk, and financial risk (leverage, cash flow, etc.). The more one or other of these factors are a concern the more the lenders will want to explore the deal—and the more costly and time consuming will be the due diligence process.

11.5.4 The advisor perspective

Advisors to private equity firm bidders have a number of conflicting issues to contend with. The client is the private equity firm that hired them, so it is in the private equity firm's interests to provide good advice and ample warning of key risks, but if that advice is overly cautious about every conceivable risk the private equity firm is unlikely to invest and will over time question whether the advice is too cautious, especially when they see competitors outbidding it. Similarly, the advisor is in many cases mindful of potential fees from getting to know the management team well. There may be future work to support the management if a deal goes through.

Underlying these tensions, there is the real and considerable risk of being sued, since the advice provided is typically "relied upon". Providing advice on such a reliance basis essentially means the advisor agrees to give a degree of indemnity to the recipients of this advice by ensuring the advice is not false or fraudulent. When due diligence fees ranging from £150,000 to over a £1mn are set against potential suits that could range into many tens or hundreds of millions, there is a disproportionate risk to the profit and reputation of the advisor.

A private equity firm would be well advised to understand these pressures when it demands certain forms of reassurance from advisors, particularly when this advice is going to be passed to banks. The simple rule of thumb is: the more you insist on creating reliance, the more bland the advice will be. If you want to get no-holds-barred advice from a consultant, then get it off the record on a non-reliance basis; if you want reliance, then expect little more than a low-risk base case from them.

12

Leveraged buyout transactions

12.1 INTRODUCTION

A leveraged buyout (LBO) is the acquisition by a private equity (PE) fund of a company, business unit, or group of assets (the target) using debt to finance the majority of the purchase price and equity for the remainder. If the target is a public company, the private equity firm may pay a premium of 15% to 50% over the current stock price (e.g., see the academic evidence provided by Kaplan, 1989; Bargeron et al., 2008). LBO transactions take many different forms with varying levels of leverage, size, required returns, or other dimensions. This chapter aims to describe the "typical" LBO transaction.

The amount of *debt* used is typically around 65% to 70% of the target's purchase price, but has reached around 90% on some deals during the peak transaction years— hence the term "leveraged buyout". The LBO buyer (also known as the *LBO sponsor*) raises the debt through bonds and/or bank loans issued by the target company. The debt is either secured against the target's assets or is unsecured, and the target's free cash flows are used to service and repay the debt. The debt almost always includes a loan portion that is senior and secured, and is arranged by a bank or an investment bank. In the 1980s and 1990s, banks were also the primary investors in these loans. More recently, however, institutional investors have purchased a large fraction of senior and secured loans.[1] The debt in leveraged buyouts also often includes a junior unsecured portion that is financed by either high-yield bonds or "mezzanine debt" (i.e., debt that is subordinated to senior debt).

The *equity* portion of the purchase price is typically provided through a PE fund. These are private investment vehicles made up of limited partners (LPs) and general partners (GPs) who manage the fund and its investments in return for a compensation structure based on fixed management fees and on the performance of the fund (carried interest). The new management team of the purchased company (which may or may not be identical to the pre-buyout management team) typically contributes to the new equity, although the amount is usually a small fraction of the equity contributed.

---

1. These investors include hedge fund investors and "collateralized loan obligation" managers, who combine a number of term loans into a pool and then carve the pool into different pieces (with different seniorities) to sell to institutional investors.

This chapter has been co-authored with Mike Glossop (MBA, London Business School) and Bjoern Koertner (MBA, London Business School).

The objective of the PE fund is to hold the target for a relatively short period, typically around 4–7 years and, then, sell the company with the scope of realizing a relatively high financial return on the original equity investment. The target return on equity, measured using the internal rate of return (IRR), is normally required to be 20%. PE funds use a combination of three principal mechanisms to achieve this financial objective:

1. Increase the target firm's value through operational improvements that boost the target's revenues and earnings.

2. Pay down the debt taken to acquire the target using the target's free cash flows from operations, thereby increasing the equity portion in the capital structure of the company.

3. Sell the target company when market conditions are favorable.

12.1.1 Historical perspective

While the first LBOs took place in 1901, when J.P. Morgan acquired Carnegie Steel Company for USD480mn, using debt for acquisitions was considered a questionable financing technique before the 1980s. Before the 1980s, in spite of some early transactions, leveraging was a rare financing technique, as most companies felt uncomfortable with high leverage.

In the early 1980s, various newly founded dedicated buyout firms emerged. These firms profited from LBOs of undervalued corporate assets and subsequent asset stripping and financial engineering. This period created a very negative public image of PE firms. They were called *corporate raiders* and books such as *Barbarians at the Gate* highlighted questionable practices. However, a new generation of managers felt more comfortable with high levels of debt, and the buyout industry thrived. While only four deals with an aggregate value of USD1.7bn were reported for 1980, 410 buyouts with an aggregate value of USD188bn took place in 1988 (Olsen et al., 2003). The first boom ended after the crash of the junk bond market and several high-profile bankruptcies of overleveraged PE-owned companies in the late 1980s.

In the early 2000s, interest rates decreased, lending standards were relaxed, especially for high-yield financing, and stock markets quickly recovered from the burst of the internet bubble. According to Roxburgh et al. (2009), worldwide PE fundraising jumped from USD71bn in 2004 to USD198bn in 2005, USD281bn in 2006, and USD301bn in 2007. These conditions fed the biggest LBO boom in history: the transactions volume jumped to USD581bn in 2007. This volume was mainly driven by so-called megadeals (LBOs with a transaction value in excess of USD3bn), that made up USD331bn or 57% of the 2007 deal volume. Some of the megadeals included high-profile companies such as the Hospital Corporation of America, Alliance Boots, TXU Energy, and Chrysler.

The financial crisis and the connected collapse of the high-yield bond market ended this second LBO boom. The credit crisis seriously hit the availability of debt and equity. LBO fundraising fell from USD301bn in 2007 to USD89bn in 2009 (Q1 annualized numbers). Even more alarmingly, the new syndicated debt issuance to PE funds fell to USD12bn in Q4 2008, which represented only 4% of its peak of USD283bn in Q1 2007 (Roxburgh et al., 2009). In addition, the cost of credit dramatically increased. As a consequence of these adverse factors, LBO activity dramatically decreased from USD581bn in 2007 to only USD150bn in 2008, with just USD18bn in Q4 2008.

Sixty-four percent of the decline was due to the virtual disappearance of megadeals (USD54bn in 2008, down 84% from USD331bn in 2007).

12.1.2   Lessons learned

Besides the presence of a favorable regulatory treatment and the availability of interesting target companies, the activity of the buyout industry depends predominantly on the availability of equity from LPs and cheap debt as well as the development of the stock market. All these elements tend to be scarce during economic downturns and available in excess in good times, thus making the buyout industry inherently dependent on economic conditions and explaining why buyouts happen in waves.

Given recent developments, the buyout industry is likely to follow three important trends:

1. *Greater focus on operational improvements*—due to the tightening of debt markets and the commoditization of value creation by financial leverage, operational improvements are becoming increasingly important. Hence, PE firms will be able increasingly to differentiate themselves based on active management capabilities and industry knowledge.

2. *Greater industry specialization of PE firms*—in the early days of private equity, many PE firms were accused of achieving their returns by asset stripping and financial engineering. Because these activities are very similar across industries, PE firms and their GPs were mostly generalists. However, recently value creation shifted to operational improvements that require deep industry knowledge and operational experience. Hence, the industry specialization of PE firms and the emergence of sector groups within large PE firms that can already be observed are likely to intensify in the future.

3. *Greater diversification of PE firms' revenues away from buyouts*—in the decade from 1998 to 2008, the buyout revenue share of the PE industry declined from 57% to 44%. The same period saw growth in infrastructure, real estate, and other investments such as distressed debt. Moreover, PE firms started to provide more advisory services to their portfolio companies. These trends are likely to continue.

12.2   LBO EXECUTION: THE DEAL PROCESS

The analysis of LBOs requires knowledge of many concepts, theories, and instruments. For example, knowledge of the different debt and equity instruments as well as ways to determine the debt capacity of a company is needed to understand the capital structure of buyouts. Even more importantly, LBO values and financing structures are built on a huge number of assumptions and decisions that interact with each other in very complex ways. Understanding these complex interactions is critical to understanding and structuring an LBO.

We start with a very basic description of the five stages of an LBO deal transaction process, as shown below and in Exhibit 12.1.

Stage 1.   *Screening of deal opportunities*. The first stage is to source and screen opportunities. Potential deals are sourced by the general partners in the PE firm, using personal networks including experts, CEOs, and investment bankers. Once a potential deal is sourced an initial screening is conducted to shortlist opportunities. This screening is based on readily available information (which varies between public and private companies).

EXHIBIT 12.1

THE FIVE STAGES OF AN LBO TRANSACTION

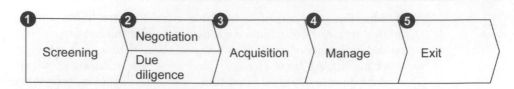

Due to the very specific characteristics of an LBO, a potential LBO target must be able to service a high leverage, have potential exit opportunities within a 5-to-10-year horizon, and have the potential to achieve a 20%+ IRR. Hence, choosing appropriate companies is a central element of the work of a PE firm.

Finding a suitable target for an LBO is mostly about finding companies that have unused debt capacity. The following characteristics are typical for a strong LBO candidate:

1. *Low current leverage*—a company with low current leverage allows the PE investor to benefit from the value created by higher leverage. However, given that this effect is a commodity and every financial investor can benefit from it, the value created by financial leverage might be included in the sale price already. In this case, the seller is benefiting from it and not the PE firm.

2. *Predictable and strong cash flows*—high leverage with acceptable interest rates and risk is only possible if the company can reliably service the interest and principal repayments. In theory, the value of the equity in the target will increase as debt is amortized. Thus, the ideal targets have strong and especially predictable free cash flows which are normally consequences of the following characteristics:

   - A long history of stable operating cash flows
   - The company's market is at a mature stage
   - The firm has a leading and defensible market position
   - The firm owns strong brand names
   - The firm's customers have a stable demand
   - The firm sells its products and services through long-term sales contracts
   - Low capital expenditure requirements are needed to service the customers.

The target should have a leading and defensible market position. This is often the case in industries where extensive R&D, investments, technology, or patents are needed in order to enter the market. Another significant entry barrier is the brand name. Being a well-known and respected brand often means a larger market share and, therefore, stronger sales figures than the competitors. Companies with a strong market position and brand name are often able to generate steady cash flows.

3. *Strong asset base*—an asset base is strong if it includes a large amount of tangible assets that have a high market value and are liquid. High market values and liquidity require assets that are not too specific to the company's business and

have a large number of potential buyers. A strong asset base can be used as collateral when taking on bank debt. Hence, it facilitates achieving high leverage at reasonable interest rates. A strong asset base also acts as a barrier to entry for competitors and, therefore, makes cash flows more predictable and secure. However, while a strong asset base is helpful, it is not a necessary precondition for an LBO. Companies with a weak asset base might still be good LBO candidates if their cash flows are so strong and predictable that debt can be secured against these cash flows.

4. *Operational improvement opportunities*—while financial leverage was the key value driver of PE returns for a long period of time, operational improvements are becoming more important in the current market. Hence, the PE firm needs to identify opportunities for operational improvements that have not yet been exploited or that competitor buyers cannot see.

5. *Growth opportunities*—growth opportunities that are not fully included in the purchase price or that can be generated by the improvements the PE firm introduces also make a company a stronger LBO candidate. Realizable growth opportunities ensure that it is possible for the company to grow during the holding period. Above-expectation growth helps to pay back the debt earlier, generates a higher EBITDA and exit value, and might positively affect the exit multiple. It also makes it possible for the company to take on more debt and still meet the covenants. Beyond that, high growth makes it easier for the company to benefit from economies of scale and, therefore, get better profit margins. Further, it increases the chances of an IPO, an often more lucrative exit option. However, this characteristic is more important for the growth capital sector of the PE industry than it is for the LBO sector.

6. *Exit options*—because the funds raised by PE firms are usually time bound and because their performance is largely evaluated based on the time-weighted IRRs, having a variety of potential exit options in a time horizon of 2 to 7 years is critical. Hence, being attractive to potential strategic buyers, having the potential to do an IPO (due to location, operational history, maturity of processes, etc.), and being located in an active PE market with multiple financial buyers supports the suitability of a company for an LBO.

7. *Availability of a strong management team*—a strong management team is absolutely critical to deliver under the high-leverage, fast-pace, and high-exit pressure. The high levels of debt in the financial structure of portfolio companies after an LBO transaction place greater demands on management to operate the company more efficiently. If the existing management is strong enough to deliver under these conditions, the PE investor will typically keep them and closely align management's incentives with large equity stakes or ratchets. However, if the PE firm considers the existing management weak, it will bring in new management with experience in LBOs and in the respective industry. Hence, a strong LBO candidate either has a strong management team in place or is in an industry and situation for which the PE firm can replace them.

Other considerations

Firm size. While we have now seen seven characteristics a strong LBO candidate should have, some other characteristics still have to be discussed. Strong LBO candidates exist in various different sizes. The use of debt and the existence of large buyout funds enable

PE firms to buy very large companies. However, the maximum size of buyouts that can be financed by PE funds highly depends on the availability of debt and the availability of equity from LPs. In the boom buyout period between 2005 and 2007 the cheap debt and large amount of abundant capital led to large LBO deals.[2]

The targeted minimum and maximum size of buyouts is an element of the strategy of individual funds. The maximum size is usually limited by the size of the fund, rules that only allow GPs to invest a specific percentage of the fund in one target (e.g., 20%), and the debt capacity of the target. However, club deals (cooperation of multiple PE firms in one deal) and co-investments enable even larger deal sizes.

The effort it takes to manage an LBO used to be relatively independent of the size of the buyout. Hence, PE firms and, especially, the supporting investment banks that are paid based on deal value, used to prefer big deals. However, with the emerging focus on operational improvements instead of financial leverage, the effort per deal seems to be much more size driven than before. Hence, a priori preference towards big deals is getting less prominent.

Ownership structure. In order to acquire a company for a reasonable price, the ownership structure of the target plays an important role. A suitable LBO candidate should have concentrated ownership with few major stockholders. As owners with less than 10% of the shares cannot affect the premium level of the deal, the focus of the PE firm is on getting an acceptance on the bid price from the majority owners. Being able to discuss the premium with fewer shareholders increases the possibility of reaching an agreement at a lower cost.

Geography. PE firms can find strong LBO candidates in various geographies. However, in practice, the U.S. and U.K. are the countries with the most active buyout market. This is not due to the characteristics of the targets, but due to the maturity of the PE industry and the regulatory environment.

Industry. Strong buyout candidates can in theory exist in nearly all industries. However, some industries show a significantly higher activity of buyouts because they better enable the fulfilment of the seven favorable characteristics listed above. For example, consumer products/services and business products/services as well as telecommunication and energy are sectors with very high LBO activity, mainly due to vast tangible assets and strong and predictable cash flows. In contrast to this, high-tech companies are very rarely LBO targets due to the mainly intangible assets and a fast-changing business environment that does not allow making predictable cash flow forecasts. PE firms are increasingly specialized on one industry or at least internally structured along industries to assess companies based on detailed industry knowledge and to enable operational improvements after the acquisition.

Stage 2. *Due diligence and negotiation.* Due diligence is the investigation of a target's business by the potential acquirer(s). The information used depends on the type of transaction, as shown in Exhibit 12.2.

Friendly deals typically involve a two-stage process consisting of an initial 2-to-3-week due diligence to submit a non-binding offer for shortlisting, followed by a more in-depth due diligence and, possibly, exclusivity. Hostile deals involve a shorter single-stage process and, clearly, there is no information provided by the target. Many LBOs are hostile and the due diligence process must rely on publicly available

2. For example, the buyout of TXU Energy in 2007 for USD45bn, the buyout of Equity Office Properties Trust in 2007 for USD39bn, and the buyout of the Hospital Corporation of America for USD32.7bn in 2006 (Sorkin, 2007; CNNMoney.com, 2007). In contrast, after the financial crisis in 2009, the so-called megadeals (more than USD3bn value) disappeared.

EXHIBIT 12.2

DUE DILIGENCE INFORMATION SOURCES BY DEAL TYPE

	Friendly	**Hostile**
Public	• Information memorandum	• Public accounts
	• Management and statutory accounts	• Annual reports
	• Management team	• Analyst reports
	• Analyst reports	• Company website
	• Expert opinion	
Private	• Information memorandum	• Press coverage
	• Management accounts	• Expert opinion
	• Management team	• Insider contacts
	• Expert opinion	• Company website

---

information or expert advisors to form assumptions and forecasts for the analysis of the deal.

Due diligence is a complicated process where every aspect of the target company is evaluated in order to understand how the company works and what potential risks are associated with the investment. Complete due diligence is seldom done in-house. Here most firms contract consultants such as Alix Partners, McKinsey, Bain, BCG, etc. Sometimes PE firms have the competence to carry out certain parts of the due diligence process while others are outsourced. Due diligence can normally take 2 to 6 months but can be done faster (and imperfectly) if there is time pressure to get a deal before other bidders. Due to the fact that due diligence is a costly and time-consuming process, a *letter of intent* is written before the PE firm starts to engage in full due diligence. This letter gives the PE firm the exclusive right to buy the target during a specific timeframe. The due diligence process can be split into four different areas (see Rosenbloom, 2002 for a more detailed presentation and Exhibit 12.3):

1. *Strategic due diligence* for LBOs aims to understand the target's market, competitive position, and customers, with a focus on future growth, margins, and free cash flows for debt repayment. This could include an analysis of market size, growth rate, lifecycle (i.e., emerging, mature, or declining), and an understanding of who the customers are and how they are segmented. It should also analyze the competitive environment, market shares, strategy, and potential response to the deal. The acquirer will also want to understand the potential barriers to entry, such as high capital expenditure, and the potential exit opportunities or barriers to exit. Finally, there should be an analysis of regulatory and technology issues and risks.

2. *Operational due diligence* is often combined with strategic due diligence under the umbrella term of *commercial due diligence*. The main purpose is to develop sound and defendable assumptions as the basis for deal structuring and to identify potential areas for value creation through operational improvements. The latter is normally achieved using a benchmarking study of close competitors, based on key

EXHIBIT 12.3

THE FOUR STAGES OF THE DUE DILIGENCE PROCESS

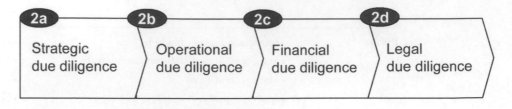

ratios specific to each industry. For example, does the target have a very high COGS compared with other similar retail businesses, and does this present a risk which should be incorporated in the purchase price or a value creation opportunity? Finally, this stage in the due diligence process will evaluate the incumbent management team and their ability to deliver the proposed strategy for the deal, identifying any key positions that the acquirer will need to fill.

3. *Financial and accounting due diligence* includes corroborating the target's historic financial statements and supporting the development of future assumptions. The acquirer must first check the financial information the target has provided or, in the case of a hostile deal, make estimates using experts and third parties. Accounting due diligence aims to verify the reasonableness of the judgments the target has made in presenting its financial statements. This is particularly important in a friendly deal where the target has prepared itself for sale. In this case many sellers are tempted to inflate their performance by using very aggressive accounting judgments.

4. *Legal due diligence* is like detective work to analyze the target's contractual obligations to all third parties (e.g., customers, suppliers, debtors, creditors, government, etc.) in order to uncover any negative aspects of the deal or potential future liabilities.

Overall, the focus of the due diligence process will vary depending on time, available information, the target's business area, and the importance of the deal to the acquirer. The combination of the different due diligence activities should be well coordinated to provide coherent and robust analysis of the characteristics of the LBO candidate, the potential structuring of the deal, and sensitivity analysis regarding operational, entry, and exit assumptions.

Stage 3. *Acquisition of the target*. The acquisition process varies depending on the type of deal. For proprietary deals where the buyer has exclusivity, the process will involve the GPs of the PE firm, their buy-side advisors, and the target's management team and sell-side advisors. For competitive deals the management team are normally less involved, but may be allied with a particular buyer.

The buyer must creatively structure financing to maximize returns and align stakeholder interests. The acquisition price will be a balance between achieving the required return of the fund and the competition for the deal or the expectation of the seller. The price the buyer needs to pay is normally defined by the market conditions, the competition for the deal, and the relative power of the seller (i.e., is it a forced seller or can it negotiate hard on the deal?). In this stage, the PE firm will create an LBO model to support the deal-structuring process and to ensure that, given the price the buyer needs to pay in order to close the deal, the required return on equity will be achieved (see Chapter 13 on LBO modeling).

To find the optimal structure for the deal, in-depth knowledge about typical legal and financial structures and available debt instruments (sources) is required.

Financial structure

The debt structure of an LBO varies depending on the target, the investor, and market conditions, but a typical structure, depending on market conditions, would be 50% to 70% debt and 50% to 30% equity. We illustrate in Exhibit 12.4 a structure with 70% debt and 30% equity.

While high leverage has benefits in terms of enhancing equity returns, it also has negative consequences related to the costs of financial distress. High leverage means targets that were previously investment grade are downgraded to non-investment grade by the ratings agencies, thus increasing the cost of debt financing.

As shown in Exhibit 12.4, the debt structure incorporates a range of instruments with varying degrees of risk and return to suit a range of different investors. In general, higher seniority and security equates to lower risk and a lower required return (interest rate) for debt investors. Bank loans that finance the LBO are typically issued by investment banks through a syndicate of lenders which can include institutional investors such as hedge funds, collateralized loan obligations (these are vehicles that

EXHIBIT 12.4

EXAMPLE OF AN LBO CAPITAL STRUCTURE

Standard and Poors' computed averages for the period 1999-2008				Seniority
Debt 70%	Senior	45%	Revolver facility Senior term debt Tranche A Tranche B Tranche C Tranche D	High
	Junior	20%	Subordinated debt High-yield bonds	
	Mezzanine	5%	Convertible debt	
Equity 30%			Preferred stock Common stock	Low

buy loans and issue bonds to finance the purchases), or pension funds.[3] Their interest rates are floating and are computed as LIBOR plus a margin that reflects a credit premium. Such spread margins are negotiated for each debt facility and are affected by conditions in the debt market as well as the risk associated with each loan. Typically, interest rates would be around LIBOR + 3% for the revolver and senior debt, LIBOR + 6% for the subordinated debt, and higher for mezzanine debt. These levels depend, of course, on the financial health of the target company but also on the covenants and other terms attached to each debt instrument.

The senior bank debt will contain more stringent debt covenants which require the target company to maintain a designated credit profile based on financial ratios such as the leverage ratio, interest service coverage ratio, and debt service coverage ratio. In addition, the covenants may severely restrict the operational flexibility of the company by not allowing asset dispositions, additional debt, or changes in ownership. Senior debt is somewhat flexible with varying collateral and covenant packages as well as amortization schedules. It generally covers 25% to 50% of the total financing needed for the deal.

The issuance of corporate bonds is an additional more expensive source of financing if senior debt is used up. Because of the inherently high leverage levels associated with an LBO, these bonds are usually rated non-investment grade by rating agencies. Thus, bonds issued through an LBO are often referred to as "high-yield" or in some cases "junk" bonds because of the relative high risk associated with this type of investment. The typical term of these bonds is 6 to 10 years (they usually mature after the senior debt). They have yearly payments of interest and the repayment of the principal is at maturity. This form of debt is often structured as 20% to 40% of the total deal cost. The main buyers of these bonds are pension funds, insurance companies, hedge funds, or other institutional and private investors.

Mezzanine debt is a highly negotiated instrument between PE firms and their debt providers. It is typically tailored to meet the financing needs of the specific LBO transaction and needs to meet a certain return level for its investors. As such, it allows for great flexibility in structuring terms. Mezzanine debt typically has embedded warrants attached to it and provides between 0% and 10% of the total funding needed. This incremental capital comes at a cost below that of equity, with the purpose of enabling PE firms to stretch the leverage level and pay a higher purchase price when alternative capital sources are inaccessible.

The equity capital in an LBO comprises 20% to 60% of the total capital. This figure varies over time and is highly dependable on conditions in the debt market and the preferred level of financial risk. This equity contribution provides a cushion to lenders and bondholders in the event that the financial condition of the LBO target deteriorates. The management often invests in equity with the PE firm. For very large LBOs several PE firms may team up to create a consortium of buyers, thereby reducing the amount of each individual PE fund's equity contribution (these are known as club deals).

Exhibit 12.5 shows a breakdown of the debt elements of an LBO transaction into four categories: senior, revolver, subordinated, and mezzanine debt. There may also be an existing debt element, but this is usually repaid as part of the transaction. Exhibit

---

3. Institutional investors have become increasingly important lenders in the past few years. Their position as buyers of leveraged pay-in-kind bonds has also been used in the financing structure. These instruments give the issuer the option of meeting interest payments either in cash or through the issuance of new bonds.

EXHIBIT 12.5

COMPARISON OF CHARACTERISTICS OF DEBT INSTRUMENTS

	Senior bank debt	Revolver	Subordinated/ Junior debt	Mezzanine debt
Description	Bank debt, normally has 3–4 tranches with varying risk/return	Flexible loan which can be repaid and reborrowed at any point during the facility (similar to a bank overdraft)	High-yield debt—non-investment grade loans	Hybrid instrument—between debt and equity
Source	IBs and institutional investors	IBs and institutional investors	IBs, institutional investors, hedge funds, etc.	Specialist mezzanine funds or syndicated by the senior debt providers
Secured	Yes—fixed or floating charge over the target assets	Yes	No	No
Seniority	Highest	After senior bank debt	After senior bank and revolver	After senior and high-yield debt
Covenants	Yes—highly restrictive	Possibly	No	No
Interest rate	Floating rates based on a benchmark rate (e.g., LIBOR) plus a spread (margin). Spread is dependent on various factors including the amount of leverage, quality of security from the assets, and credit profile	On the drawn-down portion—rates are similar to senior debt and based on benchmark plus spread	High coupon rates to compensate for the higher risk level	Higher interest rates compared with high-yield bonds—expected returns on mezzanine debt are in the mid to high teens
Maturity and repayment schedule	Long-term debt with a defined repayment schedule for interest and principle	Ongoing facility	Interest only with a "bullet" principle repayment at the maturity date (7-to-10-year maturity)	Interest only. Option to convert to equity
Fees	Arrangement fee	Arrangement fee and commitment fee on the undrawn portion	Arrangement fee	Arrangement fee
Additional information		Used to fund working capital requirements and occasionally funds part of the purchase price	Enables the issuer to significantly increase leverage beyond what is available in the secured loan market. Option of payment-in-kind (PIK) interest—paying interest in the form of additional notes—enables issuer to preserve cash during downturns or initial investment/growth periods	Quasi-entity to prioritize new owners ahead of existing equity owners in the event of bankruptcy. For the investor it offers the potential to share in any equity upside due to the convertibility option

12.5 shows a summary of these main debt elements with their characteristics. The financing structure is initially determined using estimates based on the breakdown in Exhibit 12.4, the determination of debt capacity rules employed by the banks, and the lenders' requirements regarding covenants and debt service ratios. The structure is then optimized using the LBO model as described in Chapter 13 on LBO modeling.

Legal structure

A certain legal structure that facilitates LBO transactions has developed over time. As can be seen in Exhibit 12.6 which presents the typical structure, in a first step the equity contributed by the LBO fund is invested in a new "parent company". This

---

EXHIBIT 12.6

TYPICAL LEGAL STRUCTURE OF AN LBO

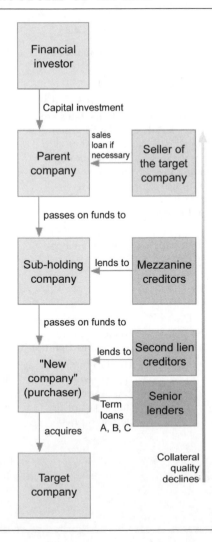

company then purchases a 100% stake in a "subholding company", which, in turn, takes over the "new company". This latter company is formed for the sole purpose of acquiring the target portfolio company.

This legal setup facilitates the financing structure of the LBO where different providers of debt capital in the transaction receive different levels of protection. Senior loans are granted to the "new company", which makes it easier to gain quick access to the cash flows and the collateral provided by the target company. Although of equal rank to term loan tranches in respect of cash flow, second-lien loans entitle their holders only to subordinated claims to collateral. They are less well secured but they are still typically granted to the "new company". Subordinated and mezzanine debt instruments are the least protected, especially as they are typically raised by the "subholding company". Finally, if any seller loans are received they are usually unsecured and are received by the "parent company". These loans can be regarded as a deferred claim to the payment of the purchase price.

Stage 4. *Active ownership/Manage the target.* The trend towards strategic active ownership and operational improvement looks set to continue as a driver for LBO value creation. Active ownership is described very succinctly in a book by two Bain & Co. partners, Orit Gadiesh and Hugh MacArthur. Their book, *Memo to the CEO: Lessons from Private Equity Any Company Can Use* divides the active ownership stage into six substages, which are described in Exhibit 12.7.

1. *Define the full potential of the firm*—this substage draws on the due diligence to establish a maximum value for the firm. It will identify strategic opportunities and optimize strategic decisions in the modeling to provide a benchmark of future potential and what can be achieved in the proposed holding period.

2. *Develop the blueprint—100-day plan*—the 100-day plan is a detailed blueprint of how that potential will be achieved, from what will be done differently on Day 1 to longer term changes in strategy. The strength of the PE firm over many corporately run firms is its ability to identify the "few" activities that add most of the value and focus obsessively on those activities. This avoids wasting time on low-value-added activities and enables the PE firm to exit in a short timeframe and maximize returns. The relationship between time and returns is discussed in more detail in Section 12.4.1.

3. *Accelerate performance*—accelerating performance involves "molding" the organization to the blueprint. This includes structural changes, matching talent to key initiatives, and monitoring a few key metrics. Again, it is important to

EXHIBIT 12.7

THE SIX SUBSTAGES OF ACTIVE OWNERSHIP

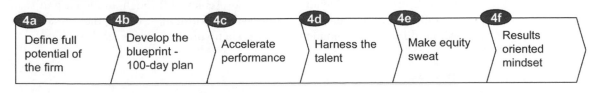

4a Define full potential of the firm
4b Develop the blueprint - 100-day plan
4c Accelerate performance
4d Harness the talent
4e Make equity sweat
4f Results oriented mindset

Source: Gadiesh and MacArthur (2008).

focus on one or two metrics that really measure performance and encourage value-adding activity. Many firms overmonitor too many metrics, some of which encourage management to destroy rather than add value.

4. *Harness the talent*—the principal mechanism for harnessing talent is to align the investor's and management's incentives through a rewards structure that will encourage managers to embrace the blueprint and undertake value-adding activities. It also incentivizes management to be proactive, pre-empting changes in the business environment, and being strategically agile. Finally, it is important to create a flexible and agile culture and a value-adding board of directors who can really advise and drive the firm in the right direction.

5. *Make equity sweat*—this requires the application of LBO economics, which brings financial discipline and the aggressive management of working capital. But, it must be implemented with caution due to uncertainty of future cash flows and the ability to service debt. If the target is unable to pay dividends to equity holders it can continue as a going concern, but failure to pay coupons on debt can lead to bankruptcy.

6. *Results-oriented mindset*—this links back to the culture and incentives of management. PE firms in LBO deals focus on earnings, margins, and cash and reward proactivity by management. The performance hurdles are closely monitored and continually adjusted to provide ongoing incentives for achievement.

Stage 5. *Exit*. The average holding period (time between buyout and exit) is 5 years, and typically ranges from 3 to 7 years. The holding period is short because the success of a fund is measured on its IRR return, which incorporates the time value of money (see the IRR formula on p. 273). The decision to exit is typically a balance between current market conditions and additional opportunities to create future value. However, due to the time value of money and downward pressure on IRR, subsequent value creation opportunities would need to be significant to justify delaying the exit. In other words, while holding an investment longer may generate additional cash on cash returns, it could simultaneously reduce the IRR. A lower IRR lowers the PE firm's standing in the returns tables and could demote them from the top quartile, thus negatively affecting its ability to raise future funds.

Objectives to achieve before exit

This should fit with initial target screening and due diligence and will include some or all of the following:

- *Increase in EBITDA*—through acquisition, organic growth, and efficiency improvements
- *Reduced debt*—use of cash flows to pay down debt and increase equity
- *Multiple expansion*—higher exit multiple. Achieved through an increase in size, operational improvements, better growth opportunities, timing the market, and exiting during an economic upturn or when your company's stock is "hot".

Exit options

There are three broad categories of exit options, but we discuss in detail exit opportunities in Chapter 15.

1. Sale of the business to a strategic buyer (*trade sale*) or another PE firm (*secondary buyout*):

    a. A strategic buyer will normally be the highest bidder due to perceived synergies and a lower cost of capital (it normally has a higher credit rating because it has low leverage). However, it is dependent on finding a buyer either with a good strategic fit or one that believes diversification can add value. With 38% of exits between 1970 and 2007, this is the most common exit (Kaplan and Strømberg, 2009).

    b. Sale to a PE firm is dependent on the funding markets, as the next buyer will need high leverage and good debt terms to make the deal work a second time around. Some companies have gone through multiple rounds of PE ownership. This can be explained partly by the need to offload the company within a short time horizon in order to maintain a high IRR. Sales to financial buyers accounted for 24% of the exits between 1970 and 2007 (Kaplan and Strømberg, 2009).

2. *Initial public offering* (IPO): an IPO involves selling a percentage of the company's shares on the stock market and typically involves only partial monetization at the first offering, followed by subsequent secondary offerings. The advantage of this approach is that it enables the PE fund to take part in future growth and provides a liquid market for existing equity investors. In addition, if market conditions are favorable, IPOs may offer a higher valuation per share than a strategic or secondary sale. IPOs account for 14% of all exits between 1970 and 2007 (Kaplan and Strømberg, 2009).

3. The final option is *recapitalization*, which is not an "exit", but rather a monetization event. The company relevers and uses the proceeds from the new debt to pay large dividends to the equity holders. This is achieved by either (i) extending existing debt facilities or loans if the covenants allow or (ii) issuing new debt at a holding company level, to avoid covenant restrictions at the target level. This option is often utilized if the PE firm wants to partially monetize its investment and either (i) wants to retain an upside potential in business (the sponsor retains 100%) or (ii) cannot achieve the required value for the company value due to poor market conditions.

12.3 LBO STAKEHOLDERS

Over the lifetime of an LBO, 11 different main stakeholder groups are involved or at least affected. The following sections describe the goals and activities of each of these stakeholders. Exhibit 12.8 shows the involvement of each stakeholder by phase in a typical LBO process.

Sellers/Pre-deal shareholders

The goal of pre-deal shareholders is to sell the company and achieve a maximum selling price. In the case of a private company, the ability to liquidate the otherwise illiquid shareholding in the company is the main motivation to sell. Pre-deal shareholders either actively offer their company to potential buyers, or they get called by investment banks or PE firms. Pre-deal shareholders arrange the selling process: a competitive auction between multiple bidders or a proprietary negotiation with only one bidder. Furthermore, they perform or assist actual negotiations and bidder selection. Specialized

---

EXHIBIT 12.8

LBO STAKEHOLDERS ARE ACTIVE AT DIFFERENT STAGES AND HAVE DIFFERENT LEVELS OF INVOLVEMENT

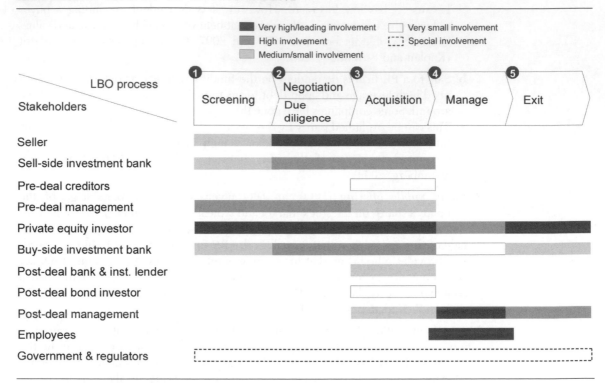

---

consultancies or sell-side investment banks often support the activities of pre-deal shareholders.

Sell-side investment banks

If the seller engages an investment bank, the bank typically markets the company to prospective buyers, sets up the selling process, and acts as an advisor in the negotiations with buyers. The investment bank's goals are to make sure the deal goes through, to maximize fees, and to establish relationships with the involved parties as a potential basis for future business.

Pre-deal creditors

Pre-deal creditors do not play an active role in the LBO process, but ensure that existing covenants are not breached. Pre-deal creditors have an incentive to thoroughly check this because if their covenants do not protect them, they could lose out as a result of the transaction (wealth transfer from creditors to shareholders by risk shifting). This is because they receive the same return as before the LBO, but are exposed to higher credit risk due to the higher leverage.

Pre-deal management

The goals and activities of pre-deal management highly depend on the type of deal. Depending on the involvement of the management, LBOs are classified into the following types:

- *Management buyout (MBO)*—the existing management invests its own money, often a significant amount of their own net worth, to buy the company or unit. They often invest alongside PE funds. They have the advantage of insider knowledge about the company. Their goal is to win the deal to be an investor in their own company and to significantly increase their own net worth within a limited timeframe.

- *Management buyin (MBI)*—a team of outside managers replaces the existing managers. These managers invest their own money, often a significant amount of their own net worth. The goal of the existing management is often to either stop the MBI or, at least, to negotiate a good severance package.

- *Buyin management buyout (BIMBO)*—this type of LBO is a combination of an MBO and MBI. The existing management stays in place and invests its own money. However, other managers join the company and invest their own money too. In many cases, a new CEO buys in and the pre-deal management represents the second management level.

PE firm/post-deal shareholder/financial sponsor

The PE firm is the only stakeholder that is actively involved in every phase of the LBO process. The PE firm leads the screening, leads the due diligence, is one of the two leading stakeholders in the negotiations and deal making (alongside the seller), supervises and controls the management phase, and leads the efforts to find a suitable exit. The PE firm's goal is to achieve a high IRR and money multiple, which drive the amount of carry the GPs receive on exit. Furthermore, the firm's success determines if future funds can be raised and, therefore, also influences future carry options and management fees.

Buy-side investment banks

Buy-side investment banks provide a variety of services in several phases of the LBO process. Their goals are the same as the goals of sell-side investment banks: earn high fees and build long-lasting relationships to support future business. In the sourcing period, investment banks support with expertise, relationships, and resources. Afterwards, they support the negotiations and perform financial due diligence on targets. They check the target's ability to service a highly levered structure and validate the target's business plan using their internal credit processes. Investment banks lead the construction of a finance structure tailored for the target. After the bank's internal credit team approves the financial structure, the bank can also provide a financial commitment to support the sponsor bid and guarantees this in a sequence of documents. When using underwritten financing, investment banks guarantee funding for the debt portion of the deal. Typically, buy-side investment banks also keep in close contact with the portfolio company during the management phase and support potential refinancing rounds if necessary. The buy-side investment bank also tends to support the exit at the end of the LBO process, where they serve as sell-side investment banks.

Post-deal bank and institutional lenders

Bank and institutional lenders act as capital providers for the debt part of the capital structure. Their goal is to invest their money with a good risk/return structure. Banks typically provide the revolver and amortizing term loans. Institutional lenders—in particular, hedge funds, pension funds, and insurance companies—typically provide longer term loans with limited amortization. Banks and institutional lenders perform their own due diligence on the proposed transaction and often negotiate specific covenants. So-called "bank meetings" are the platform for discussion between the portfolio company, the financial sponsor, the investment bank, and the bank or institutional lender.

Post-deal bond investors

The goal of bond investors is to achieve an attractive risk-adjusted return on their investment. Bond investors are normally high-yield mutual funds, hedge funds, pension funds, and insurance companies. They purchase high-yield bonds after attending roadshow presentations (one-to-one meetings with the company's management).

Post-deal management

In LBOs, the post-deal management have high incentives in the form of a high equity stake or ratchets that align their interest to that of the PE firm. Their goal is to achieve high compensation and to prove themselves. The post-deal management lead the management phase in the LBO process. In this phase, they must be able to execute based on extremely ambitious plans, to encourage change, and to handle multiple projects at the same time. In addition, the post-deal management are highly involved in the preparation and execution of the exit phase.

Employees

Employees do not have an active role in most phases of the LBO. They only actively take part in the management phase, when often very ambitious operational improvement programs are implemented. An LBO seriously affects employees if a headcount reduction is part of the operational improvement program. However, research shows that PE-owned companies do not have a statistically higher tendency to reduce the employee headcount than non-PE-owned companies (e.g., see Amess and Wright, 2007).

Governments and regulators

Governments and regulators are usually not actively involved in any of the phases of the LBO process. However, their laws and regulations influence each step. Hence, the goals of governments and of regulators are very important for PE firms. The main areas of interest for governments and regulators are the effects of LBOs on employment, taxes, and strategically important industries such as defense and infrastructure. Governments around the globe have varying opinions about the PE industry. Hence, it is crucial for a PE firm to be aware of current regulations in any country they operate in and to pay close attention to regulatory potential.

12.4   VALUE CREATION IN AN LBO

12.4.1   Measurement of LBO returns: A short overview

Before we discuss value creation in an LBO transaction, we present the most common measures of performance, which are the internal rate of return (IRR) and the cash multiple (or cash-on-cash) return (COC). These performance measures are discussed in greater detail in Chapter 3.

Internal rate of return (IRR)

The IRR measures LBO returns by factoring in the time value of money, meaning that it is important to have a relatively short holding period. However, returns are not risk adjusted, so care must be taken when comparing the performance of different LBO transactions. The IRR captures the total return during the investment period, including interim cash inflows and outflows such as dividends paid to equity holders or additional investments.

The IRR is easy to calculate using the IRR function in Excel. It is, however, important to understand what it really means. The IRR can be thought of as the discount rate that would make the NPV zero. The equation is:

$$\sum_{n=0}^{N} \frac{CF_n}{(1 + IRR)^n} = 0$$

For example, if the PE fund buys a company for 100 in Year 0 and sells it for 250 in Year 5, with no interim cash flows, the IRR return would be given by:

$$-100 + \frac{0}{(1 + IRR)^1} + \frac{0}{(1 + IRR)^2} + \frac{0}{(1 + IRR)^3} + \frac{0}{(1 + IRR)^4} + \frac{250}{(1 + IRR)^5} = 0$$

Solving for IRR $= 0.201$ or 20.1%.

It is, therefore, important to have a relatively short holding period, as a longer investment horizon puts increasing downward pressure on the IRR. In the above example, if the holding period moved to 10 years as opposed to 5, the IRR would be just 12.1% as opposed to 20.1%.

There are a number of important characteristics and a specific terminology relating to PE LBO returns, which deserve closer discussion:

1. The *J-curve* refers to returns during the life of a buyout fund, which could include a number of LBO transactions over a period of 10 or more years. A buyout fund is a series of uncertain cash inflows and outflows. Initially, the cash outflows dominate and the fund returns a negative IRR in the early years. As the fund matures and cash dividends are returned to investors, the inflows will at some point match the outflows, meaning the IRR will be zero. In the latter years and the final year when the cash is returned to investors the fund will, hopefully, achieve positive returns. The J-curve is illustrated in Exhibit 12.9, which shows typical returns for a 12-year buyout fund.

2. *Vintage year* refers to the year a PE fund was formed; vintage year returns cover the returns from that vintage year to a specified year following the formation of the fund. As a rule, the greater the number of years over which a vintage year return is calculated, the more robust the IRR calculation becomes. This is in contrast to the returns from most other investments, which can be calculated accurately on Day 1 (e.g., bonds, assuming no default).

EXHIBIT 12.9

THE J-CURVE EFFECT

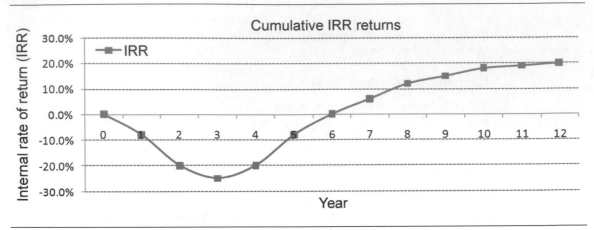

3. *Upper-quartile returns* refers to the return of the 75th percentile fund—not the average returns of the top 25% of funds. In other words, top-quartile returns could be 33%, which means the 75th percentile fund achieved an IRR of 33%, but there could be a significant range above that, with the top 1% to 2% of funds achieving IRRs of over 100%.

4. *Returns are not risk adjusted*, which means care must be taken when comparing the performance of different buyout funds.

Cash on cash (COC)

The COC return is simply a multiple of the initial equity investment in the LBO transaction. It does not factor in the time value of money and, therefore, is not affected by the investment horizon. Therefore, COC and IRR should be considered in combination to provide a more complete picture of performance. In the above example of 100 invested in Year 0 and 250 realized (after debt repayment) in Year 5, the COC multiple would be 2.5×.

12.4.2 Sources of value

Buyout funds managed by PE firms aim to achieve an IRR in excess of 20%, depending on the individual fund and its risk profile. There are three principal ways PE firms can create and capture value to achieve these return targets:

A. Operational improvements (value creation)

B. Multiple expansion (value arbitrage)

C. Financial leverage (value transfer from government).

A   Operational improvements

Improving the operational performance of the portfolio company is a key lever for the PE firm to create and capture value. When ignoring the effects of multiple expansion, financial leverage, and value transfers, the value created by boosting the EBITDA from $\text{EBITDA}_{\text{before}}$ (i.e., EBITDA of the company at the time of the LBO transaction) to $\text{EBITDA}_{\text{after}}$ (i.e., EBITDA of the company at the time of the exit) by operational improvements can be described as:

$$V_{\text{ops}} = \frac{(\text{EBITDA}_{\text{after}} - \text{EBITDA}_{\text{before}}) * \text{Purchase multiple}}{(1 + \text{Discount rate})^{\text{years to exit}}}$$

where the *purchase multiple* is the acquisition multiple computed as the ratio of the purchase price to EBITDA.

As in every company, boosting the EBITDA can be achieved in three ways: (1) increasing the quantities sold, (2) increasing prices, and/or (3) cutting production and overhead costs.

While all three approaches might be valuable in a buyout situation, in most cases the emphasis is on cutting costs. The most prominent improvement approaches are:

- Cutting overhead costs
- Consolidating sourcing/suppliers
- Streamlining operations and the supply chain
- Adding new management information systems
- Better controlling the working capital, especially inventory
- Terminating some investments, starting others into new markets/products
- Selling some assets
- Reducing complexity
- Investing in product development and other organic growth initiatives
- Quick analysis and decision making.

B Multiple expansion

The multiple a PE firm pays when buying a company is called the "purchase or entry multiple" and the multiple the PE firm receives upon exit is called the "exit multiple". Typically, the multiples used in buyout situations are EBITDA multiples. Multiple expansion describes a situation where the exit multiple is higher than the purchase multiple. When ignoring the effects of financial leverage and operational improvements, the value captured by multiple expansion can be described as:

$$V_{\text{mult}} = \frac{\text{EBITDA}_{\text{after}} * (\text{Exit multiple} - \text{Purchase multiple})}{(1 + \text{Discount rate})^{\text{years to exit}}}$$

Multiple expansion has two drivers. However, both are either very unreliable or a very small source of value:

- *Market timing (multiple arbitrage)*—the PE firm buys the company in a bearish market and sells it in a bullish market for a higher multiple. In this case, the PE firm did not create value, but benefited from value arbitrage. However, when believing in semi-efficient capital markets, consistently benefiting from market timing over time is unlikely. Hence, multiple arbitrage is not considered a reliable source of value creation.
- *Improved future prospects (value creation)*—a multiple reflects the buyer's expectations about the future potential of a company. If the PE firm is able to

EXHIBIT 12.10

VALUE CREATION FROM AN INCREASE IN FIRM VALUE

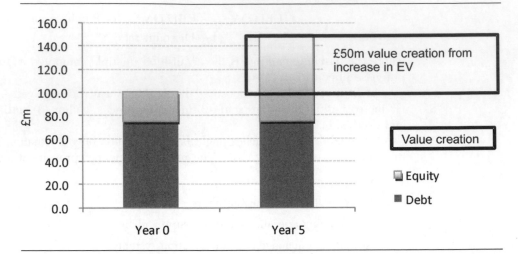

improve this future potential, the multiple should increase. However, given that LBO targets typically have a strong and leading position in their industry, improving their future prospects above previous expectations is challenging. Most improvement levers focus on immediate EBITDA effects and, therefore, do not affect the multiple. Multiple expansion due to value creation is much more important for PE firms operating in the growth capital sector.

As an example, Exhibit 12.10 illustrates a scenario in which no debt is repaid and returns on equity are generated through an increase in enterprise value, which can be a result of operational improvements and/or multiple arbitrage.

C Financial leverage

Financial leverage directly affects the returns and risks of the PE firm. If the return a company creates is higher than the cost of debt, these excess returns are captured by the PE firms and, therefore, increase its financial returns. However, it also increases the risk. If the return of the target LBO company falls below the cost of debt, high leverage leads to lower returns for the PE firm. In terms of the effect on equity return, paying off the debt increases the equity's share in the target's capital structure:

$$V_{debt} = \frac{Debt_{after} - Debt_{before}}{(1 + Discount\ rate)^{years\ to\ exit}}$$

The effect of debt on value creation is actually more complex. In the Modigliani–Miller world that assumes no taxes, no cost of financial distress, no asymmetric information, and no inefficiencies in the market, financial leverage does not affect company value. However, in reality, financial leverage does affect company value: it builds a tax shield, it increases the probability of financial distress, and it generates agency costs of debt. Hence, the effect of financial leverage on the company value is positive as long as the expected tax shield exceeds the two kinds of expected costs.

EXHIBIT 12.11

VALUE CREATION FROM DEBT REPAYMENT (DE-LEVERAGING)

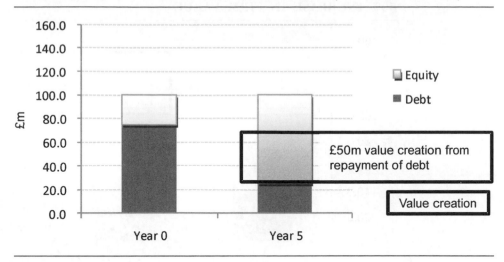

Exhibit 12.11 illustrates a scenario in which a firm is bought and sold for the same price. The firm's EBITDA is the same in Year 5 and the exit multiple is equal to the purchase multiple. The return on equity is generated through the repayment of debt from cash flows.[4]

Example

Assume that a company is bought for £100mn and sold 5 years later for £150mn. All free cash flows are used to service the interest on the debt and no debt is repaid. The only difference between the two deals is the initial level of leverage. In Exhibit 12.12, Scenario 1, the transaction has a low leverage of 25%, meaning an equity investment of £75mn. This deal produces an IRR of 10.8% and a return multiple of 1.7×.

In Exhibit 12.13, Scenario 2, the transaction has a higher leverage of 75%, meaning an equity investment of only £25mn. The transaction is identical in all other respects. This deal produces an IRR of 24.6% and a return multiple of 3.0×.

There are two important issues to highlight. First, this comparison does not consider the potential costs of financial distress associated with higher leverage. The IRR in Scenario 2 should be adjusted for this increased risk. Second, the analysis assumes that the remaining £50mn that is not invested in Scenario 2 can be invested elsewhere for a return greater than 10.8%.

Other sources of value

Transfers of value from other stakeholders are another potential source of value captured by PE firms. However, while these transfers might be of high importance in specific cases, on average they are not significant. For existing creditors and preferred shareholders, increasing leverage often leads to higher risk (if new debt has the same or higher seniority), which is not compensated by higher returns. Covenants may be in

---

4. This simplified illustration of value creation ignores the time value of money.

EXHIBIT 12.12

LEVERAGE SCENARIO 1—25% DEBT, NO DEBT REPAYMENT, 50% INCREASE IN FIRM VALUE

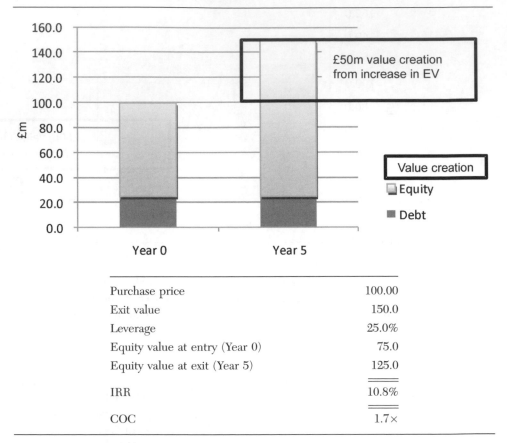

Purchase price	100.00
Exit value	150.0
Leverage	25.0%
Equity value at entry (Year 0)	75.0
Equity value at exit (Year 5)	125.0
IRR	10.8%
COC	1.7×

---

place to prevent this risk shifting and, hence, existing debt is often retired in an LBO to avoid infringement of these covenants.

Implicit and legally non-binding contracts may determine employee bonuses or wages. Breaching these implicit contracts might lower costs and, therefore, transfer value from employees to the PE firm. However, it can be argued that the possible negative effects such as lower employee morale and higher turnover would destroy more value for the PE firm than what can be transferred to employees in wages. In line with this counterargument, there is no systematic scientific evidence for a value transfer from employees to PE firms by breaching implicit contracts.

12.4.3 The differentiators of the PE approach

Unlike a strategic buyer, PE firms cannot benefit from synergies unless there are similar companies in the portfolio. Also, the levers PE firms use—in particular, operational improvements, high leverage, and possibly multiple expansion—are also available to the previous management. So, why do top PE firms achieve relatively high returns? Do they just exploit bad management, the so-called *management arbitrage*?

EXHIBIT 12.13

LEVERAGE SCENARIO 2—75% DEBT, NO DEBT REPAYMENT, 50% INCREASE IN FIRM VALUE

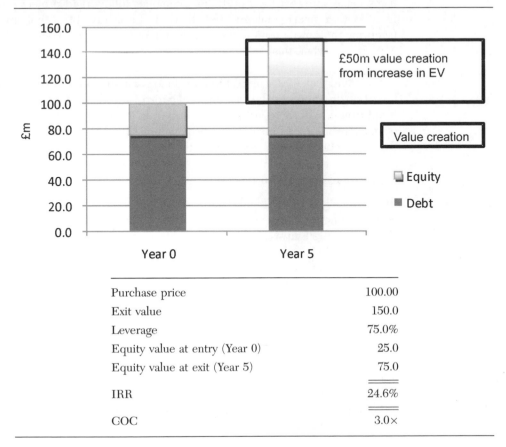

Purchase price	100.00
Exit value	150.0
Leverage	75.0%
Equity value at entry (Year 0)	25.0
Equity value at exit (Year 5)	75.0
IRR	24.6%
COC	3.0×

While management arbitrage is one underlying reason that enables PE firms to achieve high returns, there are at least three more elements that characterize the *PE approach of managing* and underlie the success of the industry: (1) the PE governance model, (2) PE firms' access to extraordinary talent, and (3) the knowledge and experience of PE firms.

1   PE governance model

The PE governance model promotes a value creation mindset, high incentives, and alignment of stakeholder interests. To achieve this, PE firms incentivize portfolio company managers with equity stakes and ratchets. Given that a large proportion of managers' actual or potential net worth is tied to the company's success and given that the liquidity of this net worth is tied to a successful exit, their interests are well aligned and focused on economic value creation. Also, PE firms often expand the system of high incentives to board members, thereby creating value (see Braun and Latham, 2007).

The focused mindset around value appreciation eliminates some non-value-adding management practices, especially in mature companies. For example, many companies with strong disposable cash flows may not have value-creating investment opportunities. However, managers still tend to invest instead of paying dividends to shareholders. PE firms make sure that their portfolio companies follow rigid project portfolio management. Other managerial practices that PE firms do not accept are entrenchment (securing their own position to the detriment of the company), empire building (growth is more important than value creation), and the quiet life approach (postponing tough decisions).

Beyond that, CEOs of PE fund portfolio companies only have to report to their own board of directors. In the case of public-to-private deals, the target's management is freed from quarterly reporting duties and from the pressure of meeting analysts' short-term expectations. In the case of business unit LBOs, the target's management is freed from limitations from headquarters, the resource drain, and costs of reporting.

2   PE firms' access to talent

PE firms have access to highly talented employees (e.g., Gadiesh and MacArthur, 2008). Many legendary managers such as former GE CEO Jack Welsh work for PE firms. Furthermore, PE firms are among the most desired employers for the top students from elite universities and business schools around the world. There are two reasons for this: the type of work and the compensation structure. GPs in PE firms are principals, not agents, which is desirable for most high achievers. Furthermore, the work of GPs is diversified and interesting, covering all phases of an LBO deal and allowing them to concentrate on multiple companies at any point in time.

Given that the main income element of PE firms is, or at least should be, the carry (usually 20% of the appreciation of the investors' money above a specified hurdle rate), GPs are usually paid depending on the size of this carry. This enables GPs in PE firms to obtain very high compensation on large and successful deals.

Beyond the access to talent in the PE firm itself, PE firms are also very successful in attracting high-profile managers to join their portfolio companies due to the exciting prospects and excellent incentives.

3   Knowledge and experience of PE firms

PE firms are experts in change and optimization. In all their portfolio companies, propagating and supporting change and optimization is their key activity.

12.5   REFERENCES

AMESS, K., AND WRIGHT, M. (2007) "The wage and employment effects of LBOs in the UK," *International Journal Economics of Business*, **14**(2), 179–195.

BARGERON, L., SCHLINGEMANN, F., STULZ, R., AND ZUTTER, C. (2007) "Why do private acquirers pay so little compared to public acquirers?" *Journal of Financial Economics*, **89**(3), 375–390.

BRAUN, M.R., AND LATHAM, S.F. (2007) "The governance of going private transactions: The leveraged buyout board of directors as a distinctive source of value," *Management Decision*, **45**(5) 866–882.

CNNMONEY.COM. (2007) "PE power list: Top ten deals," available at *CNNMoney.com* (last accessed April 4, 2010).

DAMODARAN, A. (2008) *The Anatomy of an LBO: Leverage, Control, and Value*, CFA Institute, *cfapubs.org*

GADIESH, O., AND MACARTHUR, H. (2008) "Lessons from private equity any company can use," Harvard Business School Press, Boston.

KAPLAN, S.N. (1989) "Management buyouts: Evidence on taxes as a source of value," *Journal of Finance*, **3**, 611–632.

KAPLAN, S.N., AND STRØMBERG, P. (2009) "Leveraged buyouts and private equity," *Journal of Economic Perspectives*, **23**(1) 121–146.

MEYER, T., AND MATHONET, P-Y. (2008) *Beyond the J-Curve*, Wiley Finance, Hoboken, NJ.

OLSEN, J., GAGLIANO, S., WAINWRIGHT, F., AND BLAYDON, C. (2003) *Note on Leveraged Buyouts*, Tuck School of Business at Dartmouth Center for PE and Entrepreneurship, Case #5-0004.

ROSENBAUM, J., AND PEARL, J. (2009) *Investment Banking*, Wiley Finance, Hoboken, NJ.

ROSENBLOOM, A.H. (2002) *Due Diligence for Global Deal Making*, Bloomberg Press, Princeton, NJ.

ROXBURGH, C., LUND, S., LIPPERT, M., WHITE, O.L., AND ZHAO, Y. (2009) *The New Power Brokers: How Oil, Asia, Hedge Funds, and PE Are Faring the Financial Crisis*, McKinsey Global Institute, San Francisco, CA.

SORKIN, A.R. (2007) "Private Equity Buyout of TXU is Enormous in Size and in its Complexity," *New York Times*, February 27.

STANDARD & POOR'S (2009) "Recent LBO stories: High leverage, low ratings, and bad timing, available at *www.standardandpoors.com/ratingsdirect*

VOLPIN, P. (2010) "Merger, MBOs, and other corporate restructurings: Leveraged Buyouts," London Business School, lecture slides.

13

Leveraged buyout modeling: An Excel application

13.1 OVERVIEW

To illustrate the LBO modeling process with real data, we have recreated the *LBO of Toys R Us* in 2005, which was bought by a consortium led by Bain Capital and KKR. The consortium invested USD1.3bn of new equity to complete the USD6.6bn LBO.

In our analysis, we have used historic financial data for 2001–2004, from *Toys R Us* publicly available annual reports. Our base case analysis, which forecasts forward using historic ratios and uses a leverage ratio of 70% debt, gives an IRR of 24% and a money multiple of 3× assuming a 5-year holding period.

When a PE firm structures an LBO deal, it must satisfy at least two conditions: it must be acceptable to the seller and it must achieve acceptable returns to all relevant investors with a manageable level of risk. To judge whether these conditions are fulfilled, the following output measures are taken into consideration:

- *Purchase price*, often compared with previous transactions based on EBITDA multiples. In public-to-private transactions, the premium over the market price is compared with previous transactions, and in competitive bids the purchase price relative to other bidders is key

- The *IRR* and *money multiple* for each investor

- The *interest* and *debt service coverage ratios* (ISCR and DSCR), *EBITDA to the debt level*, and the *fixed coverage ratio*.

A deal has multiple dimensions: the amount of leverage, the choice of debt instruments, the choice of equity instruments, and the purchase price. These degrees of freedom influence the output measures in complex ways. Hence, to be able to take all the information and dependencies into consideration and structure an optimal LBO deal, an *LBO model* is created. An LBO model is usually an Excel file that contains the relevant information, assumptions, and decisions of an LBO deal. The LBO model is a tool to structure an optimal LBO by enabling the user to test the consequences of different decisions and assumptions.

This chapter has been co-authored with Mike Glossop (MBA, London Business School) and Bjoern Koertner (MBA, London Business School).

EXHIBIT 13.1

THE LBO MODELING PROCESS CAN BE BROKEN DOWN ON THREE LEVELS OF DETAIL TO TWO, SIX, AND THIRTEEN STEPS

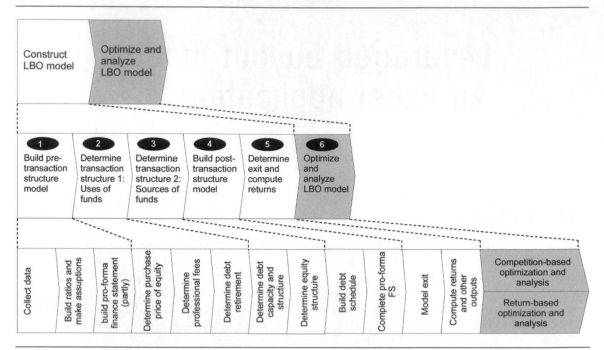

Without an LBO model, it would be nearly impossible to understand all the consequences of a given set of decisions and assumptions that are necessary in LBO deals. Consequently, the LBO modeling described is of the highest importance. It is, however, critical to keep in mind that the LBO model is merely a tool that does not provide any intelligence. The basic modeling principle of "garbage in, garbage out" also applies to LBO models. In other words, it is important to understand the sensitivity of the results to the assumptions made and ensure the highest data quality possible.

As shown in Exhibit 13.1, there are two main phases of LBO modeling:

- *Construction of the LBO model*—initially, the Excel file that models the LBO must be created. This phase contains multiple work steps and some assumptions. The steps include locating historic financial statements, formatting them in an appropriate way, and calculating relevant ratios based on these statements. These work steps do not require an advanced amount of judgment or opinion. However, the creator of the LBO model must make some initial assumptions (e.g., the future growth rate of a specific industry). These assumptions will be reviewed and optimized in the next phase. After the construction, the PE firm has an Excel file that automatically calculates the relevant output measures based on the available information and dependencies, assumptions, and decisions.

- *Optimization and analysis of the LBO model*—the decisions are the degrees of freedom the PE firm has to optimize the deal structure. In this phase, the PE firm analyzes output measures and considers which decisions it can change to improve the output measures and, therefore, optimize the overall deal structure. This is an iterative process that is repeated several times. The assumptions made must be defendable and based on facts wherever possible. Sensitivity analysis should be done to test the effect of assumptions. An LBO model contains a large amount of decisions (e.g., the purchase price, the debt structure, and the equity structure). A single decision is neither wrong nor right. The PE firm must analyze the output measures of the model and evaluate whether it has to change these decisions.

As highlighted in Exhibit 13.1, the two LBO modeling phases can be broken down into six steps. These can be further broken down into 13 steps. In the following, we will describe each of the six steps in a separate subsection. Furthermore, we visualize these steps in the LBO Excel model template that we created, using real-world Toys R Us data.

13.2 BUILD A PRE–TRANSACTION STRUCTURE MODEL

A pre–transaction structure model is a set of pro forma financial statements forecasting the next 7 to 10 years of the target.[1] These statements contain assumptions about future developments including the expected effects of operational improvement levers the PE firm plans to pull. However, this pre–transaction structure model does not contain the effects of the transaction structure of the LBO. In particular, the effects of the finance structure and debt schedule are not included. Hence, the pro forma financial statements that make up the pre–transaction structure model will contain "gaps" to be filled later. However, it is important to complete the structure and ensure the model balances at this point. The forecast financial statements for Toys R Us are shown in Exhibits 13.2–13.4.

The pre–transaction structure model is built from historic financial statements and forecasts based on historic ratios, expert opinion, and the due diligence process. It contains the expectations of the PE firm about the future operational development of the target if the LBO takes place. Given the increasing importance of operational improvements to generate high returns, a considerable amount of resources is devoted to the due diligence process and pre–transaction structure model.

The creation of the pre–transaction structure model can typically be subdivided in three substeps:

1. Collect data and build historic income statement.

2. Build ratios and make assumptions.

3. Build pro forma financial statements as shown in Exhibits 13.2–13.4.

Step 1. *Collect data.* As a basis for the forecasts, data about the targets market, industry, and other macroeconomic conditions must be collected. The most important data are the historic financial statements of the company over the last 3 to 4 years. While these data are easily accessible for public companies, for private targets PE firms must rely on disclosure of the data or make assumptions based on scant public information and expert opinion. In a friendly deal, the target prepares an information memorandum that provides historic financial statements, financial forecasts, and other information and analysis prepared by the sell-side team to support the transaction. Clearly, any

---

1. The typical time horizon of the forecast model should match the longest maturity of utilized debt instruments; typically, this is 7 to 10 years.

EXHIBIT 13.2

TOYS R US PRE–TRANSACTION STRUCTURE INCOME STATEMENT.

Toys "R" Us LBO Model - Income Statement ($m)

	Hist. 2001	Hist. 2002	Hist. 2003	Hist. 2004	1 Proj. 2005	2 Proj. 2006	3 Proj. 2007	4 Proj. 2008	5 Proj. 2009	6 Proj. 2010	7 Proj. 2011	8 Proj. 2012	9 Proj. 2013	10 Proj. 2014
Sales	11,332.0	11,019.0	11,305.0	11,320.0	11,546.4	11,777.3	12,012.9	12,253.1	12,498.2	12,748.2	13,003.1	13,263.2	13,528.4	13,799.0
% growth	—	(2.8%)	2.6%	0.1%	2.0%	2.0%	2.0%	2.0%	2.0%	2.0%	2.0%	2.0%	2.0%	2.0%
Cost of Goods Sold	7,815.0	7,604.0	7,799.0	7,646.0	7,793.8	7,949.7	8,108.7	8,270.9	8,436.3	8,605.0	8,777.1	8,952.6	9,131.7	9,314.3
Gross Profit	3,517.0	3,415.0	3,506.0	3,674.0	3,752.6	3,827.6	3,904.2	3,982.3	4,061.9	4,143.2	4,226.0	4,310.5	4,396.7	4,484.7
% margin	31.0%	31.0%	31.0%	32.5%	32.5%	32.5%	32.5%	32.5%	32.5%	32.5%	32.5%	32.5%	32.5%	32.5%
Selling, General & Administrative	2,801.0	2,721.0	2,724.0	3,026.0	2,886.6	2,944.3	3,003.2	3,063.3	3,124.5	3,187.0	3,250.8	3,315.8	3,382.1	3,449.8
% sales	24.7%	24.7%	24.1%	26.7%	25.0%	25.0%	25.0%	25.0%	25.0%	25.0%	25.0%	25.0%	25.0%	25.0%
Other Expense / (Income)	—	186.0	—	63.0	115.5	117.8	120.1	122.5	125.0	127.5	130.0	132.6	135.3	138.0
EBITDA	716.0	508.0	782.0	585.0	750.5	765.5	780.8	796.5	812.4	828.6	845.2	862.1	879.3	896.9
% margin	6.3%	4.6%	6.9%	5.2%	6.5%	6.5%	6.5%	6.5%	6.5%	6.5%	6.5%	6.5%	6.5%	6.5%
Depreciation & Amortization	290.0	308.0	339.0	368.0	288.7	294.4	300.3	306.3	312.5	318.7	325.1	331.6	338.2	345.0
EBIT	426.0	200.0	443.0	217.0	461.9	471.1	480.5	490.1	499.9	509.9	520.1	530.5	541.1	552.0
% margin	3.8%	1.8%	3.9%	1.9%	4.0%	4.0%	4.0%	4.0%	4.0%	4.0%	4.0%	4.0%	4.0%	4.0%
Interest Expense														
Existing Debt														
Revolving Credit Facility														
Senior Long Term Debt														
Subordinated Debt (Mezz)														
Commitment Fee on Unused Revolver														
Agent Fees														
Cash Interest Expense														
Amortisation of Deferred Financing Fees														
Total Interest Expense														
Interest income														
Net Interest Expense														
EBT (Earnings Before Tax)					461.9	471.1	480.5	490.1	499.9	509.9	520.1	530.5	541.1	552.0
Income Tax Expense					175.5	179.0	182.6	186.2	190.0	193.8	197.6	201.6	205.6	209.7
Net Income					286.4	292.1	297.9	303.9	310.0	316.2	322.5	328.9	335.5	342.2
% margin					2.5%	2.5%	2.5%	2.5%	2.5%	2.5%	2.5%	2.5%	2.5%	2.5%

LEAVE BLANK IN STEP 1

TO BE COMPLETED IN STEP 4 - LINKED FROM <u>FINANCE STRUCTURE AND DEBT SCHEDULE</u>

Income Statement Assumptions

	Hist. 2002	Hist. 2003	Hist. 2004	1 2005	2 2006	3 2007	4 2008	5 2009	6 2010	7 2011	8 2012	9 2013	10 2014
Sales (% YoY growth)	(2.8%)	2.6%	0.1%	2.0%	2.0%	2.0%	2.0%	2.0%	2.0%	2.0%	2.0%	2.0%	2.0%
Cost of Goods Sold (% margin)	69.0%	69.0%	67.5%	67.5%	67.5%	67.5%	67.5%	67.5%	67.5%	67.5%	67.5%	67.5%	67.5%
SG&A (% sales)	24.7%	24.1%	26.7%	25.0%	25.0%	25.0%	25.0%	25.0%	25.0%	25.0%	25.0%	25.0%	25.0%
Other Expense / (Income) (% of sales)	1.7%	—	0.6%	1.0%	1.0%	1.0%	1.0%	1.0%	1.0%	1.0%	1.0%	1.0%	1.0%
Depreciation & Amortization (% of sales)	2.8%	3.0%	3.3%	2.5%	2.5%	2.5%	2.5%	2.5%	2.5%	2.5%	2.5%	2.5%	2.5%
Interest Income	2.6%	3.0%	3.0%	4.0%	4.0%	4.0%	4.0%	4.0%	4.0%	4.0%	4.0%	4.0%	4.0%
Tax Rate				38.0%	38.0%	38.0%	38.0%	38.0%	38.0%	38.0%	38.0%	38.0%	38.0%

EXHIBIT 13.3

TOY R US PRE–TRANSACTION STRUCTURE BALANCE SHEET

Toys "R" Us LBO Model - Balance Sheet ($m)

	Actual 2004	Incr / (Decr)	Pro Forma 2004	1 2005	2 2006	3 2007	4 2008	5 2009	6 2010	7 2011	8 2012	9 2013	10 2014
								Projection Period					
Cash and Cash Equivalents	2,003.0		2,003.0	2,326.1	2,679.4	3,039.8	3,407.4	3,782.3	4,164.7	4,554.8	4,952.7	5,358.5	5,772.5
Accounts Receivable	146.0		146.0	158.2	161.3	164.6	167.9	171.2	174.6	178.1	181.7	185.3	189.0
Inventory	2,094.0		2,094.0	2,135.3	2,178.0	2,221.6	2,266.0	2,311.3	2,357.5	2,404.7	2,452.8	2,501.8	2,551.9
Prepaid Expenses	486.0		486.0	461.9	471.1	480.5	490.1	499.9	509.9	520.1	530.5	541.1	552.0
Total Current Assets	**4,729.0**		**4,729.0**	**5,081.4**	**5,489.9**	**5,906.4**	**6,331.4**	**6,764.8**	**7,206.8**	**7,657.8**	**8,117.7**	**8,586.8**	**9,065.4**
PPE Beginning Balance	--		--	4,439.0	4,381.3	4,322.4	4,263.3	4,201.1	4,136.6	4,074.8	4,009.8	3,943.5	3,875.8
CapEx	--		--	230.9	235.5	240.3	245.1	250.0	255.0	260.1	265.3	270.6	276.0
Depreciation and Amortisation	--		--	(288.7)	(294.4)	(300.3)	(306.3)	(312.5)	(318.7)	(325.1)	(331.6)	(338.2)	(345.0)
PPE Ending Balance	4,439.0		4,439.0	4,381.3	4,322.4	4,263.2	4,201.1	4,138.6	4,074.8	4,009.8	3,943.5	3,875.8	3,806.9
Goodwill and Intangible Assets	348.0		348.0	348.0	348.0	348.0	348.0	348.0	348.0	348.0	348.0	348.0	348.0
Other Assets	749.0		749.0	749.0	749.0	749.0	749.0	749.0	749.0	749.0	749.0	749.0	749.0
Deferred Financing Fees	--		--	--	--	--	--	--	--	--	--	--	--
Total Assets	**10,265.0**		**10,265.0**	**10,559.7**	**10,909.2**	**11,265.8**	**11,629.4**	**12,000.3**	**12,378.7**	**12,764.6**	**13,158.2**	**13,559.7**	**13,969.2**
Accounts Payable	1,022.0		1,022.0	1,024.9	1,045.6	1,066.3	1,067.7	1,109.4	1,131.6	1,154.2	1,177.3	1,200.9	1,224.9
Accrued Liabilities	866.0		866.0	923.7	942.2	961.0	980.3	999.9	1,019.9	1,040.2	1,061.1	1,082.3	1,103.9
Other Current Liabilities	976.0		976.0	923.7	942.2	961.0	980.3	999.9	1,019.9	1,040.2	1,361.1	1,082.3	1,103.9
Total Current Liabilities	**2,864.0**		**2,864.0**	**2,872.4**	**2,929.8**	**2,988.4**	**3,048.2**	**3,109.1**	**3,171.3**	**3,234.7**	**3,299.4**	**3,365.4**	**3,432.7**
Existing Debt	2,349.0		2,349.0	2,349.0	2,349.0	2,349.0	2,349.0	2,349.0	2,349.0	2,349.0	2,349.0	2,349.0	2,349.0
Revolving Credit Facility													
Senior Long Term Debt					LEAVE BLANK IN STEP 1 - TO BE COMPLETED IN STEP 4: LINKED FROM DEBT SCHEDULE								
Subordinated Debt (Mezz)													
Other Debt													
Other LT Liabilities	1,078.0		1,078.0	1,078.0	1,078.0	1,078.0	1,078.0	1,078.0	1,078.0	1,078.0	1,078.0	1,078.0	1,078.0
Total Liabilities	**6,291.0**		**6,291.0**	**6,299.4**	**6,356.8**	**6,415.4**	**6,475.2**	**6,536.1**	**6,598.3**	**6,661.7**	**6,726.4**	**6,792.4**	**6,859.7**
Shareholders' Equity	3,974.0		3,974.0	4,260.4	4,552.4	4,850.3	5,154.2	5,464.2	5,780.3	6,102.8	6,431.7	6,767.2	7,109.5
Total Shareholders' Equity	**3,974.0**		**3,974.0**	**4,260.4**	**4,552.4**	**4,850.3**	**5,154.2**	**5,464.2**	**5,780.3**	**6,102.8**	**6,431.7**	**6,767.2**	**7,109.5**
Total Liabilities and Equity	**10,265.0**		**10,265.0**	**10,559.7**	**10,909.2**	**11,265.8**	**11,629.4**	**12,000.3**	**12,378.7**	**12,764.6**	**13,158.2**	**13,559.7**	**13,969.2**
Balance Check	*0.000*		*0.000*	*0.000*	*0.000*	*0.000*	*0.000*	*0.000*	*0.000*	*0.000*	*0.000*	*0.000*	*0.000*
Net Working Capital	(138.0)		(138.0)	(117.0)	(119.4)	(121.8)	(124.2)	(126.7)	(129.2)	(131.8)	(134.4)	(137.1)	(139.9)
(Increase) / Decrease in Net Working Capital				(21.0)	2.3	2.4	2.4	2.5	2.5	2.6	2.6	2.7	2.7

Balance Sheet Assumptions
Current Assets

	Actual 2004		Pro Forma 2004	2005	2006	2007	2008	2009	2010	2011	2012	2013	2014
Days Sales Outstanding (DSO)	4.7		4.7	5.0	5.0	5.0	5.0	5.0	5.0	5.0	5.0	5.0	5.0
Days Inventory Held (DIH)	100.0		100.0	100.0	100.0	100.0	100.0	100.0	100.0	100.0	100.0	100.0	100.0
Prepaid and Other Current Assets (% of sales)	4.3%		4.3%	4.0%	4.0%	4.0%	4.0%	4.0%	4.0%	4.0%	4.0%	4.0%	4.0%

Current Liabilities

	Actual 2004		Pro Forma 2004	2005	2006	2007	2008	2009	2010	2011	2012	2013	2014
Days Payable Outstanding (DPO)	48.8		48.8	48.0	48.0	48.0	48.0	48.0	48.0	48.0	48.0	48.0	48.0
Accrued Liabilities (% of sales)	7.7%		7.7%	8.0%	8.0%	8.0%	8.0%	8.0%	8.0%	8.0%	8.0%	8.0%	8.0%
Other Current Liabilities (% of sales)	8.6%		8.6%	8.0%	8.0%	8.0%	8.0%	8.0%	8.0%	8.0%	8.0%	8.0%	8.0%

Text boxes in the Incr / (Decr) and Pro Forma columns:
- LEAVE BLANK IN STEP 1
- TO BE COMPLETED IN STEP 3: FOLLOWING CONSTRUCTION OF SOURCES AND USES OF FUNDS

EXHIBIT 13.4

TOYS R US PRE-TRANSACTION STRUCTURE CASH FLOW STATEMENT

Toys "R" Us LBO Model - Cash Flow Statement ($m)	1	2	3	4	5	6	7	8	9	10
	Proj. 2005	Proj. 2006	Proj. 2007	Proj. 2008	Proj. 2009	Proj. 2010	Proj. 2011	Proj. 2012	Proj. 2013	Proj. 2014
Operating Activities										
Net Income	286.4	292.1	297.9	303.9	310.0	316.2	322.5	328.9	335.5	342.2
Depreciation & Amortization	288.7	294.4	300.3	306.3	312.5	318.7	325.1	331.6	338.2	345.0
Amortisation of Deferred Financing Fees	--	--	--	--	--	--	--	--	--	--
Sub Total	575.0	586.5	598.2	610.2	622.4	634.9	647.6	660.5	673.7	687.2
Changes in Working Capital Items										
Accounts Receivable (DSO)	(12.2)	(3.2)	(3.2)	(3.3)	(3.4)	(3.4)	(3.5)	(3.6)	(3.6)	(3.7)
Inventory (DIH)	(41.3)	(42.7)	(43.6)	(44.4)	(45.3)	(46.2)	(47.2)	(48.1)	(49.1)	(50.0)
Prepaid Expenses	24.1	(9.2)	(9.4)	(9.6)	(9.8)	(10.0)	(10.2)	(10.4)	(10.6)	(10.8)
Accounts Payable (DPO)	2.9	20.5	20.9	21.3	21.8	22.2	22.6	23.1	23.5	24.0
Accrued Liabilities	57.7	18.5	18.8	19.2	19.6	20.0	20.4	20.8	21.2	21.6
Other Current Liabilities	(52.3)	18.5	18.8	19.2	19.6	20.0	20.4	20.8	21.2	21.6
(Inc.) / Dec. in Net Working Capital	(21.0)	2.3	2.4	2.4	2.5	2.5	2.6	2.6	2.7	2.7
Cash Flow from Operating Activities	554.1	588.9	600.6	612.6	624.9	637.4	650.1	663.1	676.4	689.9
Investing Activities										
Capital Expenditures	(230.9)	(235.5)	(240.3)	(245.1)	(250.0)	(255.0)	(260.1)	(265.3)	(270.6)	(276.0)
Other Investing Activities	--	--	--	--	--	--	--	--	--	--
Cash Flow from Investing Activities	(230.9)	(235.5)	(240.3)	(245.1)	(250.0)	(255.0)	(260.1)	(265.3)	(270.6)	(276.0)
Free Cash Flows	*323.1*	*353.3*	*360.4*	*367.6*	*374.9*	*382.4*	*390.1*	*397.9*	*405.8*	*414.0*
Financing Activities										
Existing Debt					LEAVE BLANK IN STEP 1 -					
Revolving Credit Facility				TO BE COMPLETED IN STEP 4: LINKED FROM FINANCING STRUCTURE AND DEBT SCHEDULE						
Senior Long Term Debt										
Subordinated Debt (Mezz)										
Other Debt	--	--	--	--	--	--	--	--	--	--
Dividends	--	--	--	--	--	--	--	--	--	--
Equity Issuance / (Repurchase)	--	--	--	--	--	--	--	--	--	--
Cash Flow from Financing Activities	--	--	--	--	--	--	--	--	--	--
Excess Cash for the Period	323.1	353.3	360.4	367.6	374.9	382.4	390.1	397.9	405.8	414.0
Beginning Cash Balance	2,003.0	2,326.1	2,679.4	3,039.8	3,407.4	3,782.3	4,164.7	4,554.8	4,952.7	5,358.5
Ending Cash Balance	2,326.1	2,679.4	3,039.8	3,407.4	3,782.3	4,164.7	4,554.8	4,952.7	5,358.5	5,772.5
Cash Flow Statement Assumptions										
Capital Expenditures (% of sales)	2.0%	2.0%	2.0%	2.0%	2.0%	2.0%	2.0%	2.0%	2.0%	2.0%

document prepared by the seller must be treated with caution; the due diligence process should verify and challenge management forecasts.

Step 2. *Build ratios and make assumptions.* Typically, the PE firm calculates financial and operational ratios and analyzes the developments of these ratios in the last 3 years. The key ratios are calculated in the tinted boxes at the bottom of the financial statements in Exhibits 13.2–13.4. These ratios form the basis of the future forecasts used to build the pro forma financial statements.

These assumptions are influenced by the specific operational improvement initiatives the PE firm plans to launch. The PE firm decides which initiatives are appropriate for the target and models the effects of these initiatives by including different operating scenarios in the forecasts. The forecasting assumption sheet for the Toys R Us model is shown in Exhibit 13.5. Usually, PE firms forecast several scenarios: an *expected* or *base scenario*, a *pessimistic scenario*, an *optimistic scenario*, and a *management scenario* which contains the management forecasts from the information memorandum.

Step 3. *Build pro forma financial statements ready to incorporate the transaction structure.* Based on forecast financial ratios, the PE firm creates pro forma financial statements for the next 7 to 10 years (the duration should match the debt instrument with the longest maturity). In general, all three financial statements (income statement, cash flow statement, and balance sheet) are forecast. This is considered best practice. However, in specific situations, PE firms simplify this step and do not forecast all elements of the balance sheet. For example, in the case of infrastructure investments only fixed assets are forecast, instead of the full balance sheet.

At this point in time, the financial statements are incomplete, as the transaction structure of the deal needs to be incorporated. However, the transaction structure is not yet defined. Hence, in the pro forma financial statements in this pre–transaction structure model, there are some "gaps", as shown by the white boxes in Exhibits 13.2–13.4, which also indicate where and at what point to obtain the inputs to these sections.

13.3 DETERMINE TRANSACTION STRUCTURE: USES OF FUNDS

There are three uses of funds in an LBO deal: (1) purchase price of equity, (2) professional and financing fees, and (3) retirement of existing debt.

Use 1. *Purchase price of equity.* Setting the purchase price of equity is a very important decision in an LBO. It highly influences two competing objectives:

- Purchase price must be high enough to win the bid
- Purchase price must be low enough to make a good return for investors.

At this point in the modeling process, the purchase price decision is only an initial estimate based on a multiple of EBITDA or an offer price per share for public companies. But the decision will be reviewed in the optimization and analysis phase. To set the initial purchase price, we can utilize three approaches:

1. The *market-based approach* tries to set the price based on previous comparable transactions, often based on EBITDA or PE multiples. For public companies, the purchase price can be calculated based on the share price plus a premium (in percent) of previous comparable transactions.

EXHIBIT 13.5

TOYS R US PRE–TRANSACTION STRUCTURE FORECASTING ASSUMPTIONS

Toys "R" Us - Forecasting Assumptions

Income Statement Assumptions

Legend:
1. Base Case
2. Sponsor
3. Management
4. Optimistic
5. Pessimistic

Sales (% YoY growth)

	1 Proj. 2005	2 Proj. 2006	3 Proj. 2007	4 Proj. 2008	5 Proj. 2009	6 Proj. 2010	7 Proj. 2011	8 Proj. 2012	9 Proj. 2013	10 Proj. 2014
1 Base Case	2.0%	2.0%	2.0%	2.0%	2.0%	2.0%	2.0%	2.0%	2.0%	2.0%
2 Sponsor	3.0%	3.0%	3.0%	3.0%	2.0%	2.0%	2.0%	2.0%	2.0%	2.0%
3 Management	4.0%	4.0%	4.0%	3.0%	3.0%	2.0%	2.0%	2.0%	2.0%	2.0%
4 Optimistic	5.0%	5.0%	5.0%	4.0%	3.0%	2.0%	2.0%	2.0%	2.0%	2.0%
5 Pessimistic	1.5%	1.5%	1.5%	1.5%	1.5%	1.5%	1.5%	1.5%	1.5%	1.5%

Cost of Goods Sold (% margin)

	1 2005	2 2006	3 2007	4 2008	5 2009	6 2010	7 2011	8 2012	9 2013	10 2014
1 Base Case	67.5%	67.5%	67.5%	67.5%	67.5%	67.5%	67.5%	67.5%	67.5%	67.5%
2 Sponsor	67.5%	67.5%	67.5%	67.5%	67.5%	67.5%	67.5%	67.5%	67.5%	67.5%
3 Management	67.5%	67.5%	67.5%	67.5%	67.5%	67.5%	67.5%	67.5%	67.5%	67.5%
4 Optimistic	65.0%	65.0%	65.0%	65.0%	65.0%	65.0%	65.0%	65.0%	65.0%	65.0%
5 Pessimistic	68.0%	68.0%	68.0%	68.0%	68.0%	68.0%	68.0%	68.0%	68.0%	68.0%

SG&A (% sales)

	1 2005	2 2006	3 2007	4 2008	5 2009	6 2010	7 2011	8 2012	9 2013	10 2014
1 Base Case	25.0%	25.0%	25.0%	25.0%	25.0%	25.0%	25.0%	25.0%	25.0%	25.0%
2 Sponsor	25.0%	25.0%	25.0%	25.0%	25.0%	25.0%	25.0%	25.0%	25.0%	25.0%
3 Management	25.0%	25.0%	25.0%	25.0%	25.0%	25.0%	25.0%	25.0%	25.0%	25.0%
4 Optimistic	24.0%	24.0%	24.0%	24.0%	24.0%	24.0%	24.0%	24.0%	24.0%	24.0%
5 Pessimistic	25.5%	25.5%	25.5%	25.5%	25.5%	25.5%	25.5%	25.5%	25.5%	25.5%

Other Expense / (Income) (% of sales)

	1 2005	2 2006	3 2007	4 2008	5 2009	6 2010	7 2011	8 2012	9 2013	10 2014
1 Base Case	1.0%	1.0%	1.0%	1.0%	1.0%	1.0%	1.0%	1.0%	1.0%	1.0%
2 Sponsor	1.00%	1.00%	1.00%	1.00%	1.00%	1.00%	1.00%	1.00%	1.00%	1.00%
3 Management	1.00%	1.00%	1.00%	1.00%	1.00%	1.00%	1.00%	1.00%	1.00%	1.00%
4 Optimistic	0.50%	0.50%	0.50%	0.50%	0.50%	0.50%	0.50%	0.50%	0.50%	0.50%
5 Pessimistic	1.25%	1.25%	1.25%	1.25%	1.25%	1.25%	1.25%	1.25%	1.25%	1.25%

Depreciation & Amortization (% of sales)

	1 2005	2 2006	3 2007	4 2008	5 2009	6 2010	7 2011	8 2012	9 2013	10 2014
1 Base Case	2.5%	2.5%	2.5%	2.5%	2.5%	2.5%	2.5%	2.5%	2.5%	2.5%
2 Sponsor	2.5%	2.5%	2.5%	2.5%	2.5%	2.5%	2.5%	2.5%	2.5%	2.5%
3 Management	2.5%	2.5%	2.5%	2.5%	2.5%	2.5%	2.5%	2.5%	2.5%	2.5%
4 Optimistic	2.0%	2.0%	2.0%	2.0%	2.0%	2.0%	2.0%	2.0%	2.0%	2.0%
5 Pessimistic	3.0%	3.0%	3.0%	3.0%	3.0%	3.0%	3.0%	3.0%	3.0%	3.0%

Interest Income

	1 2005	2 2006	3 2007	4 2008	5 2009	6 2010	7 2011	8 2012	9 2013	10 2014
1 Base Case	4.0%	4.0%	4.0%	4.0%	4.0%	4.0%	4.0%	4.0%	4.0%	4.0%
2 Sponsor	4.0%	4.0%	4.0%	4.0%	4.0%	4.0%	4.0%	4.0%	4.0%	4.0%
3 Management	4.0%	4.0%	4.0%	4.0%	4.0%	4.0%	4.0%	4.0%	4.0%	4.0%
4 Optimistic	6.0%	6.0%	6.0%	6.0%	6.0%	6.0%	6.0%	6.0%	6.0%	6.0%
5 Pessimistic	2.0%	2.0%	2.0%	2.0%	2.0%	2.0%	2.0%	2.0%	2.0%	2.0%

Balance Sheet

Current Assets

Debtor Days - DSO (Days Sales Outstanding)

Base Case	5.0	5.0	5.0	5.0	5.0	5.0	5.0	5.0	5.0	5.0
Sponsor	5.0	5.0	5.0	5.0	5.0	5.0	5.0	5.0	5.0	5.0
Management	5.0	5.0	5.0	5.0	5.0	5.0	5.0	5.0	5.0	5.0
Optimistic	4.0	4.0	4.0	4.0	4.0	4.0	4.0	4.0	4.0	4.0
Pessimistic	6.0	6.0	6.0	6.0	6.0	6.0	6.0	6.0	6.0	6.0

Inventory Days - DIH (Days Inventory Held)

Base Case	100.0	100.0	100.0	100.0	100.0	100.0	100.0	100.0	100.0	100.0
Sponsor	100.0	100.0	100.0	100.0	100.0	100.0	100.0	100.0	100.0	100.0
Management	100.0	100.0	100.0	100.0	100.0	100.0	100.0	100.0	100.0	100.0
Optimistic	90.0	90.0	90.0	90.0	90.0	90.0	90.0	90.0	90.0	90.0
Pessimistic	110.0	110.0	110.0	110.0	110.0	110.0	110.0	110.0	110.0	110.0

Prepaid and other current assets (% of Sales)

Base Case	4.0%	4.0%	4.0%	4.0%	4.0%	4.0%	4.0%	4.0%	4.0%	4.0%
Sponsor	4.0%	4.0%	4.0%	4.0%	4.0%	4.0%	4.0%	4.0%	4.0%	4.0%
Management	4.0%	4.0%	4.0%	4.0%	4.0%	4.0%	4.0%	4.0%	4.0%	4.0%
Optimistic	5.0%	5.0%	5.0%	5.0%	5.0%	5.0%	5.0%	5.0%	5.0%	5.0%
Pessimistic	3.0%	3.0%	3.0%	3.0%	3.0%	3.0%	3.0%	3.0%	3.0%	3.0%

Current Liabilities

Creditor Days - DPO (Days Payment Outstanding)

Base Case	48.0	48.0	48.0	48.0	48.0	48.0	48.0	48.0	48.0	48.0
Sponsor	48.0	48.0	48.0	48.0	48.0	48.0	48.0	48.0	48.0	48.0
Management	48.0	48.0	48.0	48.0	48.0	48.0	48.0	48.0	48.0	48.0
Optimistic	50.0	50.0	50.0	50.0	50.0	50.0	50.0	50.0	50.0	50.0
Pessimistic	45.0	45.0	45.0	45.0	45.0	45.0	45.0	45.0	45.0	45.0

Accrued Liabilities (% of Sales)

Base Case	8.0%	8.0%	8.0%	8.0%	8.0%	8.0%	8.0%	8.0%	8.0%	8.0%
Sponsor	8.0%	8.0%	8.0%	8.0%	8.0%	8.0%	8.0%	8.0%	8.0%	8.0%
Management	8.0%	8.0%	8.0%	8.0%	8.0%	8.0%	8.0%	8.0%	8.0%	8.0%
Optimistic	7.0%	7.0%	7.0%	7.0%	7.0%	7.0%	7.0%	7.0%	7.0%	7.0%
Pessimistic	9.0%	9.0%	9.0%	9.0%	9.0%	9.0%	9.0%	9.0%	9.0%	9.0%

Other Current Liabilities (% of Sales)

Base Case	8.0%	8.0%	8.0%	8.0%	8.0%	8.0%	8.0%	8.0%	8.0%	8.0%
Sponsor	8.0%	8.0%	8.0%	8.0%	8.0%	8.0%	8.0%	8.0%	8.0%	8.0%
Management	8.0%	8.0%	8.0%	8.0%	8.0%	8.0%	8.0%	8.0%	8.0%	8.0%
Optimistic	7.0%	7.0%	7.0%	7.0%	7.0%	7.0%	7.0%	7.0%	7.0%	7.0%
Pessimistic	9.0%	9.0%	9.0%	9.0%	9.0%	9.0%	9.0%	9.0%	9.0%	9.0%

Cash Flow Statement

CapEx (% of Sales)

Base Case	2.0%	2.0%	2.0%	2.0%	2.0%	2.0%	2.0%	2.0%	2.0%	2.0%
Sponsor	2.0%	2.0%	2.0%	2.0%	2.0%	2.0%	2.0%	2.0%	2.0%	2.0%
Management	2.0%	2.0%	2.0%	2.0%	2.0%	2.0%	2.0%	2.0%	2.0%	2.0%
Optimistic	1.5%	1.5%	1.5%	1.5%	1.5%	1.5%	1.5%	1.5%	1.5%	1.5%
Pessimistic	2.5%	2.5%	2.5%	2.5%	2.5%	2.5%	2.5%	2.5%	2.5%	2.5%

2. The *expectation-based approach* sets the initial purchase price onto the level that the seller expects. This approach requires good information about the seller's true expectations.

3. The *value-based approach* tries to set the initial purchase price depending on the real value of the company. Often, the real value is approximated by using trading multiples of comparable companies.

Exhibit 13.6 shows the calculation of the purchase price for Toys R Us using the market-based approach of both an EBITDA multiple and a share price. The model calculates the enterprise value based on a 7.5× EBITDA multiple. For the share price method, instead of adding a premium to the 2004 share price, which we believe gives an inflated valuation due to market imperfections and the share price being too high, the price per share is an implied share price backed out from the enterprise value calculated in the EBITDA multiple method. The remainder of this section sets the model as a private transaction using the EBITDA multiple to calculate the firm's value, as we believe this is a more robust methodology for calculating the purchase price and value of equity.

Use 2. *Professional and financing fees*. There are three kinds of fees: investment banker/lender fees (normally calculated as a % of the deal value or % of each debt instrument), legal fees (based on billed hours), and consulting fees (based on billed days).

Depending on the desired accuracy, there are two options for modeling these fees: rules of thumb or explicit modeling:

1. As a rule of thumb, in big deals professional fees make up 3% to 6% of the uses of funds. In small deals, this can increase to 10%, because some work items have the same complexity independent of the size of the deal.

2. Explicit modeling is more accurate, but is also much more time consuming. Given that the differences between explicit modeling and rules of thumb are relatively small compared with the effects of other decisions, the rule of thumb is normally sufficient (see Exhibit 13.7).

Use 3. *Retirement of debt*. In most cases the pre-LBO debt must be retired when the deal takes place, due to covenants that protect the existing debt against LBOs and the downgrading of the target's credit rating which normally breaches these covenants. The PE firm must determine the amount of debt that must be retired and the early repayment costs that the debt contracts might require.

13.4 DETERMINE TRANSACTION STRUCTURE: SOURCES OF FUNDS

The uses of funds must be covered by the sources of funds. There are three main sources of funds: debt, new equity, and the existing cash on the balance sheet of the target. As with the uses of funds, at this point in the modeling process, we will not produce final numbers for the sources of funds, but will produce a functioning model with a reasonable starting assumption.

The three steps to determine the sources of funds are: (1) determine debt capacity, (2) determine debt structure, and (3) plug in the required equity contribution.

Step 1. *Determine debt capacity*. The amount of debt a company can take on is limited based on the fact that it must be able to service the interest payment and debt repayment. In practice, debt capacity is determined by the buy-side investment bank. However, to double-check their results and to have a good view on how much risk the proposal of

---

EXHIBIT 13.6

PURCHASE PRICE ASSUMPTIONS

Type of target (public/private)	Private	Type of target (public/private)	Public
Entry EBITDA multiple	7.50×		
		Offer price per share	$19.00
2008 EBITDA	585.0	Fully diluted shares outstanding (million)	213
Enterprise value	**4,387.5**	**Equity purchase price**	**4,041.5**
Less: Total debt	(2,349.0)	Plus: Total debt	2,349.0
Less: Preferred securities	0.0	Plus: Preferred securities	0.0
Less: Non-controlling interest	0.0	Plus: Non-controlling interest	0.0
Plus: Cash and cash equivalents	2,003.0	Less: Cash and cash equivalents	(2,003.0)
Equity purchase price	**4,041.5**	**Enterprise value**	**4,387.5**

---

the investment bank involves, PE firms should also use the following rules of thumb and methods:

- *Debt capacity = 5 * EBITDA multiple*—as a rule of thumb, the debt capacity of a company is approximately 5× its annual EBITDA. Unfortunately, this rule does not take the variability of the company's cash flows into account (the higher the variability, the lower the debt capacity).

- *Debt capacity = 100% cash sweep in ~8 years*—another rule of thumb says that debt capacity equals the amount of debt that the company could service and pay back in 8 years assuming a 100% cash sweep.[2] As shown in Exhibit 13.8, the debt structure in the Toys R Us model pays down senior debt in 8 years based on 70% leverage and a 4.2× debt/EBITDA ratio.

- *Debt capacity = ISCR and DSCR*—another driver of debt capacity is the interest and debt service coverage ratios. In particular, lending institutions will require the target to remain within predefined bounds, governed by these debt covenants.

- *Optimal amount of debt based on tradeoff theory*—based on the tradeoff theory (Kraus and Litzenberger, 1973), it is possible to calculate the optimal amount of debt for a company. The amount of debt is optimal if the benefits of debt (e.g., tax shields) equal the cost of debt (e.g., financial distress).

Step 2. *Debt structure.* The PE firm must decide on the debt instruments to use and on the quantity of these debt instruments. A typical debt structure for an LBO contains around 45% of bank debt, 25% of high-yield bonds, 5% of mezzanine debt, and 30% equity.

Step 3. *Equity structure.* Equity makes up the difference between the debt and the uses of funds; it is a plugged value in the model. Structuring equity involves deciding which investors to include, how much each investor invests, and at what valuation the investors

---

2. A cash sweep is a debt covenant that requires the paydown of the outstanding debt with available free cash flows. A 100% cash sweep requires the use of the entire free cash flow to retire the debt with this covenant.

EXHIBIT 13.7

TOYS R US FINANCING STRUCTURE AND FEES ASSUMPTIONS

Toys "R" Us LBO Model - Financing Structure and Fees Assumptions

Purchase Price Assumptions

Type of Target (Public/Private)	2 0 Private
Entry EBITDA Multiple	7.5x
2004 EBITDA	585.0
Enterprise Value	**4,387.5**
Less: Total Debt	(2,349.0)
Less: Preferred Securities	0.0
Less: Noncontrolling Interest	0.0
Plus: Cash and Cash Equivalents	2,003.0
Equity Purchase Price	**4,041.5**
Fully Diluted Shares Outstanding (End 2004)	214.0
Offer Price Per Share	$19.0

Financing Structure

	Structure 1	Structure 2	Structure 3	Structure 4	Structure 5	Active Case: Structure 2
Sources of Funds						
Revolving Credit Facility Available	100.0	100.0	100.0	100.0	100.0	100.0
Revolving Credit Facility Drawn Down	50.0	50.0	25.0	25.0	--	50.0
Senior Long Term Debt	1,800.0	2,000.0	2,200.0	2,400.0	1,625.0	2,000.0
Subordinated Debt (Mezz)	1,200.0	1,250.0	1,300.0	1,300.0	800.0	1,250.0
Equity Contribution	1,537.5	1,337.5	1,112.5	912.5	2,212.5	1,337.5
Cash on Hand	2,003.0	2,003.0	2,003.0	2,003.0	2,003.0	2,003.0
Total Sources	**6,640.5**	**6,640.5**	**6,640.5**	**6,640.5**	**6,640.5**	**6,640.5**
					0.70	
Uses of Funds						
Purchase Equity	4,041.5	4,041.5	4,041.5	4,041.5	4,041.5	4,041.5
Re-Pay Existing Debt	2,349.0	2,349.0	2,349.0	2,349.0	2,349.0	2,349.0
Deferred Financing Fees	100.0	100.0	100.0	100.0	100.0	100.0
Other Fees and Expenses	150.0	150.0	150.0	150.0	150.0	150.0
Total Uses	**6,640.5**	**6,640.5**	**6,640.5**	**6,640.5**	**6,640.5**	**6,640.5**
Check	0.0	0.0	0.0	0.0	0.0	0.0

Deferred Financing Fees

Financing Structure 2

	Amount	Fees %	Fees £
Revolving Credit Facility	100.0	1.75%	1.8
Senior Long Term Debt	2,000.0	1.75%	35.0
Subordinated Debt (Mezz)	1,250.0	2.25%	28.1
Other (Bridging Loan)	1,250.0	1.00%	12.5
Other Financing Fees and Expenses			22.6
Total Financing Fees			**100.0**

Amortisation of Deferred Financing Fees

	Year	Term	1.0 31-Dec-05	2.0 31-Dec-06	3.0 31-Dec-07	4.0 31-Dec-08	5.0 31-Dec-09	6.0 31-Dec-10	7.0 31-Dec-11	8.0 31-Dec-12	9.0 31-Dec-13	10.0 31-Dec-14
Revolving Credit Facility		6.0	0.3	0.3	0.3	0.3	0.3	0.3	--	--	--	--
Senior Long Term Debt		7.0	--	--	--	--	--	--	--	--	--	--
Subordinated Debt (Mezz)		10.0	2.8	2.8	2.8	2.8	2.8	2.8	2.8	2.8	2.8	2.8
Other (Bridging Loan)		10.0	1.3	1.3	1.3	1.3	1.3	1.3	1.3	1.3	1.3	1.3
Annual Amortisation			4.4	4.4	4.4	4.4	4.4	4.4	4.1	4.1	4.1	4.1
Agent Fees (Revolver)			0.15	0.15	0.15	0.15	0.15	0.15	0.15	0.15	0.15	0.15

invest. Furthermore, the exact equity instruments (e.g., common shares, preference shares) must be determined. The structuring of equity should:

- *Ensure control*—PE firms in LBOs want to control the target. But they need to be mindful that control is influenced by both the ownership of the majority of shares and the terms and conditions of the transaction.

- *Align management incentives*—as part of the PE governance approach, the management should get a large equity stake that should represent a significant part of the management's net worth. Furthermore, ratchets connected to either operational measures or exit events can be created.

- *Reduce risk*—equity structure is especially important if the buyout fails. For example, owning a significant stake of preferred shares pays off more than a significant stake of common shares (due to the owner's position in the pecking order).

- *Enable high returns*—obviously, the equity structure has a direct effect on investor returns.

Exhibit 13.7 shows the financing structure and fees section from the Toys R Us model. This section should include the purchase price calculation, financing and other fees, and the sources and uses of funds. The sources and uses section is a summary of the flows of cash required to complete the transaction. Notice there is also functionality to include a number of alternative financing structures, which will be linked and operated by a toggle switch on the transaction summary page (see Section 13.6).

The final part of this stage is to link the sources and uses section of the model to the adjustments column in the balance sheet, shown blank in Exhibit 13.3. The main adjustments are as follows:

- (−) Cash and cash equivalents if these have been used as part of the sources for the deal

- (+) Goodwill, which is equal to the equity purchase price minus the book value of existing shareholder equity

- (+) Deferred financing fees calculated in Section 13.3 and Exhibit 13.7

- (+) Cash from new debt instruments

- (−) Retirement of existing debt (if retired)

- (+) Net equity contribution, which equals the equity contribution from sources of funds, less other fees and expenses

- (−) Existing shareholder equity.

The completed adjustments section of the balance sheet is shown in Exhibit 13.10.

13.5 BUILD A POST–TRANSACTION STRUCTURE MODEL

At this stage, the effects of the financing structure must be fed back into the pre–transaction structure model to generate a post–transaction structure model. This phase only requires work steps, so no assumptions or decisions are needed.

Building the post–transaction structure model is comprised of four substeps: (1) build the debt schedule, (2) complete the income statement from EBIT down to net income, (3) complete the balance sheet, and (4) complete the cash flow statement.

Step 1. *Build the debt schedule*. The first step is to build the debt schedule as illustrated in Exhibit 13.8. The debt schedule calculates the free cash flows available for mandatory and optional debt repayment. It is constructed in order of paying down the loans, so excess cash flows can drip through to pay down debt.

The free cash flows calculated from the cash flow statement are available for debt repayment. Following mandatory debt repayments the remaining funds plus cash from the balance sheet are available for optional debt repayments. A switch is added to the transaction summary options selector to enable the user to switch the cash flow sweep from the balance sheet on and off. This is a useful functionality allowing a proportion of the excess cash to be paid out as a dividend as opposed to paying down debt, should this be required by the investors.

The debt schedule calculates the interest and principal payments for each tranche of debt as follows:

- Beginning balance (linked from the ending balance from the previous year)
- (−) Mandatory repayments
- (−) Optional repayments
- (=) Ending balance (which will be the beginning balance for the subsequent year)
- The interest rate is LIBOR plus the spread or a fixed coupon rate
- The interest expense is equal to the interest rate multiplied by the average of beginning and ending debt balances.

Step 2. *Complete the income statement from EBIT down to net income*. Complete the cash interest expense section of the income statement from the debt schedule (Exhibit 13.8) and financing fees and assumptions sheet (Exhibit 13.7). The completed income statement is shown in Exhibit 13.9.

Step 3. *Complete balance sheet*. Now complete the debt section of the balance sheet from the ending balances of each debt instrument on the debt schedule. Shareholders' equity is equal to the previous year's shareholders' equity plus the current year's net income from the income statement. The completed balance sheet is shown in Exhibit 13.10.

Step 4. *Complete cash flow statement*. Finally, complete the financing activities section of the cash flow statement by linking the optional and mandatory repayment lines in the debt schedule, for each debt instrument. The completed cash flow statement is shown in Exhibit 13.11.

13.6   DETERMINE EXIT AND COMPUTE RETURNS

The PE firm must model the exit and calculate output measures such as the returns for each stakeholder.

EXHIBIT 13.8

TOYS R US DEBT SCHEDULE

Toys "R" Us LBO Model - Debt Schedule ($m)

	1	2	3	4	5	6	7	8	9	10
	Pro forma 2004	Proj. 2005	Proj. 2006	Proj. 2007	Proj. 2008	Proj. 2009	Proj. 2010	Proj. 2011	Proj. 2012	Proj. 2013	Proj. 2014
LIBOR Forward Rates	3.00%	3.00%	3.15%	3.30%	3.60%	4.00%	4.35%	4.80%	4.85%	5.10%	5.25%
FCFs Available for Debt Repayment		183.6	220.1	235.2	250.2	266.4	285.1	305.7	329.5	350.0	367.0
Minimum Excess Cash on BS	--										
Total Mandatory Repayments		(20.0)	(20.0)	(20.0)	(20.0)	(20.0)	(20.0)	(20.0)	(20.0)	0.0	0.0
Cash from Balance Sheet		0.0	0.0	0.0	0.0	0.0	0.0	0.0	0.0	25.8	375.8
Cash Available for Optional Repayments		163.6	200.1	215.2	230.2	246.4	265.1	285.7	309.5	375.8	742.7

		2005	2006	2007	2008	2009	2010	2011	2012	2013	2014
Revolving Credit Facility											
Amount Available (Credit Limit)	100.00										
Spread	3.25%										
Remaining Term	6 years										
Commitment Fee on Unused Portion	0.5%										
Beginning Balance		50.00	--	--	--	--	--	--	--	--	--
Drawdown/(Repayment)		(50.00)									
Ending Balance		--									
Interest Rate		6.25%	6.40%	6.55%	6.85%	7.25%	7.60%	8.05%	8.10%	8.35%	8.50%
Interest Expense		1.56	--	--	--	--	--	--	--	--	--
Commitment Fee on Unused Balance on Revolver Facility		0.38	0.50	0.50	0.50	0.50	0.50	0.50	0.50	0.50	0.50

		2005	2006	2007	2008	2009	2010	2011	2012	2013	2014
Senior Long Term Debt											
Size	2,000.00										
Spread	3.50%										
Remaining Term	8 years										
Repayment Schedule	1.0%	Per Annum, Bullet at Maturity									
Beginning Balance		2,000.00	1,866.42	1,646.28	1,411.10	1,160.88	894.49	609.40	303.68	--	--
Mandatory Repayment		(20.00)	(20.00)	(20.00)	(20.00)	(20.00)	(20.00)	(20.00)	(20.00)	--	--
Optional Repayment		(113.58)	(200.14)	(215.17)	(230.22)	(246.39)	(265.08)	(285.72)	(233.68)	--	--
Ending Balance		1,866.42	1,646.28	1,411.10	1,160.88	894.49	609.40	303.68	--	--	--
Interest Rate		6.50%	6.65%	6.80%	7.10%	7.50%	7.85%	8.30%	8.35%	8.60%	8.75%
Interest Expense		125.66	116.80	103.95	91.31	77.08	59.03	37.89	12.68	--	--

(continued)

EXHIBIT 13.8 (cont.)

Existing Debt

			2005	2006	2007	2008	2009	2010	2011	2012	2013	2014
Size	—											
Spread	3.00%											
Remaining Term	0 years											
Repayment Schedule	1.0%	Per Annum, Bullet at Maturity										
Beginning Balance			—	—	—	—	—	—	—	—	—	—
Mandatory Repayment			—	—	—	—	—	—	—	—	—	—
Optional Repayment			—	—	—	—	—	—	—	—	—	—
Ending Balance			—	—	—	—	—	—	—	—	—	—
Interest Rate			6.0%	6.2%	6.3%	6.6%	7.0%	7.4%	7.8%	7.9%	8.1%	8.3%
Interest Expense			—	—	—	—	—	—	—	—	—	—

Subordinated Debt (Mezz)

		2005	2006	2007	2008	2009	2010	2011	2012	2013	2014
Size	1,250.00										
Coupon	8.00%										
Term	10 years										
Beginning Balance		1,250.00	1,250.00	1,250.00	1,250.00	1,250.00	1,250.00	1,250.00	1,250.00	1,250.00	1,250.00
Repayment											
Ending Balance		1,250.00	1,250.00	1,250.00	1,250.00	1,250.00	1,250.00	1,250.00	1,250.00	1,250.00	1,250.00
Interest Expense		100.00	100.00	100.00	100.00	100.00	100.00	100.00	100.00	100.00	100.00

EXHIBIT 13.9

TOYS R US COMPLETED INCOME STATEMENT

Toys "R" Us LBO Model - Income Statement ($m)

	Hist. 2001	Hist. 2002	Hist. 2003	Hist. 2004	1 Proj. 2005	2 Proj. 2006	3 Proj. 2007	4 Proj. 2008	5 Proj. 2009	6 Proj. 2010	7 Proj. 2011	8 Proj. 2012	9 Proj. 2013	10 Proj. 2014
Sales	11,332.0	11,019.0	11,305.0	11,320.0	11,546.4	11,777.3	12,012.9	12,253.1	12,498.2	12,748.2	13,003.1	13,263.2	13,528.4	13,799.0
% growth	--	(2.8%)	2.6%	0.1%	2.0%	2.0%	2.0%	2.0%	2.0%	2.0%	2.0%	2.0%	2.0%	2.0%
Cost of Goods Sold	7,815.0	7,604.0	7,799.0	7,646.0	7,793.8	7,949.7	8,108.7	8,270.9	8,436.3	8,605.0	8,777.1	8,952.6	9,131.7	9,314.3
Gross Profit	3,517.0	3,415.0	3,506.0	3,674.0	3,752.6	3,827.6	3,904.2	3,982.3	4,061.9	4,143.2	4,226.0	4,310.5	4,396.7	4,484.7
% margin	31.0%	31.0%	31.0%	32.5%	32.5%	32.5%	32.5%	32.5%	32.5%	32.5%	32.5%	32.5%	32.5%	32.5%
Selling, General & Administrative	2,801.0	2,721.0	2,724.0	3,026.0	2,886.6	2,944.3	3,003.2	3,063.3	3,124.5	3,187.0	3,250.8	3,315.8	3,382.1	3,449.8
% sales	24.7%	24.7%	24.1%	26.7%	25.0%	25.0%	25.0%	25.0%	25.0%	25.0%	25.0%	25.0%	25.0%	25.0%
Other Expense / (Income)	--	186.0	--	63.0	115.5	117.8	120.1	122.5	125.0	127.5	130.0	132.6	135.3	138.0
EBITDA	716.0	508.0	782.0	585.0	750.5	765.5	780.8	796.5	812.4	828.6	845.2	862.1	879.3	896.9
% margin	6.3%	4.6%	6.9%	5.2%	6.5%	6.5%	6.5%	6.5%	6.5%	6.5%	6.5%	6.5%	6.5%	6.5%
Depreciation & Amortization	290.0	308.0	339.0	368.0	288.7	294.4	300.3	306.3	312.5	318.7	325.1	331.6	338.2	345.0
EBIT	426.0	200.0	443.0	217.0	461.9	471.1	480.5	490.1	499.9	509.9	520.1	530.5	541.1	552.0
% margin	3.8%	1.8%	3.9%	1.9%	4.0%	4.0%	4.0%	4.0%	4.0%	4.0%	4.0%	4.0%	4.0%	4.0%
Interest Expense														
Existing Debt														
Revolving Credit Facility					1.6									
Senior Long Term Debt					125.7	116.8	104.0	91.3	77.1	59.0	37.9	12.7	--	--
Subordinated Debt (Mezz)					100.0	100.0	100.0	100.0	100.0	100.0	100.0	100.0	100.0	100.0
Commitment Fee on Unused Revolver					0.4	0.5	0.5	0.5	0.5	0.5	0.5	0.5	0.5	0.5
Agent Fees					0.2	0.2	0.2	0.2	0.2	0.2	0.2	0.2	0.2	0.2
Cash Interest Expense					227.7	217.4	204.6	192.0	177.7	159.7	138.5	113.3	100.7	100.7
Amortisation of Deferred Financing Fees					4.4	4.4	4.4	4.4	4.4	4.4	4.4	4.1	4.1	4.1
Total Interest Expense					232.1	221.8	209.0	196.3	182.1	164.0	142.6	117.4	104.7	104.7
Interest Income					--	--	--	--	--	--	--	(0.5)	(8.0)	(22.4)
Net Interest Expense					232.1	221.8	209.0	196.3	182.1	164.0	142.6	116.9	96.7	82.3
EBT (Earnings Before Tax)					229.8	249.3	271.6	293.8	317.8	345.9	377.5	413.7	444.5	469.6
Income Tax Expense					87.3	94.7	103.2	111.6	120.8	131.4	143.5	157.2	168.9	178.5
Net Income					142.4	154.6	168.4	182.2	197.1	214.5	234.1	256.5	275.6	291.2
% margin					1.2%	1.3%	1.4%	1.5%	1.6%	1.7%	1.8%	1.9%	2.0%	2.1%

Income Statement Assumptions

	Hist. 2001	Hist. 2002	Hist. 2003	Hist. 2004	2005	2006	2007	2008	2009	2010	2011	2012	2013	2014
Sales (% YoY growth)	--	(2.8%)	2.6%	0.1%	2.0%	2.0%	2.0%	2.0%	2.0%	2.0%	2.0%	2.0%	2.0%	2.0%
Cost of Goods Sold (% margin)	69.0%	69.0%	69.0%	67.5%	67.5%	67.5%	67.5%	67.5%	67.5%	67.5%	67.5%	67.5%	67.5%	67.5%
SG&A (% sales)	24.7%	24.7%	24.1%	26.7%	25.0%	25.0%	25.0%	25.0%	25.0%	25.0%	25.0%	25.0%	25.0%	25.0%
Other Expense / (Income) (% of sales)				0.6%	1.0%	1.0%	1.0%	1.0%	1.0%	1.0%	1.0%	1.0%	1.0%	1.0%
Depreciation & Amortization (% of sales)	2.6%	1.7%	3.0%	3.3%	2.5%	2.5%	2.5%	2.5%	2.5%	2.5%	2.5%	2.5%	2.5%	2.5%
Interest Income				4.0%	4.0%	4.0%	4.0%	4.0%	4.0%	4.0%	4.0%	4.0%	4.0%	4.0%
Tax Rate				38.0%	38.0%	38.0%	38.0%	38.0%	38.0%	38.0%	38.0%	38.0%	38.0%	38.0%

EXHIBIT 13.10

TOYS R US COMPLETED BALANCE SHEET

Toys "R" Us LBO Model - Balance Sheet ($m)

	Actual	Incr/(Decr)	Pro Forma	1	2	3	4	5	6	7	8	9	10
				Proj.	Proj.	Proj.	Proj.	Proj.	Proj.	Proj.	Proj.	Proj.	Proj.
	2004		2004	2005	2006	2007	2008	2009	2010	2011	2012	2013	2014
Cash and Cash Equivalents	2,003.0	(2,003.0)	--	--	--	--	--	--	--	--	25.8	375.8	742.7
Accounts Receivable	146.0	146.0	146.0	158.2	161.3	164.6	167.9	171.2	174.6	178.1	181.7	185.3	189.0
Inventory	2,094.0	2,094.0	2,094.0	2,135.3	2,178.0	2,221.6	2,266.0	2,311.3	2,357.5	2,404.7	2,452.8	2,501.8	2,551.9
Prepaid Expenses and Other Current Assets	486.0	486.0	486.0	461.9	471.1	480.5	490.1	499.9	509.9	520.1	530.5	541.1	552.0
Total Current Assets	**4,729.0**		**2,726.0**	**2,755.3**	**2,810.4**	**2,866.6**	**2,924.0**	**2,982.4**	**3,042.1**	**3,102.9**	**3,190.8**	**3,604.1**	**4,035.6**
PPE Beginning Balance	--	--	--	4,439.0	4,381.3	4,322.4	4,262.3	4,201.1	4,138.6	4,074.8	4,009.8	3,943.5	3,875.8
CapEx	--	--	--	230.9	235.5	240.3	245.1	250.0	255.0	260.1	265.3	270.6	276.0
Depreciation and Amortisation	--	--	--	(288.7)	(294.4)	(300.3)	(306.3)	(312.5)	(318.7)	(325.1)	(331.6)	(338.2)	(345.0)
PPE Ending Balance	4,439.0		4,439.0	4,381.3	4,322.4	4,262.3	4,201.1	4,138.6	4,074.8	4,009.8	3,943.5	3,875.8	3,806.9
Goodwill and Intangible Assets	348.0	67.5	415.5	415.5	415.5	415.5	415.5	415.5	415.5	415.5	415.5	415.5	415.5
Other Assets	749.0		749.0	749.0	749.0	749.0	749.0	749.0	749.0	749.0	749.0	749.0	749.0
Deferred Financing Fees	--	100.0	100.0	95.6	91.3	86.9	82.6	78.2	73.9	69.8	65.8	61.7	57.6
Total Assets	**10,265.0**		**8,429.5**	**8,396.7**	**8,388.6**	**8,380.4**	**8,372.1**	**8,363.7**	**8,355.3**	**8,347.1**	**8,364.5**	**8,706.1**	**9,064.6**
Accounts Payable	1,022.0		1,022.0	1,024.9	1,045.4	1,066.3	1,087.7	1,109.4	1,131.6	1,154.2	1,177.3	1,200.9	1,224.9
Accrued Liabilities	866.0		866.0	923.7	942.2	961.0	980.3	999.9	1,019.9	1,040.2	1,061.1	1,082.3	1,103.9
Other Current Liabilities	976.0		976.0	923.7	942.2	961.0	980.3	999.9	1,019.9	1,040.2	1,061.1	1,082.3	1,103.9
Total Current Liabilities	**2,864.0**		**2,864.0**	**2,872.4**	**2,929.8**	**2,988.4**	**3,048.2**	**3,109.1**	**3,171.3**	**3,234.7**	**3,299.4**	**3,365.4**	**3,432.7**
Existing Debt	2,349.0	(2,349.0)	--	--	--	--	--	--	--	--	--	--	--
Revolving Credit Facility		50.0	50.0	--	--	--	--	--	--	--	--	--	--
Senior Long Term Debt	2,000.0	2,000.0	2,000.0	1,866.4	1,646.3	1,411.1	1,160.9	894.5	609.4	303.7	--	--	--
Subordinated Debt (Mezz)	1,250.0	1,250.0	1,250.0	1,250.0	1,250.0	1,250.0	1,250.0	1,250.0	1,250.0	1,250.0	1,250.0	1,250.0	1,250.0
Other Debt														
Other LT Liabilities	1,078.0	1,078.0	1,078.0	1,078.0	1,078.0	1,078.0	1,078.0	1,078.0	1,078.0	1,078.0	1,078.0	1,078.0	1,078.0
Total Liabilities	**6,291.0**		**7,242.0**	**7,066.8**	**6,904.1**	**6,727.5**	**6,537.1**	**6,331.6**	**6,108.7**	**5,866.4**	**5,627.4**	**5,693.4**	**5,760.7**
Shareholders' Equity	3,974.0	(2,786.5)	1,187.5	1,329.9	1,484.5	1,652.9	1,835.0	2,032.1	2,246.6	2,480.6	2,737.1	3,012.7	3,303.8
Total Shareholders' Equity	**3,974.0**		**1,187.5**	**1,329.9**	**1,484.5**	**1,652.9**	**1,835.0**	**2,032.1**	**2,246.6**	**2,480.6**	**2,737.1**	**3,012.7**	**3,303.8**
Total Liabilities and Equity	**10,265.0**		**8,429.5**	**8,396.7**	**8,388.6**	**8,380.4**	**8,372.1**	**8,363.7**	**8,355.3**	**8,347.1**	**8,364.5**	**8,706.1**	**9,064.6**
Balance Check	*0.000*		*0.000*	*0.000*	*0.000*	*0.000*	*0.000*	*0.000*	*0.000*	*0.000*	*0.000*	*0.000*	*0.000*
Net Working Capital	(138.0)	(138.0)	(138.0)	(117.0)	(119.4)	(121.8)	(124.2)	(126.7)	(129.2)	(131.8)	(134.4)	(137.1)	(139.9)
(Increase) / Decrease in Net Working Capital				(21.0)	2.3	2.4	2.4	2.5	2.5	2.6	2.6	2.7	2.7

Balance Sheet Assumptions

Current Assets

	Actual	Incr/(Decr)	Pro Forma	2005	2006	2007	2008	2009	2010	2011	2012	2013	2014
Days Sales Outstanding (DSO)	4.7		4.7	5.0	5.0	5.0	5.0	5.0	5.0	5.0	5.0	5.0	5.0
Days Inventory Held (DIH)	100.0		100.0	100.0	100.0	100.0	100.0	100.0	100.0	100.0	100.0	100.0	100.0
Prepaid and Other Current Assets (% of sales)	4.3%		4.3%	4.0%	4.0%	4.0%	4.0%	4.0%	4.0%	4.0%	4.0%	4.0%	4.0%

Current Liabilities

	Actual	Incr/(Decr)	Pro Forma	2005	2006	2007	2008	2009	2010	2011	2012	2013	2014
Days Payable Outstanding (DPO)	48.8		48.8	48.0	48.0	48.0	48.0	48.0	48.0	48.0	48.0	48.0	48.0
Accrued Liabilities (% of sales)	7.7%		7.7%	8.0%	8.0%	8.0%	8.0%	8.0%	8.0%	8.0%	8.0%	8.0%	8.0%
Other Current Liabilities (% of sales)	8.6%		8.6%	8.0%	8.0%	8.0%	8.0%	8.0%	8.0%	8.0%	8.0%	8.0%	8.0%

EXHIBIT 13.11

TOYS R US COMPLETED CASH FLOW STATEMENT

Toys "R" Us LBO Model - Cash Flow Statement ($m)	1 Proj. 2005	2 Proj. 2006	3 Proj. 2007	4 Proj. 2008	5 Proj. 2009	6 Proj. 2010	7 Proj. 2011	8 Proj. 2012	9 Proj. 2013	10 Proj. 2014
Operating Activities										
Net Income	142.4	154.6	168.4	182.2	197.1	214.5	234.1	256.5	275.6	291.2
Depreciation & Amortization	288.7	294.4	300.3	306.3	312.5	318.7	325.1	331.6	338.2	345.0
Amortisation of Deferred Financing Fees	4.4	4.4	4.4	4.4	4.4	4.4	4.1	4.1	4.1	4.1
Sub Total	435.5	453.3	473.0	492.8	513.9	537.5	563.2	592.1	617.8	640.2
Changes in Working Capital Items										
Accounts Receivable (DSO)	(12.2)	(3.2)	(3.2)	(3.3)	(3.4)	(3.4)	(3.5)	(3.6)	(3.6)	(3.7)
Inventory (DIH)	(41.3)	(42.7)	(43.6)	(44.4)	(45.3)	(46.2)	(47.2)	(48.1)	(49.1)	(50.0)
Prepaid Expenses	24.1	(9.2)	(9.4)	(9.6)	(9.8)	(10.0)	(10.2)	(10.4)	(10.6)	(10.8)
Accounts Payable (DPO)	2.9	20.5	20.9	21.3	21.8	22.2	22.6	23.1	23.5	24.0
Accrued Liabilities	57.7	18.5	18.8	19.2	19.6	20.0	20.4	20.8	21.2	21.6
Other Current Liabilities	(52.3)	18.5	18.8	19.2	19.6	20.0	20.4	20.8	21.2	21.6
(Inc.) / Dec. in Net Working Capital	(21.0)	2.3	2.4	2.4	2.5	2.5	2.6	2.6	2.7	2.7
Cash Flow from Operating Activities	414.5	455.7	475.4	495.3	516.4	540.0	565.8	594.7	620.5	642.9
Investing Activities										
Capital Expenditures	(230.9)	(235.5)	(240.3)	(245.1)	(250.0)	(255.0)	(260.1)	(265.3)	(270.6)	(276.0)
Other Investing Activities	--	--	--	--	--	--	--	--	--	--
Cash Flow from Investing Activities	(230.9)	(235.5)	(240.3)	(245.1)	(250.0)	(255.0)	(260.1)	(265.3)	(270.6)	(276.0)
Free Cash Flows	183.6	220.1	235.2	250.2	266.4	285.1	305.7	329.5	350.0	367.0
Financing Activities										
Existing Debt	(50.0)	--	--	--	--	--	--	--	--	--
Revolving Credit Facility	--	--	--	--	--	--	--	--	--	--
Senior Long Term Debt	(133.6)	(220.1)	(235.2)	(250.2)	(266.4)	(285.1)	(305.7)	(303.7)	--	--
Subordinated Debt (Mezz)	--	--	--	--	--	--	--	--	--	--
Other Debt	--	--	--	--	--	--	--	--	--	--
Dividends	--	--	--	--	--	--	--	--	--	--
Equity Issuance / (Repurchase)	--	--	--	--	--	--	--	--	--	--
Cash Flow from Financing Activities	(183.6)	(220.1)	(235.2)	(250.2)	(266.4)	(285.1)	(305.7)	(303.7)	--	--
Excess Cash for the Period	--	--	--	--	--	--	--	25.8	350.0	367.0
Beginning Cash Balance	--	--	--	--	--	--	--	--	25.8	375.8
Ending Cash Balance	--	--	--	--	--	--	--	25.8	375.8	742.7
Cash Flow Statement Assumptions										
Capital Expenditures (% of sales)	2.0%	2.0%	2.0%	2.0%	2.0%	2.0%	2.0%	2.0%	2.0%	2.0%

13.6.1 Model the exit

To model the exit, two decisions are required:

1. First, the exit year must be decided. Typically, LBOs have a time horizon of about 2 to 7 years.

2. Second, the expected price at exit must be modeled.

Usually, PE firms assume the same entry and exit EBITDA multiple. Multiple arbitrage, where a higher exit multiple is achieved, is a function of market conditions and cannot be controlled directly by the PE firm. It is therefore not prudent to assume a higher exit multiple to make the deal work or factor this into the returns. However, PE firms may assume a lower exit multiple, if the entry multiple is higher than the historic multiple of the industry.

13.6.2 Compute returns and other output measures

After all assumptions and decisions are included in the model, the most important output measures can finally be calculated. The return from an LBO is measured using the IRR and the money multiple (or cash-on-cash return, COC). A screenshot of how we modeled the returns for the Toys R Us deal is shown in Exhibit 13.12.

Assuming the base case operating scenario, 70% leverage, and entry and exit multiples of 7.5×, the Toys R Us deal would return an IRR of 24.2% and a COC multiple of 3×, assuming an exit after 5 years. The first sensitivity analysis at the bottom left of Exhibit 13.12 shows how different entry and exit multiples affect the IRR. For example, if the exit occurs under favorable market conditions and an exit multiple of 8.5× is achieved, the IRR will go up to 28.9%. However, exiting under unfavorable conditions at 6.5× would reduce the IRR to 18.6%. The second sensitivity shows the effect of varying the exit year. This clearly shows the negative effect on IRR of a delayed exit, all other parameters remaining constant. These are the most common sensitivities for an LBO transaction, but other analyses can be added based on the sponsor's requirements.

One final warning about the use of IRR as a measure for returns: The best return is achieved in Year 1, at 87.8%. However, withdrawing at this point would only make financial sense if the amount withdrawn could be re-invested immediately at a relatively high return, higher than the 5-year IRR return. In practice, putting money to work in a PE LBO environment is not straightforward, and investors must often commit funds for a long period of time before they are eventually drawn down and earn the relatively high returns associated with top-quartile funds investing in LBO transactions.

13.6.3 Transaction summary sheet

Finally, a transaction summary sheet, as shown in Exhibit 13.13, is added to the model. This is also known as the *LBO model dashboard*. The transaction summary shows the most important decisions, assumptions, and output measures, and enables the user to make changes to the assumptions or scenarios and see the immediate effect on the returns and debt service coverage ratios. This is done using the toggle switches in the "options selector" box in the top right-hand corner of the sheet.

EXHIBIT 13.12

TOYS R US—RETURNS ANALYSIS

Toys "R" Us LBO Model - Returns Analysis
CoC and IRR Returns

	Pro forma 2004	1 Proj. 2005	2 Proj. 2006	3 Proj. 2007	4 Proj. 2008	5 Proj. 2009	6 Proj. 2010	7 Proj. 2011	8 Proj. 2012	9 Proj. 2013	10 Proj. 2014
Entry EBITDA Multiple	7.5x										
Exit EBITDA Multiple	7.5x										
EBITDA		750.5	765.5	780.8	796.5	812.4	828.6	845.2	852.1	879.3	896.9
Enterprise Value at Exit		5,628.9	5,741.4	5,856.3	5,973.4	6,092.9	6,214.7	6,339.0	6,435.8	6,595.1	6,727.0
Total Debt		(3,116.4)	(2,896.3)	(2,661.1)	(2,410.9)	(2,144.5)	(1,859.4)	(1,553.7)	(1,250.0)	(1,250.0)	(1,250.0)
Cash and Cash Equivalents		–	–	–	–	–	–	–	25.8	375.8	742.7
Net Debt		(3,116.4)	(2,896.3)	(2,661.1)	(2,410.9)	(2,144.5)	(1,859.4)	(1,553.7)	(1,224.2)	(874.2)	(507.3)
Equity Value at Exit		2,512.5	2,845.2	3,195.2	3,562.5	3,948.4	4,355.3	4,785.3	5,241.6	5,720.9	6,219.7
Initial Equity Investment	1,337.5										
Cash on Cash (CoC) Return		1.9x	2.1x	2.4x	2.7x	3.0x	3.3x	3.6x	3.9x	4.3x	4.7x

	1 Proj. 2005	2 Proj. 2006	3 Proj. 2007	4 Proj. 2008	5 Proj. 2009	6 Proj. 2010	7 Proj. 2011	8 Proj. 2012	9 Proj. 2013	10 Proj. 2014
Initial Equity Investment	(1,337.5)	(1,337.5)	(1,337.5)	(1,337.5)	(1,337.5)	(1,337.5)	(1,337.5)	(1,337.5)	(1,337.5)	(1,337.5)
Equity Value at Exit	2,512.5	2,845.2	3,195.2	3,562.5	3,948.4	4,355.3	4,785.3	5,241.6	5,720.9	6,219.7
IRR	87.8%	45.9%	33.7%	27.8%	24.2%	21.7%	20.0%	18.6%	17.5%	16.6%

IRR Sensitivity Analysis

Assuming Exit in 2013E

Entry Multiple \ Exit Multiple	6.5	7.0	7.5	8.0	8.5
6.5	33.0%	36.3%	39.3%	42.1%	44.6%
7.0	24.6%	27.7%	30.5%	33.0%	35.4%
7.5	18.6%	21.5%	24.2%	26.6%	28.9%
8.0	14.0%	16.8%	19.4%	21.7%	23.9%
8.5	10.3%	13.0%	15.5%	17.8%	19.9%

Assuming 7.5x Exit Multiple

Exit Multiple \ Exit Year	2007	2008	2009	2010	2011
6.5	21.8%	19.9%	18.6%	17.5%	16.7%
7.0	28.0%	24.0%	21.5%	19.7%	18.4%
7.5	33.7%	27.8%	24.2%	21.7%	20.0%
8.0	38.9%	31.2%	26.6%	23.6%	21.4%
8.5	43.8%	34.4%	28.9%	25.3%	22.8%

EXHIBIT 13.13

TOYS R US—TRANSACTION SUMMARY SHEET

Toys "R" Us LBO Model - Transaction Summary

Financing Structure

Sources of Funds

Revolving Credit Facility	50.0
Senior Long Term Debt	2,000.0
Subordinated Debt (Mezz)	1,250.0
Equity Contribution	1,337.5
Cash on Hand	2,003.0
Total Sources	**6,640.5**

Uses of Funds

Purchase Equity	4,041.5
Re-Pay Existing Debt	2,349.0
Deferred Financing Fees	100.0
Other Fees and Expenses	150.0
Total Uses	**6,640.5**

Purchase Price

Equity Purchase Price	4,041.5
Exiting Net Debt	346.0
Enterprise Value	4,387.5

Returns Analysis

Exit Year	2009
Entry Multiple	7.5x
Exit Multiple	7.5x
IRR	24.2%
COC	3.0x

Options Selector

Operating Scenario	1	Base Case
Public / Private Target	2	Private
Financing Structure	2	70% Leverage
Interest Calculation	1	Average
BS Cash Flow Sweep	1	Yes

Checks

Balance Sheet	OK
Sources and Uses	OK

Summary Financial Data ($m)

	Hist. 2001	Hist. 2002	Hist. 2003	Hist. 2004	Proj. 1 2005	Proj. 2 2006	Proj. 3 2007	Proj. 4 2008	Proj. 5 2009	Proj. 6 2010	Proj. 7 2011	Proj. 8 2012	Proj. 9 2013	Proj. 10 2014
Sales	11,332.0	11,019.0	11,305.0	11,320.0	11,546.4	11,777.3	12,012.9	12,253.1	12,498.2	12,748.2	13,003.1	13,263.2	13,528.4	13,799.0
% growth		(2.8%)	2.6%	0.1%	2.0%	2.0%	2.0%	2.0%	2.0%	2.0%	2.0%	2.0%	2.0%	2.0%
Gross Profit	3,517.0	3,415.0	3,506.0	3,674.0	3,752.6	3,827.6	3,904.2	3,982.3	4,061.9	4,143.2	4,226.0	4,310.5	4,396.7	4,484.7
% margin	31.0%	31.0%	31.0%	32.5%	32.5%	32.5%	32.5%	32.5%	32.5%	32.5%	32.5%	32.5%	32.5%	32.5%
EBITDA	716.0	508.0	782.0	585.0	750.5	765.5	780.8	796.5	812.4	828.6	845.2	862.1	879.3	896.9
% margin	6.3%	4.6%	6.9%	5.2%	6.5%	6.5%	6.5%	6.5%	6.5%	6.5%	6.5%	6.5%	6.5%	6.5%
Capital Expenditures	402.0	705.0	395.0	262.0	230.9	235.5	240.3	245.1	250.0	255.0	260.1	265.3	270.6	276.0
% sales	3.5%	6.4%	3.5%	2.3%										
Cash Interest Expense					227.7	217.4	204.6	192.0	177.7	159.7	138.5	113.3	100.7	100.7
Total Interest Expense					232.1	221.8	209.0	196.3	182.1	164.0	142.6	117.4	104.7	104.7
Free Cash Flow														
EBITDA					750.5	765.5	780.8	796.5	812.4	828.6	845.2	862.1	879.3	896.9
Less: Cash Interest Expense					(227.7)	(217.4)	(204.6)	(192.0)	(177.7)	(159.7)	(138.5)	(113.3)	(100.7)	(100.7)
Plus: Interest Income					0.0	0.0	0.0	0.0	0.0	0.0	0.0	0.0	0.0	0.0
Less: Income Taxes					(87.3)	(94.7)	(103.2)	(111.6)	(120.8)	(131.4)	(143.5)	(157.2)	(168.9)	(178.5)
Less: Capital Expenditures					(230.9)	(235.5)	(240.3)	(245.1)	(250.0)	(255.0)	(260.1)	(265.3)	(270.6)	(276.0)
Less: Increase in Net Working Capital					(21.0)	2.3	2.4	2.4	2.5	2.5	2.6	2.6	2.7	2.7
Free Cash Flow					**183.6**	**220.1**	**235.2**	**250.2**	**266.4**	**285.1**	**305.7**	**328.4**	**333.9**	**322.2**
Cumulative Free Cash Flow					183.6	403.7	638.9	889.1	1,155.5	1,440.6	1,746.3	2,074.8	2,408.7	2,730.9
Capitalisation Table														
Cash					--	--	--	--	--	--	--	25.80	375.76	742.72
Revolving Credit Facility				50.00	--	--	--	--	--	--	--	--	--	--
Senior Term Loans				2,000.00	1,866.42	1,646.28	1,411.10	1,160.88	894.49	609.40	303.68	--	--	--
Existing Term Loan				--	--	--	--	--	--	--	--	--	--	--
Other Debt				--	--	--	--	--	--	--	--	--	--	--
Total Senior Secured Debt				**2,050.00**	**1,866.42**	**1,646.28**	**1,411.10**	**1,160.88**	**894.49**	**609.40**	**303.68**	**--**	**--**	**--**
Subordinated Debt				1,250.00	1,250.00	1,250.00	1,250.00	1,250.00	1,250.00	1,250.00	1,250.00	1,250.00	1,250.00	1,250.00
Total Debt				**3,300.00**	**3,116.42**	**2,896.28**	**2,661.10**	**2,410.88**	**2,144.49**	**1,859.40**	**1,553.68**	**1,250.00**	**1,250.00**	**1,250.00**
Shareholders' Equity				1,187.50	1,329.95	1,484.51	1,652.88	1,835.04	2,032.11	2,246.56	2,480.62	2,737.09	3,012.65	3,303.81
Total Capitalization				4,487.50	4,446.37	4,380.79	4,313.98	4,245.92	4,176.60	4,105.97	4,034.30	3,987.09	4,262.65	4,553.81
% of Bank Debt Repaid														
Debt Service Coverage														
Leverage Ratio (Debt/Total Capitalisation)					70.1%	66.1%	61.7%	56.8%	51.3%	45.3%	38.5%	31.4%	29.3%	27.4%
EBIT					461.9	471.1	480.5	490.1	499.9	509.9	520.1	530.5	541.1	552.0
Interest Payments					227.2	216.8	204.0	191.3	177.1	159.0	137.9	112.7	100.0	100.0
Mandatory Principal Repayments					70.0	20.0	20.0	20.0	20.0	20.0	20.0	20.0	--	--
Debt Service Requirements					**297.2**	**236.8**	**224.0**	**211.3**	**197.1**	**179.0**	**157.9**	**132.7**	**100.0**	**100.0**
ISCR					2.0x	2.2x	2.4x	2.6x	2.8x	3.2x	3.8x	4.7x	5.4x	5.5x
DSCR					1.6x	2.0x	2.1x	2.3x	2.5x	2.8x	3.3x	4.0x	5.4x	5.5x
Total Debt / EBITDA					4.2x	3.6x	3.4x	3.0x	2.6x	2.2x	1.8x	1.4x	1.4x	1.4x

EXHIBIT 13.14

THE OPTIMIZATION AND ANALYSIS OF AN LBO MODEL IS AN ITERATIVE PROCESS

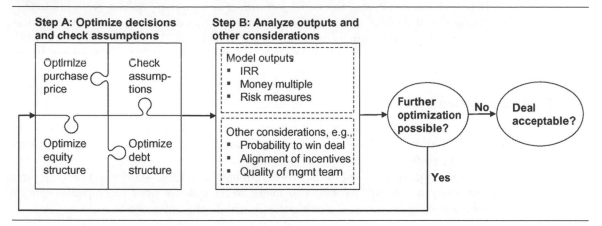

13.7 OPTIMIZATION AND ANALYSIS OF THE LBO MODEL

At the beginning of this phase, the LBO model is fully functional. All relevant information is included and all decisions, assumptions, and output measures are modeled. Changes to decisions and assumptions immediately affect the output measures. However, the modeled decisions are just preliminary so far and have not yet been optimized.

This phase is about optimizing the LBO transaction structure. As shown in Exhibit 13.14, this is an iterative process. In Step A, the PE firm checks the assumptions and attempts to optimize decisions regarding the purchase price, the debt structure, and the equity structure. In Step B, the PE firm analyzes explicit model outputs such as the IRR and COC and risk measurements such as the ISCR. Furthermore, the PE firm has other considerations in mind, such as the probability of winning the deal and the alignment of stakeholder incentives. Finally, if further optimizations could be achieved, the process is repeated. If no further optimization is possible, the transaction structure is defined and the PE firm and other stakeholders must decide whether the proposed deal is acceptable.

The optimization of decisions can be done following two different logics: competition-based optimization or return-based optimization.

13.7.1 Competition-based optimization

When following competition-based optimization, the basic question is: *Given the specific purchase price required to win the deal, can we make the transaction acceptable to all investors?*

This approach is generally used if the PE firm is aware of the approximate purchase price required to win the bid. This is often the case in public-to-private transactions or in industries with lots of comparable PE transactions. Following this approach, the optimization of decisions in each iteration of Step A is normally done in the following order:

1. Set the purchase price to the level that can probably win the bid.

2. Update the debt level and debt structure.

3. Update the equity structure.

It is very important that the initial forecasting assumptions do not get optimized to "make the deal work", although this is a common bad practice in many LBO transactions. In Step B, the main focus of the PE firm is on the IRR and COC. Normally, when deciding whether the deal is acceptable, the transaction IRR is compared with the hurdle IRR rate of the different investors.

13.7.2   Return-based optimization

When following return-based optimization, the basic question is: *Given that the investors want to achieve at least a specific hurdle IRR, what is the maximum price we can pay for the equity?*

This approach is used in the absence of any knowledge about the purchase price that is required to win the bid. This might be the case for private companies with no comparable transactions. Following this approach, the optimization logic is:

- In Step A: If current IRR < target IRR, then consider a lower purchase price, more debt, or a more investor-friendly equity structure. If current IRR > target IRR, then consider a higher purchase price, less debt, or a less investor-friendly equity structure

- In Step B: Stop if current IRR = target IRR.

13.8   ANALYSIS OF THE TOYS R US LBO

Was Toys R Us a good LBO candidate? Overall, Toys R Us 2005 was a good target in 2005, based on the characteristics of strong LBO candidates described in Chapter 12 on LBO transactions. But, it does have a major negative point. We discuss the characteristics below.

Positive characteristics

- It has strong cash flows as shown in the historic income statement in Exhibit 13.2. Although growth has been stagnant, the cash flows are stable. In addition, debtor days are much lower than creditor days—4.7 vs. 48.8, respectively, in 2004 (see Exhibit 13.3). This means Toys R Us, like most retail businesses, is cash flow positive. This is advantageous when maximizing working capital efficiency to pay down debt.

- It has a strong asset base as shown by the opening balance sheet in Exhibit 13.3. Inventory, accounts receivable, and PPE, which are common sources of debt security, have a book value of USD6.6bn, vs. a proposed leverage of around USD3bn. This will increase the target's debt capacity and reduce risk and interest rates.

- It is not possible to analyze the growth and operational improvement opportunities without thorough due diligence, but the company was having operational difficulties and had attempted a repositioning before the deal, which had been unsuccessful. The brand name is strong and there could be scope for a PE firm to create value using the techniques of active ownership. There may be a case for replacing some of the management team given the recent strategic problems the company has experienced.

Negative characteristics

- The current leverage is very high. The company has over £2bn of debt which means the benefits of LBO economics may already be included in the share price. Sensitivity analysis shows that a deal based on the 2004 closing share price of USD27 would produce a negative IRR and COC return. This is why our analysis is based on an EBITDA multiple, despite Toys R Us being a public company.

Value creation

Operational improvements

This can be achieved by increasing sales (price or quantity, depending on elasticity) or reducing costs. Most PE activity is focused on cutting costs and making organizations more efficient. In the case of Toys R Us, if we assume COGS can be reduced by 1.5% from 67.5% to 66%, the IRR would jump from 24.2% to 35.1%, and the COC return from 3× to 4.5×! This demonstrates the powerful effect of successful operational improvement strategies.

Multiple expansion

In the event the PE firm can achieve multiple expansion through market timing or improved future prospects, the value creation effect can also be substantial. However, it is mostly beyond the control of the PE firm, so our base case assumes the same entry and exit multiple of 7.5×. If the exit multiple were to increase to 8.5×, the IRR would increase from 24.2% to 28.9% and the COC to 3.6×.

Financial leverage

The powerful effects of leverage can be illustrated by increasing it from 65% (the base case) to 80%. This increases the IRR from 24.2% to 39.9% and the COC to 4.6×. But there is no account taken of the increasing costs of financial distress, so it is only a benefit as long as the target can continue to service the debt and avoid bankruptcy. This omission is one important criticism of many LBO models. In practice, this is controlled in an LBO deal by the coverage ratios the bank sets and the debt covenants which enforce them. As discussed above, a maximum of 5× EBITDA is a good guide. Leverage of 80% in this deal would lead to a debt/EBITDA ratio of 4.7×, an ISCR ratio of 1.8×, and a DSCR of 1.5×, all of which were acceptable ratios in 2004.

A combination of the above value creation measures (i.e., COGS reduction, exit multiple of 8.5×, and 80% leverage), would lead to an IRR increase from 24.2% to 48% and a COC increase from 3× to 7.1×. This demonstrates the power of LBO economics and how very high relative returns can be achieved if operational improvement and fortunate market timing is included. The dashboard for this scenario is shown in Exhibit 13.15.

However, conditions can also deteriorate, as happened following the recent financial crisis. A recession will have negative effects on both the exit multiple and the sales of the company. If we assume the exit multiple drops to 6× and the company's sales decrease by 3% in the 2 years prior to exit, the IRR would drop to 10.4% and the COC to 1.6×, a relatively low return given the risks associated with private equity investment;

EXHIBIT 13.15

DASHBOARD FOR OPTIMISTIC TOYS'R'US LBO RETURNS (REDUCED COGS BY 1.5%, 8.5× EXIT MULTIPLE, AND 80% LEVERAGE)

Purchase price		Options selector		
Equity purchase price	4,041.5	Operating scenario	1	Base case
Exiting net debt	346.0	Public/Private target	2	Private
Enterprise value	4,387.5	Financing structure	4	80% leverage
Returns analysis		Interest calculation	1	Average
Exit year	2009	BS cash flow sweep	1	Yes
Entry multiple	7.5×	**Checks**		
Exit multiple	8.5×	Balance sheet	OK	
IRR	*48.0%*	Sources and uses	OK	
COC	*7.1×*			

Debt service coverage	Year	1.0	2.0	3.0	4.0	5.0
Leverage ratio (debt/total capitalization)		77.5%	71.3%	64.5%	56.9%	48.6%
EBIT		**635.1**	**647.8**	**660.7**	**673.9**	**687.4**
Interest payments		251.8	234.7	215.2	195.1	172.2
Mandatory principal repayments		49.0	24.0	24.0	24.0	24.0
Debt service requirements		**300.8**	**258.7**	**239.2**	**219.1**	**196.2**
ISCR		2.5×	2.8×	3.1×	3.5×	4.0×
DSCR		2.1×	2.5×	2.8×	3.1×	3.5×
Total debt/EBITDA		3.7×	3.3×	2.9×	2.5×	2.0×

and, with an exit multiple below 5× (as has been the case during recession), the returns would be negative.

13.9 REFERENCE

KRAUS, A., AND LITZENBERGER, R.H. (1973) "A state-preference model of optimal financial leverage," *Journal of Finance*, **28**(4), 911–922.

ROSENBAUM, J., AND PEARL, J. (2009) *Investment Banking*, Wiley Finance, Hoboken, NJ.

14

Post-deal operational improvements

14.1 WHAT OPERATIONAL IMPROVEMENTS ARE MADE POST DEAL?

The answer is, it depends. It depends on the company and its circumstances. The answer is also anything and everything that is required to achieve the target investment returns. Often this is referred to as the full potential program (FPP). Private equity firms with funds that have performed in the top quartile have, over the years, consistently delivered high returns by improving their value creation from post-deal operational improvements. Higher purchasing multiples for target companies have resulted from increased competition, so the need to "create more value" under private equity ownership to support lucrative exit returns became more important.

Any company encountering a change in ownership, whether it's public or private will experience some form of transition. What is it, however, that private equity firms do differently when they acquire a business? Three key underlying factors exist identifying the opportunity; the projection of EBITDA growth; and the full utilization of its assets including its human capital.

There is no deal if there is no opportunity. Post-deal plans are interlinked to the investment thesis adopted around the identified opportunity at the pre-acquisition phase, which is covered in Chapter 11 on deal due diligence. No successful private equity firm would venture into a transaction without a clear strategic roadmap for the future of the company with identified opportunities for success. This could be in many forms, stemming from internal strategic advantages to external market factors favorable to the future of the company. PE funds will tend to have a longer term outlook when considering opportunities compared with publicly listed companies which are constantly scrutinized by the markets and need to announce results on a quarterly basis. This could provide alternative unique options for the company. The accurate identification of the opportunity leads to a sound investment thesis, and the implementation activities involved for its achievement naturally follow.

Another crucial element which dictates the post-deal operational improvement implementation is EBITDA growth, which in turn results in cash availability of the business to fund bank debts and returns for shareholders. Every operational improvement will be measured based on the impact it would have on EBITDA. Margin

This chapter has been written by John Maloney and Kay Nemoto.

improvements through leaner operations, reduction in working capital, and cost reduction efforts are all examples to improve EBITDA, often seen post deal.

A less obvious but no less important factor that drives operational improvement is the assets of the company and how private equity extracts maximum value from them, whether it be from the sale and leaseback of property or even from getting more out of the management of the firm. By putting in place clear incentive structures, general partners (GPs) motivate management to deliver according to plan. Incentives alignment may not be considered an operational improvement but, in fact, it is one of the most effective operating models that private equity firms have introduced. Getting management to work and deliver results is a key component of the post-deal private equity operational improvement.

In this chapter we will explore some examples of operational improvement options around these three key drivers. However, it is by no means a comprehensive list as there are many options that could differ for each portfolio company and its circumstances. Nor will it be a step-by-step guide on how operational improvements are made. They are also not unique to a private equity–owned business. It is a well-known fact that most private equity firms—or, more accurately, the portfolio companies—will appoint advisors and management consultants to support their post-operational improvement initiatives and each will have its own frameworks and methodologies on implementation. The larger the portfolio company, the more likely there will be specialist advisors helping the management along the way in achieving post-deal operational improvements. GPs will work alongside operational advisors and steer strategic direction, but it will be management and the board of the portfolio company who will ultimately be responsible for key decisions and implementation.

14.1.1 Background

Within the last decade, private equity has boomed, benefiting from a surge in funding. It has rapidly grown to a sizable industry with some major billion dollar funds becoming commonplace, enabling them to acquire companies with household names. Among private equity firms, competition gradually intensified, making it challenging to find good target companies at low acquisition multiples. The banks also spurred this on by supporting transactions with large amounts of affordable debt.

The rapid development and success of the industry that had operated relatively discreetly until then also brought unwanted attention. Policymakers started to take notice, calling upon industry panels to explain the private equity business model and debate the introduction of new disclosure policies and capital gains tax. In Germany, they were labeled "locusts", and media hype across many countries about the fat cats of the private equity industry slightly tainted the perception of the activities of private equity firms.

Unraveling how private equity—in particular, the large and mature private equity firms—made handsome returns and grew became a focus of debate. Acharya, Hahn, and Kehoe (2010) attempt to understand and quantify value creation at the enterprise level and attribute this to financial engineering, systematic risk, and operational engineering. The research found "abnormal performance"—compared with quoted peers, in particular—in "organic" deals that focus exclusively on internal value creation programs and improve margins. However, "inorganic" deals with an M&A focus grew EBITDA multiples more substantially. They conclude that abnormal performance is partly due to differences in human capital factors. GPs with an operational background (ex-consultants or ex-industry managers) generate significantly higher outperformance in organic deals. In contrast, GPs with a background in finance (ex-bankers or ex-accountants) generate higher outperformance in deals with M&A events, thus suggesting that the background of GPs is correlated with deal performance.

If post-deal outperformance is in fact correlated to the background of GPs, the success should be attributable to the investment thesis they developed for the target portfolio company. Here, we will explore only the operational engineering efforts that are made by PE professionals.

14.2   IDENTIFYING THE OPPORTUNITY

High-level post-deal operational improvement plans start taking shape well before the transaction. GPs will start to develop hypotheses on the opportunities for the company and start to explore them in more detail. It is critical to identify the key opportunities accurately by analyzing and challenging them in the pre-transaction due diligence stage, thus the inseparable nature of the processes.

Most target companies will present a 3-to-5-year business plan developed by the incumbent management team. This plan often becomes the basis of calculating the company's value and the foundations of the investment thesis, identifying operational synergies and growth opportunities. This has been covered in more detail in Chapter 11 on deal due diligence. A typical business plan would provide a detailed explanation of the corporate strategy, historical events and milestones, market and competitor overview, and planned developments for the business over the coming years to support projected growth. The incumbent management team that has issued the business plan would be questioned thoroughly about details in the due diligence process and would also be assessed for the assumptions made and capabilities required to deliver the projected growth or strategic direction.

GPs, often with the support of advisors, will start formulating opportunities over and beyond what has been presented by the incumbent management team. This would then form the investment thesis and the post-deal strategy of the company. As there will be hypotheses and assumptions behind the investment thesis, these will be scrutinized and challenged in detail by the investment committee of the private equity firm. If the investment thesis has flawed hypotheses and assumptions or key risk factors have not been identified, there would be grave consequences in the road ahead for implementation.

Private equity firms are often given exclusive access to the company during the final due diligence process allowing them to better understand the business and challenge the thinking of the company's management around their investment thesis and plans. They must ensure the feasibility of their calculated synergies which may or may not be shared with the management at the pre-transaction stage.

Successful private equity firms map out the full execution strategy from deal to exit with target investment returns in mind as they complete the deal. They are fully ready to execute their strategy by the time the deal is complete and detailed planning around the execution and implementation of the strategy starts in earnest. The "how" becomes the main focus.

14.2.1   Organic top-line growth strategy

An acquired business that has shown solid organic growth over recent years and projects similar strong growth in the future could be an attractive investment. Once the growth story has been carefully analyzed and accepted, the immediate concerns should be about its operational sustainability.

The prime focus of a private equity firm is in EBITDA growth. This could be delivered through top-line growth if costs grow in proportion to revenue, as a worst case scenario, or by obtaining cost benefits from economies of scale. Understanding the fine balance of growth and increased costs associated to deliver projected revenue growth becomes crucial.

Business expansion

Business expansion is the most common approach to organic growth. Many successful examples can be found in retailers increasing the number of shops to capture a larger consumer base or manufacturers increasing their production capacity. The underlying business may remain the same, but gross margins and profitability could be improved by scaling up the business. As simple as it sounds, expansion needs to be carefully planned and managed with consideration of investment requirements, market demand, risks, and many other factors. This is, of course, not unique to private equity–backed companies, but private equity firms would be particularly focused on returns to investment.

If it is a manufacturing business, focus is required on capital expenditure and whether there is enough capacity to sustain production growth and at what point further investment would be required for things such as new land, building, factories, machinery, and employees. Existing processes would need to be reviewed so that the company has the highest productivity to keep cost increases to a bare minimum despite growth.

A higher risk generated by business expansion would be from entering new markets. This could be in the form of international expansion or a completely new segment of the market with a new product or service offering. Again, this will be an investment that would require careful research and planning, adding further complexity to the business. Failed market entries and new products are commonplace.

Sales force effectiveness

A more subtle approach to increasing the top line without the requirement of major upfront investment is by increasing sales force effectiveness. The performance of the sales team will have an immediate and direct impact on the top line.

Typically, there is a sales team in a company that offers products or services. Are the number of salespeople sufficient? Do they have the right tools and information to sell and are they in the right locations? Do they have the right marketing support? How are they managed? Are they incentivized to be successful salespeople? Can they sell more? Are they selling the right products or services? Can they cross-sell a mix of other products and services? There are plenty of questions that need to be asked and analyzed to ensure a business has an effective sales force. Again sufficient market research and analysis are required to form the best approach in improving sales effectiveness. Adequate key performance indicators (KPIs) need to be in place to measure sales force efficiency and benchmarking with the sales force of competing peers could also provide comparisons on the effectiveness of one's sales force.

Pricing

There is an opportunity to increase revenue by addressing the pricing model if this has not already been done by the company. Every company will have a logical pricing matrix used to sell its products and services, but there could be a more advantageous pricing model to directly boost revenues. For instance, a company can increase the price of a product by a couple of cents with a great positive impact on the bottom line, without customers noticing the change. Thus, analyzing the pricing model could be well worth the effort.

Addressing churn

In a business where there is recurring income from customers, growing the top line only works if you are not losing existing revenue. If there is high churn, efforts need to be addressed to stop the loss of revenue by identifying the root causes and addressing them. Churn analysis involves understanding customer issues and finding solutions to resolve them.

14.2.2 Bolt-on growth by acquisition strategy

A private equity firm may acquire a business to bolt on to an existing portfolio company, either larger or smaller. Operational benefits could range from increased market share, access to new markets, product diversification, cost benefits, valuable assets, and even acquiring a new management team. It is usually followed by a post-merger integration project with multiple work streams managing the integration process to extract synergies, often with full oversight from the management.

If the acquisition involves employees, employment laws in the applicable jurisdictions need to be sensibly considered while pursuing the most optimal solution with the highest return on investment. It could involve site closures, integration and migration of multiple sites. Alternatively, it may be concluded that keeping the businesses separate and doing little integration work is the best option for the combined entity. The latter is fairly common, but it could also lead to potential issues and criticism of not acting sooner regarding issues of higher costs and duplication of processes. Cultural issues could also arise if two businesses are not integrated well. To avoid later issues from non-activity, it would be advisable to address operational integration issues immediately rather than taking too long and allowing issues to fester.

14.2.3 Manufacturing footprint optimization to low-cost countries (LCCs)

Towards the complex end of operational improvements are found the major change management transformation projects such as site closures, site integrations, and migration into the manufacturing sector, often called manufacturing footprint optimization (MFO). This involves complex program management and careful financial planning to make sure that synergies and assumptions are not overestimated to begin with, only to disappoint after the heavy lifting work is complete. Such changes are not unique to a private equity–backed company.

In recent years, site migrations and outsourcing to low-cost countries have become common. Often, very high savings are initially estimated based on low labor cost but, with more case examples and lessons learned, it has become clear that cost savings need to be properly analyzed to get a fair and more realistic estimate of savings based on distance to the markets and supply of materials. Import and export tariffs, transportation costs, cross-border treaties, and trade agreements should be taken into account before actual migration takes place. As in any major project, careful analysis and planning is required. Corporate advisors are at hand to support the decision-making and implementation process for the company management.

14.3 EBITDA GROWTH

The prime focus of a private equity firm is in EBITDA growth. EBITDA is one of the most important financial measures that is monitored closely by private equity firms. All operational changes in plans will be evaluated based on their impact on EBITDA and will dictate the selection and priority of implementation.

Banks will also monitor EBITDA closely as most buyout transactions are leveraged. Acquired companies will be saddled with new debt backed up by a detailed facilities agreement supporting it, stipulating all the details around the repayment schedule, covenant calculations, and the periodic (monthly, quarterly, semi-annual, and annual) reporting that needs to be sent to the bank or bank syndicates. Covenants are set and agreed with the banks at the point of transaction and are based on future forecast financial performance submitted at that point, namely EBITDA. Facility agreements are provided on the basis of the growth story, and agreed covenants are ratcheted up based on the projected financial performance of the company. Such covenants also act as a key driver to make operational improvements an essential requirement to deliver the projected financial results.

Some of the more common operational improvements post deal are cost reduction and working capital reductions. Private equity firms should identify opportunities to immediately improve EBITDA by having leaner and better managed operations. Again, such opportunities are identified at the pre-acquisition stage by methods such as benchmarking gross margins and overhead costs against close competitors or identifying cost-cutting opportunities by changing existing operating models and processes.

If some cost reduction opportunities are evident at the outset, post transaction this is one of the first areas that will be implemented or done in parallel with top-line revenue growth efforts.

14.3.1 Gross margin improvement

Gross margin improvement could involve different types of opportunities such as improvements in the supply chain, procurement, and internal operational process streamlining.

Supply chain management and procurement

Improving the supply chain could lead to savings for a company. This could be based on geographical distance between the company and its suppliers and market, which could impact transportation costs and time, from end to end. It could also be about rationalizing the number of parties involved in the supply chain—the fewer involved, the higher the efficiency. Some processes could be brought in-house or outsourced to a supplier to be more cost effective. Each business needs careful consideration to have the most optimal end-to-end supply chain.

Almost all businesses need to make purchases. Let us use the example of a manufacturer: in order to produce goods the manufacturer needs to purchase materials and energy from other suppliers. The procurement manager would need to negotiate the best price possible for such purchases. The timing and quantity of purchases will play a crucial role in reaching the best price. For materials sourced internationally, currency exchange rates will also impact procurement costs. Is the procurement function efficient? Are materials bought at the best price possible? Is the business susceptible to fluctuations in commodity prices or is it hedged to protect itself? Could it put in place a long-term contract at fixed prices? Should it? Again, there are many areas to identify possible cost savings for the business.

In recent years, some private equity firms have started adding scale to their margin improvement efforts. Examples of shared supply chain and procurement functions across portfolio companies are emerging, creating cost-saving opportunities for the companies. This is particularly successful when a private equity firm has a concentrated industry focus and holds a portfolio of similar businesses.

Operational structure and processes

A business, for example, may be operating out of multiple small sites. Synergies could possibly be identified by consolidating them into one big site. As businesses grow, they tend to shift from a dispersed localized model to a centralized model or a hub-and-spoke model. Yet, a GP would need to understand why they have been operating in such a fragmented manner to begin with. Was it past acquisitions and post-merger integration that had just not been addressed or was it a crucial strategic decision to be close to a fragmented market? If the latter, does the business need to remain operating as it is or are there elements that could be consolidated while leaving crucial elements near the fragmented geographies? Could the company outsource elements of the process for greater efficiency? Could it reduce headcount? There are many questions to ask and decisions to be made prior to execution. Alternatively, there might not be a need to change the status quo if the additional return that can be obtained is minimal. Ultimately, the key question to answer is, "Is the existing business model and infrastructure the optimal solution?"

If changes in the business operation model are to be made, they will likely cause major disruption to day-to-day business and would need to be planned and implemented carefully to reap the benefits of a major transition.

IT systems

IT systems have become an integral part of most businesses. Thus, assessing whether the company has adequate IT systems in place is a must. If the right systems are adopted, significant cost savings can be obtained. We will not explore this in detail here, however we recognize that IT is an area that requires careful scrutiny to identify the optimal solution.

14.3.2 SG&A cost reduction

Reducing overhead costs may be the most common form of post-acquisition quick wins where savings would immediately impact EBITDA. The actions taken could be as minimal as putting in place a hiring freeze waiting for natural attrition in headcount; or it could be !s drastic as operational changes such as introducing shared services where internal consolidation of back offices would contribute to headcount reductions and cost savings. Back-office functions could even be outsourced reducing overall costs.

Again, when looking at the possibility of a reduction in headcount, local employment laws need to be considered to understand what can and cannot be done. The cost of involuntary redundancy also needs to be taken into account to understand the economics of such decisions. However, more important than the economics, the overall impact of draconian cost cutting on an organization and its employees need to be considered. People are the most important element of a business and, when considering changes to an organization, however small those changes may be, the impact on its people and the business need to be fully taken into account.

Reducing marketing or R&D expenses could also be considered if these costs are proving to be too high for the company. Better usage of marketing expenditure could be explored by measuring the effectiveness and contribution to sales. Looking at the investment returns of R&D costs will also result in understanding their importance. It may be that existing R&D capabilities are too weak and ineffective that, in the long run, it would be more economical to buy externally. These are key strategic decisions which could have major impacts on the business and require careful consideration.

14.3.3 Working capital reduction

The same could be done for working capital, looking at receivables and payables, and inventory levels. Key measurements such as days inventory outstanding, days sales outstanding, and net working capital are calculated to gain an understanding of how much cash is tied up in working capital. Benchmarking against industry peers is a tool often used to estimate the financial upside potential of implementing such improvements. Inventory levels could be optimized to ensure large amounts of inventory are not sitting in warehouses. Finance departments could improve collection of late payments or incentivize early payment. If they are paying too early, they could stretch the payment terms to ensure they pay only when required. This will ensure the greatest efficiency in working capital.

14.4 MAXIMIZING ASSETS—HUMAN CAPITAL

Any income-generating asset the company holds could provide better returns in some circumstances. For instance, property assets can be sold and leased back via an opco/propco deal thus unlocking a lot of resources. Where possible, this is likely to be explored, but as it is more of a financial engineering tactic than an operational improvement effort, we will refrain from going into detail here.

Instead, we would like to focus and explore the human capital resources in this section. Any business will tell you how important its people are and extol them as being the greatest asset of the company. Private equity firms have definitely placed a strong emphasis on selecting the right management team and have skillfully aligned them to their benefit beyond other ownership models.

14.4.1 Relationship with the management team

Assessing the incumbent management team is an important aspect of acquisition. Many private equity firms choose not to proceed with a transaction if they find the incumbent management team has a weak track record of delivery or seems incapable of steering the future of the company on the basis of the proposed strategy. Alternatively, prior to acquisition, they have already identified a new management leadership to take over.

The relationship with the management will play an important part of a successful ownership. If the incumbent management team has a clear track record of implementing operational improvements and has a roadmap of new initiatives, there may be a case for the private equity firm not to interfere with operations and allow the incumbent management to progress with the changes. This will be based on the trust relationship built between the private equity firm and management as well as clear accountability tied to future incentives.

Results-driven culture

The actual operational improvements made within portfolio companies may not be unique to private equity–owned businesses and could be applied to businesses with other ownership models, but the focus on an exit plan from Day 1 gives companies under private equity ownership a unique sense of urgency and a strict culture of delivery, where failure would not be acceptable. Where companies are laden with a high level of debt with covenants and repayment schedules, again this keeps management working hard to deliver agreed results according to projections.

GPs may suggest the appointment of management consulting and advisory firms to support management to implement the full potential plans set out for the company, whether they be cost reduction plans, procurement and supply chain improvements, and/or a multitude of other EBITDA improvement efforts. This would allow management to continue with their current responsibilities of running the business while operational improvements are being made with minimal disruption and time involvement.

In recent years, some PE firms have also adopted internal operational teams that operate among the portfolio companies (Hemptinne and Hoflack, 2009). Although operational management of companies is not the core function of a PE firm, its importance has increased.

Incentivizing management

Incentive schemes are introduced as effective tools to ensure management is driven to succeed and only rewarded when agreed targets are met. They draw out the entrepreneurial behavior by making responsibility and accountability clear. Incentive tools do not stop at the management of the portfolio company but apply to the private equity firms as well. It may be naive to stereotype private equity investment professionals but, in general, they are well-educated, competitive, and demanding individuals. They are unlikely to accept mediocrity and are unforgiving of failure. They too are heavily incentivized to bring success to their private equity fund, and this would require the portfolio companies under their responsibility to perform and generate returns for their shareholders.

The portfolio company management will constantly remain under the scrutiny of GPs and are likely to receive regular calls and requests for financial performance information, keeping management "on their toes".

Operational involvement at arm's length

Investment professionals involved in the deal from the private equity firm will take up board positions to have visibility of the company and to be involved in actively steering its direction. In some cases, that could be the only involvement if they decide not to get actively involved with the operations of a business, as long as the company is performing or even overdelivering on agreed financial targets. The management would be entrusted to continue leading the company to achieve financial performance targets as projected in the business plan that was used as the basis of the transaction.

Good corporate governance

Investment professionals who take up board positions in the acquired company are likely to have been involved in the deal-screening and due diligence process, with a clear understanding of the historical performance of the company, and understand the future plans and vision for the company. They are responsible for monitoring the newly acquired business, bring professional rigor and challenge, and with the help of management steer the direction of the company. They will be unlikely to take a passive approach at board level. This should immediately strengthen the corporate governance process and, if there are emerging issues with the company, it would allow PE firms to quickly identify and receive an early warning. PE firms may also identify and introduce key leaders from the industry to joint the board alongside them.

14.4.2 Prioritizing execution

The post-deal operational plans are unlikely to involve a single change but a list of initiatives that could be undertaken. They could range from quick wins that can be implemented in the short to medium term to more complex long-term transitions. It is by no means an easy transition and would require both financial and operational muscle.

Do you tackle low-risk and easy-to-implement initiatives first or do you challenge high-risk and difficult projects first? Do you tackle both simultaneously? These are questions that need careful consideration in the implementation of operational improvements—most likely involving more than one initiative. Timely and swift execution is critical for new ownership to signal necessary change across the organization and to lay out expectations for the future—all carefully balanced with detailed planning.

As in any business, all strategic elements of the portfolio company would need to be addressed. Incumbent competitors in the marketplace need to be understood and monitored. Threats from new entrants or substitute products or services need to be considered. Without fail, the supply chain, suppliers, and buyers need full consideration.

The motivation for selling a company to private equity has been discussed in Chapter 11 on due diligence, but in many cases there are other reasons: maybe the road ahead is likely to be difficult and having a strong private equity firm with wide experience would enhance and support the next stages of the company's development. Also, for some take-private deals, the company's management would likely prefer not to deal with complex operational transitions constantly under the glare of public scrutiny and the noise of stock price volatility distracting them through the transition.

14.5 WHEN THINGS GO WRONG

The severe banking crisis–led global recession from 2007 has put many PE portfolio companies off course from their forecast financial projections. In particular, the highly leveraged transactions with procyclical businesses have been the first to feel the brunt of the downturn. Starting with real estate–related companies, other sectors such as consumer goods, retail businesses, financial services, and leisure businesses suffered, and criticisms were made of being overleveraged and private equity firms paying too much at the boom of the markets.

Private equity firms that had not calculated the possibility of an economic downturn experienced turbulent times. Some were caught unprepared with highly leveraged underperforming portfolio companies in a marketplace where liquidity had dried up.

Many private equity firms rushed to revisit the original business plan to adjust it to a more realistic scenario and looked at further options for operational improvement—namely, cost reduction. Restructuring advisors were appointed to support portfolio companies negotiate financial restructuring, either by means of a covenant reset or debt restructuring. Often, in parallel, cash flow management and diagnostics for operational improvement to support a new business plan took place. If a portfolio company reaches this stage, the banks will also take an active role, appointing their own advisors to review the company and report back. This is called an investment bank review and is conducted by accountants and restructuring advisors working on behalf of the banks.

The recession weeded out the winners from the losers. Well-managed portfolio companies emerged unscathed or weathered the recessionary pressures well, recovering quickly, whereas those that had not improved their operations or had not prepared their downside risks had difficulties.

14.6 CONCLUSION

In earlier chapters, it has been demonstrated how successful private equity firms diligently identify attractive opportunities and invest in companies by means of a strategic plan and roadmap for their exit. The investment thesis then develops into detailed execution of operational improvement or organizational change, which lies at the core of value creation and, more specifically, EBITDA margin improvement within the enterprise.

The operational improvement plan itself may not be too different from what could be done for any peer publicly owned company, but would be executed without distraction from constant market speculation impacting share prices.

What successful private equity firms have repeatedly demonstrated is pure focus and drive to create a lean and efficient mode of business and not waste time in setting up a target model, without bureaucratic slow decision making or internal politics slowing down the process, ultimately extracting value for the company and its shareholders.

Clear articulation of the investment strategy, careful and detailed planning, and a results-driven culture with incentive schemes aligning the interests of the private equity firm with those of company management are all essential components in coming up with a successful private equity formula.

14.7 REFERENCES

ACHARYA, V.V., HAHN, M., AND KEHOE, C. (2010) "Corporate governance and value creation: Evidence from private equity," Working Paper No. FIN-08-032, New York University.

HEMPTINNE, C., AND HOFLACK, V. (2009) *The Value of In-house Operations Teams in Private Equity Firms*, INSEAD, France.

15

Harvesting private equity investments

15.1 INTRODUCTION

The principal vehicle through which private equity investments are made is the limited partnership. This structure typically has a finite life of 10 years from its establishment (with life extensions of up to 4 further years frequently included in limited partnership agreements). Although the repayment to the limited partners (LPs) with illiquid securities of the portfolio companies is sometimes unavoidable, it is highly undesirable, as individual LPs will receive neither liquidity nor control. Consequently, general partners (GPs) that manage the fund are expected to exit the companies in the fund's portfolio within the life of the fund in order to return the LPs' investments. Value is realized either part way though the life of an investment via a recapitalization or when the business is ultimately sold. As serial sellers of businesses, private equity funds have well-developed sales skills and are able to draw upon a variety of exit routes to maximize cash returns to investors. Given that private equity investors know that there is an imperative to divest their investments within the life of the fund, exit considerations figure prominently in any investment case that a GP builds.

In the private equity market, an *exit* is the process by which private equity funds realize the return on their investments in companies. Through an exit, the private equity fund not only obtains financial returns but also allows the portfolio companies to receive infusions of capital and/or a different strategic direction from their new investors.[1] The timeframe from investment to exit can be as little as 2 years or as much as 10 or more years. If, at the time of exit, the private equity fund does not sell all the shares it holds, it is termed a *partial exit*. Partial exits are most commonly seen when the private equity fund sells shares into the public equity market. In this instance, the private equity fund is unlikely to be able to sell more than 50% of the equity in the business.

The exit phase is a key stage in the private equity value generation process. Up until then investors have indications of value creation only through the periodic valuations

---

1. The portfolio company's articles might specify *drag rights*. These rights indicate that, when the private equity fund sells its shareholding, management or other shareholders in the company need to sell their shareholding at the same time and on similar terms.

This chapter has been co-authored with Fardeen Nariman (MBA, London Business School).

produced by the GP. Only at exit does value crystallize and cash generated get received. The need to ultimately exit investments shapes every aspect of the private equity investment cycle, from the opportunity to raise capital to the types of investments that are made (e.g., see Gompers and Lerner, 2000). In the first stage, to make an investment, money has to be raised by finding LPs willing to invest. Successful exits made by the PE fund in the past have a strong influence on the ability to raise follow-on funds and, thus, are of major importance. In the second stage, appropriate investment targets are selected. Private equity firms consider their exit opportunities while structuring the deal. In the third phase, the value-adding phase, private equity funds contribute to the potential exit success of an investment by providing knowhow, offering informal advice, and exposing the portfolio company to their huge network. In the last phase, harvesting, private equity funds realize returns by selecting the most appropriate route that satisfies the needs of all stakeholders and then delivering on the exit itself. These alternative exit routes depend on a variety of factors, which can also change over time. Besides the actual profit that can be realized at the date of exit, factors such as the company's size, the goals of the management, and the current market environment need to be considered as well.

There are important differences between venture capital and buyout funds in terms of exit strategy and liquidity. Although both types of investment are generally made via a limited partnership structure (and, thus, are limited in time), venture capital investments are typically characterized by a number of "rounds" of investment, made by an investor "syndicate." Serial investments are made at, hopefully, rising underlying entity valuations. Moreover, the underlying investment is typically funded wholly by equity before an exit is achieved. Exit can be achieved via a sale to another private equity investor with skills to develop the business further, via a trade sale to a corporation, or via an initial public offering (for large and successful investments).

By their nature, buyout investments are somewhat different, as they see investors acquire interests in mature businesses where the initial acquisition is funded by a mixture of debt and equity (a so-called *leverage buyout*). In this scenario, investors have access to additional options regarding realizing liquidity, as they may be able to recapitalize their investment and "dividend out" proceeds without actually reducing their equity ownership in the company.

In summary, there are six possible exit routes available to private equity funds:

1. *Trade sale*—the portfolio company is merged with another company or is acquired by another company, either public or private.

2. *Initial public offering (IPO)*—the portfolio company's shares are offered to the general public on a public exchange.

3. *Secondary buyouts*—the portfolio company is sold to another private equity fund. The portfolio company's shares can also be sold via private placements to accredited or institutional investors that are not classified as private equity funds.

4. *Recapitalizations*—the private equity fund takes on additional debt and possibly outside investors' equity capital in order to redeem a portion of the existing equity base of the portfolio company.

5. *Share repurchase*—the portfolio company's shares are bought back by the company and/or its management from the private equity fund.

6. *Breakups and liquidations*—the portfolio company is liquidated and sold piecemeal. This is usually the case when the company fails and becomes a drain on the private equity fund's resources.

Using a sample of buyout transactions in the U.S., Kaplan and Strømberg (2007) record that the most common exit route is the sale of the company to a strategic (i.e., non-financial) buyer: this occurs in 38% of all exits. The second most common exit route is the secondary leveraged buyout (24%). This exit route has increased considerably over time. Initial public offerings, where the company is listed on a public stock exchange (and the private equity firm can subsequently sell its shares in the public market), account for 14% of exits. This exit route has decreased significantly in relative importance over time.[2]

With respect to venture investments, the National Venture Capital Association, which represents more than 400 venture capital firms in the U.S., estimates that over the period from 2004 to 2010 the most likely exit route was via a trade sale. These transactions were almost seven times more likely than an IPO.[3] This is unsurprising as, by their very nature, few startup businesses reach sufficient scale to be viable candidates for an IPO. However, when a venture capital–backed business does become a legitimate candidate for an IPO, it often attracts extremely high valuations, particularly in a "hot" IPO market. A transatlantic comparison of the importance of different exit routes shows an interesting difference. Trade sales are about the only viable exit route for European venture funds with a large share of all exits, whereas in the U.S. venture funds realize many exits through IPOs.

Each exit route has different ramifications for the LPs, the GPs, and the company's management. As mentioned above, an IPO may result in the highest valuation of a company, but the financial sponsor is very unlikely to be able to exit 100% of their investment, and the after-market performance of IPOs is notoriously poor. A further consideration is that the portfolio company's management may favor an IPO over a trade sale where the company simply becomes a division of a larger enterprise, because it preserves the firm's independence. Equally, the management team may prefer a sale to another financial sponsor (i.e., a secondary buyout) able to support the next phase of the company's development. A trade sale can be a very attractive exit route for the private equity fund, as it provides payment in cash or marketable securities, and a clear end to the involvement with the company. The trade sale might have different consequences for the company's management, though, to the extent that the company is merged with or acquired by a larger company, and cannot remain independent. Consequently, management may prefer an exit to another financial sponsor via a secondary buyout, as this guarantees their ongoing involvement with the business.

Given today's volatile economy, and the difficult IPO market, financial sponsors frequently seek to explore multiple exit options simultaneously. They elect to employ a so-called *dual-track* strategy, whereby one team looks for potential acquirers while the other team prepares for an IPO. Under this strategy, the company

---

2. The approach to exits is fundamentally different between private equity funds in the U.S. and in Europe. In the U.S., private equity funds are more likely to exit through an IPO than in Europe. In Europe, on the other hand, the focus on exit to corporate or new private equity buyers has increased the effort directed to selling.

3. Cumming and Johan (2007) investigate the exits of Canadian venture capitalists and find that the investment holding period is lower for companies exited via IPO than for those exited through trade sales or other exit methods.

tries to better position itself to take advantage of either exit route should the opportunity arise.

Several market factors affect the increase of activity in the acquisitions and the IPO markets, the two markets that provide the main exit routes. The acquisitions market is buoyed by overcrowding in some sectors and maturing product lines that are encouraging consolidation; by large cash-rich trade buyers taking advantage of low asset values; or by improvements in operating performance that make both buyers and sellers more enthusiastic to engage in transactions.

The IPO market gets a boost when there is an increase in investor confidence and appetite for risk due to improved returns in financial markets, when private companies have gone a long time without new capital and have had time to mature and grow stronger, or when large institutional investors such as hedge funds or mutual funds are leading the way.

15.2   STEPS TO EXITING A PRIVATE EQUITY INVESTMENT

Private equity firms evaluate potential exit strategies with the aim of maximizing the return on their investments. Planning how to exit an investment is just as important as preparing to make one. Private equity firms typically make an attempt to consider all options and invest proactively in pre-sale diligence to expedite the sale process, maintain control and credibility, and enhance exit value.

Exit planning should start early, with considerable thought being given to structuring and positioning the business to make it attractive to likely buyers, as well as networking and relationship development with these buyers. A lot of preparation should go into the robustness of the management plans, the detail of due diligence, and other reports. Efforts should be made to "warm up" the market, by making potential buyers aware of the upcoming sale several months before the formal process starts. In addition, the private equity funds are expected to time the market by exiting the portfolio companies when the market conditions are favorable. In the case of an IPO, which is a good indicator of favorable market conditions, the private equity fund may sell few, if any, shares. While the fund does not benefit directly from the higher exit price it can benefit indirectly by suffering less dilution.

Strategic considerations

The exit thesis normally forms a key part of the investment approach for any investment contemplated by the pivate equity firm. GPs need to understand the exit potential of the underlying business, not only to be able to model returns, but also to understand any elements of the proposed investment strategy that may actually detract from value creation. When deciding whether to exit or keep the company in the portfolio for a longer period, a GP should consider several strategic factors:

- *What are the financial motives behind the pursuit of an exit strategy?* Most likely, a successful exit strategy balances the company's need for additional growth capital with the need to provide returns on capital to the fund's LPs. The private equity fund should evaluate the timing of the exit and assess whether it benefits shareholders to continue to strengthen the company as a standalone entity and fetch a higher valuation at a later time, or whether now is the optimal time to exit. In other words, does the potential for expansion and access to additional capital outweigh the potential dilution of ownership that comes with the exit?

- *Does the GP see the company approaching the potential exit from a position of strength or weakness?* It is important to understand whether the company is able to manage throughout the exit process by itself. Execution of an exit strategy can involve a significant amount of time and money to pay for advisors, especially during an IPO process. Also, the management team and the board of directors should have the ability and qualifications to lead the company through the process. Is the company ready for the intense scrutiny of its management and operations that accompanies the exit process? Before conducting an exit strategy, a company will be subjected to a stringent due diligence process to ensure that all of the proper systems and controls are in place. A company is in a position of strength if its track record shows it consistently meets or beats its goals and performance targets.

- *What is the state of the market?* How accessible is the market, given the current conditions? For instance, public markets can be volatile, and a successful exit strategy depends largely on market timing. Many IPOs have been pulled at the last minute at a high cost, because of unfavorable market conditions. The private equity fund should also try to understand whether the marketplace wants the company at a significantly larger scale, which could be gained through an IPO or a trade sale. Alternatively, have the market conditions deteriorated such that selling the company is a means of survival?

- *What will be the impact on the company?* It is necessary to assess whether or not the exit will enhance the portfolio company's core competencies. Will the exit route provide the company with the best opportunity to expand and gain additional market share? Are the founders and initial shareholders ready to relinquish their leadership and control of the company, if necessary? What will be the impact on the management and employees? Retention of key management and personnel can be critical. Furthermore, employees often become nervous upon hearing rumors of a sale, especially since it can lead to downsizing and layoffs. In fact, "employee problems" are responsible for a large number of exit failures.

Sell-side due diligence

If a GP believes that an IPO is the exit vehicle of choice, she or he needs to evaluate the likelihood (early on) of the company being able to survive as a standalone entity. A GP may assess whether potential buyers exist at the outset to believe that a trade sale or a secondary buyout are viable.

There are, however, no guarantees that the exits will be as timely or as profitable as the GP would hope or require. Strategically preparing for an exit is critical not only for executing the sale efficiently, but also for maximizing its value. An important step that the GP should take prior to engaging in a transaction is to perform a thorough *sell-side* or *vendor due diligence*. This is a particularly valuable component of any exit strategy in today's uncertain economic environment. As credit markets have tightened and transactions have become subject to heightened scrutiny, it has become even more critical that GPs looking to sell anticipate the risks and issues that might arise and potentially disrupt a deal, or lower its value. Taking an in-depth look at the company in advance helps prevent unwanted surprises and allows the GP to proactively address all associated transaction risks. It may even expedite the transaction process.

A well-executed sell-side due diligence includes thorough assessments of (1) the strategic attractiveness of the company; (2) the financial health of the company;

(3) the operational performance relative to its peers; (4) the technological edge over competitors; (5) human resource issues; and (6) the need for further capital. Sometimes, companies that are put up for sale are unprepared or lack the resources to address the critical pressures that come with the transaction process. For instance, a small company might lack the financial and accounting infrastructure to respond to the buyers' informational needs.

GPs can counter transactional risks by taking a proactive approach to mitigating anticipated deal-breaking issues through sell-side due diligence. Before moving forward with a potential deal, they should:

- Evaluate the profitability of the company by assessing the quality of earnings and identifying any non-recurring charges or credits to maximize the company's value. Also, GPs should analyze trends in revenues and EBITDA to identify key value drivers and measure the impact of fixed vs. variable costs, capital expenditure requirements, and the importance of certain administrative activities.

- Assess the quality of assets to be sold and liabilities that would be assumed. As part of this analysis, the GPs should evaluate the required working capital and develop a target working capital level in advance of the purchase agreement.

- Identify internal management and operational weaknesses, as well as any potential transitional issues.

- Identify tax risks, including federal, state, and sales tax obligations. As part of this analysis, the GP should determine the optimal tax structure before the deal and evaluate its impact on potential buyers. We discuss more about these issues below.

- Assess the impact of regulations on the company at the time of exit. For instance, an exit in the U.S. by listing the shares on a public exchange is affected by the Sarbanes–Oxley 2002 Act. Complying with Sarbanes–Oxley can take up a significant portion of a portfolio company's CEO's time and needs to be prepared well in advance.

It is critical that companies confirm to GAAP (generally accepted accounting principles), since discrepancies between reality and what has been reported in financial statements are likely to be unveiled during the transaction process. Accounting estimates such as bad debt reserves, inventory reserves, and other contingency reserves should be carefully reviewed. GPs should be aware that buyers may have a differing view of what constitutes an appropriate estimate for these reserves. This differing view can result in a post-closing purchase price adjustment dispute.

The effect of taxes

Whether the exit involves an IPO, a recapitalization, or a strategic/financial acquisition, tax matters can and do drive valuation, particularly when valuable tax assets such as net operating losses and tax credits exist. Two primary areas require attention: the deal structure and optimization of the underlying tax assets residing within the target.

It is essential to structure the sale from a local government income tax perspective, evaluating ways to allocate income to low-tax locations. For instance, the sale can be negotiated as an asset sale or as a sale of stock. If it is an asset sale, it is important to get a premium on the asset, to put the private equity fund in the same after-tax cash position.

It is also important for GPs to consider tax exposures prior to the sale. One way to quantify the tax risk and mitigate that concern is to conduct a *nexus analysis*. Such an analysis would need to address state income and franchise taxes, sales and use taxes, and property taxes. The seller and the buyer have to come to terms on which party is responsible for all unfiled tax returns. The analysis might result in a requirement for an escrow account for potential taxes. An additional consideration is whether business licenses and permits can be transferred.

An agreement between the parties related to taxes on a pre and post-transaction basis should be drafted. Issues related to taxes such as documentation related to basis, net operating losses, and credits come up several years after transactions are completed, and it is important to identify the responsibilities of both the seller and the buyer. This includes tax triggers through change-of-control payments.

15.3   EXIT STRATEGIES

The divestment phase is crucial for the overall performance of a private equity investment, as pointed out above. Recognizing the difficulty of assuring a successful and timely exit, private equity funds sometimes build arrangements into their financing structure instruments that allow a payout in the absence of a full exit opportunity. One approach is to structure the investment as *subordinated debt*, with an interest rate and repayment schedule that provide at least a minimally acceptable return. The debt is coupled with *warrants*, which allow the investors to realize a full equity return if the investment is successful.

Another approach for investors purchasing a minority interest in a business is to demand an *equity put* from the majority holder under certain stated conditions. For example, such a right to put the shares might be exercisable if the majority holder refuses to accept a bona fide offer by a qualified prospective buyer to acquire the company. These devices, which are common in developed markets, may not be available or enforceable under the laws of some emerging countries. In many situations, however, they are attractive to the majority owner who wants to retain control of the enterprise.

In the following subsections, we provide a brief overview of the three main exit routes. We also discuss alternative exits such as recapitalizations, share repurchases, and liquidations. The popularity of an exit route depends mainly on the prevailing economic conditions.

15.3.1   Trade sales

Trade sales (also referred to as *acquisitions*) are achieved by selling the entire share capital or the assets of a portfolio company to another firm that is typically in the same industry. Basically, trade sales involve selling the portfolio company to a strategic investor. This is the most common exit route.

In a *share sale* the acquiring firm purchases all or substantially all of the common stock of the portfolio company for a specified price. The buyer replaces the selling private equity fund as the owner of the target company. This type of trade sale is the most common form of private equity exit unless there are strong reasons against it. In an *asset sale* the acquiring firm buys only specific assets and perhaps some liabilities that are explicitly detailed. The tax and accounting basis of the assets, including any goodwill being purchased, is the purchase price. The acquisition can also be done via a *forward merger*, where the portfolio company that is sold merges into the acquirer's company and the private equity fund gets acquirer's stock in return.

Private equity firms may prefer a trade sale over other exit routes, as it provides more control over the exit process, and they can maximize the value of the investment through sale negotiations. They also tend to favor the trade sale exit route over an IPO, because they can realize their investment in cash, or cash and shares where the shares can be sold for cash. In a trade sale there is only one purchaser to deal with (except in an auction sale), making the preparation and negotiations easier and more efficient.

When pursuing a trade sale, the private equity firm should attempt to understand what the acquirer has to offer, how these attributes would benefit the portfolio company, and the motive behind the desire to merge or acquire. Common motives can be strategic (i.e., the company has a technology or service that the acquirer cannot or will not develop on its own), defensive (i.e., the company offers too much competition to the acquirer) or just growth (i.e., the acquirer has the capital, a well-developed distribution network, and more expertise to further develop the company).

Preparation of a trade sale

Preparation for a trade sale exit involves the appointment of advisors, the carrying out of due diligence on the company, and the preparation and negotiation of transaction documentation. At least two advisors are appointed: the investment bank and the law firm. The investment bank might be needed to provide help with the valuation, to find buyers, or just to run the auction sale. The lawyers' role is to prepare the *data room* (i.e., a set of all the documents that any purchaser might want to see to complete an analysis of the business being sold) and to draft the share purchase agreement. The share purchase agreement documents the agreement between the parties and includes any warranties, indemnities, consideration, conditions precedent, restrictive covenants, completion arrangements, and other matters such as the transfer of pension rights.

The private equity firm should also decide whether or not it will pursue an *auction sale*. In an auction sale, the private equity fund will seek competing bids for the company. A sale through an auction depends on the appetite for the company in the market. As a first step, on receipt of a signed confidentiality agreement from the buyers, the company will circulate to prospective buyers an *information memorandum* summarizing the key investment considerations, recent financial information, sales analyses, and other key information about the company. Recipients of the memorandum may then submit indicative bids. A shortlist of bidders is then given access to the data room to complete their due diligence, and offers are submitted with a marked-up version of the seller's proposed share purchase agreement. Auction sales can be attractive to private equity funds, as competition reduces the buyers' bargaining positions and a higher valuation of the company can be achieved.

The auction process can last 6 to 9 months, although "aggressive" auction processes often take far less time. The first few months are spent preparing for the formal marketing phase, which then lasts 3 to 4 months (as short as possible to maintain competitive tension among the prospective purchasers). The lengthier process involved may also be reduced, at a cost, if the private equity fund carries out the due diligence exercise itself.

Warranties and indemnities

The seller usually produces a disclosure letter, which qualifies the *warranties* if any are provided. Private equity firms try to resist giving warranties on a sale (other than as to title to the shares, and capacity and authority to enter into the sale agreement), primarily because it prevents distribution of the full amount to the LPs in the fund.

The sale proceeds cannot be distributed, due to fear of any clawbacks. However, purchasers will generally be unwilling to proceed without warranties, so usually the management of the portfolio company is called upon to provide the warranties and take much, if not all, the residual risk, despite taking only a relatively small percentage of the sale proceeds.

At the time of the original investment, in the investment agreement, management will have provided warranties to the private equity fund, usually to the effect that they have made full disclosure to it of all material information and have taken reasonable care in preparing the business plan. On the basis that significant value is being realized at the exit, the management may well be persuaded to repeat these wide-ranging warranties.

Indemnities have become a common mechanism for parties in private equity transactions to deal with price adjustments. The company sold is valued by reference to a balance sheet as at a date prior to closing (usually an audited balance sheet from the last year-end, or a specific one drawn up for the deal). The mechanism is based on the idea that the economic interest in the business effectively transfers at that date, after which the buyer assumes the risk. The private equity seller is expected to provide a contractual indemnity that no cash or other benefits have been taken out of the business since that balance sheet.

Alternatives to management warranties can include (1) escrow arrangements, where all exiting shareholders participate in funding any claim pro rata, subject to the limit of the escrow; (2) the purchase of warranty and indemnity insurance by the selling shareholders on behalf of the purchaser; and (3) the provision of further financial incentives to management to take greater contingent risk on the warranties.

Most trade sales these days involve the private equity fund sellers having to give warranties and indemnities to the purchaser. Often these warranties and indemnities are a 7-year obligation. Insurance provides a good solution. For a one-off premium, the seller can purchase a policy with significant benefits: a policy period of up to 7 years; defense costs cover and settlement protection; and protection for all of the warrantors. This insurance can remove a large amount of risk and uncertainty from a transaction.

Advantages and disadvantages of a trade sale

The general advantages of trade sales often mentioned are:

- *The possibility to exit fast*—negotiations with one strategic buyer can be very efficient and fast, especially if interests are aligned. Ultimately, only one buyer needs to be convinced of the deal. In an IPO, investment bankers and the public at large have to be handled.

- *Ability to have a clean exit*—the private equity seller sells not only the title to the company's assets, but also the burden of underlying liabilities.

- *Better value*—although there is a widespread belief that IPOs provide the best returns, a trade buyer may be willing to pay a premium, for reasons such as synergies, market share, or market entry.

- *Fewer restrictions compared with IPOs*—trade sales do not involve additional disclosure costs, which are typical for companies that are publicly listed.

- *The possibility to influence the investment* according to the needs of strategic investors.

- *Access to additional capital*—an acquisition usually gives the target company access to additional resources that it did not have as a standalone entity, thus giving it more opportunity for growth.

- *Ability to save on taxes*—a sale of shares in the company may be tax free for some private equity funds (if non-taxpaying) or involve a capital gains tax disposal.

However, a trade sale may be less attractive for several reasons:

- *Management opposition*—there is the potential for the managers to lose their positions and roles within the company post acquisition. Alternatively, the sale could put them back in the position they were in prior to the private equity buyout. The acquirer might blend management teams together or dismiss current management, depending on the terms of the deal. Also, existing management may not fit into the management culture of the acquirer.

- *Closures and job losses*—after a merger or acquisition, the surviving entity may attempt to achieve synergies resulting from the combination. These synergies are often attained by downsizing in areas now deemed to be unnecessary, duplicated, or extravagant, which often results in facility closures and job losses.

- *Loss of confidentiality*—in many cases the best candidate buyers are often close competitors of the portfolio company. The due diligence process might result in the disclosure of confidential information that, notwithstanding good confidentiality agreements, can be used by the competition against the company.

- *Involves additional liabilities*—trade buyers might demand warranties and indemnities that can be costly to the seller.

15.3.2   Listing on an exchange or an initial public offering (IPO)

An *initial public offering* (IPO), also known as a *flotation* or *listing*, involves the quotation of the company on a stock market (e.g., the London Stock Exchange or the Alternative Investment Market in the U.K., or NASDAQ and NYSE in the U.S.). Companies intending to conduct an IPO must file a detailed registration statement with the local securities regulatory body, which usually includes in-depth financial, management, and operational information about the company.

An IPO is the most visible exit and is often perceived to be the most remunerative for the private equity fund. IPOs are usually exit channels for highly profitable portfolio companies that have high growth prospects. In fact, venture capital funds are more likely to pursue an IPO strategy during the portfolio company's growth phase than buyout funds. For buyouts, which are in a mature development stage, the probability of exiting via an IPO is generally smaller than through other exit routes. Das et al. (2001) find that the probability of an IPO decreases when companies move from early-stage to later-stage investments and is the smallest for buyouts. There is, however, a subcategory of buyout-backed IPOs called *reverse LBOs* (see Cao and Lerner, 2006 for more detail).

Preparation for an IPO

There are several requirements a portfolio company must fulfill as well as steps it can take to better position itself for a potential IPO. Depending on the exchange where the securities will trade, the company will have to meet a minimum market valuation. The ability to raise a sufficient amount of capital in its offering and the achievement of a minimum growth rate are also keys to a successful IPO.

If a portfolio company is to conduct an IPO, it needs to begin operating like a public company well beforehand. Some GPs note that it should be fully functional as a public company at least two quarters before the IPO. The company needs to have in place tight accounting, financial, and legal internal controls, and accurate financial statements. Some actions the private equity fund can take prior to conducting an IPO include:

1. Cleaning up the financial records of the company and ensuring they are free of material misstatements.

2. Creating an investor relations department to prepare to deal with investors and analysts.

3. Establishing controls to ensure the timely and accurate preparation of the upcoming disclosures required of a public company.

4. Setting up a sound and qualified board of directors. Depending on the exchange, a public company must adhere to strict corporate governance standards. Mandatory rules might specify the number of directors that must be independent. GPs who serve on the boards of their portfolio companies may be forced to resign as they do not meet the current independence standards.[4]

5. Replacing the management team of the portfolio company. Different skillsets and teams are often needed to manage a public company. It is important to anticipate when these management changes are necessary, rather than waiting until it is too late and a crisis develops. These personnel changes will likely be confined to a handful of key people.

In addition to preparing the company, the GPs of the private equity fund should give consideration to the optimal structure of the IPO at the outset of discussion. In addition, they should identify how soon the capital is required, and the best time of year for strong demand in the IPO market. The factors that will be taken into account in deciding on the structure of the offering, and the market on which to commence trading, include the size and nature of the company and its business, the breadth of the shareholder base being sought, and the likely level of demand for the company's shares. Another factor is the amount of money the company, the PE house, and the selling shareholders want to raise from the IPO. Will the offering be of existing shares only or will more capital be raised by the issue of new shares?

An IPO may be structured as (1) *an institutional offering*—the shares are placed privately to a selected base of qualifying institutional investors; or (2) *a retail offering*—the shares are offered to members of the public resident in selected jurisdictions and who satisfy certain criteria. Retail offerings entail significantly higher transactional costs, as a result of the increased complexity of the compliance requirements. Thus they are undertaken only for larger transactions, particularly where the company has a high public profile. Both institutional and retail offerings are usually coupled with an employee offering that rewards and incentivizes key personnel in the portfolio company.

---

4. In the U.S., the Sarbanes–Oxley Act has created stricter rules for listed companies. For instance, five of a company's directors must be financially literate and at least two must have had a CPA license at one point.

The IPO process

The timeline of events associated with an IPO consists of several steps. One of the first steps in conducting an IPO is the selection of an *underwriting firm*. An underwriting firm assists throughout the whole IPO process, from the preparation of the registration statement to setting a price for the company's securities. With its access to capital markets, the underwriting firm can help distribute the company's shares to institutional and retail clients. The GPs often select the underwriter, as they try to limit the involvement of the company's management team in the whole process. Both the IPO and M&A processes can be very distracting to management and take up too much of their time, if they are too closely involved.

When evaluating an underwriter, it is important to consider the size and types of IPOs the firm has handled in the past, as well as its client base. The underwriting firm needs to have experience in the relevant industry sector and should have a wide client base that will allow the distribution of shares to a range of institutional and individual investors. Other important factors are the pricing of the company, the sell-side coverage offered by the underwriter, and the strategy to position the company.

Depending on the size of the portfolio company, the GPs might hire more than one underwriter, to gain access to a larger pool of public investors. The group of underwriters working on the deal is called a *syndicate*.[5] One firm is usually designated as the lead underwriter, with heightened responsibilities, including setting the final price before the IPO, entering into the underwriting agreement, and controlling advertising. In recent years the formation of an underwriting syndicate has been common, given the large size of many IPOs.

Once the underwriter or underwriting syndicate has been selected, a non-binding *letter of intent* is drafted. This includes a description of the security, the tentative number of shares to be issued, a tentative price range, underwriters' compensation, the type of underwriting (firm commitment or best efforts), and which expenses the company will be responsible for if the offering does not succeed.

The company also develops a *share prospectus*, which is basically a document trying to sell the company. The prospectus is very valuable to the company, because after it has submitted a request to the regulator to go public there is a "quiet period" after the stock begins trading (approximately 25 days in the U.S.). The prospectus should provide a full representation of the company, its products, its competitors, and its objectives. The prospectus also contains valuable historical financial information (typically for 5 years) that will assist investors and others in learning more about the profitability of the company and its financial position.

Advantages and disadvantages of an IPO

The general advantages of an IPO are:

- *It can generate exceptional returns*—if an IPO is very successful, the private equity firm may generate greater returns than in a trade sale.

- *It gives the company its independence and flexibility*—an IPO exposes a company to a significant number of investors, giving it access to a larger pool of capital to use. The company will be able to issue more shares, which can be used as

---

5. The underwriting syndicate is paid out of the spread, the difference between the price the issuing company receives from the lead underwriter and the offering price to the public.

consideration in acquisitions of other companies. In addition, a floating gives the company flexibility to offer share options to employees.

- *It provides greater visibility*—because of the increased media and analyst coverage of public companies, an IPO results in increased visibility for both the company itself and the private equity firm that has listed it.

The main disadvantages of an IPO are:

- *Lock-up agreements increase the risk of losses*—the private equity firm will typically be required by the underwriting firm to maintain a significant part of its holdings for a certain period (the so-called lockup period). During this period the fund cannot have an exit and it faces the risk of a drop in the share price, depending on market conditions.

- *It is expensive*—the preparation of documents, due diligence, and the long process take up a significant amount of management's time. Furthermore, advisors such as lawyers, accountants, underwriters, and other counsels charge high fees to assist with the process. The company also needs to meet costly regulatory requirements. Over the last few years there has been an increase in regulations required by governments and various exchanges. In the U.S., the cost of taking a company public has increased substantially, largely as a result of the Sarbanes–Oxley Act of 2002.[6]

- *It reduces control*—the GPs and the management lose exclusive control of the company after conducting an IPO. Shareholder approval is required for certain activities, such as issuing new stock, M&A activity, or instituting an employee stock purchase plan.

- *It increases scrutiny*—public companies are required to disclose more about their operations through press releases, filings with regulators, and annual reports. These financial documents must be available for public access. With this increased visibility comes intense scrutiny of financial information and management behavior.

Dual-track process

The dual-track process is an exit strategy that combines an IPO of the company with a trade sale or a secondary buyout (we discuss this exit route below). This creates competitive tension between stock market investors and trade buyers, which can enhance the price and sale terms. The private equity seller engages in this dual-track process until it becomes clear which exit route will achieve the higher value. Although this exit strategy is potentially favorable to both the private equity firm and the management team, it is not suitable in every exit scenario and is usually considered only where the company has a strong brand, low levels of debt, strong cash flows, prospects for

6. The Act requires chief executives and chief financial officers of companies registered with the U.S. Securities and Exchange Commission (SEC) (including foreign companies with securities listed on a U.S. exchange or quoted on Nasdaq) to make certain certifications regarding financial and other information contained in annual and quarterly financial reports. These certifications include, for instance, responsibility for internal controls, ensuring that they know of all material information, or that the relevant report does not contain any untrue statement or omission. Providing a knowingly false certification will lead to fines and criminal sanctions. These provisions were enacted as a result of the Enron and WorldCom scandals in the U.S.

growth, and a strong management team. Planning is crucial, and the market conditions must be stable, particularly in view of the IPO.

15.3.3   Secondary buyouts

Secondary buyouts refer to the sale of portfolio companies from one financial private equity fund to another.[7] Initially, secondary buyouts were rare, because private equity firms were reluctant to sell a portfolio company to another private equity firm. There was a stigma of failure associated with not being able to take a company public or sell it to a strategic partner. However, investors now understand that a secondary buyout may be appropriate during the expansion phase of a portfolio company. Different financial investors engage in different lifecycle phases of a company. As a result, the acquiring investor may still be able to use his or her different expertise in order to maximize firm value.

In addition, the timing of exits by private equity investors is sometimes influenced by the need to pay out LPs when funds are close to the end of their life. This leaves an opportunity for secondary buyout private equity investors to exploit market-timing opportunities. In a growing market and low-cost-of-debt environment, secondary investors can buy a target in industries with high multiples, financing the deal with high levels of leverage. Because of industry-driven multiple expansion, the target can then be sold at a higher multiple, after having paid down part of the debt. The attractiveness of this strategy is enhanced by the positive track record of the potential targets, which have already proven to be able to cope with high levels of leverage. Additionally, the management of the company has already gained expertise in dealing with private equity investors, and enhanced governance and monitoring systems are already in place. As a result, secondary buyouts can provide follow-up private equity buyers with a less risky, quicker, and possibly more lucrative alternative to first-round acquisitions. Consistent with this argument, the volume of secondary buyouts, calculated as a percentage of total value transacted in buyouts, reached its peak at 26% in 2006–2007, in correspondence with the preceding credit boom.[8]

In general, secondary buyouts are seen as a less preferable option for private equity funds and are associated with periods during which other exit mechanisms are less accessible.[9] Secondary buyouts are also increasingly being used as private equity exit routes, because of private equity firms wanting to shorten the deal lifetime. They offer the opportunity of recapitalizing the business while also releasing cash to the management team to incentivize them to continue to work hard.

In a primary buyout, a conflict of interest exists between the target's management team and the private equity fund acquirer. The management team has a desire to achieve a successful sale, which might conflict with their future plans for the company once acquired. For secondary buyouts these conflicts of interest are magnified, given that the management team needs to manage the relation with both the selling and the acquiring private equity fund. The alignment of managers is harder to achieve, because the windfall in share sale proceeds generated by the secondary buyout puts managers in a good position to negotiate. One way to achieve alignment is for the buying private

---

7. Kaplan and Strömberg (2009) report that this route is responsible for up to 24% of buyout exits.

8. Strömberg (2007) provides evidence that secondary buyouts are significantly more likely to lead to successful exits than public-to-private deals.

9. For instance, research provided by Nikoskelainen and Wright (2007) suggests that this exit mechanism is associated with returns that, albeit positive, are significantly lower than the returns from exits via IPOs or trade sales.

equity fund to seek to defer the consideration payable to the management, by paying less upfront cash and maximizing the amount put into a loan note that is repayable on a later exit.

Secondary buyouts are no different from trade sales with respect to the buyer's demand for protection against unknown liabilities and other matters that could diminish the value of the target after acquisition. However, the selling private equity fund will almost certainly refuse to provide full warranty and indemnity insurance. The target's management will normally agree to provide it, except in cases when managers will not participate in the business going forward. In this case, the sellers may agree to put a proportion of their proceeds into an escrow account for an agreed period of time.

15.3.4 Recapitalizations

A private company *recapitalization* (or *recap* or *refinancing*), in its simplest form, involves a company borrowing money and using the proceeds to purchase some of the owner's equity ownership or to pay special dividends. A leveraged recapitalization involves relevering the portfolio company, based, for example, on the company's earnings. The residual portion of the equity that exceeds the total firm value at that time flows back to the private equity fund that owns the company. In such a transaction the private equity fund pulls out the equity invested *without* selling the company. Since special dividends generate tax consequences, private equity investors may prefer share repurchases. However, some companies use a combination of the two, repurchasing some shares and distributing the remainder of the recap as a special dividend.

Leveraged recapitalizations are highly controversial in some countries. For example, some unions are concerned that payment of special dividends, especially from companies' cash reserves or financed by borrowings, might make their employment positions more vulnerable. In some countries there is a minimum capital regime in place to protect against insolvency that may make recapitalizations difficult to implement.

Recapitalization criteria

Leveraged recapitalizations are generally financed based upon the future potential of a company. The exit route is appropriate especially for companies with high free cash flows. However, not every business is a viable leveraged recapitalization candidate. The primary requirement is the ability to utilize debt, including asset-based and cash flow–based (mezzanine) financing, to fund the transaction. This means that companies that already have a highly leveraged capital structure, or which operate in an industry where debt is difficult, will not be able to pursue a recapitalization transaction.

Debt used for recapitalizations

Releveraging of portfolio companies can be realized via securitizations, high-yield debt offerings, or sales and leasebacks. Thus, a recapitalization can be seen as a way of recycling capital, since no new "real" value is added by the transaction.

Most recaps rely on bonds, but some private equity funds turn to bank debt or term debt as an alternative or in addition to bonds. When used for a recap, bonds often include buyer protections, absent in most bond issuances. In certain circumstances, immediate redemption can be triggered at slightly above face value. The bond's interest rate can be tied to credit ratings or to changes in control. The company faces downside risk if conditions worsen, but these investor protections make financing cheaper and are attractive for solidly profitable companies. Hybrids are sometimes used to reduce the cost of debt, even though they carry very long terms. Convertibles may also be used to reduce costs, although they pose the additional risk that investors will exercise their right to acquire stock.

Bank debt is less often used than bonds, but it can be a good choice when the GPs of the private equity fund do not want to be tied to a fixed term for some or all of their debt needs. Bank debt can be prepaid and, in favorable markets, is relatively cheap.

Advantages and disadvantages of recapitalizations

Some advantages of recapitalizations are:

- *They provide earlier returns and liquidity*—the proceeds of a recapitalization are distributed through share repurchase plans and special dividends to their private equity owners before the company is sold. Therefore, recapitalizations enable private equity owners to achieve partial liquidity without having to sell their ownership.

- *They provide tax-related benefits*—all things being equal, tax-efficient debt beats other sources of financing, because its interest is tax deductible.

- *They discipline the management*—with so much additional debt, private equity fund owners can be fairly sure that management will act in a more focused and disciplined manner than if they had excess cash.

However, recapitalizations have some disadvantages:

- *Higher financial risk*—after a recapitalization, the company is left with more leverage, which increases the probability of failure. Highly leveraged companies may no longer have the financial resources to weather unexpected economic conditions or even carry on their business. Moreover, creditors will have a claim on the company's assets if the company becomes insolvent and no longer has the capacity to repay its debts.

- *Loss of flexibility*—the leverage associated with recapitalization decreases the flexibility of the company because of restrictive covenants that are usually attached to the debt instruments. For instance, the company may not be allowed to sell assets, or a change in the company's ownership might trigger forced repayment of the debt.

15.3.5 Repurchases

A repurchase involves the buying back of private equity investors' shares by the company and/or its management. The repurchase can also be a mandatory redemption in the case of preferred shares. Sometimes private equity investors demand exit options to the owners of the company at the time of the initial investment. *Buyback rights* cause the company to buy back the private equity investors' shares, whereas *put option rights* cause the management of the company to purchase the private equity investors' stake at an agreed return. For many investments, however, share buybacks by the firm are considered a backup exit route and are used primarily when the investment has been unsuccessful.

Usually the firm's management specify a price at which they will buy back shares, the number of shares they intend to repurchase, and the period of time for which they will keep the offer open. Equity repurchases may offer tax advantages to the private equity fund, since dividends are usually taxed at higher rates. Furthermore, the private equity fund has the option not to sell its shares back to the firm and, therefore, does not have to realize capital gains in the period of equity repurchases.

15.3.6   Exits of unsuccessful investments: Liquidations and breakups

Private equity firms generally try to minimize their portfolio failure ratio, owing to their negative effect on performance and reputation. Nevertheless, underperforming investments do occur and, sooner or later, have to be written down or written off. Hence, this exit channel has to be regarded as a constraint rather than an option.

Liquidations are sales in circumstances where the banks have taken control because the company has been unable to support the bank debt that was injected as part of the original acquisition. These tend to be relatively rare, because in these circumstances there is usually a "workout" or restructuring whereby the capital structure, including the debt, is restructured to make it serviceable.

The *breakup* exit strategy involves reorganizing the company and separating it into independent businesses, which are sold by individual trade sales. This divestment strategy can result in a lengthier process, but sometimes the total disposal proceeds can be in excess of the initial purchase price.

Certain factors will be taken into consideration in determining whether the company is suitable for breakup. Subsidiaries that operate as separate legal entities and are individually financed are self-contained and will be easy to sell on. Alternatively, a reorganization of the company can be undertaken to divide the group into easily disposable companies. There might be significant overlap in the due diligence and data rooms provided for each sale. A standardized approach should be taken for each disposal, reducing fees, expenses, and time taken on each sale. Running simultaneous transactions may further reduce cost and maximize efficiency.

15.4   SUMMARY

The exit is probably the most important part of the private equity process. As mentioned earlier, all private equity funds conduct an exit review as early as the time of considering making an investment. This gives them a view of what the potential exit method will be and who the likely buyers will be. The value created by the private equity fund is embedded in the sale price of the portfolio company. This profit is then passed on to the funds' investors.

Of late, given the depression in the markets and the contraction of credit, secondary buyouts have become a popular means of exit. However, trade sales remain the preferred route for most private equity funds.

15.5   REFERENCES

CAO, J., AND LERNER, J. (2006) "The performance of reverse leveraged buyouts," NBER Working Paper 12626, National Bureau of Economic Research.

CUMMING, D.J., AND JOHAN, S.A. (2007) "Preplanned venture capital exits," working paper, York University.

DAS, S., JAGANNATHAN, M., AND SARIN, A. (2001) "The private equity discount: An empirical examination of the exit of venture backed companies," working paper.

GOMPERS, P., AND LERNER, J. (2000) "Money chasing deals? The impact of fund inflows on private equity valuation," *Journal of Financial Economics*, **55**(2), 281–325, February.

KAPLAN, S.N., AND STRÖMBERG, P. (2009) "Leveraged buyouts and private equity," *Journal of Economic Perspectives*, **23**(1), 121–146.

NIKOSKELAINEN, E., AND WRIGHT, M. (2007) "The impact of corporate governance mechanisms on value increase in leveraged buyouts," *Journal of Corporate Finance*, **13**(4), 511–537, September.

STRÖMBERG, P. (2007) "The new demography of private equity," working paper, Swedish Institute of Financial Research.

PART 3

Early-stage investing

16

Angel investing

16.1 WHAT IS ANGEL INVESTING?

As job growth and economic prosperity in both developed and emerging markets continue to become less dependent upon large firms, the economic importance of small firms is receiving increased attention. It is now accepted that the small-firm sector will provide the main vehicle for recovery from recessions and will be the main provider of jobs for the next decade at least. One of the most important considerations that new and small firms face in the transformation from entrepreneurial ideas to revenue-generating companies is the procurement of capital. Because traditional avenues of finance, such as debt, are often not available, young firms must seek risk capital by relying on two sources of outside equity: venture capital and business angel financing.

A *business angel investor* is a high-net-worth individual, who typically provides capital, in the form of debt or equity from his or her own funds to a small private business owned and operated by someone else who is neither a friend nor a family member. The term "angel investor" originates from the financiers of Broadway shows in the early 1900s. These were wealthy individuals who provided capital to help launch new theatrical productions. As patrons of the arts, these investors were considered by theater professionals as "angels." Angels are informal investors, but not every informal investor constitutes an angel. Informal investors are made up of two different groups of investors: angels, and friends and family.

The typical business angel investment is carried out either through close friends— by introducing entrepreneurs to potential investors with the help of relatives, friends, colleagues, or professors—or through "angel networks", when one angel investor gets other angel investors interested in investing. Angels typically offer value-added services to entrepreneurs such as seasoned advice on early-stage venture development. Their participation usually happens informally, although sometimes angels enter into a formal employment or consulting relationship with the venture.

The significance of business angels arises for several reasons:

- Business angels represent one of the oldest and largest sources of seed and equity capital. Their investments substantially dwarf investments made by professionally managed venture capital (for more details see Wetzel, 1987; Gaston, 1989; Sohl, 2003; Mason and Harrison, 2000). The funding importance of angels has become even greater in recent years, as venture capitalists in the main markets (the U.S.

341

and U.K.) have started to shift their investment focus away from startups and early-stage firms in favor of safer and more mature ventures.

- Business angels do not incur the transaction costs of venture capital firms: thus, they are able to make smaller seed and startup-stage investments, well below the minimum deal sizes considered by venture capital fund managers. Angels fill a critical capital gap between "friends and family" and venture capitalists. Friends, family, and the entrepreneur's own efforts may provide some funding (up to $100,000 or so), but this is hardly enough to sustain a rapidly growing startup for very long. When a startup requires more than $100,000 but less than about $1.5mn to $2mn, angels are a viable source of capital. This level of funding is usually below the radar screen of most venture capitalists.[1] Venture funds attract large amounts of capital from investors, and spending this capital efficiently requires making larger investments than may be appropriate for very young companies.

- Business angels are much more geographically dispersed than venture capital funds. Venture funds are overwhelmingly located in just a small number of major financial technology centers and concentrate their investments in a relatively small number of locations. By contrast, business angels tend to make the majority of their investments in firms located within 50 to 100 miles of where they live (e.g., Harrison et al., 2003).

- Business angels invest across various sectors, whereas venture capitalists tend to focus on high-tech and bio-tech industries. Several low-technology companies founded in industries in which most startups are not high growth have generated extremely high financial returns on angel investments (e.g., Starbucks and Kinko's).[2]

The aggregate angel market is estimated to be as large as, or even larger than, the venture capital market. Although it is difficult to estimate the total size of the angel market, owing to its informality, some studies estimate the size of angel investments to be at least twice that of the institutional venture capital market (e.g., Wetzel, 1987; Freear et al., 1994; Mason and Harrison, 1994). Since angel investments are, on average, of a much smaller size, it is also "guesstimated" that angels fund between 30 and 40 times the number of entrepreneurial firms financed by the formal venture capital industry (e.g., Wetzel and Freear, 1996).

The European Business Angels Network (EBAN) estimates that the number of business angels in Europe is around 75,000, a small number in comparison with the U.S., which has an estimated 250,000. The size of the European angel market is approximately 25% that of the U.S. angel market and consists of approximately 350 organized networks and groups. These groups receive about 40,000 business plans, on average, every year.

1. There are exceptions, such as specific venture funds devoted to early-stage investments, but early-stage investments are not the industry norm. Even during the height of the dotcom era, when venture capitalists were said to be investing heavily in earlier stage investments, still less than 30% of all venture capital was allocated to early-stage deals (e.g., Van Osnabrugge and Robinson, 2000).

2. The most famous angel investment in recent years was probably the $100,000 check that Sun Microsystems co-founder Andy Bechtolsheim made out to Google after watching Larry Page and Sergey Brin demonstrate their search engine software. The check was uncashable at first: Google did not yet exist as a legal entity. That check made hundreds of millions of dollars for Andy Bechtolsheim. Other famous business angels are Iain McGlinn, who invested in Body Shop, and Thomas Alberg, one of the angel investors in Amazon.com.

Angels fill the capital gap by providing appropriate amounts of funding to early-stage startups. By doing so, they function as a "conveyor belt" that moves some young startups along toward venture capitalists. This financing allows early-stage companies to accomplish a variety of objectives that will make them attractive to venture capitalists, including proving a concept through product development, beginning marketing, securing customers, and obtaining patent protection.

Angel investors are a heterogeneous group. Angels come from diverse backgrounds: some are financially sophisticated, whereas others are relatively inexperienced. In addition to making a financial investment, some angels actively participate in the firm's operations, but such participation varies by angel. The different types of angel investors affect the range of businesses in which they invest, the organizational arrangements that they employ, their investment criteria, their decision-making processes, and a host of other things that make it quite difficult to describe business angels. We discuss in detail below some of the main classifications.

Accredited vs. unaccredited business angels

Accredited angel investors in the U.S. are individuals who meet the Securities and Exchange Commission's (SEC) accreditation requirements and who use their own money to provide capital to a private business owned and operated by someone else, who is neither a friend nor a family member. SEC Rule 501 of Regulation D states that an accredited investor is an individual who has a net worth of more than \$1mn or an expected individual (household) yearly income of more than \$200,000 (\$300,000). In the UK, a certified sophisticated angel investor needs to have an annual income of £100,000 or more and to have net assets of the value of £250,000 or more during the financial year immediately preceding the certification date. Net assets for these purposes do not include the property that is the primary residence, or any loan secured on that residence, or any benefits (in the form of pensions or otherwise) that are payable on the termination of service or on retirement.

Unaccredited angel investors in either the U.S. or U.K. are individuals who do not meet the accreditation requirements above and who use their own money to provide capital to a private business owned and operated by someone else, who is neither a friend nor a family member.

Active vs. passive business angels

Active angel investors use their own money to provide capital to a private business owned and operated by someone else, who is neither a friend nor a family member, and also invest time in the development of the company. These investors are usually cashed-out entrepreneurs who continue to yearn for the next high-growth venture. They perform their own due diligence, typically invest in ventures in familiar industries, and get actively involved with the companies that they finance. This type of investor has relevant industry expertise, a strong rolodex of contacts, and the experience to add substantial value to the company.

Active angels provide value-added services to entrepreneurs. These are non-financial services of a different type than venture capitalists provide. Venture capitalists take a more formal role and offer benefits such as connections to professional managers, but active angels provide informal advice and counseling. Because they are usually ex-entrepreneurs themselves, they can provide seasoned advice and empathize with the many difficulties that entrepreneurs face in advancing an early-stage venture. Many entrepreneurs believe that an active angel's advice and industry connections are as important as her or his financial capital.

Passive angel investors are individuals who use their own money to provide capital to a private business owned and operated by someone else, who is neither a friend nor a family member, but do not invest time in the development of the company. Passive investors may provide early-stage investments without looking at the entrepreneur's business plan and perform little or no due diligence on investments that they make. Passive angel investors include both passive investors who co-invest with other active investors and passive investors who invest alone without any active involvement with the portfolio company. A passive angel might be a wealthy doctor, an attorney, or similar professional who must focus on his or her day-to-day career. This type of investor is willing to invest, but usually does not have the time or specific expertise to be of much help to a startup.

The investment capacity of passive angels is usually lower than that of active angels. In addition, the proportion of business owners and entrepreneurs is higher amongst active angels (80% of active angels vs. 37% of passive angels).

Other business angel types

There is also a significant minority of *virgin angels*. These are angels who are actively looking to make their first investment. Their inactivity is associated with their lack of knowledge of the investment process or with the limited number of business proposals that meet their requirements. Another category is *dormant angels*. These are individuals who have made one or more investments but are not currently looking to make new investments, either because they have no further liquidity or because they have invested and have withdrawn from the market as a result of bad experiences, poor results, or unmet expectations.

16.2 WHAT MOTIVATES BUSINESS ANGELS?

- *Financial returns*—achieving a substantial financial return on the investment is a significant motivation for business angels to invest, but it is not the only consideration.

- *Employment opportunities*—some angels are looking to work on a regular basis at their investments. Often, angels will work part time, with periods of full-time commitment, to help entrepreneurs through challenging issues. For this reason, the angel investment often becomes more personal to both the investor and the entrepreneur.

- *Altruism*—many angels enjoy helping another entrepreneur build a business. They often express the desire to "give back" to the entrepreneurial community that made them wealthy doing what they loved. This altruism can take the form of helping emergent entrepreneurs become successful, investing in startups seeking to commercialize socially useful technology (e.g., green/clean technology), or investing in startups that will create jobs in the angel's community.

- *Tax incentives*—governments and other public entities have implemented various policy initiatives to improve access to informal equity financing for small and new technology businesses. The most common policy is to offer tax relief on the amount invested in early-stage ventures, which has an immediate effect on the annual income tax of the angel investor.[3] Also, a large number of countries are abolishing capital gains tax for this type of investment. In a recent U.K. study by Wiltbank (2009), 80% of investors surveyed had made use of the Enterprise Investment Scheme at least once. Also, investors said that 24% of their investments would not have been made without tax incentives.

16.3 ANGEL INVESTMENT PROCESS

In terms of investment focus, business angels tend to invest in smaller amounts, and at earlier stages of development, than venture capitalists. Business angels place capital at risk in situations where:

- A high degree of uncertainty exists as to how the company will develop over time
- The quality and motivation of the entrepreneur cannot be accurately assessed
- Time and financial resource constraints inhibit the ability to undertake extensive due diligence
- Other sources of financing are largely absent.

Business angels have less costly structures, even if they operate in syndicates, and, hence, they face low transaction costs. Also, they are accountable only to themselves and have no need to refer decisions to others for approval: this, combined with their more limited "due diligence", results in a much shorter decision cycle.

16.3.1 Investment process

Many deals do not progress smoothly, and the process can easily stall as a result of any number of factors. For example, raising the full amount of capital required for a business may involve funding from several angels and, while some may be willing to invest, others may be more reluctant or uncomfortable with the terms. Similarly, an angel may delay the process in order to carry out more screening. An angel can easily withdraw from the process by terminating discussions with the entrepreneur at any time prior to making an investment.

We discuss the angel investment process in several stages.[4] These stages highlight the importance of an angel's personal investment objectives. These objectives may be financial, such as income and capital growth, but they can also include personal goals.

Screening stage

This stage of the investment process involves learning about the opportunity and meeting the entrepreneur. The investment opportunities may come through various sources, such as friends, colleagues, business associates, accountants, lawyers, banks, or organized angel networks.

---

3. For example, the U.K. and France have promoted tax measures, such as the U.K.'s pioneer Enterprise Investment Scheme (EIS) and the recent SUIR (Société Unipersonnelle d'Investissements à Risque) (translated as Individual Company for Risk Capital Investments), which were created to facilitate investment by individuals in small and young companies. In the Netherlands, the Tante Agaath ("Aunt Agatha") scheme, set up in 1996, also proved to be popular with angel investors.

4. Paul et al. (2007) present this process based on interviews with a large number of active angel investors.

At this early stage in the process, angels usually receive a summary business plan. The opportunity is analyzed, based on the location and on industry sector key considerations. Angels usually prefer to invest close to home and in familiar industries. However, they may be prepared to examine proposals that do not meet their preferences, particularly if a trusted person has referred the proposal to them or if they are investing alongside an informed investor.

In the early stages of a venture's development, assets are often intangible and knowledge based and the trading track record is limited. Therefore, business angels work with little historical performance data on which judgments about investments can be based. Against such a background, they have little option but to place relatively greater weight on the personal attributes of the founders of a business.

While more information may be gathered about the business opportunity, assessment at this stage focuses mainly on the entrepreneur or team behind the business. Arthur Rock, a legendary venture capitalist, who was an early investor in major firms including Intel, Apple Computer, Scientific Data Systems, and Teledyne, once said, "Nearly every mistake I've made has been in picking the wrong people, not the wrong idea."

Entrepreneurs need to be able to present not only their ideas but also themselves effectively. While the business idea may be exciting, the person who runs the business is key to its success. The most important issue for angels is to assess whether they can work with the entrepreneur. Angels use their own business networks to check the background and performance track record of the entrepreneur.

Investors look for entrepreneurs who show passion. Entrepreneurs who demonstrate this quality typically receive more interest than those who may have a better business model or product, but lack enthusiasm. Entrepreneurs without great commitment and enthusiasm are less likely to succeed. Angels also appreciate it if the entrepreneur has made money in past careers and has put up a significant amount of his or her own money to start the company. Each interaction between the entrepreneur and the angels is an opportunity to build trust. Entrepreneurs who appear to provide contradictory answers lose credibility and trust.

Angels should always try to understand whether the management team is appropriate for the project. Angels are usually less concerned about the team being in place for startups that are not very far along. However, as the company grows, the entrepreneur is not expected to be able to do everything. The entrepreneur should know the shortcomings of the current team and what team members need to be added. An important aspect that should be discussed is the team's commitment. Investors like teams that struggle through hard times and show persistence.

At the screening stage, angels should also try to understand who the potential acquirers may be for the company. A startup might demonstrate profitability, have a solid business plan, and be led by an entrepreneur with a proven track record, but it might not be a good investment opportunity if there is no clear exit path. The focus should be on who might want to purchase the startup and why.

Throughout the screening stage many business-planning themes could emerge. These may include barriers to the entry of competitors, intellectual property, growth potential, competition, profitability, advisors, the domain knowledge of the investor, and the expected return.

Bargaining stage

During this stage, the business plan is thoroughly studied. Business angels are also likely to be assessing how they can contribute to the business beyond the scope of their financial investment. Foreseeing a satisfactory post-investment role can be a key factor in ensuring that the investment process unfolds smoothly, as consideration of this issue makes it more likely that angels will achieve good "matches" with appropriate entrepreneurs.

At this stage, some form of due diligence is also completed. It is often not a formalized process and, frequently, it is carried out by angels themselves. The actual level of due diligence will vary, depending upon factors such as the size of the investment, the nature of the business, its prior trading history, and the angel's level of familiarity with such deals. A basic due diligence exercise will commonly cover some or all of the following:

- *Legal*—for example, checking that the company has been properly incorporated; reviewing any major commercial contracts that may be in place; checking whether employees have appropriate employment contracts; and ascertaining ownership of intellectual property (particularly important for companies operating in the technology sector).

- *Financial*—ensuring that there are no errors or missing numbers in the accounts and assessing the company's future projections and forecasts.

- *Commercial*—understanding the company's target market and, possibly, speaking with key customers.

Negotiations are finalized on the value of financial investment in equity terms. A key issue is how much an angel should expect to receive for varying levels of investment. In part, this is difficult, because angels invest early in the entrepreneurial process, when there is often little to value. However, if the entrepreneur has already established a business and made an outlay of time and money, this provides the angel with something to which an approximate value can be more readily attached. There are no real guidelines: angels just have to exercise their judgment.

The initial valuation has a significant impact on the return on investment, because investing at the early stage implies that the venture, if successful, will attract follow-on rounds of equity financing from the venture capital industry or from other investors. Each of these subsequent rounds requires an independent valuation. If the valuation at the seed or startup stage is judged too high, then in subsequent rounds the extent of stock dilution of early-stage investors becomes acute. Thus, accurate valuations take on added importance, especially in declining markets.

Consideration may also be given to how and when additional investment funds will be made available. Usually, this is not set out in a formal agreement. The conclusion of the bargaining stage is a formal agreement between the entrepreneurs and angels, setting out the detail of the agreement reached.

Value creation stage

Angel investors usually have much experience in business and entrepreneurship and many are fairly active in this stage of the investment process. In addition to providing the much-needed capital, most angel investors assume the role of advisors in the firms. Angel investors take an active post-investment role in the business, because they can make a contribution to it. They can help the entrepreneur with contacts and with advice on how to run the company.

Many angel investors take full-time or part-time jobs in companies they invest in. However, business angels' participation usually does not interfere with these firms' autonomy.

During this stage, angels typically expect to take a role that enables them to contribute not only strategically but also operationally, by interacting with the entrepreneur on an ongoing basis. Regardless of whether the business angel is employed permanently or on a temporary "as needed" basis, the presence of an investor–employee affords business angels the opportunity to more closely interact with management, participate in decision making, and observe venture performance in real time.

Typically, active investors limit the number of businesses in which they invest. While the overall level of funds available for investment is a limiting factor, time is also a critical resource.

Exit stage

An exit mechanism means that the angel investor has a means to cash out on the investment. Angels have no clear preference about how an exit should be achieved, other than estimating that it would most likely be an acquisition of the angel's position, or the entire company, by a third party. An initial public offering or management buy-back is unlikely and rare. In fact, most angel investors do not specify a particular exit mechanism. Usually, what they want to see is a company that is run professionally enough to create value, and to attract investments from other sources such as venture capitalists. In addition, exit timescales tend to be very flexible, although some angels might wish to keep their investment for at least as long as is necessary to maximize their tax advantages.

16.3.2   Characteristics of angel investment contracts

Business angels rarely obtain majority ownership of their portfolio companies. Most studies show that the angels who invest in the initial financing round of a startup collectively acquire between 20% and 35% of the company in which they are investing. An angel investment usually results in the following documents:

1. *Investment and shareholders' agreement*—this document sets out the terms of the investment and regulates the relationship of the shareholders once the investment has been completed. It addresses the specific rights of the angel investor(s), such as rights to appoint directors, to receive information on the business, and to veto certain actions of the company.

2. *Articles of association*—a company's articles of association set out its internal regulations and dealings with its management and administration. They guide on matters such as transfers of shares, dividends, and voting rights, and complement the investment and shareholders' agreement.

3. *Disclosure letter*—the disclosure letter sets out disclosures against the warranties contained in the investment and shareholders' agreement.

4. *Other documents*—for example, assignments of intellectual property (the intellectual property should be assigned to the company not to the entrepreneur) and service agreements (if the senior management team does not have employment contracts in place).

Little data are available from representative samples on the term sheet provisions used by angel investors. The data usually come from sophisticated angel investors and suggest that relatively little angel investing involves the use of venture capital–like term sheet provisions.

Investment staging

Angels usually do not stage their investments. A survey in Wong (2002) found that, when a venture capital round follows an angel round, angels are unlikely to participate. These findings confirm the conventional wisdom that angels provide early-stage funding to grow the startup for the first year or so, after which venture capitalists or other investors take over. When an angel does follow on his or her own investment in a later round, it correlates with a lower return, suggesting that the angel provided the subsequent funding as a last resort to keep a struggling venture afloat, rather than to obtain a larger piece of a good investment.

Stock received

Angels usually receive common instead of preferred stock in exchange for their investment. Common equity claims do not provide any protection in the event of bankruptcy or liquidation. Wong's (2002) survey found that the greatest number of angels took straight common stock, which is consistent with anecdotal evidence.

Board seats

While board seats are commonly granted in venture capital rounds, they do not appear common in angel rounds. Most angel investments are made without the angel receiving a seat on the board of directors. When board seats are allocated, the founders usually retain board control, indicating that board control is not the primary control mechanism utilized by angels (e.g., Wong, 2002).

Anti-dilution clauses

Anti-dilution protection is the name given to provisions, usually in the articles of association, to protect an investor from suffering dilution of his or her shareholding, which would otherwise occur when additional shares in the company are issued after the date of the investor's contribution.

Angel investments are less likely than venture capital investments to use anti-dilution clauses. Moreover, when sophisticated business angels do use anti-dilution provisions, the terms of their provisions are much more favorable to entrepreneurs than similar provisions used by venture capitalists. Such protection can take the form of a ratchet mechanism that retrospectively reprices the investor's stake if further shares are issued by the company at a lower price. Angels use full ratcheting much less frequently than institutional investors do.

More usually, in angel investments anti-dilution protection takes the form of pre-emption rights over the issue of new shares, such that no new shares can be issued until they have first been offered to the existing shareholders, pro rata to their existing shareholding.

Liquidation clauses

Angel investment agreements are much less likely than venture capital investment contracts to include a liquidation provision. For example, one study found that only about half of the contracts written by sophisticated accredited angel investors have a liquidation provision, as opposed to the vast majority of venture capital contracts (Von Osnabrugge and Robinson, 2000). Wong's (2002) study found that a provision granting angels the right to force bankruptcy was included in only 4.6% of angel contracts (this includes both sophisticated and unsophisticated angels).

Why do angels demand fewer rights than venture capitalists, despite investing in highly risky firms? A first possible explanation is that angels are unsophisticated investors, who are willing to settle for few protections because they do not know any better. However, although a lack of sophistication may partially explain angel contract design, it is unlikely to be the primary explanation for two reasons. First, many angels are high-net-worth individuals or "accredited investors", who are not the sort of investors generally considered unsophisticated. Second, many angels are ex-entrepreneurs, which suggests that they not only understand investing as a general matter, but also understand startup investments, in particular. This is because they made their fortunes after going through the very same funding process on the other side.

A second explanation is that angels—as the first, but not the last, source of outside funding for startups—need to build the financial bridge from the funds received from friends and family to venture capital. Angels must entice venture capitalists to follow their investments to have any hope of profit. This need for venture capital sets de facto limits on the terms of the angel investment contract. This is because venture capitalists are flooded with funding proposals, but accept perhaps only 1% to 3% of them. Funding proposals might be rejected in the presence of an aggressive or overreaching angel. Angels need to keep the terms of their investment simple, because nothing prevents follow-on funding more effectively than an overly complicated angel investment contract, which a venture capitalist needs to unwind.

A third explanation is that angels might rationally choose to forgo preference-laden contracts, because the costs entailed would be disproportionately high relative to the amount of investment and because angels do not have the same need for some provisions (e.g., regarding exit, because they do not face the same downstream pressures as venture capitalists). Not only is there a cost of negotiating with the entrepreneur, but also it is very costly to prepare a contract that is verifiable by a third party, such as a judge, if and when it is violated and in dispute. In addition, the potential ex post legal costs related to having the contract verified and enforced by a third party might be very high.

On the other hand, venture capitalists have pressure to behave competently for their limited partners: therefore, they have to spend more on contracting costs and on screening, before they make an investment (i.e., they use comprehensive contracts and a thorough and formal due diligence process).

16.3.3 Returns

Angels use their own capital and are fully exposed to both the risk and the reward of any investment. In addition, they usually do not have fixed targets in terms of return and timescales and are beholden only to themselves. Consequently, business angels are less risk averse and more patient than venture capitalists. One reason for these preferences is that angels have the flexibility to invest for non-financial as well as financial reasons if they so choose.

Only a small portion of angel investments have a positive exit. An angel's financial payoff comes from a small number of startups that go on to attract venture capital and then exit through an initial public offering (IPO) or a private sale. The best financial returns for investors in startup companies tend to come from investments in companies that go public. However, only a small proportion of angel-backed companies go public.

Shane (2008) calculates that from 1980 through 2006 only about 100 companies with potential angel backing went public in the U.S. every year, out of the many thousands of investments made annually by angels.

Wiltbank and Boeker (2007) examine the investment returns of 539 angel investors from 86 groups of angels in the U.S. who had made 3,097 investments, from which they had experienced 1,137 exits. An average investment in the sample (mean investment) generated a profit of $295,000 on an initial investment of $191,000 in 3.52 years. However, even these highly successful angels lost money on more than half (52%) of their investments. In fact, the median angel investment made by this sample of very experienced and successful angels involved an investment of $50,000 that returned $40,000, or 80 cents in the dollar. Moreover, just 7% of the investments accounted for three quarters of financial returns.

In a U.K. study, Wiltbank (2009) finds that the most likely outcome in a given angel investment is failure: 56% of exits failed to return the capital invested. However, "winning" investments are very attractive. He calculated the overall return to business angel investing in the U.K. to be 2.2 times the invested capital. Given the holding period of just under 4 years, the gross internal rate of return is estimated to be approximately 22%. In fact, the top 9% of the investments generate more than 10 times the capital invested.

To measure the rate of return on angel investing properly, the opportunity cost of the angel's time must be taken into consideration, because such investing is not passive, unlike putting money into a mutual fund, a venture capital limited partnership, or a hedge fund. It has proved to be difficult to obtain the rate of return on angel investments net of opportunity costs.

Another issue relates to obtaining a large representative sample of angel investors. Unfortunately, this information is not readily available. Consequently, studies have focused on investment performance data from business angels affiliated with angel groups. These are unrepresentative samples, given that they capture more active and sophisticated angels. Many angels are not part of these groups, thus the data might suffer from survivorship bias.

16.3.4 Success factors

Given the constantly changing environment in which the firms receiving angel investing operate, it is difficult to draw definitive conclusions about the golden rules that guarantee business angels' success. Luck always plays a central role. There are, however, some factors that appear to be systematically related to better outcomes. We discuss several of them in the list below, but the discussion is not intended to be comprehensive.[5]

Angel investors are more likely to obtain a good return on their investment if they:

1. *Build a network to source good deals*—one way to do this is to become a member of an angel network (see Section 16.4.1) or to be part of an informal network. These networks facilitate contact and the exchange of best practice and experience between angels, venture capitalists, and other sources of early-stage funding through networking events and regular communication.

2. *Invest in a business sector they thoroughly understand*—angels often have networks in particular industries that can be great sources of valuable information.

5. We thank Andrew Dixon, founder of ARC InterCapital and serial angel investor, for suggesting some of these factors to us.

Angel investors who are familiar with an industry are more likely to realize when major trends are shifting and can better see possible risks.

3. *Do some due diligence*—even a relatively small amount of due diligence helps avoid failure. Expertise is relevant only when it is used to evaluate the details and potential of many ventures before ultimately choosing the attractive opportunity. Wiltbank (2009) finds that the investments on which the investor spent at least 20 hours of due diligence prior to investing were less likely to fail than those on which less (or no) due diligence had been performed.

4. *Are realistic about the business opportunity*—one thing is certain about any business plan for a new venture: it will be wrong. Projections, teams, and competitors change. Most successful companies make radical modifications to their initial business plans, as entrepreneurs discover the reality of their situation compared with their original expectations. As a result, the experience of the management team is critical in order to handle sudden changes in strategy. Active angel investors are expected to play a critical role in helping management teams make adjustments and prepare for venture funding.

5. *Are not necessarily judging the product/idea but are judging the people*—in the early stages of a venture, when angels make investments, assets are often intangible and knowledge based. Also, the products or the ideas might be untested in the market. Therefore, angels should place a relatively greater weight on the attributes of the founders of the business and the team running it. They are ultimately investing in a team. The management should be tested with critical milestones even prior to the investment.

6. *Are passionate but view the investment process as more than a hobby*—angels should assess appropriately not only the amount of money required to break even, but also the amount of time they need to allocate to their investment. They should participate in the venture after the investment has been made. This participation can come through coaching, board membership, introductions, or even operational involvement.

7. *Focus on the winners, not the losers*—angel investors should be very careful when making additional investments into the same company, since this does not always work to their advantage. One of the reasons for investing more is protection against dilution. However, in many cases the commitment escalates because the venture generates losses and runs out of cash. These ventures are more likely to be failures, so these additional investments only magnify the losses. Also, they consume valuable time that could be allocated to more successful investments.

8. *Diversify the risks*—one way to diversify the risks is to invest smaller amounts in more ventures. Each investment should be less than 10% of an angel's portfolio, because of the risks of potential losses. The portfolio approach is very important: estimates suggest that angel investors lose some or all their investment in over half of the companies they fund. Also, angels should set aside at least the same amount that they have invested in a startup so that they can make follow-up investments in future funding rounds if the company becomes successful. This will allow them to mitigate dilution. Another way to diversify risks is to invest as a part of a syndicate of angels.

16.4 RECENT DEVELOPMENTS AND TRENDS

Angels typically invest through informal networks, but a recent trend has been for angels to also invest through formal networks. The informal personal networks to which an angel may turn for advice and support include friends, co-investors, and business associates. The formal networks include communities of practice that actively support angel activity, such as business angel networks, syndicates, and economic development agencies. We discuss each of these formal networks below.

16.4.1 Business angel networks

Angels are increasingly abandoning informal operation in favor of professional organizations. Nevertheless, some angels believe that the best deals are picked up sooner, before they reach these professional organizations. Although angels are still investing personal funds, greater numbers of them are screening and pooling their investments through regional *angel groups*. There are various advantages of working in groups, including networking, easier access to pre-qualified deal flow, leveraging the intellectual capital and expertise of individual members, and learning from each other regarding deal evaluation skills.

A recent development in angel investing has been the emergence of organized angel groups that are a part of *business angel networks* (BANs). These combine the startup investment activities of multiple accredited investors and may be organized in various ways, as public or private organizations, regional, local, or national, based on direct contact, magazines, or the internet.

Major BANs

The oldest organized angel group, the *Band of Angels*, is only 16 years old. It was started in 1994 by Hans Severiens (now deceased) in Silicon Valley. The Band of Angels began with 12 members, but by 2010 it had grown to more than 100 members. The Band of Angels' annual report in 2009 indicates that the network examines more than 700 plans a year in some depth; selects 33 to present before the group as a whole (akin to a partners' meeting at a VC firm); and generally invests in about eight deals per year. So far, the group has invested $186mn in more than 200 companies. Of these, 45 have been acquired for a gain and 9 have gone public on Nasdaq. The cumulative IRR for all band investments since inception, including the losses suffered through the bust, is a positive 18%. Not only did the Band of Angels' membership grow, but also the idea of formally organizing regional angels caught on throughout the world.

In the U.S., many angel groups have banded together to form a trade association—the *Angel Capital Association* (ACA)—to help facilitate information exchange and to develop policy related to angel investing. The ACA survey indicates that angel groups are quite varied in size, in terms both of the number of investors and of the number of full-time staff. The median age of an angel group that is a member of the ACA is only 3 years. In terms of the number of investors, the smallest group has only 3 members, while the largest has 280. For the 122 groups that reported their size, the average group has 47.6 members, while the median group has 37. Only 84 groups reported their number of full-time staff. However, we still see considerable variation in size based on the number of full-time staff, from a low of 0 to a high of 7, with an average of 0.98.

The European early-stage investment market has changed significantly over the last 10 years. When EBAN was created as the *European Business Angel Network* in 1999, only 50 angel networks were operating in Europe, half of which were located in the

U.K. As EBAN closes its 2010 annual research on the market, over 350 organized networks and groups have been identified. These groups gather some 20,000 angels and receive 40,000 business plans on average every year. Moreover, there is now a clear interest from business angels—traditionally, local investors—to look at collaboration (including investment) opportunities in different countries throughout Europe and beyond.

Created in 2004 with backing from the British government, the *British Business Angels Association* (BBAA) has grown rapidly into a vibrant community of like-minded organizations. It now represents almost 100 organizations, including the vast majority of business angel networks across the U.K., over 20 early-stage venture capital funds, and professional service providers and advisors, including accountancy and law firms, corporate finance firms, banks, regional development agencies, universities, and public policy-makers. The BBAA has direct links to the government to ensure that the requirements of the early-stage industry are not only heard but also acted upon.

Unlike traditional angels, BANs are not difficult to find. Most have websites that provide information about the organization for potential members and entrepreneurs. However, members' identities may be more carefully guarded. In terms of membership, some BANs require members to be accredited investors. Others, including the Band of Angels, require technical knowledge and expertise, and therefore exclude the likes of lawyers and accountants. Industry-specific BANs will, unsurprisingly, require substantial knowledge of the industry.

How BANs function

BANs introduce a more arm's length relationship with entrepreneurs, thus reducing the angel's ability to rely on informal substitutes to contract. BANs' desire for a more consistent deal flow means that fewer entrepreneurs and business plans will be known by the angel beforehand: therefore, BANs potentially sacrifice some of the familiarity and intimacy that such pre-existing knowledge brings. Moreover, some BAN angels may be less active participants in venture development post investment than traditional angels.

Many of these BANs run on a non-regulated basis whereby the gatekeeper, acting as a facilitator, reads the business plans and meets the entrepreneurs, and subsequently decides which propositions should be presented to the investors, but does not get engaged in the deal process or give investment advice. The investors can invest alone within the network or can form a syndicate of high-net-worth/sophisticated individuals taking their own individual decisions.

BANs were conceived to respond efficiently to information in the market. They provide a channel of communication between investors and entrepreneurs in order to minimize the cost of the entrepreneurs' search for capital and to enable investors to examine a larger number of investment opportunities and, hence, facilitate their access to proposals that meet their investment criteria. BANs are also important instruments for raising awareness about the market on both sides: both for entrepreneurs seeking external capital and for potential investors.

BANs can play the role of intermediaries in the informal investment marketplace. In particular, they reduce the search costs of entrepreneurs and investors by enabling them to connect with each other more easily. Some act as mere intermediaries, introducing the parties and leaving them alone to pursue the closing of deals. Others are active in bringing the venture to an investment-ready stage and working towards completion of a deal. It is likely that BANs will evolve into knowledge-based intermediaries, providing training and coaching to entrepreneurs and business angels in the process of raising capital and investing in new ventures.

Some groups require that a member meet with the entrepreneur and determine whether the plan is viable before allowing the entrepreneur to present to the group. Other groups allow the administrative staff and managing director to review the plan and invite the entrepreneur to present without a "champion". Once the presentation has been made (usually in 10 to 45 minutes, including a question-and-answer period), the entrepreneur is asked to leave the room. The angels discuss the opportunity and, if one or more angels are interested, then, depending on the group, either the entrepreneur is invited back at a later date for a more thorough review of the plan or an initial term sheet is developed within a week and presented to the entrepreneur.

What BANs provide to business angels

BAN angels resemble venture capitalists more closely than traditional angels in a number of important ways. First, they are more professional and allow for higher capital commitments and later-stage investments. In that sense, they start to resemble early-stage venture capitalists. Second, their opportunities for informal screening and monitoring are fewer than for traditional angels, owing to the more arm's length relationship role between BAN angels and entrepreneurs. This increases levels of uncertainty, information asymmetry, and agency costs, which must then be mitigated by contract. Finally, BAN angels' higher transaction costs are justified by higher investment amounts and a longer duration for preferences.

BANs perform a number of roles:

- They provide a steadier stream of deal flow to angel members by matching ventures looking for capital with business angels
- They facilitate interaction between angels, venture capitalists, and service providers such as lawyers and consultants
- They facilitate funding for larger deals through the pooling of member angels' resources
- They facilitate due diligence
- They provide consulting services to young ventures in order to make them "investment ready"
- They promote angel and venture capital as the primary mechanism to fund the capital requirements of new and high-growth firms
- They engage in regular dialogue with governments, to help shape policy for the benefit of the industry
- They develop codes of conduct for angels, to promote best practice.

16.4.2 Syndications

Syndication is an increasingly important element in the business angel market. Syndicates arise when more than two angels pool their funds and make a joint investment. Syndication affords the opportunity for business angels to diversify risk and benefit from the combined base of experience of a group of individuals by bringing new and inexperienced investors alongside more experienced ones. A broader base of experience may be of particular benefit to the entrepreneur, but it could also be argued that the perceived level of risk faced by individual business angels is lower when "many eyes are looking at the deal" and "many hands are available to help" post investment.

Generally, angels invest in syndicates in order to group their smaller investments to create the level of financing that a business needs. Thus, syndications allow young companies to obtain the necessary funding in subsequent rounds when they grow rapidly. One investor will generally act as a lead angel on behalf of the syndicate.

Syndicates are more likely to carry out due diligence and draw up legal agreements to protect their investment relationship with the business. They craft tighter contracts, because they tend to be run more professionally than solo business angel investments.

16.4.3   Government support

Many governments in developed countries have announced plans to support small businesses. Such businesses are vital to the economy, because they provide most of the jobs and make the highest contribution to gross domestic product (GDP). One way to help these businesses is to provide policies that improve their access to early-stage financing.

The European Commission launched a significant effort in 1998 to support BANs. In 1990 there were only 52 BANs in Europe, 48 (92%) of them in the U.K. (e.g., EBAN, 1998). The positive results in terms of the cost-effectiveness of a pioneer program in the U.K. encouraged the European Commission to promote business angels as a strategic policy objective at the European level. The European Commission launched a 3-year-horizon call for proposals offering support to the creation of business angel networks, feasibility studies on their establishment, and dissemination actions. The Commission also encouraged the use of regional funds to facilitate the creation of BANs.

Similarly, governments started to provide significant tax incentives. In the U.S. there is a 50% reduction in personal capital gains tax from investing in a qualified small business if the shares are held for 5 years. The tax on the gains from the sale of these shares can be deferred, provided the proceeds are re-invested in other qualified small businesses within 60 days of the day of sale.

In the U.K. the Enterprise Investment Scheme (EIS) has proven to be very successful.[6] It is designed to encourage investments in small unquoted companies carrying on a qualifying trade in the U.K., by providing angels with income tax and capital gains tax relief. The tax relief is intended to offer some compensation for the risk these investors take. Business angels qualify for 20% income tax relief on up to £500,000 of investment per year, and an exemption from capital gains tax on disposal of EIS shares after 3 years.[7] They also obtain unlimited capital gains tax deferral on amounts re-invested in EIS shares.

The U.K. also started a venture capital trusts (VCT) scheme in April 1995. This is designed to encourage individuals to invest indirectly in a range of small higher risk trading companies whose shares and securities are not listed on a recognized stock exchange, by investing through VCTs listed on the London Stock Exchange. These VCTs need to be approved by the government. Investing in these trusts allows investors to spread their investment risk over a number of companies. VCTs provide income tax relief at the rate of 30% of the amount subscribed for shares, which can be offset against

---

6. For more information please visit *www.eisa.org.uk* (Enterprise Investment Scheme Association).

7. Not all companies qualify for EIS status. EIS companies need to have gross assets of not more than £7mn pre investment, have fewer than 50 employees, and be independent.

any income tax liability that is due (the maximum amount allowed in tax relief is £200,000). In addition, there is no chargeable gain (or allowable loss) for capital gains tax purposes on selling ordinary shares in a VCT.

The newest form of government intervention to support the business angel market comes in a form of co-investment schemes. The purpose of co-investment schemes is to stimulate the investor's appetite for the early-stage segment by improving the appeal of early-stage deals. Specifically, given the increasing size of the equity gap and the preference of venture capital funds for larger deals, these programs seek to complement the scarce financing available from active business angels.

This type of direct intervention in the financing of an entrepreneurial firm usually takes the form of loans or equity, with the public sector's contribution to a single deal limited to matching the financing provided by the business angel. Mixed packages of debt and equity are very attractive for investors. The larger the share of debt in an operation, the higher is the return obtained by investors. If a loan is a part of the deal, schemes of this type bring some of the attractiveness of management buyout deals to the earlier and riskier investment stages. For instance, several funds are in place in the U.K.:

- *DTI Capital Fund Program*—launched in 2006, this program is open to business angel investors. It is designed as a loan facility equaling twice the private money invested. In addition to a market-conforming interest rate, a small share of the profits (10–25%) has to be paid out as a return to the government (to compare with the two thirds they have in the "capital").

- *London Seed Capital*—this is a £4.8mn early-stage venture capital fund launched in December 2002 as the first of the U.K. government's early-growth funds. The fund exclusively co-invests amounts of £50,000 to £100,000 alongside business angels. The total equity investment must be less than £400,000, including the fund's investment. The co-investment facility is applicable to deals that have secured financing for at least £50,000 from business angels and have identified a lead business angel investor.

- *Scottish Co-Investment Fund*—this fund totals about £45mn. The fund can complement investments made by corporate ventures, institutional investors, professional fund managers, smaller unregulated fund managers and investors, business angel syndicates, and private individual investors who have been approved by the co-investment fund manager. In contrast to London Seed Capital, this fund does not find and negotiate investment deals on its own or take any part in deciding whether the company is a good opportunity or whether it has been valued at the right level. The private investor makes the investment decision, and the public funding will automatically follow if the business passes the basic criteria (based largely on size, location, and sector). After the deal is closed, the fund does not become involved in post-deal monitoring or decision making. The private sector partner is responsible for the monitoring and control of the investment.

16.5 SUMMARY

The market for angel investing emerged to bridge the gap between the capital provided by the entrepreneur or his friends and family and the capital provided by venture funds. Angels are typically high-net-worth individuals who invest their personal funds into early-stage companies. In addition to providing capital, these investors also tend to contribute management and industry expertise to the startup firms.

Considering that an angel's investments are smaller in size than a venture capital investment, more startup businesses depend on angel financing than on venture financing. As a result, understanding angel activities has important implications for the efficient allocation of private capital and the success of many new small businesses.

16.6   REFERENCES

EBAN (1998) *Dissemination Report on the Potential for Business Angels Investments and Networks in Europe*, European Business Angel Network, Brussels.

FREEAR, J., SOHL, J.E., AND WETZEL, W.E. (1994) "Angels and non-angels: Are there differences?" *Journal of Business Venturing*, **9**, 109–123.

GASTON, R.J. (1989) *Finding Venture Capital for Your Firm: A Complete Guide*, John Wiley & Sons, Inc.

HARRISON, R.T., MASON, C.M., AND ROBSON. P.J.A. (2003) "Determinants of long distance investing by business angels," in W.D. Bygrave, C.G. Brush, P. Davidsson, J. Feit, P.G. Greene, R.T. Harrison, M. Lerner, G.D. Meyer, J. Sohl, and A. Zacharakis (Eds.), *Frontiers of Entrepreneurship Research*, Babson College, Wellesley, MA.

MASON, C.M., AND HARRISON, R.T. (1994) "The informal venture capital market in the UK," in A. Hughes, and D.J. Storey (Eds.), *Financing Small Firms*, Routledge.

MASON, C.M., AND HARRISON, R.T. (2000) "Informal venture capital and the financing of emergent growth businesses," in D. Sexton, and H. Landstrom (Eds.), *Handbook of Entrepreneurship*, Blackwell.

PAUL, S., WHITTAM, G., AND WYPER, J. (2007) "Towards a model of the business angel investment process," *Venture Capital: International Journal of Entrepreneurial Finance*, **9**(2), 107–125.

SHANE, S. (2008) "Angel groups: An examination of the Angel Capital Association survey," working paper.

SOHL, J.E. (2003) "The private equity market in the USA: Lessons from volatility," *Venture Capital*, **5**, 29–46.

VON OSNABRUGGE, M., AND ROBINSON, R. (2000) *Angel Investing: Matching Startup Funds with Startup Companies: The Guide for Entrepreneurs, Individual Investors, and Venture Capitalists*, Jossey-Bass.

WETZEL, W.E. (1987) "The informal risk capital market: Aspects of scale and efficiency," *Journal of Business Venturing*, **2**, 299–313.

WETZEL, W.E., AND FREEAR, J. (1996) "Promoting informal venture capital in the United States: Reflections on the history of the venture capital network," in R. Harrison, and C. M. Mason (Eds.), Woodhead-Faulkner, Hemel Hempstead, U.K.

WILTBANK, R. (2009) *Siding with the Angels. Business Angel Investing: Promising Outcomes and Effective Strategies*, National Endowment for Science, Technology and the Arts/British Business Angels Association, London.

WILTBANK, R., AND BOEKER, W. (2007) "Returns to angel investors in groups," working paper, Ewing Marion Kauffman Foundation.

WONG, A. (2002) "Angel finance: The other venture capital," working paper, Analysis Group, Chicago, IL.

17

Venture capital

17.1 INTRODUCTION

"Someone, somewhere, is making a product that will make your product obsolete"

—Georges F. Doriot, *America's First Institutional Venture Capitalists*

Venture capital involves investing in nascent early-stage private companies and making them profitable by injecting both financial and human capital into these businesses. The capital is most commonly provided by venture capital (VC) firms, who work closely with the incumbent founder/entrepreneur, with the hope of achieving monetary success by backing only the most innovative and commercially interesting ideas.

VC raised in the U.S., the largest venture market globally, comprises only 0.2% of the GDP according to a study completed by the U.S.-focused National Venture Capital Association (NVCA). Yet, in spite of this small relative size, the economic impact of VC is disproportionally much more significant—venture investments have been credited with creating more jobs, driving more innovation, generating more revenues, and contributing more to economic growth than the equivalent capital investments in non-venture-backed firms. According to statistics produced by the NVCA, 11% of U.S. private sector jobs come from venture-backed companies and venture-backed revenue accounts for 21% of U.S. GDP. In Europe, VC firms invested more than €270bn in over 56,000 companies and venture-financed companies created 1 million new jobs between 2000 and 2004 (EVCA, 2005).

Most readers would be familiar with VC success stories; however, there are thousands of other VC success stories that are less well documented and have produced a great benefit to broader society through improved innovation, as measured by the volume and quality of new patents (Kortum and Lerner, 2000). Examples include the development of new drugs, new biotechnology devices, and other specific life-changing and life-enhancing technologies that are less well known because they do not exist under a single globally recognized brand name.

Notwithstanding many post venture successes and the prospect of further successes in the future, the VC sector is attracting less capital commitments from investors. In 2009, USD30bn capital was directed to VC, a full one fifth of the capital committed to

This chapter has been co-authored with William Lamain (MiF, London Business School) and Rebecca Zimmerman (MiF, London Business School).

VC at the peak of the market in 2000 (NVCA, 2010). Institutional investors such as pension funds, insurance companies, endowments, and foundations have long recognized the benefit of including VC in their portfolios. Of this group, pension funds are by far the largest provider of capital to the venture industry, accounting for 20% of all VC commitments from 1985 to the second quarter of 2010. While commitments in recent years have been affected by the global financial crisis, the average amount committed between 2005 and 2008 was USD57bn, which is still some way off the average of USD97bn between 1999 and 2001 (NVCA, 2010).

LP surveys, such as the Coller Capital Global Private Equity Barometer, document that many institutional investors that have historically committed to the VC asset class are reconsidering their allocations to this segment. The primary reason for the reconsideration in capital commitments and this investor sentiment is because the aggregated average returns produced by VC funds are underwhelming and strong-performing funds are concentrated across a very small universe of managers. Moreover, these strong-performing managers are very difficult to access as their funds seek to raise relatively modest amounts of capital and are frequently multiple times oversubscribed.

In addition to dedicated VC funds other investors who provide VC to finance early-stage businesses include angel investors and corporate venture capitalists. As discussed in Chapter 16, angel investors are those who contribute their own personal capital to seed investments prior to VC backing. Corporate venture capital, typically found in companies where research and development are critical to the business model, is provided by in-house venture corporate divisions to facilitate better innovation and growth.

17.2   WHAT IS VENTURE CAPITAL

Definition

Venture capital is early-stage equity funding provided to potentially high-growth private companies. Venture capital, commonly known in its abbreviated form as VC, generally follows after a founder's self-funding and seed-funding stages from business angels and is used to facilitate growth, increase scale, and ultimately monetize the investment through a liquidity event. As consideration for VC funding, which is provided in cash, the investor providing the capital receives a portion of the firm's equity. This is one reason VC investors often are heavily involved in portfolio companies, both in daily operations and as strategic advisors to the company. They can be involved in coaching, guidance, recruiting, networking; this involvement differentiates VC investors from other types of equity investors.

Individuals, VC investment firms, governments, and corporations can all be sources of early-stage funding. While no demarcation definitively separates early-stage investment stages, progression of the financing often follows a predictable pattern. Entrepreneurs typically self-fund the development of a concept, technology, or product. To attract additional investment and accompanying commercial expertise, an entrepreneur partners with a "business angel" investor, who after assessing the underlying commercial concept or product and business plan provides initial equity funding, called *seed capital*. This is usually when an official legal entity is formed for the business and when the entrepreneur's idea is shaped into a marketable product. However, the product has likely not generated any revenue at this stage. Following progression at this seed capital stage and perhaps initial marketing success, the company will need additional capital for research and development, staff salaries, operations expansion, marketing and customer attraction, or other expenses—which require additional capital and business expertise beyond what a typical business angel can offer. VC fills this funding void between business angels and access to private equity, capital markets, or bank lending. VC investments are typically undertaken in several key sectors: technology, healthcare, sustainability, and communications. Each of these sectors attracts different types of VC investments and offer specific opportunities and challenges.

Historical background

In terms of the genesis of the industry, VC was an informal function until it grew and was formalized during the Second World War in the United States. The first U.S. VC fund was the American Research and Development Corporation, formed in Boston in 1946. This was a publicly traded company which invested in small firms that had developed technology for the Second World War. The first British VC fund was the International and Commercial Financial Corporation, which was founded in 1945 and later became 3i. The formalized VC concept spread across Europe and Asia, growing during the post–Second World War economy of the 1950s while focusing primarily on technology companies.

The most famous VCs post Second World War were known as the "Traitorous Eight", a reference to eight engineers who resigned from Shockley Semiconductor Laboratory in 1957. These individuals then founded Fairchild Semiconductor with USD1.5mn in VC funding from Arthur Rock, an early and successful VC investor, and subsequently invented the first commercially practical integrated circuit. Seven of these eight individuals later left Fairchild and proceeded to found new companies. Between 1957 and 1976, at least 23 out of the 67 entrants to the semiconductor industry had at least one founder who worked for Fairchild, including Advanced Micro Devices, Intel, Teledyne, Xicor, National Semiconductor, and related entities such as Kleiner Perkins (Braun and Macdonald, 1982).

Through the 1970s, investments were primarily provided by wealthy individuals, causing the industry to develop slowly through 1974, when the Employee Retirement Income Security Act (ERISA) was revised by the U.S. Department of Labor. This allowed pension funds to invest in certain risky investments such as private companies as the "prudent man" rule outlined that risky assets should be viewed in the context of total portfolio risk rather than individual assets risk. This change caused large pools of previously unavailable capital to be directed toward VC investments. Several headline success stories during the late 1970s attracted many new entrants—VC firms and limited partners—to the industry. Returns across geographies skyrocketed during the 1995 to 2000 dotcom boom, when valuations peaked in line with market indexes due to investor focus on the internet and other technological innovations. While VC has always been impacted by the cyclicality in exit markets and limited partner commitments, VC is currently a well-developed industry in North America, Western Europe, and several Asian geographies and continues to expand and develop in emerging economies.

VC fund structure

VC funds are structured as a partnership, similarly to buyout funds. This involves passive limited partners (LPs) supplying the capital, and the general partner (GP) investing and managing the fund. The primary difference between buyout funds and VC funds is the amount of funds being managed: a VC fund will rarely exceed

USD500mn due to the typically smaller deal sizes and extensive post-investment involvement by VCs in portfolio companies.

Each VC fund typically has a specific focus to differentiate itself from other VC funds given that it is very competitive to raise capital from institutional investors. The differentiating factors could be the industry or sector of the target company, the investment size, geographical location, or the development stage.

Similarly to buyout funds, most VC funds have a fixed 10-year lifetime, with potential extensions to liquidate investments. A GP may spend one year fundraising, depending on investor interest, with investors committing a fixed amount to the GP for a specific VC fund. Exceptions include most funds raised by the top VC firms, which have historically been many times oversubscribed with many investors having their requested commitments scaled back. In these situations, the fundraising period is much shorter than the industry average. The fund is initially unfunded, but investor commitments are called as suitable investments are found. After the fundraising period ends, VC funds typically spend the next 5 years sourcing and completing investments. Years 5 through 8 are spent harvesting—that is, managing the investments and improving value in portfolio companies with the main focus on preparing for an exit. The last 2 years, the exiting phase, involve exiting the investments via trade sales, IPOs, or stock buybacks. These timeframes in a fund lifecycle are subject to many factors including the GP's track record, the team of venture professionals, and the stability of this team, market conditions, and types of investment strategy.

Relatively speaking, smaller VC funds are disadvantaged when compared with larger VC funds. First, larger funds are able to attract better talent to source, evaluate, and execute investments. This talent attraction feature often causes more favorable returns on investments through application of experienced managerial skill, which in turn attracts larger amounts of capital due to prior successes. Thus, the cycle tends to continue, with success typically breeding further success, especially since portfolio company success can be highly reliant on the VC's managerial input. Second, smaller VC firms often lack the financial wherewithal to provide significant follow-on financing to successful companies. As larger investors step in to provide these funds, the original but smaller investors can become severely diluted. Third, smaller VC funds may lack appropriate diversification if funds are constrained to only a few core investments. While diversification is important in any portfolio, it is especially important in a VC fund's portfolio as only a fraction of the fund's investments will contribute very high-performance returns. Fourth, since smaller firms tend to make smaller and, therefore, more early-stage investments, these investments by definition carry additional risk. These smaller investments can be more costly to manage and tend to have higher uncertainty and longer periods before exit.

VC drivers

Today, VC ranks as an important asset class for a diversified investor although it remains minute compared with other types of asset classes. Because VC investments are high risk, only a small number of firms successfully attract VC funding. Estimates indicate that approximately 3,000 U.S. firms get VC investment each year, including 500 start-ups; nearly all are in the high-tech field (Shane, 2008).

The U.S. has the largest and most developed VC industry. Over the last 10 years the U.S. VC market has comprised on average 57% of the global VC market as measured by capital committed to the asset class (see Exhibit 17.1). Over the same time period, Europe comprised, on average, 20% of this capital, with the U.K. comprising the bulk of

EXHIBIT 17.1

FUNDRAISING BY YEAR TO Q3 2010 ($ MILLION)

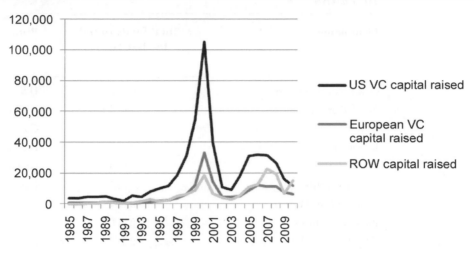

Source: Thomson One Venture Expert.

this. The rest of the world (ROW in Exhibit 17.1) comprised the remaining 23%. By sector, the VC industry in both the U.S. and U.K. directs the majority of its capital to the technology sector, including software, medical devices and equipment, and biotechnology.

Since VC is the key medium for institutional funding for startup companies, governments play a crucial role in a country's VC activity:

- Tax rates for capital gains and carried interest have a large bearing on the level of VC investment activity.

- A stable and investment-friendly regulatory framework can encourage VC activity with policies that provide continued funding of research. Given the relatively long time horizon, VC investments are disproportionally exposed to higher risk than other similar investments.

- Pension fund regulations that allow pension funds to commit funds to the VC industry.

- A healthy exit market (public markets and appropriate incentives for larger firms to acquire smaller firms such as VC-backed companies) is also critical to the continued success in the industry.

Geographies where government policies are more conducive to VC have been able to raise more capital and invest in more new ventures. This is evidenced by the Exhibits 17.1 and 17.2, the latter shows the VC firms that have raised the largest amounts of capital in the last 10 years. Nine of the ten largest VCs reside in the U.S.

VC clusters

Another phenomenon that is unique to the VC industry is that VC firms are commonly based and operate in a few geographical areas called *clusters*. Broadly defined, a cluster

EXHIBIT 17.2

VENTURE FUNDS BY SIZE OF TOTAL FUNDS RAISED IN THE LAST 10 YEARS

Firm name	Total funds raised in the last 10 years ($ million)	Primary region	Primary region
Oak Investment Partners	6,426	U.S.	Diversified
Accel Partners	4,657	Global	Diversified
New Enterprise Associates	3,600	Global	Diversified
Kleiner Perkins Caulfield & Byers	3,235	Global	Diversified
Matrix Partners	3,074	Global	Seed/Early
Austin Ventures	2,925	U.S.	Early
U.S. Venture Partners	2,831	U.S.	Early
Battery Ventures	2,800	U.S.	Early/Growth
DFJ Tamir Fishman Ventures	2,792	Global	Diversified
InSight Venture Partners	2,751	U.S.	Late/Growth

Source: VentureXpert (2010).

is a local concentration of related companies that both cooperate and compete. Most clusters expand and are concentrated around geographical areas defined by high levels of education, research, and entrepreneurialism. Often, large universities or public economic development agencies will foster research of new concepts and products through business incubators, which offer resources to entrepreneurs to develop concepts or products. Entrepreneurs often work together with developers and researchers as they seek to develop and commercialize these concepts.

Geographical concentration is important to VC investors to remain involved in daily operations of portfolio companies and to have an ample source of new investment opportunities. The network of deal team participants also grows due to the number of deals being created from the incubator and the economic benefits created through the VC-investing process. The concentration of talent in time attracts more talent to support the deal team. The "spillover effect" or "ripple effect" from job creation and economic ramifications supports the additional population. The VC industry also benefits from sharing unique resources, such as intellectual property attorneys, specialized labs for biotech research, etc.

Currently, the most well-known venture clusters exist in the U.S. and are most geographically concentrated in the southern part of the San Francisco Bay area (more commonly known as Silicon Valley), Route 128 near Boston (Massachusetts), and in New York, although more recently also in Austin (Texas) and the Research Triangle in North Carolina. As evidence of this clustering effect, close to 50% of all U.S. VC-backed companies are located in San Francisco, Boston, and New York (Chen et al., 2009). Outside the U.S. these clusters exist in Israel in Tel Aviv and Herzliya and in the UK in Oxford and Cambridge. In more recent years there has been rapid expansion of VC firms in India and China, and research suggests it is set to continue. An LP survey conducted by Deloitte has suggested that an increasing number of LPs expect to shift some of their VC allocations to emerging markets (Deloitte, 2010). This is in part due to high economic growth in these regions but also because of the evolution of the VC ecosystem in these markets.

17.3 THE VC INVESTMENT PROCESS

17.3.1 Investment stages

VC can be provided through two types of financial arrangements: milestone financing (also known as full financing) or round financing. *Milestone financing* is where the VC firm contractually commits to providing all capital upfront, provided specific financial and non-financial hurdles (e.g., revenue hurdles, clinical test FDA approvals, licensing agreements, etc.) are met. *Round financing* involves the staging of capital, where a discrete and smaller pool of capital is provided for a specific stage or round of financing. In round financing the onus is on the entrepreneur to raise subsequent capital after the capital from a particular round has been exhausted. However, even within round financing the capital is provided gradually on a contingent basis, subject to specific milestones.

The reasons that capital is provided on a milestone or contingent basis are twofold. First, it gives the VC fund an exit option with respect to providing additional capital. Second, it minimizes opportunistic behavior by the entrepreneur. For the purpose of this chapter, we intend to focus more heavily on round financing given its peculiarity and prevalence in the VC industry.

The financing stages (Exhibit 17.3) will typically require multiple rounds of financing to develop and grow a company for an eventual exit. The exit is necessary for the VC fund to monetize value, which is the ultimate goal. Within the VC industry, the multiple rounds of finance can be broadly split into pre-revenue and post-revenue rounds and, then more specifically, into startup, seed, early, mid, and late-stage

EXHIBIT 17.3

VENTURE CAPITAL FINANCING STAGES

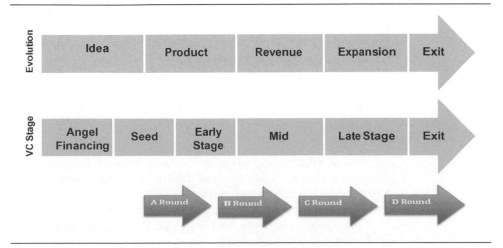

financing. The startup, seed, and early stages are typically pre revenue, while the mid and late stages are typically post revenue.

Startup and seed stages

The start-up and seed stages are primarily concerned with financing the initial concept or product introduced by the founder. These financings will most commonly be provided by founders, friends and family, and angel investors—not VC funds. VC funds do not typically invest in these earlier rounds because the equity requirements and resulting upside potential are too small to justify a VC firm's resources.

Early stage

With respect to round financing, a more straightforward method of categorizing rounds is by categorizing the early stage as the A-round (or Series A). This is the first round in which a VC firm provides capital. This initial stage of financing will incur the highest level of risk as there is least visibility into potential for success.

Moreover, the amount of capital provided in the early stage tends to be smaller as the business is still unproven and, therefore, capital is supplied more cautiously. The investment at this stage is typically still pre revenue. As visibility improves and specific hurdles are achieved a VC firm comes to have more conviction in the opportunity and more capital is provided.

The amount of capital to be committed is reflective of the size of the VC fund and the number of investments the GP wants to include in a fund (the average is between 20 and 30 investments). On average, the amount of capital provided in the A-round varies between USD1mn and USD5mn, which is expected to finance the company for between 6 months to 2 years. The capital from this round is used to pay for the hiring of additional professionals, building a distribution network to execute the sales plan, and make progress on marketing the firm or product. Prior to this point of financing, the management team will already be in place and the product will be ready or close to being ready for distribution. The objective for the VC firm at the end of this stage of financing is to produce a revenue-generating firm.

Mid stage

After the A-round capital is provided, a VC firm will realize relatively early on whether there is justification for providing further follow-on capital for subsequent rounds or, alternatively, if it makes commercial sense to abandon the investment. If the initial VC firm or another investor decides to provide additional capital as needed by the company, this is termed the B-round of investing, which occurs at the mid stage. The key objective of this round of financing is to convert top-line growth into profits. Capital will typically be directed to many of the areas from the A-round but with emphasis on the areas that are more critical in reaching profitability.

Late stage

Later stage financing occurs after the A-round and B-round when a company has produced consistent sales, revenue growth, and profits and there is visibility into an exit. Exits are typically achieved through an IPO, a sale to a strategic investor, a merger with another firm, or a sale to a larger financial buyer, such as a small-sized buyout fund.

Consequently, because later stage financing is the round closest to exit, terms will have become tighter to allow for maximum monetization by later stage investors.

If prospects for the firm are particularly strong a number of prior round investors will want to exercise pre-emption or right-of-first-refusal rights to allow them to provide further capital and, therefore, mitigate the possibility of being diluted before a potentially large wealth creation opportunity.

Exit stage

A VC firm also creates value through exit. The firm has the ability to influence the timing and method of exit and often has the relevant contacts to better facilitate this Company exits in the VC industry can occur through three primary avenues:

1. IPO.

2. Acquisition by a financial buyer.

3. Acquisition by a trade buyer.

The method for exit will depend very much on the appetite of the buyers and the macroeconomic environment at the time prior to exit. It is certainly much more difficult to exit through the public markets during more difficult trading conditions as appetite from public markets is very much reduced. It is also more challenging for VC firms to exit their investments in geographies that have less established markets for smaller cap companies.

More VC firms are looking to exit through acquisitions; historically, a greater percentage of companies have been exited through acquisition than through IPO. However, this is predicated on the acquirers wanting to acquire the business. Moreover, returns from acquisitions have historically been lower.

17.3.2 Syndications

In round financing, each round of financing will typically involve between one and two VC firms—one lead investor and one co-investor. Multiple VC firms offer multiple perspectives and increased industry contacts. Clubbing together provides incrementally more capital, distributes the undertaken risk, and provides an independent valuation. The strategic positioning of a venture-backed firm is further enhanced as there is a greater possibility that at least one VC firm decides to participate in the B-round. If there is only one VC firm that elects not to participate in the next round, first-time B-round investors may become suspicious about the prospects for the company, resulting in either no financing or a less attractive valuation if they do invest.

Naturally, there is a tradeoff in involving more than one VC firm. The tradeoff is that each VC firm will want to take some of the equity in the business and the more investors, particularly over subsequent financing rounds, the more the founder's share of the business will be diluted. Negotiations of each party's interests and transaction terms can become increasingly protracted and complex when involving multiple VC firms, and an equity-sharing mechanism can be equally intricate. These factors need to be balanced with the additional value derived from the VC firms involved.

The abovementioned complexity has in fact become more pronounced in recent years due to the subdued exit environment, which has resulted in more VC firms clubbing together and more rounds taking place.

It should be noted that most VC firms will not commit capital from more than one underlying VC fund. For example, the VC firm will rarely commit to the same company from VC Fund I and VC Fund II owing to obvious conflicts of interest issues centering on valuation. Investors from Fund II would be concerned that the valuation is too high and that they are being asked to subsidize losses on Fund I. Investors from Fund I would be concerned that a lot of the upside would accrue to Fund II investors due to dilution to Fund I investors. In the limited scenarios where a cross-fund investment has taken place the GPs of the VC firm would have had to engage a third-party valuation to substantiate the investment in question.

17.3.3 The due diligence process

The depth of due diligence is necessary due to the riskiness of a potential investment, recognizing that a majority of early-stage companies will fail and investment will be written off. Commonly quoted statistics indicate that 20% to 90% of portfolio companies typically fail to provide the fund's required return. Therefore, the typical fund is highly reliant on a small number of very successful investments that may return perhaps 10× the original investment to subsidize those that fail or do not meet the required return metrics. This also may be cause a misalignment of incentives. While entrepreneurs may be looking for a likelihood of success with a smaller payoff, VC firms are looking for that huge payoff despite only a small probability of it occurring. Therefore, the due diligence process is thorough and exhaustive. Several aspects are analyzed:

1. The company must offer a scalable and innovative product, protected by either proprietary technology or patents. A company may be taking advantage of a dislocation in a market that has customers demanding its product. VC firms need to see a viable market for any product and then understand the cost and revenue drivers of how the product can satisfy a market's need.

2. The VC firm must have confidence in the management team, who are subject matter experts, have extensive industry expertise, and/or have proven track records in comparable situations. The management team must be committed to ensure continuity through the term of the VC investment. For this reason, experienced management teams with strong entrepreneurial track records are likely to be more successful at the early stages of a firm than beginning entrepreneurs.

3. The company and management team must have a comprehensive and defined business strategy for minimal operational execution risk. This will include a close look at the market structure and validation, as well as competitors, substitute products, potential new entrants, suppliers, and product buyers. Additionally, product-specific factors such as the length of the sales cycle, customer switching costs, repeat sales record, stability of pricing, and value proposition to customers will be taken into account. Comprehensive due diligence will allow a VC firm to quantify an expected potential for growth which will provide an attractive return on capital invested.

Additionally, VC firms examine the rate at which a company is projected to use cash (called "cash-burn") and the track record of the company to date. For later stage VC investments, a small company that has a healthy financial position is more attractive to an investor than a company that needs an immediate cash injection to remain solvent. Therefore, where possible, a company should initiate its proposition to VC investors when it experiences positive developments and when the financial condition is relatively healthy.

VC firms will typically favor founders who are financially committed to their firm via a sizable investment as a proportion of their wealth. This implies that the success of the company is intricately linked to their own personal success and, thus, a source of motivation. Any sign of insiders selling shares implies questionable prospects for the firm, unless a convincing financial need arises. Therefore, only in extenuating circumstances will a VC purchase a founder's shares.

The product of this extensive due diligence is a positive or negative decision to invest in the subject company and the appropriate amount to invest. Once a VC firm decides to invest in a company, both parties need to agree on several issues. First, the firm's pre-money, or pre-investment, valuation is important. The uncertainty of future cash flows from a new product can make this a difficult exercise. We discuss a valuation method commonly used in Section 17.3.4. Second, both parties need to decide on the amount and terms of the investment. Third, both parties need to agree on the future strategy of the company. Fourth, both parties need to agree as to what extent the investor will be involved and have a direction in the company's operations. These negotiations can be protracted and difficult, as the entrepreneur may be having discussions with several interested VC firms. The company must also complete its due diligence on the investor, as the arrangement represents a partnership for the future. Once complete, consideration for the cash infusion is transferred to the investors via partially equity ownership or interest, dividends, royalties, or similar payments.

17.3.4 Pre and post-money valuations

The typical techniques for valuing companies such as discounted cash flows and comparable multiples are difficult to implement for startup companies. A company looking to receive venture backing is a nascent business with limited operating history and often no revenues. The key value in an early-stage firm lies in the intangible assets—the ideas, the technology, the entrepreneur's experience and knowledge—and the expected future value of these intangible assets. To this end, the preferred method to use is a VC method that incorporates the abovementioned factors and adjusts for the multiple rounds of VC financing. This method is presented in Chapter 10 which discusses private equity valuation.

Pre-money valuation refers to the value of the firm prior to any financing round. *Post-money valuation* reflects the value of the firm after the financing has been provided and is calculated by summing the pre-money valuation with the value of the financing that has been provided. The ownership stake is calculated by taking the value of the financing and dividing it by the post-money valuation:

$$\text{Post-money valuation} = \text{Pre-money valuation} + \text{Investment}$$

$$\% \text{ Ownership} = \text{Investment}/\text{Post-money valuation}$$

If a VC firm decided to contribute £50,000 in return for a 50% stake in a firm, this would suggest that the value of the entire firm to the investor would be £100,000 (£50,000/0.50). The post-money valuation in this case would be £100,000 and is the representative value of the firm after the money has been injected. This would also suggest that the value of the firm prior to the £50,000 capital injection was £50,000 (£100,000 − £50,000). The VC method is most reflective of the value of a firm at the time co-inciding with capital injection. This firm would not be valued at £100,000 if the capital injection did not take place nor if the capital injection took place some time ago under different circumstances.

The next question to answer is how the VC firm decided that £50,000 for a 50% stake would be appropriate. There are several steps to arrive at these data points. First, the VC firm could decide how much it can commit to a single deal and the typical level

EXHIBIT 17.4

TARGET RATES BASED ON STAGE

Stage of development	Typical target rates of return (%)
Startup	50–70
First stage	40–60
Second stage	35–50
Bridge/IPO	25–35

of ownership required to be incentivized to invest. Second, the VC firm could make assumptions about the exit value, the discount rate, time to exit to arrive at the ownership percentage required given the typical equity ticket of the VC fund managed. With the inherently high level of risk in investing in early stage forms, the cost of capital for a venture capitalist can vary from 25% to 70%. This is largely because the loss rate on a single venture investment is high and the VC firm is looking to achieve an overall fund return of between 25% and 30%. Exhibit 17.4 presents the approximate target rates based on the stage.

In reality, valuing an early-stage firm is considered to be more of an art than a precise science. While a VC firm would use discount rates and apply the various valuation assumptions as outlined above, it will become more confident in the pricing range as more deals are priced and invested in. The VC firm may also be guided by comparing valuations of similar deals recently completed in the same segment.

The way VC firms model the valuation of a venture is through a *capital (cap) table*. The cap table will include detailed information about the expected rounds of financing, when the capital was provided, how much was provided, in which security types, level of ownership, and the corresponding pre- and post-money valuations at each round. It allows a VC firm to model various assumptions including the holding period, level of equity ownership, exit value, expected IRR outcomes. It is the output from these cap tables which forms the basis of negotiations between a VC and the entrepreneur. This is illustrated in Exhibit 17.5.

In Exhibit 17.5 we have four rounds taking place and have assumed that in each round there is only one VC firm investing. In the founder round, all of the new shares are issued to the founders and they have a 100% stake in the firm.

In the first round, the VC firm contributes USD1mn in return for 818,182 preferred ordinary shares (voting shares that have priority claim over the founder's ordinary shares), resulting in the VC firm taking a 45% share in the business. The issue of these shares has resulted in the founder being diluted from having a 100% ownership stake to having a 55% ownership stake. However, by issuing shares in return for capital the value of the business can be calculated. The pre-money value of the business is taken by multiplying the price per share (which is calculated by the capital provided in a round divided by the number of shares issued in a round, USD1mn/818,182) by the number of shares outstanding in the prior round (1,000,000). The post-money value is the sum of the pre money and the capital provided. The methodology for the second round and third rounds is similar.

EXHIBIT 17.5

A SAMPLE CAP TABLE

	Founder round		Round 1		Round 2		Round 3		Round 4	
	Shares	**% owned**	**Shares**	**% owned**	**Shares**	**% owned**	**Shares**	**% owned**	**Shares**	**% owned**
Founder's ordinary shares	1,000,000	100.0	1,000,000	55.0	1,000,000	42.0	1,000,000	25.0	1,000,000	21.1
VC Round 1			818,182	45.0	818,182	34.4	818.182	20.5	818,182	17.2
VC Round 2					562,771	23.6	562,770	14.1	562,770	11.8
VC Round 3							1,619,048	40.5	1,619,048	34.1
VC Round 4 preferred ordinary shares									750,000	15.8
VC Round 4 redeemable preferred shares										
Total ordinary shares	*1,000,000*	*100.0*	*1,818,182*	*100.0*	*2,380,953*	*100.0*	*4,000,000*	*100.0*	*4,750,000*	*100.0*
Ordinary share capital			1,000,000		1,000,000		1,700,000		1,200,000	
Redeemable preferred capital									500,000	
Total capital									*1,700,000*	
Share price (capital/total shares outstanding)			1.22		1.78		1.05		1.60	
Pre money			1,222,222		3,230,767		2,500,000		6,400,000	
Capital			1,000,000		1,000,000		1,700,000		1,700,000	
Post money			2,222,222		4,230,767		4,200,000		8,100,000	

In the fourth round, the VC firm has provided USD1.7mn of which USD1.2mn comprises preferred ordinary shares and USD0.5mn comprises redeemable preferred shares. The capital from the redeemable preferred shares influences the post-money valuation; however, as this share class does not have any voting rights attached at this point in time (only once redeemed) it has no impact on the level of equity ownership in the business.

The number of shares issued in each round is arbitrary and the price per share is not the best indicator for value creation. This is because the number of shares is frequently reverse-engineered to decide on the ownership percentage given an investment amount.

To understand if valuations have been increasing, we must compare the pre-valuation price in one round with the post-valuation price in the prior round. If there is price appreciation between the pre-financing in the current round and post-financing in the prior round this demonstrates value creation. In the example above, there has been value destruction between Rounds 2 and 3—the pre-money valuation in the third round (USD2.5mn) is less than the post-money valuation from the second round (USD4.23mn).

The cap table is helpful in demonstrating how the stages of financing impact the value of the business, the level of dilution, and the increasing level of complexity that occurs over successive rounds of investment. Being aware of the valuations and dilution dynamics before negotiations commence is critical, as is understanding which security types are most conducive to protecting an investor's interest (preferred ordinary equity).

17.4 THE VC CONTRACT

17.4.1 Security types and specific terms

An investment in an early-stage company often presents agency problems and asymmetric information. Often entrepreneurs have an information advantage over VC investors with respect to the company, while VC investors frequently have an information advantage with respect to the external environment. To mitigate against these risks, a VC firm will structure the investment contract so it specifies cash flow (how residual cash flows are split), liquidation (priority of payment), and control rights (voting rights and board rights) of the founder and the VC fund.

In each round of investment, VC firms negotiate investment terms with the previous parties—founders, CEO (if other than the founder), business angels, and the VC firms who invested in prior rounds. These negotiations are on both valuation and terms. Typically, the (frequently higher) valuation forms the basis of the discussions. However, as the new investors have the strongest position of negotiation, certain benefits accrue by way of downside protections and warrants.

The majority of capital that is provided by a VC firm is in the form of equity, usually as convertible preferred stock. Preferred equity not only gives a position that is senior to or "ahead of" the common stock if the company is sold or liquidated, getting their capital out prior to the founders, but also allows VC firms to participate in the "upside" with the common stock when the company starts to take off. This is also why the inclusion of convertible ordinary shares and warrants are a common feature together with convertible preferred stock in a financing round. Below we have outlined commonly used VC security structures and VC-specific terms that feature in the legal documentation.

Security types

- *Ordinary shares (common shares)*—ordinary shares confer ownership and are attached with voting rights. A capital gain is more common than dividends given the limited cash flows of early-stage businesses. Typically, it is the founders, management, and employees who own the common stock. The claims of ordinary shareholders are ranked below those of preferred shareholders. In some VC financings, there will be different classes of ordinary shares. It is not uncommon for founders to have ordinary shares that are attached with voting rights, while VC firms receive ordinary shares that are attached with different voting and board rights and sometimes even a different vesting schedule (i.e., VC stock vests immediately).
- *Preferred shares*—these rank ahead of ordinary shares in the capital structure and will frequently be attached with a fixed rate dividend. If the dividend cannot be paid for whatever reason it accrues and forms part of the liquidation preference (see below), ensuring that the VC firm is able to take its capital out ahead of the founders.
- *Convertible shares*—these allow VC firms to participate in the upside by being able to convert the shares into ordinary shares at a pre-determined conversion price. This is particularly helpful if a company is about to experience a liquidity event.
- *Convertible preferred shares*—these are similar to preferred shares in that they rank higher in the capital structure than ordinary shares (protect the downside) but they also allow the owner to participate in the upside by being able to convert the shares into ordinary shares at a pre-determined conversion price. Frequently, this conversion price can vary depending on underlying performance. In the event of an IPO these shares automatically convert into ordinary shares. Convertible preferred is the most common tool for VC firms to invest in companies.
- *Participating preferred/Participating convertible preferred*—upon liquidation, the VC fund receives the proceeds of the preferred shares and also receives additional ordinary shares.
- *Warrants*—a warrant can be converted into ordinary shares at a pre-agreed price. The objective of warrants is to increase upside participation.

Contract terms

- *Liquidation preference*—this ensures that VC is returned first in case of liquidation of the company. The liquidation preference is stated in terms of the original capital invested. It is not uncommon for some VC firms to insert terms that provide a liquidation preference that is a multiple of the original capital invested. This is particularly destructive to the founders, especially following a down-round.
- *Drag-along rights*—the VC firm has the right to sell the company and force the rest of the shareholders to also sell the company by dragging them along. This is dilutive to the founders if the drag-along rights are combined with a liquidation preference.
- *Vesting rights*—to further ensure the founder's interests are aligned with those of the VC firm, the shareholding will often have a vesting schedule attached (i.e., shares are only awarded after a pre-agreed time period). If an entrepreneur were

to leave the firm, the unvested shares would be transferred to the venture capitalist. Vesting is more common in earlier rounds, when the venture capitalist is more reliant on the entrepreneur for value creation or when information asymmetry is large (see Kaplan and Strömberg, 2001).

- *Non-compete clauses*—these clauses prohibit the entrepreneur from initiating a new venture in the same industry for a pre-specified period of time, were he or she to leave the current VC-backed entity.

- *Anti-dilution measures*—this clause protects VC firms from dilution in subsequent equity offerings. It usually comes into effect in a down-round so that the price paid by VC firms in early rounds will be adjusted according to the conversion formula. We discuss them below.

Anti-dilution ratchets

There are two types of anti-dilution adjustments: a full ratchet and weighted average ratchet. The *full ratchet* is the most onerous from the founder's viewpoint. If the company issues even one share of stock at a price below the price paid by the VC investors, then the conversion price drops fully to that price. The *weighted average ratchet* anti-dilution adjustment is better from the founder's viewpoint. Although the formulas used differ in some ways, the basic approach is to adjust the conversion price to the average price received by the company for stock issuances taking into account the amount of money raised at different prices. A typical formula is as follows:

$$NCP = \frac{(OB * OCP) + New\$}{OA}$$

where

$$NCP = \text{new conversion price}$$
$$OB = \text{all outstanding shares before offering}$$
$$OCP = \text{old conversion price}$$
$$New\$ = \text{amount raised in offering}$$
$$OA = \text{all outstanding shares after new offering, before the ratchet.}$$

The ratchets are illustrated below with a realistic example. Assume that the Series A VC investor buys 300,000 shares of the company for USD2 per share when the founder owns 700,000 shares. Later, the Series B VC investor buys 100,000 shares from the company for USD1 per share. A full ratchet would give the Series A VC investor 300,000 new shares for free in order to reduce his average price per share to USD1.

Under the weighted average method, the Series A investor's 300,000 shares are added to management's 700,000 shares and then multiplied by USD2. The USD2,000,000 product of this calculation is then added to the USD100,000 paid by the Series B investor giving a sum of USD2,100,000. This amount is divided by the total number of shares outstanding after the second sale, 1,100,000, to give USD1.91 which becomes the new average price for the Series A investor. When divided into the USD600,000 invested by the Series A investor this yields 314,286 total shares to which the Series A investor is entitled. Thus, it is required that the company issues him or her 14,286 free shares.

We present in Exhibit 17.6 the computations for the share ownership of Series A investors after exercising their anti-dilution rights under the two types of ratchets.

EXHIBIT 17.6

SHARE OWNERSHIP COMPUTATIONS FOR A SERIES INVESTORS

Type of security	Invest-ment (USD)	Original purchase price (USD)	Shares before conversion (#)	Conver-sion price (USD)	Shares after conversion (#)	Owner-ship (%)
Initial ownership structure of the venture						
Series A investors Convertible preferred stock	600,000	2.00	300,000	2.00	300,000	30
Founders Common stock			700,000		700,000	70
One year later, the company issues 100,000 new convertible preferred stock at $1.00 per share to Series B investors						
Full ratchet						
Series A investors Convertible preferred stock	600,000	2.00	300,000	1.00	600,000	43
Series B investors Convertible preferred stock	100,000	1.00	100,000	1.00	100,000	7
Founders Common stock			700,000		700,000	50
Weighted average ratchet						
Series A investors Convertible preferred stock	600,000	2.00	300,000	1.91	314,286	28
Series B investors Convertible preferred stock	100,000	1.00	100,000	1.00	100,000	9
Founders Common stock			700,000		700,000	63

Milestones

Another method that VC firms will use to ensure their capital is protected is to provide capital that is contingent on specific milestones (or hurdles), both financial and non-financial. This way the VC firm has the option to terminate or force the liquidation preference when milestones are not achieved. This provision is included in the majority of contracts and has a typical maturity of 5 years (Kaplan and Strömberg, 2001). Similarly, when a VC firm is more heavily reliant on the founder for value creation, the liquidation preference is a less effective risk mitigation mechanism and, therefore, the contract is structured so that the founder's ownership stake is subject to vesting provisions. Typically, when asymmetric information risks are more pronounced, the entrepreneur is more likely to be subject to vesting and have his or her equity stake tied to specific performance hurdles being achieved.

17.4.2 Roles in the VC contract

The legal documentation will clearly outline the roles of the VC firm and the entre-preneur, the composition of the board, which is formed by representatives from both the VC firm and entrepreneur, and board and voting rights. In a VC deal, two main forms of documentation exist—the term sheet and the share and purchase agreement. The *term sheet* outlines the key terms in summarized format while the *share and purchase agreement* will provide additional depth with respect to these terms. The objective of these documents is to clarify the parameters of financing and how the business will be run with respect to the roles of the VC firm, the entrepreneur, and the board.

Role of the VC firm

- The VC firm is primarily focused on ensuring the likelihood of monetization is maximized.

- VC firms influence business decisions through their board representation and voting rights. In some cases VC firms may have a majority of voting rights and, therefore, they may be better positioned to influence venture-related decisions, including changes to management and whether or not to appoint an outside CEO.

Role of management

- Day-to-day management of the business and ensuring performance hurdles are achieved.

Role of the board

- The board is the governing body of the firm and will be represented by management (1–2 seats), VC professionals (1–3 seats), and outside parties (1–2 seats) which have been agreed to by both the founders and the VC firm. In early rounds, VC majority board seats are less common; however, after a number of rounds, VC majorities become more common. In some situations when the entrepreneur has not achieved certain performance metrics, VC firms may obtain full control of the board.

- The number of board members increases as additional financing rounds take place.

- Hiring and firing the management team.

- Providing strategic input to business.

- Signing off on all business-related decisions.

17.4.3 VC expertise

In contrast to mainstream providers of financial capital, who do not get involved beyond providing capital, VC firms also expect to provide human capital—providing input, through their influence, into how the venture in which they have injected capital is governed and developed. As referred to repeatedly throughout this chapter, the primary objective of the VC firm is to monetize the investment for a higher value. The probability of success is increased when the VC firm is involved in shaping the business.

Most VC firms prefer to specialize in what they do, typically either by stage and/or sector of investment. This deep level of domain expertise allows them not only to assess the merit of an opportunity relatively quickly but also provide help to the founder after an investment has been given the "green light". This hands-on approach and continued monitoring together with their ability to professionalize a business are key elements in the value creation process.

VC firms are heavily involved in the company they have decided to back through assuming board seats, providing strategic input to the firm, providing valuable input into the development of the product or technology, using their deep networks to negotiate with buyers and suppliers, making customer introductions, professionalizing the firm through appointing professionals at both the senior management level and further down in the organization (e.g., sales and marketing professionals), creating human resource policies, and adopting stock option plans for employees to increase employee incentives. VC firms will often appoint individuals for specific roles within the firm and, in some cases, remove individuals from the firm (including the CEO, if the founders' skills are less relevant for the firm's next stage of development).

VC firms whose reputation precedes them, as measured by experience and past successes, have historically produced more successful exits, strengthening the argument that a VC professional is not just about providing capital to early-stage firms but also about adding value. Further evidence of this value-add is that an offer from a more successful VC firm is three times more likely to be accepted by an entrepreneur. This is because being affiliated with a successful VC firm is often more important than the valuation and quantum of capital received due to the potential for further upside in the future through working with that VC firm.

17.5 ALTERNATIVE SOURCES OF VC FINANCING

17.5.1 Corporate venture capital

Corporate venture capital (CVC) is the direct equity investing undertaken by larger established corporations into independent early-stage entities in a related line of business. CVC investing differs from traditional VC investing in that the investment is made directly into an early-stage company—not via a third-party VC firm. Additionally, CVC's reasons for investing are strategic as well as financial. Similarly to traditional ventures, the CVC investor may offer strategic advice and other support services to the startup to help foster its development. In many cases, CVC operates alongside traditional VC as an additional source of finance for the early-stage company.

The CVC market ranges from approximately USD20bn to USD25bn annually, or an estimated 6% to 8% of the entire VC market (MacMillan et al., 2008). While CVC is primarily focused in the largest VC arenas such as biotechnology, communication, and software, it also extends to other sectors that typically are shunned by traditional VC, such as financial services.

One of the primary factors of CVC is for a corporate to gain competitive advantage by obtaining early access to a new concept or product. By becoming an investor in a promising young entity, a large corporate can monitor developments on new concepts or products and gain a first-mover advantage for any joint venture or licensing schemes. CVC also avoids costly and uncertain M&A transactions, although a corporate may subsequently acquire developed entities which are familiar through previous CVC investments. Additionally, CVC may allow entities to grow and develop what would otherwise be limited in the environment of a large, structured corporate.

The due diligence and financing process of CVC is nearly identical to that of VC, although evaluation of the strategic interests of CVC occurs concurrently. Additionally, corporations may have inside industry knowledge that may aid the due diligence evaluation of new ventures.

17.5.2 Venture lending

Venture lending is defined as debt offered by either a bank or a non-bank to any company that is still reliant on VC support. Venture debt can be secured by future cash flows or collateral; collateral-based lending can include venture leasing, receivables and inventory factoring, asset finance, and supply chain financing. The stage, size, assets, and growth of the company will dictate which type of lending is available. Additionally, venture lending may offer bridge financing between various equity rounds. For early-stage companies, venture debt can be a crucial component of the capital structure to ensure the company has an appropriate amount of cash to stay solvent. This can provide funding to sustain the company through product development and testing, marketing campaigns, or other similar phases which are necessary to expand the company.

The providers of venture debt often receive equity warrants in addition to interest payments and fees as consideration, which makes venture debt similar to mezzanine finance. This adds an equity component to the debt to compensate venture debt providers for the risk undertaken, thus resulting in a debt–equity hybrid. The warrants, which offer the holder the right but not the obligation to purchase equity at a pre-determined date and price, will dilute existing shareholders, so proper structuring and consideration of the all-in cost is important.

When equity holders are considering venture debt as another source of liquidity, management must have a specific use for the funds and know how much is required. Repayment terms, tenors, covenants, collateral, and warrants differentiate venture lending from traditional bank finance.

The primary motivation to obtain venture debt instead of venture equity is to limit shareholder dilution, thereby increasing the return to existing shareholders via leverage. Venture debt may also finance certain equipment "soft costs", such as installation, testing, and pre-delivery payments that would otherwise consume a portion of the company's cash reserves. For companies that are almost at significant milestones, venture debt can be a resource to help fill the funding gap and, by achieving certain milestones, look more attractive to other investors and aid the company in obtaining more favorable terms.

Venture debt, however, comes at a cost to the company given the amount of risk involved. First, while returns required by providers will be less than other pure equity investors, the all-in rates from the interest, fees, and warrants will be considerably higher than commercial bank lending rates. Second, dilution will occur from the warrants, although it will likely be less than dilution of adding a pure equity investor. Third, complying with venture debt requirements can prove burdensome from an administrative perspective. Fourth, strict financial or operational covenants may restrict the activities of the business. Finally, certain types of debt can restrict access to more debt in the future.

17.6 CONCLUSION

Since its creation, the VC industry has been instrumental in creating jobs and driving economic growth and innovation. VC-backed companies have produced many products that have become household names and are now considered essential to daily life. What is particularly remarkable is the speed at which these companies have evolved from being early-stage businesses to becoming large organizations and the speed in which these companies' new products and services have been accepted and incorporated into the mainstay of society.

The VC industry has proven its ability to add value to early-stage companies for more than 50 years, and this is demonstrated in a number of ways. First, VC funding has a successful track record in having had some level of involvement with most of the major and successful technology companies in existence today. This is due to the professional, operational, and financial expertise VC professionals offer after seeing many companies transition through the same challenges. Second, VC firms are able to take far greater risks than other funding sources and, therefore, fulfill a crucial funding gap in the market. Third, due to the early-stage nature of the typical VC-backed company, VC firms utilize strict corporate governance structures compared with non-VC-backed companies. Fourth, empirical evidence shows that VC-backed companies grow more quickly and generally bring products to market more quickly than non-VC firms (Hellmann and Puri, 2002; Strömberg, 2009).

In aggregating all of the abovementioned points, what is clear is that the VC industry will continue to be a driver of innovation globally, a powerful economic engine, and an essential asset class for institutional investors.

17.7 REFERENCES

BRAUN, E., AND MACDONALD, S. (1982) *Revolution in Miniature: The History and Impact of Semiconductor Electronics Re-Explored*, Updated and Revised Second Edition, Cambridge University Press, New York.

CHEN, H., GOMPERS, P.A., KOVNER, A., AND LERNER, J. (2009) "Buy local? The geography of successful and unsuccessful venture capital expansion," NBER Working Paper No. w15102.

DELOITTE (2010) *Global Trends in Venture Capital: Outlook for the Future.*

EVCA (2005) *Employment Contribution of Private Equity and Venture Capital in Europe.*

HELLMANN, T.F., AND PURI, M. (2002) "Venture capital and the professionalization of start-up firms: Empirical Evidence," *Journal of Finance*, **57**(1), February.

HSU, D. (2004) "What do entrepreneurs pay for venture capital affiliation," *Journal of Finance*, **59**(4), 1805–1844.

KAPLAN, S.N., AND STRÖMBERG, P. (2001) "Characteristics, contracts, and actions: Evidence From venture capitalist analyses," *Journal of Finance*, **59**(5), 2177–2210.

KORTUM, S., AND LERNER, J. (2000) "Assessing the contribution of venture capital to innovation," *RAND Journal of Economics*, **31**(4), 674–692, Winter.

MACMILLAN, I., ROBERTS, E., LIVADA, V., AND WANG, A. (2008) "Corporate venture capital seeking innovation and strategic growth," working paper.

NVCA (2010) *National Venture Capital Association Yearbook*, Thomson Reuters, New York.

SHANE, S. (2008) *The Illusions of Entrepreneurship: The Costly Myths that Entrepreneurs, Investors and Policy Makers Live By*, Yale University Press, New Haven, CT, p. 90.

STRÖMBERG, P. (2009) "The economic and social impact of private equity in Europe: Summary of research findings," working paper.

PART 4

Case studies

Chapter	Case study	Key themes
18	*Realza Capital* Region: Spain	The Realza case study examines the motivations and challenges of raising a first-time private equity fund in Spain. Key themes: • What LPs would typically look for before investing into a fund • Measuring GPs' track record • Pros and cons of captive vs. independent funds • Fundraising process: strategy, due diligence, and role of the placement agent • Term sheet negotiation between a GP and LP • Timing of the fund's first investment and fund closing.
19	*Swicorp* Region: MENA	The Swicorp case study examines the activities of a private equity fund in the Middle East and North Africa (MENA) region, from its entrance to the market, through its operation and execution of deals in the region. Key themes: • Unique characteristics of private equity in the MENA region, including the role of sovereign wealth funds • Strategic positioning in the MENA market • Investment strategy and deal selection • Two specific acquisitions—Step (Turkey) and JATE (Jordan): structure and negotiation.
20	*Mekong Capital* Region: Vietnam	The Mekong case study recounts the story of the foundation and growth of a Vietnamese private equity firm, set up by an American expatriate, which has three funds under management. Key themes: • Issues and challenges faced when creating and growing a private equity firm in an emerging market • Contesting several "myths" of investment in an emerging market • Insight into different investment themes and processes employed over time, including detailed examples of two investments • Challenges associated with the corporate culture in Vietnam and the introduction of a corporate transformation process.

Chapter	Case study	Key themes
21	*Bloomsbury Capital* Region: Europe	The Bloomsbury case study focuses on the deal selection process through a detailed examination of three investment opportunities at the preliminary stage of screening. Key themes: • Issues faced by a private equity firm in defining its deal box • Business valuation and investment analysis of potential opportunities • Identifying critical success factors and key issues for due diligence • Determining the fit with the fund • Characteristics of the deal-screening process within a private equity firm.
22	*Edcon* Region: South Africa	The Edcon case discusses Bain Capital's acquisition of Edcon, the leading retailer in South Africa. This has been so far the biggest acquisition in Africa. It examines the complex issues faced by Bain Capital in its due diligence and ultimate bid. Key themes: • Detailed deal analysis in an emerging market—opportunities and risks • Discussion of factors influencing the risk premium paid for an investment • Financial structuring—bank vs. bond financing • Bid strategy in an auction scenario.
23	*FiberNet Communications* Region: Hungary	The FiberNet case examines a proprietary opportunity sourced by Warburg Pincus with respect to a secondary buyout of a Hungarian cable TV operator. The case study is accompanied by a buyout modeling spreadsheet. Key themes: • Characteristics of a secondary buyout transaction • Business and financial analysis in a secondary buyout transaction • Working through a financial model of a buyout transaction • Post-acquisition issues.
24	*Seat Pagine Gialle SpA* Region: Italy	The Seat case examines a combined public-to-private and privatization transaction with respect to Seat SpA, the dominant publisher of directories in Italy. Key themes: • Working through an investment proposal from initial screening to valuation metrics and commercial due diligence • Investment considerations endemic to an unfamiliar country and the potential value-add of partnering with a local firm • Financial structure of the deal.
25	*Ducati & Investindustrial* Region: Italy	The Ducati case looks at the transformation of Ducati, the legendary motorcycle manufacturer, under the stewardship of Investindustrial, the largest private equity firm in South Europe. Key themes: • Investing in a listed company to acquire a minority position • Implementing a turnaround plan for the business, including brand repositioning, efficiency improvements through operations focus and management turnaround • Consideration of options subsequent to a minority investment, including exit to a trade buyer, taking the company private or keeping the existing equity stake.

Chapter	Case study	Key themes
26	*Styles & Wood* Region: U.K.	The Styles & Wood case is a sequence of case studies that follow the lifeline of a business in the shopfitting industry in the U.K., including a business turnaround, a management buyout, the buyin by private equity group 3i, a secondary buyout by Aberdeen Asset Management, a recapitalization, and finally an IPO. Key themes: • Turnaround of a lackluster business—focusing on leadership, staff, business model, and customer base • Design of the secondary buyout transaction • Governance styles • Analyzing incentives and aligning management and investors • Assessment of a multitude of alternatives to grow or exit the business • Designing of a refinancing transaction • The dynamic interplay between managers and investors before an IPO.
27	*SunRay Renewable Energy* Region: Southern Europe	The Sunray case recounts the story of the spectacular growth of an entrepreneurial venture focused on solar energy projects. Since its foundation in 2006, the firm attracted the interest of private equity firm, Denham Capital, and was subsequently bought out by Sunpower, an international supplier of solar power technology, in 2010. Key themes: • Analysis of solar technologies, value chain of a solar photovoltaic developer, and government incentive schemes in Europe • Issues faced in market entry • Funding of the business—seed funding, private equity, project finance, and the advantages and disadvantages of each • Analysis of SunRay's first project in Italy and how it established a relationship with Sunpower which eventually made an offer to acquire SunRay.
28	*Debenhams* Region: U.K.	The Debenhams case looks into the high-profile acquisition of a major U.K. retail chain, Debenhams, by a private equity consortium in what has become a blockbuster success. Key themes: • Role of innovation in a bidding competition • Conflicts of interest of management in a buyout situation • Investment thesis and valuation • Pros and cons of bidding as a consortium • Implementation of a post-acquisition plan, including the separation of a company via an opco/propco structure • Attribution analysis • Criticism of private equity.
29	*Optos* Region: U.K.	The Optos case looks into an early-stage startup of a retinal-imaging technology business from concept design through product development, manufacturing, financing, and eventually flotation of the business on the London Stock Exchange. Key themes: • Issues associated with a new startup faced by the entrepreneur • Role of angel investors and venture capital • Building up cash flow projections • Exit by way of flotation including the selection of underwriting advisers • Criteria for choosing a stock exchange for listing.

Chapter	Case study	Key themes
30	*Capital for Enterprise U.K.* Region: U.K.	The Capital for Enterprise case delves into the Enterprise Capital Funds (ECF) program set up by the U.K. government to bridge the SME early-stage finance gap to enable startup businesses and high-growth potential small and medium-sized firms to raise financing. Key themes:
		• Rationale for setting up the program where previous public schemes failed
		• Specific elements in the design and delivery of the ECF scheme
		• The first experience gained from its operation during the first years of the program and next steps for future development
		• Detailed comparative information on government programs around the world designed to stimulate seed, venture capital, and other growth-oriented SMEs.

18

Realza Capital

DECEMBER 2006

It was a cold night in Madrid in December 2006 as Alfredo Zavala and Martin González del Valle walked back to the 10-square-meter office they were subletting from a venture capital firm in Madrid. The partners of Realza Capital (Realza), a fledgling mid-market private equity fund, had just returned from the company's Christmas dinner and things were not going according to plan. Their cornerstone investors, who had verbally committed the initial €40mn for Realza's first fund, had just called Zavala to say they were pulling out of the deal.

Realza's goal had been to raise €150mn to €200mn for the fund. The process of raising money was well underway and Zavala and González del Valle had already built a small team. They had recruited Catherine Armand as administrative assistant and had just convinced Pedro Fernández-Amatriain to take a risk, forego a steadier career in corporate finance and join them as an analyst. With the promise of future success, Armand joined for free and Amatriain for a very moderate sum for the next 6 months. But Armand and Amatriain were not the only ones with everything on the line. Zavala and González del Valle had both left lucrative jobs at leading Spanish private equity firms to pursue this entrepreneurial venture, which now appeared to be at risk. Three alternatives presented themselves to the partners. The first was that a major European private equity group was trying to convince them to join and create a south European private equity fund. The second was that they had an indication of a serious offer to become an asset manager for Spain for a high-net-worth individual. The last option was that a major European private equity firm had approached the partners to join as co-heads for a new Spanish office. But while these offers represented viable and immediate alternatives to the founders' original ambitions, Zavala and González del Valle needed to carefully weigh all the variables.

Attractiveness of the Spanish Market Landscape

Macroeconomic Environment (2000–2006)

Zavala and González del Valle realized that the Spanish economy was performing extremely well in 2006 and that the country's business landscape offered unique opportunities for private equity. Real GDP growth in Spain had averaged 3.7% annually

This case was co-authored with Jo Coles and Vijay Sachidanand (Executive MBA 2009). We have benefited from valuable comments by Jim Strang (Jardine Capital) and Hans Holmen (Executive Director, Coller Institute of Private Equity, London Business School).

in the period from the first quarter of 2000 until the end of 2006. By comparison, the average GDP growth in the European Union (EU) during the same period had been a little over 2% per year. Spain had almost consistently outperformed its Eurozone neighbors during this time by as much as 3.5%, even during the recessionary period triggered by the "dotcom" crash of 2002 (see Exhibit 18.1 for real GDP growth in Spain vs. EU 2000–2006).

This had not always been the case for Spain. When the country joined the EU in 1986, it was a laggard compared with existing member states and over the next two decades, it received billions of euros in EU development funding to boost growth. Between 1994 and 2005, increased construction investment and private consumption, reduced inflation, high levels of foreign investment, liberalization of the Spanish labor market, and significant immigration fed each other in a virtuous circle of wealth creation for the country.

The low end of the mid-market—the partners' target segment

Zavala and González del Valle considered their target segment to be the low end of the mid-market, which consisted of businesses with an enterprise value (EV) in the range of €15mn to €100mn. They recognized that Spain was a land of family-owned, small-to-medium-size enterprises. Many SMEs were facing the challenges of succession planning for the first time in their history. Within this segment, when transactions occurred, they tended to take place without a financial adviser. Financial advisers were only used in 34% of all M&A transactions in the SME segment during 2006, whereas 90% of the 50 largest buyout transactions used a financial adviser.[1] In addition, acquisition financing in this segment tended to be sourced from local banks at debt/EBITDA levels which rarely exceeded 3–4×.

The SME segment had many dynamic companies with capacity for growth, but generally these lacked good governance mechanisms as well as financial sophistication. Furthermore, SMEs needed to strengthen their management teams, business processes, and information systems. These types of companies presented attractive opportunities for private equity investors who were prepared to be hands on and to undertake a buy-and-build strategy.

Private equity in Spain

The potential for private equity in Spain was clear to Zavala and González del Valle. Spain had a long history of risk capital dating back to the 1970s, but it was in the latter part of the 1990s that private equity and venture capital became significant. The Spanish private equity market grew by a factor of almost 3 between 2002 and 2006. And according to the Spanish Private Equity Association (ASCRI),[2] €1,118mn was raised during the first 6 months of 2006, up 107% from the first half of 2005 (see Exhibit 18.2 for PE investment in Spain and Exhibit 18.3 for the number of PE deals in Spain).

The two partners also knew that the Spanish government recognized the key role private equity could play in helping to develop the country's economy and improve

1. *Source:* Thomson Financial Research, 2006.
2. ASCRI, founded in 1986, states its purpose as "representing, managing and defending the professional interests of its members, as well as promoting and encouraging the creation of entities whose objective is the taking of temporary stakes in the capital of non-financial enterprises that are not quoted on a stock market."

productivity. In 2005, a private equity regulatory bill was passed through parliament.[3] It sought to simplify regulation of the private equity industry. In particular, the bill stipulated

- Reduction of the administrative burden on private equity firms and funds
- Expansion of funds' areas of activity
- Permission to invest in other private equity firms, funds of funds, and public-to-private transactions
- Creation of special regimes for closed-end entities and qualified investors that do not require "small investor" protection rules.

The Partners—Alfredo Zavala and Martín González del Valle

Alfredo Zavala and Martín González del Valle were both recruited in 1989 by Mercapital, a merchant bank involved in private equity investments and corporate finance. Though they had only casually known each other before joining Mercapital, they had taken strikingly similar directions in life; both studied economics at Madrid University, and then obtained an MBA from INSEAD before moving on to spend some years working in industry (see Exhibit 18.4 for Realza founding partners' CVs).

In 1995, González del Valle left Mercapital to become Deputy General Manager and Head of Investment Banking at Banque Indosuez. Then in 2000, he was recruited as a partner by InvestIndustrial to head and build a private equity business in Spain. Zavala, on the other hand, remained at Mercapital for 17 years, where he became one of the founding partners when Mercapital carried out a management buyout in 1996 before leaving in 2006.

Their combined track record in private equity and investment banking over the years resulted in total investments of €427mn in 22 companies that generated €568mn in proceeds from 16 exits. They led 14 of the 22 deals and exited 10 of these companies. These 10 exits generated an average multiple of 2.9× (see Exhibit 18.5 for the track record of realized and unrealized investments and Exhibit 18.6 for case studies of prior investments).

Launching Realza Capital

Background, motivation, and vision

One afternoon in November 2005, the two met at the home of González del Valle in Madrid to discuss where their respective private equity careers were heading. As they reflected on the opportunities that might follow, they agreed that the environments at their respective firms were changing. As Zavala put it, "Mercapital was moving into the upper end of the private equity market. Martín and I felt we had exhausted our opportunities to grow at our current firms." González del Valle added, "We realized that, at heart, Alfredo and I are entrepreneurs. We wanted to be part of something we could start and build from the beginning." With this in mind, the two decided to start Realza Capital. "Realza" means "to enhance" in Spanish.[4] They felt the name succinctly captured their vision for the new company.

This vision was to create value for investors by leveraging their own prior

---

3. Law 25/2005 simplifies the regulatory burden, allows acquisition of listed firms in order to de-list them, and permits the creation of private funds of funds aimed at institutional investors.

4. The word also has "regal" implications; *real* means royal in Spanish.

experience and making primarily control investments in Spanish SMEs. Initially, they sought to raise €150mn for their first fund, with a target portfolio of 8 to 12 companies. The equity investment was expected to be anywhere from €5mn to €25mn per portfolio company. As a key feature, their strategy for creating value was not based primarily on leverage. Within a segment comprised of companies sorely lacking in management expertise, they sought to bring their significant operating experience to bear, moving their portfolio companies into "the next stage of their development".

Strategic positioning, organization, and team

Zavala and González del Valle chose to focus on the SME segment described above for a number of reasons:

- Companies in this segment accounted for a significant portion of the economic "value-added" in Spain (see Exhibit 18.7 for "value added" by SMEs within the Spanish economy).

- Both founders had spent the majority of their careers building a successful track record in this segment.

- The vast majority of companies in this segment were family owned, lacking sophisticated operational strategies, processes, and structures; therefore, this segment represented an opportunity to add value upon acquisition.

- Deal transactions in this segment were most often proprietary (as opposed to auctioned) deals, thus offering the opportunity for more favorable acquisition prices.

- The sheer number of companies in this segment ensured a wealth of "buy and build" investment opportunities and a good quality deal flow. Both partners were familiar with this type of investment, given their prior experience.

- There was virtually no competition in this segment, either from Spanish funds (very few with comparable experience) or international funds.

Once a fund was successfully raised, the partners anticipated having a team of six investment professionals (two partners, two investment managers, and two analysts) and two administrative staff. As the number of companies in the portfolio were to grow, the partners planned to strengthen the team accordingly, intending to hire an additional investment manager and analyst within 2 to 3 years after Realza's final closing.

Another crucial component of Realza's organization was an informal advisory board, comprised of a network of seven to ten senior managers and sector experts with whom Zavala and González del Valle had worked in the past. For each portfolio company, one or more members of this board would be designated to support the team in reviewing the due diligence and executing the business plan. These professionals would be compensated via a combination of "directors' fees", stock options, and the opportunity to participate in the investments in which they were involved.

Competitive landscape

In Spain, the private equity market in 2006 was stratified into three levels (see Exhibit 18.8 for an illustration of competitive landscape). The first tier was a large buyout fund, which targeted investments greater than €300mn in EV and was represented by global organizations with operations in Spain. This highly competitive tier was populated by both top-tier U.S. and pan-European funds.

The mid-level competitors were a more mixed group. Some global organizations such as 3i rubbed shoulders with the larger Spanish firms—Mercapital being a prime example. Deal sizes ranged from €100mn to €300mn in this mid-level. Zavala and González del Valle had observed that the size of these organizations' deals had been increasing significantly, and that more of them were being completed through advisers and auction processes.

Finally, the closest competitors to Realza were the small buyout funds, typically targeting €100mn or less in deal size. In this segment, having a strong local team and network was vital for deal origination. As the partners recognized, competition was limited in this space.

Realza's investment strategy

During their time in private equity and industry, Zavala and González del Valle had developed an extensive network that gave them excellent access to the business community in Spain. As their former firms moved away from the smaller transactions, the newly formed Realza could capitalize on the opportunities in the market that were left behind. In particular, Zavala and González del Valle directly approached the intermediaries they had dealt with before, given their deep expertise in the smaller transactions that no longer interested Mercapital and InvestIndustrial.

Realza's strategy was to invest in buyouts in the low end of the mid-market in Spain. 76% of Spanish companies are family owned and 97% of companies have a headcount greater than 10, but less than 200. The partners felt strongly that this strategy offered some uniquely attractive opportunities. The SME companies are generally less structured, which allows experienced investors to make a significant contribution to value creation by working closely with the existing management teams.

Realza shared the view, which is widely consistent in PE, that creating value by providing not only financial, but also strategic business partnership was the key. Zavala and González del Valle had also proven themselves to be adept at this. Exhibit 18.9 illustrates how the partners created value during the 22 investments they were involved in prior to forming Realza. Business plan development and implementation, professionalization, and strengthening of management were persistent themes, even more so than execution of the acquisition and financial restructuring. From the outset, it was agreed that Realza would not invest in startups or distressed companies. Family-owned, SME enterprises seemed to be the right fit.

The partners determined that Realza would invest with a target outlook of 3 to 5 years, a reasonable period in which to generate value. Disinvestment in companies would principally be through sale to strategic (trade) buyers and, to a lesser degree, through secondary transactions to private equity (financial) investors interested in furthering the business project underway and supporting the management teams.

The return on investment was to be achieved through the following factors, listed here in order of importance to Realza:

- Expansion of operating profit (EBITDA), through organic growth and acquisitions.

- Increase in the EV/EBITDA multiples, compared with the corresponding multiples paid at acquisition. While GPs in general have little control over market multiples, these multiples usually reflect expected growth opportunities for the company and GPs do have control over improving the company's ability to pursue these growth opportunities.

- De-leveraging/Financial restructuring—using the cash flow of the business to pay down a portion of the debt on the company's balance sheet.

Realza's investment process and portfolio management

Realza's investment process would involve the deal team (one partner, one investment manager, and one analyst) visiting the potential target, deepening their knowledge of the company, and writing a "preliminary investment memorandum" on the opportunity. Once the potential deal was agreed internally, a "letter of intent" would be issued between Realza and the target company, giving Realza a period of exclusivity on the deal (around 3 months, but varies from deal to deal). Realza would then conduct the more costly, in-depth due diligence on the company, before completing the deal.

The intention of the partners was to have the same team that did the acquisition remain in place to monitor and manage the investment, and eventually to undertake any buy-and-build acquisitions. Realza would also work very closely with its Industrial Board in this regard.

Conclusion

Just after 2 A.M., Zavala and González del Valle resigned themselves to returning home to try and get some sleep. The following day they would need to begin re-engaging vigorously with potential investors. How should they promote the fund and reach the right investors? Would they be able to successfully close the fund and achieve the €150mn to €200mn target size? Or should they more seriously consider, for the sake of stability for themselves and their team, the three alternatives that currently were available to them?

Madrid was just coming to life with evening revelers braving the cold as they walked to their cars. Although the partners had a clear vision of where they wanted Realza Capital to go, they knew they were still far from being able to celebrate success.

DECEMBER 2008

As Martin González del Valle and Alfredo Zavala (the partners) discussed where to hold Realza Capital"s Christmas party in December 2008, they reflected on the events of the past 2 years. They recalled how grim the mood had been at their Christmas dinner in late 2006. Key investors had withdrawn their commitments and a wealthy family had offered the partners a fallback from their dream of setting up and running their own, independent fund.

How times had changed since then. At the end of 2005, they resolved to create Realza Capital. By the end of 2006, they had made three further decisions; first, to reject the alternative offers that had presented themselves. Second, despite a difficult beginning they had decided to pursue an international base of limited partners (LPs) rather than just domestic Spanish companies. Third, in order to successfully attract international LPs and raise funds, Zavala and González del Valle engaged a placement agent. Just 3 months ago, Realza had completed its fourth and final closing. Overall, the fund had raised €170mn, well within the desired range. The mood within the firm as 2008 came to a close was buoyant.

Yet, as they entered 2009 the partners knew there were new challenges on the horizon. The Realza team, so intensely focused on fundraising until now, needed to quickly shift gears into "investing and operating mode" and start realizing value for its investors. This would have to happen against the backdrop of a deteriorating economic climate in Spain. The country was now truly starting to feel the effects of the global financial crisis.

While the turn of the year was surely a time to celebrate the achievements of the past 2 years, Zavala and González del Valle knew that the real challenges still lay ahead.

Placement agents

Zavala and González del Valle knew that private equity funds often use placement agents, or intermediaries, to connect them with investors. The agent is typically compensated based on a percentage of funds raised. The agent's role includes

- Working with the partners of the fund to create investor due diligence materials, including a private placement memorandum (PPM), sales presentation, due diligence questionnaire (DDQ), and references to support the partners" track records
- Finding potential investors, primarily through personal contacts
- Scheduling the investor "roadshow", a process whereby the partners (usually accompanied by the placement agent) "sell" the fund to potential investors
- Providing advice and support to the partners on how to effectively present the investment opportunity during the roadshow.

The larger the fund being raised, the larger the placement agent because typically larger agents work with the bigger investors that large funds are targeting.

Etienne Deshormes and Elm Capital

Etienne Deshormes, a native of Brussels, had a diverse career including managing directorships at both JP Morgan and later Zurich Capital. He also had a short stint founding an internet startup, just before the dotcom crash, to help corporations select financial advisors (see Exhibit 18.10 for Etienne Deshormes' CV).

After the demise of the startup, Deshormes had been considering his next career move, when a former colleague approached him to ask for help in raising money for a first-time fund in Italy. The venture was challenging but ultimately successful, with the fund closing within 6 months of Deshormes becoming involved in the process. He realized that a gap existed in the market for a placement agent with his background and a track record in raising money for first-time funds As Deshormes put it, "First-time funds have no existing investor base or direct track record to leverage ... and this is a difficult story to tell to relatively risk-averse investors. In addition, raising a country-specific fund is tough, as there are fewer investors with an allocation in their portfolio for country-focused investments." With this in mind, Deshormes established Elm Capital in 2001 and went on to place a further six funds, before being introduced to Zavala and González del Valle by a mutual acquaintance.

Realza engages Elm Capital

In November 2006, Deshormes flew to Madrid to meet with the partners of Realza. Deshormes recalls, "As I sat in their sublet office, I noticed that the main meeting room was also the only route for everyone in the office to get to the bathroom ... I hoped that they had an alternative meeting room for visiting investors! Nevertheless, the meeting was great and I felt confident that I could work with Martín and Alfredo."

As he boarded the flight back to London, Deshormes reflected further on the appeal of working with Zavala and González del Valle. He recalls "Both Alfredo and Martín had significant experience in the Spanish market, and a strong track record and reputation in the mid-market in particular. In the context of the Spanish economic environment at the time, I felt that the best deals [in terms of potential to create value] were the smaller ones. Also, given that larger private equity funds in Spain had recently shown pretty erratic performance, I felt that investors were looking for a fund with this type of focus."

Meanwhile, Zavala and González del Valle also considered their options. In the European marketplace, they assessed the merits of working with placement agents across the three broad tiers:

- Large market (large funds, typically more than €1bn in funds raised)—examples included Credit Suisse, Merrill Lynch, and UBS.

- Mid market (mid-size funds, typically €500mn to €1bn in funds raised)—examples included MVision, Campbell Lutyens, Helix, JP Morgan Cazenove, and Lazard.

- Small market (small funds, typically less than €500mn in funds raised)—examples included Capstone, Accantus Advisers, Triago, and Elm Capital.

Although Zavala and González del Valle felt they would get more attention and focus from a smaller agent, they realized that one possible downside of working with a smaller agent could be lack of resources to dedicate to producing due diligence materials for potential LPs. However, in the case of Realza, this was less of a concern, as the partners had already generated most of the required information.

Zavala and González del Valle decided to partner with Elm Capital as a placement agent and quickly settled on terms. As per the typical placement agent model, they agreed that Elm would get compensated via a fee based on a percentage of funds raised. As it turned out, Deshormes and Elm would spend the ensuing 18 months working exclusively with Realza.

Overview of the fundraising process

Deshormes outlined the fundraising process to the Realza team, taking them through the following three broad phases:

- Preparation of due diligence materials
- Conducting the roadshow
- Conducting follow-up meetings and finalizing terms with the LPs.

Preparation of due diligence materials

Deshormes explained to Realza that there are certain documents investors typically require to enable them to make a decision on whether to invest in the fund. These include a presentation for the roadshow meetings, a private placement memorandum (PPM), a due diligence questionnaire (DDQ), and references for the partners of the fund. The partners and the placement agent typically work together in preparing these materials and, where possible, customizing them to address particular investor "hot buttons".

The roadshow presentation is typically a slide presentation outlining the macroeconomic and competitive landscape, the partners' motivations for setting up the fund, the fund's investment strategy and structure, and the backgrounds of the key investment professionals working for the fund. Deshormes knew from experience that a crucial piece of the background of the founding partners is their track record. A significant portion of the presentation is usually devoted to describing the track record, both at an overall performance level over their careers and for each deal separately. The goal of the presentation is to excite potential investors in the relatively short period of time available at the introductory roadshow meeting. Typically, the PPM is a more detailed, "leave behind" booklet version of the presentation, while the DDQ aims to answer all further questions a potential LP might have. Exhibit 18.11 contains an outline of the key topics covered in Realza's PPM and DDQ.

Deshormes was impressed by the fact that Zavala and González del Valle prepared many of the presentations and the due diligence material in advance. This reflected well on their professionalism and understanding of the private equity process. They were also aware that potential investors want to see references and gathered the information from several CEOs of the portfolio companies with whom they had worked in the past, two of which are shown for illustration in Exhibit 18.12.

Conducting the roadshow

Deshormes played a key role in contacting target investors and arranging the roadshow for Realza. Through his network, Deshormes approached close to 300 potential LPs. Deshormes, Zavala, and González del Valle were soon on the road; they embarked upon an intensive 3-week European trip, meeting more than 40 potential investors in 16 countries. Typically, the Realza partners were the main presenters on the day, with Deshormes playing the main role before (preparation, packaging, tailoring the messages, and delivery) and after the meetings (providing feedback).

After each roadshow presentation, Zavala and González del Valle sent investors who had expressed an interest a copy of the DDQ and, facilitated by Deshormes, followed up with the investors regarding specific queries. Once their interest became serious, the investors were invited to visit Realza's office in Madrid and spend the day with Zavala, González del Valle, and their team.

Deshormes recalls some of the concerns prospective investors had at the time. "They were concerned about attribution. How much of the value that Alfredo and Martín had created had been due to them as opposed to market conditions, leverage, or other factors? And how much of it was accurate? We had to show them numerous references from the CEOs with whom the partners had worked. And, even if the track record was to be believed, there was some concern around the fact that the partners had been in the private equity market for about 20 years and had only completed 22 deals. Finally, there were some reservations expressed about the ability of Zavala and González del Valle to work together to reproduce their track record. The two had of course worked together before, but that had been quite a long time ago."

Deshormes and Realza knew that, after the office visit, potential investors who wanted to proceed usually had to present the opportunity to their own investment committees, often multiple times. During this process, Deshormes and the partners did their best to answer questions and support these internal presentations. Once the prospective investors gained approval from their internal committees, the lawyers representing Realza and the potential LPs would meet to hammer out the term sheets and legal agreements (Exhibit 18.13 provides a summary of principal terms for Realza).

First investment and fund closing

By the spring of 2007, Zavala and González del Valle knew it was going to be important to demonstrate to potential investors that Realza had the right network of contacts to originate a solid deal flow in the SME segment. Zavala put the issue succinctly: "Without the money you can't do the deal, but without the deal you may not be able to attract the investors and close." Clínica Perio, Spain's largest chain of high-end dental clinics, offered just such a chance for Realza.

Zavala and González del Valle found the dental market in Spain highly attractive. First, it had demonstrated double-digit growth consistently for the past two decades. Second, it was highly fragmented with 24,000 dentists and 14,000 clinics (i.e., an average of 1.7 dentists per clinic). Realza's investment thesis was to consolidate the market by building a national chain. Such a chain would enjoy massive scalability of common back office and procurement. Furthermore, existing clinics lacked the ability to borrow money and, therefore, were unable to reduce their cost of capital. Clearly, a national chain would be able to enjoy far superior terms. Finally, the rationale for acquisitions was supported by the lack of a secondary market for selling or buying clinics.

The Clínica Perio opportunity also demonstrated an ability to be a majority investor alongside existing management. Realza negotiated to acquire 62% of the equity from its three founders, who reinvested to take the remaining stake.[5] Realza signed the stock purchase agreement (SPA) with Clínica Perio (subject to due diligence) on July 10, 2007.

Unusually, Realza actually signed the SPA prior to the first close (hence before being able to make the actual capital call). However, this was not as risky at it might appear, as the only step remaining to complete the first close was final approval for the fund's incorporation from the Comisión Nacional del Mercado de Valores (CNMV— the Spanish financial services regulator). Most of the soon-to-be LPs had already signed letters of commitment and the SPA for Clínica Perio contained a clause making the deal contingent upon a successful first close.

---

7. No debt existed on the company's balance sheet or was used to finance the investment.

With an investment under their belts, the Realza Capital story became a more tangible proposition to potential investors. A €43mn first close in August 2007 was followed by a second close at €87mn in January 2008 and a third close at €142mn in May of the same year. Meanwhile, the overall economic picture in Spain had continued to worsen. Real GDP growth in Spain had been vigorous since 2003 but by 2008 forecasters were expecting to see the first contraction since 1993. The housing sector was showing significant signs of decline and the levels of corporate debt across the Spanish economy were at almost 115% of total GDP. Despite these concerning signs, demand from investors for Realza's fund meant they were able to exceed their target €150mn and reach €170mn by the final close in September 2008.

Conclusion

González del Valle and Zavala knew the Realza team had accomplished a tremendous amount over the past 2 years. The partners had begun with an ambition to start their own fund and stay independent, and had stuck to their guns in the face of investor withdrawals and fallback options they really did not want to entertain. They successfully raised €170mn, well within their original target range.

But meanwhile, Spain was not immune to the global financial crisis. Zavala and González del Valle were acutely aware that Spain was beginning to show the telltale signs of an overheating economy. The country was entering a new phase in its downturn, and it was in this context that Realza needed to shift from "fundraising mode" to "investing and operating mode" to start delivering value to its LPs; and they needed to do this quickly.

Would Realza have the right balance of skills on their team to source and invest in portfolio companies in the current environment? Would the managers on their Industrial Board have the right skills to create value within the portfolio companies during a time of considerable economic distress? And how might the evolving (largely worsening) macroeconomic conditions impact the exit strategy for their portfolio companies?

Zavala and González del Valle had much to think about as the winding road of 2009 stretched out ahead of them.

APPENDIX

EXHIBIT 18.1

REAL GDP GROWTH IN SPAIN VS. EU 2000–2006

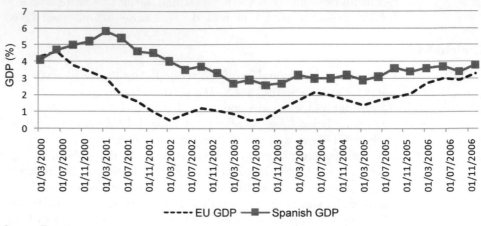

Source: Datastream.

EXHIBIT 18.2

PE INVESTMENT IN SPAIN (€ MILLIONS) 1995–2006

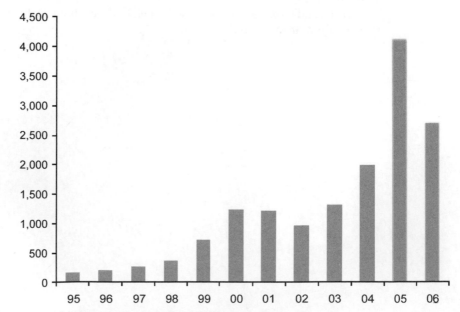

Source: Spanish Private Equity Association, ASCRI.

EXHIBIT 18.3

NUMBER OF PE DEALS IN SPAIN

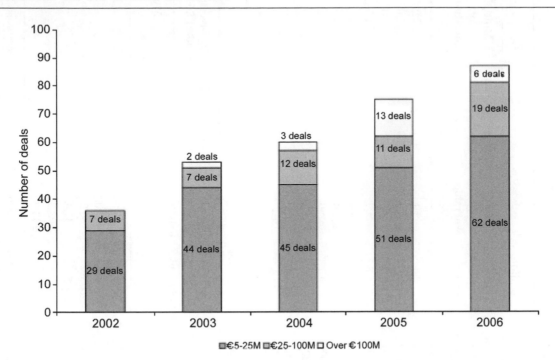

Source: ASCRI.

EXHIBIT 18.4

REALZA FOUNDING PARTNERS' CVS—ALFREDO ZAVALA AND MARTÍN GONZÁLEZ DEL VALLE

Martín González del Valle

- 2006: Advised Charterhouse on the buyout of Levantina

- 2000–2005: Investindustrial, Madrid, Partner and Managing Director in Spain (four deals)

- 1995–2000: Credit Agricole Indosuez, Madrid, Deputy GM, Head of Corporate Finance and Capital Markets

- 1989–1995: Mercapital, Madrid, Senior Director, Member of Management Committee (five deals + corporate finance)

- 1986–1988: Socelec, Madrid, Sales Director, Member of Management Committee

- 1984–1986: Baxter Travenol, Valencia, Head of Home Care Products

- 1980–1983: Sociedad Metalúrgica Duro Felguera, Internal Auditor

- BA in Law (Madrid 1980) and Economics (Madrid 1981), MBA (INSEAD 1984).

Alfredo Zavala

- 1996–2006: Mercapital, Madrid, Partner (15 deals in total)

- 1989–1996: Mercapital, Madrid, Senior Director

- 1985–1987: Editorial Gráficas Espejo, Madrid, Director, Assistant to General Manager

- BA in Economics (Madrid 1985), MBA (INSEAD 1988).

EXHIBIT 18.5a

TRACK RECORD OF REALIZED AND UNREALIZED INVESTMENTS WHERE ZAVALA AND GONZÁLEZ DEL VALLE WERE PRIMARILY RESPONSIBLE FOR THE TRANSACTION

Realized investments[1] (performance as of December 31, 2005; figures in € million)

Company	Partner	Industry	Year of initial investment	Total investment amount	Initial equity ownership (%)	Realized proceeds	Year realized	Multiple of investment	Gross IRR (%)
Mesa	MGV	Electrical equipment manufacturer	1989	2.8	61	6.1	1990	2.2	269
Mesa Gatica	MGV	Electrical equipment manufacturer	1989	2.4	59	4.9	1990	2.0	212
Barón de Ley	AZ	Rioja wine	1991	16.4	65	61.8	1997	3.8	25
Intermédica	MGV	Medical products	1992	6.7	99	10.7	1997	1.8	13
Parques Reunidos	AZ	Amusement parks	1994	12.7	66	101.7	1999–2000	6.0	51
Frida	AZ	Frozen food	1995	8.6	46	2.0	1997	2.3	63
Santos	AZ	Logistics services	1999	20.5	60	68.0	2005	3.3	22
Grupo Care	MGV	Nursing homes	2001	10.6	98	19.9	2006	1.9	17
Logic Control	MGV	Computer software	2002	38.3	100	72.4	2005	1.9	22
System[2]	AZ	IT training and education	2003	11.1	47	11.1	2005	1.0	0
Subtotal realized				*130.1*		*358.6*		*2.8*	

Unrealized investments (performance as of December 31, 2005; figures in € million)

Company	Partner	Industry	Year of initial investment	Total investment amount	Initial equity ownership (%)	Estimates by investment bank (end of 2006)	
						Equity value	Multiple
Ydilo[3]	AZ	Speech recognition	2000	3.6	24	9.2	2.6
Recoletos	MGV	Publisher of newspapers and magazines	2005	22.0	5	45	2.0
Saprogal	AZ	Animal feed	2005	30.2	75	37	1.2
Inaer	MGV	Helicopter onshore services	2005	47.4	74	77	1.6
Subtotal unrealized				*103.2*			
Total realized and unrealized				**233.3**			

Notes: 1. When the deal was led by Mercapital Group or Investindustrial, the investment figures also include co-investors. Otherwise data only reflect investments by Mercapital Group or Investindustrial (for Ydilo shareholding by financial investors was 68% and for Recoletos the MBO was for 100% of the company).
2. Contract declared null and void. Investment cost recovered.
3. Shareholding reflects position as at December 31, 2005.

EXHIBIT 18.5b

TRACK RECORD OF REALIZED AND UNREALIZED INVESTMENTS WHERE ZAVALA AND GONZÁLEZ DEL VALLE WERE MEMBERS OF THE INVESTMENT TEAM

Realized investments (performance as at December 31, 2005; figures in € million)

Company	Partner	Industry	Year of initial investment	Total investment amount	Initial equity ownership (%)	Realized proceeds	Un-realized proceeds	Total proceeds	Year realized	Multiple investment	Gross IRR (%)
Midesa	AZ and MGV	Periodical distribution	1988	27.2	43	51.0	—	51.0	1989–1997	1.9	35
Avidesa	AZ	Ice cream manufacturer	1988	35.6	26	42.3	—	42.3	1989–1992	1.2	23
Cantonajes Suñer	AZ and MGV	Packaging	1989	13.8	43	11.1	—	11.1	1992–1993	0.8	n.a.
Comelectric	AZ and MGV	Electrical equipment distributor	1989	19.6	50	0.2	—	0.2	1993	0	n.a.
Cope	AZ	Radio broadcasting	1993	3.3	6	4.6	—	4.5	1997	1.3	12
Record	AZ	Car rental	1999	37.5	56	73.0	9.8	82.8	2003–2008	2.2	n.a.
Subtotal realized				*137.0*				*191.9*		*1.4*	
Total realized				**267.1**				**550.5**		**2.1**	

(primarily responsible and members of the investment team)

Unrealized investments (performance as at December 31, 2005; figures in € million)

Company	Partner	Industry	Year of initial investment	Total investment amount	Initial equity ownership (%)	Estimates by investment bank (end of 2006) Equity value	Multiple
Jofel	AZ	Hygienic accessories	2001	33.2	54	82	2.5
Lasem	AZ	Frozen dough and oleochemicals	2003	23.4	42	48	2.1
Subtotal unrealized				*56.6*			
Total realized and unrealized as members of the investment team				**193.6**			
Total combined investment performance				***426.9***			

Source: Realza Capital.

EXHIBIT 18.6

CASE STUDIES OF PRIOR INVESTMENTS

I Grupo Santos (investment led by Alfredo Zavala at Mercapital)

Deal description

- Integrated provider of logistic services
- Strong reputation for service quality (owned by the Santos family)

Investment rationale

- The logistic services sector
    - experienced strong growth as a consequence of the trend towards subcontracting
    - was poised to undergo a concentration process at a European level
    - was increasingly demanding in the quality of the services
- Santos was deemed to be the appropriate platform from which to create a national leader
- Opportunity to grow through organic growth and acquisitions
- Opportunity to create value by strengthening the management team and implementing management systems.

Value creation

- Appointing a CEO, a CFO, and other middle managers
- Carrying out a corporate restructuring, conceiving a new brand and a corporate image
- Introducing information systems (SAP) and management systems (budgeting financial controls, etc.)
- Defining for the first time in its history a strategic plan, including acquisitions
- Leading four acquisitions of competitors
- Optimizing financial structure through financial leverage.

	Sales	EBIT	Multiple	Enterprise value	Net debt
Entry	54.0	5.0	7.6	38.2	4.0
Exit	204.3	13.6	9.7	132.5	13.2

II Logic Control (investment led by Martín González del Valle at Investindustrial)

Deal description

- Leading software company specializing in accounting and business management software for small and medium-sized companies
- Originated as part of the divestment program of its parent company, Service Point Solutions

Investment rationale

- The industry offered high barriers to entry (due to national and regional tax and accounting policies)
- Leader in its industry with wide brand awareness and an installed base of 22,000 active customers
- High cash flow visibility due to maintenance contracts
- Low acquisition multiple compared with listed companies
- Clear exit opportunities.

Value creation

- Stopped hardware business line
- Reduced workforce and expenses related
- Strengthened management team, sales network, and the distribution network (VARs)
- Created incentive plan
- Migrated the existing customer base to more value-added services, while increasing customer loyalty
- Started vertical expansion to reach related market segments
- Increased the recurrent revenues stream through the introduction of additional maintenance services
- De-leveraged through stable cash flow generation.

	Sales	EBIT	Multiple	Enterprise value	Net debt
Entry	36.6	0.7	85.7	60.0	21.7
Exit	43.6	3.1	22.8	70.8	(1.6)

EXHIBIT 18.7

VALUE ADDED BY SMES WITHIN THE SPANISH ECONOMY

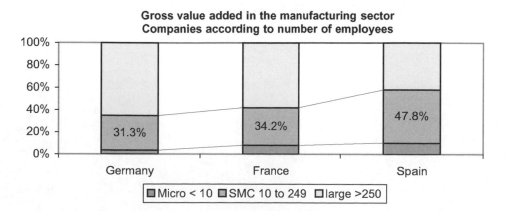

Source: Realza Prospectus.

EXHIBIT 18.8

ILLUSTRATION OF COMPETITIVE LANDSCAPE

Transaction value (EV)	+ €300mn	€100mn to €300mn	€15mn to €100mn
Number of buyouts in 2006	6	7	19
PE firms with an office in Spain		Mercapital	
	CVC	3i	*Realza*
	Apax	Advent	Nazca
	PAI	Bridgepoint	Corpfin
	Carlyle	Vista	Espiga
	Candover	N + 1	Catalana
	Doughty Hanson	Impala (excluding Suala)	Proa
		Ibersuizas	
		Investindustrial	
		MCH	
		Magnum	

Source: Capital & Corporate Magazine and Realza Capital.

EXHIBIT 18.9

VALUE CREATION BY ALFREDO ZAVALA AND MARTIN GONZÁLEZ DEL VALLE IN PRE-REALZA INVESTMENTS

Company	Business plan development and implementation	Transformation of family companies into professionally run companies	Strengthening of management	Improving companies' structures and processes	Identifying and executing acquisitions	Optimizing financial structures	Succession plans and management incentives
Mesa	✓	✓					
Mesa Gatica	✓	✓					
Barón de Ley	✓		✓		✓		✓
Intermédica	✓		✓	✓			
Parques Reunidos	✓		✓	✓	✓	✓	✓
Frida	✓		✓	✓		✓	✓
Santos	✓	✓	✓	✓	✓	✓	✓
Grupo Care	✓	✓	✓	✓	✓	✓	✓
Logic Control	✓	✓	✓	✓		✓	✓
System	✓		✓				✓
Ydilo	✓		✓				
Recoletos	✓					✓	✓
Saprogal	✓				✓	✓	✓
Inaer	✓	✓	✓		✓	✓	✓
Midesa	✓	✓	✓	✓			
Avidesa	✓	✓	✓	✓			
Cartonajes Suñer	✓	✓	✓	✓			
Comelectric	✓	✓	✓	✓			
Cope	✓		✓			✓	
Record	✓	✓	✓			✓	✓
Jofel	✓	✓	✓				✓
Lasem	✓	✓	✓	✓			✓

Source: Realza Capital.

EXHIBIT 18.10

ETIENNE DESHORMES' CV

Career

Nov. 2001–Current Elm Capital Associates Ltd., London—Founder and Chief Executive Officer

- Advisory to private equity funds assisting in the fundraising process and in negotiating acquisitions or divestitures of companies and funds.

- Raised over €700mn for private equity funds in Italy, France, Spain, Germany, the U.K. and the U.S.

May 2000–Sep. 2001 Global CFO Ltd., London—Founder and Chief Executive Officer

1998–2000 Zurich Capital Markets, London—Managing Director

1996–1998 JP Morgan, London—Managing Director Head of Equity Capital Markets for France and Belgium

1992–1996 JP Morgan, Brussels—Vice President Head of Corporate Finance

1987–1992 Euroclear, Brussels—Account Officer

1986 Cabinet of the Minister for Small and Medium Industry, Belgium

1985 International Monetary Fund and World Bank, Washington D.C.

Academic background

1979–1984 Degree in Economics with Grande Distinction, Université libre de Bruxelles, Belgium

1978–1983 Degree in Contemporary History with Grande Distinction, Université libre de Bruxelles, Belgium

1966–1978 European School, Brussels, Belgium.

EXHIBIT 18.11

OUTLINE OF THE CONTENTS OF THE PRIVATE PLACEMENT MEMORANDUM AND DUE DILIGENCE QUESTIONNAIRE

Private Placement Memorandum contents

- Executive summary
- The market opportunity
- Investment strategy
- Organization
- Partners' track record
- Case studies
- Summary of principal terms
- Risk factors
- Tax considerations
- Certain U.S. tax, Employee Retirement Income Security Act (ERISA), and securities law matters
- Selling restrictions.

Due Diligence Questionnaire

- Investment strategy
- Deal flow/Deal origination
- Investment process
- Investment performance/Track record
- Personnel
- Litigation check
- Investor reporting and relations
- Legal status, structure, and organization
- Appendix
  - internal due diligence checklist
  - partners' CVs
  - sample report to investors.

Source: Realza Capital

EXHIBIT 18.12

EXAMPLES OF REFERENCES FOR REALZA PARTNERS

Attribution letter: Logic Control

To whom it may concern: Barcelona, September, 2006

As CEO and Managing Director of Logic Control until July 2005, I've had the opportunity to develop a very close professional relationship with Martín González del Valle from 2001, at which time InvestIndustrial led the acquisition of Logic Control in a leverage buyout operation, until June 2005, when the company was sold to the British Sage Group.

Martín was InvestIndustrial's CEO in Spain and we both designed the strategic plan as well as the company's goals for the following five years. Also, together we established new remuneration packages for the management team and other key personnel, establishing a stock option plan, bonus policies, etc.

Once the investment group's entry had been finalised, Martín regularly attended the monthly meetings of the Board of Directors, in which he participated actively in overseeing the different areas of the company. Additionally and when necessary, I had personal meetings with Martín to review specific matters regarding the performance of the company in distinct areas. In fact, all of the relevant decisions I took in Logic Control during this period were formerly negotiated and agreed with Martín.

In the final state, along with his team and the investment bank that organised the competitive tender, he led and was responsible for this process until the sale was completed with the entry of Sage Group.

During these years, Martín has been for me a highly professional collaborator and his opinions and good judgement have had a positive effect on the company's results.

Carlos Grau Serra

Reference letter: Grupo Recoletos

Joaquín Güell Ampuero, Managing Director

To whom it may concern: Madrid, 31 August, 2006

The Leverage buy out—LBO—staged by the management team of Recoletos in the first months of 2005 attracted a lot of interest (we received 8 firm offers from interested parties) among the leading national and international players in the world of private equity.

As CFO of Grupo Recoletos, I played a particularly intense role throughout the whole process. Given the interest the operation aroused, our goal was to choose the best partner: one who would contribute to the project's creation of value and maximise the investment's value. To do so, we designed a highly competitive selection process, making special emphasis on qualitative factors such as experience, professionalism, team prestige, sector knowledge and differentiating factors.

As the CEO of InvestIndustrial in Spain, Martín showed great interest in the operation from the very beginning of the process and played an active role in all of the entry negotiations, convincing us in the management team and our advisers of the differentiating and enriching factors for the project that his team could provide. Additionally, we personally knew his worth, and professional reputation, which were very relevant factors we took into consideration when we made the final decision to bring InvestIndustrial into the Recoletos project. Later on, he was involved in the investment for a few months until October 2005. During this period, his contribution to defining the company's strategy and monitoring the management was very valuable.

Sincerely

Source: Realza Prospectus.

EXHIBIT 18.12

SUMMARY OF PRINCIPAL TERMS FOR REALZA

Legal structure The Fund will be formed as a Spanish regulated simplified scheme private equity fund (the "FCR") established under the Private Equity Act and registered with the CNMV, and any parallel investment vehicles as required, subject to substantially the same terms and conditions (the "Parallel Funds"). Each vehicle will participate proportionately in all investments on substantially the same terms and conditions.

Management company Realza Capital SGECR, SA, a Spanish regulated private equity management company (*Sociedad Gestora de Entidades de Capital Riesgo*) duly incorporated under the Private Equity Act and registered with the CNMV, will be the management company of the FCR and any other Parallel Funds established in Spain. The Management Company will be responsible fo identifying, making and realising suitable investments for the FCR and the Parallel Funds and for the administration of the FCR and any other Parallel Funds established in Spain.

Promoters Alfredo Zavala and Martín González del Valle or their successors from time to time.

Size of the fund Total Commitments of the FCR and the Parallel Funds are targeted to be €150mn with a maximum of €200mn.

Investment period Commitments will cease to be available for draw-down 5 years after the final closing of the Fund (the "Investment Period"), provided that Commitments may be drawn down thereafter to the necessary extent:

(a) to make investments where a letter of intent or agreements have been entered into before the end of the Investment Period;

(b) to pay the Management Fee, expenses and liabilities of the Fund; and

(c) to make investments other than New Investments (provided however that in this latter case, such investments shall not exceed the lower of: (i) 15% of Total Commitments; or (ii) total undrawn Commitments).

Commitment The minimum investor's Commitment to the Fund, subject to the Management Company's discretion, will be €3mn.

Promoters' commitment The Promoters will commit to the Fund an amount equivalent to 2% of aggregate total commitments which shall be allocated as follows:

(i) 1.5% shall be co-invested, *pari passu*, with the Fund in all portfolio company investments; and

(ii) 0.5% shall be directly invested in the Fund through the subscription of the corresponding Commitment.

Term The Fund will terminate ten years from the date of the final closing, but, subject to prior approval of the Supervisory Committee, it may be extended for up to two additional one year periods, at the discretion of the Management Company to provide for the orderly realisation of investments.

Drawdowns Commitments will be drawn down in euros on an "as needed" basis on no less than 10 business days' notice.

Management fee As of the First Closing and until the end of the Investment Period the Management Company will receive an annual management fee (the "Management Fee") equal to 2.0% of Total Commitments. After the end of the Investment Period and until the liquidation of the Fund, the Management Fee will reduce to 2.0% of the following:

(i) Total Commitments drawn down;

(ii) plus undrawn amounts corresponding to the reserve for investments other than New Investments which the Supervisory Committee has authorised the Management Company to take into account for the purposes of calculating the Management Fee;

(iii) less the acquisition cost of investments realised or written off. The Management Fee, or drawings on account thereof, will be payable semi-annually in advance.

Investment-related fees The fees received by the Management Company as transaction fees, break-up fees and other investment-related fees from the making of Fund's investments, for an amount equivalent to the abort costs incurred by the Fund not previously recovered, will be offset against the Management Fee for the relevant accounting period. 80% of the remaining investment-related fees received by the Management Company will be for the benefit of the Fund (by credit against the Management Fee).

Establishment costs All preliminary expenses (including but not limited to travel, legal, accountancy, printing and other costs) incurred in relation to or in connection with the establishment of the FCR and the Parallel Funds (the "Establishment Costs") will be borne by the FCR and the Parallel Funds up to 1% of Total Commitments (plus any VAT). The Management Company will bear any Establishment Costs in excess of this amount. No placement fees will be borne by the Fund.

Operating expenses   The Fund will bear its own operating expenses (inter alia legal, tax, audit and insurance fees) and costs arising from uncompleted transactions (abort costs).

Carried interest   The Promoters will be entitled to a carried interest equal to 20% of the aggregate Fund's profits, subject to investors first receiving repayment of drawn down Commitments and the Preferred Return.

Preferred return   An amount equivalent to interest at an annual rate of 8% (compounded annually) on Commitments drawn down and not repaid (the "Preferred Return").

Distributions   All income and realisation proceeds will, after satisfying any expenses and liabilities of the Fund and subject to payment of the Management Fee and the re-investment rights described below, be distributed as follows:

(a)   first, to the investors in repayment of their Commitments drawn down;

(b)   second, to the investors in payment of an amount equal to the Preferred Return;

(c)   third, to the Promoters until they have received 20% of all amounts distributed after repayment of the Commitments.

Carried interest escrow   Prior to the date:

(a)   when the investors have received distributions of the drawn down and undrawn Commitments and the Preferred Return; or (if earlier);

(b)   the termination of the Fund;

the Management Company shall retain within the Fund the following percentage amount of the carried interest distributions which would have been made to the Promoters:

(i)   30% during the first two years as from the final closing;

(ii)   thereafter, 20% during the third and fourth years as from the final closing; and

(iii)   thereafter, 10% during the fifth year as from the final closing

Clawback   The Promoters will be subject to clawback provisions with respect to any excess of carried interest received.

Re-investment   The Management Company shall not be obliged to distribute Fund's proceeds where the Fund is entitled to re-invest these amounts. The Management Company shall be entitled to reinvest the following amounts:

(a)   those amounts received by the Fund from divestments of bridging investments or underwriting transactions (up to the amount of their acquisition cost in each case) where such commitments or investments are sold down within 12 months of making the commitment, bridging investment or underwriting transaction;

(b)   those amounts received by the Fund on the realisation of any investment arising within 12 months of the making of the investment (up to the amount of its acquisition cost); and

(c)   proceeds from deposits or short-term negotiable instruments made or acquired for management of cashflows and other liquid assets of the Fund.

Co-investment opportunities   The Management Company, at its sole discretion and in the best interests of the Fund, may offer co-investment opportunities to investors in the Fund or to third party investors (including strategic investors), if the Management Company considers it to be in the best interests of the Fund. In case they are offered to investors in the Fund, they shall be offered in accordance with the following order of preference:

(a)   in the first place, to those investors whose commitment is greater than or equal to €15mn, pro rata to their respective commitments;

(b)   if in accordance with section (a), above, any one of the investors does not accept the co-investment opportunity offered thereto in its entirety, the other investors whose commitment is greater than or equal to €15mn may accept the offer of the remaining co-investment opportunity, pro rata to their commitments;

(c)   in the event that, in accordance with the provisions of sections (a) and (b), above, there should be a remainder of the co-investment opportunity, this may be offered, at the discretion of the Management Company, to any other investors and/or third party investors.

The co-investment opportunities shall, in any case, be offered and made in the same terms and conditions as the investment made by the Fund.

Key executives   Alfredo Zavala and Martín González del Valle will be the key executives (the "Key Executives"), primarily responsible for the Fund. In the event that during the Investment Period, any of the Key Executives cease for whatever reason to devote substantially all of their business time to the Fund, the Investment Period will be automatically suspended and Commitments may only be drawn down thereafter in order to settle prior liabilities and ordinary expenses of the Fund. The Management Company shall give notice of this event to investors which may resolve by means of an Investors' Special Consent that:

(a) the suspension of the Investment Period shall be resumed;

(b) the Investment Period shall be terminated; or

(c) the Fund shall be liquidated.

Investments, as well as the remainder of obligations, shall be shared by the Fund and the co-investors, pro rata to the amount invested by each one of them. The Management Company shall make reasonable efforts to ensure that co-investors do not dispose of any investment in a portfolio company before the Fund disposes of its investment in such portfolio company. Any disposal of an investment in a portfolio company shall be made at substantially the same time as the Fund unless the co-investors desire to hold the investment until a later date and the Management Company considers that it would not be contrary to the best interests of the Fund.

Source: Realza Prospectus.

19

Swicorp: Private equity in the MENA region 2009

Rilwan Meeran sat in his office high above Dubai and gazed out at The World, the iconic mega-project that replicated a map of the world with man-made islands. It was January 2009 and he was thinking about his ongoing deal in Jordan. Going over the main points once again, he knew he would have to bring it to Swicorp's Investment Committee soon. As he mentally enumerated the various risks of the venture, a well-established aircraft leasing business in Amman, and the mitigations his team had comprehensively detailed, Meeran realized that he was actually asking himself whether the deal ought to go ahead given the revised performance in other recent investments brought about by the economic downturn.

Looking out to the island that represented the northeastern United States, Meeran thought back to his decision, in the spring of 2006, to leave his senior position at Finstar Global Partners in New York and move halfway round the world. At the time Swicorp had made Meeran a tempting offer and he thought back to the reasons why he had decided to relocate, first, to Tunis to gain an understanding of Swicorp's culture, spending an intensive 2 months in the Swicorp office there, and, then, to Dubai to join the Intaj private equity team. He had liked the fact that Swicorp was an international company with a regional focus already 20 years old, had an established brand, and a good mix of international and local talent. With its current team he could see himself remaining with the firm for the foreseeable future.

SWICORP—A SHORT HISTORY

Founded in 1986 by Kamel Lazaar as a corporate advisory firm, Swicorp was initially based in Geneva. The founding brought together a number of European-educated francophone business partners. Before setting up the company Lazaar had held the position of Vice President with Citibank in North Africa and Europe and was on the Citibank team that set up Samba, the Saudi-American Bank in Saudi Arabia.

The case was co-authored with Richard Harvey and Geoff Leffek (LBS Dubai London Executive MBA 2009).

The initial activities of Swicorp concentrated on merger and acquisition and strategic advisory services to several large family-owned business groups. These groups, effectively family conglomerates, were common in the Middle East, and particularly Gulf countries such as Saudi Arabia. Swicorp made use of its relationships, in the Middle East and North Africa in particular, through business contacts established in Saudi Arabia.

The move into private equity

In 2003, Swicorp was engaged to advise a consumer products group on potential investment opportunities in the Saudi market. This group considered involvement in the bottling sector in the MENA region and, jointly with Swicorp, they set up a fund targeting potential acquisitions such as bottling plants and retail operations. The venture, however, did not proceed as planned and was ultimately abandoned. But the experience had provided a steep learning curve for Swicorp which resulted in the creation of an equity fund in 2004. A private equity group was set up under the leadership of Nabil Triki. Triki recognized the importance of finding a good team to kick off the fundraising. The fund was to concentrate on investment opportunities in the Middle East region tied to the large and growing consumer market, a market dominated by a young population.

At this time Swicorp undertook a group restructuring to reflect new business lines, relocated its head office from Geneva to the Saudi Arabian capital Riyadh to be closer to its main contacts and clients. The restructuring clearly split the company's banking and equity activities, with the Geneva office continuing to provide corporate advisory services. Over the following years, additional regional offices were opened in Tunis, Algiers, Jeddah, and Dubai. The Tunis office contained the research and other support services, where well-educated and relatively low-cost talent was at ample supply. By the end of 2008 Swicorp had 120 staff with the majority in the Riyadh and Tunis offices. Staff working on the consumer sector fund were concentrated in Dubai and Saudi Arabia.

The Swicorp private equity funds

In addition to its concentration on consumer-driven markets, Swicorp worked with the Saudi Arabian Government Investment Authority to set up a fund targeting energy and energy-intensive industries. The two resulting funds were "Intaj" for the consumer sector and "Joussour" in energy. In addition, a further fund was created, "Emerge Invest", an open-ended fund focused on greenfield and early stage projects. By 2006 the Joussour fund reached USD1bn in committed capital, while Intaj gained commitments of around USD250mn. The funds shared services, pooling research, finance, and other functions. Limited partners in funds (LPs) and co-investors had generally been corporate banking clients.

The Intaj fund

The Swicorp Equity team members believed themselves to be in a unique position in the regional private equity investment market, with a number of attributes that differentiated the team from other operations in the MENA market. A local presence with good access and long-standing relationships built on the advisory side with the business community was evident, and the makeup of the team, in terms of backgrounds and nationalities, provided a high level of understanding of the regional landscape.

The Intaj Capital I fund succeeded in raising USD250mn, as part of a total of USD1.4bn raised for all funds, from 50 MENA region investors including a concentration from the Gulf Cooperation Council (GCC) countries.[1] Key investors included a number of large, private investment groups from North Africa and the GCC, as well as a number of high-net-worth individuals. Efforts were made to attract institutional investors from outside the MENA region. One such investor, a European financial development institution that specialized in providing private investment in developing countries, committed the relatively small sum of USD15mn as an initial "tryout" with Intaj.

Swicorp saw the importance of attracting institutional investors from Western countries and prepared itself to go through an extensive and arduous due diligence process that Western institutional investors require. Exhibits 19.1–19.3 display information on Intaj investments.

THE MENA REGION

Spanning from Morocco to the Levant and the Gulf states, the MENA region covers over 20 countries. As a standalone economy it was the world's fifth largest with GDP growing at 4.5–6% per annum from 2000 to 2007 (see Exhibit 19.4 for GDP data). Whilst not the fastest growing region in the world, its growth rate had increased incomparably since the early to mid-1990s. Job creation had increased and unemployment had declined during that period. With a rise in foreign direct investment the private sector had grown, although not evenly across all countries. In terms of private equity investment, with billions of dollars of petroleum earnings and liberalizing economies, money had flowed freely into private equity firms over the 4 to 5 years to 2008. Following the worldwide financial crisis triggered in summer 2007 the availability of cash was significantly reduced, although some was still flowing. The *Financial Times* noted that "[In 2007] Middle East private equity funds raised USD5bn but in the first half of 2008 only USD1.1bn was committed."[2]

Within the region, countries shared a cultural affinity and comparable consumption trends and habits existed. There were two types of legal and institutional frameworks within the region, however. The North African region of the Maghreb (Morocco, Tunisia, Algeria) had a legal and institutional civil law framework aligned with French law. In the Levant, Syria was transitioning from French-influenced systems to follow more closely the Gulf countries as Gulf wealth funds and family conglomerates invested in the slowly liberalizing Syrian economy. The Gulf countries generally followed common law principles and British institutional frameworks, as did Jordan.[3] To undertake business in the MENA region as a whole, therefore, companies with cultural affinity to both systems had tremendous advantages.

Turkey is often included when considering MENA, although to a large extent it may be argued that Turkey is more aligned with Europe than the neighboring MENA

---

1. The Gulf Cooperation Council is a unified economic community of Gulf states comprising Saudi Arabia, Bahrain, Kuwait, Oman, Qatar, and the U.A.E. The U.A.E. consists of Abu Dhabi, Dubai, Sharjah, and four other emirates.

2. "Private Equity: Credit Crunch Deflects Upward Trajectory," *Financial Times*, November 24, 2008, Robin Wrigglesworth.

3. British common law is also more similar to Islamic law. In fact, it is widely suggested by scholars that fundamental English common principles were derived from similar legal institutions in Islamic law and introduced to England by the Normans.

countries of Iraq and Syria or the wider Middle East and Gulf region. To the east of MENA, Pakistan is also considered, by some, an extension of the region, particularly as a result of the proximity of Pakistan's commercial centre, Karachi, to the Gulf states.

As one professional commented:

> "Despite diversity in frameworks, MENA countries display a certain uniformity, which from a private equity perspective offers a number of advantages, such as critical mass for a diversified private equity portfolio and transferable value creation strategies."

In terms of language, for countries in the Maghreb French was the language of regulation and governance and was required to undertake business. English was the main business language, alongside Arabic, in the Gulf.[4] English or standard Arabic was generally used for communicating in business in this part of the region. Swicorp, with its background and cultural mix, was able to operate in both frameworks.

Demographics

The population of the MENA region in 2008 was approximately 360 million. If Turkey was included then the total population was 430 million at that time. The projected MENA population for 2010 was 376 million, and growth of around 2% was expected per annum until 2010, and 1.7% thereafter (see Exhibits 19.5 and 19.6).

The MENA population was dominated by the younger age groups. In Saudi Arabia, the median age was 21.5 years, and was 24.5 years in Egypt. Median age in France and Sweden, by comparison, was around 40 years.[5]

Despite a significant GDP growth in the past few years which persisted even during the financial downturn of 2008, and despite gradually improving incomes, many issues faced the population of the MENA countries. Even with increasing growth, the level of unemployment was high in North Africa. The MENA region had a sound educational establishment, but to enable high growth, particularly in the Gulf states, many highly trained professionals had to be from other Arabic countries, such as Egypt and Lebanon, or had to be expatriate professionals from outside the region.

THE MENA PRIVATE EQUITY LANDSCAPE

Private equity activities had grown to significant levels in the last few years pre the global credit crunch. Since 2005, average fund size had increased from approximately USD100mn to about USD300mn in 2008. The number of firms prior to 2006 was 29, rising to 44 at the beginning of 2008. The financial crisis had shaken activities in the region, but most firms were still in existence, weathering the financial storm (see Exhibits 19.7 and 19.8).

Middle East private equity firms were made up of local, regional, and global players (see Exhibits 19.9 and 19.10). Local and regional firms had been established with headquarters in most of the Gulf capitals—Abu Dhabi, Kuwait City, Manama, Doha,

---

4. Arabic dialects differ between countries, so it may be that Arabic is not the easiest language of communication between nationals of geographically disparate nations; Moroccan and Gulf nationals, for example. In these cases English may be used by two native Arabic speakers, or discussion is facilitated if both know modern standard Arabic. English and French nevertheless provide many of the technical words needed to conduct modern business.

5. *Source:* U.S. government surveys.

and Riyadh. Most of the firms also had a presence in Dubai, as Dubai served as an important business and financial hub for the region. The presence may have been for operational reasons, such as fundraising, or may have been for representation purposes. In addition to private equity firms, sovereign wealth funds from the Gulf also made significant investments in the region.

In terms of investors, high-net-worth individuals (HNWIs) comprised a notable portion of equity investment. It was difficult to gauge the exact proportion of equity investment by HNWIs, as their investments were often channeled through family businesses or private investment houses, but 20–30% was not unrealistic. Private investment firms pooled individual wealth, and business conglomerates also invested. Institutional investors from outside the region, such as Europe and the U.S., were also beginning to invest—partly because they were reassured by increasing transparency and local firms' improving ability to undertake meaningful due diligence, and partly because the region was still growing, despite the financial crisis of 2008, unlike most other regions of the globe.

THE ROLE OF SOVEREIGN WEALTH FUNDS (SWFS)

Sovereign wealth funds were found mainly in the Gulf states and were significant investors in companies and commercial developments in the region. Some funds in the region were relatively new, although a small number had been established for several decades. All had enormous financial weight, created predominantly from oil wealth. The strategies of the SWFs differed from country to country (and emirate to emirate in the U.A.E.).

Two main strategies are worthy of remark—one was an opportunistic approach to investment based on maximizing returns. The second was investing with a view to gain technical knowhow and knowledge to improve the skills base of the local populations concerned. The Abu Dhabi–owned Mubadala had a portfolio of investments and joint ventures in conventional and green energy, healthcare, engineering/manufacturing, and infrastructure projects, following the second model. Both strategies attempted to cushion the effects of reduced oil revenues anticipated in the future—either through returns generated by financial diversification or through gradually improving the intellectual capital of the country's nationals (Exhibit 19.11).

SWFs were gradually coming under pressure by regulators to become more transparent; those based in the Gulf were no different.[6] Adia had issued a Code of Conduct to reduce concerns over lack of transparency. Transparency had become an issue for governments of the home countries of companies in which the SWFs had acquired stakes, such as Adia's and Kuwait Investment Authority's investments in Citigroup and Morgan Stanley, as a result of the "unknown" nature of the funds. A major political storm was created in the U.S. in 2007 when SWF Dubai World subsidiary DP World purchased the ports of P&O. The U.S. government intervened and refused to allow the control of P&O's U.S. ports to be ceded to DP World. In the case of the acquisition of stakes in Citigroup and Morgan Stanley, the SWFs aimed to be good global citizens by helping to stabilize the U.S. banking system, as well as anticipating financial gain. At the beginning of 2009, many of the SWFs experienced the impact of their first major global financial downturn.

6. "Sovereign Funds Sign Up to Code of Conduct," *Financial Times*, September 4, 2008, Krishna Guha.

SWICORP'S INTAJ INVESTMENT STRATEGY

Buy and build

Like any other private equity firm, Swicorp aimed to create value through the means of multiple arbitrage, financial leverage, and operational growth (see Exhibit 19.12). Although optimization of capital structure was carried out, this was not the predominant method of wealth creation, nor was multiple arbitrage. Swicorp preferred its "buy and build" strategy, including regional or international expansion, and vertical or horizontal integration, improved operations, and enhanced corporate governance. In addition, Swicorp believed in building value through synergies with other portfolio companies, cooperation with strategic investors and through long-term partnerships with other firms. Swicorp prided itself on its distinctive and consistent investment strategy: proprietary deals requiring hands-on value creation with international standards of governance and operations. Potential acquisitions, often already local leaders in their market with high growth potential, were targeted for development into acquisition targets for global players (attractive through their strength or their potential to compete). Swicorp provided the financial resources and management reinforcement to unlock that growth potential of purchased firms, connected the acquired firm to its MENA network, raised debt, assisted with recruitment and talent retention, and worked to optimize the value chain.

Private equity firms in the Middle East had faced several challenges including scarcity of debt (even before the worldwide economic downturn) and inflated acquisitions prices since around 2005. In an attempt to fight the latter challenge, Swicorp largely avoided auctions. Limited leverage was employed in Swicorp deals. More than 40% of the money invested was internal or co-investors' money.

While Swicorp focused exclusively on the MENA region for acquisitions, it looked to Europe for possible exits. Swicorp believed its competitive advantage in MENA to be a thorough understanding of the cultures of both the GCC region and North Africa. In addition to many other nationalities, Swicorp employed among its staff a number of professionals of North African descent, fluent in both French and English, who had an innate understanding of the French–Arabic culture. Their understanding of the cultures of the people they were doing business with was both natural and profoundly deep. Few other firms could operate in North Africa west of Egypt; as one Swicorp professional remarked, "you can't [easily] do business in Tunisia, Algeria or Morocco without French language and culture" and Swicorp's "French connection" made it arguably the only player operating in the entire MENA region.

A major obstacle in the region was the imbalance between the supply and demand of capital. With limited mid-size deals, there weren't enough targets of that size in the GCC for the number of private equity firms operating there. As commented by a seasoned professional, with long experience of fundraising in the region: "The Gulf states have a limited capacity to absorb capital."[7] But while there was global interest in the region, there was low private equity penetration. This fact, coupled with favorable trends that included liberalization, privatization, family successions, and a growing internationally competitive talent pool, made the region an attractive place to do business.

Typically Swicorp restricted investment to no more than 25% of target commitments in a single country, or a single sector, providing diversification in both

---

7. Mounir Guen, founder of globally leading private equity placement agency MVision, quoted in *Private Equity International*, July/August 2003.

geography and industry. Deals were periodically reanalyzed as macroeconomic conditions changed and as appropriate deals were restructured.

The deep dive

An important aspect of Swicorp's corporate strategy was the concept of the "deep dive" in which one sector was analyzed right across the MENA region looking for gaps between MENA and Europe. When Swicorp analyzed flexible packaging they discovered one such gap. They bought the market leader in Tunisia, a small company with low margins that could be substantially improved through economies of scale, together with a packaging manufacturing facility in Europe. Swicorp shipped partially manufactured flexible packaging products from Tunisia to their plant in France where the manufacturing process was completed. The Tunisian plant was scaled up to meet the European demand; products completing manufacture in France allowed greatly enhanced margins. Reanalysis, in light of falling energy prices, revealed an ever improving bottom line. The final benefit of this scheme was that the combined flexible packaging manufacturer, having gained a not insubstantial market share, quickly became an acquisition target for its larger competitors in Europe.

The flexible packaging acquisition epitomized Swicorp's "model", one that included proximity of market, a diversified investor base, and diversification across the region. Proprietary deals were sourced by capitalizing on Swicorp's regional networks through their local offices and their multinational team. To vary from the model would always cause great concern to the investment committee of any private equity firm expecting difficulties in the implementation strategy post acquisition as well as risking to be perceived by investors as lacking focus.

Deal makeup

Co-investors figured most prominently in the Middle East. Because of the scarcity of debt, co-investors' funds were used in lieu of leverage, silent money that was brought in deal by deal—this was direct investment often provided by selected LPs, invited to co-invest in addition to their LP stake. Co-investors included institutional investors, high-net-worth individuals, and other funds. Their prime interest was in growing the company value and reinforcing Swicorp's essential buy-and-build value creation strategy.

Swicorp allocated considerable time to agreeing valuations with the seller—this was often the most protracted portion of an acquisition negotiation—as certain key concepts, such as EBITDA, were not well understood. Multiples, comparables, and discounted cash flow methods were all used to establish a range from which the final valuation could be negotiated. Target firms were gradually coming to understand these concepts in the MENA region.

DEAL SELECTION PROCESS

Once preliminary research had been commenced on a potential deal, research was carried out by the extensive back office in Tunis. Swicorp's private equity teams in the various branches had weekly conference calls to discuss their ongoing pipelines, with each team generating in advance a deal entry form so to ensure a well-informed and challenging discussion. Output from these discussions resulted in a short memo for a further peer review and for comments from the Head of Private Equity, Nabil Triki. Assuming a green light to continue, a detailed financial model was built and the actual negotiation and deal terms would be finalized. Finally, an investment memorandum, a comprehensive analysis of the target and a detailed description of the proposed deal structure, was produced for the benefit of detailed review and subsequent discussion by the Investment Committee.

The Investment Committee comprised five to six members and included Swicorp's Chairman, Kamel Lazaar, the Head of Private Equity, Nabil Triki, representatives from the fund's LPs and on occasion peer professionals not employed by Swicorp. Meetings were held on an ad hoc basis, usually by conference call, and it was unusual for there to be a formal presentation. Committee members were expected to have carefully studied the investment memoranda prepared for that meeting. Typically, the deal would be discussed for 15 to 45 minutes followed by a vote to determine whether to proceed with the deal.

STEP CARPET GROUP

In July 2008 Swicorp closed a deal with a Turkish company, Step Carpet Group, to acquire in stages a majority of each of Taftel, the manufacturing arm, and Step/Stepevi, the retailing arm. From a third-generation Istanbul-based family business dating from 1919, the Step Group was restructured in 1998 with the objective of redefining the traditional carpet industry in Turkey. Carpets targeted style-conscious middle and upper-middle class customers through contemporary designs, vibrant colors, and differentiated fabrics. By 2008, the Turkish carpet group had already established an international brand and held a significant share of the quality carpet and rug market, as a result of aggressive marketing and steady expansion, and had a strong reputation as a provider of quality carpets and associated accessories. With over 60 shops and "sales corners" located in department stores across Europe, the Middle East, and South Africa, both wholly owned and franchised, Step had achieved an impressive penetration within a short time for global market share in various carpet categories (see Exhibit 19.13). In addition, Step Group had a special projects division that designed and provided carpets for high-end residential complexes, hotels, yachts, offices, airport lounges, and quality stores.

Mass customization

Step's unique concept of "mass customization" was based upon its revolutionary robotic hand-tufting manufacturing technology that was linked to proprietary CAD/CAM systems. This technology, developed in house, permitted Step to achieve high precision in mass production with a significantly lower cost structure than its competitors. It permitted production runs ranging from one to infinity. Step's delivery time of 3–4 weeks was significantly lower than its competitors (hand-made designer carpets were typically delivered in 10–14 weeks). This enabled a much faster combined delivery, which tied up well with high-end furniture stores such as Natuzzi, Selfridges, and Roche Bobois, stores that would themselves normally require 3–4 weeks to deliver furniture. The customer, having selected complementary furniture, carpets, and accessories, could expect a single delivery of their new household.

Entering Turkey

The acquisition of Step Carpet Group represented Swicorp's first foray into the Turkish market. Meeran recalled that when he joined the company it seemed that each team leader had staked out a target country, but that no one was yet operating in Turkey. He started to build his contacts in Istanbul through an old contact from New York, now relocated to Turkey. It was through this friend that Meeran made contact with the Turkish investment banker acting as Step's sell-side adviser. The adviser was impressed by both Meeran and the Swicorp approach and endorsed the firm in discussions with Step. The main shareholder and founder as well as Chairman of the Board and General Manager of the Step Group, Mr. Cem Şengör, had been exploring ways of injecting capital into the group. Step was already speaking to a number of private equity firms when Meeran, representing Swicorp, was introduced by the adviser. Step Group comprised two companies that were each controlled by the Şengör family. The Group's ownership structure at the time of the transaction is shown in Exhibit 19.14.

Step's intention was for IS Venture Capital to cash out entirely, in accordance with IS's exit strategy, while the other shareholders' stakes were to be substantially reduced. Step wanted to set up an auction and sell to the highest bidder. After early stage negotiations Meeran convinced Step to go with Swicorp and the full auction was circumvented.

An attractive alliance

There were a number of reasons for the Step/Swicorp alliance to be attractive to both parties. Step wanted to move into the U.S. and Middle East markets and, although Swicorp had no office in Turkey, Step appreciated their network of branches and consequent strong presence across the MENA region. Swicorp's willingness to cross borders and the fact that it was supported by Step's sell-side adviser were also determining factors. For Swicorp, Meeran thought Step to be an attractive investment opportunity due to solid fundamentals, aggressive growth strategy, quality products, and clean books, the latter a consequence of IS Venture Capital's involvement. Traditionally, bookkeeping in Turkish firms, particularly as the vast majority were family companies, was more art than science; Step was in the first wave of companies moving, partly due to Turkey's gravitation towards the European Union and the accompanying regulatory requirements, to GAAP compliance. Step was not typical of Turkish firms at that time as it did not entertain black market sales and had an efficient reporting system. In particular, Swicorp liked Step's fast growth, strong local market position, successful export strategy, clear competitive advantages, brand name, retail network, and the sound management team.

The share acquisition deal was closed formally on July 21, 2008. The enterprise value of the Step Group was agreed at 8× the estimated 2008 EBITDA of Step and Taftel consolidated, of which equity comprised just over USD44mn.[8] The initial intention was to execute three ratcheted tranches with Swicorp acquiring 40% of each company in Tranche 1 and, altogether, could obtain up to 75% of each company. Performance ratchets were commonly employed in Swicorp deals. Meeran explained that the ratchet worked well to align the target owners' interests with Swicorp's. Details of the transaction structure are found in Exhibit 19.15. Within a few weeks of Tranche 1 of the transaction for Step (but not yet for Taftel), in the wake

---

8. All valuation figures and ownership percentages hereinafter are indicative approximations.

of the continuing worldwide economic downturn, Swicorp renegotiated the structure such that its stake would grow to 46% of each company. No additional capital was injected as the company was revalued—the entrance multiple was reduced from 8× to 6.3× of the estimated 2008 EBITDA and the value of equity adjusted accordingly. In return, the renegotiation eliminated the ratchet thresholds imposed upon Step. In fact, equity ratchets were offered to management based on annual earning thresholds. Although the Swicorp 46% equity was a minority position, it came with substantial blocking powers. As Meeran remarked, it is best to close in a bull market, then restructure in a bear market. Details of the renegotiated deal are found in Exhibit 19.16. Selected financial data and forecasts for the Step Group are found in Exhibit 19.17.

Buy and build in practice

The acquisition of Step represented a typical example of buy and build for Swicorp. Within the first 6 months Swicorp had helped Step to reduce cash burn by 20%, had introduced Step to a large retail chain in the Middle East, representing a significant increase in the volume of business through channel partners, and had assisted Step to increase production by 30% without increasing manpower.

Risks

Prior to entry, Swicorp's Investment Committee had been concerned about a number of risks, particularly keyman risk and the dependence upon the yarn supplier, Ipliksan. The Committee had reasoned, however, that with Step becoming a global brand the founder was less critical to the operation; in effect, any talented and dedicated executive could run the companies effectively. The concern regarding the concentration of supply from one yarn supplier was eased because Ipliksan itself was in good shape through sales of high-end yarns. Ipliksan had reduced costs by outsourcing much of its production to Croatia, a country with cheaper labor costs than Turkey; and, with Ipliksan retaining a large portion of Taftel's shares, its interests were more aligned with those of Step and Swicorp. Ipliksan, as a yarn manufacturer, was not dependent upon Taftel— it was the largest hand-knitting yarn manufacturer in Europe with $40,000\,\mathrm{m}^2$ of covered facilities and an annual output of 5,000 tonnes; Taftel's custom represented only a tiny proportion of Ipliksan's total sales.

One risk that was not given much weight at entry was currency risk, as the days of wild currency fluctuation were considered to be long gone. Unfortunately, this confident prediction was not borne out and the Turkish lira lost 30% of its value against the U.S. dollar in the fourth quarter of 2008. The decision to outsource production to Croatia for both domestic and international sales turned out to be quite detrimental.

Despite the global economic downturn in market demand Step was projected to achieve net sales of approximately USD30mn and 19% EBITDA for 2008, representing a year-on-year growth of 25% in net sales and 22% in EBITDA. Meeran pointed to Step's solid performance through aggressive sales promotion and significant cost reductions that had driven sales volume growth of 16% in the domestic market and 27% in the international market.

Swicorp's hope was to exit the Step Group in 2012, based upon 2011 financials, through either a trade sale or an IPO, on the basis of having taken the company from being a regional to an international player.

JORDAN AVIATION LLC

The next deal being considered was for an aviation leasing business in Jordan. The main added value considered was to use Swicorp's Saudi contacts to grow the business by sourcing new revenue streams.

Relationships in Jordan

Hoping to sell 20–25% of the company, the owners of Jordan Aviation LLC (JATE), Hazem Al Raekh and Captain Mohammed Al Khashman, came to Dubai to meet potential investors in August 2008. As a private investor and the second largest shareholder, Al Raekh decided to bring an adviser with him to the investor meetings. Meeran, through other business dealings in Jordan, knew Al Raekh's adviser and was able to initiate discussions directly and openly with him. These discussions concentrated on the purchase of Al Raekh's stake and the talks progressed well. As the discussions continued other shareholders learnt of the plan and they also expressed interest to take part in the sale transaction.

Meeran flew to Jordan and talked through a proposed term sheet for the purchase of a portion of each shareholder's stake. Over two long days, Meeran convinced the shareholders that Swicorp was a good fit with JATE and would be a reliable and useful partner. The deal structure was tentatively agreed late on the second day with a handshake, after running through the term sheet many times.

The deal

Al Raekh and Captain Al Khashman owned 91% of the company between them but were looking to purchase additional aircraft to allow expansion. One potential growth area they had studied was the increasing number of passengers, bound for Mecca, undertaking the Hajj pilgrimage—these passengers were fueling a demand for charter flights. Meeran had spent time with JATE's owners showing the potential valuations that could be achieved based on comparables from similar deals. He argued that Swicorp was ideally placed to offer significant business contacts to JATE through its Saudi connections; Swicorp also had excellent relations with JATE's banks in Jordan.

Jordan Aviation was incorporated in 1998 and commenced operations in the aviation leasing sector in October 2000. By the end of 2007 JATE's fleet consisted of eight aircraft and it had a workforce of over 300 employees involved in various business segments. In early September 2008, JATE added two new planes to its fleet assigning them to the wet-lease subsector (see Exhibit 19.18 for JATE financials).

Comparing JATE with other deals

It was difficult to find similar MENA companies that were comparable with JATE. Swicorp's analysts used comparables from other emerging markets, as well as from the U.S. and Europe, "normalized" to cater for differences in growth, margins, and returns.

Genesis Lease Ltd. was considered to be a similar deal—a global commercial aircraft leasing company, incorporated in Bermuda and headquartered in Ireland, the company acquired and leased commercial jets to passenger and cargo airlines around the world. Genesis went public on NYSE in December 2006 raising USD720mn in one of the largest IPOs ever for an aircraft-leasing company. It also issued USD810mn in floating rate notes backed by aircraft leases. The transactions helped

Genesis to pay for 41 large passenger aircraft, acquired from other leasing companies. Genesis' sales grew by 30% in 2006 to USD153mn.

The aviation leasing market

The aircraft-leasing sector underpinned commercial aviation and was the fastest growing sector in the aerospace industry. The most significant trend was the anticipated growth of the aircraft-leasing market. The total worldwide market in 2008 was worth USD129bn, generated through 5,000 leased aircraft worldwide, and with an anticipated market growth of approximately 6% per annum; leased aircraft numbers were expected to reach 7,200 by 2011. As of September 2008, over 30% of the global commercial aircraft fleet was leased, compared with just 5% in 1990 and 3% in 1980. It was thought that aircraft leasing was set to mushroom over the next decade as airlines scrambled to serve the fast-growing economies of the Middle East, Asia, Latin America, and Eastern Europe.

Subsectors served

JATE served a number of subsectors, namely passenger and cargo charters, dry and wet leases. Under a dry lease, aircraft-financing entities provide aircraft without insurance, crew, ground staff, supporting equipment, and maintenance. Wet leases involve the lease of an aircraft, complete crew, maintenance, insurance, fuel, and airport fees paid by hours operated. A wet lease is typically utilized during peak traffic seasons, annual heavy-maintenance checks, or to initiate new routes. A wet lease typically generates a net revenue of USD4,000 to USD6,000 per hour per plane. The charter areas covered were:

- *U.N. charters*—54% of JATE's revenues in 2006 were generated by contracts with the U.N. and two of JATE's aircraft were dedicated for this purpose. JATE had been the largest vendor for the U.N. for the past 4 years. These contracts were made on a monthly basis and had no long-term legally binding commitment. The U.N. charter business was considered to be a non-cyclical year-round business.

- *U.N. cargo*—the U.N. cargo charters subsector was similar to the U.N. charters segment with regard to getting contracts and revenue generation.

- *Air taxi*—this subsector was similar to a private on-demand jet service.

- *Program charters and tours*—program charters concern the operation of charter flights, similar to those operated by a scheduled airline. This subsector catered for tours to Mecca for the Hajj and Umrah seasons. The tours and air taxi services were booked on an ad hoc basis and, therefore, were difficult to forecast. JATE was in discussions with a third-party airline and planned to focus future aircraft utilization on Saudi Arabia by opening more routes to Mecca.

Structure of the proposed deal

A special purpose vehicle (SPV), Intaj JATE Invest Holding, was formed as a leveraged investment vehicle for the JATE transaction. Intaj put USD30mn for a 30% stake in the SPV and invited three investors from the Swicorp network to be co-investors. Consequently, family offices from North Africa and the Gulf invested around 20%. An additional sum of around 10% was provided by another PE firm (a non-fund based equity) and an individual investor made up the remaining amount of the planned 65%

Swicorp share of the investment. JATE's owners agreed to provide the remaining 35%. With USD100mn equity and an additional planned debt of nearly USD90mn also at the SPV level, this would be the biggest private equity deal in 2008 in the MENA region.

Al Raekh and Captain Al Khashman's direct ownership of JATE was to be reduced from 91% to around 42% in the original transaction in September 2008. The Swicorp controlling stake through its SPV was to be gained through two purchases:

- 12 million of JATE's 40 million existing shares from Al Raekh and Al Khashman for USD73mn
- 17 million new shares issued by the company for USD115mn.

Meeran turned his mind to reviewing the Swicorp deals completed to date. It looked like JATE, with its business based on U.N. charters and Hajj pilgrimage, should be safe in the downturn even if new business streams were slow to take off. More pressing issues were coming to the fore in Turkey where it was clear Step was starting to experience problems meeting its revenue targets. Meeran knew he would need to take action on Step and started to plan how he could safeguard Swicorp's investment and keep the Step management motivated and on-side. As he sat back looking out of the office at The World islands once more, he wondered what the main issues with Step should be in an upcoming meeting on the way forward. He also knew Swicorp would need to exit some deals as planned in order to build credibility with new investors once the pressure of the downturn had subsided. With the downturn, was the oil-rich MENA region really the best place to be?

APPENDIX

EXHIBIT 19.1

INTAJ FUND I—INVESTMENTS

Company	Initial investment date	Country	Industry	Intaj commitment (USDmn)	Ownership (%)
Al Arabia	Nov-06	Egypt	Textile	27	ca. 25
Altea Packaging	Dec-06	Tunisia	Packaging	30	ca. 80
Economic City	Apr-07	Saudi Arabia	Development project	20	ca. 5
Amlak	Jun-07	Saudi Arabia	Mortgage finance	16	ca. 40
Uniceramic Holdings	Oct-07	Qatar/Algeria	Ceramics/Tiles	35	ca. 90
Consumer/Retail	Feb-08	Confidential	Confidential	30	ca. 50
Petroser	Apr-08	Algeria	Speciality Retail	15	ca. 45
Saggaf	Pending	Saudi Arabia	Pharmacy Retail	35	ca. 70

EXHIBIT 19.2

INTAJ FUND PORTFOLIO

Geographic diversification (%)

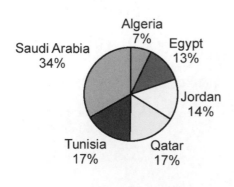

Sectorial diversification (%)

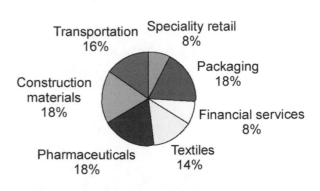

Algeria	USD15mn	Speciality manufacture and retail
Tunisia	USD35mn	Textile
Egypt	USD25mn	Textile
Jordan	USD30mn	Aviation
Saudi Arabia	USD71mn	Financial services/Pharmaceuticals
Qatar	USD35mn	Construction materials

EXHIBIT 19.3

INTAJ DEALS—EXAMPLES

	Uniceramic Holding	**Altea Packaging**
Investment vehicle	Intaj Capital Ltd.	Intaj Capital Ltd.
Investment date	2006	2006
Equity investment	USD35mn	USD30mn
Business description	Uniceramic is the first ceramic tile manufacturer in the Middle East. Swicorp acquired a majority stake to build the company into a leading player in the ceramic tiles and sanitary ware industries in the MENA region. Current projects include a new plant in the GCC and acquisitions in Algeria	Swicorp invested in partnership with Tuninvest with the objective to consolidate the packaging sector in North Africa and southern Europe
Investment rationale	The ceramic tiles and sanitary ware industries in MENA are expected to grow significantly, driven by real estate and consumer demand. The region currently imports nearly 70% of its ceramic tiles. Given ready access to low-cost energy, raw materials, and siting in the region, there is an opportunity to build a regional player	The sector is fragmented with several players in each country. Opportunity exists to consolidate the sector to create a leading pan-North Africa player in the sector to benefit from economies of scale and scope
Transaction type	Buy and build	Buy and build
Exit strategy	IPO planned by 2011	Trade sale or IPO planned by 2011

Source: Company documents.

EXHIBIT 19.4

REAL GDP GROWTH 1996–2007 (PERCENTAGE PER YEAR)

Country	1996–99	2000–03	2004	2005	2006	2007
MENA region (including Iraq)	n.a.	4.0	6.5	5.9	6.2	5.7
MENA (excluding Iraq)	3.6	4.6	5.9	5.9	6.3	5.7
By resource-based classification						
Resource-poor, labor-abundant	4.7	3.9	4.8	3.8	5.6	5.4
Djibouti	(0.7)	2.1	3.8	3.2	4.2	4.8
Egypt	5.2	3.8	4.2	4.6	6.9	7.1
Jordan	2.9	4.9	8.4	7.3	6.3	6.3
Lebanon	2.6	3.4	6.3	1.0	−5.5	1.0
Morocco	4.2	4.0	4.2	1.7	7.3	2.3
Tunisia	5.9	4.2	6.0	4.2	5.3	6.3
West Bank and Gaza	n.a.	(6.4)	6.2	6.0	(12)	n.a.
Resource-rich	3.2	4.8	6.2	6.6	6.5	5.8
Resource-rich, labor-abundant (including Iraq)	—	2.8	7.3	4.6	4.3	5.7
Resource-rich, labor-abundant (excluding Iraq)	3.8	5.0	4.9	4.6	4.3	5.7
Algeria	3.1	4.1	5.2	5.3	1.4	3.0
Iran	4.0	5.8	5.1	4.4	5.8	7.6
Iraq	NA	(16.6)	46.5	3.7	4.0	2.8
Syria	4.1	3.4	3.9	4.5	5.1	3.9
Yemen	5.5	4.0	2.6	3.8	3.9	3.1
Resource-rich, labor-importing	3.3	4.7	6.9	7.5	7.5	5.8
Bahrain	4.3	5.6	5.4	6.9	7.0	6.6
Kuwait	1.9	5.9	6.2	8.5	6.2	4.6
Libya	1.6	4.8	8.2	8.4	8.1	5.4
Oman	3.4	4.4	5.6	5.6	6.4	6.9
Qatar	11.8	7.1	11.4	11.0	12.1	14.2
Saudi Arabia	2.7	3.3	5.2	6.6	5.8	4.1
United Arab Emirates	5.2	7.1	9.7	8.5	9.4	7.7
Israel and Turkey						
Israel	n.a.	8.7	7.0	6.5	5.2	5.3
Turkey	n.a.	6.8	7.2	8.4	6.9	4.5
By geographic subregion						
Maghreb	3.2	4.2	5.8	5.1	5.0	3.8
Mashreq (excluding WBG, Iraq)	3.2	3.7	5.7	3.7	1.4	3.4
GCC	3.5	4.7	6.7	7.5	7.4	5.9
Other	4.6	4.8	4.6	4.5	6.2	7.2
By oil trade group						
Oil-exporting countries (excluding Iraq)	3.8	4.7	6.0	6.4	7.0	6.0
Oil-importing countries (excluding WBG)	3.7	4.0	5.6	2.8	4.0	3.4

Country	1996–99	2000–03	2004	2005	2006	2007
Comparator regions						
MENA (excluding Iraq)	3.6	4.6	5.9	5.9	6.3	5.7
All developing countries	4.0	4.5	7.3	6.6	6.9	7.4
East Asia and the Pacific	6.2	7.7	9.1	9.0	9.1	10.0
Europe and Central Asia	2.0	4.7	7.2	6.0	6.4	6.7
Latin America and the Caribbean	3.0	1.3	6.0	4.5	5.0	5.1
South Asia	5.7	5.1	8.0	8.1	8.2	8.4
Sub-Saharan Africa	3.4	3.7	5.2	5.5	5.2	6.1

Source: World Bank staff estimates up to 2006. From 2007 World Bank and authors' estimates.

Note:

—Due to data limitations, the West Bank and Gaza are not included in regional or subregional aggregates.

—In addition to the resource-based classifications, aggregates are presented for groups based on geography and trade. The Maghreb consists of Algeria, Libya, Morocco, and Tunisia.

—The Mashreq is comprised of Iraq, Jordan, Lebanon, the Arab Republic of Syria, and the West Bank and Gaza. "Other" consists of Djibouti, the Arab Republic of Egypt, the Islamic Republic of Iran, and Yemen.

—Net oil importers of the region include Djibouti, Jordan, Lebanon, Morocco, and Tunisia. All others are considered net exporters.

EXHIBIT 19.5

FDI AND POPULATION DATA FOR MENA

	1996–9	2000–4	2005	2006	2007
Nominal MENA GDP (USD billion)	658.1	838.9	1,225.8	1,421.4	1,593.4
Foreign direct investments MENA (USD billion) excluding Iraq	6.1	10.9	30.6	51.6	44.9

Population (million)

MENA population data	1990	2000	2005	2010	2020
MENA region total	250.2	311	342.3	375.8	444.9
MENA region age 15–64	134.2	184.5	213.9	241.8	291.2

Growth per year (%)

MENA population data	1990–2000	2000–05	2005–10	2010–20
MENA region total	2.2	1.9	1.9	1.7
MENA region age 15-64	3.2	3	2.5	1.9

Source: World Bank Economic Developments and Prospects Survey for MENA region 2007 and 2008

EXHIBIT 19.6

SELECTED DATA ON GDP, POPULATION, AND FOREIGN DIRECT INVESTMENT (FDI)

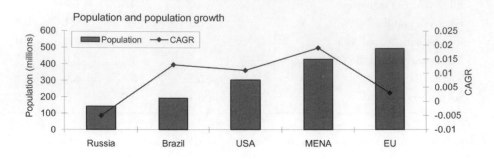

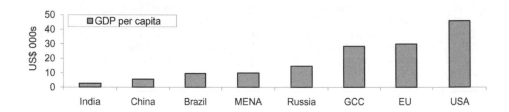

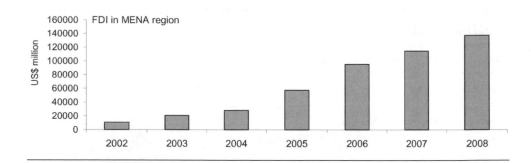

EXHIBIT 19.7

MENA PRIVATE EQUITY FUNDS COMPARISON 2004–2008 (USD MILLION)

	2004	2005	2006	2007	2008
MENA	270	3,980	4,300	7,000	2,800
U.S.		166,000	233,000	29,000	286,000
Global	127,000	259,000	362,000	449,000	425,000

Source: MENA data—empea; for 2008, authors' estimate; US and global data—Thomson Venture Economics/Carlyle Group presentations.

EXHIBIT 19.8

PRIVATE EQUITY INVESTMENTS IN THE MENA REGION

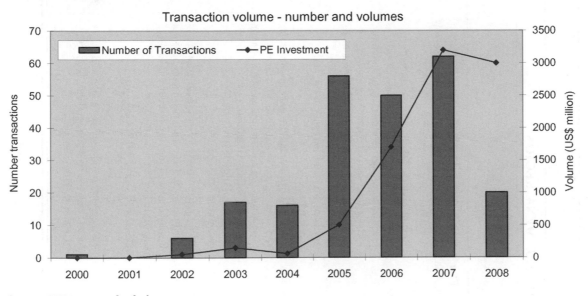

Source: GVCA, empea for deal size.

EXHIBIT 19.9

MAJOR PRIVATE EQUITY FIRMS IN THE MENA REGION

Firm	Location	Region covered	Focus	Capital in PE (across all funds)	Firm/Parent founded	PE fund activities began
Abraaj	Dubai	MENASA (Middle East, North Africa, South Asia)	Buyouts/buy and build/services such as private education providers/consumer sector/financial sector investments	$7.5bn	2002	2002
Investcorp (Gulf Growth Fund)	Bahrain (regional base)	U.S. and Europe, one fund in MENA	Buyout opportunities/corporate divestitures of non-core assets/family business divestures/privatizations/joint ventures in partnership with regional corporations. Sectors: downstream hydrocarbons and intermediate and derivative industries; medium-size infrastructure and manufacturing; and service sector	$1bn	1982	2007 (this fund)
Dubai International Capital	Dubai	Global—Gulf, Europe, U.S., Asia, and Latin America	Regional buyouts, listed equity investments, and seed capital investments for startup businesses. Not focused on particular sector—enterprise values USD500mn to USD2.5bn/industry leader/stable cash generation		2004	2004
Global Investment House	Kuwait	GCC and MENASA regions including Turkey, India, and China	Broad range of sectors with high growth attributable to increasing per capita income, favorable demographics and consolidation opportunities	$3bn	1998	1998
Amwal Al Khaleej	Saudi Arabia	Saudi, Egypt, U.A.E.	Consumer sector, MENA regional bias	ca. $650mn	2004	2004
Millennium Private Equity	Dubai	MENA/India	Energy sector and telecom media and technology in emerging markets. Tech-VC in $5mn to $10mn range	$350mn (to date)	2005	2005

EXHIBIT 19.10

FOCUS IN THE REGION—MAJOR FIRMS AND THEIR REGIONAL PRESENCE

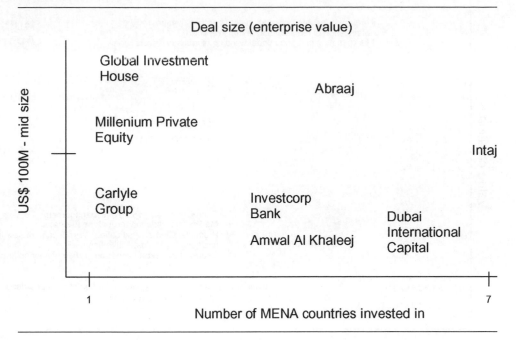

EXHIBIT 19.11

A SAMPLE OF MENA SWFS 2008

Country	Sovereign wealth fund	Controlled sum (USD billion)	Year established
U.A.E.	Abu Dhabi Investment Authority (Adia)	875	1976
Saudi Arabia	Sama Foreign Holdings	365	1952
Kuwait	Kuwait Investment Authority	265	1982
Qatar	Qatar Investment Authority	60	2003
U.A.E.	Emirates Investment Authority	20	2007
Bahrain	Mumtalakat Holding Company	14	2006
Iran	Oil Stabilisation Fund	13	1999
U.A.E.	Mubadala Development Company	10	2002

Source: "Hungry Funds Lose Their Appetite", *Emirates Business 24-7*, October 11, 2008, Ryan Harrison.

EXHIBIT 19.12

SWICORP STRATEGY

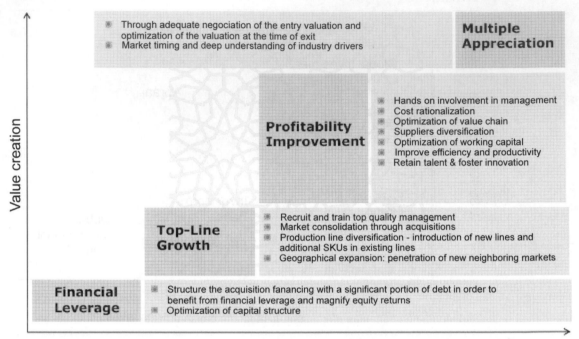

Source: Company documents.

EXHIBIT 19.13

GLOBAL MARKET SHARE OF STEP (MAIN CARPET PRODUCT CATEGORIES)

Product main category	Price range for a standard size carpet[1] (USD)	Share in carpet sales[2] 2006 (%)	Share in carpet sales[2] 2007 (%)	Carpet sales[2] 2008 (11 months)
Category Special	—	9.0	8.6	13.0
Category A	>1,915	5.6	10.8	9.7
Category B	915–1,915	58.7	61.8	55.3
Category C	438–914	4.5	4.9	7.2
Category D	<438	19.3	13.0	6.8
Other	—	2.6	0.9	8.0

Note: 1. Standard size is $170 \, \text{cm} \times 240 \, \text{cm}$.
2. Share in carpet sales is value based.

EXHIBIT 19.14

OWNERSHIP STRUCTURE AT STEP GROUP

Step (retail)	Taftel (manufacture)
Şengör family: 67%	Şengör family: 50%
IS Venture Capital: 33%	Ipliksan: 50%

Note: IS Venture Capital was the VC/PE arm of IS Bank, the largest bank in Turkey. Ipliksan was a Turkish yarn manufacturer that supplied Taftel with the majority of its yarn.

EXHIBIT 19.15

ORIGINAL SHAREHOLDING STRUCTURE OF STEP ACQUISITION

Percentage stake	Prior to transaction	Post Tranche 1	Post Tranche 2	Post Tranche 3[1]
Year	2008	2008	2009	2010
Step				
IS Venture Capital	33.3	0	0	0
Cem Şengör	66.7	60	40	25
Intaj Capital Ltd.	0	40	60	75
Taftel				
Ipliksan	50	30	20	12.5
Cem Şengör	50	30	20	12.5
Intaj Capital Ltd.	0	40	60	75

Note: 1. Tranche 3 required Swicorp to purchase a further 15% stake in Step if the company achieved an EBITDA target; if the target was not achieved Swicorp had the option to purchase the additional 15% stake. A downside protection mechanism was stipulated whereby the sellers would be obliged to give away equity to Intaj in 2009. If the threshold for the combined EBITDA of Step and Taftel was not achieved the equity ratchet schedule would be:

Realized EBITDA below targets by (%)	0–6.99	7–9.99	10–14.99	15–19.99	>20
Additional Equity to Intaj (%)	0.0	2.0	4.5	7.5	10.0

EXHIBIT 19.16

STEP SHAREHOLDING STRUCTURE FOLLOWING RENEGOTIATION

Stake (%) Year	Initial 2008	Post Tranche 1 2008	Post Tranche 2 2009
Step			
IS Venture Capital	33.3	0	0
Cem Şengör	66.7	60	54
Intaj Capital Ltd.	0	40	46
Taftel			
Ipliksan	50	50	26.1
Cem Şengör	50	50	27.9
Intaj Capital Ltd.	0	0	46

Note: Taftel was converted from a limited liability company to a joint stock company on December 28, 2006. Under Turkish law its shares could not be transferred for a period of 2 years following conversion. Consequently, Tranche 1 of Taftel occurred after the transaction structure was renegotiated.

EXHIBIT 19.17

STEP GROUP SELECTED FINANCIAL DATA IN EARLY 2008 (ACTUAL AND FORECAST)

Step Group: Consolidated Balance Sheet

USD (million)	2006A	2007A	2008E	2009E	2010E	2011E
Current assets	8.3	13.2	18.9	22.5	26.5	32.2
Cash and cash equivalents	0.1	0.3	2.8	3.3	3.9	4.5
Excess cash	0.1	0.6				2.3
Trade receivables (net)	3.1	4.2	5.9	7.1	8.4	9.5
Inventories (net)	3.7	6.0	7.7	9.3	11.0	12.4
Other	1.3	2.1	2.5	2.8	3.2	3.5
Non-current assets	4.3	7.8	7.7	7.7	7.5	6.8
Tangible fixed assets	2.2	4.8	4.7	4.7	4.5	3.8
Intangible	1.6	2.6	2.6	2.6	2.6	2.6
Other	0.5	0.4	0.4	0.4	0.4	0.4
Total assets	**12.6**	**21.0**	**26.6**	**30.2**	**34.0**	**39.0**

Current liabilities	5.9	8.5	9.9	9.9	9.2	7.9
Trade payables (net)	3.0	3.4	2.6	3.1	3.7	4.2
Short-term debt	2.8	3.4	5.9	5.4	4.1	2.2
Other	0.1	1.7	1.4	1.4	1.4	1.5
Non-current liabilities	2.6	4.6	3.3	3.3	3.3	3.3
Long-term debt	2.0	4.5	3.3	3.3	3.3	.3
Other	0.6	0.1				
Equity	4.1	7.9	13.4	17.0	21.5	27.8
Total liabilities and equity	**12.6**	**21.0**	**26.6**	**30.2**	**34.0**	**39.0**

Step Group: Consolidated Profit and Loss, selected data

USD (million)		2006A	2007A	2008E	2009E	2010E	2011E
Sales		14.3	24.4	30.6	36.3	43.0	48.6
Gross profit		9.2	15.7	18.7	22.4	26.6	30.2
EBITDA		0.7	5.5	6.7	8.6	10.5	13.2
Net income		−0.9	1.8	2.0	3.3	4.2	6.0
g domestic =	16%		Exit Assumptions:		March 2012		
g international =	27%				7×2011 EBITDA		

Step Group: Consolidated CAGR/2007

%	2008E	2009E	2010E	2011E
Sales	24.0	22.0	21.0	19.0
Gross profit	19.0	19.0	19.0	18.0
EBITDA	21.0	25.0	24.0	24.0
EBIT	20.0	26.0	24.0	25.0
Net income	12.0	35.0	33.0	35.0

Step Group: Consolidated P&L margins

%	2007	2008E	2009E	2010E	2011E
Gross profit	64.4	61.6	61.8	61.9	62.0
EBITDA	22.7	22.1	23.8	24.4	27.1
EBIT	17.2	16.7	18.2	18.8	21.3
Net income	7.4	6.7	9.0	9.8	12.3

Note: 1. The underlying assumption of the business plan is that Taftel's gross margin remains relatively stable at 28% (due to significant increase in capacity in 2007, implementation of proper cost analysis structure, and execution of supply agreement between Step and Taftel).

2. Gross margin depends upon sales channel mix. Exports were expected to grow faster than other channels and since its gross margin was 37% it was anticipated that this growth would pull down the combined gross margin from 54% in 2007 to 50.5% in 2011. Consolidated gross margin was also anticipated to fall, for the same reason, from 64.4% in 2007 to 62% in 2011.

3. Conversely, the EBITDA margin was anticipated to grow due to the relatively lower profitability of stores (higher operating expenses in stores accounted for 40–60% of store sales). The EBITDA margin was anticipated to rise from 23% in 2007 to 27% in 2011.

EXHIBIT 19.18

JATE FINANCIALS—ACTUAL AND FEASIBLE AT TIME OF ORIGINAL DEAL (USD MILLION)

	2005A	2006A	2007A	2008F	2009F	2010F	2011F	2012F
Aggregate revenues	67.24	83.78	72.91	90.38	205.51	259.8	322.08	353.26
Net income	22.35	21.86	23.42	27.66	69.61	94.32	121.37	120.61
Total assets	96.18	125.24	109.43	194.84	249.42	299.57	351.3	416.29
Total liabilities	16.8	42.85	42.26	39	63.43	72.62	83.81	88.5
Common stock	56.38	56.38	56.38	86.38	86.38	86.38	86.38	86.38
Shareholders' loan	—	—	—	31	26.35	20.15	—	—
Total equity	79.39	82.41	67.17	155.83	185.99	226.95	267.49	327.79
Number of aircraft			8					29

Note: Share capital raised from USD56mn in 2007 to USD86mn in 2008. Selling shareholders re-injected USD31mn back into the company as a shareholder loan in 2008 from USD35mn received. Dividend payout during peiod 2009 to 2012 estimated at USD203mn, based on 50% payout policy, USD69mn of which was atributed to JATE Intaj.

20

Mekong Capital: The importance of corporate culture in emerging market private equity

As Chris Freund, Managing Director and Founder of Mekong Capital ("Mekong"), parked his motorcycle at his office building in downtown Ho Chi Minh City, he was thinking about the report he was eagerly waiting for from his Director of Investments, Dr. Thomas Lanyi. It was early February 2010 and his team was finishing the 2009 annual results for all of Mekong's portfolio companies.

The year 2009 had been a busy one for Mekong, a Vietnamese private equity fund manager founded by Chris in 2001. After raising three funds over the past 8 years, Mekong Capital was ramping up the launch of its fourth fund, Mekong Enterprise Fund III, this time seeking USD150mn. If successful, this would result in Mekong virtually doubling its funds under management, and continuing the firm's impressive growth story. Despite the challenging economic climate, Mekong had received growing interest during fundraising but had not yet closed the fund. Chris knew that meeting the aggressive 2009 net profit targets was critical to closing the fund in 2010.

However, the net profit targets were also important to Chris for internal reasons. In November 2007, Chris had decided to undertake a radical overhaul of Mekong's internal working structure and culture. At that point in time, Mekong's performance had been below expectations. The Mekong team had spent a lot of time improving its investment strategy and was certainly building a strong brand name in the market, but Chris was frustrated by the internal dynamics of his team:

> "We could see that our IRRs were much lower than what we really wanted. They were good, but not great. And when we looked internally, we saw so much that wasn't working in Mekong Capital. Although we were investing a lot of time and effort to help companies, we weren't effective at causing the companies to deliver the returns expected by our

The case was co-authored with Richard Turner and Adolfo Vinatea (LBS MBA 2010).

shareholders. Instead, our staff were often making explanations for why a particular company is too difficult to deal with, why the market environment is no good or they don't have the resources or information they needed internally. One of the things that is cultural in Vietnam is a tendency to be indirect in communication. And that existed in our company. There was not enough accountability or direct communication. I also had some doubts about my leadership style—even though I had been living in Vietnam for more than 9 years, I wasn't sure if I could lead local Vietnamese people as effectively as I needed to."

With the help of a corporate business consultant, Chris launched an ambitious corporate transformation program in November 2007, which aimed to energize the working culture of Mekong with a focus on individual accountability and direct communication. Chris knew that the transformation would involve the loss of some staff, but he was stunned when his two most senior investment managers handed in their resignations within weeks of the launch of the transformation process in late 2007. Despite further staff losses in 2008 and 2009, the monthly performance data in 2009 indicated that Mekong portfolio companies had improved remarkably throughout the year. Chris expected that the 2009 year-end report would provide quantitative proof that Mekong's new systems and culture were working successfully.

FOUNDING MEKONG CAPITAL

Mekong was founded in 2001 by Chris Freund, a U.S.-born expatriate with considerable investment experience in Vietnam and South-East Asia. In 1995 Chris joined Templeton Asset Management (the emerging markets arm of the Franklin/Templeton Group) and became its first full-time employee in Vietnam (Exhibit 20.1 contains bios for the main employees of Mekong). Chris immediately fell in love with the Vietnamese food, the pervasive energy and optimism of the Vietnamese, as well as the experience of being a pioneer in a newly emerging economy. After 3 years in Ho Chi Minh City (formerly Saigon), Chris moved to Templeton's Singapore office in 1998, when Templeton closed its Vietnam office in the midst of the Asian financial crisis. In Singapore, he covered the technology sector in emerging markets, focusing on Taiwan, Israel, and Korea. Although Chris enjoyed Singapore, he hoped to return to Vietnam at some point to establish his own investment management business.

Meanwhile, in 1999 a World Bank program named the Mekong Private Sector Development Facility (MPDF)[1] was performing a feasibility study on the prospects for a small and medium enterprise (SME) fund in the Mekong region, and with the support of the Asian Development Bank (ADB), decided to go ahead with the idea. So, when the General Manager of the MPDF, Mario Fischel, contacted Chris to ask for feedback on the idea of launching a fund to invest in private companies in the Mekong region, Chris jumped at the opportunity.

Chris was thrilled and, together with the MPDF and the ADB, immediately started work on launching the fund. After much hard work, Mekong Capital Ltd. was incorporated in the Cayman Islands in March 2001 and opened a representative office in

1. The Mekong Private Sector Development Facility was a subsidiary of the International Finance Corporation (an arm of the World Bank) which promoted small and medium enterprise development at the macro, meso and micro levels of the economies in Vietnam, Cambodia. and Laos PDR. Donor support came from the Asian Development Bank and 10 OECD countries.

Ho Chi Minh City shortly thereafter. Chris remembers walking into the office on day one thinking: "I have established the company, found a location, and now all I need are some skilled and motivated staff." Chris wasn't aware at the time how challenging this would be. How would he go about finding these people? The professional recruitment industry in Vietnam was undeveloped at the time, and Chris couldn't find any people in Vietnam who fit the typical profile of mid-level or senior-level private equity professionals in other countries—such as people who had already built careers at successful private equity firms, top-tier strategy consulting firms, or investment banks. He would have to advertise in the local newspapers. And what sort of people to hire? Should they be MBAs? People with local political connections? People with a finance or auditing background? How important is it to recruit some senior figures, or "gray-hairs", to help with the fund's public image in Vietnam? Should he recruit from overseas? These were issues that Chris would wrestle with in the years ahead.[2]

With the help of a small team hired through newspaper advertisements, Mekong closed the Mekong Enterprise Fund I (MEF I) in April 2002 with USD18.5mn of commitments (Exhibit 20.2 lists the investors in MEF I). MEF I had an investment mandate to take minority equity stakes in SMEs, with an intended investment split of 65% in Vietnam and 35% in surrounding developing countries (Laos and Cambodia). MEF I was the first Vietnam-focused fund to be launched after the Asian financial crisis of 1997/1998.

VIETNAM AND THE PRIVATE EQUITY INDUSTRY

The now Socialist Republic of Vietnam has undergone intense political and economic transformations over the past 60 years. Vietnam declared independence from the French after the Second World War, but France continued to rule until the 1954 defeat by Communist forces under Ho Chi Minh. Following the Geneva Accords of 1954, Vietnam was divided into the Communist North and anti-Communist South. U.S. economic and military aid to South Vietnam grew through the 1960s in an attempt to bolster the West-friendly government, but U.S. armed forces were withdrawn following a horrific war and the subsequent ceasefire agreement in 1973. Two years later, North Vietnamese forces overran the South, reuniting the country under Communist rule which has continued until the present time.[3] In 1986, the Communist Party of Vietnamdecided to change its economic policy and begin reforms of the private sector similar to those in China. Since then, Vietnam has enjoyed substantial economic growth and a relatively stable political environment.

Vietnam is a densely populated country, with approximately 90 million inhabitants of a median age of only 26 and 29 years for males and females, respectively. The young population, together with historical ties to the U.S. and Europe, has created a fertile base of eager and entrepreneurial-minded youth who have been at the forefront of Vietnam's recent economic growth.

Vietnam's GDP growth and other macroeconomic data over the period 2007–2010 can be seen in Exhibit 20.3. Of note is the fact that its GDP growth rate was consistently

2. In 2001, Chris was also a non-executive co-founder, along with his high-school friend, Jonah Levey, of a Vietnam-focused recruitment services company called Navigos Group, which launched the website *vietnamworks.com* After a slow start, Navigos eventually became the largest recruitment service company in Vietnam.

3. Excerpt from *CIA World Fact Book* (*https://www.cia.gov/library/publications/the-world-factbook/geos/vm.html*).

higher than its ASEAN peers Indonesia, Thailand, the Philippines, and Malaysia over this period.[4] Many commentators and investors attribute this strong growth to the decision by the government, in the mid-1980s, to shift economic policy towards liberalization and international trade. The landmark of this process was the acceptance to accede to the World Trade Organization (WTO) in January 2007. In parallel, Vietnam's export-driven economy has modernized and diversified away from traditional industries such as agricultural exports and crude oil. Vietnam's main exports are crude oil, garments, footwear, rice, tea, coffee, rubber, consumer electronics, and marine products. The country's major trade partners are the U.S., Germany, South Korea, Japan, China, Singapore, Hong Kong, and Taiwan.[5] The world economic crisis of 2008/2009 affected Vietnam's economy, with GDP growth slowing in 2009 to 4.6%, well below the average of the previous decade and not enough to absorb the over one million Vietnamese entering the workforce each year.

Vietnam has a nascent and growing private equity industry. During the early 1990s, foreign investors were attracted to Vietnam by its strong growth potential and promises of economic reform, in addition to the general industry-wide investment interest in the growing Asian economies. However, the Asian economic crisis in 1997 scared away the vast majority of international investors and forced most of the early private equity players out of business. At the time of the launch of the MEF I fund, the only other locally based private equity investor was Dragon Capital's Vietnam Enterprise Investments Ltd. Founded in 1995, initially with USD20mn, and listed on the Irish Stock Exchange, the fund focused on public equities as well as unlisted investments.

MEF I AND THE INITIAL INVESTMENT PHILOSOPHY

MEF I, launched in 2002, is a commercial fund and as such aims to provide a net IRR above 20% to its limited partners (LPs). Yet, the fund also takes into consideration certain developmental objectives from its Development Finance Institution (DFI) investors such as providing capital to underfunded companies, helping develop the Vietnamese private sector, and creating employment.

Although MEF I had a broad investment mandate to take minority equity positions in SMEs, Chris formulated some investment ideas which he wanted to explore. He was initially attracted to manufacturing companies, particularly companies with an export focus, based on the success of Taiwan:

> "Vietnam appeared at that stage to be the next Taiwan. Everyone knew how successful Taiwan had been in the manufacturing sector, and how much wealth this created for the successful firms and investors. Vietnam had many of the same characteristics of Taiwan 30-40 years earlier, particularly its low cost, but relatively skilled workforce which could be counted on for quality, reliability, and strong entrepreneurial tendencies.However, Vietnam was a lot earlier in its development path, and therefore presented some great investment opportunities. When we

---

4. The Association of South East Asian Nations (ASEAN) is a geopolitical and economic organization of 10 countries located in South East Asia, which was formed on August 8, 1967 by Malaysia, the Philippines, Singapore, and Thailand. Since then, membership has expanded to include Brunei, Burma (Myanmar), Cambodia, Laos, and Vietnam. Its aims include the acceleration of economic growth, social progress, cultural development among its members, the protection of the peace and stability of the region, and to provide opportunities for member countries to discuss differences peacefully.

5. ASEAN, *Export in Vietnam, http://aseancooperation.com/export-import-in-vietnam/291/*

investigated this further in the 2001–2004 time frame, we found the private companies making the most money in Vietnam were indeed in manufacturing and export. So, we decided to focus more on those areas. Importantly, these companies would also have a positive development impact due to the large blue-collar workforce and the ability to have a positive impact on the community."

Concurrently, Mekong targeted companies where there was significant opportunity for operational improvement. In the following years, Mekong went on to establish a process improvement team, which included a number of operations and manufacturing experts, whose role was to create and apply lean manufacturing and other operational benefits to portfolio companies. A summary of the MEF I portfolio and performance as at December 31, 2009 can be found in Exhibit 20.4.

MEF I went on to make 10 investments (all in Vietnam) between March 2003 and December 2005.

MEF I CASE STUDY: AA CORPORATION

One of the first two investments of MEF I, AA Corporation (AA), was a typical early deal focused on the manufacturing and export sector. Formerly known as AA Construcion Architecture Co., Mekong invested in 2003 a total of USD1.7mn for a 24.3% interest in the company.

AA is a leading furniture and interior contracting company, based in Ho Chi Minh City. The company was founded in 1993 by Mr. Nguyen Quoc Khanh, a prominent figure in the local business community and widely considered as the "social mayor" of Vietnam's capital. Mr. Khanh successfully built and expanded the business initially focusing on the interior design of large hotels and office buildings. Over time, AA developed three business lines:

- *Interior construction (39% share of 2001 revenue)*—leading interior design contractor for large international standard hotel and building projects in Vietnam, whose customers included Intercontinental, Park Hyatt, Sofitel, Sheraton, and Novotel.

- *Furniture retail (38% of 2001 revenue)*—leader in the design, manufacturing, and retailing of high-quality indoor furniture for the domestic furniture market (as of February 2010, AA had five retail outlets in HCMC and one in each of Hanoi and Danang).

- *Furniture export (23% of 2001 revenue)*—manufacturing and export of high-quality indoor furniture. Initially, AA mostly exported furniture to Japan but with increasing focus on Europe and the U.S.

The furniture is manufactured at its 12.4 ha site in the Duc Hoa District of the Long An Province, a 1-hour drive from downtown Ho Chi Minh City.

Mekong invested in AA with two objectives: first, to grow the business further by boosting furniture export, based on its strong brand name and significant expertise; and, second, Mekong believed that operations consulting would improve efficiencies across all three business lines.

After a promising first 12 months of ownership, the AA investment started to show signs of trouble. By 2006, it was clear that significant changes needed to be made to AA: revenue in 2006 had dropped 20% from 2005, leading AA to a lower net profit in 2006 than it had in 2003 when Mekong first invested. Exhibit 20.5 contains summary financial information for AA.

Chris realized that AA faced a number of challenges: the lack of good financial systems and management, the need to write down old and expired inventory, obvious gaps in management capability, and the loss of some key customers. Mekong identified and proposed an American expat, Chad Ovel, for the role of MD of the export division. Chad was a great choice, having lived in Vietnam for over 10 years, and successfully grown a similar export business from USD20mn in sales and 70 employees to over USD150mn and 6,000, respectively. Chad joined AA in November 2006, with a clear understanding that he would have the opportunity to progress to CEO once he demonstrated his ability to lead the manufacturing division (see Chad's bio in Exhibit 20.1). According to Chad: "When Chris hired me he made it clear this was a turnaround story. When I asked where does AA sit in your portfolio, he said last. Tenth out of 10."

After three years of very hard work, Chad had turned around the export division and had made sweeping changes to the factory operations—including the reduction of the factory headcount from 2,000 to 1,200 while increasing total output due to improvements in productivity. Along the way AA had to incur USD2mn of inventory writedown, substantially affecting 2007's net profit performance. Mekong supported Chad and AA throughout the process; however, Mekong did rotate through three different deal partners for AA during that period. In late 2009, the shareholders agreed that the founder, Mr. Khanh, would hold the office of Executive Chairman and Chad would be promoted to CEO of the company. Although profitability is improving, the Mekong holding period (now over 7 years) means that a high IRR is going to be very difficult to obtain.

By the time the final investment of MEF I was made (December 2005), it was becoming clear, through the AA experience and other investments in the MEF I portfolio, that there were considerable challenges when scaling a manufacturing business, as the capacity of the plant limited the business's ability to grow. Furthermore, dealing with a founder who lacked the experience of working for an international company was more difficult in contrast to the younger entrepreneurial founders of some of Mekong's more recent investments, who tended to have experience working at multinational companies or outside Vietnam. Chris made a mental note that changes in the investment philosophy and approach of Mekong were required.

MEF II AND A NEW INVESTMENT PHILOSOPHY

At the end of the MEF I investment period, Mekong launched the USD50mn Mekong Enterprise Fund II (MEF II) in June 2006 as a successor fund to MEF I, with a similar mandate to invest in the minority equity positions of SMEs, but with an updated strategy to reflect key lessons learned from MEF I. In addition to the new committed capital, Mekong was able to expand its investor base. While some original DFIs from the MEF I investor base were present, half of the new fund was provided by American family offices and private institutional investors. The shift in the investor base was welcomed and seen as indicative of Mekong's positioning and maturity, as well as a reflection of an international appetite for investing in private equity in South East Asia.

In connection with the launch of this fund, Mekong opened its second office in Hanoi and scaled up its overall team to 27 people. The Hanoi office was led by Tran Thi Thu Hong, who was Mekong's most accomplished deal partner based on the performance of the companies for which she was accountable.

Investor interest in Vietnam was based largely on its high economic growth, which was being driven by the rising incomes of a young and rapidly growing middle class, rapid growth in domestic consumption from a low base of per capita consumption, a stable pro-reform government, and high inflow of foreign direct investment. Opportunities had expanded well beyond exporting, due to a surge in domestic purchasing power, which has largely been fueled by skyrocketing property values and has caused home-grown branding, retail, and consumer product businesses to crop up in response.

Chris was fully convinced that Vietnam was exhibiting many characteristics similar to China, albeit at an earlier stage. Structurally, they are similar economies with steadily increasing disposable income and consumption levels.

In terms of deal sourcing, by 2008 Mekong introduced a top–down investment strategy in order to predict which would be the future high-growth sectors in Vietnam, based on examples from China and other regional countries such as Indonesia and Thailand. The idea was to narrow in on sectors that have the proven ability to scale up and generate wealth. Accordingly, MEF II involved a fundamental shift in investment policy away from manufacturing and export towards internal demand or consumer-facing targets. The approach is summarized in the following steps:

- Research high growth sectors in China and analyze which corresponding sectors in Vietnam would be likely to follow the same growth path
- Identify the top performers in these chosen sectors, so as to focus investment on the top companies of each segment
- Select preferred companies based on key criteria including which company in each sector has been developing the strongest management and leadership, and is most likely to continue doing so
- Meet with the short-listed companies.

Given that Mekong had decided to pursue the market leaders in each segment, the need for institutional private investment at a realistic price was not an easy sell. To counteract these difficulties, Mekong implemented an innovative and highly proactive process called "enrollment' for engaging potential targets. The enrolment process involved interacting with corporate senior leaders in ways in which they were touched, moved, and inspired by new possibilities that were created in the meeting. This was important when Mekong approached companies that were not otherwise looking for investors. Thomas Lanyi, current Director of Investments (see his bio in Exhibit 20.1) emphasized the importance of being "unstoppable" in the pipeline process:

> "A company that does not want to see you is very likely to also not want to see others. If you're pursuing a bottom–up approach the logical response is to say 'we'll stay in touch' and move on to the next guy. Our approach is different; we select our targets carefully and pursue them vigorously. If I have to sleep in front of the factory gates to get a meeting I'll do that. That's sometimes really challenging. It means people have to go to the target's offices and look into whatever ways to set up a meeting and get a foot in the door."

After establishing contact, the Mekong deal partners urge the companies to think of long-term (5-year) objectives and possibilities. Mekong inspires them to create their own vision, which includes an IPO or an exit event and a clear value creation target which is a multiple of the valuation at which Mekong would invest. These long-term targets should be ambitious, but feasible, through a dedicated long-term growth plan. While this may sound obvious to Western investors, many of Vietnam's most successful emerging companies operate on a year-to-year basis and do not have a robust strategy or long-term value creation plan. Lastly, the deal partners present the value that Mekong Capital will bring to the table in the pursuit of the new vision and objectives. This process of focus, hard work, and ambitious planning has allowed Mekong to leverage into minority investment opportunities in leading companies which were originally not necessarily looking for investment partners. A summary of the MEF II portfolio and performance as at December 31, 2009 can be found in Exhibit 20.6.

By year-end 2009, MEF II had made eight investments.

MEF II CASE STUDY: INTERNATIONAL CONSUMER PRODUCTS

The first investment of MEF II, International Consumer Products (ICP), was representative of the shift in investment strategy away from manufacturing and towards domestic consumer-driven targets.

ICP was co-founded by Phan Quoc Cong in Ho Chi Minh City in Septmber 2001 with a USD0.2mn initial cash investment split between him and a local partner (see Cong's bio in Exhibit 20.1). Having previously been a manager at Nestle and Smithkline Beecham in Vietnam, Cong had extensive consumer products marketing experience and identified a dynamic, yet challenging market opportunity to establish a local company that could compete against "gray market" products in the fast-moving consumer goods (FMCG) sector. Cong represented the type of co-owner Mekong wanted to work with—young, educated, entrepreneurial, and open to applying the latest business thinking and management methods to his business.

ICP manufactures and markets a wide range of household and personal care, food, and beverage products. Within a few years, the company developed some of Vietnam's most reputed brands such as Veggy (vegetable-washing concentrate liquid), Ocleen (oven, kitchen, and floor cleaners), X-Men (personal care products for men), Q'Girl and L'Ovité (cosmetics and personal care range for teen girls and women).

Cong rooted ICP's success in four key factors: product innovation, consumer communication, low-cost operations, and product availability. ICP's first large success came in 2004 with the launch of its X-Men line of personal care products for men. The brand quickly became a market leader, fighting for market share among industry giants such as P&G and Unilever. The growth was supported by a production strategy that combined both in-house manufacturing (most of their high-volume products) and outsourcing (low-volume products). The company also draws strength from a proprietary nationwide distribution system, directly reaching mom and pop stores as well as supermarkets and hypermarkets nationwide. This direct distribution system allows ICP to bypass intermediaries, while at the same time transfer financing risk to third-party financiers found locally across Vietnam (essentially, the financiers assume the working capital requirements of the distribution and the credit risk of the end customers). See Exhibit 20.7 for further information. Hence, ICP created an innovative, cash flow–positive, low-risk business model in the high-growth consumer product sector.

In 2005 ICP was interested in a partner in order to help fund its expansion into new product lines (Q'Girl and L'Ovité). At this time, Mekong approached ICP, as did other investors. Cong was impressed by Mekong's prompt approach, clear vision for ICP, and hands-on operational experience. He became convinced in Mekong's ability to help ICP execute its growth objectives. In November 2006 MEF II invested USD6.25mn for a 26.9% stake in ICP, by buying shares from the two existing shareholders. In its base case, Mekong calculated an upper twenties IRR on the back of an IPO listing prospect in 3 years' time.

ICP closed the year 2006 with sales of VND185bn.[6] After the investment by MEF II, the salesforce for personal care and household products was strengthened, and through reinvesting in the business revenues grew rapidly to VND354bn in 2008. In 2009, the company acquired control of Thuan Phat, a spices and sauces company, at the same time that it spun out its beverage business into an independent unit, MFB. Exhibit 20.8 contains summary financial information for ICP.

VIETNAM AZALEA FUND

Despite not having fully invested MEF II, Mekong decided to launch a new fund in 2007 on the back of the strong appetite of its existing investors towards privatizations and pre-IPO investments, areas outside Mekong's previous focus. Mekong launched the USD100mn Vietnam Azalea Fund (VAF) in June 2007, which takes minority investments in formerly state-owned enterprises (SOEs) and large private companies which have imminent listing plans or, in some cases, have been recently listed. Under current practices in Vietnam, the privatizations of SOEs often occur through one or many auctions of shares owned by the state. VAF's primary strategy was, and is, to buy shares of companies at a discount to public equity valuations prior to their public listing and to capture the liquidity premium created by a public listing. VAF aims to take small minority stakes (5–10%) and use its reputation and collaborative approach to ensure the investee companies achieve consistently high-net-profit growth.

To date, VAF has made eight investments for a total capital outlay of USD65.5mn, with the majority of investments occurring before the height of the global financial crisis in October 2008. While absolute returns were impacted significantly by the subsequent drop in the market, VAF has maintained outperformance against key comparable benchmarks. Exhibit 20.9 contains VAF performance data as of December 31, 2009.

2007—SEARCHING FOR ANSWERS FROM WITHIN

By late 2007, Mekong had grown into a mature private equity fund manager, with USD168mn of committed capital and a portfolio of 18 companies across Vietnam. It had benefited from the country's fast economic growth and firmly established itself as one of the leading players in the local private equity industry.

In terms of results, the MEF I fund was fully invested and looking to make its first exits. At year-end 2007, Mekong valued the MEF I portfolio at 2.46× invested capital. While this return seemed solid, Chris knew that much of the value stemmed from the increase in multiples of comparable trading companies on the Ho Chi Minh Stock Exchange (see Exhibit 20.10 for stock market information) which were used to benchmark the value of the portfolio. This worried him as he knew that continued increases in the valuations were more likely to be driven by the rate of net profit growth than continued increases in valuation multiples. Internally, the aggregate net profit of

---

6. VND = Vietnam dong. As at July 1, 2010 there were VND19,065 to USD1.

MEF I portfolio companies had only grown 6.2% in 2007. This was nowhere near the growth level that was necessary in order to meet the fund's gross IRR target.

The MEF II fund had invested in five companies for an aggregate amount of USD22mn (44% of the fund's committed capital) by the end of 2007. While it was still too early to predict an outcome, mixed results were already emerging. For example, one company had received a third-party investment at a 52% valuation premium to Mekong's investment, hence providing a basis for Mekong to increase the valuation of its holding. On the other hand, the aggregate net profits of the MEF II portfolio in 2007 had dropped 14% in comparison to the prior year.

As for the internal structure, Mekong had organized the investment staff into three teams, one for each fund (Exhibit 20.11). Recruitment had been busy, with total staff leaping from 27 at the end of 2006 to 48 in late 2007, resulting in more than 50% of the team members having worked there for less than 1 year. Mekong relied on an internal HR team to handle recruitment of both its staff and for key positions in its portfolio companies. After raising the VAF fund in mid-2007, Chris had turned to examine more closely the internal operations of Mekong to assess the optimal structure and culture. He was very concerned that agreed operating and financial targets were often missed year after year for many of the portfolio companies. Every time Chris inquired into the reasons, he encountered explanations from Mekong's investment team, or from the companies themselves, about circumstances rather than individuals taking responsibility for the poor performance and doing something to ensure the targets were achieved: "the CEO doesn't listen . . .", "the competitors launched a price war . . .", "the market isn't growing this year . . .", "our biggest customer went bankrupt . . .", "a key manager resigned . . .", "it's impossible to recruit a strong management team in Vietnam . . .", etc.

Chris was also aware that the root of the problem in some cases was cultural: the indirect method of communication—such as a reluctance to speak in a direct way to authority figures (e.g., CEOs) due to concern about offending them. For example, if a CEO of a portfolio company is an older and respected member of the community, it was hard for a younger deal partner to hold him or her accountable for poor results. However, the private equity model relies on fund managers being able to cause its portfolio companies to adapt to an ever changing business environment faster than traditional firms. Excuses and cultural issues were denying Mekong the very skills that should be its strength!

Lastly, the growth in funds under management and the number of portfolio companies had necessitated an accelerated pace of external recruitment and internal promotion. Significant time was spent getting new hires up to speed instead of focusing on the portfolio. Had the rapid growth led to an overall decrease in deal partner effectiveness due to lack of experience? Last, but not least, the entrepreneurs who were Mekong's fellow shareholders in the portfolio companies were not happy about seeing so many new faces—they preferred consistency as it took years to build solid work relationships with deal partners. As in the AA case mentioned above, it was not unheard of for a deal partner to last less than 1 year.

THE CORPORATE TRANSFORMATION PROCESS

Armed with all this information Chris decided in late 2007 that, without changing Mekong's corporate culture—no matter how good the investment strategy, the growth of assets under management, or the size of staff—Mekong would not be able to deliver to its full potential. He set about transforming Mekong's corporate culture with the help of Business Breakthrough Technology Pty. Ltd.[7] Chris expected this major initiative to be complete by the year-end 2009. However, not everyone thought that this effort was necessary nor embraced it. Only 1 month into the plan, in December 2007, Mekong's second and third most senior investment staff members informed Chris of their resignations as a result of their disagreement with the transformation plan.

Chris went to the market in order to find a suitable replacement and hired Dr. Thomas Lanyi as Director of Investments during 1Q 2008. Thomas was a talented and highly educated investment professional, with 8 years' asset management experience focused on South East Asia. He shared a common background with Chris as they both used to work at Templeton Asset Management Ltd. (see Exhibit 20.1 for Thomas' bio). Thomas was already established in the country and was soon to be married to a local woman who was also a successful entrepreneur in the retail sector.

While Thomas had the professional and academic credentials for the job, he was another expatriate. Selecting a foreigner to be his second in command was not a trivial move, as many thought it was the exact opposite of what Chris should be doing. Nevertheless, Chris was impressed by Thomas and expected that he would be able to manage the team of local talent. The timing was critical, as Thomas would be entering during the beginning of the culture transformation and thus would need to get on board quickly.

The corporate culture transformation process began by identifying, exposing, and handling persistent complaints and excuses within the company and to get people to start taking responsibility for them—thus removing them as obstacles. The second stage of the process involved transforming the culture around a shared set of values and developing a new investment framework which would lead to improved business results. Initially, a list of 14 key values for Mekong was introduced, but after much deliberation the list was narrowed down to five:

- Responsibility
- Integrity
- Results
- Leadership
- Communication.

Responsibility was the value that was key and penetrated all aspects of Mekong's operations. Thomas and Chris saw it as a form of empowerment, where deal partners and other team members saw themselves at the source of what happens, not as a victim of external circumstances. Other values such as results and integrity imposed a level of accountability to deliver results that was unfamiliar and uncomfortable to some team members. It was a significant change from the way Mekong had worked before and encountered much skepticism. Collectively, the directness and perceived aggressiveness of the new culture occurred to some as being in conflict with the Vietnamese practices of respect, patience, and subtlety.

Thomas remarked on the importance of deal partners assuming responsibility:

> "If you attribute responsibility for something to an external circumstance
> you're taking it away from yourself and you're likely to be an outcome of

7. The Asian business consulting arm of Landmark Education, a global training and development organization.

the circumstances rather than really being a person in power and control of your outcome."

Mekong researched best practices to ascertain how the most successful private equity firms were organized, modified Mekong's organizational structure (see Exhibit 20.12), and eliminated the separate fund teams in 2008. Instead, the function of deal partner was consolidated by giving them responsibilities for companies across all funds, allowing for more efficient allocation of resources. Recently, Hong was promoted to the new role of Director of Post Investments, with all deal partners now reporting to her for post-investment functions. All deal sourcing and pre-investment deliverables are led by Thomas, with deal partners reporting to him when their companies are at the pipeline stage through investment completion.

At the third stage of the transformation process, a shared vision for the future of Mekong Capital was created, with the aim of ensuring that the company's strategy, plans, and operations were all aligned with that vision. Mekong applied a 14-day "alignment" process to ensure that each employee participated in generating the vision, really understood the vision, and owned it as his or her own. Mekong's future success was dependent on every staff member becoming aligned with the plan, which Chris appreciated would be an uphill battle against years of built-up inertia and reluctance to change. Chris commented:

> "We had a lot of people leave during the transformation process. Initially, there was a lot of resistance, and I wasn't able to inspire some people to be accountable for producing results, or to let go of excuses or points of view which were obstacles to producing results. Some others were sitting on the sidelines, not actively resisting but also not supporting what we were up to—and I wasn't able to inspire some of them to get into the game and really empower what Mekong was doing. We really needed our company to work together as a team in which each person is responsible for the success of the team, and the team is organized around a common goal."

WILL IT WORK?

It is now February 2010, and Chris is eagerly awaiting the 2009 year-end performance results. Chris wanted to see the most recent valuation of Mekong's portfolio companies and, in particular, how they had fared against their 2009 net profit targets. Chris used this last metric to evaluate the effectiveness of his deal partners and that of the corporate transformation as a whole. Positive results would not only provide tangible evidence that Mekong's culture transformation was working, but would also be a huge step towards proving to investors that Mekong was ready for a fourth, new fund.

However, the worldwide image of the alternative assets class had been seriously damaged over the past 18 months. While the impact of the global financial crisis was less severe in Vietnam than in other regions, asset values had been deflated—in particular, Ho Chi Minh City Stock Exchange multiples had dropped dramatically, bringing down the fair market valuation of Mekong's portfolio, with most investments being carried at single-digit PE multiples.[8]

---

6. Mekong applies the *International Private Equity and Venture Capital Valuation Guidelines*, September 2009 edition, to set out the valuation principles for the funds' investments. The fair value is the price at which an orderly transaction would take place between market participants at the reporting date.

Internally, the alignment of Mekong staff to the five key values of the transformation plan had been more difficult than anticipated and was still an ongoing process. During implementation, the cultural transformation had resulted in many long-time employees leaving the company. While the streamlined organizational structure justified a reduction in staff, the overall turnover had been higher than expected. Total staff dropped from a high of 52 at the end of 2008, to just 37 one year later. As at December 2009, average staff tenure at Mekong was only about 2 years—only a few deal partners had spent more than 3 years at the firm. While the bulk of the staff had been indoctrinated to private equity and had already embraced Mekong's core values, the team members (with the exception of Chris and Thomas) were relatively inexperienced.

During 2009, Chris had ambitiously started the process of raising MEF III, with a target of USD150mn in commitments. MEF III would be a successor fund to MEF II, sharing a similar investment policy, but would be allowed to invest more per transaction and, hence, to target larger firms. Despite the adverse economic climate and the internal transformational issues, Chris was hoping to close the fund promptly as the MEF II fund was almost fully invested and there was a risk of running out of "dry powder". At times, Chris wondered whether spending so much time and effort on corporate culture was worth the sacrifice and whether investors actually saw any value in it, as it was not a common industry practice.

When Chris reached his office, the year-end report was already posted on the public bulletin board. As he reviewed the data, it became evident that, as a whole, Mekong's portfolio companies had exceeded their net profit targets and posted very encouraging net profit growth. It now seemed like the right time for fundraising as international investors were once again flocking to Vietnam, attracted by the recent resurgence in the local capital markets and internal demand growth. Determined to push on with MEF III, Chris reached for his phone and opened his address book . . .

APPENDIX

EXHIBIT 20.1

SELECT BIOS (APRIL 2010)

Mekong Capital senior management

Mr. Chris Freund—Managing Partner (Ho Chi Minh City) Prior to forming Mekong Capital (Mekong) in 2001, Chris was a vice president and Portfolio Manager with Templeton Asset Management Ltd., the emerging markets arm of the Franklin/Templeton Group. His involvement with Vietnam dates from mid-1994 when he was doing a research project for Harris Associates, a Chicago-based fund management firm. Chris worked for Templeton in Vietnam from early 1995 until mid-1998. In mid-1998, Chris relocated to Templeton's Singapore office, where he covered the technology sector in emerging markets, focusing on Taiwan, Israel, and Korea. He moved back to Ho Chi Minh City in April 2001 to establish Mekong Capital, as the first private equity firm in Vietnam. Chris holds a bachelor's degree in psychology, with honors, from the University of California at Santa Cruz. His education also focused on religious studies, psychology, and economics.

Dr. Thomas Lanyi—Director of Investments (Ho Chi Minh City) As Director of Investments, Thomas oversees all investment activities at Mekong. The investment team reports directly to Thomas on the deal sourcing, appraisal, and implementation process. Thomas is in charge of portfolio management for the Vietnam Azalea Fund (VAF) and is a member of Mekong's internal Management Committee. Thomas has 9 years of direct investment management experience, most of which he gained working in Asia. He started his career in asset management with Singapore-based Templeton Asset Management Ltd. where he was solely responsible for strategic listed and unlisted investment opportunities in South East Asia, including Vietnam. Prior to joining Mekong, Thomas worked with Hanoi-based BIDV-Vietnam Partners Investment Management as a portfolio manager. Thomas earned a doctorate in economic sciences and capital markets theory with distinction from the Vienna University of Economics and a master's degree in international management in exchange with Hautes Etudes Commerciales in Paris. Thomas holds the CFA designation.

Ms. Tran Thi Thu Hong ("Hong")—Director of Post Investment (Hanoi) As Director of Post Investment in Mekong, Hong overseas all investment activities related to post investment. The investment team reports directly to her on post-investment value creation activities for portfolio companies of the funds. Hong is a member of Mekong's internal Management Committee. Hong was previously a business development manager with IKEA, where she was in charge of creating a sourcing network in South East Asia, building up supplier competences and setting up business strategy. Before that she worked for IBM Indochina as a procurement and distribution specialist. Hong earned a master's degree in business administration at IMPAC University, Florida.

Ms. Truong Dieu Le ("Le")—Director of Operations (Ho Chi Minh City) Le is Director of Operations and is responsible for supervising all operational activities including finance, accounting, human resources, investor relations/communications, IT and administration. Le is a member of Mekong's internal Management Committee. Before joining Mekong in 2003, Le worked as Assistant to the General Director of Huy Hoang Garment & Construction Co. Prior to that, she worked in the tax consulting practice of KPMG in Ho Chi Minh City and as Assistant to the Vice President of the Venetian Blind Company in Montclair, California. She received her MBA from the California State Polytechnic University in Pomona, California.

Ms. Truong Ngoc Phung ("Phung")—Chief Empowerment Officer (Ho Chi Minh City) Truong Ngoc Phung was previously an investor relations assistant and Special Assistant to the CEO, both in Mekong Capital. As Chief Empowerment Officer, Phung is responsible for disseminating the new corporate culture at Mekong Capital by assisting in the process of empowering employees to see how they are fully responsible for delivering results and for generating the necessary actions to deliver those results.

Mekong Capital deal partners

Deal partners have overall responsibility for the success of specific portfolio companies; they are also involved in appraising potential investments for Mekong's funds.

Ms. Ngo Thi Ngoc Anh ("Anh")—Senior Associate (Hanoi) Anh was previously a management trainee with British American Tobacco Vietnam where she rotated through various functions in the marketing department. Before that, she worked as a financial analyst and project assistant with IDG Ventures.

Ms. Nguyen Thi Dieu Thuy ("Thuy")—Senior Associate (Hanoi) Thuy was previously a sales manager for Vertu, a luxury mobile phone brand, with FPT Distribution Company, where she was in charge of the Hanoi market.

Ms. Pham Vu Thanh Giang ("Giang")—Senior Associate (Ho Chi Minh City) Giang was previously an account executive at Aon Vietnam Ltd., a non-life insurance broker, and also a member of the Risk Management Accounts team. Thanh Giang earned the executive master of finance and banking at the University of Applied Sciences Northwestern Switzerland.

Mr. Le Tuan—Senior Associate (Hanoi) Tuan previously worked for Macquarie Group in its New York office as an investment banking analyst, where he was involved in a number of M&A and capital-raising transactions. Tuan graduated at Bucknell University in Lewisburg, Pennsylvania. with a bachelor's degree in economics.

Ms. Vu Thu Thuy, CPA ("Thu Thuy")—Senior Associate (Ho Chi Minh City) Thu Thuy previously worked with Sankaty Advisors, a credit subsidiary of Bain Capital in Boston, MA, as a senior finance associate. Thuy was primarily responsible for the analysis and financial reporting of investment activity and the performance of multiple credit opportunity funds. She joined Mekong in March 2010.

Source: Mekong Internal documents and website.

Investee company CEOs

Mr. Chad Ovel, CEO, AA Corporation (MEF I case study) Chad was appointed Managing Director of AA Furniture Division in November 2006, and then became Managing Director of the AA Corporation at the end of 2009. Chad moved to Vietnam in 1996 to work for the San Diego–based venture capital fund, Pacifica Vietnam. From 1997 to 2000, he served as the Development Director of the World Wide Fund for Nature Indochina. From 2000 to 2006, Chad worked at ScanCom Vietnam where he served as the Managing Director of 6,000 employees. At ScanCom, Chad led the aggressive and innovative growth of the company to a turnover of USD150mn, making it the largest furniture exporter in Vietnam in 2006. Chad holds a BA from Carleton College, Minnesota and an executive MBA from the Booth School of Business, University of Chicago (graduated 2008).

Mr. Phan Quoc Cong, co-founder and CEO, International Consumer Products (MEF II case study) Phan Quoc Cong co-founded International Consumer Products (ICP) in 2001 and has served as CEO since then. Cong has extensive consumer product–marketing experience through stints at Smithkline Beecham (where he built Panadol as the No. 1 pain reliever in Vietnam) and at Nestlé (where he was responsible for the growth of the MILO brand and restructuring of the Vietnamese marketing department). Cong holds a graduate degree in business administration.

EXHIBIT 20.2

LIST OF INVESTORS IN MEF I

Name	Amount (USD)	Ownership (%)
Asian Development Bank	4.0	22
Nordic Development Fund	4.0	22
Finnish Fund for Industrial Cooperation	3.0	16
State Secretariat for Economic Affairs of Switzerland	3.0	16
Belgian Investment Company for Developing Countries	2.5	14
Private investor[1]	2.0	11

Source: Mekong Internal Fund document.

Note: 1. The private investor is the U.S.-based former CEO of one of the world's most respected money and asset management firms.

EXHIBIT 20.3

VIETNAM SELECT MACROECONOMIC DATA

Select Asian economies' economic data: real GDP, consumer prices, and current account balance (annual percent change unless noted otherwise)

	Real GDP				Consumer prices[1]				Current account balance[2]				
	2007	2008	2009	2010	2007	2008	2009	2010	2007	2008	2009	2010
Emerging Asia	**9.8**	**6.7**	**5.0**	**6.8**	**4.9**	**7.0**	**2.7**	**3.2**	**6.7**	**5.6**	**5.2**	**5.3**
Newly industrialized Asian economies	*5.7*	*1.5*	*−2.4*	*3.6*	*2.2*	*4.5*	*1.0*	*1.9*	*5.7*	*4.4*	*6.4*	*5.9*
Korea	5.1	2.2	−1.0	3.6	2.5	4.7	2.6	2.5	0.6	−0.7	3.4	2.2
Taiwan Province of China	5.7	0.1	−4.1	3.7	1.8	3.5	−0.5	1.5	8.6	6.4	7.9	8.0
Hong Kong SAR	6.4	2.4	−3.6	3.5	2.0	4.3	−1.0	0.5	12.3	14.2	10.7	10.8
Singapore	7.8	1.1	−3.3	4.1	2.1	6.5	−0.2	1.6	23.5	14.8	12.6	12.5
Developing Asia[3]	*10.6*	*7.6*	*6.2*	*7.3*	*5.4*	*7.5*	*3.0*	*3.4*	*7.0*	*5.9*	*5.0*	*5.2*
China	13.0	9.0	8.5	9.0	4.8	5.9	−0.1	0.6	11.0	9.8	7.8	8.6
India	9.4	7.3	5.4	6.4	6.4	8.3	8.7	8.4	−1.0	−2.2	−2.2	−2.5
ASEAN-5	*6.3*	*4.8*	*0.7*	*4.0*	*4.3*	*9.2*	*2.6*	*4.6*	*4.9*	*2.6*	*3.3*	*2.0*
Indonesia	6.3	6.1	4.0	4.8	6.0	9.8	5.0	6.2	2.4	0.1	0.9	0.5
Thailand	4.9	2.6	−3.5	3.7	2.2	5.5	−1.2	2.1	5.7	−0.1	4.9	2.7
Philippines	7.1	3.8	1.0	3.2	2.8	9.3	2.8	4.0	4.9	2.5	3.2	1.2
Malaysia	6.2	4.6	−3.6	2.5	2.0	5.4	−0.1	1.2	15.4	17.9	13.4	11.0
Vietnam	8.5	6.2	4.6	5.3	8.3	23.1	7.0	11.0	−9.8	−11.9	−9.7	−9.4
Other developing Asia[3]	*6.5*	*3.9*	*3.3*	*4.1*	*10.1*	*12.8*	*11.6*	*8.3*	*0.0*	*−2.3*	*−1.0*	*−1.4*
Pakistan	5.6	2.0	2.0	3.0	7.8	12.0	20.8	10.0	−4.8	−8.3	−5.1	−4.8
Bangladesh	6.3	6.0	5.4	5.4	9.1	7.7	5.3	5.6	1.1	1.9	2.1	1.0

Source: IMF World Economic Outlook, October 2009.

Notes: 1. Movements in consumer prices are shown as annual averages.
2. Percent of GDP.
3. Includes Afghanistan, Bhutan, Brunei, Cambodia, Fiji, Kiribati, Laos, Maldives, Myanmar, Nepal, Papua New Guinea, Samoa, Solomon Islands, Sri Lanka, East Timor, Tonga, and Vanuatu.

USD/VND 10-year historical exchange rate

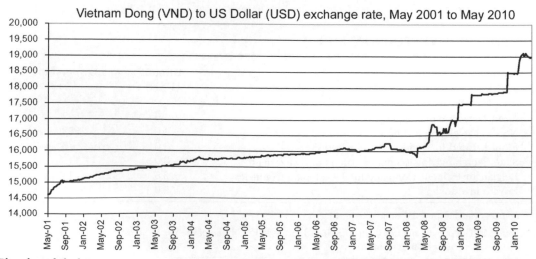

Vietnam Dong (VND) to US Dollar (USD) exchange rate, May 2001 to May 2010

Source: Bloomberg daily data.

EXHIBIT 20.4

MEF I PORTFOLIO AS OF DECEMBER 31, 2009

Active investment	Percent stake[1] (%)	Sector	Industry	Date of initial investment	Date of exit	Cost of investment (USD)	Gross IRR (%)
1 AA	12.0	High-end furniture for leisure industry (local and export)	Manufacturing	Mar-03		1,675,740	7.0
2 Lac Viet	28.0	IT hardware and software solutions	Business services: IT	Oct-03		745,650	−8.1
3 Ngo Han	20.7	Industrial magnetic wire	Manufacturing	Apr-04		1,850,000	30.6
4 Nam Hoa	25.0	Wooden toys for export	Manufacturing	Jun-04		900,000	1.3
5 Minh Phuc	30.0	Printing labels and adhesives	Business services: printing	Nov-04		1,247,517	2.4
6 Minh Hoang[2]	18.3	Athletic wear for export	Manufacturing	Apr-05		1,850,000	n.a.
7 Goldsun	25.1	Kitchenware and packaging	Manufacturing	Dec-05		1,550,000	−7.1

Exited investment	Percent stake[1] (%)	Sector	Industry	Date of initial investment	Date of exit	Cost of investment (USD)	Gross IRR (%)
1 Saigon Gas	26.4	Gas distribution	Business services: energy and gas	Nov-05	Dec-08	1,842,615	25.9
2 Duc Thanh	20.2	Wooden household products and furniture for export	Manufacturing	Feb-05	Aug-09	1,750,010	7.9
3 Tan Dai Hung	14.4	Polypropylene woven bags (local and export)	Manufacturing	Jul-03	Aug-09	1,600,000	10.8
Grand total						*15,011,532*	*9.80*

Notes: 1. Current stake as at 4Q 2009.
2. 100% writeoff, yet liquidation sale value is possible in future.

Annual value progression chart for MEF I (as of December 31, 2009)

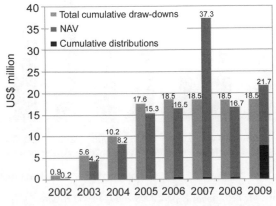

Source: Mekong internal document—MEF 4Q09 Report.

EXHIBIT 20.5

AA SUMMARY FINANCIALS (USD)

AA historical P&L, balance sheet, and employee data as of December 31, 2009

	2002	2003	2004	2005	2006	2007	2008	2009
Revenue	9,322,980	12,631,760	14,052,832	19,316,678	15,609,199	19,209,989	20,221,195	27,051,516
Gross profit	2,184,434	1,690,716	3,509,236	4,629,153	4,284,700	3,837,552	6,713,410	7,701,832
EBITDA	497,408	1,690,716	895,429	1,306,565	1,961,087	(722,202)	2,041,366	2,506,906
NPAT	(61,963)	753,452	102,463	404,767	665,732	(2,070,181)	51,746	856,012
Revenue growth	n.a.	35%	11%	37%	(19%)	23%	5%	34%
Gross profit margin	23%	13%	25%	24%	27%	20%	33%	28%
EBITDA margin	5%	13%	6%	7%	13%	(4%)	10%	9%
NPAT margin	(1%)	6%	1%	2%	4%	(11%)	0%	3%
Total assets	7,788,328	9,512,502	18,117,928	17,763,088	16,802,202	20,122,732	23,214,145	28,113,441
Shareholders' equity	1,181,791	2,623,778	2,659,276	3,680,985	4,283,569	2,210,712	6,038,363	6,325,230
Net debt	1,316,349	1,958,902	4,561,821	6,331,231	6,106,624	3,762,801	5,043,675	6,079,841
No. of employees	1,424	1,436	1,662	3,358	2,100	2,000	1,785	1,300

AA historical financial performance

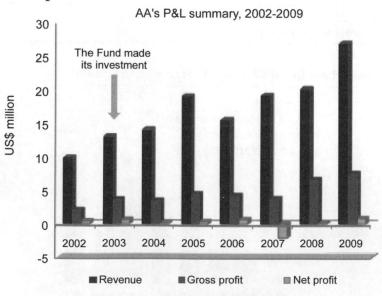

Source: Mekong internal document—*MEF I Annual Report 2008* and *Q4 2009 Report*.

EXHIBIT 20.6

MEF II PORTFOLIO AS OF DECEMBER 31, 2009

Active investment	Percent stake[1] (%)	Sector	Industry	Date of initial investment	Date of exit	Cost of investment (USD)	Gross IRR (%)
1 ICP	21.0	FMCG	Consumer goods	Nov-06		5,661,011	18.6
2 MFB[2]	21.0	Beverages retail	Consumer goods	Nov-06		588,989	−23.2
3 Ngo Han	9.0	Industrial magnetic wire	Manufacturing	Jan-07		1,910,142	21.3
4 The Gioi Di Dong	34.4	Retail of portable electronics	Consumer goods	May-07		3,500,000	67.0
5 VIVCO	35.0	Workwear and personal garments for export	Manufacturing	Oct-07		6,240,000	24.5
6 MK Smart	26.1	Smartcards for loyalty programs	Business services: consumer goods	Dec-07		4,000,000	31.2
7 Maison[3]	33.3	Retail of high-end apparel	Consumer goods	Mar-08		5,000,484	−18.5
8 Golden Gate	15.0	Restaurant	Consumer service	Apr-08		1,500,000	79.2
9 Digiworld	19.0	IT hardware distribution	Consumer goods	Nov-08		5,000,000	3.4
Total active investments						***33,400,626***	***25.8***

Source: Mekong internal document—*MEF II 4Q09 Report* (modified).

Notes: 1. Current stake as of 4Q 2009.
      2. This is a spinoff from ICP.
      3. Was 100% writeoff, yet liquidation sale was achieved.

Annual value progression chart for MEF II (as of December 31, 2009)

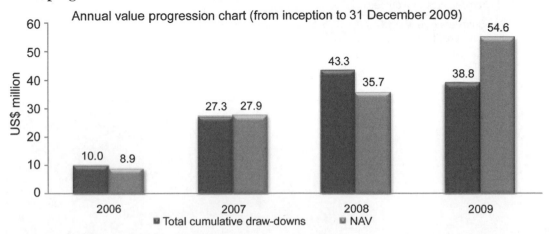

Annual value progression chart (from inception to 31 December 2009)

US$ million

2006: 10.0 / 8.9
2007: 27.3 / 27.9
2008: 43.3 / 35.7
2009: 38.8 / 54.6

■ Total cumulative draw-downs　■ NAV

Source: Mekong internal document—*MEF II 4Q09 Report.*

EXHIBIT 20.7

ICP INNOVATIVE DISTRIBUTION MODEL

- • ICP directly reaches 60,000 stores, without using arm's length intermediaries.
- • The exclusive distributors take on the working capital requirement and credit risk of distribution to the shops (i.e., ICP delivers to the distributors, the distributors pay ICP and then have responsibility for delivery and collecting payment from the shops). ICP pays an additional margin for this service.

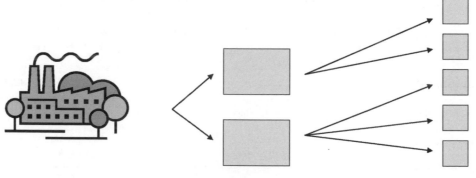

- • ICP produces goods at its HCMC factory: 60% own factory, 40% outsourced

- • Suppliers give ICP 45 – 60 days credit

- • 100 exclusive Distributors, managed by ICP

- • Responsible for invoicing and billing local shops (ICP transfers credit risk)

- • Pays cash to ICP up-front, in return for additional margin

- • 60,000 shops nationwide

- • Pays back credit to Distributor

- • Provides market intelligence to ICP

EXHIBIT 20.8

ICP SUMMARY FINANCIALS (VND)

ICP historical P&L, balance sheet, and employee data as of December 31, 2009

VND (million)	2006	2007	2008	2009
Profit and loss				
Sales	185,037	245,001	354,191	471,437
Gross profit	101,165	123,898	200,139	263,576
Net profit	36,420	31,619	29,563	40,729
Gross margin	*54.70%*	*50.60%*	*56.50%*	*55.91%*
Net margin	*19.70%*	*12.90%*	*8.30%*	*8.64%*
Balance sheet				
Current assets	77,448	98,470	253,676	195,438
Non-current assets	20,632	28,052	43,652	133,522
Total assets	*98,080*	*126,522*	*297,328*	*328,960*
Current liabilities	29,623	35,142	40.061	84,860
Non-current liabilities	754	668	1,708	9,757
Shareholders' equity	67,703	90,712	255,559	228,674
Total liabilities and shareholders' equity	*98,080*	*126,522*	*297,328*	*328,960*
Employees	**200**	**320**	**641**	**846**

Source: Mekong internal document—*2008 Annual Report, Q4 2009 Report.*
Note: 1. MFB was spun out of ICP during 2009.

ICP historical financial performance

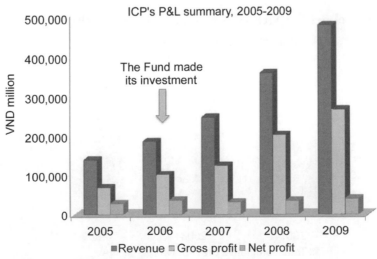

Source: Mekong internal document—*Q4 2009 Report.*

EXHIBIT 20.9

VIETNAM AZALEA FUND PORTFOLIO AND PERFORMANCE

Performance of VAF vs. VN-index from inception to December 31, 2009

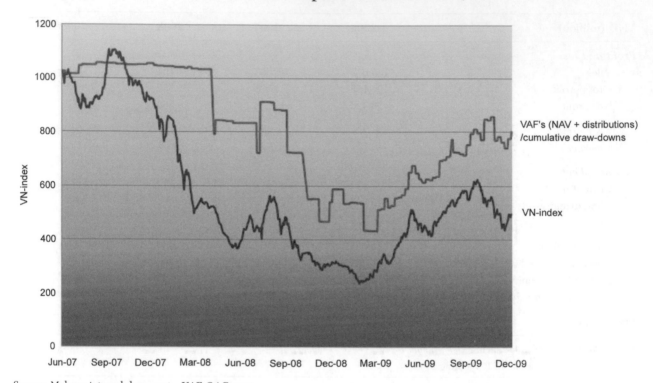

Source: Mekong internal document—*VAF Q4 Report.*

Annual value progression chart for VAF (as of December 31, 2009)

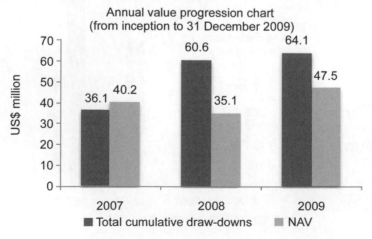

Source: Mekong internal document—*VAF Q4 Report.*

EXHIBIT 20.10

STATISTICS OF HCMC STOCK EXCHANGE (HOSE)

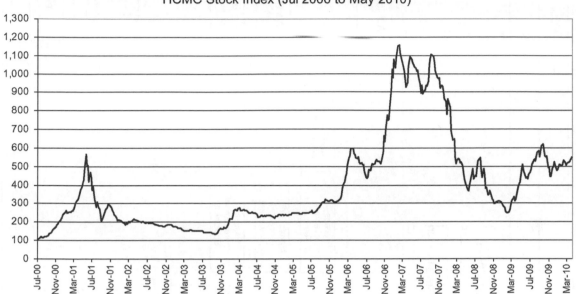

HCMC Stock Index (Jul 2000 to May 2010)

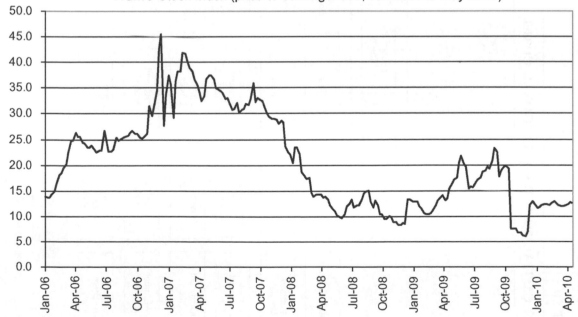

HCMC Stock Index (price-to-earnings ratio, Jan 2006 to May 2010)

Source: Bloomberg weekly data.

Note: Data weighted by market capitalization.

EXHIBIT 20.11

MEKONG CAPITAL 2007 ORGANIZATIONAL CHART

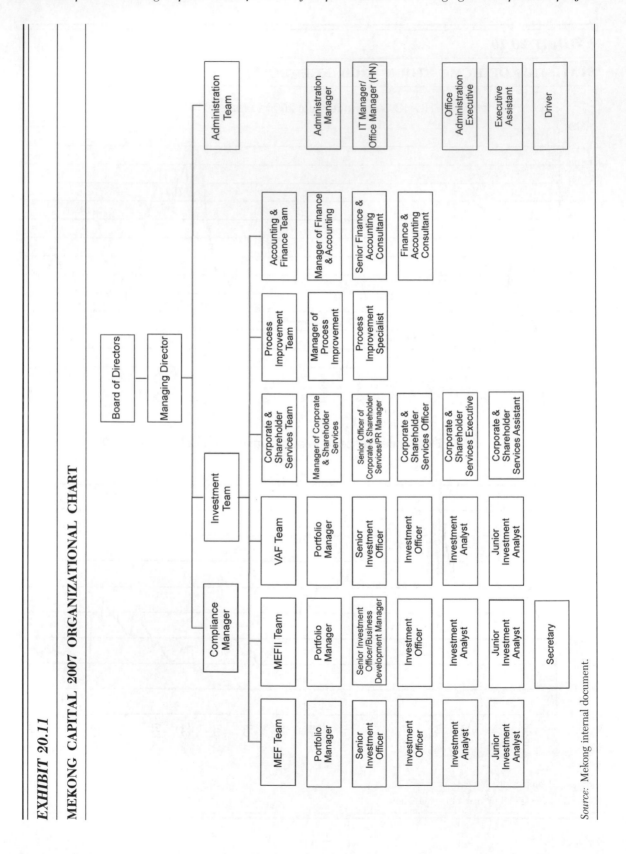

Source: Mekong internal document.

EXHIBIT Appendix 20.12

MEKONG CAPITAL 2010 ORGANIZATIONAL CHART

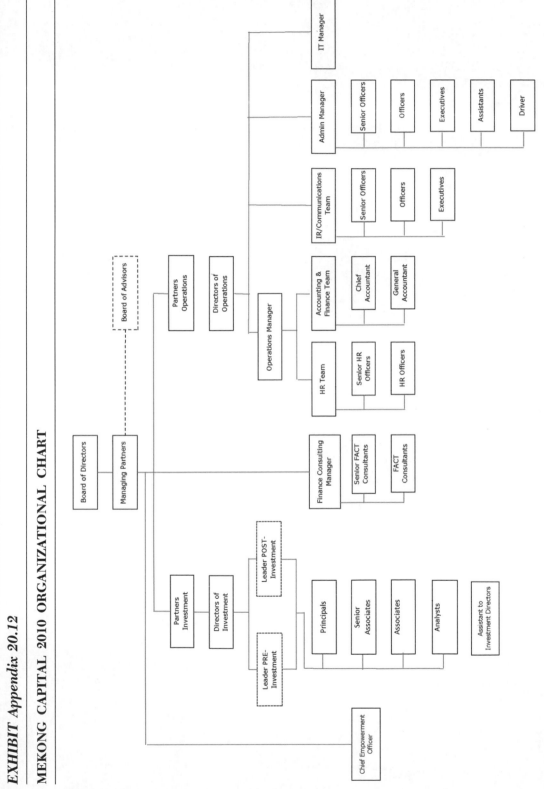

Source: Mekong internal document.

21

Bloomsbury Capital: June 2007

Pauline Cornioley felt a tinge of regret as she realized she would have to miss tonight's performance at the Royal Opera House in Covent Garden. She wondered whether she would get any sleep at all that night as she reluctantly put aside her orchestra stall tickets, a luxury she was finally able to afford after just graduating from business school and joining Bloomsbury Capital, a leading European private equity firm. Cornioley was scheduled to deliver her first presentation at Bloomsbury's partnership meeting on Monday morning and only had the weekend left to prepare. After only two months with the firm, she knew the significance of this opportunity.

Cornioley was one of the fortunate few in her graduating class who had managed to land a job in the highly sought after private equity industry. She allowed her mind to drift back to the by chance encounter with Victor Lewis, Managing Director of Bloomsbury Capital, while he was a guest speaker at her private equity class lecture. Cornioley''s second year MBA project was the perfect excuse to contact Victor Lewis, which led to further discussions and, miraculously, a job opportunity. Cornioley, however, realized her grace period may be over and that Victor Lewis and other senior partners of the firm would not hesitate to ask her difficult questions on Monday. She turned back to her workstation and the stack of documents spread out on her desk.

BLOOMSBURY CAPITAL

Bloomsbury Capital was a highly respected investor in the European private equity market. It was the successor to Sunflower Private Equity, which was founded in 1985, and acquired by a top-tier U.S. investment bank in 1997. It then went through an MBO in December 2000, and was renamed Bloomsbury Capital (Bloomsbury), in homage to the innovative group of early 20th-century British intellectuals, which included the world-famous economist John Maynard Keynes and the feminist writer Virginia Woolf. Total funds under management at the time Cornioley joined stood at €2.4bn.

Bloomsbury serviced over 200 institutional clients and managed Bloomsbury Trust plc, an investment trust listed on the London Stock Exchange that participated in all of Bloomsbury's investments. It boasted consistent long-term performance and outperformance of both the index and quoted peers (see Exhibit 21.1).

Bloomsbury's philosophy was built on three fundamental pillars. As Victor described in his presentation at London Business School:

The case was co-authored with Edward M. Gera (LBS Executive MBA 2008).

"First, Bloomsbury relies on its experience and expertise in all types of buyouts, whether the targets are divisions, companies, business assets, public-to-private transactions or turnarounds, and always works constructively with incumbent and/or new management. Second, through a diverse group of managers and investment professionals, Bloomsbury has a deep sector knowledge that enables us to invest with a high degree of confidence in companies, and build partnerships with management that are fundamental to positive performance. Last but not least, Bloomsbury prides itself in maintaining considerable resources that can be deployed in a proactive manner to help managers and companies achieve their goals."

Further to this philosophy, the firm's investment strategy was to target mid-market, pan-European, and sector-specific investments, primarily targeting the U.K., Ireland, Germany, and the Benelux region. Bloomsbury targeted companies with enterprise values between €50mn and €500mn, and was willing to consider majority or minority stakes in the companies in which it invests; however, there was a strong preference and pressure from several senior partners to focus on investments where Bloomsbury could influence changes through ownership control. Exhibit 21.2 displays the distribution of portfolio companies by main sectors: (i) consumer and leisure; (ii) industrials; (iii) healthcare; and (iv) telecommunications, media, and technology (TMT).

Headcount at Bloomsbury had increased during the past few years, with eight new investment professionals being hired during 2006, bringing the total number of employees across Europe to 79. Bloomsbury was still headquartered in London and now had offices in Frankfurt and Amsterdam, enabling it to better source and execute on deals on the Continent. By the end of 2006, the portfolio of investments had a 54% exposure to Continental Europe, up from 46% in 2005, and less than 30% in 2004. This was very much in line with the goals set by the partners, who were concerned about the U.K. competitive environment for mid-market buyouts, where making deals was more difficult and less attractive than on the Continent.

2006 was a record year for both realizations (successful exits) and new investments; and 2007 was set to be even bigger. By June 2007 Bloomsbury VI, a niche fund aimed at expansion capital opportunities, which was less than a quarter of the size of the previous buyout-focused fund raised merely a year earlier, was close to 70% invested (€280mn). In this buoyant environment the fund had partaken in more than a dozen investments and 10 fruitful realizations (see Exhibits 21.3 and 21.4, respectively). Bloomsbury's partners had begun planning for another round of fundraising before the end of the year. Most felt the strain of the many deals and transactions in such a booming time, yet they all preferred it to the dreaded investor roadshows that are the inevitable part of raising money for a new fund.

Every Monday morning the partners would meet to review potential investments or to discuss the existing portfolio. Once a decision is made to go forth with a potential investment, a deal team will be formed headed by one of the partners to take the case further and to eventually present it once more for final approval. Cornioley was intent on impressing the partners, most of whom she had only briefly interacted with before.

Investment opportunities

By Saturday morning Cornioley was still busy preparing two investment cases—a German software company and a Brussels-based industrial company that also had advanced embedded software solutions with strong IP. Then, the phone on her desk rang. It was Victor Lewis with a last minute additional opportunity, which was forwarded to him by one of the fund's long-standing LPs. He was sending her the relevant slides on a Swiss private bank and a name of a VP in Goldman Sachs's FIG team, who she could contact for information and help anytime over the weekend.[1]

Cornioley thanked Lewis, put the phone down, and sighed deeply. The next 48 hours were going to be tough. She needed to summarize her thoughts and prepare the presentation about investment cases in industries that were totally new to her.

AP Software

AP Software was founded in 1997 by Arnold Pfizermann, a serial entrepreneur from Munich. With a mere €500,000 from the proceeds of the 1995 sale to Oracle of his previous firm, ServerSolutions, Pfizermann established AP Software in order to realize his vision for changing the way large enterprises manage the way they design, present, and process-for-output all their documents. Development started with a small team of software developers, two of whom had previously worked for Pfizermann, and grew over a decade to more than 80 programmers and IT professionals. By 2007 AP Software had more than 4,200 clients across a dozen industry verticals in Europe, and everyone believed there was much room for further growth and expansion, especially entering, first, the U.S. and, then, the Asian markets.

Tragically, in January 2007 Pfizermann had a stroke and shortly after passed away leaving behind him a 24-year-old son, an 18-year-old daughter, and a widow. His son Hans had recently been awarded a B.Sc. (Honours) in computer science and management science from the Technical University Munich and joined Nortel's graduate program. Given the circumstances, Hans decided to leave Nortel and to assume the management of AP Software.

Within a couple of months a storm was brewing in the firm and it was clear that, unless some drastic change happened, the firm wouldn't survive under Hans' inexperienced management. Following a suggestion of his mother, Hans arranged to meet with his father's former partner, Frederick Braun, Marketing Director for Cognos in Germany.[2] As much as Hans wanted to be involved with the management of his father's firm, he conceded that it would be best to bring in new experienced professional management. Braun got along well with Hans and the two set to work on preparing information about AP Software to take to potential investors (see Exhibit 21.5). It was clear to both that what they were looking for was someone to come in fast with capable management and funds to fuel growth. They also wanted to make sure that whoever takes over would preserve Arnold Pfizermann's legacy and allow Hans to remain involved.

In terms of valuation, Braun showed Hans that with an EBITDA multiple of 5×, which he thought would be fair, AP Software would be worth c. €44mn, and if Hans were to sell 60% keeping 22% (a further 18% was held by several members of management and one distant relative) he could stay involved with the firm and yet generate significant cash out to the family. This seemed rather attractive to Hans, especially when he started playing with the model and using different multiples and EBITDA margins.

Cornioley reviewed the facts and felt concerned over how little she actually really knew about the firm. Arnold Pfizermann clearly knew what he was doing, but how much

---

1. FIG is the acronym for the Financial Institutions Group within the Investment Banking Division. This M&A team advises on all banking deals.

2. Cognos is a business intelligence and corporate performance management software company with 23,000 customers.

damage had been done since he passed away? It seemed that he was involved in every single aspect of management, except for R&D which was in the hands of Helmut Reichert, the firm's CTO since 2000. How easy would it be to parachute new management into such a firm? Could Bloomsbury's expertise and resources be the key to a great investment in this case?

Niras Technologies

Niras Technologies is a leading firm selling proprietary systems to the diamond industry. A Belgian firm founded in 1988, Niras develops, manufactures, and markets advanced evaluation, planning, and laser-marking systems that increase the profit margins of firms at all stages in the diamond industry value chain. Headquartered in Brussels, the company employs 120 people internationally.

Revenues in 2006 were in excess of €31mn and profit after tax was €8.3mn (40% CAGR over the past 5 years). More than 70% of Niras's revenue came from India. Management believed revenue would reach €55mn by 2009. The firm had no debt and sat on a war chest of €23mn in cash, which it believed could be used for acquisitions. This appeared to be a suboptimal financial structure. Niras had more than 60% market share in the diamond planning and grading products market. In the laser sawing and cutting products market, Niras's market share was much weaker. However, in both segments, most of its competitors were price players with inferior products.

Niras is managed by Maarten Steenhaut, aged 48, who has been with the firm for 11 years. The management team's average tenure with the firm is more than 7 years. The majority of the firm's founding scientists and engineers are still with the firm. Management sees much room for growth, both organically (positive market trends, new products, and expanding new markets such as retail), and through acquisitions that would leverage Niras's existing brand name and distribution network amongst the diamond industry. However, it would seem that this acquisitions strategy has not found a suitable target for quite some time. Some quality issues have also been brought to light, in particular with the new Nano product line.

Cornioley's preliminary research focused on the determinates of diamond pricing and the economic benefits of products that improve yield and production efficiencies. The value of a diamond is determined by several factors, known as the four Cs: carat (weight), cut, clarity, and color. For instance, a 1-carat, round, brilliant-cut, D color, IF (internally flawless) clarity, well-proportioned, well-made diamond a retail value of up to £20,000 could be expected; whereas at the bottom end a rejection quality stone of the same size would be worth around £100.

The deal came to the attention of Bloomsbury through Jeremy Stiles, a director at one of the leading U.S. investment banks in the City of London. Stiles outlined that the company was the brainchild of two groups, a group of scientists and engineers and another group of strategic investors from the industry. Some 11% equity had been distributed to management and ESOP. Growing disparity between the two sides had led to industry investors searching for as quiet and amicable an exit as possible. They were keen for Niras Technologies to continue current supplier contracts to their firms. Furthermore, one of the founding engineers intended to retire next year and she might consider selling her shares too. Thus, in total, there would be 58% of the equity on offer. Stiles pointed out that Niras' main competitor, with a 30% leverage ratio, trades on the London Stock Exchange (AIM) at a P/E multiple of 16× (14.5× average over the last 90 days). Stiles felt therefore that an enterprise value in the region of €100mn would be fair, considering Niras' leading market position, expected income this year, and potential for raising debt. He had also sent Bloomsbury a preliminary information deck on Niras, which his bank had prepared (see Exhibit 21.6).

The deal seemed quite attractive on the face of things, but Cornioley needed to understand the fund's competitive edge. She was also mulling over the degree of exposure to the Indian rupee.

Banque Pierre Malland

Cornioley felt somewhat uncomfortable to present Banque Pierre Malland. She had never before analyzed a private bank, or any other financial institution for that matter. Nor did she have anyone within the firm to call and discuss an acquisition of a financial institution. However, Julian Pitts from Goldman Sachs proved to be extremely resourceful and helpful. The stack of material Lewis sent, coupled with several long phone conversations with Pitts, gave Cornioley a fairly clear picture of what seemed like a rather attractive opportunity (see Exhibit 21.7).

Banque Pierre Malland was managed by Jerôme Lager. Apparently, there was some personal connection between Lager and one of Bloomsbury's LPs, which is how this proprietary deal reached the firm. A certain U.S. family conglomerate currently owned the Swiss private bank and felt that, on the one hand, it was not core to their business and, on the other hand, managing Lager from afar proved cumbersome. Lager was interested in finding a new partner with whom to spin off the bank—a partner who would allow his experience of more than two decades to manage the bank as he saw best. Lager currently owned 5% and wanted to increase his stake to at least 10%. Moreover, Lager believed that he could negotiate an acquisition price of CHF190mn (€115mn), which was a substantial discount to Cornioley's valuation.

In valuing the bank, Pitts told Cornioley that the easiest rule of thumb would be 4–6% of assets under management. Pitts suggested Cornioley also value the bank through both earnings multiples and a price-to-book value. Pitts had marginally different numbers to the comps table in Lewis' book. Pitts described the current M&A market for private banks as "fairly hot", given that private banking margins have been the highest within financial institutions and that banks felt there could be many synergies between retail banks, investment banks, and private banks.

APPENDIX

EXHIBIT 21.1

LONG-TERM PERFORMANCE (FIGURES AS ANNUALIZED)

	1 year to December 31, 2006 (%)	3 years to December 31, 2006 (%)	5 years to December 31, 2006 (%)	10 years to December 31, 2006 (%)
Net asset value	21.2	25.9	16.8	14.7
Share price	27.5	39.5	23.6	18.8
FTSE all-share	16.8	17.2	8.5	7.9
FTSE small cap	20.6	18.9	11.2	8.7

EXHIBIT 21.2

INVESTMENT PORTFOLIO BREAKDOWN BY SECTOR AS AT DECEMBER 31, 2006

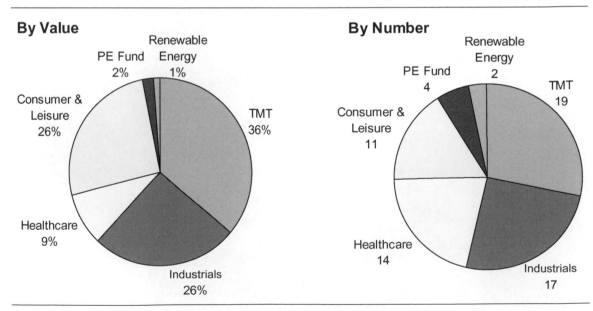

By Value

Renewable Energy 1%
PE Fund 2%
Consumer & Leisure 26%
TMT 36%
Healthcare 9%
Industrials 26%

By Number

Renewable Energy 2
PE Fund 4
Consumer & Leisure 11
TMT 19
Healthcare 14
Industrials 17

EXHIBIT 21.3

NEW INVESTMENTS (NOT EXHAUSTIVE LIST)

Company	Sector	Activity	Location	Deal type	Portfolio value (%)	Size (€mn)
1	TMT	Accounting and business software	Nordic	Buyout	8.8	580
2	Healthcare	Care homes	U.K.	Buyout	5.8	520
3	Industrials	Crash test dummies	Germany	Buyout	5.4	110
4	TMT	Security software	U.K.	Buyout	4.9	138
5	Consumer and leisure	Plastic toys	Germany	Buyout	3.3	165
6	Renewable	Renewable energy fund	Benelux	Fund	2.9	21
7	Industrials	Measuring and weighting systems	Benelux	Buyout	2.4	60
8	Consumer and leisure	Pastry retailer	France	Expansion	2.4	95

EXHIBIT 21.4

RECENT REALIZATIONS (NOT EXHAUSTIVE LIST)

Company	Sector	Exit route	IRR (%)	Multiple of original cost
A	Healthcare	Trade sale	46	2.5×
B	Consumer and leisure	Financial sale	−2	0.9×
C	Consumer and leisure	Financial sale	11	1.9×
D	Healthcare	Financial sale	78	5.8×
E	TMT	Trade sale	39	2.2×
F	TMT	Sale to management	29	1.4×

EXHIBIT 21.5

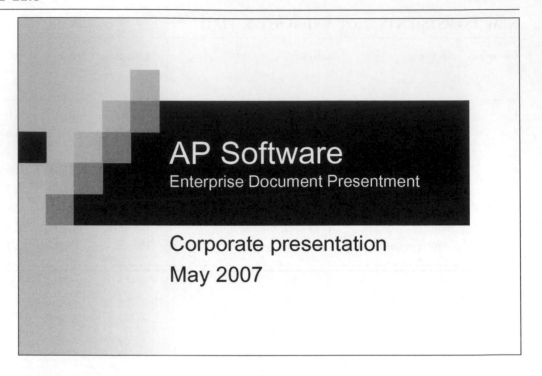

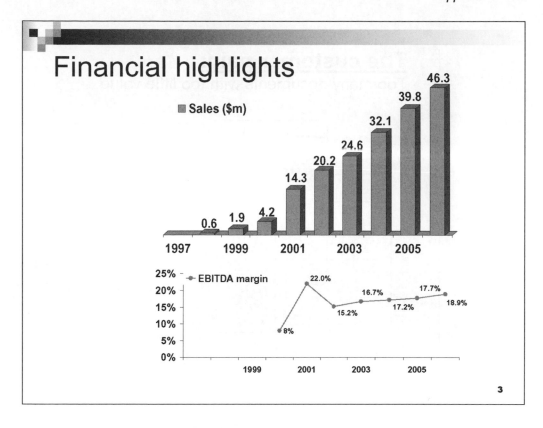

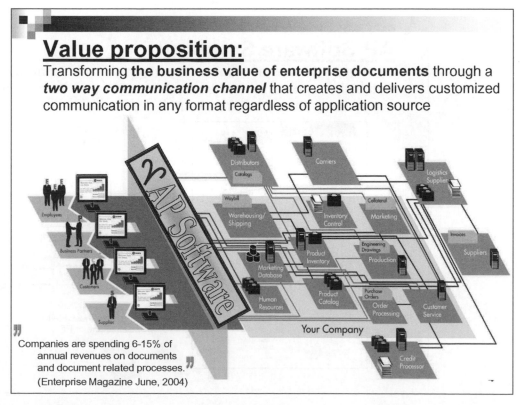

The customer pain:
Too many documents with too little value...

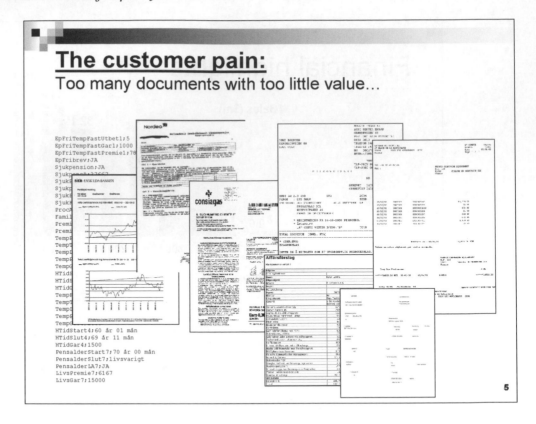

AP Software Solution:
All-in-one solution that enables the composition, personalization, distribution, and archiving of business documents -- from the enterprise application to the ultimate recipient

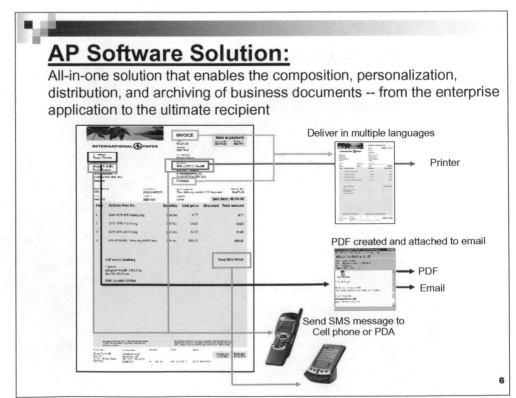

AP Software Solution:

Provides all five essential capabilities for extending effective document presentment across the last mile separating enterprise systems and customers, partners, suppliers and employees

Monitor

Manage

Present

Compose

Collect

Existing Environment & Architecture

- Seamless connectivity to ERP, legacy, and other strategic applications
- Automated design and composition of business documents
- Forms-based interaction with documents and applications
- Personalized messages in mass communications
- Recipient-specified distribution of business documents
- Electronic archiving
- End-to-end document distribution tracking

AP Software - Corporate Presentation -
May, 2007

7

The market

- Information growing at unprecedented rates
- Emergence of multiple communication channels
- Information infrastructure rapidly evolving
- Cost management fuelling profitability
- Customer satisfaction a key contributor to lifecycle management
- US represents significant market opportunity

* **ERP** - Enterprise Resource Planning,
CRM - Customer Relations Management,
KM - Knowledge Management
ECM - Enterprise Content Management.

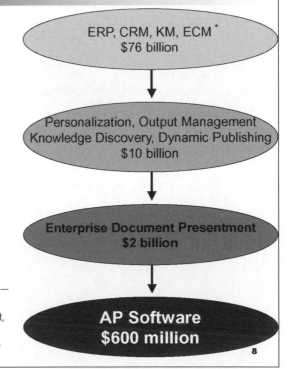

ERP, CRM, KM, ECM *
$76 billion

Personalization, Output Management
Knowledge Discovery, Dynamic Publishing
$10 billion

Enterprise Document Presentment
$2 billion

AP Software
$600 million

8

AP Software saved companies over $100 million USD worldwide in the last 12 months

- Cut paper consumption on average by 60%

- Cut company development costs by 80%

- Helped increase sales by 20%

- With over 1.3 million EDP combinations

- Utilities clients received 1 million less customer support calls

AP Software - Corporate Presentation -
May 2007

9

Targeting vertical markets

Financial Services	Utilities & Telcos	Retail & Dist.	Manufacturing
Market pressures: • Customer Churn • Market Consolidation • Commoditization of services **Solution(s):** • Statement Consolidation • Bill Presentment • E-Statements • Customer Self-Service • Correspondence **Value:** • Improve customer experience at lower cost; Increase customer retention rates, improve profitability	**Market pressures:** • Deregulation • Regulatory Compliance • Cost Management **Solution(s):** • Statement Consolidation • Production Printing • Bill Presentment **Value:** • Improve customer experience at lower cost; improved profitability	**Market pressures:** • Intense Competition • Slim Margins • Customer Loyalty • Labeling Compliance • Expanding Product Catalogs **Solution(s):** • Real-time Article Pricing • Dynamic Messaging/ Merchandising • Consolidated Shipping Documents & Labeling **Value:** • Competitive Advantage, Reduce Lost Sales, Deliver Right Product-Right Place-Less Time	**Market pressures:** • Time to Market • One Face To Customer • Low Asset Utilization • Low Profitability • Complex Supply Chains • Regulatory Compliance **Solution(s):** • Dynamic Document Branding • Automated Private Labeling • Consolidated Shipping Documents & MSDS **Value:** • Improve Cust Service • Reduce Direct Costs • On Time Delivery Of Perfect Order

AP Software - Corporate Presentation -
May 2007

10

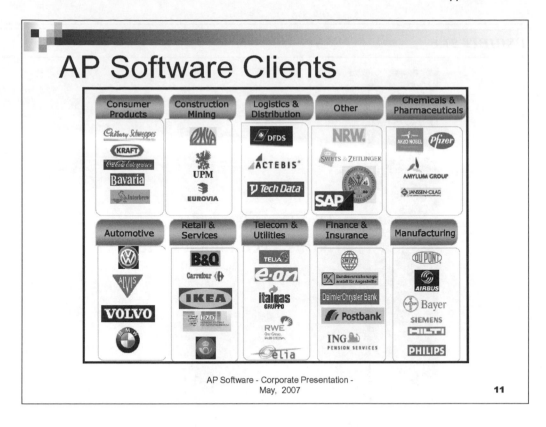

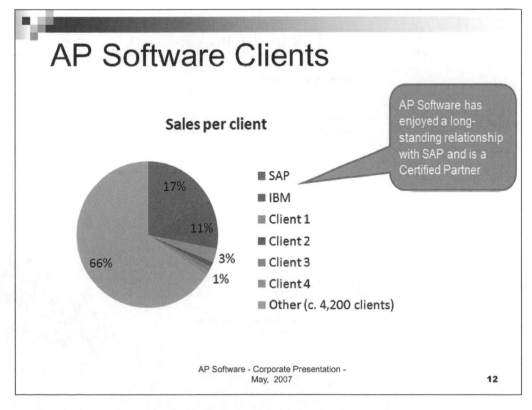

EXHIBIT 21.6

May 2007

Investment opportunity:

Niras Technologies Ltd

---

1. Introduction

The Investment opportunity

- A global leader in the development, manufacturing and marketing of advanced evaluation, planning & laser marking systems to the diamond manufacturing industry
- Opportunities for
  - leveraging
  - growth organically and through acquisitions
  - potential new addressable market
- Strong management team separate from owners with extensive experience and motivation
- Company strengths lie in positive cash flow, patents, and world-wide reputation and brand name
- On offer a proprietary sale of a controlling 58% stake by group of founders

Niras Technologies

2. Company overview

Background
- Founded and headquartered in Belgium in 1988
- A leading company with proprietary technology specifically applied to the diamond industry
- Focused on centres of diamond manufacturing and trading worldwide, including India, Belgium, Israel, USA, Russia, China, and South Africa
- Niras develops, manufactures and sells technology products that have revolutionised the diamond manufacturing industry
- Niras currently employs 123 people, including 19 in development and engineering

Highlights
- Estimated 67% market share in the diamond planning & grading products
- Established brand name and reputation in the industry
  - product of choice of market opinion leaders
- Strong industry and corporate growth potential and clear strategy
- Revenue has seen a CAGR of 37% between 2002 and 2006

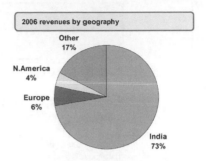

2006 revenues by geography

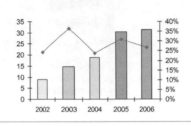

Turnover ($m) and net profit margin

Niras Technologies

3

3. Niras products

Products
- Proprietary precision mechanics, optics, electronics, laser and colour technology with sophisticated software embedded in computerized systems that
  - maximize yield of rough diamonds
  - grade quality of rough & polished diamonds according to 4Cs (carat, cut, clarity & colour)
  - inscription solutions to affirm authenticity and enhance branding
- A strong pipeline of new products
  - for new market segments ("nano")
  - for new addressable markets (retail)
  - consumable products with recurring revenues (polishing discs)
  - improved software and algorithms (fully automated inclusion mapping system in late R&D stages)
- Niras products and solutions are specifically used to increase profit margins of our customers across all levels of the diamond industry value chain
  - typical payback is 200 to 300 stones, less than 1 month turnover of an average Indian manufacturer

Niras Technologies

4

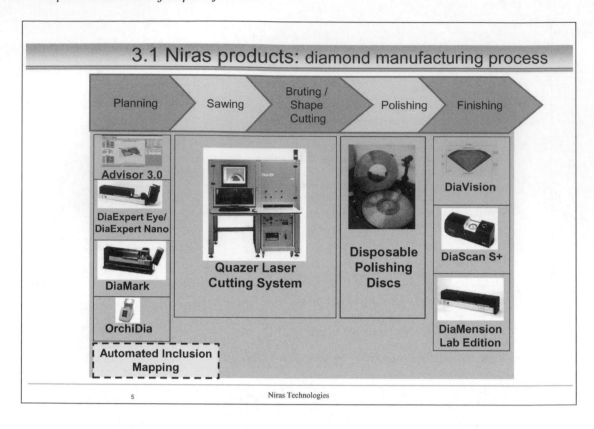

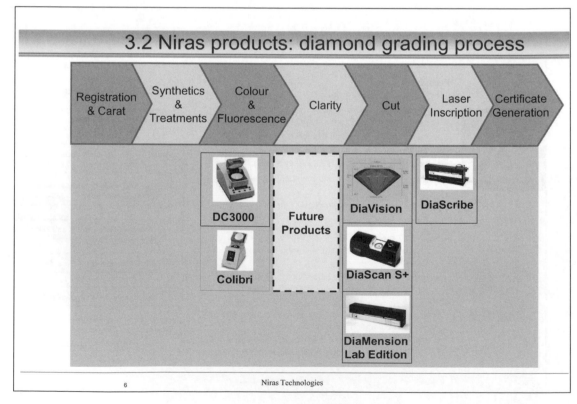

4. The market and industry

Value chain

- The diamond industry value chain starts with the site holders, such as De Beers, which controls about 50% of rough diamond mining in the world

> In 2006 an estimated **$12bn** of rough diamonds output

⇩

- Next come the manufacturers and the wholesale traders, of which India accounts for more than 90% by volume; Russian, China and South Africa are emerging as important manufacturing centres

> In 2006 there was an estimated **$13bn** in rough diamond sales and **$19bn** in polished diamond output

⇩

- Gemmological laboratories are strategic customers and industry standard setting bodies
- Retailers are at the bottom of the value chain – the US accounts for ~50% and Honk Kong just under 25% of sales

> In 2006 there was an estimated **$68bn** of retail diamond jewellery sales

Niras Position and Competition

In diamond planning and grading products

- Niras controls in excess of 60% market share
- An Israeli firm (TCS Systems) is established in the market with a global presence and is a *price* player with a range of cheap low-end products
- There is also a Russian company that has been a competitor in the high-end rough equipment space
  - has recently launched new price-driven product
  - legal conflicts over IP
- A new firm has emerged as a marketing and distribution specialist in this sector in India (a former Niras Indian representative)

In laser sawing and cutting machinary

- TCS Systems that has launched a "green laser product"
- Other competition consists mainly of Indian firms with limited international presence, and low-tech solutions
- A Canadian firm has recently developed their first laser sawing product
  - limited market penetration to date

5. Financials and KPIs

	Audited figures						Forecast		
P&L (€k)	2002	2003	2004	2005	2006	CAGR	2007E	2008E	2009E
Revenue	8,909	14,694	18,822	30,291	31,327	37%	38,532	46,239	55,486
Gross profit	5,910	10,222	12,673	20,742	20,413	36%	24,661	30,518	37,731
PBT	2,654	5,919	6,323	11,709	8,915	35%	13,486	14,334	18,311
PAT	2,158	5,329	4,467	9,350	8,378	40%	9,440	12,947	14,426
B/S (€k)									
Shareholder's equity	1,315	5,809	7,186	21,693	26,907	113%			
Total assets	3,950	8,147	12,026	29,551	32,841	70%			
Cash and equivalents	1,384	3,965	5,498	11,700	13,386	76%			
Interest bearing debt	3	6	0	0	0	nm			
Financial ratio (%)									
Gross profit margin	66.3%	69.6%	67.3%	68.5%	65.2%		64.0%	66.0%	68.0%
PBT margin	29.8%	40.3%	33.6%	38.7%	28.5%		35.0%	31.0%	33.0%
PAT margin	24.2%	36.3%	23.7%	30.9%	26.7%		24.5%	28.0%	26.0%
Revenue from India	69.3%	67.2%	69.5%	77.4%	72.3%				
Efficiency ratio (%)									
RoAE				69%	65%	34%			
RoAA				44%	45%	27%			
Operational activity ratio (days)									
Average Debtors Turnover			21days	27days	34days				
Average Payables Turnover			90days	53days	74days				
Average Inventory Turnover			63days	53days	45days				

Notes:
1. Return on Average Equity
2. Return on Average Assets

6. Prospects

Organic growth
- Management is confident in the growth prospects of the firm
- Revenues and PAT have shown a CAGR of 37% and 40% respectively over last 5 years
- Niras's brand name and market leading position are seen as positive drivers of growth

New products
- Strong R&D team with proven track record of coming to market with new technologies
- Recent launch of "Nano" product range, catering for smaller diamonds
- Recurring-sales (consumable) products, such as the disposable polishing discs
- New and improved versions of proprietary software

New markets
- Accelerating consumer demand for polished diamonds in China, India and the Middle East
- New manufacturing centres in Southern African countries
- Retail diamond sellers – "selling aid products"

Acquisitions
- Potential for acquisitions of complimentary products targeted at diamond and gem industry
  - leverage both Niras's brand name, and
  - extensive distribution network and client services infrastructure

Leverage
- Niras has a strong balance sheet with negative debt
  - no interest bearing debt; cash and equivalents to the tune of €23.4 million
- The firm is operating with a positive FCF, which it has sustained for several years

9   Niras Technologies

EXHIBIT 21.7

Investment presentation:

Banque Pierre Malland & Cie

June 2007

1. Introduction

Investment opportunity

Description

- A Swiss private bank that has evolved since the 19th Century through mergers and acquisitions
- Currently owned by the US group – Richardson Family Enterprises
- Opportunities for both organic growth and M&A in the local market
- Strong management team separate from owners with extensive experience and motivation
- Company strengths lie in its brand reputation, existing client base, senior management and self-proclaimed expertise in alternative asset management
- The bank has sustained a high dividend payout policy for several years
- On offer is a spin-off of the Swiss bank from the US group that considers it non-core

$\mathcal{PM}$

Banque **Pierre, Malland** & CIE SA

Richardson Financial Group

2   Banque Pierre Malland

2. Company overview

PM
Banque **Pierre, Malland** & CIE SA
Richardson Financial Group

PM Background

- A Swiss based private bank focused entirely on wealth management – the bank does not take on any commercial or merchant banking risk
- Headquartered in Geneva, with offices in Lausanne, Neuchâtel and Nyon. The bank is strategically focused on the on-shore market of French speaking Switzerland
- The bank employs 86 people, including 22 senior client advisors
- EUR 2.6bn (CHF 4.3bn) assets under management (AuM), as of June 2007
- Solely engaged in portfolio management for its private clients, and out-sources all of its payment transactions to an external firm (subject to a service contract)
- PM maintains a culture of a family business, with strong CSR efforts, donating c. 5% of profits

PM History

- Part of the American, independently-owned, Richardson Family Enterprises, Banque Pierre Malland ("PM") was formed in November 2003 when Banque Pierre bought Banque Malland & Cie from Banque Cantonale Burgy
- Banque Malland was founded in Lausanne in 1889 and specialised in wealth management for local and European private clients
- Banque Pierre was established in Geneva in 1969 as a subsidiary of the US based Richardson Financial Group

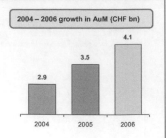

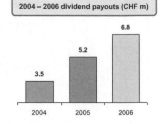

3   Banque Pierre Malland

2. Company overview

PM
Banque **Pierre, Malland** & CIE SA
Richardson Financial Group

Key developments

- The bank's clientele is balanced between Swiss and European clients, following recent focus and growth in the domestic market
- The bank claims to have developed an expertise in alternative investments
- AuM have more than quadrupled since 2002
- Two senior members of management recently retired, including the CFO
- In Jan-Feb 2007 the bank acquired and expanded its offices in Lausanne in the canton of Vaud
- In May 2007 PM opened a new branch in Nyon
- 12 new employees have been hired in 2007

Transaction potential

- PM is run independently from its US parent company. Jerome Lager, PM's Managing Director, is also a member of the executive committee of the Richardson Financial Group
- PM is considered to be non-core to its American parent
- In addition, It is rumoured that the parent company has experienced difficulties running the business
- We therefore believe that if an interesting offer was made, the parent would enter discussions. Furthermore, Lager would be keen to remain with the bank, and further increase his equity stake

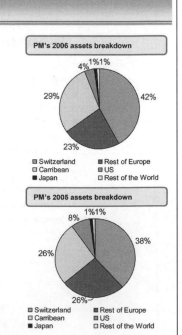

4   Banque Pierre Malland

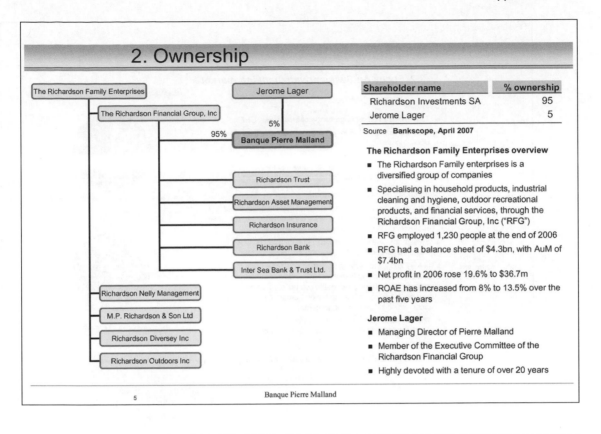

2. Ownership

| The Richardson Family Enterprises |
| The Richardson Financial Group, Inc |

95%

Jerome Lager

5%

Banque Pierre Malland

Richardson Trust

Richardson Asset Management

Richardson Insurance

Richardson Bank

Inter Sea Bank & Trust Ltd.

Richardson Nelly Management

M.P. Richardson & Son Ltd

Richardson Diversey Inc

Richardson Outdoors Inc

Shareholder name	% ownership
Richardson Investments SA	95
Jerome Lager	5

Source **Bankscope, April 2007**

The Richardson Family Enterprises overview

- The Richardson Family enterprises is a diversified group of companies
- Specialising in household products, industrial cleaning and hygiene, outdoor recreational products, and financial services, through the Richardson Financial Group, Inc ("RFG")
- RFG employed 1,230 people at the end of 2006
- RFG had a balance sheet of $4.3bn, with AuM of $7.4bn
- Net profit in 2006 rose 19.6% to $36.7m
- ROAE has increased from 8% to 13.5% over the past five years

Jerome Lager

- Managing Director of Pierre Malland
- Member of the Executive Committee of the Richardson Financial Group
- Highly devoted with a tenure of over 20 years

5   Banque Pierre Malland

---

3. The wealth management market

3.1 *Market size and growth*

Worldwide HNWI wealth market

- Number of High Net Worth Individuals ("HNWIs") around the world grew by 8.3% in 2006 to 9.5m
- Worldwide HNWI wealth market is estimated at $37.2tn in 2006, representing growth of 11.4% during the year.*
- There are three main locations where HNWIs direct their funds : New York, Switzerland and Singapore
- Growth of HNWIs is particularly prominent in Latin America, Eastern Europe, Asia-Pacific, Africa and the Middle East

> 13.1% median growth in assets under management in base currency terms (18.6% in 2005)

HNWI population by region (millions)

2004: 2.7 / 2.6 / 2.2 / 0.3 / 0.3 / 0.1
2005: 2.9 / 2.8 / 2.4 / 0.3 / 0.3 / 0.1
2006: 3.2 / 2.9 / 2.6 / 0.3 / 0.4 / 0.1

■ North America ■ Europe ■ Asia-Pacific
■ Middle East ■ Latin America ■ Africa

European HNWI wealth market

- European HNWI wealth market was estimated at $10tn in 2006
- # HNWIs in Europe grew by 6.4% in 2006 to 2.9m

Asia-Pacific HNWI wealth market

- Asian HNWI wealth was worth at $8.4tn in 2006
- Number of HNWIs in the area grew by 8.6% in 2006 to reach 2.6m

HNWI wealth by region (USD trillions)

2004: 9.3 / 8.9 / 7.1 / 0.3 / 0.3 / 0.1
2005: 10.2 / 9.4 / 7.6 / 4.2 / 1.3 / 0.8
2006: 11.3 / 10.1 / 8.4 / 5.1 / 1.4 / 0.9

■ North America ■ Europe ■ Asia-Pacific
■ Middle East ■ Latin America ■ Africa

* Individuals holding financial assets in excess of $1m

Source: **World Wealth Report 2007** (Merrill Lynch, Cap Gemini)

6   Banque Pierre Malland

3. The wealth management market

3.2 *Focus on Swiss private banking market*

Overview

- Total Swiss asset management = approximately US$6tn
- Total Swiss private banking = approximately US$4tn of which US$2.1tn offshore
- With GDP per head of approximately US$30,000 Switzerland is one of the world's wealthiest countries and therefore offers non-negligible "onshore potential"

Banking secrecy and tax programs

- Banking secrecy, introduced in Switzerland in the mid-1930s, provides protection for the privacy of both Swiss and non-Swiss customers with regard to financial matters
- Swiss banks are legally bound to ensure client confidentiality with criminal penalties for bankers who break the law
- In May 2004, Switzerland signed an agreement with the EU to settle a long running disagreement over tax fraud. In return for an opt-out on sharing information on tax evasion, Switzerland agreed to levy a withholding tax on European residents savings income held in Swiss bank accounts
- The tax, starting at 15% from 1 Jan 2005, will rise to 35% by 2010, with 75% of revenues going to the country of origin

> Other European offshore banking centres are also bound by this agreement

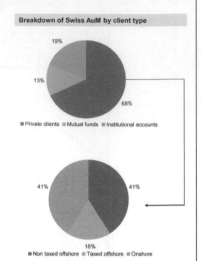

Breakdown of Swiss AuM by client type

68%
19%
13%

■ Private clients ■ Mutual funds ■ Institutional accounts

41%
41%
18%

■ Non taxed offshore ■ Taxed offshore ■ Onshore

Source **Deutsche Bank**

Mid-sized Swiss private banks likely to struggle for growth in the medium term

7   Banque Pierre Malland

---

3. The wealth management market

3.3 *Investment class spread*

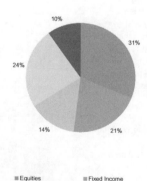

Breakdown of global AuM by investment class (2006)

31%
21%
14%
24%
10%

■ Equities   ■ Fixed Income
■ Cash/Deposits   ■ Real estate
■ Alternative Investments

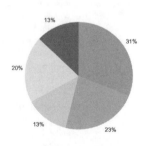

Breakdown of global AuM by investment class (2008F)

31%
23%
13%
20%
13%

■ Equities   ■ Fixed Income
■ Cash/Deposits   ■ Real estate
■ Alternative Investments

Source **World Wealth Report 2007** (Merrill Lynch, Cap Gemini)

8   Banque Pierre Malland

4. Understanding the industry

4.1 Economics, value drivers and KPIs

The attractiveness of the industry's economics

- Large and growing
  - 80% of the financial services profit pool in Europe
  - 20% of global financial services revenue (Citigroup)
  - Highest growth area in the industry (UBS)
- Profitability
  - High net profit margins, with most players achieving 25+ basis points, compared to 5 for institutional AM
  - Regulatory and economic capital requirements are low, little credit and market risk, limited need for branch network
- Stable revenue stream
  - High proportion of fees in the revenue mix, in contrast to more volatile net interest or trading income
  - Traditionally loyal client relationships
- High stock market rating
  - A premium P/E ratio of about 1.2 is the norm, compared with 0.8 for the financial sector as a whole (compared with the market as a whole)
  - EFG Int. was valued at 12% of AuM at its 2005 IPO

Value drivers

- Wealth management has four components:
  - Assets; Leverage; Fees; and Costs
- There are two key value drivers: (i) net profit margin ; and (ii) assets under management
- The ideal client will borrow against existing assets to increase the leverage of their investments. Sophisticated clients can be effectively managed with little time devoted to their portfolio
- A McKinsey (European) report indicates that (i) revenue generation, rather than cost efficiency, has been most critical; and (ii) for AuM, market performance rather than net new money or greater share of wallet

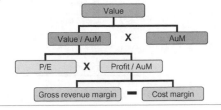

4. Understanding the industry

4.2 Competitive landscape

- Broadly there are two main models:
  - North American model: dominated by full-service discount brokerages and money managers, with strength in investment areas rather than traditional deposit gathering. Emphasis is on commission-based model
  - European model: universal and traditional (Swiss) private banks dominate, offering a comprehensive range of wealth management products and services. Emphasis is on fee-based model
- There have been cycles of consolidation in the market (Swiss case)
- Yet still very fragmented amongst tier-2 players
- Top 10 command >60% market share

Top 10 players' market share and growth in 2006

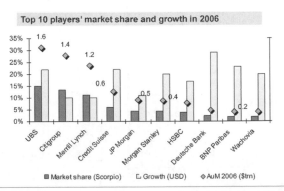

4. Understanding the industry

4.3 *Implied valuation of Key Swiss private banking transactions since 2001*

Date	Target	Buyer	Goodwill / AuM	Price / AuM	Net rev	Op profit	Net profit	Book
Dec-06	Swissfirst AG's PB	Banque Pasche SA	na	na	na	na	na	na
Sep-06	Banca Gesfield SA	Fondiaria - SAI SpA	na	na	na	na	16.0x	4.1x
Aug-06	Bagefi AG's private client base	P&P Private Bank AG	na	na	na	na	na	na
Sep-05	Banque Baring BrothersSA	Mr Eric Sturdza	na	na	na	na	na	na
Sep-05	UBS Private Banks and GAM	Julius Baer	4.6%	5.5%	4.9x	12.5x	26.9x	6.5x
Mar-05	BNY - Inter Maritime Bank (GV)	Bank Hapoalim	0.5%	3.4%	3.2x	29.8x	20.4x	1.2x
Dec-04	CaixaBank Banque Privee	BNP Paribas Private Bank	na	na	na	na	na	na
Jul-04	Bank Jenni & Cie	MBO back by Mirabaud	na	na	na	na	na	na
Jun-04	Vontobel Group	Swiss Reiffesen Group	1.7%	3.6%	3.9x	9.5x	17.7x	1.9x
May-04	Trafina Privatbank AG	Bauman & Cie	na	na	na	na	na	na
Nov-03	Notz Stucki	Banque Ferrier Lullin (UBS)	na	na	na	na	na	na
Oct-03	Bank von Ernst (HVB)	Coutts (RBoS)	3.2%	4.8%	3.8x	11.8x	18.7x	2.9x
May-03	Compagnie Bancaire Geneve	Société Générale	2.2%	3.9%	na	na	na	2.2x
May-03	Banque Edouard Constant	EFG Private Bank	1.2%	4.4%	3.7x	na	na	1.4x
May-03	IBI Bank AG	Banca Intermobiliare	1.9%	8.8%	6.1x	na	na	1.3x
May-03	STG	LGT Group	1.8%	2.8%	na	na	na	2.7x
Feb-03	Rud, Blass & Cie AG	Deutsche Bank	0.6%	2.8%	na	na	na	1.3x
Jan-03	IntesaBci Bank (Suisse)	Crédit Agricole Indosuez	3.1%	6.7%	6.6x	nm	nm	1.9x
Jan-03	Bank Thorbecke	St Galler KB	na	na	na	na	na	na
Nov-02	PBS Private Bank	Clariden Bank	na	na	na	na	na	na
Jun-02	Darrier Hentch	Lombard Odier	na	na	na	na	na	na
Mar-02	Bank Sarasin	Rabobank	2.1%	3.7%	4.1x	13.1x	20.5x	2.4x
Feb-02	Discount Bank & Trust Co	Union Bancaire Privee	1.7%	5.0%	na	na	10.5x	1.5x
Feb-02	Hyposwiss	St Galler KB	na	na	na	na	na	na
Mar-01	Bank of Austria (Schweiz)	Aargauische Kantonalbank	na	na	na	na	na	na
Jan-01	West LB (Schweiz)	Banca del Gottardo	5.3%	8.5%	6.9x	20.0x	25.6x	2.7x
Mean			**2.3%**	**4.9%**				
Median			**1.9%**	**4.4%**				

Source: La Banca Jura

An estimated value range between 3-6% of assets under management (AuM)

5. Financials and KPIs

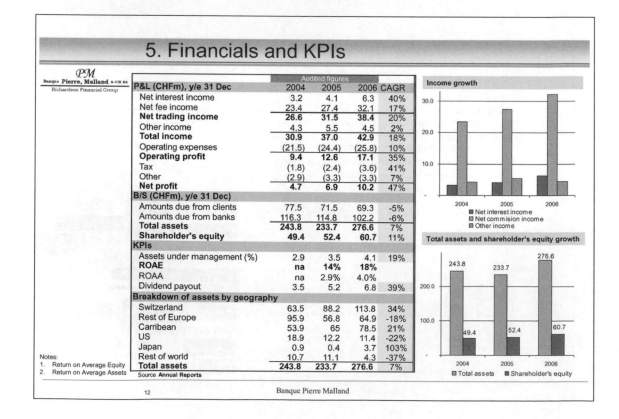

PM
Banque Pierre, Malland & CIE SA
Richardson Financial Group

P&L (CHFm), y/e 31 Dec	2004	2005	2006	CAGR
Net interest income	3.2	4.1	6.3	40%
Net fee income	23.4	27.4	32.1	17%
Net trading income	26.6	31.5	38.4	20%
Other income	4.3	5.5	4.5	2%
Total income	30.9	37.0	42.9	18%
Operating expenses	(21.5)	(24.4)	(25.8)	10%
Operating profit	9.4	12.6	17.1	35%
Tax	(1.8)	(2.4)	(3.6)	41%
Other	(2.9)	(3.3)	(3.3)	7%
Net profit	4.7	6.9	10.2	47%
B/S (CHFm), y/e 31 Dec)				
Amounts due from clients	77.5	71.5	69.3	-5%
Amounts due from banks	116.3	114.8	102.2	-6%
Total assets	243.8	233.7	276.6	7%
Shareholder's equity	49.4	52.4	60.7	11%
KPIs				
Assets under management (%)	2.9	3.5	4.1	19%
ROAE	na	14%	18%	
ROAA	na	2.9%	4.0%	
Dividend payout	3.5	5.2	6.8	39%
Breakdown of assets by geography				
Switzerland	63.5	88.2	113.8	34%
Rest of Europe	95.9	56.8	64.9	-18%
Carribean	53.9	65	78.5	21%
US	18.9	12.2	11.4	-22%
Japan	0.9	0.4	3.7	103%
Rest of world	10.7	11.1	4.3	-37%
Total assets	243.8	233.7	276.6	7%

Source **Annual Reports**

Notes:
1. Return on Average Equity
2. Return on Average Assets

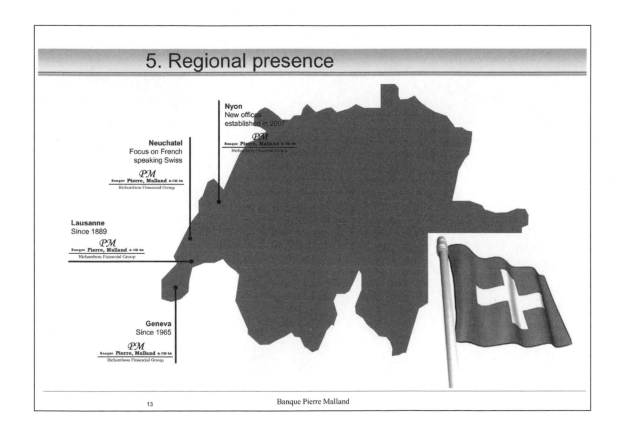

23

FiberNet Communications

Norbert Kovacs, a new associate in the London office of Warburg Pincus, was reading an investment report at his desk in early 2004, when one of the firm's partners, William Knott, walked into his office. Unfortunately, Knott brought gloomy news: it turned out that Kovacs and Knott had just lost one of their deals in a heated auction. Both of them spent many weeks investigating this investment opportunity and were working relentlessly on the financial analysis in order to construct a winning bid. However, now the deal process came to a complete halt, as another firm in the market came up with a higher bid. Kovacs was very disappointed: he joined Warburg Pincus, one of the world's prominent private equity firms (Exhibit 23.1), several months ago and was very eager to execute a transaction from start to finish. He worked very hard on this transaction and could not even find the time to have a proper telephone conversation with his childhood friend Peter Szepesi, who recently tracked him down and wanted to catch up.

Kovacs knew Szepesi from the elementary school in Hungary, where both of them grew up. The two shared a number of interests and stayed in touch, even after Kovacs left the country in 2002 to pursue an MBA. Now, when Kovacs finally had some time, he decided to distract himself from the pessimistic thoughts about the lost deal and finally returned Szepesi's call. To Kovacs' surprise, it turned out that his friend had a business proposition: Szepesi's father was a CEO of FiberNet Communications, a major Hungarian cable company. The original investor in FiberNet was ARGUS Capital Partners—a CEE private equity firm, whose strategy was to quickly assemble together a major cable company through acquisitions of numerous local cable operators. Now the firm wanted to exit this investment because their fund was approaching the end of its life, thereby pushing the firm to seek a buyer for FiberNet and other investments in the portfolio. Since FiberNet was one of the winners in the portfolio, the fund's asking price for the company was 8.5× 2003 EBITDA. Szepesi knew that Kovacs was working in the private equity industry and, therefore, wanted Kovacs and his colleagues to review this opportunity. In Szepesi's opinion, Kovacs could benefit by bringing an attractive deal to Warburg Pincus, while Szepesi's father would have less uncertainty about the future of his company, as now there would be a personal connection between FiberNet and the new investor. With this in mind, Szepesi sent the background materials to his friend.

Kovacs initially became interested in FiberNet, especially given the fact that he just lost a transaction earlier in the day and was eager to begin working on a different

The case was prepared by Tamara Sakovska (LBS MBA 2004) under the supervision of Eli Talmor.

investment opportunity. He knew that the Hungarian cable market was potentially very attractive, as it had been growing explosively over the past several years. Kovacs also realized that FiberNet was a fairly young company that was able to become one of the major cable operators in the industry in a relatively short timespan. In addition, Kovacs knew that his friend's father, FiberNet's CEO, was a very hard-working, intelligent, and savvy businessman who conducted a number of successful acquisitions that allowed FiberNet to gain market share.

However, Kovacs hesitated about a number of aspects relating to the potential deal. First, the transaction was probably going to be small for Warburg Pincus. The firm generally invested in companies with a revenue of several hundred million dollars, whereas FiberNet's revenue was projected to be approximately USD37mn for 2004. A transaction of this size must provide compelling returns in order to capture sufficient interest within the firm. Second, the company was located in a less developed European country, which would complicate the due diligence process and potentially create obstacles in obtaining debt financing. Third, Kovacs was unsure whether the personal relationship with the CEO would prove to be a blessing or a curse: on the one hand, it would allow Warburg Pincus to gain additional transparency on the investment opportunity while, on the other hand, it may give rise to a number of uncomfortable situations that could compromise Kovacs' relationship with his childhood friend. Kovacs ultimately presented the investment opportunity to William Knott, who became enthusiastic about FiberNet and asked Kovacs to gather information about the industry and the company in order to perform a preliminary analysis of the potential deal.

HUNGARIAN HISTORY AND ECONOMY

From its location at the heart of Europe, Hungary shares borders with seven Central and Eastern European as well as Balkan countries. The Hungarian population was slightly over 10 million in 2003 and could be characterized as relatively homogeneous in ethnic terms when compared with other countries in Europe. Following imposition of a communist regime in 1947 and a crushed revolt in 1956, Hungary began in 1968 liberalizing its economy by increasing the autonomy of enterprises and by introducing competitive mechanisms in the marketplace. After the collapse of communism, Hungary held its first multiparty elections in 1990 and initiated a fully fledged free market economy. It joined NATO in 1999 and acceded to the EU along with nine other states in May 2004.

Hungary's domestic market is relatively small, although the country's economy is third largest in Central Europe (after Poland and the Czech Republic). Post-socialist Hungary significantly benefited from the political stability and high levels of foreign direct investment. As a result of an extensive privatization of the mid-1990s, major stakes in the telecommunications, utilities, banking, and television sectors were given to private investors. In 2003 the private sector accounted for almost 80% of GDP and represented one of the highest shares in the region. Service industries had traditionally been neglected under the socialist regime, however Hungary rapidly redirected its focus from manufacturing to services in the early 1990s in order to make its economy similar to those in other EU countries. Hungary's economy experienced significant growth in the past decade, allowing Hungarians to significantly improve their standard of living, as the country's GDP per capita became third largest in Eastern and Central Europe by 2002 (after Slovenia and the Czech Republic). A summary of Hungary's economic data is provided in Exhibit 23.2.

HUNGARIAN TELEVISION BROADCASTING MARKET

Before the collapse of the socialist regime, commercial broadcasting did not exist in Hungary, and the state-controlled Magyar Televízió (MTV—Hungarian Television) enjoyed a monopoly. MTV transmits two channels: its main channel, m1, offers general entertainment programming, while the second channel, m2, provides news and information programming. The Hungarian Broadcasting Act of 1996 paved the way to broadcasting competition and transformed MTV from a state-controlled monolith to a public service channel. Private national terrestrial television did not launch until October 1997; however, when the competition did arrive, MTV suffered extensively from a loss of both viewers and advertising revenues. Moreover, when national private channels launched, m2 was forced to give up its terrestrial frequency and is now available only via cable or satellite. MTV's market share gradually declined from 83.7% in 1993 to 27.5% in 1998, and further slipped to a mere 14.3% in 2001. Apart from suffering from diminishing audiences and recurring threats of bankruptcy, MTV faces political allegations. Under Hungarian law, MTV's board must represent both the current government and the opposition equally; however, in the past the ruling coalition used the broadcaster for promoting its own agenda.

In addition to MTV, there are two private national terrestrial channels in Hungary, TV2 and RTL Klub. TV2 was launched in 1997 and is owned by the Scandinavian Broadcasting System (49%), the Hungarian production company MTM Kommunikációs (38.5%), and the German productions company Tele-München (12.5%). The channel aims at the younger urban viewer and offers mostly entertainment programming, such as soap operas, chat shows, game shows, and comedy. TV2 is one of the most successful channels in Hungary: its market share approached 31.2% after a year of operation, peaked at 39.7% in 2000, and fell slightly to 38.2% in 2001. Like TV2, the other private terrestrial channel RTL Klub was launched in 1997 and is owned by RTL Group (49%), Hungary's telecommunications operator Matav (25%), the U.K.-based media group Pearson (20%), and the Hungarian bank Unicbank Raiffeisen (6%). RTL Klub offers entertainment programming, such as celebrity shows, chat shows, and recently won the rights to broadcast Formula 1 racing.

Hungary's television broadcasting also features many commercial channels that are accessible via cable or satellite, as well as a number of local stations that cater to the local information need of their audiences. Multichannel penetration in Hungary is one of the highest in Central and Eastern Europe, with 48.1% of TV households subscribing to cable by the end of 2003. MTV's prolonged monopoly in the national terrestrial space contributed to the popularity of cable and satellite channels; however, the demand for multichannel television has been growing steadily even since the launch of private terrestrial channels in 1997. Exhibit 23.3 provides an overview of Hungary's major television channels.

CABLE TV INDUSTRY

Cable is the dominant multichannel platform in Hungary because it offers greater availability and attractive pricing when compared with satellite and digital TV. The Hungarian cable industry is highly fragmented, although it has begun consolidating in the past several years. During the socialist regime, the cable TV industry was money losing and virtually non-existent.

The first basic cable networks were laid in the late 1980s and early 1990s by local municipalities and owners of apartment blocks. Capital expenditure was generally subsidized by the government, allowing municipalities to keep the prices at a level that was sufficient to cover operating costs. During the early 1990s, average revenue per user (ARPU) was very low and ranged from USD1 to USD3. The technical capacity of cable networks was rather limited: the narrowband nature of networks restricted the number of television channels available, thereby allowing the provider to offer only one basic package for all. Moreover, the networks were built as a local loop, which made it difficult for providers to enforce subscription payments as pirated connections could not be cut.[1] The technical inadequacy of the networks restricted the services that could be provided and, as a result, the fees that could be charged. The cable TV market grew mostly in local clusters during the 1990s and still remains highly fragmented, with more than 400 operators in 2003.

The consolidation of the Hungarian cable industry was initiated in the late 1990s by the three largest players: UPC Hungary, MatávkábelTV, and FiberNet. All three operators employed similar strategies: (1) acquire local loop networks; (2) upgrade networks from loop to star in order to combat piracy and offer more services, such as broadband internet;[2] (3) increase prices as much as possible without breaching regulations; (4) improve the content and continue increasing ARPU. Although such a strategy resulted in some customer churn, the operators were broadly successful in raising prices, often in conjunction with network upgrades and improved content offerings. By 2003, ARPU from cable services reached between USD7 and USD10 and was broadly in line with the average figure for other Eastern European countries. Moreover, most cable providers began offering a broadband internet srvice, with ARPU ranging from USD35 to USD39 in 2003.

However, price hikes in the cable TV industry did not go unnoticed by the regulators: Hungary's Competition Office performed an ex-post price review based on customer complaints, but so far has accepted most of price increases in the market. The National Communications Authority is another regulatory body that, since January 2004, is entitled to review the level of market dominance by individual operators. Moreover, Hungary's recent membership in the EU implies that its regulatory environment may become tighter because its regulatory regime is expected to come in line with EU requirements. As a result, it was unclear how further price increases in the cable industry would be received by the regulators.

The evolution of the Hungarian cable industry implies that operators behave like local monopolies virtually everywhere, apart from the capital city of Budapest, where there are parallel cable networks. All cable operators have access to the same content at broadly comparable prices, as they are supplied through a Hungarian cable association that negotiates with content providers on their behalf. Since content providers are significantly larger in size than the largest operators, only the three large players could go directly to the major content suppliers to negotiate specific subscriber volume-based discounts that amount to approximately 10% to 30%. Although there are no regulatory barriers to entry, the emergence of new players is unlikely because of very high capital expenditure requirements. The new entrant will inevitably be confronted by price competition from the incumbent and most likely will find it virtually impossible to earn an adequate return on capital investment. The cable industry in Hungary faces little threat from substitute offerings, such as satellite or digital TV. Although satellite TV has better content, it is significantly more expensive than cable TV and is popular among

---

1. A loop network is built as a ring connecting multiple subscribers via one cable.
2. A star network links individual subscribers via a direct connection that can be easily cut in case of piracy.

high-income families or people living in rural areas. Digital TV is unlikely to grow significantly over the next few years given the investment required by broadcasters as well as consumers.

Since the cable industry in Hungary enjoyed heavy state subsidies in the 1980s and later experienced explosive growth driven by the three large operators, the country is characterized by a relatively high cable TV penetration when compared with other Eastern European markets. In 2003, 57% of all households had access to cable TV,[3] and 76% of these households actually had a subscription to the cable service. Cable networks can be further extended to cover more households in additional residential areas, although this effort may not be economically viable for most established operators. Further growth in the industry is expected to come from developers of apartment complexes, as the government continues subsidizing capital requirements for installation of cable networks in the new apartment blocs. Exhibit 23.4 provides key historical data and projections for the Hungarian cable TV market. Exhibit 23.5 provides comparative statistics for Hungary and other European markets.

FIBERNET'S KEY COMPETITORS

Although the cable TV market in Hungary is very fragmented, it is dominated by a handful of operators, with the Top-3 players accounting for 66% of the market (Exhibit 23.6). FiberNet is the third largest player, behind UPC Hungary and MatávkábelTV.

UPC Hungary

The operator entered the Hungarian cable market in 1993. Netherlands-based UPC is the largest cable operator in Hungary: as of September 2002 it passed 952,800 households and attracted 674,100 subscribers, which was equivalent to a 71% connection rate. UPC Hungary operates in the cities of Budapest, Miskolc, Debrecen, and Pécs. The operator recently made significant investments for network upgrades in order to allow full two-way interaction. The connection fee for reception of analog TV service is about HUF25,500, although discounts are frequently available. Exhibit 23.7 shows the cable TV packages offered by UPC Hungary.

UPC Hungary launched a broadband internet service in November 2000 in Budapest, just 2months after the telecommunications provider Matáv launched the country's first high-speed internet service via ADSL transmission. Such timing ensured that no one standard became dominant in Hungary during the early adoption of a broadband internet service. By September 2002 UPC Hungary extended its services to other cities, passing 482,000 homes with subscriptions amounting to HUF20,000, which was equivalent to a 4% connection rate. The operator offered only one high-speed internet package (see Exhibit 23.8).

MatávkábelTV

Telecommunication operator Matáv provides cable services through its subsidiary MatávkábelTV, which was formed in 1998. Since then Matáv has sold 25% of its equity and 75% of its shareholder voting rights to insurance company Hungaria Biztosito in order to comply with stricter regulations relating to the cross-ownership of cable and telecommunication interests. MatávkábelTV offers cable services mainly in Budapest

---

3. According to industry convention, this metric is labeled as percent of "households with cable passing".

and some rural areas. As of September 2002, the operator passed approximately 360,000 households and attracted 325,989 subsribers, which was equivalent to a 90% connection rate. Like UPC, MatávkábelTV recently upgraded its networks in order to improve its offering to customers. The connection fee for reception of analogue TV services is about HUF25,000 for a residential subscriber, or HUF40,000 for a business subsriber. The operator offers the cable packages shown in Exhibit 23.9.

MatávkábelTV offers a broadband internet service in Budapest and three other cities: as of the beginning of 2002, the operator passed about 70,000 homes and attracted about 1,900 subscribers, which was equivalent to a connection rate of approximately 3%. The operator provided two offerings: Otthon, a basic package, and Profi, a package that allows up to five concurrent users (see Exhibit 23.10).

THE FIBERNET OPPORTUNITY

Company

FiberNet entered the Hungarian cable industry only in 1999 and, as a result, was in a weaker position than its rivals UPC Hungary and MatávkábelTV. FiberNet provides services to small towns and operates in only one of Hungary's Top-12 cities, compared with 11 cities served by UPC and 9 cities served by MatávkábelTV. The operator's strategy to date has been to focus on acquisitions and upgrades of small cable TV players in the regions. Going forward, the company hopes to combine organic growth with further acquisitions.

More than 90% of FiberNet's networks are not overlapped by other cable networks (Exhibit 23.11), thereby allowing the operator to experience substantial growth. As of early 2004, the company passed about 330,000 homes and attracted about 210,000 subscribers, which was equivalent to a connection rate of 64%. FiberNet recently undertook a series of technical upgrades, with a superior star/broadband network representing over 70% of all networks by subscribers in 2004. Most remaining networks are scheduled for an upgrade over the next 2 years. The content provided by FiberNet is broadly comparable with rival offerings (see Exhibit 23.12).

FiberNet recently entered the broadband market, passed about 97,500 homes, and was able to attract approximately 6,150 customers as of the beginning of 2004, which was equivalent to a connection rate of about 6%. The operator offers multiple broadband internet packages (see Exhibit 23.13).

The more expensive Otthon package offers additional email addresses, while Otthon Plusz provides 5 MB of web space.

Management

FiberNet's management team was quite good, although some team members were stronger than others (the organizational chart is shown in Exhibit 23.14). The operator's CEO, Jozsef Szepesi, has been with the company since 1999. During his tenure at FiberNet, Szepesi built a loyal team around him and overall demonstrated a solid track record as a business builder. Szepesi had a superb knowledge of the cable industry in Hungary and had a clear vision about how to aggressively grow FiberNet in the future. FiberNet's CFO, Istvan Magyar, had a very good understanding not only of business, economics, and financials, but also operational specifics of the cable industry. Even though he was younger than other members of the team, he proved himself to be highly reliable, intelligent, and resourceful.

Certain other members of the management team were less impressive and were likely to be replaced. Moreover, the positions of COO Laszlo Mokos and Marketing Director Zoltan Kemeny were likely to be reviewed, as their roles in the organization were not clearly defined. Apart from reviewing the roles of certain team members, FiberNet needed to hire a business development director to support the CEO and COO and focus on identifying suitable acquisition targets.

Overall, the management team at FiberNet was functional yet incomplete. It was clear that it would be challenging to continue business as usual while replacing key executives at the same time. In addition, it would be difficult to find high-quality Hungarian managers who possessed deep market knowledge and were able to execute FiberNet 's ongoing strategy.

Financials

During the past 2 years, FiberNet has enjoyed explosive revenue growth averaging 47% per annum, with an EBITDA margin averaging 42%. Management's projections (shown in Exhibit 23.15) assumed that revenue growth would slow in the future to approximately 10%. Future growth was assumed to come from both increased cable TV prices and a greater number of subscribers. In addition, management assumed improvements in EBITDA margins, as they hoped that the price increases would not require significant content enhancements, thereby keeping costs at approximately the same level. Moreover, FiberNet's executives expected capital expenditure to decrease, as most of the networks had already been upgraded.

Exhibit 23.16 provides information about private cable transactions that took place in 2002 and 2003, whereas Exhibit 23.17 provides information on the yield curve in Hungary. As Kovacs researched the opportunity of investing in FiberNet, he wondered whether Warburg Pincus should go ahead at all with the transaction. He was worried about the risks that the Hungarian deal posed and did not know how he would resolve the potential conflict of interest when friendship and business had to be mixed.

APPENDIX

EXHIBIT 23.1

WARBURG PINCUS

Since 1971 Warburg Pincus has built an institution that currently operates on a worldwide basis. The firm is headquartered in New York and has offices in Menlo Park, London, Munich, Hong Kong, Seoul, Singapore, Mumbai, Beijing, and Tokyo. Warburg Pincus is organized by business sectors, with more than 100 professionals focusing on business services, communications, financial institutions, healthcare, media, information technology, energy, and real estate. The firm invested more than $12.2bn of capital, of which $4.7bn was invested in buyouts, recapitalizations, and special situations, $3.6bn was provided as development capital, and $3.9bn was devoted to venture capital transactions. The firm's latest fund, Warburg Pincus Private Equity VIII, was raised in 2001 and has a total size of $5.3bn.

Warburg Pincus was the first U.S. private equity firm to make a commitment to Europe. Since the firm's first transaction in Europe in 1983, Warburg Pincus has invested more than $2.5bn in 64 transactions in 14 European countries. The firm has committed as much as $500mn to a single transaction and has provided more than $150mn to a single European startup company. Warburg Pincus has more than $7.5bn available for additional investment, which includes one of the largest pools of available private equity capital in Europe.

Warburg Pincus is an experienced investor in Eastern Europe, most notably in Slovakia and the Czech Republic. The table below details the firm's recent investments in the region.

Company	Notes
Leciva	• Leading branded generic pharmaceutical company in the Czech Republic and Slovakia with a broad product portfolio; sales of $160mn in 2001 and 13% market share by value in the Czech Republic, 10% in Slovakia • Acquired from the National Property Fund in 1998 in a $125mn buyout • Represents the largest private equity investment in Central and Eastern Europe to date
APP	• Largest independent, indigenous IT consulting and implementation services business in the Czech Republic; • Transformed itself under Warburg Pincus's ownership to ERP and CRM business solutions provider • Warburg Pincus invested in APP between 1997 and 1998 and subsequently sold its stake to Ness Technologies in 2002
Slovakofarma	• Leading Slovak pharmaceutical company with sales of $163mn in 2001 • Slovakofarma merged with Leciva to create a leading player in the Central and Eastern European pharmaceutical market
Systinet	• Web services application platform provider based in the U.S. and the Czech Republic in which Warburg Pincus invested during 2002 • Warburg Pincus backed leading Czech technology entrepreneur Roman Stanek, formerly with Sun Microsystems

Source: Warburg Pincus brochures, internal documents, VentureXpert.

EXHIBIT 23.2

ECONOMIC AND DEMOGRAPHIC DATA FOR HUNGARY, ACTUAL AND PROJECTED

Year	Total GDP (USDmn)	Annual disposable income (USDmn)	Annua rates of inflation (%)	Unemploy- ment rate (%)	Exchange rates (HUF per USDmn)	Population ('000)	Urban population (%)	Rural population (%)
1997A	38,261	22,922	18.3	8.7	186.79	10,174	63	37
1998A	45,190	26,023	14.2	7.8	214.4	10,182	64	36
1999A	51,041	28,638	10.0	7.0	237.15	10,190	64	36
2000A	59,010	32,625	9.8	6.4	282.18	10,197	64	36
2001A	66,524	37,022	9.2	5.7	286.49	10,178	64	36
2002A	76,069	40,202	5.3	5.2	257.89	10,158	64	36
2003A	82,033	43,096	4.7	5.6	223.22	10,139	65	35
2004E	89,574	46,861	5.5	6.4	209.00	10,120	66	34
2005E	97,195	49,770	4.6	6.7	—	10,100	66	34
2006E	104,491	53,321	3.9	7.5	—	10,081	67	33
2007E	111,550	57,823	3.2	7.7	—	10,062	67	33
2008E	118,605	62,966	2.5	6.8	—	10,043	68	32
2009E	126,174	66,584	2.8	6.7	—	10,024	69	31
2010E	134,306	70,057	2.9	5.7	—	10,005	69	31
2011E	143,001	74,798	3.1	5.3	—	9,986	70	30
2012E	150,624	81,786	2.7	5.8	—	9,967	70	30

Source: Euromonitor (2004); SNL Kagan Eastern European Cable TV Guide.

EXHIBIT 23.3

HUNGARIAN TERRESTRIAL AND NON-TERRESTRIAL TELEVISION CHANNELS

Terrestrial channels

Channel	Household penetration (%)	Daily hours of transmission	Advert minutes per week	Year of first transmission
Public				
m1	100	20.0	—	1957
Private				
TV2	94	21.0	1,784	1997
RTL Klub	93	19.5	1,638	1997

Cable and satellite channels

Channel	Household penetration (%)	Daily hours of transmission	Advert minutes per week	Year of first transmission
Public				
m2	58	20.0	—	1998
Duna TV	60	19.0	—	1992
Spektrum	35	16.0	—	1996
Private				
Magyar ATV	43	14.5	1,218	—
Viva+	30	17.0	1,428	1997
Minimax	27	11.0	924	2000
HBO	8	24.0	2,016	1995
Viasat3	32	18.0	1,512	2000

Source: "Television in Central and Eastern Europe to 2011," *ZenithOptimedia*, February 2003.

EXHIBIT 23.4

KEY STATISTICS FOR HUNGARIAN CABLE TV MARKET, ACTUAL AND PROJECTED

	1997A	1998A	1999A	2000A	2001A	2002A	2003A	2004E	2005E	2006E	2007E	2008E	2009E	2010E	2011E	2012E
Population ('000)	10,174	10,182	10,190	10,197	10,178	10,158	10,139	10,120	10,100	10,081	10,062	10,043	10,024	10,005	9,986	9,967
Households ('000)	3,928	3,947	4,012	4,095	4,104	4,113	4,122	4,130	4,140	4,149	4,158	4,167	4,177	4,186	4,196	4,205
TV households ('000)	3,513	3,555	3,596	3,631	3,664	3,692	3,719	3,746	3,773	3,792	3,810	3,828	3,845	3,863	3,881	3,898
Cable																
Homes passed ('000)	1,965	2,040	2,070	2,100	2,100	2,226	2,338	2,408	2,456	2,505	2,555	2,606	2,632	2,659	2,685	2,712
Homes passed as % of TVHH	55.9	57.4	57.6	57.8	57.3	60.3	62.9	64.3	65.1	66.1	67.1	68.1	68.5	68.8	69.2	—
Basic subs ('000)	1,277	1,428	1,511	1,605	1,596	1,692	1,788	1,854	1,903	1,954	2,001	2,049	2,074	2,100	2,127	2,153
Basic subs growth (%)	—	11.8	5.8	6.2	−0.6	6.0	5.7	3.7	2.6	2.7	2.4	2.4	1.2	1.3	1.3	1.2
Homes passed (%)	65.0	70.0	73.0	76.4	76.0	76.0	76.5	77.0	77.5	78.0	78.3	78.6	78.8	79.0	79.2	79.4
TVHH (basic subs) (%)	36.4	40.2	42.0	44.2	43.6	45.8	48.1	49.5	50.4	51.5	52.5	53.5	53.9	54.4	54.8	55.2
Avg. monthly basic rate ($)	3.37	3.47	3.58	4.00	5.93	6.70	7.23	7.67	8.05	8.45	8.88	9.32	9.69	10.08	10.48	10.90
Basic ARPU growth (%)	—	3.0	3.2	11.7	48.3	13.0	7.9	6.1	5.0	5.0	5.1	5.0	4.0	4.0	4.0	4.0
Pay cable																
Total pay TV cable subs ('000)	43	51	57	71	80	93	107	121	135	156	180	205	228	252	276	301
Growth (%)	—	18.6	11.8	24.6	12.7	16.3	15.1	13.1	14.6	15.6	15.4	13.9	11.2	10.5	9.5	9.1
Avg. rev./sub/month ($)	5.86	5.86	6.74	7.28	9.38	10.86	11.94	12.78	13.54	14.36	15.07	15.83	16.62	17.28	17.98	18.69
Pay cable ARPU growth (%)	—	0.0	15.0	8.0	28.6	16.0	9.9	7.0	5.9	6.1	4.9	5.0	5.0	4.0	4.1	3.9
Broadband internet																
Ethernet/Cable internet (subs) ('000)	—	—	—	10	20	35	58	87	126	177	234	285	333	370	407	436
Growth (%)	—	—	—	—	100.0	75.0	65.7	50.0	44.8	40.5	32.2	21.8	16.8	11.1	10.0	7.1
Avg. rev./sub/month ($)	—	—	—	24.25	39.82	39.82	35.84	28.67	25.80	24.51	23.53	22.59	21.69	20.82	20.20	19.59
ARPU growth (%)	—	—	—	—	64.2	00.0	−10.0	−20.0	−10.0	−5.0	−4.0	−4.0	−4.0	−4.0	−3.0	−3.0

Source: SNL Kagan Eastern European Cable TV Guide.

EXHIBIT 23.5

COMPARATIVE CABLE TV STATISTICS FOR HUNGARY AND OTHER EUROPEAN MARKETS

Homes passed as percent of TV households 1997–2001 (actual and projected)

	1997A	1998A	1999A	2000A	2001A	2002A	2003A	2004E	2005E	2006E	2007E	2008E	2009E	2010E	2011E
Austria	57.1	58.1	58.5	58.6	59.0	59.1	59.1	58.9	58.8	58.7	58.6	58.5	58.5	58.4	58.3
France	31.3	32.4	35.0	37.6	37.8	38.4	39.4	40.6	41.7	42.8	43.7	44.5	45.2	45.5	45.8
Germany	81.3	83.7	83.7	82.6	82.7	83.2	83.8	84.3	84.8	85.4	85.9	86.5	87.1	87.7	88.3
Italy	4.3	5.1	5.1	5.4	6.5	8.3	9.7	10.8	12.0	13.1	14.2	15.3	16.4	17.6	18.7
Portugal	33.9	41.4	50.0	57.9	63.8	67.2	71.0	74.0	76.3	78.3	80.0	81.3	82.3	82.9	83.5
Spain	8.0	8.3	14.2	18.4	33.9	41.7	47.9	52.6	56.2	58.9	60.9	62.2	62.9	63.5	64.1
Czech Republic	55.9	57.4	56.5	57.2	56.9	57.1	57.7	58.6	59.4	60.0	60.6	61.2	61.8	62.4	63.1
Poland	44.8	57.4	67.8	73.1	76.9	78.4	79.2	79.7	79.9	80.1	80.1	80.1	80.0	79.9	79.9
Hungary	*55.9*	*57.4*	*57.6*	*57.8*	*57.3*	*60.3*	*62.9*	*64.3*	*65.1*	*66.1*	*67.1*	*68.1*	*68.5*	*68.8*	*69.2*

Penetration of homes passed 1997–2011 (actual and projected) (percent)

	1997A	1998A	1999A	2000A	2001A	2002A	2003A	2004E	2005E	2006E	2007E	2008E	2009E	2010E	2011E
Austria	65.7	65.9	66.4	66.1	65.1	64.5	64.6	64.7	64.8	64.9	65.0	65.1	65.2	65.3	65.4
France	34.2	36.3	36.4	35.8	38.1	41.0	44.0	47.0	49.0	51.0	52.0	53.0	54.0	55.0	56.0
Germany	66.5	66.4	66.8	66.8	67.5	67.8	68.0	68.2	68.4	68.6	68.8	69.0	69.2	69.4	69.6
Italy	5.9	6.2	5.5	4.3	5.6	9.4	14.3	25.5	29.0	31.5	33.3	34.5	35.4	36.0	0.0
Portugal	26.1	32.6	33.7	35.3	38.3	40.0	41.5	43.0	44.5	45.5	46.5	47.3	48.1	48.8	49.4
Spain	14.9	15.7	11.2	12.1	12.7	15.5	18.0	21.0	24.0	26.5	28.4	29.8	31.0	32.0	32.8
Czech Republic	30.4	31.4	32.8	32.2	32.0	32.3	33.4	34.5	35.6	36.6	37.5	38.4	39.3	40.0	40.7
Poland	60.4	48.2	42.0	42.0	42.4	42.8	43.6	44.5	45.4	46.2	46.9	47.5	48.1	48.8	49.5
Hungary	*65.0*	*70.0*	*73.0*	*76.4*	*76.0*	*76.0*	*76.5*	*77.0*	*77.5*	*78.0*	*78.3*	*78.6*	*78.8*	*79.0*	*79.2*

Penetration of TV households (basic subscriptions) 1997–2011 (actual and projected) (percent)

	1997A	1998A	1999A	2000A	2001A	2002A	2003A	2004E	2005E	2006E	2007E	2008E	2009E	2010E	2011E
Austria	37.5	38.3	38.9	38.7	38.4	38.1	38.1	38.1	38.1	38.1	38.1	38.1	38.1	38.1	38.1
France	10.7	11.8	12.8	13.5	14.4	15.8	17.3	19.1	20.5	21.8	22.7	23.6	24.4	25.0	25.7
Germany	54.0	55.6	55.8	55.2	55.8	56.4	57.0	57.5	58.0	58.6	59.1	59.7	60.3	60.9	61.5
Italy	0.3	0.3	0.3	0.2	0.4	0.8	1.4	2.8	3.5	4.1	4.7	5.3	5.8	6.3	0.0
Portugal	8.9	13.5	16.8	20.5	24.4	26.9	29.5	31.8	33.9	35.6	37.2	38.5	39.6	40.5	41.3
Spain	1.2	1.3	1.6	2.2	4.3	6.5	8.6	11.0	13.5	15.6	17.3	18.5	19.5	20.3	21.0
Czech Republic	17.0	18.0	18.6	18.4	18.2	18.5	19.3	20.2	21.2	22.0	22.7	23.5	24.3	25.0	25.7
Poland	27.0	27.7	28.5	30.7	32.6	33.6	34.5	35.4	36.3	37.0	37.6	88.1	88.5	39.0	39.5
Hungary	36.4	40.2	42.0	44.2	43.6	45.8	48.1	49.5	50.4	51.5	52.5	53.5	53.9	54.4	54.8

Source: SNL Kagan Eastern European Cable TV Guide.

EXHIBIT 23.6

MARKET SHARES BY NUMBER OF SUBSCRIBERS OF KEY CABLE OPERATORS, 2002–2003

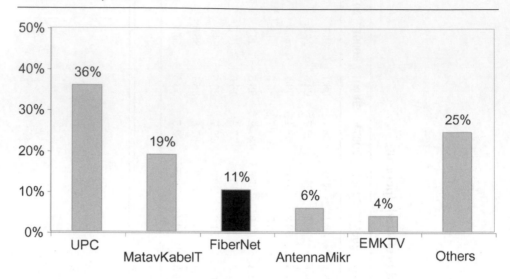

Source: Warburg Pincus Transaction Documents.

EXHIBIT 23.7

UPC HUNGARY ANALOGUE PACKAGES, BUDAPEST TYPICAL

Package	Monthly price (HUF)	Channels
Basic	550	m1, m2, Duna TV, Helyi TV, Képúszág
Standard	1,970	Basic plus Mozaik, SAT1, TV%, TVE, Pro7, Eurosport, CNN, 35at, Fashion TV, RTL2, Rai Uno, VH!, Euronews, RTL, Fix TV, CCTV 4, ERT Sat, Pax TV, Viva+, RTL Klub, Vox, Mezzo, Super RTL, Fox Kids, Cartoon Network/TCN, Animal Planet, BP TV, tv2, Viasat 3, Club, Extreme Sports, Nickelodeon, BBC World
Extended	2,840	Basic plus Standard plus NTV, Discovery Channel, MCM, Spektrum, National Geographic Channel, Magyar/ATV, Travel Channel/Private Gold, MTV Europe, CNBC, Filmmúzeum, Romantica, SATeLIT, Sport1, Reality TV, Minimax
Premium	2,750	HBO

Source: SNL Kagan Eastern European Cable TV Guide.

EXHIBIT 23.8

UPC HUNGARY HIGH-SPEED INTERNET PRICE PROFILE

Package	Monthly price (HUF)	Download speed (Kbps)	Upload speed (Kbps)	Surcharge threshold (MB)
Chello	10,900	512	128	Unlimited

Source: SNL Kagan Eastern European Cable TV Guide.

EXHIBIT 23.9

MATÁVKÁBELTV ANALOGUE PACKAGES, BUDAPEST TYPICAL

Package	Monthly price (HUF)	Channels
Mini-Basic	550	XMedia, MusicBox, Fix TV, Zenit TV/Helyi TV2, Deutsche Welle/Helyi TV1, Information Channel, Duna TV, m2, m1
Basic	1,920	Basic plus ATV, Eurosport, BP TV, TV5, SATeLIT TV, SAT1, Fonix TV, Sport1, Reality TV, RTL, Filmmúzeum, Viva+, CNN, tv2, RTL Klub, Viasat 3
Extended	3,000	Basic plus ORT1, Discovery Channel, VH1, Private Blue, Mezzo, Romantica, Minimax, Spektrum, Cartoon Network/TCM, National Geographic, MTV Europe, Hallmark, Le Cinema, Fox Kids, Rai Uno, TVE
Premium	2,880	HBO

Source: SNL Kagan Eastern European Cable TV Guide and ZenithOptimedia (2003).

EXHIBIT 23.10

MATÁVKÁBELTV HIGH-SPEED INTERNET PRICE PROFILE

Package	Monthly price (HUF)	Download speed (Kbps)	Upload speed (Kbps)	Surcharge threshold (MB)
Otthon	17,900	512	128	Unlimited
Profi	35,240	512	128	Unlimited

Source: SNL Kagan Eastern European Cable TV Guide.

EXHIBIT 23.11

GEOGRAPHICAL COVERAGE OF KEY CABLE OPERATORS IN HUNGARY

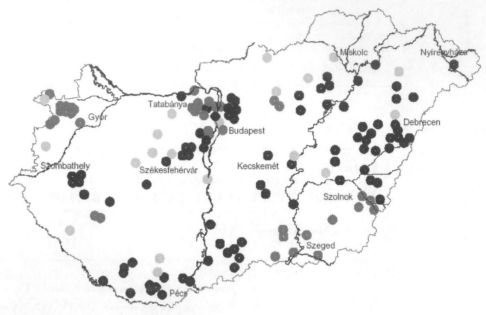

Source: Warburg Pincus Transaction Documents.

EXHIBIT 23.12

FIBERNET ANALOGUE PACKAGES

Package	Monthly price (HUF)	Channels
Basic	250–799	m1, m2, Duna TV, Képúszág, BBC World, Ferencvárosi TV
Standard	1,900–2,900	Basic plus RTL Klub, ATV, tv2, National Geographic, Pro 7, CNN, 35at, Cartoon Network/TCM, TV5, Vox, Rai Uno, TVE, SAT1, ERT, Mezzo, RTL II, NTV, MTV Europe, Minimax, Discovery Channel, RTL, Hallmark, Fashion TV, Private Gold, Viasat 32, Fox Kids, Romantica, Animal Planet, Filmmúzeum, SATeLIT, Spektrum, RTP, Sport1, Deutsche Welle, Kabel 1, MCM, Viva+
HBO	2,399	HBO

Source: SNL Kagan Eastern European Cable TV Guide.

EXHIBIT 23.13

FIBERNET HIGH-SPEED INTERNET PRICE PROFILE

Package	Monthly price (HUF)	Download speed (Kbps)	Upload speed (Kbps)	Surcharge threshold (MB)
Alap	5,900	512	128	1.5 GB
Otthon	11,120	512	128	Unlimited
Otthon Plusz	14,400	512	128	Unlimited

Source: SNL Kagan Eastern European Cable TV Guide.

EXHIBIT 23.14

FIBERNET'S ORGANIZATIONAL CHART

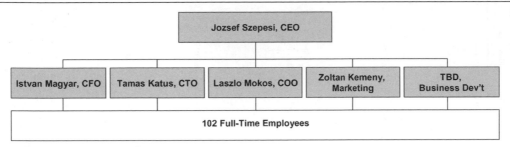

Source: Warburg Pincus transaction documents.

EXHIBIT 23.15

MANAGEMENT PROJECTIONS FOR FIBERNET, FEBRUARY 2004

	2002A	2003A	2004E	2005E	2006E	2007E	2008E	2009E
Revenue (USD million)	18.8	25.1	37.6	45.1	54.1	64.3	72.8	80.4
Revenue growth (%)	58.5	33.3	49.9	20.0	19.8	18.9	13.2	10.5
EBITDA (USD million)	7.8	10.8	14.4	18.0	21.9	26.4	30.2	33.8
EBITDA margin (%)	41.4	43.0	38.3	40.0	40.5	41.0	41.5	42.0
EBIT (USD million)	4.1	5.6	8.4	11.3	14.9	19.3	23.7	28.1
EBIT margin (%)	21.5	22.1	22.3	25.0	27.5	30.0	32.5	35.0
CAPEX (USD million)	9.6	12.0	17.6	5.7	5.7	5.7	5.7	5.7
No. of CATV subscribers, EOY	184,091	195,872	220,403	224,801	231,968	238,340	244,826	251,246
No. of internet subscribers, EOY	615	4,037	14,327	21,804	32,351	40,941	47,906	57,207
ARPU CATV (USD)	7.7	10.0	12.4	14.0	15.5	17.5	19.0	20.0
ARPU internet (USD)	42.9	31.0	31.0	31.0	31.0	31.0	31.0	31.0

Source: Warburg Pincus transaction documents.

Notes: Revenue: the total figure includes connection and installation fees.

   EOY: end of year.

EXHIBIT 23.16

CABLE TRANSACTIONS 2002–2003

Announcement	Name	Type date	Country	Buyer	Seller	EV (million)	EBITDA (million est.)	Multiple	Company notes	Transaction notes
April 30, 2003	TeleColumbus Group	Secondary buyout	Germany	BC Partners	Deutsche Bank	EUR510	EUR90	5.7×	TeleColumbus Group is a cable service provider all over Germany with more than 2.3 million cable customers, revenues of EUR235mn, and a profit margin above 30% in 2002. The group offers broadband cable television programs, high-speed internet and security services	The debt package amounted to EUR375mn loans and a EUR60mn mezzanine tranche. Total net debt to EBITDA is less than 4×, while senior net debt to EBITDA is about 3.2×
April 24, 2003	Com Hem	Buyout	Sweden	EQT Partners	TeliaSonera	SKR2,150	SKR53	40.6×	Based primarily in Stockholm, Com Hem is the largest cable TV operator in Sweden and provides cable TV to 1.4 million households and has 72,000 broadband subscribers. Net sales amounted to SKR1,017mn in 2002	The debt package amounted to SKR800mn. The company turned EBITDA positive only in Q3 2002. FX conversion: SKR1 = EUR0.1096
February 5, 2003	Eutelsat	Buyout	France	Eurazeo	France Telecom	EUR1,930	EUR506	3.8×	Paris-based Eutelsat provides capacity on 23 satellite infrastructures offering services including television and radio broadcasting, professional video broadcasting, corporate networks, internet services, and mobile communications. With its fleet of satellites, it reaches four continents and has achieved sales of EUR659mn	Eurazeo purchased a 19% stake in Eutelsat for EUR379mn
February 1, 2003	Est Vidéocommunication	Buyout	France	SG Capital, Péchel Industries	Fipares	EUR50	EUR17	2.9×	Strasbourg-based Est Vidéocommunication operates a cable network in eastern France, with 150,000 subscribers of analogue and digital TV and high-speed internet services. Sales were EUR34mn in 2002	Seller is a subsidiary of Electricité de Strasbourg
December 9, 2002	Casema	Buyout	Netherlands	Providence, Carlyle, GMT Communications	France Telecom	EUR665	EUR85	7.8×	Casema is the third largest cable operator in The Netherlands with 1.3 million subscribers. Services, available now or in the near future, include internet, pay per view, alarm systems, home shopping, telephony, data communication, and video on demand	Providence Equity and Carlyle have each acquired 46% ownership of Casema, with GMT owning the remaining 8%
November 25, 2002	Aster City Cable	Buyout	Poland	Argus, Emerging Markets Partnership, and Hicks Muse	Elektrim Telekomunikacja	EUR110	EUR9.9	11.1×	Aster Cable Television Network, created in 1994, is the cable operator in the Warsaw region, reaching more than 500,000 households. It also offers it customers internet access	The consortium acquired the cable TV operations of Elektrim Telekomunikacja, the Polish joint venture between Elektrim SA and Vivendi Universal SA for a total consideration of EUR110mn

Source: MergerMarket, Factiva.

EXHIBIT 23.17

INTEREST RATES AND FORWARD YIELD CURVE IN HUNGARY

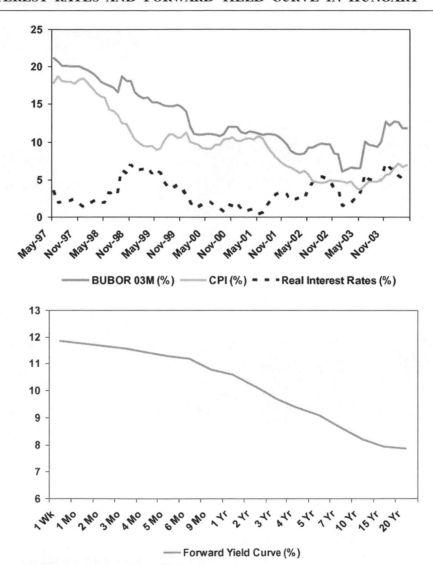

Source: Warburg Pincus transaction documents.

Note: BUBOR: Budapest Interbank Offered Rate; the key benchmark rate fixed daily based on rates
contributed by eight leading banks

24

Seat SpA

On Saturday May 10, 1997, Jonathan Lavine, a principal at Bain Capital, a U.S. private equity firm, was preparing an investment memorandum for Bain Capital's credit committee to make a bid for Seat SpA, the largest publisher of *Yellow Pages* and *White Pages* in Italy. Seat was being sold as part of the Telecom Italia privatization process undertaken by the Italian government. He had just reviewed the paper with Mark Nunnelly, the Managing Director with whom he was working on the investment. They were both excited about the opportunity, but were also cautious, as this deal was in a country with which they had little or no experience. Adding to the complexity was the fact that Seat would be one of the largest investments the firm had ever made.

Bain Capital had joined a local Italian consortium assembled by Investitori Associati and included Banca Commerciale Italiana, De Agostini, BC Partners, and CVC Capital Partners. Bids were due to be submitted in one month.

As Jonathan contemplated the deal, several issues came to mind. Bain Capital did not have much deal-making experience in Italy, or Europe for that matter, although it had taken part in investment discussions with local Italian partners in the past. Since Bain Capital was an American private equity firm, Jonathan was concerned about Italian country risk exposure and how it could affect cash flows and expected returns. Apart from the economic risks, there were political considerations that were harder to measure. Seat was a government-owned company and there was resistance, mainly from opposition parties, to the privatization process in general. One overarching question was how traditional methods and metrics used by a U.S. investor in its diligence process would translate to this large deal in Italy. Assuming Bain and its consortium partners were successful in the bid process, Jonathan was well aware of the difficulties in changing Seat's public company organizational culture to a more market-driven one. A change that was critical to realizing Bain Capital's expected returns.

To complicate matters further, these changes had to be made while simultaneously dealing with Pagine Utili, a competitive *Yellow Pages* offering. This directory was launched at the beginning of 1997 by Italian media investor and former prime minister Silvio Berlusconi, through his Fininvest Group. There were of course more questions to

The case was co-authored with Enrique Ho-Fernández (LBS MBA 2005), Oriol Juncosa (LBS MBA 2005), and Dwight Poler, Managing Director at Bain Capital. Thanks are due to Jonathan Lavine, Managing Director at Bain Capital, Aditya Kotibhaskar (LBS MBA 2006), and Michael Geary (LBS Sloan Fellow 2006) for their comments and assistance.

answer: How would the recent entry of Pagine Utili affect the performance of Seat? Would the directory market expand or contract? What was the likelihood of a price war? The answers to these questions would ultimately affect investment returns and exit options.

Jonathan contemplated the Italian investment consortium with whom Bain Capital was partnered, in preparation for the Seat bid. Bain Capital brought international expertise and high investment capacity, while the Italian partners brought extensive local knowledge regarding economic, political, and regulatory issues that Bain Capital lacked. Investment consortiums were a relatively new phenomenon and Jonathan understood the fundamental importance of aligning incentives among the different investors in the group to achieve the common objective of maximizing returns. If these objectives diverged in the future, the likelihood of shareholder disagreements would increase, affecting Bain Capital's expected returns negatively.

Apart from these issues there were also opportunity costs to consider. The Italian government had announced its intentions to sell Seat back in September of 1996 but, mainly because of political opposition to the deal, the process had taken longer than expected. There had initially been more than 18 bidders for Seat but, by the time Jonathan was preparing the internal investment memorandum, only the consortium including Bain Capital and a strategic buyer, GTE, a U.S. telecommunications and directory company, were left in the process. The Bain Capital consortium had been analyzing the transaction since late 1996 and had already spent considerable resources during the due diligence process, nevertheless doubts remained. Was Seat really worth all the trouble? Was Bain Capital better off concentrating on other deals where the risks were more manageable? How could they prevent an escalation of the bidding process, which could dramatically reduce returns? The most precious asset in private equity is time; and Jonathan knew that time spent on Seat was time Bain Capital was not using on analyzing other deals. The opportunity costs, as well as the stakes, were high.

Finally, there was a reputation issue. The Seat deal was a high-profile transaction, potentially becoming one of the largest leveraged buyouts in European history. Operating out of Boston, Bain Capital was an American firm with only one deal done in Europe in the early 1990s. This transaction would surely define the firm's European reputation for the future, leading to more investments in Europe, or an end to investments—this transaction being a one-time episode. Even though this transaction had firm-wide commitment, Jonathan felt a certain personal responsibility for the outcome, while also reflecting on the potential impact of this deal on his own career.

Jonathan and Mark had expended considerable effort in evaluating not only how much to pay, but how much leverage was appropriate for the transaction. While considering the bid price, Jonathan fully recognized the difference between financial buyers and strategic buyers like GTE. In general, strategic buyers are in a good position to bid higher than financial buyers because the former can realize synergies across complementary businesses. However, strategic buyers also have substantial leverage constraints. After all these months of preparation and dedication to the deal, Jonathan still wondered what price would be high enough to beat GTE but low enough to realize a good return on the investment.

It was his wife's birthday and Jonathan left the office to buy her a present. As he was walking to nearby Newbury Street, Jonathan used the brief repose to crystallize his assessment of the key issues in the transaction and complete the memorandum for the credit committee.

CHRONOLOGY OF SEAT TRANSACTION

1996

- May: Pagine Utili, a unit of Fininvest Group (Berlusconi) entered the directory market by launching its first directories.

- September: Italian government announced its intention to privatize Seat in order to continue liberalization of the telecommunications market in Italy:
  - Seat was 100% owned by the Italian public phone company (STET—Telecom Italia);
  - STET was 61.3% owned by IRI, the government holding company that grouped its industrial participations, and 38.73% was listed on the Italian stock market and owned by a large number of small shareholders.

- October: Bain Capital agreed to partner with a group assembled by Investitori Associati that included Banca Commerciale Italiana, De Agostini, Investitori Associati, BC Partners, and CVC Capital Partners in order to bid for Seat.

1997

- January: Seat was de-merged from STET on December 31, 1996 and listed on the Milan Stock exchange on January 2, 1997:
  - The de-merger and listing of the company were completed to facilitate the privatization of the business. Moreover, listing the company gave an immediate minimum value for the stock that the government still owned. In parallel, the Italian Treasury put its 61.3% stake in Seat up for sale.

- February: four consortiums were shortlisted to bid for Seat (in the end only two bidders remained, Bain Capital and GTE).

- May: The consortium including Bain Capital concluded the business due diligence.

BAIN CAPITAL: BACKGROUND

In 1997 Bain Capital was a leading U.S. private equity firm with headquarters in Boston. It had no offices in Europe. The firm was formed in 1984 by a group of professionals from Bain & Co., an international consulting firm. Even at the time of the Seat transaction, a number of the senior professionals at Bain Capital were former consultants from Bain & Co. Bain Capital was highly successful in implementing a business-and-industry-focused consulting approach to investing. Consequently, the firm was well regarded within the private equity industry as an expert in the due diligence process and in creating value through business improvement, rather than financial engineering only.

Although two separate firms, given their common heritage, Bain Capital had a close relationship with Bain & Co. There was a particularly close relationship with Bain, Cuneo e Associati, which was Bain & Co.'s subsidiary in Italy and the largest strategy consulting firm in that country. Both firms had explored deal opportunities in the past, but Bain Capital had not participated in any Italian deals until 1997. Also, Investitori Associati, with whom Bain Capital partnered, had its roots in Bain & Co., having been formed by a group of former Bain, Cuneo e Associati professionals. With a common approach, Bain Capital and Investitori Associati decided to join forces when the Seat transaction came about.

THE GLOBAL AND EUROPEAN DIRECTORY MARKET

Directory products and services consisted of ordinary telephone directories (*White Pages*) and classified directories (*Yellow Pages*). *White Pages* provides information on residential, professional, and company telephones. *Yellow Pages* provides information on all businesses and professionals in specific geographical areas. In 1997, the U.S. was the largest directory market in the world, with 51% of the total. The Italian market was the fourth largest in the world and the second biggest in Europe. The world market for directory services was worth USD21bn in 1996 (Exhibit 24.1A).

In most markets, *Yellow Pages* provided the bulk of revenues. In Italy, however, *Yellow Pages* was not introduced until 1966, which explained why *White Pages* was an important source of revenues in comparison with other countries. Historically, directory publishers were wholly owned subsidiaries of the main telecom carriers. Even independent publishers were reliant upon a specific telecommunication company for access to the telecommunications listings database.

From 1995 until 1997, the fixed line telecommunications market was deregulated in many parts of the world. However, deregulation did not lead to a substantial increase of new entrants into the directory sector (Exhibit 24.1B), due to its industry structure and its inherent network externalities.

The more customers advertised and the higher the usage rate, the more people were attracted to advertise. Rapidly building up a large customer base was therefore a key strategic objective. In addition, consumers were reluctant to stockpile multiple directories at home (one or two served their needs). This customer behavior limited the potential level of competition in any given geographical market. It was also difficult to establish and maintain the database required to enter the business, since this aspect usually needs a partnership with a telecommunications company. Lastly, advertising renewal rates were in excess of 80%, which was a substantial constraint on the volume of customers anyone could take from the existing players.

A new competitor had to sustain substantial losses over the medium term in order to establish critical mass in terms of customers, thereby attracting the level of advertising required for success. This case was illustrated by Thomson's entry into the U.K. directory market. Thomson suffered 7 years of losses after entering the U.K. market in 1980 as a competitor to the Post Office. In 1997, Thomson had achieved a market penetration of 16%. In contrast, in Belgium the new directory entrant became the market leader after signing a contract to supply directories to Belgacom, the incumbent telecommunications operator, and displacing the former directory provider.

The characteristics of the directory market translated into high operating margins and low capital employed, which in turn generated high returns and strong free cash flow (Exhibit 24.2). EBITDA margins were usually much higher on *Yellow Pages* than on *White Pages*. Margins on *White Pages* tended to be capped by the database fees that had to be paid to local telecommunications companies. Furthermore, *White Pages* directories attracted much less advertising than *Yellow Pages*.

Expenditure on directories proved to be less sensitive to the economic cycle than other forms of advertising. Directory revenue growth slowed but revenues did not decline during economic downturns. The strong cash generation of these businesses, in the context of a relatively stable operating environment, allowed for very high dividend payouts and a high degree of financial leverage, increasing IRRs for investors.

THE ITALIAN DIRECTORY MARKET

Seat was the only *Yellow Pages* publisher in Italy until 1996. Pagine Italia, a subsidiary of the Fininvest Group, launched Pagine Utili jointly with Mondadori in 1996. Similar to most directory markets, the introduction of competition, at least initially, was expected to stimulate growth in the directory market. By mid-1997 it was not clear, however, whether Pagine Utili could overcome the difficulties associated with generating an economic return. However, Pagine Utili had already gained over 8% market share in less than a year.

While total advertising expenditure as a percentage of Italian GDP was lower than that for other European countries, directory advertising expenditure as a percentage of total advertising was higher (Exhibit 24.3). The net effect was that directory advertising expenditure as a percentage of GDP appeared to be in line with the European average (Exhibits 24.4A and 24.4B). Breaking down these figures further, while having a much higher than average revenue per client, the Italian market was characterized by a much lower than average penetration rate: customer penetration at 20% in Italy was well below the average of 27% for Western Europe (Exhibits 24.5A and 24.5B).

Although the directory business is relatively resilient in times of economic downturn, the rate of growth of any *Yellow Pages* operation is a function of the economic cycle and the secular trend in domestic advertising growth. According to Bain & Co., the Italian *Yellow Pages* market could grow by over one or two percentage points above inflation from 1997 to 2000. This growth of the Italian *Yellow Pages* industry was consistent with the growth experienced in other countries where a new entrant came into the market. In countries—such as the U.K., Belgium, The Netherlands, and the U.S.—where *Yellow Pages* monopolies had been removed, the overall market grew faster than inflation as new entrants attempted to compete by pricing below the incumbent. In all cases, the new entrant built a salesforce to gain customers from the incumbent and attempted to generate potential new advertisers (increasing *Yellow Pages* advertising penetration). The entrenched player was usually able to avoid a price war because its advertisements were accessed by more customers. After gaining significant market share, the two competitors coexisted with stable prices and a more modest growth (Exhibit 24.6).

SEAT BUSINESS DESCRIPTION

Seat's core business was the publishing of *Yellow Pages* and *White Pages* throughout Italy (around 81% of sales). In 1996, 42% of revenue and 55% of operating profit were derived from *Yellow Pages* and 39% of sales and 42% of operating profits were generated by *White Pages*. The balance of revenues and profits was driven by direct marketing services, tour guides and city maps, free press advertising, online services, and other products. These revenues were derived from a customer base of over 600,000 advertisers. *Yellow Pages* and *White Pages* products currently generated a disproportionately high margin and accounted for an estimated 98% of group EBIT in 1996.

Main products of Seat

- *Pagine Gialle* (*Yellow Pages*) was available in two versions: *Pagine Gialle Casa* (Home) and *Pagine Gialle Lavoro* (Work). These products met the promotional needs of small and medium-sized businesses that operated at a regional or a local level. *Pagine Gialle Casa* was printed annually and delivered free of charge to 22 million households. There were 253 different editions, which were tailored to suit the relevant geographical area. *Pagine Gialle Lavoro* was distributed to 9 million corporate customers and included the details of 3 million Italian businesses. Independent market research found that the home and work editions of *Yellow Pages* were consulted by almost 2 million people per day. In 71% of cases, the user then proceeded to contact an advertiser, and in 3 cases out of every 4 contacts, a purchase was made. Thus, more than 50% of all consultations translated into business for the advertiser.

- *The A-Z Telephone Directory* or *White Pages* (*Pagine Bianche*) contained the name and telephone numbers of all Telecom Italia's subscribers. Upon request, and for payment of a fee, additional information could be inserted. Around 32 million copies were produced each year, covering nearly all of Italy's 109 provinces. The product was consulted, on average, more than 2.8 million times per day. Seat published *White Pages* on behalf of Telecom Italia and its revenues were regulated by a contract that was to expire in 2007.

- *Annuario Seat* (*Seat Annual Trade Directory*) was a publication divided into 12 industry-specific volumes (covering clothing, food, furnishings, chemicals and medicine, culture and recreation, construction, electronics, machinery, transport, trade associations, and banks). It contained a list of more than 1.8 million businesses divided into 1,700 categories. Seat distributed 415,000 copies of this directory, free of charge, to 200,000 companies. The information was presented according to the stage of the production cycle, and included macroeconomic and sector-specific analysis.

- *Europages* was the leading pan-European business guide containing data on the largest European exporting companies, classified by activity and country of origin. The directory was published in six languages (English, French, German, Spanish, Dutch, and Italian) and was distributed to 600,000 manufacturing and distribution enterprises in 27 European countries. It principally targeted companies and businessmen that lacked the resources and infrastructure to open branches or offices overseas. Seat had the exclusive right to sell advertising space in Italy. *Europages* was distributed free of charge and was available in three formats: print, CD-ROM, and internet. The paper product contained information on 150,000 companies split by category and business sector. Internet consultations were running at around 400,000 per year.

- *Tuttocittà* was a color map of the local city, which was distributed free of charge every year as a supplement to *Pagine Gialle*. Around 28 million copies were distributed in 87 editions.

- *Seat Direct* was Seat's direct marketing arm. This service sought to leverage further Seat's fixed investment in the Telecom Italia database by offering direct mailing and telemarketing services to its customers. Direct marketing was at a very early stage of development in Italy and was growing rapidly. Seat was the second largest player in the market (estimated share of 15%), which was worth LIT200bn. Management was targeting revenues of LIT47bn in 2002, a CAGR of 9%.

- *Pagine Gialle Online* was the online version of the traditional *Pagine Gialle* or *Yellow Pages*. Launched in 1996, the website *www.paginegialle.it* was expected to receive more than 50,000 consultations per day, and by 1997 it had close to 80,000 advertisers (equivalent to 30% of the existing hard copy *Yellow Pages* customer base).

MARKET ENTRY OF PAGINE UTILI

In order to understand the competitors and customers further, the investor group commissioned a market research study to evaluate the impact of the entry of *Pagine Utili* (PU) in those areas where the two directories had competed in the current campaign. Four hundred "investors" (customers) in *Pagine Utili* were contacted in this study. The results were the following:

- Over 30% of PU's customers were new clients who were not investing in 1996, neither in *White Pages* or in *Yellow Pages*; these clients represented a net growth of the total market.

- The average investment of new and exclusive PU clients was relatively lower than those who invested in Seat only.

- Clients overlapping (PU and Seat) represented over 65% of the sample. However, the shift from exclusively Seat to exclusively PU was limited, representing only 10% of the sample.

- The average investment in Seat for those clients that were also investors in *Pagine Utili* was slightly decreased (by around 10%) contributing to an overall expansion of the market in terms of value.

THE INTERNET: THREAT OR OPPORTUNITY?

By mid-1997 the Italian internet market was still in its infancy, but growing fast. A study by IDC predicted that internet users would increase to 13.2 million in 2002, from fewer than 2 million in 1997. This increase translated into internet penetration growing from 4% to 23%.

It was not clear how the internet would affect Seat's future profitability. Would the emergence of the internet, as an alternative advertising medium, reduce the barriers to entry that Seat had so long enjoyed in the traditional *Yellow Pages/White Pages* business? Did Seat possess the right mixture of resources and capabilities to create and capture value from internet advertising and traffic? If not, how could Seat acquire these critical capabilities? What players could emerge as new competitors? Even if Seat could develop a successful online business, would that cannibalize its traditional "cash cow" business? (Exhibits 24.7 and 24.8).

According to Forrester Research (1997), "The Internet is destroying the classic divide between media and commerce. Media companies will reinvent themselves as transaction enablers, partner with resellers, and create commerce networks within content-based vertical portals." The internet had the potential to change the whole structure of the media/publishing business. Brands could become more important than in an exclusively hard copy world. Brands would be the only guarantee to users about the integrity of data obtained on the web. The real question for traditional media business companies was which of them would be successful in migrating their brands seamlessly onto the web. Those that failed would experience a substantial erosion of their competitive advantage.

Since Bain Capital would probably keep the Seat investment for a number of years, Jonathan and Mark considered how the Internet would affect the future profitability of

Seat, which in turn would impact the company's valuation. Seat had recently implemented an aggressive internet strategy, but it was too early to tell whether or not it would ultimately be successful. Whether or not this upside should be included in the valuation was also a key debate among the investors, as well as how to fund the losses the internet business would generate as it developed.

DUE DILIGENCE

Bain Capital and its partners in the consortium believed profitability could be increased at Seat by implementing clearly identified initiatives. One was cost reduction, which would result from printing and paper cost decreases, labor force efficiencies, product line rationalization, and other miscellaneous improvements. Bain, Cuneo e Associati estimated savings of approximately 5% to 10% of its operating costs. Paper and printing costs were to be reduced by a combination of the introduction of a competitive bidding process, including international operators and technological improvements at Ilte, Seat's printing subsidiary. Indeed, the group sought to explore the potential for outsourcing printing to a third party and to divest it from the business. Personnel benchmarking vs. other European directory companies revealed Seat's oversized organizational structure and suggested areas for improvement. Other cost reduction opportunities included eliminating unprofitable product lines, decreasing IT costs by upgrading technology, outsourcing non-core functions, and reducing advertising expenditures.

Revenue expansion was the other main value driver, primarily by increasing Italian directory advertising penetration to European averages, rather than by increasing prices. The recent entry of *Pagine Utili* into the Italian market blocked the price increase option. *Pagine Utili* was offering a number of services comparable with Seat's but at prices more than 30% lower. Bain Capital believed that cost reduction opportunities would compensate for expected 1997 revenue declines, due to the entry of *Pagine Utili* into the Italian market.

With regard to market evolution, Bain, Cuneo e Associati estimated that *Pagine Utili*'s entry expanded the total market by about 13%, with a 15% increase in the number of clients.

ITALIAN ECONOMIC AND POLITICAL LANDSCAPE

The Italian political scene was expected to be subject to continued instability and uncertainty in 1997–1998. The center–left coalition government, L'Ulivo, led by Romano Prodi, struggled to implement its program of structural reforms, particularly in the economic sphere. As pressure to introduce major economic reforms mounted, the government found it more and more difficult to reconcile the different positions within the ruling coalition. In addition, Mr. Prodi had staked the survival of his government on Italy's early participation in the EMU, scheduled for January 1999. Analysts believed this would be unlikely to be achieved, in spite of the progress made in reducing the budget deficit and stabilizing inflation. The general government deficit was not expected to fall below 4% of GDP in 1997, which, although well down on the figure of 6.8% for 1996, would not be close enough to the 3% reference value set in the Maastricht Treaty (Exhibit 24.9).

Failure of the government's strategy, centered on its participation in EMU, would lead to new elections and a probable defeat. However, the financial markets expected

Italy to join the EMU in 2000 or 2001, in time for the replacement of national currencies by the euro, planned for 2002.

In view of the uncertainty over the government's ability to reduce its deficit permanently, some analysts were expecting the lira to come under renewed pressure. By January 1997 Italy had amassed USD48bn in reserves and the current account continued to generate surpluses. It was therefore expected that other European central banks would support the lira, reducing the likelihood of it deviating materially from the central rate. Domestic demand would, however, remain weak in 1997, before accelerating in 1998, resulting in interest rate fluctuations (as shown in Exhibit 24.10).

PRIVATIZATION PROCESS IN ITALY

After years of debate, the dismantling of Italy's top-heavy public sector was now well under way. In late 1992 the Amato government initiated an ambitious privatization program by transforming the major state shareholdings—Istituto per la Ricostruzione Industriale (IRI), Ente Nazionale Idrocarburi (ENI), Istituto Nazionale delle Assicurazioni (INA), and Ente Nazionale per l'Energia Elettrica (ENEL)—into joint stock companies, as a preliminary step towards their whole or partial flotation. Subsequently, the Ciampi government floated the two major IRI-owned commercial banks on the stock exchange, Credito Italiano in December 1993 and Banca Commerciale Italiana in March 1994. In February 1994, the first tranche of Istituto Mobiliare Italiano, the investment bank, was also floated, with the remaining quota sold in two tranches by private treaty in 1995 and 1996.

The process slowed down in 1994 and 1995, but the flotation of the first tranche of INA did go ahead, completing in June 1996. A combination of political opposition and regulatory problems led to repeated postponements of the privatizations of STET (parent company of Seat) and ENI. In November 1995, after much wrangling, legislation providing for an independent energy authority was approved and 15% of ENI was floated on the stock market. Two further tranches were sold in October 1996 and June 1997, reducing the government's stake to just over 51%.

THE DEAL

Up to 18 individual buyers had expressed interest in the deal since mid-1996. Trade buyers and numerous large U.S. and European private equity firms had done substantial due diligence; but most withdrew from the deal because of the delays caused by Italian political uncertainty.

By late 1996 there were only three consortiums interested in the Seat deal: two industrial buyers, GTE and ITT, and one financial consortium led by Bain Capital that included Investitori Associati and the local Italian consortium. ITT dropped out from the race because it was in the process of being acquired by VNU, the Dutch publishing company. GTE was an American telecommunications company with revenues over USD22bn and operating margins of USD9.9bn. Directories represented approximately 8% of its operating margins in 1996. Outside the U.S., GTE was strong in Latin America, but had a minimal presence in Europe. GTE wanted to expand into the European telecom and directory markets.

The winning company/consortium was to acquire 61.3% of Seat's shares owned by the Italian Treasury. The remaining shares were listed on Milan's stock exchange, and the winner would have to make a tender offer at a pre-agreed price (similar to the price paid for the 61.3% share plus a small premium). Thus, this deal would be structured as a privatization and a public-to-private transaction.

Bain Capital and the Italian investment consortium had to take into consideration that Telecom Italia had the right to co-invest in the company alongside the winning party, as specified in the sale documentation. If this option was exercised, it would dilute the participation of existing shareholders. Nevertheless, it was also a way to lock in its largest client and provider of information.

To evaluate the deal, Jonathan Lavine was looking for, but struggling to find, relevant comparables. This was the first private equity transaction of a *Yellow Pages* publisher worldwide and none of which was publicly traded. As an approximation, Jonathan considered GTE because it was a stable telecom operator, even though directories only provided a small portion of its business. He also looked at Dun & Bradstreet, since it owned a *Yellow Pages* advertisement service, together with other business-marketing information products that display similar revenue stability. Key financial information for GTE and Dun & Bradstreet is provided in Exhibits 24.12 and 24.13.

Jonathan believed that its well-connected Italian consortium could use senior contacts to provide the company with necessary management depth, including a new CEO and a personnel director. Furthermore, the consortium members had familiarity with Italian laws and customs, and had experience with the relevant unions and labor councils. However, he was still deliberating on the price. The corporate, tax, and debt structure also still required serious consideration.

APPENDIX

EXHIBIT 24.1A

WORLDWIDE MARKET FOR DIRECTORY SERVICES (1996)

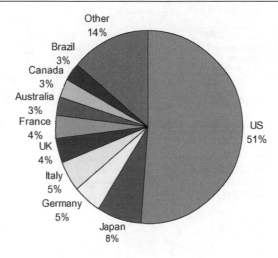

Source: Morgan Stanley.

EXHIBIT 24.1B

EUROPEAN DIRECTORY MARKET (EARLY 1997)

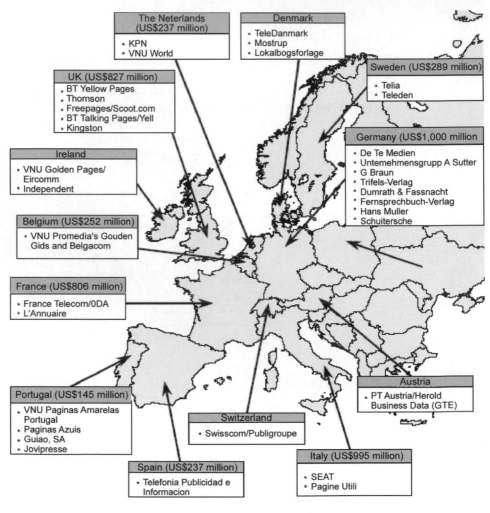

Source: Deutsche Bank.

EXHIBIT 24.2

SELECTED DIRECTORY PUBLISHERS' EBIT MARGINS

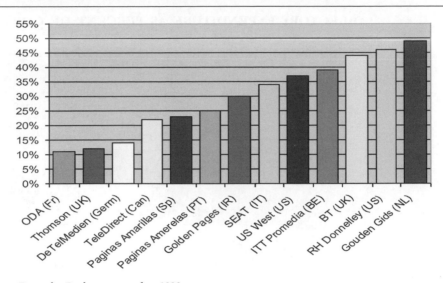

Source: Deutsche Bank, company data 1996.

EXHIBIT 24.3

TOTAL ADVERTISING EXPENDITURE AS PERCENT OF GDP, AND DIRECTORY ADVERTISEMENT EXPENDITURE AS PERCENT OF TOTAL ADVERTISEMENT EXPENDITURE

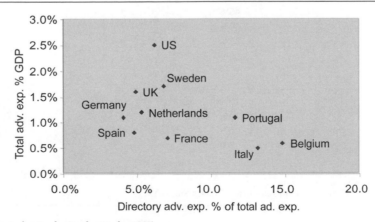

Source: Deutsche Bank, Cowles/Simba 1997.

EXHIBIT 24.4A

DIRECTORY EXPENDITURE AS PERCENT OF GDP

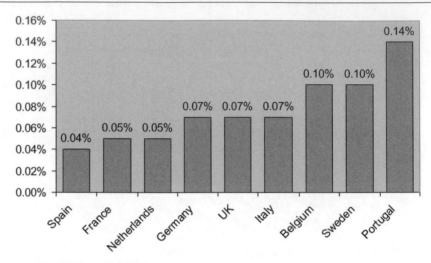

Source: Deutsche Bank, Cowles/Simba 1997.

EXHIBIT 24.4B

DIRECTORY EXPENDITURE PER CAPITA VS. GDP PER CAPITA

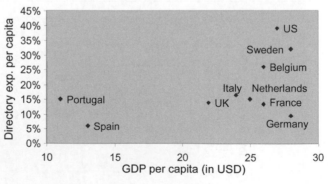

Source: Deutsche Bank, Cowles/Simba 1997.

EXHIBIT 24.5A

AVERAGE REVENUE PER DIRECTORY CLIENT (ADVERTISER) (IN USD)

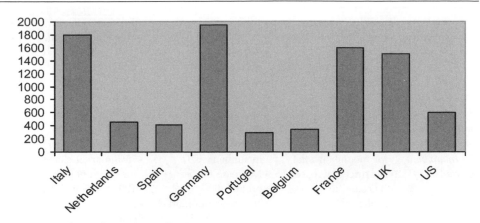

Source: Deutsche Bank, Cowles/Simba 1997.

EXHIBIT 24.5B

PENETRATION RATES OF DIRECTORIES

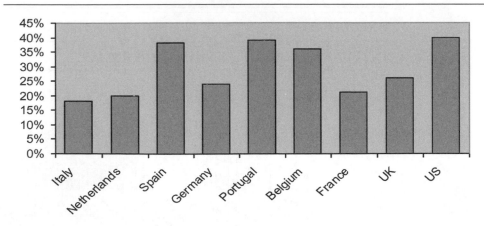

Source: Deutsche Bank, Cowles/Simba 1997.

EXHIBIT 24.6

SUMMARY ANALYSIS OF OTHER COMPETITIVE MARKETS

	U.K.	Belgium	The Netherlands	U.S.A.
Second player characteristics and strategy	• Small ex-operator • Regional smaller area • Same price • Does not cover entire territory	• Telecom operator • "Me too" product • Price discount • Face-to-face confrontation	• Telecom operator • More local product (twice the number of editions) • Little price discount • Face-to-face competition	• Small independents • "Me too" product • 50% price discount • Strategy of better client service
Results on the market and the incumbent operator	• Market growth >10% • 87% market share for incumbent, flat • No price decrease • Increase in profitability • Increase in market coverage (28%) • Expected growth of 7–8% in the next 3-4 years	• Price war market flat • 70% market share for incumbent, flat • Decrease in profitability • No change in market coverage (30%)	• Market growth (+20% in 2 years) • 75% market share for incumbent in 1996, 65% in 1997 • Expected growth to continue at around 10% in the next years	• Market still growing with each new entrant • No price decrease • Market coverage from 30% to 40%

Source: Bain, Cuneo e Associati.

EXHIBIT 24.7

INTERNET PERCENT PENETRATION IN 1997

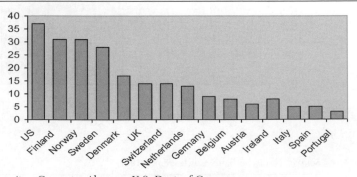

Source: Datamonitor, Computer Almanac, U.S. Dept. of Commerce.

EXHIBIT 24.8

SEAT'S INTERNET STRATEGY

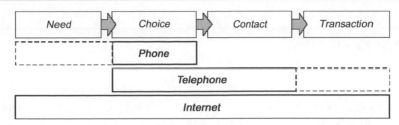

Source: Seat 1997.

EXHIBIT 24.9

KEY INDICATORS AND FORECAST GROWTH RATES FOR THE ITALIAN ECONOMY

Forecast summary	1995	1996	1997	1998
Real GDP	3.0	0.7	1.2	2.2
Consumer prices	5.4	3.9	2.5	2.5
Industrial production	5.5	−1.7	0.7	2.0
Unemployment (% of labor force)	12.0	12.1	12.3	11.8
Current account ($ billion)	25.7	40.0	38.6	33.9
General government balance (% of GDP)	−7.0	−6.8	−4.0	−3.0
Interest rates (3-month T-bill)	10.6	8.6	7.3	6.4
Exchange rates (average)				
LIT:DMK	1,137	1,026	1,000	990
LIT:USD	1,629	1,543	1,670	1,604

Source: Economist Intelligence Unit, 2Q 1997.

EXHIBIT 24.10

ITALIAN INTEREST RATES (PERCENT, PERIOD AVERAGES)

		1994	1995	1996	March 1997
Prime rate		9.3	11.7	11.0	9.5
3-month T-bills (BOT)		8.8	10.7	8.6	6.7
Long-term bond yields	Italian state	10.6	11.8	8.9	7.8
	German bund	6.9	6.8	6.1	5.9
Money market	3-month lira interbank rate	8.5	10.5	8.8	7.3
	3-month Deutschmark interbank rate	5.4	4.5	3.3	3.2

Source: OECD, main economic indicators; Banca d'Italia; *Bolletino Economico*; Deutsche Bundesbank; *Financial Times*.

EXHIBIT 24.11

FINANCIAL STATEMENTS OF SEAT (LIT MILLION)

Income statement (LIT million)	1993	1994	1995	1996	1997
Revenue	1,668,559	1,659,070	1,688,163	1,708,225	1,685,917
Cost of goods sold	(663,835)	(665,370)	(694,595)	(741,676)	(765,755)
—raw materials	(115,160)	(101,579)	(119,126)	(132,755)	(122,749)
—typesetting, printing, and packaging	(103,122)	(104,478)	(106,264)	(124,602)	(147,866)
—agents	(140,981)	(155,871)	(157,693)	(154,530)	(158,094)
—royalties to Telecom	(295,598)	(294,055)	(302,003)	(318,103)	(325,836)
—royalties to other publishers	(8,974)	(9,387)	(9,509)	(11,686)	(11,210)
General expenses	(191,210)	(198,588)	(195,196)	(199,606)	(208,966)
Labor costs	(159,043)	(172,907)	(170,097)	(188,068)	(196,162)
Reserves	(55,741)	(54,354)	(53,343)	(54,151)	(41,316)
Adjustments	12,353	12,995	3,517	0	0
EBITDA	**611,083**	**580,846**	**578,449**	**524,724**	**473,718**
Depreciation and amortization	(23,076)	(27,359)	(27,483)	(30,057)	(37,613)
EBIT	**588,007**	**553,487**	**550,966**	**494,667**	**436,105**
Reserves and provisions from subsidiaries[1]	0	(16,000)	(41,538)	(273,617)	(9,150)
Operating results and dividends from subsidiaries[1]	(41,594)	(42,760)	(12,933)	(1,172)	9,571
Interest income	9,941	(1,719)	(8,880)	16,692	29,677
EBT	**556,354**	**493,008**	**487,615**	**236.570**	**466,203**
Tax	0	0	0	0	(259,679)
Tax adjustment due to provisions	0	0	0	0	20,048
Net income	**556,354**	**493,008**	**487,615**	**236,570**	**226,572**

Source: Company data.

Notes: 1. Capital expenditure was approximately LIT10bn per annum.

Balance sheet (LIT million)	1993	1994	1995	1996	1997
Trade receivables and payables to sales agents	822,980	881,454	805,512	784,772	773,752
Inventories	31,270	25,280	21,780	23,015	22,718
Other current assets	(36,410)	15,237	19,451	5,852	0
Cash	0	0	0	54,133	496,102
Total current assets	**817,840**	**921,971**	**846,743**	**867,772**	**1,292,572**
Net tangible assets	147,970	158,180	157,410	168,279	175,672
Other fixed assets	137,187	129,924	263,803	300,581	274,367
Total fixed assets	285,157	288,104	421,213	468,860	450,039
Total assets	**1,102,997**	**1,210,075**	**1,267,956**	**1,336,632**	**1,742,611**
Trade payables	224,779	256,662	218,333	189,704	196,402
Debt for services to be rendered	436,422	400,510	363,401	281,002	288,822
Other current liabilities	16,080	16,362	10,160	18,422	18,184
Total current liabilities	**677,281**	**673,534**	**591,894**	**489,128**	**503,408**
Debt	61,070	60,166	19,725	4,452	0
Deferred taxation	0	0	0	0	245,596
Other reserves/obligations	95,637	118,689	164,749	282,646	192,614

Source: Company data.

EXHIBIT 24.12

GTE FINANCIAL INFORMATION

With 1997 revenues of more than $23bn, GTE is one of the world's largest telecommunications companies and a leading provider of integrated telecommunications services. In the U.S., GTE provides local services in 28 states and wireless services in 17 states, nationwide long-distance services and internetworking services ranging from dial-up internet access for residential and small-business consumers to web-based applications for Fortune 500 companies and a video service in selected markets. Outside the U.S., the company serves over 7 million telecommunications customers. In addition, GTE is a leader in government and defense communications systems and equipment, directories, telecommunications-based information services, and aircraft–passenger telecommunications.

Selected financial information	1997 (USD million)	Other information	Late 1997 (USD million)
Revenues		P/E ratio	13.4
Local services	6,060	EBITDA/Share	8.44
Network access services	4,618	Dividend yield	4%
Toll services	2,500	Beta equity	0.7
Cellular services	2,562		
Directory services	1,527		
Other services	4,072		
Total revenue	21,339		
Depreciation and amoritization	3,770		
EBIT	4,412		
Net income	2,798		
Long-term debt	13,210		
ROE	40.20%		

EXHIBIT 24.13

DUN & BRADSTREET FINANCIAL INFORMATION

Dun & Bradstreet consists of the Dun & Bradstreet operating company, a leading provider of commercial credit, business-marketing information, and receivables management services; Moody's Investor Service, a leading debt-rating agency and a major publisher of financial information for investors; and R.H. Donnelly, the largest independent marketer of *Yellow Pages* advertising in the U.S.

Profit & loss statement	1996 ($ million)	1997 ($ million)
Revenues	2,092	2,195
Corporate information services	1,717	1,809
Directory information services	375	368
Operating costs	507	545
Selling, general, and administrative costs	920	958
Deprection and amortization	155	164
Total costs	1,582	1,667
EBIT	510	528
Net income	285	303
EPS	1.68	1.77

Other information	Late 1997
Beta	0.9
Price/Book:	3.4
Dividend yield	4.21%
P/E ratio	12.57
5-year low P/E	36.51
5-year low P/E	11.04
Long-term debt	0

EXHIBIT 24.14

TYPES OF DEBT USED IN LEVERAGED FINANCE TRANSACTIONS

Secured debt

Type of debt	Costs (spread over lira interbank rate) (%)	Term	Purpose	Typical size	Common covenants
Senior term A	2.50	Annuity of 7 years	Acquisition funding	Up to 4× EBITDA	Max. leverage (debt to EBITDA) Min. EBITDA Fixed coverage ratio Max. CAPEX
Revolving credit facility	2.50	Short term	Fund working capital only	Max. of 1.0× working capital each year	
CAPEX/Acquisition line	Between 2.25 and 2.5 and fees of 0.25	Usually 7 years with a max. of 2–3 years to draw the total available	Fund future CAPEX/acquisitions	Depends on needs	As above, plus limits on CAPEX/acquisitions permitted
Mezzanine facility	Mezzanine investors look for IRR of 10 over interbank rate	8-year bullet	Acquisition financing	Along with senior A, total long-term debt not to exceed 5× EBITDA	Subordinated to senior term debt. Possibility to use payment in kind (PIK)—PIK debt consists of debt that does not require payment of principal or interest until maturity. Slightly looser covenants than senior.

Unsecured debt

* *Vendor debt*—vendors set aside a deposit in cash within the company to ensure funds are available to meet warranty claims.
* *Sponsor debt*—for tax reasons it may be more efficient for sponsors to make an investment in subordinated debt since interests are tax deductible. Term: 10 years or at least 6 to 12 months longer than senior.

Notes: 1. Total long-term debt (interest bearing only) as a multiple of EBITDA ranged from 3× to 5× for most transactions.
2. Equity should be at least 20% of the transaction values.

25

Ducati and Investindustrial: Racing out of the pits and over the finish line

It was a clear sunny day on June 5, 2010 in Mugello, Italy as Andrea C. Bonomi, the founder of Investindustrial, watched Team Ducati clinch the first place at the 2010 Moto GP Gran Premio D'Italia qualifications. As he ducked out of the stadium to head back to Lugano, Switzerland, Bonomi's mind moved away from Ducati's success on the track to its performance as an investment. Many events had transpired since Investindustrial uncharacteristically invested in a listed company by buying a stake in Ducati in 2005. At that time, the legendary bike manufacturer was on the verge of bankruptcy. Overleveraged and fraught with cash problems, Ducati was about to default on its existing loan obligations as the bank was unwilling to restructure the debt. Investindustrial rescued the company by injecting cash and taking over the remaining 30% equity stake of the Texas Pacific Group (TPG).

Over the next few years, Bonomi employed his hands-on style to effect a "revolution" inside the company that turned Ducati's financial position around. The changes also unleashed the passion for innovation that Ducati had always been known for and the company began revamping its dusty product line.

In 2008, as the financial crisis started to unfold, Bonomi had a choice to alter his investment in Ducati. He was contemplating his options of exiting the investment, buying the remaining 70%, or maintaining the 30% stake.

Investindustrial was the brainchild of Bonomi who started the fund in 1990 after identifying an unmet need for private equity capital in Southern Europe, particularly in Spain and Italy. He explained:

> "I noticed that the GDP of Spain and Italy combined is 1.5 times that of the U.K., yet the PE investments in these countries were less than 20% of that in the U.K. And these economies are about as advanced as the U.K. so there was a tremendous opportunity and I wanted to help create that market and lead it."

This case was co-authored with Ashish Kumar, Norman Lee, and Vishal Radhakrishnan (LBS MBA 2010). Hans Holmen and Luca Simonazzi provided valuable comments.

In the course of two decades, Investindustrial raised over €2bn to make 44 investments. With a team of 50 people focused on taking control positions, Bonomi made investments between €35mn and €200mn in companies with revenues of up to €1bn. A long-term investment horizon and an industrially driven approach had established Investindustrial as the leaders of private equity in Southern Europe. As of late 2010 Investindustrial had realized 28 exits generating a gross IRR of 39% and a money multiple of 2.4× with just one writeoff. The firm had built a successful and consistent track record through a focused investment strategy and by maintaining a moderate debt level—typically below 3× EBITDA—as a cushion against significant changes in the marketplace. Details of Investindustrial's strategy, investment team, fund history, and current status are given in Exhibit 25.1.

Inspired by the infamous radio inventor and Bologna native, Guglielmo Marconi, the Ducati family began producing radios in the city in 1926. Building upon the initial success to invent new types of cameras, movie projectors, and other appliances, the business outgrew the family villa to eventually become the second largest manufacturing concern in Italy. Forced to retool their production facilities to meet the needs of the Italian government during the Second World War, Ducati became a repeated target of Allied bombing and was razed to the ground in 1943. Barely a month after the war, the Turin firm SIATA mounted a small pushrod engine on a bicycle and named it the Cucciolo (Italian for "puppy", in reference to the distinctive exhaust sound). As the economy was recovering, The Cucciolo started to replace manual bicycles as the preferred driving vehicle for businessmen across the country. In 1950, Ducati produced its first motorized bicycles, a 60 cc bike with a tiny 15 mm carburetor delivering 85 km/L.

However, following years of hardship, the founders were left penniless and the company was rescued by the Italian government through the Institute for Industrial Reconstruction (IRI). Under IRI, the company was split into two concerns: Ducati Energia, a consumer electronics company, and Ducati Meccanica, the motorcycle company. It was Ducati Meccanica that created the Cucciolo. What really put Ducati on the map was the engine designed by Fabio Taglioni. The avant garde Taglioni design, also called the desmodromic distribution system, was partially designed out of necessity. As quality steel was unavailable in the postwar period in Italy, Taglioni invented a new type of engine that could allow valves to open and close at high revolutions without the use of springs. Over the next 40 years Ducati established itself as the premier Italian manufacturer of racing motorbikes.

In 1983 the Italian state suffered significant losses on Ducati due to management issues and sold the company to the Italian conglomerate Cagiva. Cagiva stood for "Castiglioni Giovanni Varese", and was named after the founder and the town in which the company was based. While producing its own motorcycles since 1979, Cagiva had great frames but no engine whereas Ducati had a great engine but not an outstanding body. When the two were put together, the Ducati of today was born. Run by the Castiglioni brothers, Cagiva became an organization passionate about building world-class motorcycles. Giving the engineers free reign, the brothers enlisted a design group in San Marino, a principality 85 miles from the Ducati headquarters in Bologna, to create a portfolio of bikes. The team in San Marino, driven by independent-minded designers and engineers, operated in total secrecy. Castiglioni was given very little information on the kind of bike that was being built or the timeline for the release but was simply asked to meet the ongoing funding requirements. One of the bikes this team developed was the Monster motorcycle.

The Monster, with its revolutionary minimalist design, was a runaway hit becoming

Ducati's biggest selling bike in history. In spite of success in the marketplace, Ducati suffered from serious financial and management issues. Ducati's marketing budget was a fraction of that of its competitors and its distribution channel comprised motorcycle enthusiasts who were not focused on maximizing sales or profitability. Ducati still operated like a family business with limited financial controls and poor corporate governance.

In 1996, after a challenging negotiation with the Castiglioni brothers, TPG made their debut European transaction by acquiring a 51% stake in Ducati based on the Italian lira equivalence of USD420mn transaction value of which two thirds (USD280mn) were financed by debt.[1] The TPG acquisition was completed in 1998 to make the American private equity group the sole owner of Ducati. On the operational side, TPG recruited Federico Minoli, a former Bain consultant and executive of Benetton U.S.A., to run Ducati. Setting branding as a priority over fixing operations, the first move Minoli made after taking over the beleaguered company was to build a museum; an act that caused the workforce to promptly go on strike. That first day set the tone for the next 7 years. Focused on telling a unique story to fend off intense competition from the Japanese, Minoli positioned the Ducati brand as the Ferrari of motorbikes. In a few years, "the red motorcycle from Borgo Panigale" became synonymous with high-end racing performance and Italian style.[2] TPG took Ducati public in 2000 and exited partially, leaving it with a residual 30% controlling stake in the company.

The successful turnaround and IPO gave TPG the credibility in Europe to raise its first European fund. As TPG shifted its focus towards making investments from the new fund, Ducati began to show signs of weakness. Minoli brought much needed marketing skills to augment the engineering background of Castiglioni's Ducati; however, over time the company began to move away from its core competency of making great bikes. De-emphasizing product innovation, Minoli only launched one new bike during the TPG years. For a new concept, Minoli hired the best consultants to conduct extensive market research to determine the exact product that would meet customer needs. The idea was to create a bike that was low enough for women to ride but high enough for the road—a model that had enough of a new body to be deemed new, yet given financial constraints used the same technology as existing bikes. The 999 model was Ducati's biggest flop. Looking more like a mainstream Honda than a Ducati, customers perceived the 999 as a bike of compromises without Ducati's trademark passion. The company later realized that customers do not want—in Bonomi's words—"A bike that is quiet, reliable, smooth and powerful. They want a Ducati made by a bunch of crazy passionate engineers. If it burnt your leg a little, well, isn't that cool?!" (see Exhibit 25.2 for Ducati relevant market segments and Exhibit 25.3 for customer perception of motorcycle brands in 2005).

INVESTINDUSTRIAL ACQUISITION OF DUCATI

For nearly 3 years investment bankers had repeatedly urged Investindustrial to acquire Ducati. Conceptually, it made perfect sense—Ducati was a famous Italian brand and Investindustrial was a leading private equity firm in Southern Europe. However, Bonomi questioned the upside potential since TPG had extracted the turnaround value. He was also concerned that buying a stake in a publicly listed company would likely

---

1. This acquisition figure includes USD40mn of transaction costs.
2. Borgo Panigale is the suburb of Bologna where the Ducati factories are located.

limit the ability of Investindustrial to drive a proper repositioning process. Third, there was a free-riding problem where some of Investindustrial investors might have wondered why they couldn't directly invest in the listed shares of Ducati, thereby avoiding Investindustrial management and performance fees.

Situated at the heart of the financial community of northern Italy, it was no wonder that Bonomi had close personal connections with Ducati. He repeatedly received calls from friends who sat on the board of Ducati and others close to the company to look at it on the grounds that it was a great opportunity as the company was mismanaged. Internally, Dante Razzano, a senior principal at Investindustrial who had helped TPG to acquire Ducati in 1996 and served on its board, also started to see a new opportunity emerge. Investindustrial, however, declined all invitations to invest.

The turning point came in January 2006 when a leading Italian merchant banker from Mediobanca known for his frugality insisted on taking Bonomi to the most expensive restaurant in Milan. "The company must really be in trouble," thought Bonomi. He learned that Ducati was in breach of loan covenants and would be facing bankruptcy soon and so decided to meet the CEO, Federico Minoli. During their meeting, Bonomi expected to discuss Ducati's impending bankruptcy. Instead, Minoli focused on Ducati's upcoming product placement in the new *Batman* movie. Bonomi thought:

> "Here was the CEO of a company facing bankruptcy and he's talking to me about celebrities and racing. Maybe there is a leadership problem in this company—this could be an opportunity."

He decided to approach David Bonderman, the founder of TPG. As TPG was buying Investindustrial's stake in another company, Bonomi had built a strong relationship with him and asked for exclusivity to evaluate Ducati for a possible acquisition. With no lawyers and bankers in the middle, TPG gave free access to Investindustrial. Being listed on the Milan exchange and controlled by a globally leading PE firm, Ducati's books were surely in order. Exhibit 25.4 provides key financial figures for the 1996–2001 growth phase and, then, for the latest year 2005. From a preliminary financial inspection and by talking to management, Investindustrial realized the potential value of a deal. As Razzano commented:

> "We realized that since the fundamentals of the company were still strong, that with the right people, the least we could strive to do was to bring the performance back up to 2000–2001 levels. With a few changes, like refreshing the product lineup, the company could be able to lift back the EBIT margin from nothing to a double-digit percentage over a 4-to-5-year period. That should generate a decent return."

As part of the strategic due diligence Investindustrial retained Porsche Consulting, the leading automotive manufacturing consulting firm in Europe, to prepare a comprehensive turnaround plan. This included revamping the customer acquisition model by repositioning the Ducati brand through premium models, as well as a detailed plan to improve efficiency in all areas (see Exhibits 25.5 and 25.6, respectively). The deal was completed shortly afterwards in March 2006 whereby a consortium led by Investindustrial acquired TPG's remaining 30% stake for €74.5mn. The investment was made by Investindustrial Fund III (€38.7mn),[3] where the rest of the funding

---

3. Additional shares were purchased during 2007 thereby increasing Investindustrial Fund III's investment to €41.3mn.

was shared between one of its limited partners Hospitals of Ontario Pension Plan and another Italian private equity firm, BS Investimenti. Through this structure, Investindustrial obtained a controlling position in Ducati, which by Italian corporate law enabled it to nominate all but one of the directors on the board.

Alongside €137mn of Ducati debt, the transaction represented an enterprise value (EV) of €306mn, 2.0× of forecast 2006 sales, and 22.1× of forecast 2006 EBITDA (24.8× actual 2005 EBITDA). While this may seem a high entry valuation, Investindustrial did not perceive the current performance as indicative, as it expected to triple EBITDA within a few years. Paying off the entire debt and assuming a contraction of the entry multiple to 8.0× EBITDA, Ducati would generate a 2.5× return to investors.

IMPROVING THE COMPANY (2006–2008)

With the focus on operations instilled by the new owner and implementing the due diligence plan, Minoli managed to return the company to profitability. Revenue in 2007 jumped 30% over the previous year to €398mn, driven largely by the success of the new models (the 1098 and the Hypermotard) at higher price points. Actual unit sales grew from 35,095 in 2006 to 39,687 in 2007 to almost equal Ducati's historical unit sales record achieved in 2001. Sales performance also reflected the strategic decision, taken in 2006, to lower inventory levels throughout the network which allowed fewer retail markdowns.

Previously, Ducati customers would have to wait 18 months to take delivery of the bike they ordered. By implementing the *kaizen* method popularized by Toyota, the lead time was reduced to a mere 40 days. These sweeping changes, along with the success of the new models in the marketplace, helped the company post consistent earnings over the period. The operational changes implemented to improve Ducati's performance are summarized in Exhibit 25.7.

As a result of a successful turnaround, Investindustrial understood that Ducati was ready for new management to take it forward to the next phase of growth. Minoli was replaced by Gabriele Del Torchio, who had years of experience working directly with a number of private equity houses—some spent as CEO of the global yacht manufacturer Ferretti. In August 2007, a recapitalization of the investment vehicle in Ducati generated a significant distribution to Investindustrial III, returning 118% of its investment in just 1.5 years.

THE WORLD MOTORCYCLE INDUSTRY IN 2008

The overall motorcycle market can be separated into bikes that are used as a primary means of transportation and bikes that are used for recreation. Almost all bikes with engines larger than 500 cc fall into the latter category. These recreational bikes can be broadly split into three subsegments—sport bikes, touring bikes, and cruisers. Sport bikes are aggressively styled motorcycles that closely resemble the features of a racing bike. The rider leans forwards into the wind improving aerodynamics, thus allowing higher speeds. Touring bikes are straightforward, versatile motorcycles where the rider sits upright or leans forward slightly. Cruisers emphasize comfort at the expense of performance. The rider sits at a lower seat height, leaning slightly backwards.

Worldwide sales of recreational bikes had reached an unprecedented high, primarily fueled by increasing discretionary income for a second or third vehicle. While

Europe, North America, and Japan constituted the majority of sales, the importance of Asian and South American markets was increasing (see Exhibit 25.8 for a breakdown of Ducati's sales by geography and product line). This worldwide demand was generally met by Japanese manufacturers—Suzuki, Honda, Yamaha, and Kawasaki—who dominated the market and produced the best-selling bikes in all categories. The sport bike segment was similarly dominated by Japanese manufacturers. Even in Europe, Japanese brands controlled over 70% of the sport bike market.

The Japanese manufacturers were the market leaders and catered products to the needs of the mainstream audience, with a focus on reliability and value for money. However, in each segment there were a few key niche players who defined the category and had a cult-like following. In the cruiser segment, that leader was Harley-Davidson which had built its reputation as the bike for the "wild child" in the 1960s and continued to occupy a strong place in the consciousness of the American consumer as a lifestyle product. The touring category was led by BMW which was able to apply the manufacturing principles of the automobile business to produce motorbikes that effectively balanced reliability and performance. Last, in the sport bike segment, the image leader and key niche manufacturer was Ducati, which translated technology developed by its racing subsidiary, Ducati Corse S.r.l., to produce models that captured the hearts and minds of motorcycle enthusiasts worldwide (see Exhibit 25.9 for market positioning and Exhibit 25.10 for Ducati Corse's track record).

RAISING A NEW FUND

By 2007 over 60% of the Investindustrial Fund III was invested and Bonomi was working closely with Mounir Guen, CEO of MVision, a leading global placement firm, to raise Investindustrial Fund IV. After spending 4 months on the road in Europe and the U.S., Investindustrial raised a record €1bn in 2008, twice the size of the previous fund. The strenuous process was over, as was uncertainty on Investindustrial's ability to seal the target fund size. Now was the time to initiate a new of round of investments building on Investindustrial's demonstrated accomplishment.

The new fund provided Investindustrial the capability of evaluating secondary investments in existing portfolio companies like Ducati where they held a minority stake.

A "WILD RIDE" FOR DUCATI'S STOCK

In November/December 2007, movements in Ducati's stock price caused concern to Razzano. The stock lost half of its value only to quickly regain it and then lose it once again. Unprecedented volumes of stock were affected by fluctuations in value that were not in line with general movements in the Italian stock market or for comparable motorbike manufacturers worldwide. Razzano, a seasoned investment banker, suspected that this activity might be the result of a takeover attempt on Ducati—someone could be secretly buying enough of the company to emerge with a controlling stake.

Coincidentally, there was an indirect contact by a large player in the manufacturing sector who expressed interest in buying Investindustrial's 30% stake in Ducati for a sizable premium. What started off as an exploratory conversation only a few weeks ago quickly escalated into real tangible interest. Given that Ducati had already returned Investindustrial investors their money, the extra return from an outright sale would deliver an excellent IRR.

Just a few months earlier, a number of bankers had also tried to persuade Investindustrial to take the company private. They were turned down since there were quite a few operational improvements under way and Investindustrial wanted to see them through before deciding to put any further money in. Since then, Gabriele Del Torchio, the new CEO, had done an excellent job in continuing the EBITDA growth, and Razzano felt more comfortable exploring this option. In line with a take-private practice, the bankers advised Investindustrial to offer a premium over the market price of €1.47 to ensure the success of the tender offer (see Exhibit 25.11 for Ducati's key financial performance figures during the period and forecasts and Exhibit 25.12 for its balance sheet).

Yet, at the same time the global stock market was tumbling on the back of the subprime crisis that had exploded in the U.S. several months prior. The equity market was taking a beating, with the S&P dropping 15% in just the previous 3 months. On Monday, January 21, 2008 oil prices broke the USD100-a-barrel psychological barrier for the first time. This caused a sharp drop in global equities triggered by concern that higher commodity prices would sharply impair corporate profits. With the FTSE 100 experiencing the biggest ever 1-day fall in points and European stocks closing with their worst results since September 11, 2001, some news headlines and general columnists termed it Black Monday and anticipated a global shares crash. Bonomi wondered if he should follow other private equity firms and hold off on transactions or continue to evaluate this deal on its own merit (see Exhibit 25.13 for 2008 macroeconomic parameters).

Following weeks of intensive research, Bonomi and Razzano felt they had sufficient information. They were in an enviable position where all options had strong merit. On one hand, Ducati could be exited to a trade buyer, thereby providing investors with an exceptional return. However, Investindustrial believed that Ducati had further growth potential and, thus, they might be leaving "money on the table" by exiting too early.

A second option would be to "double down" by taking the company private. They could take advantage of the market dip to acquire equity at relatively attractive valuations. The interest of a first-tier industry player to purchase the existing stake gave Investindustrial a credible reference point to determine how much to offer for the remaining 70% of the total 328 million outstanding shares. For a tender offer to succeed, it would require at least a ¢20 premium over the current €1.5 share price. To finance a possible tender offer, a short-term facility was secured from Banca Popolare di Milano and the Royal Bank of Scotland. Thereafter, Intesa Sanpaolo, leading a syndicate of Italian banks, would provide a permanent package consisting of €240mn senior debt and €35mn mezzanine (see Exhibit 25.14 for the terms). However, there were some issues they needed to address. Investindustrial, like other private equity firms, had limits on the amount it could invest from a fund in any single portfolio company. Depending on the price Bonomi had to pay to acquire the rest of Ducati, this could force him to concentrate close to 20% of the fund into just this investment. Also, since the capital would have to be drawn from the new fund, both Investindustrial III and Investindustrial IV would be investing in the company. Bonomi was worried that this might create an internal conflict of interest. A clear solution to this problem had to be presented to the investment committee before a follow-on investment could be authorized. The fact that a trade buyer had offered to buy Investindustrial's stake in Ducati for a higher price than the proposed tender offer gave Investindustrial additional comfort and an arm's length pricing benchmark.

Third, there was the option of doing nothing. This could play out in an interesting way as, in the event of a hostile takeover, the acquirer might be ready to pay a significant premium to gain control of the company. However, this strategy also came with its own set of risks as there was no certainty that an acquirer would in fact materialize, and Investindustrial might lose the opportunity to either exit its investment or buy the remaining shares at a great price.

Bonomi had spent long days working with Razzano and the bankers to closely evaluate the financials behind each of the three options. As he headed home after a marathon working session, his phone rang. The strategic buyers interested in Ducati wanted to visit the Ducati plant in Bologna before making their formal bid for the Investindustrial consortium's 30% stake in Ducati. He needed to think quickly in order to give them an answer.

JUNE 2010

Two years later, Bonomi wondered whether he had made the right decision in February 2008 when completing a public tender offer for Ducati in its entirety. At the time, the take-private had been at a much lower EV/EBITDA valuation than in the original entry, and the deal would make Investindustrial the most experienced public-to-private investor in the Italian market. Ducati had been one of four companies that Investindustrial had taken private for a combined enterprise value of €2.0bn. However, in the subsequent two years global financial markets had become profoundly jittery and in the process depressed consumption. Luxury good manufacturers were hit particularly hard. Many things that private equity had relied on were disappearing: loose credit fueling buoyant acquisitions had dried up and the IPO markets were firmly shut. In June 2010 the stability of financial markets was being tested again with Greece teetering on the brink of bankruptcy and analysts worrying about Ireland, Spain, Portugal, and Italy being next.

With €1bn of "dry powder" from its recent fund, the financial crisis felt like a perfect storm as the competition had difficulty in raising new capital. With the volume of activity in recent years, the Investindustrial team felt cohesive and experienced enough to face whatever new challenges presented themselves.

Bonomi picked up the phone to talk to Del Torchio about the sales of Ducati's recently launched Multistrada model, an important step towards hopefully making "the Red One" from Borgo Panigale also a roaring investment success.

APPENDIX

EXHIBIT 25.1A

PROFILES OF KEY PERSONNEL AT INVESTINDUSTRIAL AND DUCATI

Andrea C. Bonomi Andrea founded Investindustrial in 1990 and has served as its Chairman since then. He started his career in investment banking at the New York offices of Lazard Freres & Co. and then moved to Europe to work at Kleinwort Benson in London where he oversaw M&A transactions in Spain and Italy. Andrea made his transition into European private equity by monitoring the European and U.S. investments of the Saffa Group, an industrial holding company. During his career at Saffa, Andrea developed his thesis for a standalone private equity firm focused on Southern Europe and started Investindustrial. Andrea earned a B.Sc. in business administration from New York University in 1985.

Dante Razzano Dante is a senior principal at Investindustrial. Joining the firm in 2004, he is involved in both deal sourcing and screening in Italy. Dante moved back from New York to Italy in 1992 to join Morgan Grenfell and help start the Italian investment banking and private equity practice franchise. While in New York he headed Citicorp Italian merchant bank activities. Throughout his career, Dante has been involved in key Italian private equity deals, including the TPG-led acquisition of Ducati in 1996. Dante attended CUNY and Pace universities in New York.

Gabriele Del Torchio A Varese native, Gabriele has a degree in economics from the Sacro Cuore Catholic University in Milan. In 1973 he began his career at the Banca Commerciale Italiana and then moved to Sperry New Holland SpA, a worldwide leader in agricultural machinery, where he held various positions before becoming President and CEO of its Ford New Holland subsidiary. In 1990, Gabriele joined Fai Komatsu SpA, a European leader of construction machinery, as CEO and subsequently President. Gabriele's rich industry and operation experience includes serving as CEO of CIFA SpA, a company specializing in cement plant design and installation, to be followed by heading APS SpA, the multiutility company for the city of Padova (energy, transport, environment, and telecommunications). He then took on the role of CEO of Carraro Group, a world leader in automotive components and systems. From 2005 to 2007 he was CEO of the private equity–backed Ferretti Group, one of the leading companies in the world of design and construction of luxury motor yachts and sporting boats. Since May 2007 Gabriele has been CEO of Ducati Motor Holding SpA, the leading manufacturer of high-performance sports motorcycles, and was appointed President in January 2009.

Source: Investindustrial.

EXHIBIT 25.1B

INVESTINDUSTRIAL'S EVOLUTION 1990–2010

Investment program	Structure	Investment period	Fund size (€ million)	Investee companies
First	Evergreen	1992–1999	185	16
Second	Investindustrial Fund LP	2000–2005	323	12
Third	Investindustrial Fund III LP	2005–2008	600	10
Fourth	Investindustrial Fund IV LP	2008–current	1,000	5

Source: Source: Investindustrial.

EXHIBIT 25.1C

INVESTMENT PORTFOLIO OF INVESTINDUSTRIAL

Source: Investindustrial's *Group Overview*, April 2010.

EXHIBIT 25.2

MOTORBIKES MARKET SEGMENTS

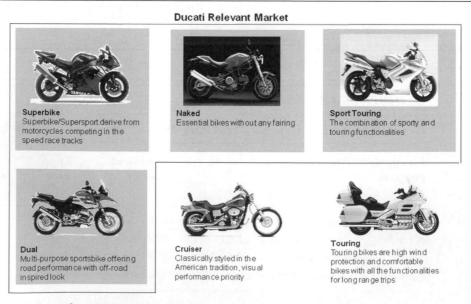

Source: Ducati's *Strategic Plan 2006–2008*, May 2006.

EXHIBIT 25.3

CUSTOMER PERCEPTION OF LEADING BRANDS IN 2005

Ducati is perceived high on bike sportiness and design

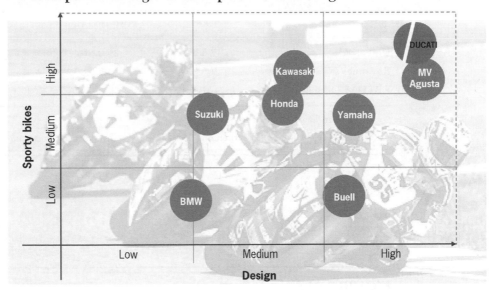

Ducati is perceived low on price/performance and technological innovation

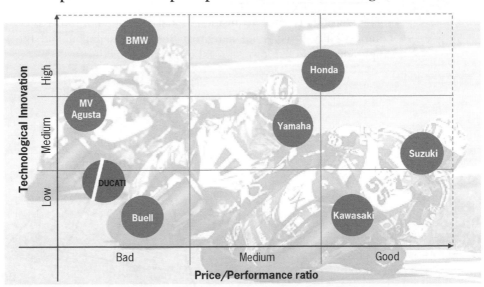

Source: Porsche Consulting, *Motorrad des Jahres 2005*, Motorrad, Motor-Presse Verlag, 2005.

EXHIBIT 25.4

DUCATI'S MILESTONES: OWNERSHIP AND KEY FIGURES

Castiglioni Bros.		TPG		70% public + 30% TPG		70% public + 30% Investindustrial
1996		2000		2005		
		1996		Post-IPO (2001)		2005
Units sold		12,639		40,016		34,500
Revenues (€ million)		105.8		407.8		320.8
EBITDA (€ million)		11.8		6.1		24[1]

Source: Ducati financial statements.

Note: 1. Adjusted for one-off restructuring accrual reserves, inventory devaluation and write off penalties.

EXHIBIT 25.5

2005 DUE DILIGENCE: REVISING THE CUSTOMER ACQUISITION MODEL

The Ducati Customer Acquisition Model developed in 1997 has deteriorated due to the impossibility to generate margin in the entry segment and the diminished rate of upgrade due to the lower appeal of premium models.

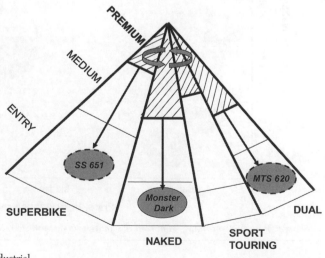

Source: Investindustrial.

EXHIBIT 25.6

2005 DUE DILIGENCE: STRONG POTENTIAL IMPROVEMENT IN ALL AREAS

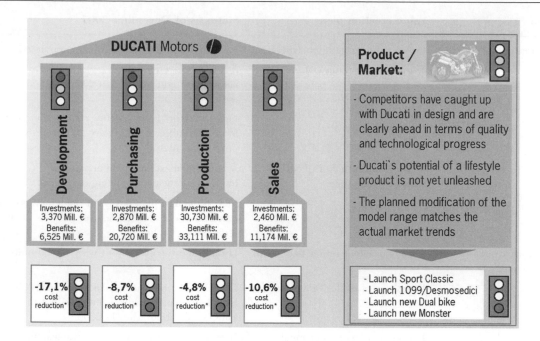

Potential effect on Ducati's cost structure over the next 3 years

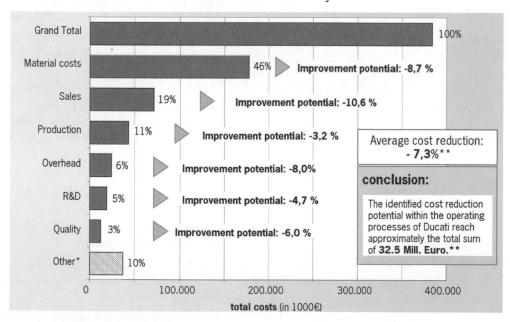

Source: Porsche *Consulting Report*, August 2005.

Notes: °Other material, net racing costs, restructuring costs, etc.
°°Based on 5% sales increase (Sport Classic).

EXHIBIT 25.7A

OPERATIONAL IMPROVEMENTS INITIATED BY INVESTINDUSTRIAL, 2006–2007

Area	Value creation plan	Status as of December 2007
Organizational structure	Review of management structure	New CEO Gabriele Del Torchio appointed
Cost reduction	Reduction in number of employees	A workforce reduction plan was agreed with the labor union and initiated in 2006 (headcount reduction by 90)
		Due to better than expected results, the company hired a number of temporary employees to meet production plan
	Reduction in number of SKUs (stock-keeping units)	A new organizational plan aimed at improving efficiency is being developed
		SKU reduction plan has been implemented with excellent results in R&D. Inventory has been reduced by €20mn
Working capital management	Focus on sellout rather than sellin	Hit all-time record sell-out with 40,000 units
	Reduction of dealer's inventory	Dealers inventory further reduced by 2,000 units reaching normal levels of fewer than 4-month sales (vs. 5-month sales in 2006)
	Reduction of working capital	Improved management of receivables and payables resulting in further reduction of working capital from 21% of sales in 2006 to approximately 10% in 2007 (a €37mn reduction)
Focus on R&D	R&D team	Faster and more efficient transfer of technology from Ducati's experience in MotoGP in commercial vehicles
	Product development	Ongoing reduction in number of engines
		Reduction of warranty costs by 10% New models require less frequent service, fewer parts, and less labor during each service reducing scheduled maintenance by 50%
		696 (new Monster) development in 24 months
	Product range	Sizable sales of three new models launched in 2006–2007
		Product range being renewed with the phaseout of low-margin family models
Procurement process	Improve quality of suppliers' base	Improvement of suppliers' quality largely achieved
	Implementation of global sourcing	Component of new Monster bike manufactured in lower cost environments
	Improve terms and conditions of agreement with suppliers	Medium-term structured agreements reached with key suppliers

Source: Investindustrial.

EXHIBIT 25.7B

TREND OF WARRANTY CLAIMS PER BIKE, 2004–2010

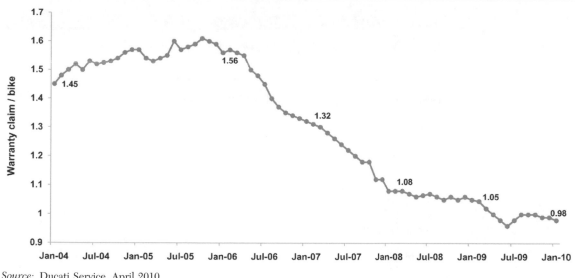

Source: Ducati Service, April 2010.

EXHIBIT 25.8

DUCATI TURNOVER BREAKDOWN

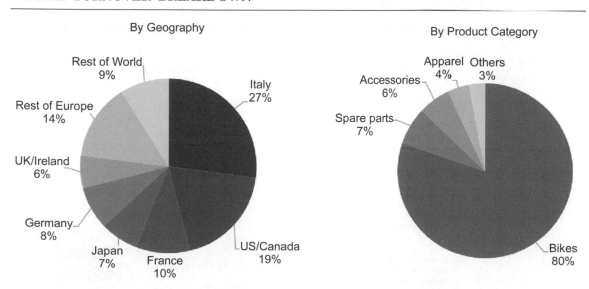

Source: Ducati, April 2010.

Note: 2009 data.

EXHIBIT 25.9A

DUCATI MARKET SHARE*

Suzuki	25.0
Honda	19.9
Yamaha	18.6
Kawasaki	14.0
BMW	9.1
Ducati	4.4
Triumph	3.2
Buell	1.5
Aprilia	1.2
KTM	1.3
MV Agusta	0.5

Source: 2005 data.

Note: *The Ducati-relevant market is defined as Superbike, Naked, Sport Touring, and Dual (all of which are above 398 cc bikes).

EXHIBIT 25.9B

DUCATI'S STRATEGIC POSITIONING—FOCUSED NICHE BRAND

- Japanese players adopt a generalist strategy competing in every segment of the market with high quality and technological products at low prices

- Ducati and Harley compete in specific niches where a **highly characterized** product can demand a premium price

- Both niche brands are pushing the boundaries of their original niche while remaining loyal to their respective DNA and heritage

- Ducati has been particularly successful expanding towards lifestyle with Monster family and towards comfort with Multistrada and Sport Touring

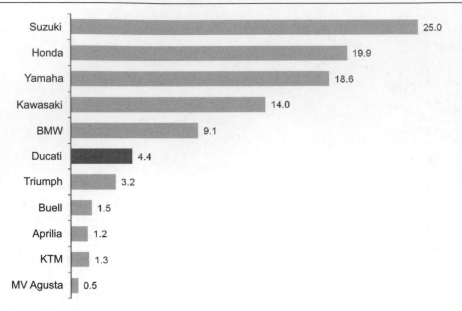

Source: Ducati's *Strategic Plan 2006–2008*, May 2006.

EXHIBIT 25.10

DUCATI'S RACING RECORD

Ducati has been providing motorbikes for racers ever since the world-famous English racer Mike Hailwood requested a machine of "superior" performance in 1958. Since then, Ducati has dominated the racing circuit, especially the SBK variety. In this format, racers use "street-legal" bikes that are manufactured and sold in large quantities in the market with little modifications. The other format, Moto GP, is more popular and uses bikes that are specially designed for racing. This is the "Formula One" of bikes and has a strong following worldwide. Ducati has been participating in SBK races for many years and entered the MotoGP category in 2003.

Competition		2002	2003	2004	2005	2006	2007	2008	Total race victories
SBK	Pilots	2nd place (Bayliss)	Champion (Hodgson)	Champion (Toseland)	4th place (Toseland)	Champion (Bayliss)	4th place (Bayliss)	Champion (Bayliss)	272[1]
	Manufacturers	Champion	Champion	Champion	3rd place	Champion	2nd place	Champion	
	Onsite attendance			1 million, increasing 10–15% per yea					
	TV viewers			2 billion, with coverage increasing 10% per year					
MotoGP	Pilots	Not present	4th place (Capirossi)	10th place (Capirossi)	6th place (Capirossi)	3rd place (Capirossi)	Champion (Stoner)	2nd place (Stoner)	24[2]
	Manufacturers		2nd place	3rd place	3rd place	3rd place	Champion	2nd place	
	Onsite attendance	n.a.	1,700,000 (approx.)	1,843,947	2,003,545	2,139,413	2,322,914	n.a.	
	TV viewers	n.a.	5.1 billion	5.2 billion	5.2 billion	5.2 billion	>5.5 billion	>5.5 billion	

Source: Investindustrial Annual Investors' meeting, November 2008.

Notes: 1. Since 1988.
2. Since 2003.

EXHIBIT 25.11

DUCATI'S KEY FINANCIAL PERFORMANCE AND FORECASTS (€ MILLION)

	2005A	2006A	2007A	2008E	2009E	2010E
Revenue	321	305	398	469	496	561
Revenue growth	*16%*	*−5%*	*29%*	*18%*	*6%*	*13%*
EBITDA	24	27	55	78.5	85	107
EBITDA margin	*7.5%*[1]	*8.8%*	*13.8%*	*16.7%*	*17%*	*19%*
Depreciation and amortization	24	22	32	37	42	47
EBIT	0	5	23	36	43	60
EBIT margin	*0*	*1.6%*	*5.8%*	*7.8%*	*8.7%*	*10.7%*
Capital expenditure	31	34	39	40	40	40
Effective tax rate[2]	n.a.	n.a.	28%	29%	30%	31%
Employees (year-end)	1,134	1,043	1,142	1,140	1,150	1,180

Source: Ducati's financial statements 2005–2007 and management projections, February 2008.

Notes: 1. 5.8% adjusted after restructuring cost.

2. Statutory tax rates of 27.5% corporate (Ires) and 3.9% regional (Irap) are envisaged under the 2008 Finance Law.

EXHIBIT 25.12

DUCATI: CONSOLIDATED BALANCE SHEET (DECEMBER 31, 2007)

Current assets		
Cash and cash equivalents	108,518	
Trade receivables, net	72,475	
Inventory	85,605	
Other current assets	11,451	
Total current assets	**278,049**	53.9%
Non-current assets		
Property, plant, and equipment, net	72,936	
Goodwill and intangible assets with indefinite useful lives	86,050	
Other intangible assets	53,128	
Equity investments	287	
Deferred tax assets	25,184	
Oter non-current assets	317	
Total non-current assets	**237,902**	46.1%
Total assets	**515,951**	100%
Current liabilities		
Short-term borrowing	13,972	
Trade payables	126,245	
Due to tax authorities	4,853	
Other current liabilities	21,955	
Provisions for risks and charges—current portion	6,443	
Total current liabilities	**173,468**	33.6%
Long-term liabilities		
Long-term borrowing	105,401	
Employee benefits	7,433	
Deferred taxation	20,474	
Provisions for risks and charges—long-term portion	1,849	
Total long-term liabilities	**135,157**	26.2%
Total liabilities	**308,625**	59.8%
Shareholders' equity		
Share capital	167,257	
Reserves	75,010	
Retained earnings (losses)	(48,207)	
Results for the year	13,257	
Total group shareholders' equity	**207,317**	40.2%
Minority interest	9	
Total shareholders' equity	**207,326**	
Total liabilities and shareholders' equity	**515,951**	100%

EXHIBIT 25.13

ITALIAN CAPITAL MARKET DATA

Equity markets

	FTSE MIB	Ducati stock price
2004	30,903	0.663
2005	35,704	0.705
2006	41,434	0.914
2007	38,554	1.412

GDP growth rates

	Italy	U.S.
2004	1.20%	6.40%
2005	0.60%	6.40%
2006	2.40%	5.40%
2007	0.30%	5.30%

EURO exchange rates

	USD
2004	1.3554
2005	1.1849
2006	1.3197
2007	1.4589

6-month interest rates

	Euribor	Libor
September 2007	4.76%	5.54%
February 2008	4.36%	3.04%

Source: Bloomberg, *www.euribor-ebf.eu*, *www.liborated.com*

EXHIBIT 25.14

BANK DEBT PACKAGE FOR DUCATI'S TENDER OFFER (FEBRUARY 2008)

Lending bank: Intesa Sanpaolo (under syndication process)

	Amount	Terms	Pricing (spread over LIBOR)	Multiple of 2008E EBITDA
	(£ million)		(%)	
Term Loan A	100	7-year amortizing	2.6	
Term Loan B	70	8-year bullet	3.1	
Term Loan C	70	9-year bullet	3.6	
Total Senior Debt	*240*			3×
Mezzanine[1]	35	10 year	4.5 + 6.5 PIK	
Total debt	*275*			3.5×
Total debt/post-completion EV	0.36			
Revolving credit facility	25	7-year bullet	2.6[2]	

Notes: 1. At the holding company level assuming 100% shareholding of Ducati.
    2. Plus 0.5% commitment fee.

Financial covenants for senior debt and expected level post-tender offer

Maintenance covenants	Senior debt/EBITDA	EBITDA/Interest payable
Threshold	4.00×	3.1×

Source: Investindustrial.

26

Styles & Wood: Behind the scenes of retail

In May 2004, Francesco Santinon saw the dome of St. Paul's Cathedral in the heart of London's finance district come in to view as he briskly walked towards his office. Santinon was Senior Investment Director at Aberdeen Asset Managers Ltd., Private Equity Division, one of the U.K.'s leading mid-market private equity investors. He was scheduled to present his investment proposal to support a secondary management buyout of Styles & Wood Ltd. (S&W).

As if it were yesterday, Santinon remembered being in the same position just 3 years earlier. Only then 3i, a major private equity competitor, had outbid him for S&W in an auction where he had underestimated the bid price of £18mn. Now, 3i was expected to double the value of its investment. S&W was no doubt a success story for its investors, led by an impressive management team. Operating out of Manchester, it was in the shopfitting business and, since 1995, had performed remarkably well increasing their turnover from around £30mn to £145mn in just under a decade. He did not want to miss out on this opportunity again, and now Aberdeen Asset Managers had to get their offer right.

STYLES & WOOD: THE HISTORY

Styles & Wood was known as a shopfitter, a business providing interior fitout services for the retail sector and seen as a segment of the construction industry. The current business dates back to the mid-1980s when it was owned by a private group, Meridian Holdings Ltd. In May 1989, the business was acquired by Wembley Stadium Group, owners of the world-renowned football stadium and other leisure sites, as part of their substantial program of diverse acquisitions in the late 1980s.

Shopfitting involved provision of the interior and exterior features of retail premises, including shopfronts, signs, counters, shelving, slotted wall cladding, and merchandise display units. The total fitout project also required flooring, lighting, suspended ceilings, financial point-of-sales equipment, security devices, automatic doors, shutters, chilled food cabinets, and decorative display units. The shopfitting

The case was co-authored with Kay Nemoto (LBS MBA 2002) and Alberto Pons (LBS Sloan Fellow 2007).

business was fundamentally dependent on the prosperity of the retail industry. Its market was considered to be heavily influenced by trends in retail sales.

Shopfitting in the mid-1990s was estimated to be approximately a £1.1bn industry in the UK. Supermarkets provided the largest shopfitting opportunities, with the non-food market segment also growing in finance, offices, hotels, and leisure facilities. The market had been hit badly by the recession, falling by 18% between 1990 and 1993 with an upturn in sales starting in 1994.

The construction industry, in general, was going through a stagnant period where late delivery of contracts became the norm, legal disputes were raging with clients in the courtrooms, and some companies were going into administration.

In the early 1990s, S&W depended heavily on its three largest customers, one of which was its new owner Wembley Stadium Group. Debenhams and Gateway (which later became Somerfield) were the other major retail clients. The three combined represented two thirds of their revenue.

GERARD QUILIGOTTI AND THE TURNAROUND YEARS

In September 1991, Gerard Quiligotti faced one of the most crucial turning points in his career by offering his resignation as Managing Director from Quiligotti plc, started by his grandfather and now a global manufacturer and supplier of floor tiles. Gerard Quiligotti had grown up with the expectation that he would lead the family business; however, when a management buyin deal was accepted, his perspective also changed and he too decided to step away from the business.

Quiligotti was immediately approached by Wembley Stadium Group to look into a recent underperforming acquisition in the Manchester area called Styles & Wood Ltd. Quiligotti craved for a new challenge. He felt the business of procuring and laying floor tiles for offices and stores may not be too different from a storefitting business and wanted to take his mind off his resignation. Quiligotti quickly agreed to the new business consulting role offered to him at S&W.

Quiligotti was in for a surprise as he walked in for his first day at S&W. What he found was a company lacking in leadership and direction and a group of completely de-motivated employees. As he walked through the office, he recognized the bored disinterested looks in his direction. He knew that it would be no easy task to pull the people together but visualized a company that could be turned around. Quiligotti rolled up his sleeves for the task ahead.

Four key issues were identified at S&W by Quiligotti—the leadership (or lack of it), the people, the business model, and the customer base. The leadership issue was arguably the easiest and became the first to be tackled. In 1992, S&W offered him the post of chief executive, which he accepted under the condition that he had "right of first refusal" should the owners wish to sell the company. The turnaround process had begun, and he determined to rebuild the company.

(i) Restoring employee morale through investors in people

One of the first projects Quiligotti embarked upon was restoring employee morale; he knew the most visible aspect of any company to customers was its people. A training and staff improvement program was put in place utilizing the accreditation process of Investors in People, a corporate qualification that helps organizations improve performance and realize objectives through the management and development of their people.

Quiligotti engaged all staff members in the rehabilitation and management change process, so that they would eventually take pride in their work and the company. With employees taking more accountability for their work, those who did not like the change were weeded out, while at the same time the process attracted new talent to the company. Though Quiligotti was able to gain the support and retain most of the management team, the Sales Director who had failed to bring in sufficient new business over the years was one of the first to depart.

His replacement, Neil Davies—previously Managing Director of a competitor BSC (U.K.) Ltd., had heard of the changes taking place at S&W and was appointed. Davies took on the role of Business Development Director working on the strategic development of S&W alongside Quiligotti with specific responsibility for the sales and marketing function of the business. It was soon apparent that the duo of Quiligotti and Davies would work beautifully.

In fact, during the 1990s the sales team—whose remit was to visit clients and potential new customers—consisted of only two people: Quiligotti and Davies. Both in nice tailored suits, they could have easily been mistaken as finance professionals from the City of London.

(ii)   Service delivery model

Frustrated by the general stagnation of the construction industry at that time, Quiligotti immediately embarked on trying to bring S&W back to business basics of "putting the customer first". He wanted to detach S&W from the traditional shopfitting business and position it more as a consultative support service provider of "integrated property services". His vision was to reposition and refocus the business as a sales and service–led organization, concentrating solely on its core skillset within the retail sector.

Shopfitting requires intricate time management and project management skills with great awareness of the retail business and its customers. The work is often started when the store closes at night and continues until it opens the following morning; sometimes work is carried out in parallel with store opening hours with areas cordoned off for shopfitting work in progress. To keep customers happy and to receive payment for completed work on time, all aspects from keeping contractors on schedule to the behavior of workers on site had to be managed very carefully.

With Quiligotti and Davies at the helm, S&W quickly transitioned from the hard hat–wearing blue-collar image to that of a business-suited white-collar consultant team. They listened to customer needs and put forward ideas based on experience from other projects. Once the planning and design stages were complete, they outsourced much of the work to partnering contractors and became efficient project managers of the supply chain.

There was also a noticeable change in customers; purchasing behavior in the 1990s. Traditionally, retail fitout contracts had been awarded on a purely price-led competitive tender basis. This process inevitably placed downward pressure on margins and gave little scope for building customer relationships. Gradually, customers were changing to a longer term procurement style called "framework" allocation. S&W quickly adapted to these changes by adopting the way their work was won. Instead of participating in constant bidding wars, they aimed to win "framework" allocations through Quiligotti and Davies's relationship-building efforts with potential and existing clients.

Quiligotti and Davies also identified that, by becoming involved with customers at the planning stage of store development, S&W would not only improve its operational delivery but also aid the development of enduring customer relationships.

This aspect of the company's strategy was most notably progressed in 1999, when the company secured an outsourcing agreement to supply design implementation services to Boots, the largest retail pharmacy chain in the U.K. with 1,400 stores. This involved transfer of the Boots in-house design team to S&W, in exchange for guaranteed exclusive work for the next 3 years. This was the beginning of a new trading division, Styles & Wood StorePlanning, an additional service offering for other clients who also wished to outsource services.

(iii) Customer target list and customers for life

S&W grew to increasingly cater for their main customers, who not only provided the majority of S&W's revenue but were also of the quality and size that suggested they would continually invest in store developments irrespective of macroeconomic trends. Such customers regenerated and evolved their store portfolios in order to maintain long-term market positions and brand strength. They were the ideal target for S&W's framework sales approach, allowing for repeat business and longer term procurement.

This prompted Quiligotti and Davies to actively focus on larger blue chip retailers and to adopt a target customer list of the 50 top retailers in the country which they named the "Premier League". It was, however, hard work to win contracts from Premier League retailers, sometimes taking over 5 years of continued sales effort. Quiligotti and Davies came up with the "customer for life" concept, which was a customer management program designed to create and maintain strength and depth in S&W's relationship with each of its customers, with a view to generating repeat business from negotiation rather than the traditional competitive tender. The importance of customer for life was apparent. S&W managed to generate over 85% of each year's turnover from its existing customer-for-life base and to secure over 60% of sales by negotiation, where price was not the sole criterion.

This also allowed the company a high degree of visibility and steady operation from one year to the next, which in turn allowed for better planning, supply chain management, and resourcing of the business.

THE MBO: THE FALL OF WEMBLEY STADIUM GROUP

It became apparent in 1995 that the owners of S&W, Wembley Stadium Group, was facing financial problems. This was the moment Quiligotti was waiting for. Based on the original agreement when Quiligotti accepted the Chief Executive position in 1992, he was presented with the opportunity to purchase S&W.

In August of that year, Quiligotti led a successful management buyout of the company, alongside the senior management team of Graham Clark (Finance Director), Martin Raftery (Commercial Director), and David Howarth (Operations Director). This was structured through a newly formed holding company, Maraq Ltd. (see Exhibit 26.1). A value of £2.25mn was agreed of which £1.5mn was financed by debt from Royal Bank Development Capital. A third external partner, Simon Fawcett, a private investor and business friend of Quiligotti, acquired 20% equity as a condition of the loan. Business Development Director Neil Davies had only started working for S&W shortly before the management buyout and, thus, was not included in the equity investment opportunity.

Quiligotti was pleased he had tied in three senior management members to S&W through this MBO. Retaining top managers was key to the ongoing turnaround process of S&W, and he could not afford to lose them. Quiligotti had convinced them to invest in the future of S&W together and saw this as a key tool for retention and incentivization. He treasured their commitment and also promoted the practice of cashing out a portion of their gains so that their personal lifestyle would improve from the growth of S&W. Quiligotti thus adopted an internal unwritten rule where he would attempt a divestment when the enterprise value doubled and allow for the next tier of senior management to participate in the scheme.

STYLES & WOOD SINCE 1996: MANAGING THE GROWTH STRATEGY

By 1996, the turnaround strategy was clearly showing results. Not only did management have a controlling stake in the company but the employees had been awarded the Investors in People accreditation, one of Quiligotti's first initiatives. Most notably, the change was reflected in their impressive sales performance, with Quiligotti and Davies constantly winning new business. Successful sales efforts led turnover to increase by 64% in 1996 compared with a year earlier from £33mn to £54mn and again by 41% the following year to £76mn (see Exhibit 26.2). This tremendous growth as a result of capturing a larger market share inevitably put a strain on operations and on service delivery.

In fact, the growth led to a major shift in S&W, where the company became a sales-led entity instead of an operational capacity-led entity that could stifle growth. Quiligotti and Davies were gradually increasing the number of attractive high-end customers for life.

By the end of 2000, they had more than 20 Premier League customers which included such household names as Sainsbury's, Marks & Spencer, Barclays Bank, and HSBC. Just as they had hoped, the major retailers and banks committed to larger and longer term projects. This allowed Quiligotti and Davies to secure approximately 40% of the following year's revenue by December. This gave S&W better visibility and accuracy of their financial forecast as well as a firm grip on their planning for the following year.

In addition to growing their customer base, another of the company's key long-term aims was to grow revenue by engaging every customer for life across each of the company's new trading divisions. StorePlanning had been created alongside StoreFit after integration of the Boots design team, and StoreCare was added for after-service care, ensuring customer satisfaction (see Exhibit 26.3). By 2003, the success of this multidivisional sales strategy was evident, with 82% of revenue representing customers for life that had engaged the company through at least two of its three service divisions.

S&W suddenly found itself at the forefront of industry change and improvement, and its innovations in service were starting to be recognized as a new approach to retail store development.

PROJECT OAK IN 2001: MANAGEMENT INCENTIVES AND REAPINGREWARDS

S&W had consistently outperformed its competitors to become the dominant player in its market since Quiligotti took over as CEO. Turnover and profit before tax had grown from £54mn and £1.4mn, respectively, in the year ended December 31, 1996 to £96mn and £2.7mn in the year ended December 31, 2000.

With the support of a local boutique investment bank, Rickitt Mitchell & Partners Ltd. (Rickitt Mitchell), discussions were held with a limited number of debt and equity providers who Rickitt Mitchell thought S&W would represent an attractive investment. They called this initiative "Project Oak".

Quiligotti wanted to ensure that Davies participated this time in the round of equity pool share. Davies had played a major role in repositioning S&W's product offering and redefining its customer relationships. He had just officially been recognized as the successor designate to Quiligotti and had been appointed Deputy Chief Executive.

An employee share pool of 5% of authorized but not issued share capital was also planned. The aim was to provide incentivization for the development of a second-tier management team.

3i Group plc investing

3i Group plc outbid other interested parties such as Francesco Santinon (then at Close Brothers Private Equity) and emerged as the winner of the auction organized by Rickitt Mitchell. 3i Group was the new and first private equity owner for S&W, which was now valued at £18mn, a multiple of 4.9× EBIT considering the £3.9mn cash on the balance sheet. 3i paid £5.15mn for a mix of loan stock and 36.5% of ordinary shares.

Quiligotti couldn't conceal his smile as he walked through the parking lot of S&W after Project Oak was completed. He recognized a few stylish cars recently purchased by his management team who had cashed out part of their equity holdings.

A non-executive director representing 3i Group was immediately appointed to the board but Quiligotti and Davies were to find out that very little demand or confrontation came from 3i Group. In fact, only quarterly meetings were held where good news of solid growth and stellar financial performances were announced. 3i seemed very pleased with S&W and became very passive investors with no meaningful involvement in the operation or strategic planning.

In 2001 the 3i Group underwent its own restructuring process following the challenging business conditions that followed the dotcom bubble crash and September 11. 3i had just announced an 18% reduction in its workforce as a result of centralizing its investment decisions and closing down regional offices, such as the Leeds Office which was responsible within the 3i Group for the S&W investment (Exhibit 26.4 reviews the history of 3i).

Subsequently, the partnership with 3i ended, but S&W continued to grow from 2001 at a rate faster than forecast. Quiligotti and Davies had secretly started "Project Oval" in which they planned their next cashout. This plan started taking shape the day after Project Oak was completed.

At the end of December 2003 the revenue had grown to £132mn and the secured order book for 2004 was already at £58mn. By the first quarter of 2004 the EBITA was expected to almost double that of 2001. Quiligotti and Davies were ready to realize some of their gains again by undertaking Project Oval. They also wanted to increase the employee share pool to 10% to support and provide incentives to the next generation of management and employees.

When 3i Group was approached with the idea, they raised no objection of divesting from S&W as they predicted a healthy return from their investment. Again working with Rickitt Mitchell, another roadshow began. They soon came across the familiar name of Francesco Santinon who had now moved to Aberdeen Asset Managers Ltd. (Aberdeen). Quiligotti and Davies were pleased to hear of his continued interest in the company which gave them a good feeling about Project Oval.

PROJECT OVAL IN 2004: FROM 3I TO ABERDEEN—SECONDARY BUYOUT DECISION

Francesco Santinon was generally pleased with the due diligence reports and its findings on Styles & Wood as there were no major surprises on the progress since 2001. In fact, he recognized that they had outperformed their forecast from 2001. Santinon noted that turnover had shown consistent growth over the period though the margins in the business remained relatively low, typical of the industry (see financial statements in Exhibit 26.5).

Santinon remembered Gerard Quiligotti of Styles & Wood very well. He stood out among the management personnel he had met, and he had come across quite a few through his work identifying companies to invest in. He was also glad to see Neil Davies taking on a leading role with Quiligotti as 3 years earlier his concern was the company's dependence on one man. In fact, Quiligotti had stepped back as Chairman and Davies was now the Chief Executive. The partnership seemed to be working extremely well and so was the company.

Through this transaction, the management proposed enlarging the employee equity pool to a total of 10% of ongoing equity (including the 4.5% already issued in 2001). Santinon appreciated incentive programs for management and employees so that their interest would be aligned with that of investors, and this proposal reinforced his view that the top management of the company was resolute about growing the next generation of talent. He highly rated the effort S&W put into managing, training, and developing its employees. In 2003, they even launched the Styles & Wood Academy in association with Manchester Business School with the objective of educating their future management personnel.

It seemed that S&W employees were now regarded as the best operators in the sector making them the prime targets of recruitment consultants and competitors. In defense, S&W made every effort possible to hold on to staff by offering them stakeholder pensions and a profit-sharing scheme, which was effective in retaining employees.

Santinon also recalled being impressed by the way in which the company functioned and its governance model. As early as 2001 the professionalism of the management and its board came across as one of the key features of the company. S&W was still a relatively small company with an EBITA well below £10mn but had processes and structures that were typical of much larger enterprises. Santinon assumed that this was the result of Quiligotti's prior experience in his much larger family business and the input from Rickitt Mitchell. One thing he knew he would change, however, was the frequency of board meetings. Santinon looked forward to attending monthly meetings and getting to know the company and all its other directors better (see management structure in Exhibit 26.6). He wanted to be more involved in reviewing and enhancing the operational performance of the business.

S&W had submitted a financial forecast for the next 3 years (see Exhibit 26.5A). Their growth strategy was based on much of the same organic growth as previous years. It was a working model with a combination of excellence in its people, targeting the right customers and retaining them long term, cross-selling different services, and continued sales efforts. There were also plans to penetrate new markets, mainly strengthening their position in financial services and food retail customers where they had not had much success in the past. Service expansion and integration were key to their growth.

Since StorePlanning was created in 1999, it had grown to a £3.4mn business in about 3 years. Following this lead, further service offerings were created through the clearly defined business divisions of StoreFit, StorePlanning, StoreCare, and StoreData (see Exhibit 26.7). The first three operated as separate business divisions, with full P&L account responsibility. The success of the expansion of its service offering beyond StoreFit was evidenced by the fact that these additional services accounted for 15% of the company's profitability in the year to December 2003 (see Exhibit 26.8).

Santinon thought that StoreData, at the time part of StoreCare, could also become a separate division as the demand for data services was increasing on the back of success stories such as Wal-Mart's data center. The Styles & Wood service offering would then cover the full lifecycle of store development with clearly recognizable divisions and brands—ranging from input to individual customers' annual strategic programs; to planning implementation of the program within each specific store; to the core business of implementation and delivery; to handover, merchandising services, and after-sales care; and, ultimately, to ongoing maintenance and care of the store. Altogether he forecast non-StoreFit to account for over 24% of profitability in 2006.

Although these service lines were in their first few years of operation—especially, StorePlanning and StoreCare—Santinon recognized the potential of these areas as they were high-margin contributors. The added value in terms of positioning the business for sale could be substantial. S&W planned to achieve greater cross-selling of its three business divisions across the customer-for-life base through the pursuit of further outsourcing agreements.

Santinon also recognized that part of the success of S&W in the fragmented and often unaccountable fitting industry was achieved by introducing a formal "smarter handover procedure", a set of processes to be observed and delivered to customers by project managers at the point of project handover, which substantially improved customer satisfaction.

Contracting and subcontractors

S&W was exposed to the inherent risks associated with any contracting business such as slippage of contract dates, slow payments from customers, and volatile working capital. However, Santinon realized that S&W had a proven track record in managing such risks and had consistently met its targets (including those set out in its business plan from the 3i deal in 2001). S&W had successfully managed working capital and generated cash. With EBITA converting every year to 1.1 to 1.2 times free cash flow, the company managed to repay £8mn of debt since the deal with 3i and was in a good position to releverage its balance sheet again in order to pay for further cash distributions to shareholders.

Furthermore, all of the shopfitting activities and, thus, the majority of the inherent risks were passed on to subcontractors. For example, if customers were late paying S&W, it would delay paying its subcontractors, providing a natural hedge against performance risks. During the past three years there had only been three notable loss-making contracts of around £40,000 to £50,000 each which represented 1% of total turnover.

Clearly, S&W had exposure to the performance of its subcontractors, and this was an area of key focus for the management. The strategy with the subcontractor base had been to establish a key pool of around 40 regular suppliers and to attempt to mirror the "partnering" concept S&W had with its customers. Commercial due diligence revealed that, whilst there were some attempts at partnering, S&W managed to exert its power over the subcontractors on issues such as pricing and payment terms. The pressure, however, was not excessive and the track record in terms of managing the risks of underperformance by the contractors was excellent. The due diligence report claimed, "We could find very few complaints from customers on quality, cost, and delivery".

MARKET AND COMPETITION

According to industry research reports, the U.K. shopfitting market had consistently grown to reach almost £2.0bn by 2004 and S&W was the market leader (see Exhibit 26.9). Santinon had some concerns about how S&W would cope in a downturn. There had in fact already been a decrease in British retail activity from 2001 (growth rate 5.9%) to 2003 (growth rate 2.3%). During this period, however, there was little evidence of a slowdown in shopfitting expenditure by the retail industry, and S&W had continued to show strong growth. Management referred to this as the "retail paranoia" of large franchises, which meant that underperformance was followed by an increase in new investment to revamp their estates.

Santinon was also pleased to see that commercial due diligence actually estimated the market to be closer to £3bn and the level of new build was helping to stimulate the market. It also identified that retail M&A activity helps stimulate investment as stores are rebranded. Legislation has also had a positive impact arising from the Disability Discrimination Act covering the requirement for access for elderly and disabled people. This was expected to continue for the next few years.

It was also inevitable that S&W would experience a degree of market concentration given the size of its customers. However, each client company seemed to have different spending patterns each year, and the risk was spread among the top 15 customers who typically accounted for over 80% of turnover. Furthermore, S&W also managed to spread the client base to retail subsectors and to non-retail activity that could prove less cyclical (see Exhibit 26.10).

"Our customer service program works and we have never lost one of our main clients," Quiligotti was quoted as proudly saying in a meeting. S&W's ability to manage growth was excellent and, though demanding, it posed little concern as the company had historically invested in its infrastructure to cope with increases in activity.

S&W was in a good position in a large market. There may be some impact on the overall market as a result of consumer slowdown, but spend is more likely to be driven by individual corporate factors and legislation. Given the blue chip nature and financial strength of its customer base, S&W should have some insulation against the negative impacts of macroeconomic factors. The company was successfully moving into other areas such as retail banking, which would further spread this risk. It also planned to increase current activity levels in leisure and commercial offices, and look to expand into new areas such as the public sector, where the directors had identified an improvement in procurement methods similar to that experienced in the retail industry.

Competition came primarily from three major sources:

- The "property solutions" divisions of major U.K. construction service companies such as Amec, Balfour Beatty, Carillion, Alfred McAlpine, and Costain
- Small independent shopfitters
- In-house property divisions engaging contractors directly.

The divisions of the construction service companies were generally much larger than

S&W, and comparisons were difficult to make as they provided slightly different services. They typically had long-term framework agreements with major retailers, and S&W would often find itself as one of the select few framework partners alongside these larger players. S&W differentiated itself from these larger players by promoting its retail specialization and its ability to act quickly.

As for competing against smaller shopfitters, S&W promoted its critical mass and ability to service customers on a national basis, its leading position in retail, and the breadth of its service offering.

S&W would always be in competition against in-house teams resourcing contractors directly, although the trend to outsourcing was compelling as customers focused more on the fixed cost bases of their businesses. The main issue was the rate at which this was likely to occur, though S&W was well placed to benefit as the practice became more widespread.

Cash out

Quiligotti proposed that, parallel with 3i cashing out, senior management will receive a sum of £8.6mn and an additional amount of £250,000 be paid out to other employees in the equity pool. Santinon knew about the big house and nice cars Quiligotti owned already. He assumed it was no longer about the money, and he was confident the management team led by Quiligotti would remain focused on growing the business. Besides, apart from Quiligotti, the management team was cashing out 50% or less of their equity holdings and should have more to gain from their re-invested amounts. The due diligence team had also spent a significant amount of time with the four senior directors, and they had demonstrated real drive and determination to take the business on to its next stage of development.

INVESTING DECISION

S&W's management could have opted for a likely trade sale but they chose to pursue the current deal, stating they believed the business could grow and develop further. From an investor's perspective, Aberdeen really liked this exceptional management team as well as the cash-generative nature of the business which was attractive for leverage. Santinon was also thinking about its exit possibilities. With its critical mass, U.K. market leading position, breadth of service offering. and customer list, S&W should represent an excellent acquisition opportunity for either one of the large construction companies or a facilities management company—and an arbitrage gain on sale would be a real possibility. A further regearing or buyout may also be possible, especially given the fact that the company had already achieved this twice before and the fact that a very strong second-tier management team was developing. The company would also meet many of the criteria for an AIM flotation, such as critical mass, a blue chip customer base, and the professional way in which it was managed. These were all highly feasible options, Santinon thought.

Of course, Santinon knew there would always be risks in investing but was now confident they were manageable. He just wanted to ensure Aberdeen would not miss the investment opportunity a second time. He was not given any indication about competition from other investors but was aware that Aberdeen would have to bid at the higher end of the price because it was very liekly that they would not be able to raise the bid at a later stage, as was the case in 2001. Santinon had to use his judgment and the little information available about listed comparable companies (see Exhibit 26.11). It seemed that S&W's management wanted to move quickly.

Santinon was well prepared for the Aberdeen investment management committee and was now ready to begin the meeting.

APPENDIX

EXHIBIT 26.1

SHAREHOLDINGS IN MARAQ LTD., AUGUST 1995

	% of ordinary share capital
Gerard Quiligotti	59
Astle Holdings Ltd.[1]	20
Graham Clark	7
Martin Raftery	7
David Howarth	7
	100

Note: 1. Investment by Simon Fawcett through his Guernsey-based investment company.

EXHIBIT 26.2

STYLES & WOOD REVENUE 1994 TO 2004

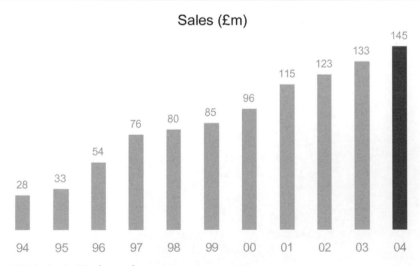

Sales (£m)

94	95	96	97	98	99	00	01	02	03	04
28	33	54	76	80	85	96	115	123	133	145

Source: 2004 Styles & Wood annual report.

EXHIBIT 26.3

CUSTOMER-FOR-LIFE REVENUE FORECAST

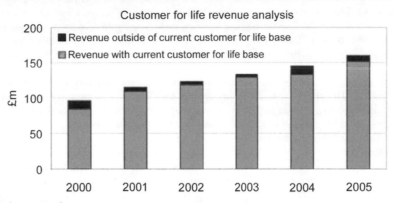

Customer for life revenue analysis

■ Revenue outside of current customer for life base
▨ Revenue with current customer for life base

Source: Styles & Wood.

EXHIBIT 26.4

HISTORY OF 3I GROUP PLC

3i Group plc is one of the oldest private equity groups in Europe. Its most direct predecessor, the Industrial and Commercial Finance Corporation (ICFC), was founded in 1945 to provide long-term capital for small and medium-sized firms helping domestic industry recover from the ravages of the Second World War and the Great Depression that had preceded it. The Bank of England and the five major clearing banks at the time funded the effort with £10mn in equity ownership, in effect establishing a future competitor.

Under Lord William Piercy, its first chairman, ICFC became somewhat of a financial maverick and an innovator, working across much of the economy and injecting a new measure of competition into London's financial circles. Starting in 1950, ICFC saw the chance to drive growth by expanding into Britain's regions, moving first into Birmingham and then, by 1953, into Manchester and Edinburgh. The local offices were encouraged to make independent investment decisions but also bore responsibility for them. This expanding branch network (29 offices by 1972) and devolved decision making contrasted with the clearing banks' strategy of centralized decision making and reduced attention to small regional businesses.

In 1973, ICFC still funded all its activities from its own cash flow. ICFC also expanded its product line. In addition to buyouts and recapitalizations, it became involved in early-stage venture investing. In 1981, the CEO, John

Foulds, decided to remake the company's image and unify the disparate names and far-flung activities under a single brand. After much debate, FFI, ICFC, and FCI became 3i ("Investors in Industry") in 1983. Foulds also expanded internationally. 3i established an office in Boston (MA) in 1982 and expanded to Paris and Frankfurt in the following years. It started a joint venture in India and entered Australia through a wholly owned subsidiary.

By the mid-1980s, 3i had become a financial conglomerate. It was active in shipping finance, plant leasing, property development, and corporate finance, in addition to consulting and venture operations. It had offices in the U.S., France, Germany, Italy, Spain, India, Japan, and Australia and a network throughout the U.K. One 3i executive might be responsible for 30 or 40 companies, a ratio that precluded close involvement and required aggressive syndication. In 1985, the clearing banks and the Bank of England finally agreed that 3i should be floated on the public market. Resolving issues around 3i's status and finding a time when the markets looked favorable delayed the flotation for 9 years.

To prepare for flotation, 3i undertook an intense analysis to determine the cost-effectiveness of its various divisions. It discovered that the core effort of making long-term capital investments in small to medium-sized companies had been carrying the rest of the firm, along with an oversized management staff. In response, 3i refocused on its core business, shed the others, and reduced the headcount by 45% to 570.

3i was floated on July 18, 1994, with a market capitalization of £1.6 billion, a 13.5% discount to the net asset values as of March 31, 1994. At that time, the U.K. was just emerging from the recession of the early 1990s. By September of that year, 3i's market cap had risen enough that it was included in the FTSE 100.

3i began to manage its first third-party fund in 1994. This effort helped to reduce the dependence of syndicate partners on the buyout business and generated a respectable fee stream. During the late 1990s the group had expanded dramatically, especially into venture capital. The dotcom bubble meltdown and the deteriorating business conditions following September 11 led to a total loss of £960mn for 2001. By 2002, 3i's six funds managed $7bn, and it was raising a $3bn Eurofund IV to invest in mid-market buyouts. At that time the 3i Group comprised

174 separate legal entities to comply with regulations in all its countries of operation. Its market capitalization was £3.5bn, down from a peak of £10.7bn in September 2000.

In 2003, after what had been a period of clear difficulty for the company, giving up the progress made in the late 1990s, and what most analysts felt was a lack of acknowledgment of its precarious position, 3i undertook internal reforms to reposition itself for the future. The changes included a reduction in headcount by 9% year on year, which was more clearly felt in some areas than others (notably technology), a change in internal deal processes, and structuring operations along product lines (early-stage technology, growth capital, and buyouts) and business sectors rather than geography.

An analyst at Credit Lyonnais commented: "This last change ensured that dealmakers with the relevant experience and ability handle industry-specific deals, rather than the previous approach which was tribal in nature".

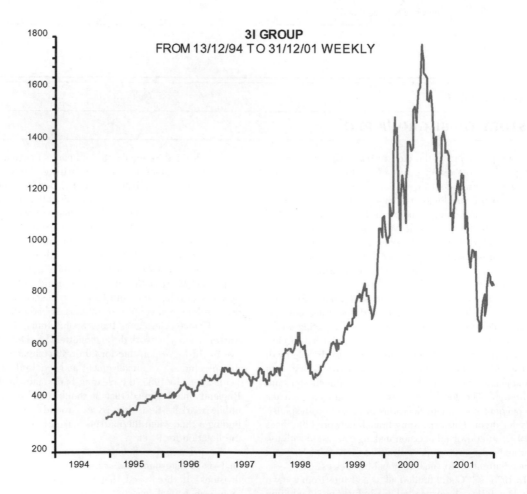

3I GROUP
FROM 13/12/94 TO 31/12/01 WEEKLY

Source: Drawn from 3i Group plc annual reports, its website, and Harvard Business School 2003 Ref. 9-803-020, Hardymon F, Lerner J, Leaman A.

EXHIBIT 26.5A

2004 STYLES & WOOD INCOME STATEMENT AND CASH FLOW AND FORECASTS

Years ending 31 Dec.	1999 (£000) Audited	2000 (£000) Audited	2001 (£000) Audited	2002 (£000) Audited	2003 (£000) Un-audited	2004 (£000) Plan	2005 (£000) Forecast	2006 (£000) Forecast
Profit and loss								
Turnover	*85,067*	*96,266*	*115,228*	*123,006*	*132,902*	*145,000*	*160,000*	*172,500*
Cost of sales	−78,495	−88,778	−106,125	−113,105	−121,871	−132,675	−146,240	−157,405
Gross profit	6,572	7,488	9,103	9,901	11,031	12,325	13,760	15,095
Overheads	−4,293	−4,990	−6,174	−6,675	−7,222	−7,795	−8,410	−9,025
EBIT	*2,279*	*2,498*	*2,929*	*3,226*	*3,809*	*4,530*	*5,350*	*6,070*
Interest receivable	130	205	354	303	239	225	250	275
PBT	**2,409**	**2,703**	**3,283**	**3,529**	**4,048**	**4,755**	**5,600**	**6,345**
Gross profit margin (%)	7.70	7.80	7.90	8.10	8.30	8.50	8.60	8.80
EBIT margin (%)	2.70	2.60	2.50	2.60	2.90	3.10	3.30	3.50
PBT margin (%)					3.10	3.30	3.50	3.70
Cash flow								
EBIT	*2,279*	*2,498*	*2,929*	*3,226*	*3,809*	*4,530*	*5,350*	*6,070*
Depreciation	164	249	363	291	408	433	433	433
(Profit)/loss on sale of fixed assets			5	−18	4			
(Increase)/decrease in debtors	−9,972	3,679	518	−4,154	−1,960	1,088	−2,240	−1,870
Increase/(decrease) in creditors	7,150	−2,888	4,711	2,960	4,606	56	2,602	2,141
Cash flow from operations	*−379*	*3,538*	*8,526*	*2,305*	*6,867*	*3,931*	*6,145*	*6,774*
Interest received	130	205	354	303	239	225	250	275
Net capital expenditure	−234	−359	−752	−408	−310	−633	−500	−564
Free cash flow (pre-tax)	**−483**	**3,384**	**8,128**	**2,200**	**6,796**	**3,523**	**5,895**	**6,485**

Source: 2003 Styles & Wood financial statements.

EXHIBIT 26.5B

STYLES & WOOD 2003 BALANCE AHEET

Unaudited balance sheet as at December 31, 2003	2002 (£000)	2003 (£000)
Fixed assets		
Plant and vehicles	1,012	910
Goodwill[1]	12,721	12,963
Current assets		
Amounts receivable on contracts	10,244	6,035
Trade debtors	7,520	14,647
Other debtors and prepayments	1,682	581
Cash deposits secured against bank guaranteed loan notes	6,054	5,865
Cash at bank and in hand	6,590	4,286
	32,090	31,414
Current liabilities		
Trade creditors	21,286	24,925
Corporation tax	334	523
Other taxation and social security	352	450
Other creditors and accruals	885	1,754
Accrued dividends and interest	325	246
	23,182	27,898
Net current assets	8,908	3,516
Long-term liabilities		
Bos Bank Loan	(5,325)	
Bank guaranteed loan notes	(6,054)	(5,865)
Unsecured loan notes	(4,217)	(2,217)
Net assets	**7,045**	**8,387**

Source: 2003 Styles & Wood financial statements.

Note: 1. Styles &Wood's policy has been to manage its intra-month working capital requirements out of cash in hand rather than using an overdraft. The company aims to keep a minimum of £2mn cash in hand at each month-end and currently has a £3mn overdraft facility to provide headroom. The cash on the balance sheet shown above of £4.3mn should therefore be seen as part of the company's working capital funding, and not as surplus cash.

EXHIBIT 26.5C

STYLES & WOOD WORKING CAPITAL ANALYSIS

	2002 (£ million)	2003 (£ million)
Revenue	123	132
COGS	113	121
Accounts receivables	19.4	21
Current assets	26	25.5
Account payable	21	25
Current liabilities	23	28
Current ratio	1.1	0.9
New working capital	−1.8	−3.7
Day sales outstanding	58	59
Average payment period	69	75

Source: 2003 Styles & Wood financial statements.

EXHIBIT 26.6

STYLES & WOOD MANAGEMENT BOARD STRUCTURE 2004

Gerard Quiligotti
Chairman

Neil Davies
Chief Executive

Andy Campbell	**Graham Clark**	**Martin Raftery**	**Ivan McKeever**	**Steve Wilton**
Operations Director	Director of Finance	Commercial Director	Service Development Director	Director of Support Services

Source: Styles and Wood.

EXHIBIT 26.7

STYLES & WOOD BUSINESS

StoreFit carries out the project management and implementation of storefitting, refurbishment, and modernization schemes. StoreFit provides customers with a single-point procurement and project delivery service.

StorePlanning provides retail design and development services, including outsourcing of property support functions such as undertaking store surveys, feasibility reports, planning, and design management.

StoreCare provides ongoing support to customers in the form of outsourcing of property support functions such as project management of small works, planned store maintenance, and store merchandising.

StoreData delivers property information management solutions that provide retailers with efficient gathering, storage, and use of property data. The product currently covers four applications that together span all aspects of the retail property lifecycle: standards, portfolio, projects, and assets.

StoreFit, StorePlanning, and StoreCare operate as separate business divisions, with full P&L account responsibility. StoreData is currently accounted for within the StorePlanning business division, but the directors believe that StoreData has the potential to develop into a

Source: Styles and Wood.

standalone high-margin trading division in its own right. This complete service offering is best illustrated by the following diagram:

The directors believe that the approach summarized above has now come to represent the industry leading model.

EXHIBIT 26.8

STYLES & WOOD TURNOVER BY ACTIVITY

	Year-end December 2001 (£000)	Year-end December 2002 (£000)	Year-end December 2003 (£000)
StoreFit	113,375	120,487	128,409
StorePlanning	1,853	2,519	3,374
StoreCare	—	—	1,119
	115,228	123,006	132,902
Gross profit by activity			
StoreFit	8,302	8,894	9,434
StorePlan	801	1,007	1,407
StoreCare	—	—	190
Gross profit	9,103	9,901	11,031
Overheads	(5,879)	(6,380)	(6,789)
EBITDA	**3,224**	**3,521**	**4,242**
Depreciation	(295)	(295)	(433)
EBITA	**2,929**	**3,226**	**3,809**
StoreFit gross margin (%)	7.3	7.4	7.3
StorePlan gross margin (%)	43.2	40.0	41.7
StoreCare gross margin (%)	n.a.	n.a.	17.0
Overall gross margin (%)	7.9	8.0	8.3
EBITA margin (%)	2.5	2.6	2.9

Source: 2003 Styles & Wood financial statements.

EXHIBIT 26.9

COMPETITION BY TURNOVER AND MARKET SHARE

Shopfitting market	Market share 2003 (%)	Turnover 2003 (£ million)
Total Market Size	—	1,870
Last 2 years average growth (%)		2.8
Styles & Wood	7.1	132
Mace	5.5	102
Havelock Europa	4.7	87
Hurst Group	3.2	60
Curzon	3.1	58
Nuttal	2.9	54
Support Services Group	2.9	54
Pearce (retail)	2.9	54
Morris & Spottiswood	2.9	54
S. Dudley & Sons	2.3	43
Barlow Group	2.2	41

Source: Keynote report 2005.

EXHIBIT 26.10

2003 STYLES & WOOD CUSTOMER SEGMENTATION

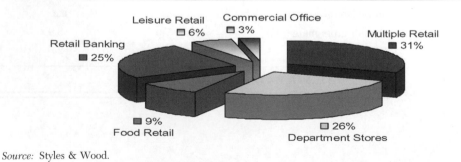

Source: Styles & Wood.

EXHIBIT 26.11

MULTIPLES FOR COMPARABLE LISTED COMPANIES

Price earnings ratio	2002	2003
FTSE 100 index	17.69	17.1
Connaught Plc	12.7	12.7
Mears Group	22.8	21.7
Mitie Group Plc	16.9	16.9
Dawson Holdings Plc	9.3	12.7
Diploma Plc	11	12.1

EV/EBIT	2002	2003
Connaught Plc	14.3	11.0
Mears Group	9.3	14.9
Mitie Group Plc	13.5	8.0
Dawson Holdings Plc	9.4	7.0
Diploma Plc	3.9	5.2

Source: Datastream.

27

SunRay Renewable Energy: Private equity in the sunshine

It was almost midnight in Tel Aviv on a Friday in January 2010, as Yael Talmor watched the heavy traffic flow towards the nightlife district from the 28th floor offices of SunRay Renewable Energy (SunRay). She was still at work, preparing documents for due diligence on SunPower Corporation's (SunPower) USD300mn takeover bid for SunRay. This acquisition would cement SunPower's vertical integration strategy by increasing its pipeline of solar photovoltaic (PV) generation projects by 1,200 megawatts (MW) in Southern Europe.[1]

Over 2,000 miles away, Tulika Raj-Joshi looked out over the Thames from the London office of Denham Capital Management (Denham). Tulika was also still at work, assembling piles of documents and coordinating closely with colleagues at SunRay and Denham Capital. She thought back at her MBA project at London Business School (LBS). SunRay, then a newly formed business, had commissioned her team to conduct a strategic review of the renewable energy market in the European Union (EU).

At the helm of SunRay was Yoram Amiga, a serial entrepreneur in private equity and property investments. Subsequent to a successful career in commodities, he shifted his interest to new ventures. Working with other investment partners closely attached to the LBS community resulted in a steady flow of graduating MBAs as full-time employees as well as students for ad hoc projects at both the holding and portfolio companies.

By mid-2006, Yoram and his investment partners were looking for opportunities in renewable energy, which was expanding rapidly in the EU. Growing environmental awareness, underpinned by the Kyoto Protocol, had spurred many European governments to establish regulatory frameworks and price supports favoring the generation of power from renewable sources.

SunRay's founders saw an opportunity to leverage their professional networks in parts of Southern Europe where much renewable energy was being developed by

1. A solar PV developer pipeline is the amount of MW for which the company has optioned land and is in the process of obtaining the permit for the development of a solar PV park. See Exhibit 27.1 for a glossary of basic solar PV terminology.

This case was co-authored with Matthias Vandepitte and Lode Van Laere (both LBS MBA 2011).
We thank Michael Barnea, Robert Belke, Giles Clark, Hans Holmen, Alba Martinez, and Andres Truuvert for most valuable comments.

relatively unsophisticated local entrepreneurs. They sought to build a professional pan-European platform, based in London, which would become a leading continental producer of renewable power. However, they first needed to evaluate renewable energy generation technology and the investment environment in various European jurisdictions.

SUNRAY'S CHOICE OF SOLAR TECHNOLOGY

The first element in developing their business strategy was the choice of a core technology. Wind, biomass, geothermal, hydroelectric, solar PV, and solar thermal technology were all mature and commercially viable, while fuel cells and tidal/wave energy were not (an overview of the different technologies is provided in Exhibit 27.2). Many of these technologies had shortcomings, however. For geothermal, hydroelectric, and solar thermal generation, these included long project timescales, a heavier engineering requirement, and limited pools of suppliers. Biomass power generation was not readily scalable and was fairly risky, requiring a supply chain for feedstock and custom technology specific to the feedstock. Energy generation from wind required a higher degree of engineering and was already a mature global business with established players at a time where turbines were in short supply.

Solar PV was found particularly attractive because of its relative simplicity and the bankability of projects. The photovoltaic effect was well understood, with no patent protection on the core technology, using silicon solar cells to convert energy from sunlight to electricity. In the right locations, sunlight is abundant and predictable.[2]

The dominant solar PV technology was crystalline silicon, which accounted for over 90% of solar PV energy generation in 2006. Other technologies, such as thin film, were in far earlier stages of engineering development and market acceptance. Exhibit 27.3 shows the basic principles of solar cell technology, and Exhibit 27.4 compares solar PV technologies.

THE VALUE CHAIN OF A SOLAR PV DEVELOPER

After choosing solar PV as the technology to pursue, attention turned to a detailed understanding of the value chain in the developer's business. Solar PV is generally installed either on the roofs of buildings or in large ground-mounted parks connected directly to transmission grids. SunRay chose to focus on ground-mounted installations, which are more readily scalable. Having settled on ground-mounted solar PV, SunRay turned to understanding the development value chain, how to enter new markets, and what obstacles they might face.

The first step in developing a solar PV park is to identify a tract of land which is available, sufficiently large, relatively flat, and close to the national electricity grid. The developer will require permits to construct the park and connect it to the grid, which involves negotiating simultaneously with the landowner, local government, and the local electricity utility, taking into account economic factors as well as technical aspects such as production projections, site constraints (slopes and shadows) and grid parameters. The developer therefore needs a deep knowledge of energy legislation, regional planning and environmental procedures, power capacity, and other intricacies of the grid infrastructure in each jurisdiction where they operate.

2. *http://re.jrc.ec.europa.eu/pvgis/*

The developer must also select the construction elements of the installation. In the most basic design, the modules are installed on fixed ground-mounted structures, facing the usual direction of the sun. The efficiency of the modules can be increased with motorized trackers which turn the panels to follow the sun on either one or two axes. The solar array is connected to an existing or new local substation belonging to the local power utility, which is in turn connected to the grid by power lines (Exhibit 27.5 outlines the basic configuration of a solar PV park). In order to actually construct the site, the developer must also choose an engineering procurement and construction (EPC) contractor to install and connect all the components, and coordinate with the local utility company, which evacuates the power to the national electricity grid once the site is commissioned and enough grid capacity is available. Finally, the developer must decide whether to operate the plant independently or sell it to investors or a utility company.

SunRay believed in its ability to establish a multiregional development platform to efficiently secure suitable land and navigate the complex permit application process. Many local businessmen were already applying for permits and grid connections, but this fledgling activity was largely ad hoc, often compromised execution, and lacked a long-term view. SunRay hoped to professionalize this process on a large scale, which would require them to develop core expertise applicable to development across multiple countries.

THE EUROPEAN RENEWABLE MARKET IN 2006–2008

With the help of the LBS student team, SunRay analyzed in detail the attractiveness of various European markets. Driven by volatile and rising energy prices, global warming, and energy security concerns, the EU's European Climate Change Program mandated the increased use of renewable energy. In 2007, the EU announced the dual goals of cutting emissions by 20% below 1990 levels and generating 20% of energy from renewable sources, both by 2020.[3]

Member states could strive for these targets through three types of support systems:

- *Direct market support*—either market volume support (e.g., renewable portfolio standards) or market price support via feed-in tariffs or tax advantages
- *Investment support*—direct government subsidies or tax credits to investors in renewable energy
- *Research and development grants*—to help develop and optimize renewable generation technology.

Governments were considered unlikely to reverse their renewables incentives, since the EU targets for 2020 were viewed as challenging. Exhibit 27.6 summarizes feed-in tariff terms for the main European solar PV countries. Exhibit 27.7 shows annual installed solar PV power in Germany, Spain, and Italy in 2000–2008.

Germany

Germany was a pioneer in renewable energy. By 2006, despite lower solar irradiation levels, the country led the world in solar PV installations and had developed into

3. *Sources for this section:* IEA, Eurostat, U.S. Energy Information Administration, Kyoto targets: *http://unfccc.int/*

Europe's most mature solar PV market. This was driven by attractive solar PV feed-in tariffs, a conducive banking environment, and well-thought-through alternative energy legislation. The feed-in tariff was continuously adapted to the diminishing prices of solar PV equipment, providing transparency for future subsidies and allowing developers to plan ahead.

Spain

High and growing dependence on external supplies of energy prompted the Spanish government to promote alternative sources of energy. In 2005, it announced the *Plan de Energías Renovables en España* (Spanish Renewable Energy Plan) intended to provide at least 12% of the country's energy from renewable sources by 2010. An annual quota feed-in tariff system entitled developers to 25 years of subsidized rates for new solar panel projects connected to the national grid during that calendar year.

This scheme was well intended but flawed, with unforeseen consequences. It made solar PV very attractive, since the tariffs were generous and Spain has ample sunshine, but the program was a victim of its own success. The government received a flood of permit applications, including many from entrepreneurs lacking the technical savvy and financial resources necessary to actually complete projects. Projects rushed to connect to the grid by the annual deadline, creating an enormous backlog of applications for connection. Developers could no longer be certain that their project would connect by the year-end tariff deadline and the consequent uncertainty of revenue made project finance impossible.

In 2007 the government saw the need for a pre-screening system and imposed an escrow deposit which would be forfeited if the developer failed to build the project and connect it to the grid.[4] This further complicated matters by tripling the upfront cost, forcing a desperate sale of pending permits into an already turbulent secondary market.

In 2008, faced with a dysfunctional allocation system and the global financial crisis, the government cut the feed-in tariff for new PV plants by 30% and restricted the higher feed-in tariff to parks built and connected to the electricity grid by September 28, 2008. This resulted in a short-term peak in the price of land and permits, and much of the world's solar PV development capacity relocated albeit temporarily to Spain. The severely reduced tariff, coupled with the escrow requirement, and a complicated application process,[5] made new permit applications unattractive and the industry crashed. Worldwide solar cell demand and, therefore, prices plummeted and thousands of jobs were lost. Tariffs were subsequently cut further as the country's economic woes deepened.

Italy

Italy has limited domestic sources of energy and depends on imports. The EU Directive set the country a target of generating 25% of its electricity from renewable sources by 2010, in partial response to which the government established a fixed feed-in tariff for solar PV, guaranteed for 20 years. The rate was uneconomic for the time, however, and failed to stimulate solar PV. It was not until new legislation in July 2006 provided an

---

4. In May 2007, the Spanish government enacted Royal Decree 661 which levied a loan guarantee (*aval*) of EUR500,000 per 1 MW requested permit, to be deposited in a government escrow account and returned to developers only when the project was operational and connected to the electricity grid.

5. The complexity arose from centralized energy legislation which each region adopted differently and from the high opacity of local levies and other hidden costs.

attractive mix of stimuli, initially for up to 500 MW of capacity, that the Italian solar PV industry took off.

Greece

Greece was faced with emissions limits, rapidly growing electricity demand, and a fleet of high-emission coal-fired power plants. Spurred by a major blackout in 2004,[6] the government announced a modernization of its energy sector and incentives for renewable energy, with 29% of electricity to be from renewable sources by 2020, including 700 MW of solar PV capacity. This program did not operate as intended, however; by the end of 2008 its backlog of applications for solar PV permits had reached about 3 gigawatts (GW) and only 36 MW of solar PV had been installed.

SunRay saw no point in entering the established and economically less attractive German market. They decided to commit the capital necessary to build a strong organization qualified to move in parallel into Spain, Italy, and Greece. They would keep other countries—in particular, France and Israel—on their radar for early market entry when conditions were suitable and internal resources allowed.

SUNRAY'S BUSINESS MODEL

To Yoram the potential business seemed too good to be true; any electricity produced was pre-sold for 20–25 years ahead at a very attractive price guaranteed by the government and a national utility company. He sought to replicate the success of pioneers in wind generation in developing and operating an international portfolio of power generation assets.

A developer would of course require access to land with a solar PV development permit. This could be achieved through *greenfield development* (finding the land, persuading the owner to sell or lease and applying for the permit), *outright purchase* of permitted land (from financially constrained local developers), or by a joint venture with a local developer.

Spain and later Italy were attractive to institutional investors such as banks and utilities. Although fully priced, only the outright purchase was a realistic land access alternative for such institutions. The economic principle of comparative advantage resulted in a classic division of labor—local developers concentrated on obtaining solar PV permits to flip into the secondary market.

SunRay took a different approach: manage multiple local teams in parallel from a professional development office in London. Yoram's many years in commodities had sensitized him to country-specific risks. He was determined to expand quickly across regions and countries, to diversify bureaucratic risks, and to build a balanced portfolio of projects in countries that are at different stages of development. SunRay's business model would be solid, leveraging on the whole value chain of solar development from permit application to the construction and connection of solar PV parks.

BUILDING THE MANAGEMENT TEAM

For SunRay to execute such a diverse process in a new market, it vitally needed to build core expertise and complementary skills. In stark contrast to many small shoestring

6. In July 2004, a severe heat wave increased demand for air conditioning, overloading the Greek grid.

regional developers, SunRay decided to spare no expense and to pursue exceptional individuals capable of executing and delivering its bold plan of multiple parks in multiple geographies. Over the course of 2007, SunRay accumulated a core team of professionals by tapping certain founders with credibility from previous ventures and through external hires.

Recognizing the importance of in-house legal expertise, the first recruit was a senior lawyer, specialized in negotiating M&A and capital market transactions with multinational companies. At the same time, SunRay met Seán Murphy, a trained electrical engineer, head of Nomura's clean technology research and one of London's best regarded authorities in the renewable sector. Seán joined SunRay as Chief Technology Officer (CTO), complementing the small team with his extensive knowledge of the renewable industry and technology. Another key hire was the then Chairman of Enemalta, Malta's state-owned utility company responsible for providing and distributing electricity, gas, and petroleum throughout the country. In addition to hands-on utility expertise, he brought with him a broader policy perspective from his experience on the board of Eurelectric, the Brussels-based association of the European electricity industry.

Looking back at how Yoram built a team of experienced professionals around him, Seán recalls: "They all stood out in their different skills, it was just incredible."

LEARNING THE SOLAR PV GAME THE HARD WAY

While the team was applying for its first permits in Greece, it learned lessons in Spain that later proved invaluable. In Spain, SunRay was intensively searching for emerging local developers to serve as joint venture partners, while simultaneously communicating with local authorities and regional offices of the power utility. They realized that they needed a country manager with language skills and on-the-ground expertise in Spanish infrastructure. In addition, SunRay teamed up with a dynamic Cordoba-based technical consulting firm that designed state-of-the-art power structures and also had daily working relations with Spanish utility companies and government authorities. SunRay developed an opportunity-hunting team of five people in London and ten in Spain, a model which they would repeat in other countries.

In less than two years, SunRay looked at well over a hundred opportunities throughout Spain. They learned how to deal with third-party agents, how to assess site-specific risks, and what core questions to ask—in the process developing a way of efficiently assessing potential sites. In the end, however, SunRay did not build a single project in Spain. Neither joint ventures nor outright acquisition permits worked out; most permits available on the secondary market did not survive their rigorous due diligence and SunRay was constrained by its core philosophy of employing high financial gearing. As Seán commented:

> "Because the founders of SunRay came from investment or financial backgrounds, we were finely tuned to the concept of bankable quality. Since we always knew that we would need bank debt to finance 80% or more of the project costs, we could only ever look at projects where we had managed risks (permit application, equipment selection, energy yield forecasts, etc.) sufficiently well that we could reliably ask a bank for finance. Our perspective was quite different to those project sponsors and investors chasing hot money where their selection criteria were more lenient than ours. Having a relentless focus on risk and a drive for quality

projects may have lost us opportunities in the raging hot Spanish market, but proved the single most valuable asset when it came to capitalizing on the Italian opportunity."

As described above, the bull market in Spanish solar PV ended in 2008. Yoram realized that SunRay had entered Spain too late. The experience influenced the team in Greece and Italy but also pushed them to commit resources to markets which were in their infancy and even lacked solar PV legislation, such as France and Israel.

SCALING UP THE BUSINESS ACROSS SOUTHERN EUROPE

SunRay had entered Greece through a partnership with the Greek Orthodox Church, which had immense political muscle and was the largest landowner in the country. Backed by a local bank, a qualified engineering company, and a well-regarded law firm, SunRay applied for a total of 69 MW of solar PV capacity in June 2007. The considerable legal expertise of SunRay London ensured that the legal structure for making the applications was economically efficient, albeit convoluted.

By mid-2007, solar PV was becoming increasingly attractive in Italy, with its ideal climatic conditions and improved fee-in tariff, although some regions were politically unstable and administratively constrained. As in Spain, SunRay's strategy was to identify local engineering consultancy groups to obtain market intelligence and identify suitable sites. A caravan of international investors seeking opportunities had already pulled up where the sun shines the brightest: Sicily and Puglia, the heel of Italy. While not underestimating the attraction of southern Italy, SunRay also looked to Lazio, the region centered on Rome, where it became a market pioneer in August 2007.

UNDER THE UMBRELLA OF PRIVATE EQUITY

The search for capital

By the end of 2007, Spain, Italy, and Greece had taught the team how capital intensive solar development can really be. Much seed capital is required even before starting construction—for permit applications, options on land, legal costs, engineering surveys, and financial deposits. While completed projects can be highly geared on the basis of their secure long-term revenues, anyone developing a pipeline of permit applications needs to spend non-recoverable money upfront. The actual construction is even more capital intensive, of course, even if a partial line of credit is available from the EPC.

SunRay wasn't finding it cheap to run a multicountry operation with uncompromising standards; it needed more funding. The founders contemplated raising money on a project basis with local partners and spoke to several family offices about funding development at a country level. Eventually, they decided to raise money at the holding company level, either from private equity or a large corporation. This would avoid the need for multiple contracts and negotiations, while providing SunRay the greatest flexibility in using the proceeds.

As the management team were quite experienced in finance, they had no trouble preparing an effective presentation and started contacting potential investors. Even though SunRay had not yet built a single solar park, it was on its way to receiving its first permit in Italy. Its key messages were:

— SunRay has in place a unique platform of centralized expertise in London (systemic processes of project development, solar engineering, and project finance), while locating more regional expertise (land sourcing, interpretation of planning regulations) "in the field".

— Achieving an after-tax leveraged IRR in excess of 20% on a pipeline of about 230 MW of potential solar developments in three different countries.

— Revenue is not at risk, as the feed-in tariffs were backed by governments for 20 to 25 years, operational risk is very limited, and construction risk would be hedged by working with blue chip EPC contractors capable of providing contractual performance guarantees.

In November 2007, SunRay met the president of a major American conglomerate which, once it understood the concept and the business plan, offered SunRay up to USD300mn. The funding would use either a classic pre-money valuation structure or a combination of project level funding and equity for general and administrative (G&A) development expenses at the holding company level. SunRay realized that a strong brand and solid balance sheet would be a tremendous boost to building the business. However, SunRay also saw that it and the conglomerate had different business philosophies and that the approval process for investment decisions would be slow. Yoram commented:

> "They saw SunRay purely as a developer business and not as a capital portfolio business, which was the opposite of what we intended to be. Secondly, we felt we would be a small fish in a big pond as they were investing in many different businesses. Finally, we looked for an investor that could make a quick decision when opportunities would arise and therefore we opted for private equity."

The private equity solution became available when Yoram pitched SunRay to Denham Capital, which had recently hired Louis van Pletsen to establish its London office. Louis was formerly Managing Director at Nomura, where he was a colleague of Seán Murphy and the investment banker to one of SunRay's founders.

Denham Capital: Unlocking value dislocation

Denham was a global private equity firm focused on energy and commodities with over USD4.25bn in assets under management in 2008. The firm was founded in 2003 by Stu Porter, its CEO and Chairman, when he left the Harvard Management Co., where he was responsible for investments in energy and commodities. Denham typically invested USD75mn to USD200mn in its portfolio companies. It was headquartered in Boston, with additional offices in Houston, Short Hills (NJ), São Paulo, and London (Exhibit 27.8 provides an overview of Denham's funds and portfolio).

Denham's business model was to continuously seek investments with dislocations of value. Tulika Raj-Joshi, now a vice president at the firm, explains:

> "Value dislocation exists between a development asset and an operating asset. It is the difference between the cost of de-risking an asset and the value of the operating asset. This is particularly the case in renewable energy, as development assets will ultimately generate a predictable earnings stream once they reach an operational stage and generate income based on long-term government-mandated feed-in tariffs. Therefore, in the case of SunRay, Denham Capital focused on intelligently mitigating the risks of the development stage assets."

Denham has a particularly keen understanding of the risks inherent in the development business, as most of its investment officers are industry experts with an operational background, which differentiates them from many purely financial investors.

In 2007, Scott Mackin, partner and head of the Power & Renewables group at Denham, was investigating solar PV as a potential investment theme. The firm had spotted the potential to capture the significant dislocation of value inherent in European solar PV. Scott and Louis saw the parallels with wind generation, which also benefited from government supports and declining equipment costs. They started evaluating a large number of European solar PV opportunities, with the key pre-requisite of a solid but highly entrepreneurial team with the skills to deliver on its promises. In January 2008, Scott flew from his office in New Jersey to meet the dozen different solar management teams identified. On Tuesday the 22nd, it was SunRay's turn to pitch their business plan to Denham.

The negotiation with Denham Capital

During the meeting it only took about 2 hours for the SunRay team to convince Scott and Louis that SunRay was the company Denham was looking for. Denham's initial reluctance about a CEO without a solar or energy background was overcome by Yoram's confidence and overall experience. Louis recalls:

> "The reason why I was attracted to financially back SunRay was because Yoram had a sense of urgency and impatience. His vision, passion and momentum make things move."

Yoram managed to reassure Denham that SunRay had strong commercial relations with project financiers, regional EPCs, and suppliers. The business was supported by strong local engineering and development teams with strong ethics and technical competence. However, what Scott found as key was "that SunRay understood how development really works—a logistical exercise which requires relentless focus and adjustment."

Denham saw that SunRay had solid technological and market knowledge, a formulated project appraisal process, and a determination to grow the business aggressively, including expansion to additional countries under investigation.[7]

By the end of their second meeting, the two firms were well on their way to striking a deal, negotiated chiefly between Denham and another founder of SunRay. The private equity firm committed to deploy USD200mn by 2012 in SunRay's development portfolio, at project level lifecycle IRRs exceeding 20%, with an expectation of exiting via a sale based on contracted cash flows to a buyer whose discount rate is about 10%. Denham considered the co-incentivized management team as highly competent and reached an agreement with Yoram to add personnel in senior solar project management and procurement. Two days after the second meeting, Yoram flew with Scott to visit SunRay's local teams and operations on the ground in the different countries.

Denham agreed to commit an immediate short-term loan of USD3mn,[8] and up to USD200mn in expansion capital within 60 days, conditional on successful completion of a due diligence program consisting of four major steps:

7. The Czech Republic, France, and Israel.

8. The short-term loan was to fund SunRay's operations until closing the definitive financing. The main commitment of USD200mn was to be drawn over time, with each draw subject to approval by Denham.

602 • *Chapter 27: SunRay Renewable Energy: Private equity in the sunshine*

1. Verify the costs, efficiencies, degradation, and market assumptions presented by SunRay, for which Denham retained CH2M HILL, a consultant with expertise in solar project development and manufacturing. Denham also asked CH2M HILL to qualify equipment vendors for early projects.
2. Verify the tariff regimes and potential land, regulatory, and tax issues in Italy, Spain, and Greece.
3. Perform a background check on key SunRay employees.
4. Verify assumptions regarding debt project finance with solar project lenders.

Denham's target return depends on the risk associated with the investment and other considerations. In this case Denham's base case was an exit wherein its investment is sold for a multiple of 3× its original investment, of which substantial amounts would go to management and founders. Denham structured its investment as preferred equity, the return on which would be realized entirely upon exit. Management and founders would receive an increasing share of the exit proceeds after certain minimum returns to Denham were achieved.

To ensure a more structured and risk-based approach at SunRay, Denham took total control of the board.[9] Scott explains:

> "We put in a process for funding projects and financing G&A expenses once requested by SunRay management. Both G&A budget and project funding requests had to be approved by Denham's investment committee (IC) in two steps—first as an 'introduction' of the request and second as a 'vote' or approval of the request. This structure forced the business development team to act less opportunistically and to apply more controls to the planning and budget. Not to hold up the process from SunRay's perspective, formal IC meetings were held weekly, and requests could be turned around very quickly for short-fuse business opportunities. When SunRay wanted to purchase a piece of land, for example, its finance team prepared the documents for discussion, including the details of the permit, and identification of the EPC provider and potential financiers."

The financial firepower provided by private equity proved more than sufficient for SunRay to roll out its business plan, recruit top-quality people, and build relationships with its suppliers.

MONTALTO DI CASTRO: BUILDING THE LARGEST SOLAR POWER PARK IN EUROPE

Getting the local community involved

SunRay used a grassroots approach to entering markets, working closely with local authorities and communities. Giora Salita, a long-time manager at several of Yoram's businesses had joined to run SunRay's operations. Giora hired regional local teams that understood the local environment and knew the basics of solar PV. Away from his home in London, he spent most of his time in the field screening sites and co-development opportunities. He introduced analytical tools and processes to efficiently advance new opportunities and compile a continuously updated map of field intelligence for manage-

---

9. The board consisted of three representatives from Denham (Scott, Louis, and Todd Bright) and two from SunRay.

ment in London. SunRay later applied these scalable project development techniques in other countries and considered them some of its main competitive advantages and differentiators.

Giora explains how SunRay managed to scale its business in multiple countries in parallel:

> "It doesn't matter how smart you are, how charismatic you are, it's an intelligence gathering, information process. and deep pockets business. Our local managers have to be there in the trenches 24/7 gathering and processing vast amounts of information. Every single day we are in the office is a waste of time. In the morning you option the land, in the evenings you dine with businessmen, decision-makers, to get market intelligence. When you manage a campaign, you double-check, day in day out, because these deals can disappear overnight and one small mistake can kill millions. People are the core of any business but particularly of this one. They need to be very fast and ultra-diligent at the same time."

The first book Giora gave his newly hired Italian managers to read was *Alexander the Great's Art of Strategy* by Partha Bose (Gotham Books, 2003). The techniques used by Alexander to move quickly and establish a vast empire set SunRay's strategy on how to engage and eventually team up with third parties, how to set up offices close to the decision makers, and how to hire reliable employees. SunRay needed self-sufficient streetwise negotiators who could be trusted, and sought to retain them with attractive performance-related incentive packages. Giora summarizes: "There is nothing complicated about what we did. It is all about people relationships, integrity, and accountability. Down to basics."

The team found a very suitable piece of land close to the electricity grid in the northern part of the region of Lazio, near Montalto di Castro and the Alto Lazio nuclear plant, which was 70% built but never used after a national referendum in 1987 prohibited nuclear generation in Italy. At the heart of the business strategy was a genuine working partnership with the local community, which would benefit in several ways; a state-of-the-art renewable energy installation would improve the image of the town and its surroundings and SunRay had committed to recruit half the construction and maintenance workforce locally and to contribute a stated share of its electricity revenues towards the construction of local hospitals and schools. Furthermore, SunRay would build a permanent visitor center at the project, allowing visitors to view the plant and the control room and learn about the project, its benefits, and solar power and renewable energy, in general. The facilities would be able to accommodate as many as 100–150 visitors at a time.

On August 4, 2008 SunRay received the exciting news that the *autorizzazione unica* permit for a 24 MW solar PV installation in Montalto di Castro had been approved. With the permit in hand, SunRay faced two more important milestones: finding a supplier and contractor to build the park and a bank to provide the debt finance.

Finding a supplier

SunRay faced a significant challenge in finding a good supplier of modules and an EPC. Many candidates had a limited understanding of solar PV technology and negotiations were difficult because demand from the Spanish market was strong at the time.

Solar modules were at a premium due to a global shortage of silicon, rooted in the 2000 semiconductor bubble. During the boom, manufacturers committed to multibillion dollar capacity expansions, which they were unable to use once the semiconductor market collapsed. As the manufacturers were reluctant to build new capacity and it took 2–3 years to build a new factory, it was not until 2009–2010 that supply met demand (Exhibit 27.9 shows polysilicon projections for 2007–2012).

In 2007, manufacturers of solar modules were clearly in the driver's seat. The industry, dominated by about 20 companies, was running at capacity and making fantastic margins. Polysilicon was in short supply, solar modules were pre-sold, and the average lead time was 18 months from order to delivery.

SunRay had started attending trade fairs to build its credibility, become familiar with the latest technology, and meet the top suppliers. One such supplier was SunPower, a top-tier manufacturer based in California with its own EPC division. It was considered the "Rolls Royce" of the solar industry and offered SunRay not just solar modules, but also credibility in the eyes of potential providers of project finance.

SunRay and SunPower verbally agreed an EPC price for Montalto di Castro Phase I (24 MW), but the crash of the Spanish solar PV market in late 2008 sharply reduced module prices. The reduction amounted to a staggering EUR400,000 per MW or EUR9.6mn for all of Phase I. Under the extreme market circumstances and in the absence of a contract, SunPower were perplexed when Yoram did not renegotiate a more realistic price. In part it was his commodity background, where your word is your commitment, and perhaps he also counted on a larger contract for the additional 60 MW of Montalto di Castro Phases II and III. Still, without a fully signed EPC contract, SunPower started building in February 2009. This was a sign to Lazio and other regional Italian communities that SunRay was delivering on its promises.

Project finance: Securing the money and the project

In parallel, SunRay had to secure project financing for Montalto di Castro, but time was against them. On September 15, 2008 Lehman Brothers filed for bankruptcy, sending global financial markets into meltdown, and freezing the supply of debt. As the firm realized that it would be extremely difficult to raise debt finance in the credit crunch, they hired Tim Corfield from Deutsche Bank, where he was responsible for debt financing for solar projects in Spain.

Tim assembled a team of current SunRay employees, retained outside consultants to help build an extremely detailed project finance model of the Montalto di Castro project, and put significant efforts into creating a formal information memorandum for the project. After Lehman, not a single bank wanted to engage with SunRay, and Tim realized that solar PV was fairly new to most banks. "SunRay only had one chance to present a compelling business case and we made it rather a good one," he told the management. The information memorandum set out extensive information regarding the project, SunRay, Denham, suppliers, and contractors, and SunRay hired a top-tier advisory team to boost its credibility.[10] In November 2008 SunRay went on a roadshow to meet 10 different banks, and in February 2009, together with Denham, decided on the banking group.[11]

10. Allen & Overy, Fichtner, and Deloitte.
11. The mandated lead arrangers were Banca Infrastrutture, Innovazione e Sviluppo, Société Générale, and WestLB AG, with SACE, the leading Italian credit insurer, participating as partial guarantor of the Société Générale tranche.

While project finance was being discussed, Denham's investment committee and SunRay's management team had to make a difficult decision. The construction schedule of Montalto di Castro was well behind schedule, because the bank group had delayed its decision due to the negative financial climate and the group's unfamiliarity with solar PV. The profitability of the project depended on the extremely favorable feed-in tariffs available only if it was connected to the grid before the end of 2009. If SunRay wanted to finalize the construction by the end of 2009, the EPC contractor had to start immediately. SunPower was already committed to the project and offered SunRay a 30-day credit facility. Tim Corfield explains:

> "It was a very stressful time and however much you push the bankers, they do what they want to do. You cannot force them because in the end you are borrowing 80 to 85% of the funds, the vast majority of the money."

By August 2009, the project schedule and projected financial returns were in jeopardy. SunPower had signed the contract for pre-construction work 3 months earlier, had commenced construction, and thus had committed a significant amount of money, which it might lose if construction were stopped. Fortunately, the interests of SunPower, SunRay. and Denham were aligned.

SunPower agreed to continue construction and granted more generous payment terms. In exchange it required the right to take possession of the park if financing did not materialize and a "no-shop" period during which it could obtain information about SunRay's business with a view to an acquisition.

This deal saved the Montalto di Castro project. The bank group finally approved EUR120mn of project finance for Phase I in September 2009—the biggest solar PV project finance deal in Europe in 2009.[12] More important, the ability of SunRay—a new company without a track record—to secure project finance during a credit crisis reaffirmed that the project counts—not just the sponsor's balance sheet. With bank funding secured, the park was completed and connected to the electricity grid well before the December 2009 deadline for securing the higher Italian feed-in tariff.

THE DECISION TO EXIT

As its business matured, SunRay required a more efficient capital structure to accommodate its reduced risk profile. Private equity had been an effective source of capital to expand the company (buying land, the permitting process, supporting business development) but was not ideal to fund recoverable assets (the construction of PV solar parks). SunRay estimated that it would have to pre-fund up to 25% of the entire cost of each project with equity capital before funding with project finance. With a weak project finance market, SunRay would eventually need to sell operating PV parks in part or in full to realize the returns that were expected.

However, for an eventual IPO to yield the maximum value, SunRay would need to own operating assets as well as its strong pipeline of projects, which would require far larger capital injections by Denham. It seemed that the company needed access to a large permanent balance sheet, such as that of an established corporate player, to best equip it to take a further leap and build a large portfolio of solar assets.

SunPower had supported the Montalto di Castro project throughout, and SunRay's management team had shown itself capable of delivering on its promises. Finally,

---

12. In February 2010 *Project Finance* magazine recognized SunRay's financing as the 2009 European Solar Deal of the Year.

Yoram received the call he had anticipated for quite a while. The President of SunPower asked if SunRay was for sale; but, only when he mentioned an indicative bid price of USD300mn did SunRay and Denham believe that his interest was serious. The 1,200 MW pipeline of solar projects that SunRay had built up over 3 years appealed to the module manufacturer and would fit perfectly in its vertical integration strategy. SunPower was not looking to own the parks it developed, but could sell completed parks to fund new projects, recognizing revenue from module sales along the way.

It was SunRay's annual gathering in Rome, with the entire management rank in attendance and where SunPower's top brass were invited to join. Chaired by SunPower's president, SunRay's managers and country heads presented in turn, brainstormed, and strategized the "day after". A new partnership was formed with Via del Babuino as a backdrop. In his taxi to the airport after the meetings, Yoram reflected on SunRay's brief but eventual life and the challenges still ahead of him.

On February 11, 2010 SunPower announced the signing of a definitive agreement to acquire SunRay Renewable Energy. By that time SunRay had a staff of 70, operating from offices in seven countries, all of whom became new employees of SunPower. Exhibit 27.10 shows the timeline of SunRay from the founding of the company till the exit.

SUNRAY'S SPIRIT STILL ALIVE

Back in the Tel Aviv office, Yael juggled her routine work and the immense paperwork for an acquisition by a publicly listed U.S. company. Although SunRay was about to be acquired, the management team continued looking for new and creative ways to finance its business,[13] and opportunities to expand it with additional focus on Israel and elsewhere.

While Israel was a pioneer in clean technology, it trailed in the number of active installations. The country was heavily dependent on imports of oil and coal and, although enormous offshore gas reserves were recently discovered, the government set a goal to diversify its energy mix to include 10% from renewable sources. With an average of 2,000 hours of sunshine per year, solar power seemed the best way to achieve this goal.

Recalling the painful experience of missing the train in Spain, SunRay decided not only to enter Israel before it had passed any legislation, but to help shape it. The company has been sharing the lessons from its experience throughout Europe to promote a liberal and well-considered legislative framework. Led by a committed CEO with energy sector expertise and backed by the company's extensive international skills and experience, SunRay, now part of SunPower, should be well positioned to develop solar PV in the home country of its founders, writing a new chapter for a venture that was shaped in the corridors of London Business School.

13. "SunPower planning to sell bonds for Italy's largest solar park," Bloomberg, October 26, 2010
http://www.bloomberg.com/news/2010-10-26/sunpower-planning-to-sell-bonds-for-italy-s-largest-solar-park.html

APPENDIX

EXHIBIT 27.1

SOLAR PV GLOSSARY

Array   Linked collection of PV modules.

Base load   The average amount of electric power that a utility must supply in any period.

Capacity   The total number of ampere-hours that can be withdrawn from a fully charged battery at a specified discharge rate and temperature.

Crystalline silicon   A type of PV cell made from a single crystal or polycrystalline slice of silicon.

Efficiency   The ratio of output power (or energy) to input power (or energy), expressed as a percentage.

Electrical grid   An integrated system of electricity distribution, usually covering a large area.

Incident light   Light that shines onto the face of a solar cell or module.

Irradiation   The solar radiation incident on an area over time. Equivalent to energy and usually expressed in kilowatt-hours per square meter.

Inverter (power conditioning unit or power conditioning system)   In a PV system, an inverter converts DC power from the PV array/battery to AC power compatible with the utility and a.c. loads.

Joule (J)   Unit of energy equal to 1/3,600 kilowatt-hours.

Module   The smallest replaceable unit in a PV array. An integral encapsulated unit containing a number of interconnected solar cells.

N-type silicon   Silicon material that has been doped with a material that has more electrons in its atomic structure than silicon.

One-axis tracking   A system capable of rotating the PV module about one axis.

Panel   A designation for a number of PV modules assembled in a single mechanical frame.

Peak load   The maximum load demand on a system.

Peak sun hours   The equivalent number of hours per day when solar irradiance averages $1,000\,\text{W/m}^2$. For example, 6 peak sun hours means that the energy received during total daylight hours equals the energy that would have been received had the irradiance for 6 hours been $1,000\,\text{W/m}^2$.

Peak watt (Wp)   The amount of power a PV module will produce under standard test conditions (normally $1,000\,\text{W/m}^2$ and $25°\text{C}$ cell temperature).

Photovoltaic system   An installation of PV modules and other components designed to produce power from sunlight and meet the power demand for a designated load.

Polycrystalline silicon   A material used to make PV cells which consist of many crystals as contrasted with single-crystal silicon.

Substation   A subsidiary station of an electricity generation, transmission, and distribution system where voltage is transformed from high to low or the reverse using transformers.

Transformer   Converts the generator's low-voltage electricity to higher voltage levels for transmission to the load center, such as a city or factory.

Two-axis tracking   A system capable of rotating independently about two axes (e.g., vertical and horizontal).

Wafer   A thin sheet of semiconductor material made by mechanically sawing it from a single-crystal or multi-crystal ingot or casting

Zenith angle   The angle between directly overhead and the line intersecting the sun; $(90°—\text{zenith})$ is the elevation angle of the sun above the horizon.

Source: http://www.pvresources.com/en/glossary.php

EXHIBIT 27.2

MAJOR WORLDWIDE RENEWABLE ENERGY TECHNOLOGIES IN 2007

	Market size 2007	Forecast growth rates	Value Chain stages	Top companies
Mature, commercial technologies				
Wind energy	74,000 MW $23bn sales	15% to 20%	Turbines, gearboxes & generators	Vestas, GE Wind, Enercon (GE), Gamesa, Suzion
Solar Energy – Silicon Manufacturing	35,000 tons $6bn sales	30% to 35%	Silane gas, silicon production, ingots and wafer sawing	Shin-Etsu, MEMC, REC, Wacker Chemie, Tokuyama
Solar Energy – Solar Cells and Modules	$18bn sales	15% to 20%	Solar panels, accessories, system installation	Sharp, Sanyo, Kyocera, SolarWInd, Suntech, SunPower, First Solar
Biomass	$20bn sales	20% to 30%	Feedstock, biofuel production, distribution	Novozymes, Verbio, Biopetrol Industries, Nova Biosource
Geothermal	<$1bn equipment sales	5% to 10%	Non-electric "Direct Heat", steam generation	Ormat, WFI Industries
Immature technologies				
Fuel Cells	$1bn sales			Ballard Power, Medis Technologies, Fuelcell Energy
Tidal / Wave power	Effectively pre-revenue			Ocean Power Technology

Source: Global Wind Energy Council, Photon International, Geothermal Industry Association, and the National Renewable Energy Council.

EXHIBIT 27.3

BASICS OF SOLAR CELL TECHNOLOGIES

The upper graph shows how energy is present in sunlight, distributed across a range of energy levels. The lower portion of the diagram shows in stylized form how a solar cell works. The simplest solar cell structure is based on a pair of complementary semi-conductor materials in which each one has a "band gap" within which photons of light knock electrons loose. These electrons can then be captured. Engineers can "mix and match" different pairs of materials into combinations of cells that capture energy from complementary portions of the available spectrum.

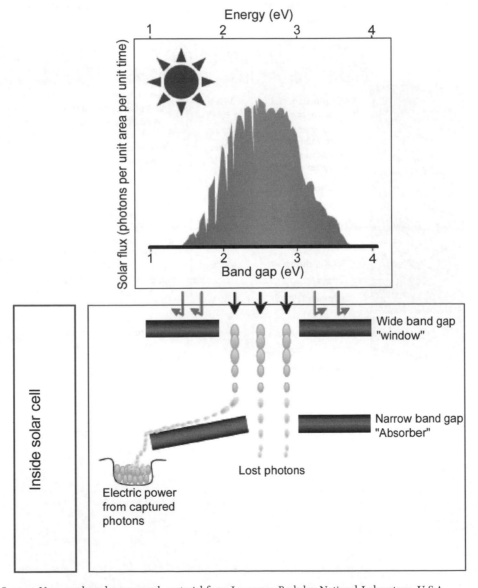

Source: Nomura, based on research material from Lawrence Berkeley National Laboratory, U.S.A.

EXHIBIT 27.4

A COMPARISON OF ALTERNATIVE SOLAR PV TECHNOLOGY SOLUTIONS IN 2007

	Technology "sub-flavours"	Typical efficiency	Manufacturing maturity	Commercial record
Crystalline silicon (poly- and mono-)	Single junction, multi- and mono- crystalline	13% to 15%*	Proven technology, scales well, accepted by customers, requires lots of silicon	Dominant technoloy (over 90% of the market)
	Heterojunction amorphous silicon on thin crystalline wafers	13% to 15%	Proven technology, good temperature gradient	
Thin film solar cells	Amorphous silicon (a-Si)	6.5%	a-Si is fully proven. Multiple other competing thin film technologies not yet proven in scale (Cadmium Telluride the closest). These technologies either use no silicon or less than 1% as much as crystalline silicon technology.	Under 10% of the market but immense R&D effort re-invigorated by demand boom and limited silicon supplies
	Micromorph (tandem junction)	10%		
	CIS/CIGS chalopyrite	10%		
	Cadmium Telluride	10%		
Next generation solutions	Dye-sensitised cells		Still at research stage. Basic physics not yet well understood. At least 5 years to full scale production	Scarcely visibile on the market, but R&D continues
	Polymer based cells			

* Efficiency goes up to 19% for high efficiency back contact modules

Source: SunRay documentation.

EXHIBIT 27.5

CONFIGURATION OF MONTALTO DI CASTRO SOLAR PV PARK

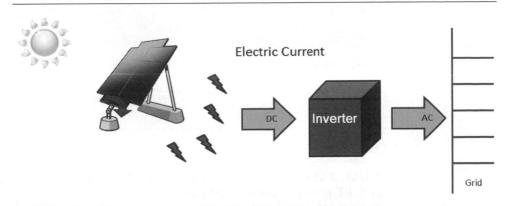

EXHIBIT 27.6

INCENTIVE PROGRAMS FOR THE MAIN EUROPEAN SOLAR PV MARKETS IN 2007

	Germany	Spain	Italy	Greece	Portugal
Peak sun hours (kWh/year)	887	1,430	1,282	1,381	1,413
Solar feed-in tariff (€/kWh)	0.59	0.44	0.49	0.4	0.317
Duration of feed-in tariff (years)	20	25	20	20	25

Source: International Energy Agency, PVGIS utility.

EXHIBIT 27.7

ANNUAL INSTALLED SOLAR PV POWER IN GERMANY, SPAIN, AND ITALY BETWEEN 2000 AND 2008

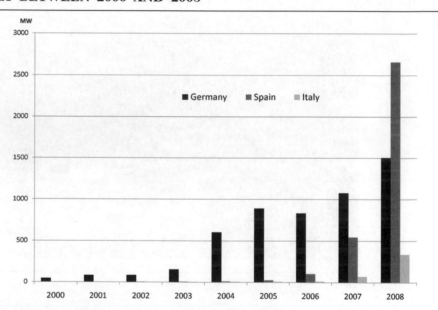

Source: International Energy Agency.

EXHIBIT 27.8

PROFILE OF DENHAM CAPITAL MANAGEMENT AS OF MAY 2008

Denham is a global private equity firm that invests in commodities, energy, and natural resources. As of May 2008, Denham had over USD4.25bn in assets under management and had committed approximately USD2bn of capital to 33 portfolio companies worldwide.

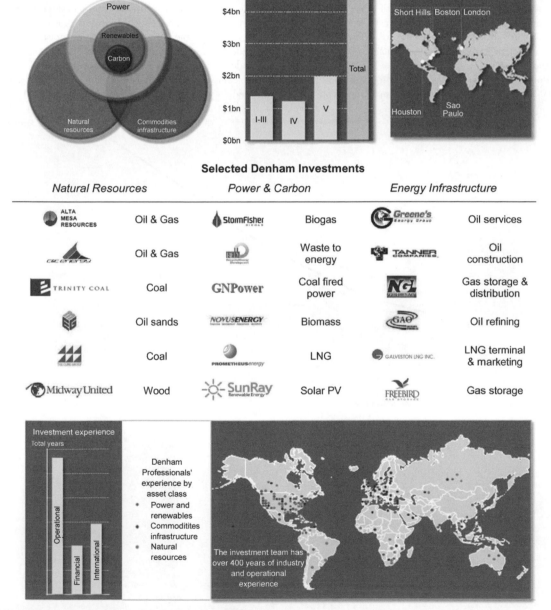

Source: Internal Denham Capital documentation (2008).

EXHIBIT 27.9

POLYSILICON PROJECTIONS IN 2007 THROUGH 2012

The increase in production of polysilicon, cells, and modules resulted in decreased prices across the supply chain. The global economic downturn and restricted access to capital was projected to limit the growth in PV installations to 4.2 GW in 2009, a year-on-year growth of only 10%. The corresponding figure for 2007 was 40%, while 2008 saw installation growth of 50%. iSuppli forecast a return in 2010 of the high growth rates that the industry had come to expect, boasting over 6 GW of installed capacity and showing potential for 10 GW in 2012. However, overcapacity was going to become a major problem for the industry.

Polysilicon production was projected to reach 100,000 Mt, or 12 GW, in 2009. Planned polysilicon capa-

city expansions saw that figure climb to over 250,000 Mt by 2012, or approximately 38 GW. The 2008 polysilicon price peak saw the cost reach approximately USD400 per kilogram, but this figure was expected to fall to an average of USD250/kg in 2009. Prices were forecast to fall to below USD150/kg in 2010, below USD100/kg in 2011, and below USD50/kg in 2012. At these low selling prices, it would be survival of the fittest, with only the most cost-efficient polysilicon producers being able to sell above cost.

A further problem was the vast discrepancy between PV module production and installations which resulted in module production reaching approximately 11 GW in 2009, compared with installations of 4.2 GW. Overcapacity in module production would exceed 160% in 2009.

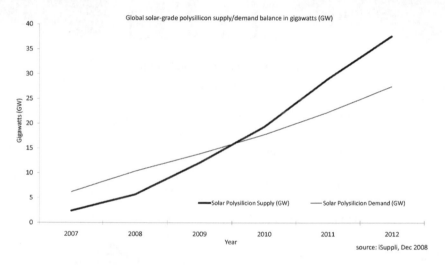

Global solar-grade polysillicon supply/demand balance in gigawatts (GW)

source: iSuppli, Dec 2008

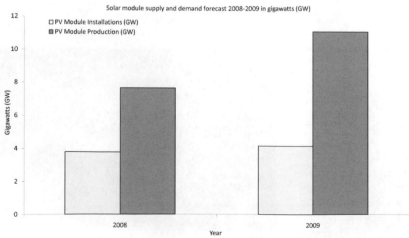

Solar module supply and demand forecast 2008-2009 in gigawatts (GW)

Source: iSuppli, 2009.

EXHIBIT 27.10

SUNRAY TIMELINE

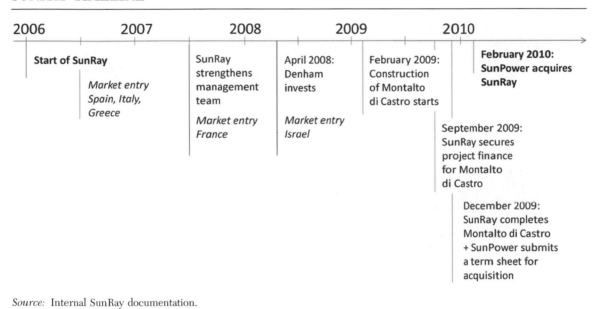

2006   2007   2008   2009   2010

Start of SunRay

Market entry Spain, Italy, Greece

SunRay strengthens management team

Market entry France

April 2008: Denham invests

Market entry Israel

February 2009: Construction of Montalto di Castro starts

February 2010: SunPower acquires SunRay

September 2009: SunRay secures project finance for Montalto di Castro

December 2009: SunRay completes Montalto di Castro + SunPower submits a term sheet for acquisition

Source: Internal SunRay documentation.

28

Debenhams

PRIVATE EQUITY GOES SHOPPING

It was October 23, 2003 as Philippe Costeletos enjoyed the California sun, but only from his hotel window. He was glued to the phone with his office back in London as the unexpected turn of events over the last few days required a swift and decisive decision from him now and could not wait for his return back to London.

Costeletos had joined Texas Pacific Group (TPG), one of the world's largest private equity buyout firms, only 6 months ago but it was already starting to feel much longer. He had instigated TPG to team up with CVC Capital Partners and Merrill Lynch Group Private Equity to create an investment vehicle called Baroness Group, a consortium to target the buyout of Debenhams, one of the UK's largest retail department stores. If they were to succeed, it would become a ground-breaking buyout deal and become, to date, the largest public company to be taken private in the U.K.

The race for Debenhams had started in February that year when Permira Advisers Ltd. (Permira), a leading European-based private equity firm, made its first offer. This was quickly dismissed by the board of Debenhams but Permira returned in early May on behalf of the newly formed Laragrove consortium with an indicative offer that the board could not brush aside. Costeletos recalled taking in this news a week before joining TPG and how he since had to constantly play catchup as he was late in joining the negotiations.

This was it, the final stage in the race for Debenhams. Did his team have the right offer price? Would they outbid their competition? After hours of deliberation, Philippe decided to give the go-ahead to announce a new offer for Debenhams, even trumping his own earlier offer made just a month ago.

U.K. retail sector

In 2003, the U.K. was enjoying a strong and growing economy. Personal disposable income (PDI) was on the rise and consumer confidence and employment levels were on the increase (see Exhibit 28.1). The real estate market was also seeing a boom with average house prices appreciating over 70% since 1999. These conditions were favorable for the retail sector fueling an increase in consumer spending activity. There

The case was co-authored with Andrew Strachan (LBS Sloan Fellow 2007) and Kay Nemoto (LBS MBA 2002). Thanks are due to Philippe Costeletos, Senior Investment Partner at TPG Capital (formerly Texas Pacific Group) and Richard Parry (LBS Sloan Fellow 2006) for their valuable comments and assistance.

were speculations, however, that 2003 was the peak and consumer spending was on the brink of a downturn. Interest rates were expected to increase and record high credit levels and increased mortgage payments were expected to start impacting consumer behavior. From late 2002, the retail sector in the U.K. was seeing increased change in ownership. Iconic U.K. retail executives such as Philip Green, Stuart Rose, John Lovering, Rob Templeman, and Terry Green, who all had prior track records in managing successful retail businesses, became active in a new wave of consolidation attempts (see Exhibit 28.2). Private equity houses were starting to team up with such renowned executives targeting stores that were household names.

The industry was now a prime target with room for consolidation, aiming to create operational efficiencies by consolidating costs such as advertising, purchasing, and head office administration functions. Some equity analyst reports were also claiming that the cash-generating sector was ripe for a shakeout as the effect of a prolonged stock market slump meant many store groups were trading at less than the value of the property, cash, stock, and goodwill they owned. They claimed there was a fundamental disconnect between the stock market values of the retail sector and their future business potential.

Most notably, the turnaround of British Home Stores (BHS), a U.K. fashion, furniture, and home accessories retail chain, led by Philip Green who acquired the store for £200mn in early 2000 and sold it for an estimated value of £1.2bn only 2 years later was setting the expectations for similar deals in the retail sector.

Debenhams' department stores: History and growth up to 2003

By 2003, Debenhams' department store chain was considered the second largest in the U.K. dominating almost a quarter of market share (see Exhibit 28.3A). As a result of recent aggressive expansion activities, it had 104 stores including 14 overseas franchise outlets in Europe, the Middle East, and South Asia (see Exhibit 28.3B).

Debenhams opened its first department store in 1905 in central London's busiest shopping district, Oxford Street, where its flagship store still stands today. Its origins date back to 1778, but the name was first used in 1813 when the Clark & Debenham Partnership was established in London's Wigmore Street, directly behind Oxford Street. The partnership had grown its business expanding retail outlets across the U.K. and even had its own clothing manufacturing operations.

In 1928, Debenhams listed its shares on the London Stock Exchange (LSE) trading as an independent company and continued to pursue an expansion strategy across the country. By 1985, it had department stores in 65 key locations across the U.K. and owned a number of other branded retail stores including Hamleys, the famous London toy store, and Harvey Nichols, London's boutique department store for high-end fashion located near the exclusive Sloane Square, Knightsbridge, where the wealthiest Londoners were known to shop.

In 1985 Debenhams was acquired for £560mn by the Burton Group, a major U.K. retail conglomerate owning mid-range fashion retail store chains such as Topshop, Evans, and Dorothy Perkins. Under new ownership, the company introduced exclusive ranges of branded items and aggressively expanded, opening its first overseas franchise store in the Middle East in 1997.

Ownership under the Burton Group did not last very long, and by 1998 Debenhams was de-merged and returned to an independently listed company on the LSE.

Following the de-merger from the Burton Group, Debenhams pursued a strategy of sustainable growth improving their brand and customer proposition. With strong operating cash flow, it had expanded and modernized the store portfolio making significant investments in its core business. Debenhams enjoyed a strong presence in key product categories which included women, men, and children's fashion, homeware, health and beauty, and accessories. By 2002, it had 22,000 employees and boasted a turnover of £1.7bn and pre-tax profits of £153mn (see financial statements in Exhibit 28.4).

Debenhams became known to consumers for its wide selection of products. It had an array of different brands including its own in-house branded goods, created by leading U.K. designers who were solicited to create product lines that were only sold in Debenhams' department stores. This exclusive selection differentiated Debenhams from competing department stores and soon it was successfully marketing 55 brands which included 25 unique brands called "Designers at Debenhams" (see Exhibit 28.5).

An online shopping site was also introduced in 1999, one of the first to be offered in the U.K.

In addition to its major department store locations, Debenhams started opening stores called "Desire by Debenhams" in smaller cities with a targeted mix of women's fashion, beauty, and accessory products. There were plans to roll out more of these smaller scale stores across the country.

Apart from its successful business growth, Debenhams had a large property portfolio as it owned most of its city center department stores. With a boom in the commercial property market, this was a major contributor for investors to eye Debenhams as a potential acquisition target, planning to unlock the value of the property portfolio.

Laragrove and its first-mover advantage

Permira made the first approach to acquire Debenhams in February 2003. Its offer, however, was simply dismissed by the Debenhams' board in early April, with Peter Jarvis, Chairman of Debenhams, commenting that the offer was "not serious".

Undeterred, Permira returned under the guise of a consortium—Laragrove. It was a bidding vehicle set up with two other major private equity firms, the Blackstone Group and Goldman Sachs Capital Partners, the private equity arm of the global investment bank. Creating a consortium (also known as "club deals") was becoming common allowing private equity houses to pool their funds and target larger companies.

Laragrove made its first indicative offer on the May 12, 2003 offering 425p per share. Debenhams' stock price a week prior to the offer announcement was trading around 330p per share. The offer was pitched so far above the prevailing share price that the board of Debenhams had to give serious consideration to the offer.

Debenhams' share price had fallen sharply in September 2000 where at one point it had plummeted to 190p per share due to a change of management. Terry Green, who had built up his reputation as Chief Executive of Debenhams for almost 9 years, departed to run another department store chain, BHS. Surprising the market, Belinda Earl was appointed as his replacement. She was relatively unknown, having joined the department store in 1985 making a slow ascent to the top job. Over the subsequent 3 years, her performance had proven stalwart and the share price had risen reflecting this (see Exhibit 28.6).

Seduction and misalignment of management interest

As part of its offer, Laragrove expressed from the onset its intention to keep Belinda Earl at the helm with her management team. This suggested that Laragrove already had

620 · Chapter 28: Debenhams

the management team successfully aligned to their interests by guaranteeing they would remain in place with further financial gains. It was revealed that Belinda Earl (CEO) and Matthew Roberts (CFO) were guaranteed to keep their jobs as well as getting a 6.9% equity stake in Debenhams. In addition, it was estimated that Belinda Earl would be guaranteed a windfall of £3mn if the bid was successful.

This led to immediate questions by the media regarding potential conflicts of interest for the management team and accusations of poor corporate governance. Belinda Earl was also accused of misleading the market as she had only weeks ago denied receiving any takeover offers when she announced positive interim results. Laragrove claimed that it had decided on its higher offer as a result of the announcement of the interim results but could not escape from being seen as having an unfair advantage.

Serious questions were raised by critics about Laragrove's open access to the management team and having an inside track on the company by guaranteeing their job status. This was seen as a strong disincentive for any other bidders to approach the deal, perhaps denying shareholders the best possible price.

Increased commitment through inducement fees

By late May, Laragrove skilfully negotiated not only the management support but gained an inducement fee agreement in which Debenhams would have to pay a penalty fee to Laragrove if they turned down their offer. It was highly unusual for such an arrangement to be agreed at such an early stage of the bidding process and prior to any due diligence taking place. Traditionally, inducement fees (also known as breakup fees) were agreed on the eve of an official signature mitigating deals falling out so late in the process. It was primarily seen as a final sign of commitment from the seller to the buyer.

Laragrove secured the following commitments:

- £6mn would be paid to Laragrove if Laragrove was willing to make an offer of 425p per share and the Debenhams' board was not willing to recommend such an offer; and
- £8.5mn would be payable to Laragrove if the Laragrove 425p offer was unsuccessful because a higher competing offer succeeded.

Laragrove was now ready to give its full attention to due diligence with the added bonus of securing the above financial commitments that would mitigate the costs of the process. Laragrove was in a strong position, not only with the inducement fees, but by having the full cooperation of both CEO Belinda Earl and CFO Matthew Roberts. In addition, there were no signs of any competition.

Searching for suitors

Laragrove was still the sole bidder for Debenhams in early June prompting the Debenhams' board to set up a committee to oversee and evaluate the private equity bid while searching for other possible bidders. This was to be chaired by a non-executive director as it emerged that the chairman of Debenhams Peter Jarvis had also created a conflict of interest by entering into an agreement with Laragrove to receive annual pay of £220,000 should Laragrove succeed in its bid and should his role as chairman disappear.

The committee began a desperate search to get a proper auction process started in order to achieve the best value for the company. This, however, was an upward struggle for the committee as rumors were rife in the press that several firms had rejected entering the deal due to the established inducement fees and the close relationship between Belinda Earl and the Laragrove consortium.

Baroness Group and the race for Debenhams

Philippe Costeletos could not have joined Texas Pacific Group at a more timely moment (mid-May 2003). He was responsible for leading TPG fund investments in the retail sector. Costeletos thought Debenhams was such a high-profile deal that—should he decide to bid—he would be risking his reputation so early after joining TPG, and Laragrove was already steaming ahead in the process. Costeletos knew that he would need to act quickly.

Debenhams was in reasonably good financial health with decent operating cash flows and profitability margins. Sector analysts, however, were forecasting a gloomy outlook ahead predicting a downturn in the U.K. economy that would affect consumer spending. Across the Atlantic, the U.S. retail sector had not fared very well in recent years either. Costeletos immediately started exploring his options with Debenhams to see if he could identify additional value potential of the department store chain to justify a competing bid to the Laragrove offer.

A new management team

As a priority, Philippe Costeletos set out to identify some leading figures in the retail sector. In a timely fashion, TPG's bankers Merrill Lynch brought his attention to John Lovering, Rod Templeman, and Chris Woodhouse (see Exhibit 28.7). The three managers had over 70 years of retail experience between them. They had worked together when Permira acquired Homebase, a major U.K. DIY store chain, and then teamed up again at Halfords, a hardware retail store chain mainly focusing on car accessories. The latter was an investment by a global private equity group, CVC Capital Partners (CVC). Costeletos liked the fact that the three key managers had previously worked with private equity firms. Furthermore, an additional candidate who knew Debenhams from the inside was identified. Michael Sharp was the effective number two and COO at Debenhams after it had de-merged from the Burton Group in 1998. He had built a solid reputation within the group as one of the strongest operators and had since become Managing Director of Principles, a U.K. retail fashion chain. Costeletos had now identified key executives to guide him through the intricate details of the retail sector and, more importantly, he had assembled the fundamental ingredients for a management buyin.

The Baroness Group consortium

As an unexpected side development for Costeletos, the management trio were also in discussions about the Debenhams deal with CVC. With the further addition of Merrill Lynch Group Private Equity, this soon developed into the creation of Baroness Retail Holdings Ltd. (Baroness Group), the consortium that would pool their resources together to compete against Laragrove.

It would, however, not be until June 29—well over a month after Laragrove negotiated an agreement for inducement fees and was lethargically involved in the due diligence process feeling confident in their solitary position—that Debenhams revealed they were in discussions with the Baroness Group, finally precipitating an expected bidding war.

TPG investment committee

In parallel with the creation of the consortium, Costeletos had to set the wheels in motion on his home turf, convincing the investment committee at TPG to support his mega-bid for Debenhams, his debut proposal upon joining TPG. Costeletos' conviction for the investment in Debenhams rested on three major arguments.

First, he made the case that comparison of U.S. retail sector investments vs. the U.K. was misleading and the U.K. market was far more favorable as it was less competitive due to government regulations that restricted new land use developments and new store openings.

Second, Costeletos argued that the gloomy outlook for consumer spending based on general economic factors would not show a slowdown as material as that predicted by analysts. He did not believe that U.K. consumer spending would drop even in a downturn and predicted a growth of 4% to 4.5% over the following two years. This was considerably higher than the 2% to 2.5% estimates by leading analysts.

His third conviction rested with his new management team and their ability to create operational efficiencies and improve profit margins. Costeletos argued that the existing management of a public company would have a short-term quarterly view failing to improve long-term margins. While analysts were predicting a 13.2% EBITDA over the following two years, Costeletos argued that it would be 16.4% (see Exhibit 28.8).

He eventually won over the support of the TPG investment committee and gained approval to continue pursuing the investment opportunity in Debenhams based on the following investment thesis:

- Stable core store cash flows and property portfolio to provide underpinning value
- Significant upside in operating/central cost, CAPEX, and working capital
- Backing of aggressive new management team with demonstrable track record
- Growth opportunity in underpenetrated product categories
- New-store and new-format growth potential
- Not a turnaround: Solid base plus upside potential.

An inducement fee and commitment fee for Baroness Group

On July 18 Debenhams' board conceded to a second and separate inducement fee agreement with Baroness Group. It was seen as an inevitable decision by the board in order to attract the Baroness Group as a second bidder. This was even more apparent by the agreement of a further commitment fee to pay Baroness Group for conducting due diligence. This was unheard of before in past private equity transactions and a novel and innovative feature which Baroness Group imposed on the board. Costeletos argued that this would at least stop Laragrove from bidding below the 425p offer:

> "Before we entered the process, there was little incentive for Permira to revise its price ... But given how far ahead the competitors were in the process, we couldn't justify going out of pocket with the diligence costs, so we asked to be compensated for it. This wasn't something that had been done before, but we felt it was the only way to move forward and as a result ... added competitive tension to the sale process."
>
> —Costeletos' comments to *Buyout* magazine, March 2004

The details of the inducement fee and the commitment fee agreed upon were as follows:

- Baroness Group would be paid £1.2mn per week over up to a 5-week period if it reaffirmed each week its "strong commitment", having consulted with its legal and financial advisors, to continue discussions regarding an offer at a price above the level of any offer made by Laragrove or another bidder and if Baroness notified Debenhams before the end of September that they no longer wished to proceed with an offer for the company. This fee would only be paid if they decided not to bid.

- A fee of £8.5mn would be payable if Baroness Group made an offer at a price higher than Laragrove's 425p per share but was deemed unsuccessful because a higher offer succeeded.

This agreement, which eventually was made public, drew criticism:

> "It sets an unwelcome precedent to fund a venture capitalist group to do due diligence on your company and we are disappointed that the management felt they had to do this. If a venture capital company is seriously interested, they should not need to be funded, it makes management appear too keen to be taken over."
>
> —David Cumming, Investment Director, Standard Life,
> *The Independent*, July 29, 2003

Costeletos was relieved at achieving this agreement tipping back some of the imbalance from Laragrove's head start while strengthening his position with the TPG investment committee. He also knew that the Debenhams' board could not afford to lose the interest of Baroness Group in order to get an auction process started between the two contending syndicates; so, as controversial as it may be viewed, he thought this to be a fair deal. Baroness Group was ready to delve into the due diligence process, almost two months after Laragrove.

The bidding war begins

Formal offer from Laragrove, July 29, 2003

The Laragrove consortium made its formal offer to the Debenhams' board on July 29, maintaining their earlier indicative offer of 425p per share. Laragrove committed £528mn in equity (arranged as ordinary income and deep discount bonds) with the remainder in debt resulting in a leverage ratio of 68% (Exhibit 28.9 provides the deal structure for Laragrove's tender offer).

Laragrove also announced its plans for immediate refinancing post acquisition by setting up a mortgage facility for £160mn secured on Debenhams' stores. Furthermore, they announced the planned sale and leaseback agreements with Legal & General, Ravenscroft, and Royal Bank of Scotland for £144mn, £22.4mn, and £145mn, respectively. Together these transactions would amount to £471.4mn. The U.K. property market was in the midst of a boom with prices appreciating quickly. In fact, the sale and leaseback offer was already higher than an estimate given by a property advisor earlier in the month.

Laragrove, in addition, pushed ahead by announcing the possible appointment of an iconic figure in the U.K. retail business, Stuart Rose, as non-executive chairman if their bid was to be successful.

The Laragrove offer was met with a lukewarm response from the Debenhams' board, commenting: "(Laragrove's offer) represents a proposal worthy of serious consideration in the absence of a higher offer being received."

There was no summer holiday for Costeletos and his team that August. "It was down to the wire and an extraordinary experience," recalls Costeletos and his team who barely slept for an entire week. They were busy conducting due diligence while in parallel configuring the financial structure of their offer, carefully planning between the three private equity firms, legal advisors, and then followed by intense negotiations with four different banks for the debt assignment: Credit Suisse, Merrill Lynch, Morgan Stanley, and Citigroup.

The financing was not dissimilar to that of Laragrove. The portfolio of property assets was the attractive part of the deal as Baroness Group had intentions to separate Debenhams' retail activity and real estate into separate property companies as well. The plan was to "carve out" the property assets from the balance sheet through a sale and leaseback.

On September 12, Baroness Group announced its offer of 455p per share. It was offering £599mn in equity, yielding a slightly lower leverage ratio than Laragrove at 66%. The offer was also made with the option to switch to an unusual form of the Takeover Code called a "scheme of arrangement".

Scheme of arrangement

Baroness Group wanted a quick resolution. It was conscious of the looming Christmas shopping months, a crucial seasonal trend in the retail sector, and did not want the auction process to drag its heels and impact the business.

Baroness Group introduced the option to switch to a scheme of arrangement where a decision could be reached much quicker. Typically, the scheme was used in distressed situations. In this uncommon use of the scheme, the panel on Takeovers & Mergers (Takeover Panel), an independent body that regulated and supervised transactions through the code of practice, became involved and mulled over the use of such a process as it would likely set a precedent for future bidding wars.

On October 13 the Takeover Panel set out the following ground rules for the scheme of arrangement:

> After 5 P.M. on the 30th of October, should one party wish to place a higher bid, this must be lodged with the Panel Executive by 4 P.M. of the following day. At 5 P.M., this offer would officially be announced. The counter-bidding could continue daily in the same manner until the 3rd of November when the open auction process would come to an end. A final sealed bid would then ensue with the last offer to be submitted to the Panel Executive by 1 P.M. on the 4th of November. The highest bidder, thus new owners of Debenhams would then be announced on the same day at 5 P.M.

Final showdown: Laragrove vs. Baroness Group

Seventeen days after Baroness Group submitted its offer, Debenhams' board announced its favorable view. Nevertheless, the deal was far from over with Laragrove still having the opportunity to counterbid. Costeletos was still not holding his breath.

Soon, news reached him that Permira, the lead investor in the Laragrove consortium had just successfully raised more capital through a staggering £5.1bn fund, one of the largest yet in Europe. This would enable Laragrove to increase its offer.

Adding even more fuel to the heated fire over Debenhams, the announcement of the financial results for the year ending August 2003 revealed stronger than expected business results. Actual turnover had increased by 7% and pre-tax profits were up by almost 10%.

Unfolding of the tender process

Expecting a counterbid any day now from the Laragrove consortium, Costeletos reluctantly boarded a flight bound for Los Angeles to attend TPG's annual investors' conference which he just couldn't miss. The only thing going through his mind was how far Laragrove would be willing to go and by how much would it increase the offer. Some analysts were predicting that the final price would settle around 490p per share.

By the time he disembarked from his 12-hour flight, everything had changed, and the race for Debenhams had taken on a peculiar turn. Goldman Sachs Capital Partners announced its pullout from the bidding process delivering a severe blow to the Laragrove consortium. It felt that the auction process would hike up the price too high and it no longer wanted to remain involved. Rumors were, however, circulating that Permira, undeterred, was now in talks with another major private equity firm.

Costeletos and his team had to act swiftly. He wanted to deliver a surprise attack with a new bid even above Baroness' own earlier offer. He knew this move would surprise both Laragrove and Debenhams. He also assumed that many Debenham shares were now in the hands of hedge funds and opportunistic investors waiting for the final deal to close and, therefore, would be happy to accept a higher price and lock in healthy year-end profits. The question was how high should the Baroness Group go?

Costeletos had now been glued to his computer and phone and has spent two sleepless nights liaising with his team in London. They at last had a new bid which hopefully would become the decisive knockout blow to the Laragrove consortium.

Finally, as he slowly placed the phone down, he was starting to sense the deal was within his grasp. Exhibit 28.10 provides the timeline for key events in the Debenhams' bidding war. Exhibit 28.11 presents comparables for U.K. retail buyouts during the period.

POST DEAL AND GOING PUBLIC AGAIN

Debenhams Plc was eventually de-listed from the London Stock Exchange (LSE) on December 5, 2003 under the new ownership of the Baroness Group which invested £607mn in equity. At Debenhams, the prior management team was swiftly replaced by the private equity–backed veterans consisting of John Lovering (Chairman), Rob Templeman (Chief Executive), and Chris Woodhouse (Finance Director). Both the new management and Baroness Group embarked upon their post-acquisition plan under private ownership.

Releasing value from the property assets, Baroness Group immediately focused on the post-acquisition financing by separating the real estate assets and creating several new property companies away from the operations of Debenhams. It prioritized refinancing the higher interest rate bridge and mezzanine facilities with mortgages and high-yield bonds which offered more attractive rates (see Exhibit 28.12).

By April 2004, both the bridge and mezzanine facilities were paid back in full, replaced with a £370mn mortgage facility and issues of deep-discounted bonds. The ultimate goal, however, was achieved in February 2005 with a sale and leaseback arrangement with British Land for £490mn for 23 of their department stores. The cash flow from this transaction along with the proceeds from the disposal of 7 other properties released £125mn which became part of Baroness Group's May 2005 dividend package.

Operational improvements

In parallel, the new management team implemented radical downsizing in Debenhams' operation. Fire sales were held to clear old inventory off the balance sheet and to drastically reduce the stock of merchandise. More attractive credit payment terms were negotiated and the large number of small suppliers was cut to much fewer numbers, which reduced the time to market for new products from 18 weeks to less than 13 weeks (see Exhibits 28.13 and 28.14). By the end of fiscal year 2005, Debenhams was showing a negative working capital. Altogether, the new strategy improved operational effectiveness by transforming the supply chain and identifying new growth sources and areas for geographical expansion. New department stores were opened while less profitable ones were closed down. A new range of smaller concept stores—labeled Desire by Debenhams and aimed at women—were introduced (see Exhibits 28.15 and 28.16).

These operational changes markedly changed the business providing strong cash generation and improved EBITDA results. On the back of this success and with the property company sale and leaseback arrangements in place, Baroness Group was ready to recapitalize the business.

In May 2005, effectively a new leveraged buyout occurred whereby the old holding company, Baroness Group Holdings Ltd., was acquired by a new company, Debenhams Retail Holdings Ltd. by means of a share-for-share exchange. This acquisition and refinancing enabled Baroness Group to extract a £1.3bn dividend payment from Debenhams in a tax-efficient manner: £1,196mn was paid to the sponsor consortium and £84mn was paid to the management and employees. The original equity investment was reshuffled to the new vehicle in the same proportions as before by the consortium, and £1.82bn of senior term loan debt was raised. Because the senior note debt was moved farther away from the operational assets of Debenhams, the banks were taking on additional risk in issuing this debt while, on the other hand, preparing Debenhams for an eventual IPO.

Baroness Group achieved its plan to improve the financial and operational performance of Debenhams and, suitably, was approached by several underwriters in late 2005 on the grounds that it was a "good window for an IPO".

On May 5, 2006, less than 3 years from being taken private, Debenhams re-emerged on the LSE with a share price of 195p where 57% of the company was floated with 37% of shares remaining with the private equity firms of the Baroness Group consortium and 6% with the management team. A further 5% was sold by the Baroness Group a couple of days later by exercising an overallotment option. Exhibit 28.17 portrays the post-IPO results on May 7, 2006. The IPO yielded handsome profits for CVC, Texas Pacific Group, and Merrill Lynch Private Equity, and was hailed as one of the largest private equity takeovers in the U.K.

Very few imagined that, in less than 18 months after this reverse LBO, the share price would drastically underperform dipping below 90p per share. Coinciding with the general furor and public scrutiny of private equity activity in both European parliaments and the U.S. Congress, the consortium members of the Baroness Group found themselves having to defend their business model and endure skepticism of the way in which they conducted themselves:

> "We have been in (Debenhams) for over three years and we can be patient and stay in for a long time. If people came in looking for a quick return they may be disappointed. The question is how patient they are."
>
> —Costeletos, quoted in the *Financial Times*, August 6, 2007

APPENDIX

EXHIBIT 28.1

U.K. GROSS NATIONAL DISPOSABLE INCOME 1990–2006 (SEASONALLY ADJUSTED 2000 = 100)

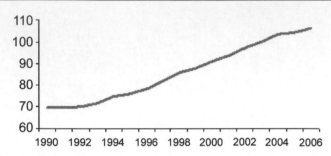

Source: Office of National Statistics.

EXHIBIT 28.2

M&A ACTIVITIES IN THE U.K. RETAIL SECTOR, AUGUST 2002–APRIL 2003

Date	Retail store	Description	Key management/ entrepreneur
Aug 2002	Arcadia	Conglomerate of mid-range fashion retail chains. Taken private by billionaire who earlier turned around failing store chain BHS making 6× turnover	Philip Green Stuart Rose
Nov 2002	Homebase	DIY home improvement superstore chain. Owned by private equity firm Permira since 1998 and managed a successful turnaround with the key management team. Trade sale to GUS for £900mn	John Lovering Rob Templeman Chris Woodhouse
Nov 2002	Harvey Nichols	Luxury lifestyle stores specializing in brand name merchandise was taken private by its largest shareholder, Hong Kong tycoon Dickson Poons for £137.5mn	
Dec 2002	House of Fraser	Large department store chain's takeover attempt failed by private equity group TBH Investments and Scottish retail entrepreneur. Taken private by Icelandic investor Baugur Group in August 2006	Tom Hunter
Feb 2002	Allders	Large department store chain. Successful LBO by Minerva, an investment vehicle by a property group. Took on top retail executive (previous CEO of Debenhams, Terry Green)	Terry Green
Mar 2003	Hamleys	Largest toy store in the U.K. Authorization given to explore a management buyout backed by Baugur Group in March 2003 but bidding war ensues	Stuart Rose appointed Exec. Chairman in Oct.
Apr 2003	Selfridges	High-end department store chain. Tom Hunter tries to acquire after failed attempt on House of Fraser. Lost to Canadian billionaire with ownership in other retail stores in the UK.	Tom Hunter Galen Weston

EXHIBIT 28.3A

U.K. DEPARTMENT STORE MARKET SHARE (%) IN 2001

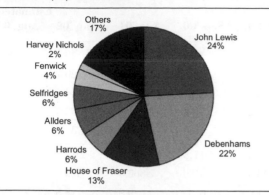

EXHIBIT 28.3B

DEBENHAMS INTERNATIONAL STORE LOCATIONS IN 2003

Bahrain	Saudi Arabia
Cypress	Turkey
Czech Republic	United Arab Emirates
Iceland	
Indonesia	
Kuwait	
Philippines	
Qatar	

Source: Deutsche Bank Securities Inc.

EXHIBIT 28.4A

DEBENHAMS: CONSOLIDATED FINANCIAL STATEMENTS (IN £ MILLION)

INCOME STATEMENT Fiscal year ending	Pro forma Aug '98	Aug '99	Sep '00	Aug '01	Aug '02	Estimated Aug '03
Group turnover/revenue[1]	1,365.8	1,378.8	1,397.2	1,606.9	1,688.5	1,810.2
Cost of sales	(1,165.4)	(1,182.0)	(1,198.3)	(1,376.0)	(1,448.1)	
Gross profit	**200.4**	**196.8**	**198.9**	**230.9**	**240.4**	
Distribution cost	(22.3)	(23.5)	(25.3)	(29.7)	(33.1)	
Administrative expenses	(32.0)	(28.1)	(37.3)	(44.4)	(43.5)	
Group trading profit	**146.1**	**145.2**	**136.3**	**156.8**	**163.6**	**175.8**
Share of trading profit in joint ventures	—	(0.2)	(1.9)	(2.5)	(3.8)	—
Total trading profit	**146.1**	**145.0**	**134.4**	**154.3**	**160.0**	**175.8**[2]
Net interest and similar charges	(7.5)	(6.2)	(4.8)	(8.2)	(6.4)	
Exceptional items	128.7	—	—	—	—	
Earnings before taxation	**267.3**	**138.8**	**129.6**	**146.1**	**153.6**	**149.1**
Taxation	(55.7)	(45.8)	(41.5)	(43.8)	(44.6)	
Profit for the finncial year	**211.6**	**93.0**	**88.1**	**102.3**	**109.0**	**104.2**
Basic earnings per share	65.8p	24.7p	23.6p	27.9p	29.8p	
Supplemental items						
EBITDA	198.0	189.4	190.1	219.4	237.0	
Weighted average basic shares out (million)	376.6	377.2	372.6	367.0	365.9	

Source: Company data, Capital IQ.

Notes: 1. Turnover comprises sales of all merchandise to third parties including the gross value of concession sales, excluding value-added tax.
2. Before restructuring costs.

EXHIBIT 28.4B

DEBENHAMS: CONSOLIDATED FINANCIAL STATEMENTS (IN £ MILLION)

BALANCE SHEET Fiscal year ending	Pro forma Aug '98	Aug '99	Sep '00	Aug '01	Aug '02	Estimated Aug '03
Cash and equivalents	8.6	14.1	10.2	12.9	29.4	18.2
Accounts receivable	13.5	12.9	14.2	16.9	20.1	18.8
Other receivables	3.5	2.3	6.0	3.3	4.5	5.2
Inventory	173.0	177.2	195.3	211.1	203.5	198.2
Pre-paid expenses	11.5	19.7	21.8	25.6	33.6	33.7
Total current assets	**210.1**	**226.2**	**247.5**	**269.8**	**291.1**	**274.1**
Net property, plant, and equipment	705.0	753.4	819.9	865.4	920.2	969.8
Long-term investments	0.8	1.0	(2.1)	9.9	18.8	—
Goodwill	—	—	—	—	—	1.9
Other intangibles	—	—	—	0.2	0.2	0.3
Loans receivable long term	—	0.2	4.2	—	—	—
Other long-term assets	—	—	4.2	—	—	—
Total assets	**915.9**	**980.8**	**1,073.7**	**1,145.3**	**1,230.3**	**1,246.1**
Accounts payable	59.6	59.4	59.9	60.3	69.8	66.8
Accrued expenses	75.8	69.5	75.8	89.8	84.7	120.6
Short-term borrowings	28.2	60.3	92.0	78.3	97.0	—
Current portfolio of long-term debt	6.8	—	—	—	—	86.6
Current income taxes payable	54.9	51.1	44.4	41.3	21.1	10.3
Other current liabilities	82.8	74.4	90.5	95.3	111.3	107.8
Total current liabilities	**308.1**	**314.7**	**362.6**	**365.0**	**383.9**	**392.1**
Long-term debt	63.4	3.4	61.9	—	—	59.4
Capital leases	—	57.7	—	59.2	59.4	—
Pension and other post-retirement benefits	—	—	—	—	—	41.5
Deferred tax liability, non-current	22.8	27.7	37.0	49.4	57.9	63.9
Other non-current liabilities	4.6	6.5	5.0	3.1	3.8	2.6
Total liabilities	**398.9**	**410.0**	**466.5**	**476.7**	**505.0**	**559.5**
Common stock	37.8	37.8	37.0	37.1	36.9	36.6
Additional paid in capital	—	0.1	0.1	2.4	3.3	19.7
Retained earnings	436.0	489.7	526.1	585.1	640.9	585.3
Comprehensive income and other	43.2	43.2	44.0	44.0	44.2	45.0
Total shareholders' equity	**517.0**	**570.8**	**607.2**	**668.6**	**725.3**	**686.6**
Total liabilities and shareholder equity	**915.9**	**980.8**	**1,073.7**	**1,145.3**	**1,230.3**	**1,246.1**

Source: Company data.

EXHIBIT 28.4C

DEBENHAMS: CONSOLIDATED FINANCIAL STATEMENTS (IN £ MILLION)

CASH FLOW STATEMENT Fiscal period ending	Pro forma Aug '98	Aug '99	Sep '00	Aug '01	Aug '02	Estimated Aug '03
Net income	**182.4**	**145.0**	**134.4**	**102.3**	**109.0**	**104.2**
Depreciation and amortization	(51.9)	(44.4)	(55.7)	(65.1)	(76.9)	(82.9)
Amortization of goodwill and intangibles	—	—	—	—	(0.1)	(0.2)
Depreciation and amortization, total	**(51.9)**	**(44.4)**	**(55.7)**	**(65.1)**	**(77.0)**	**(83.1)**
(Gain) Loss from sale of assets	—	—	(0.7)	(1.1)	—	(1.6)
Asset writedown and restructuring costs	6.6	(2.9)	(0.6)	(0.8)	(1.1)	—
Income (loss) on equity investment	—	0.2	1.9	2.7	4.0	—
Other operating activities	8.3	—	—	52.0	52.2	50.8
Change in accounts receivable	(24.9)	(4.1)	(1.6)	(9.5)	(7.9)	(1.6)
Change in inventories	(77.5)	(4.2)	(18.1)	(15.8)	9.2	5.3
Change in accounts payable	(159.4)	(4.4)	21.1	29.6	1.9	23.3
Change in income taxes	(19.8)	(48.4)	(39.4)	(35.3)	(53.4)	(44.7)
Cash from operations	**(49.0)**	**131.4**	**153.9**	**190.8**	**193.1**	**218.8**
Capital expenditure	(92.0)	(105.2)	(134.8)	(133.8)	(127.7)	(134.5)
Sale of property, plant, and equipment	2.9	1.3	7.4	16.3	—	2.3
Cash acquisitions	—	—	—	—	4.7	(2.1)
Divestitures	919.2	—	—	—	—	—
Sale (purchase) of intangible assets	—	—	—	(0.2)	(0.1)	(0.1)
Investments in marketable and equity securities	—	(0.2)	—	—	—	—
Other investing activities	(6.0)	(5.3)	(7.4)	(7.7)	(11.2)	(7.7)
Cash from investing	**824.1**	**(109.4)**	**(134.8)**	**(125.4)**	**(134.3)**	**(142.1)**
Short-term debt repaid	(19.3)	(3.4)	(7.1)	—	(3.4)	—
Long-term debt repaid	(729.4)	—	—	—	—	—
Total debt repaid	**(748.7)**	**(3.4)**	**(7.1)**	**—**	**(3.4)**	**—**
Issuance of common stock	197.2	0.1	—	2.1	0.7	8.9
Repurchase of common stock	(0.8)	(0.4)	(15.4)	(13.8)	(27.8)	(40.4)
Common dividends paid	(296.0)	(37.8)	(39.3)	(81.6)	(88.6)	(46.0)
Preference dividends paid	(0.1)	—	—	—	—	—
Total dividends paid	**(296.1)**	**(37.8)**	**(39.3)**	**(81.6)**	**(88.6)**	**(46.0)**
Cash from financing	**(848.4)**	**(41.5)**	**(61.8)**	**(93.3)**	**(119.1)**	**(77.5)**
Miscellaneous cash flow adjusted	—	—	—	47.7	54.7	—
Net change in cash	**(73.3)**	**(19.5)**	**(42.7)**	**19.8**	**(5.6)**	**(0.8)**

Source: Company data.

EXHIBIT 28.5A

MARKET POSITIONING OF DEBENHAMS COMPARED WITH THE COMPETITION

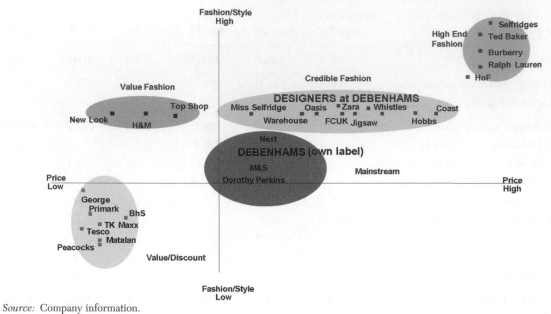

Source: Company information.

EXHIBIT 28.5B

DEBENHAMS' BRAND MIX

Source: Company information.

EXHIBIT 28.6

DEBENHAMS' DAILY SHARE PRICE MOVEMENT, SEPTEMBER 2002–OCTOBER 2003

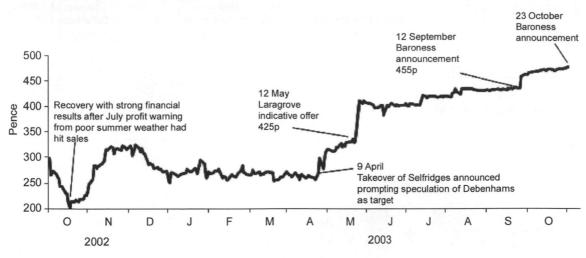

Source: Bloomberg, LBS.

EXHIBIT 28.7

BIOGRAPHIES OF KEY INDIVIDUALS ON THE BARONESS TEAM

Philippe Costeletos Prior to joining Texas Pacific Group as a partner responsible for retail, Philippe was a Member of the Management Committee at Investcorp where he worked for 8 years and was involved in a number of buyouts in Switzerland, Norway, the Netherlands and the U.K. Prior to joining Investcorp, Philippe was with JP Morgan's private equity group where he was involved in evaluating and executing private equity investments in Europe and Latin America. Previous to that, he worked with Morgan Stanley in London and New York. He is an Advisory Board Member of the London Business School Private Equity Institute.

Philippe holds a BA (Magna Cum Laude) with distinction in mathematics from Yale University and an MBA from Columbia Business School (Beta Gamma Sigma).

John Lovering John Lovering was Chairman of Somerfield Ltd. and has led several consumer-focused private equity transactions, including Homebase Group, Halfords, Fitness First, the Laurel Pub Company, Birthdays Group, Odeon Cinemas, and Fired Earth. He was previously Chief Operating Officer at Tarmac plc and Finance Director at Sears plc.

Rob Templeman Rob Templeman was Chairman of Halfords Group, Chief Executive of Homebase Group, and before that Chief Executive of Harvey's Furnishing plc.

Chris Woodhouse Chris Woodhouse was previously Deputy Chairman of Halfords Group and Commercial Director and Deputy Chief Executive at Homebase Group. He is a former finance director of Birthdays Group and Superdrug Stores. He is a Fellow of the Institute of Chartered Accountants in England & Wales and is an Associate of the Association of Corporate Treasurers.

EXHIBIT 28.8

TPG FINANCIAL PROJECTIONS BEHIND BIDDING FOR DEBENHAMS IN JUNE 2003

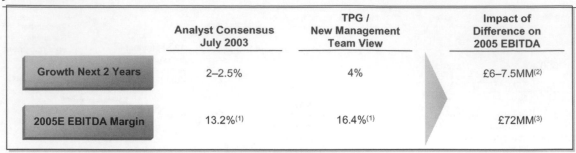

	Analyst Consensus July 2003	TPG / New Management Team View	Impact of Difference on 2005 EBITDA
Growth Next 2 Years	2–2.5%	4%	£6–7.5MM[2]
2005E EBITDA Margin	13.2%[1]	16.4%[1]	£72MM[3]

(1) Proforma for sale and leaseback
(2) Assuming constant margin
(3) Assuming TPG / New management team sales growth

Differential View on Cost Opportunity	+	Great Management Team	=	Win public bidding contest

Source: TPG.

EXHIBIT 28.9

BREAKDOWN OF DEAL STRUCTURE FOR LARAGROVE'S OFFER AT 425P (AS OF JULY 29, 2003)

Sources	(£ million)	Uses	(£ million)
Term Loan A	280	Purchase of equity	1,541
Term Loan B	120	Refinanced debt	127
Term Loan C	120	Transaction cost	55
Bridge loan	325		
Mezzanine	350		
Ordinary equity	22		
Deep discount bonds	506		
	1,723		**1,723**

Source: Debenhams.

EXHIBIT 28.10

DEBENHAMS' BIDDING PROCESS KEY EVENTS TIMELINE IN 2003

Date	Details
February	Permira makes first approach for Debenhams which is dismissed as "not serious".
April 9	Bid for Selfridges, a high-end department store by Tom Hunter sparks initial speculation of a buyout of Debenhams.
May 12	Laragrove consortium makes indicative offer of 425p per share. Committee of independent directors appointed. Inducement fee agreed by Debenhams' board.
May 19	Philippe Costeletos joins TPG to lead retail sector investments.
June 5	TPG and CVC meet introduced through John Lovering, Rod Templeman, and Chris Woodhouse
June 7	Debenhams appoint Jim Clarke, a non-executive director to lead committee to evaluate bids as it is disclosed that Chairman Peter Jarvis would receive up to £220,000 should Laragrove win.
June 10	Laragrove announces intention to appoint Stuart Rose as non-executive chairman should it win.
Mid-June	Baroness Group formed by CVC, TPG, and Merrill Lynch Private Equity.
June 29	Debenhams reveal Baroness Group's interest and agreement of commitment fee.
July 4	Laragrove asks for offer extension until July 22.
July 9	Debenhams' property portfolio estimated at £425mn by property advisor Colliers CRE.
July 18	Inducement fee agreement reached between Baroness Group and Debenhams.
July 22	Debenhams announces 3.8% growth in like-for-like sales in the first 20 weeks of the second half of the year and a 7.8% rise in sales.
July 23	Laragrove confirms 425p offer for a value of £1.54bn, which is recommended to shareholders by management who would be given a 6.9% interest.
July 29	Independent directors of Debenhams endorse Laragrove offer.
August–September	Baroness Group considers offer while conducting due diligence.
August 4	Laragrove offer presented to shareholders.
September 12	Baroness Group announces bid of 455p per share under scheme of arrangement at a value of £1.66bn. Debenhams' share stays above 455p.
September 26	Baroness Group seeks fast-track approval from Debenhams' shareholders through a "scheme of arrangement".
September 29	Debenhams' board recommends Baroness offer.
October 7	Permira closes a new £5.1bn fund.
October 14	Takeover panel rules on how contest should proceed and agrees to scheme of arrangement.
October 14	Debenhams reports strong sales with a 9.6% rise in pre-tax profits and 6.7% increase in turnover to £1.7bn for year ending August 30, 2003.
October 21	Goldman Sachs Private Equity announces their pullout from the Laragrove consortium.
October 23	Baroness Group increases its offer and submits bid.

EXHIBIT 28.11

COMPARABLES FOR U.K. RETAIL BUYOUT TARGETS 2002–2003

Date	Target	Acquirer	Price (incl. debt) (£ million)	EBIT (£ million)	EBITDA (£ million)	Post-tax profits (£ million)	EV/EBIT (×)	EV/ EBITDA (×)	Debt-free PE (×)	Actual PE (×)	Direction of profits
May-02	Debenhams	Permira	1,517	160	237.0	109.0	9.5	6.4	13.9	13.9	Up
May-02	Selfridges	Weston	628	44	64.0	31.0	14.3	9.8	20.3	19.3	Up
Nov-02	Homebase	GUS	900	102	144.5	71.4	8.8	6.2	12.6	12.6	Up
Aug-02	Arcadia	Philip Green	763	113	189	70.7	7.6	4.6	10.8	10.3	Up
Nov-02	Harvey Nichols	Dickson Poon	161	12.2	17.25	8.5	13.2	9.3	18.9	16.0	Down
Dec-02	Allders	Minerva	151.6	11.6	27.9	8.1	13.1	5.4	18.7	15.4	Down
Jul-02	Halfords	CVC	427	54.3	67.7	38.0	7.9	6.3	11.2	11.2	Down
Dec-02	Focus Wickes	Apax	1,050	115.6	147.5	80.9	9.1	7.1	13.0	13.0	Up
May-02	First Sport	JD Sports	53.2	6.2	12.3	4.34	8.6	4.3	12.3	12.3	Down
	Average						9.8	6.2	14.6	13.8	
	Average excluding Allders (because it is asset backed)						**9.2**	**6.3**	**14.1**	**13.6**	
Mar-03	JJB Sports (based on 2002/3 profits)	Dave Whelan	651	96	118.5	67.2	6.8	5.5	9.7	9.5	Down

Source: Deutsche Bank estimates.

EXHIBIT **28.12**

EFFECTIVE INTEREST RATES FROM 2003 TRANSACTION TO IPO IN 2006 (%)

Group		Aug-30 2003	Interim	Aug-28 2004	Feb-26 2005	Interim	Sep-03 2005	Mar-04 2006	Interim
New credit agreement	Bank loans and overdrafts	n.k.		n.k.	5.75		5.50	5.50	
	B loan notes	n.k.		n.k.	—		7.05	7.05	
	Term loan facility	—							
	Receiving facility	—							
Senior credit agreement	Senior term loan—Tranche A	—				LIBOR + 2.25 plus ratchet and QPO	6.85	6.84	
	Senior term loan—Tranche B	—				LIBOR + 2.75 plus ratchet and QPO	7.35	7.34	
	Senior term loan—Tranche C	—				LIBOR + 3.25 plus ratchet and QPO	7.85	7.84	
	Senior term loan—Tranche D	—					9.10	9.59	
	Multicurrency revolving credit	—				LIBOR + 2.25 plus ratchet and QPO	LIBOR + 2.25 plus ratchet and QPO	LIBOR + 2.25 plus ratchet and QPO	
Loan notes	A loan notes			—	—	n.k.	—	—	
	B loan notes			—	—	4.80	—	—	
	C loan notes			—	—	4.80	—	—	
High-yield bonds	High-yield bonds			10.3	10.30				
Mortgage facility	Mortgage facility			6.50	—				
2003 acquisition	Senior facility			n.k.	7.53				
	Deep discounted bonds		6.50	12.50	12.50				
	Bridge facilities		10.50	—	—				
	Mezzanine facility			—	—				
	Lease obligations	n.k.		n.k.	5.25		5.25	5.25	

Source: Company data, April 2006.

Note: The effective interes rate on the B loan notes includes the interest rate on the guarantee of the Tranche A of the senior term loan which amounts to 2.25%.

EXHIBIT 28.13

SUMMARY OF DEBENHAMS' FINANCIAL INFORMATION AND OPERATING DATA AS OF APRIL 2006 (£ MILLION)

	52 weeks ended Aug 30 2003 (U.K. GAAP)	52 weeks ended Aug 28 2004 (U.K. GAAP)	53 weeks ended Sep 3 2005 (U.K. GAAP)	53 weeks ended Sep 3 2005 (IFRS)	26 weeks ended Feb 26 2005 (IFRS)	26 weeks ended Mar 4 2006 (IFRS)
Gross transaction value[1]	1,810.2	1,902.9	2,086.8	2,086.8	1,113.3	1,216.8
Group turnover[2]/revenue[3]	1,435.9	1,491.8	1,608.7	1,608.7	869.2	957.8
Cost of sales	(1,187.4)	(1,235.4)	(1,272.4)	(1,294.9)	(673.2)	(755.6)
Gross profit	248.5	256.4	336.3	313.8	196.0	202.2
Distribution costs	(37.7)	(41.1)	(43.5)	(43.5)	(22.5)	(26.7)
Administrative expenses	(61.7)	(106.9)	(109.6)	(45.6)	(29.0)	(22.4)
Group operating profit[4]/operating profit before deemed disposal of a subsidiary[5]	**149.1**	**108.4**	**183.2**	**224.7**	**144.5**	**153.1**
Exceptional cost of sales	—	16.0	2.6	2.6	—	—
Exceptional distribution costs	—	2.8	—	—	—	—
Exceptional administrative expenses	14.2	30.5	1.8	1.8	—	—
Depreciation	82.9	91.3	89.1	85.4	43.2	40.4
Amortization	0.2	31.8	64.5	3.8	1.6	4.3
(Profit)/Loss on disposal of fixed assets	(1.6)	0.9	3.0	3.0	1.1	0.4
EBITDA[6]	**244.8**	**281.7**	**344.2**	**321.3**	**190.4**	**198.2**

Source: Company data, April 2006.

Notes: 1. Gross transaction value presents turnover on a gross basis, including the sales (excluding VAT) of concessions rather than just the commissions received from them. The directors believe gross transaction value represents a guide to the value of the overall activity of the group.
2. Group turnover is Debenhams' turnover in the group's U.K. GAAP financial information.
3. Revenue is Debenhams' revenue in accordance with IFRS and is equivalent to group turnover under U.K. GAAP.
4. Group operating profit is a term used in the group's U.K. GAAP financial information.
5. Operating profit before deemed disposal of a subsidiary is a term used in the group's IFRS financial information.
6. EBITDA is calculated as group operating profit before exceptional items under U.K. GAAP or operating profit before deemed disposal of subsidiary and before exceptional items under IFRS (both of which include amortization of landlord and developer contributions received), plus depreciation of tangible fixed assets and amortization of goodwill (for the purposes of U.K. GAAP), and other intangible assets, plus profits or losses on the disposal of fixed assets where these are included in operating profit.

EXHIBIT 28.14

DEBENHAMS' KEY PERFORMANCE METRICS PRE AND POST ACQUISITION

	52 weeks ended August 30 2003	53 weeks ended September 3 2005	Change
Gross transaction value (£ million)[1]	1,810.2	2,086.8	15.3%
Department store U.K. market share[2]	15.2%	18.6%	340 bp
Gross merchandise margin[3,6]	42.2%	42.9%	70 bp
Terminal stock percent of total stock[4,6]	7.2%	2.2%	(500) bp
Average trade creditor days[5,6]	27	60	33 days
Average working capital (£ million)[5,6]	25	(120)	(145)
Capital spend (£ per square foot)—new store[5,6]	178	108	(39.3)%
Capital spend (£ per square foot)—refurbishment[5,6]	30	7	(76.7)%

Source: Company data, April 2006.

Notes: 1. Gross transaction value presents turnover on a gross basis, including the sales (excluding VAT) of concessions rather than just the commissions received from them. The directors believe gross transaction value represents a guide to the value of the overall activity of the group.
   2. *Source:* Verdict 2005.
   3. Gross merchandise margin consists of gross transaction value less direct merchandise costs and reflects the direct profit made from the sale of products. In this exhibit, gross merchandise margin is expressed as a percentage of gross transaction value.
   4. Terminal stock is defined by the company as merchandise that has reached the end of its selling season.
   5. *Source:* Management accounts.
   6. Unaudited.

EXHIBIT 28.15

DEBENHAMS' STORE OPENINGS AND MODERNIZATIONS/ REFURBISHMENTS

	FY 2003	FY2004	FY2005	March 2006[1]
New department store openings	5	2	13[2]	1
Store modernizations/refurbishiments	9	6	6	11
Desire by Debenhams openings	n.a.	n.a.	1	1

Source: Company data, April 2006.

Notes: 1. Represents 26 weeks to March 4, 2006. In addition, two new department stores and one Desire by Debenhams store have been opened.
   2. Includes eight former Allders stores rebranded and traded as Debenhams. Not included under refurbishment numbers.

EXHIBIT 28.16

DEBENHAMS' EMPLOYEE NUMBERS INFORMATION

	August 30 2003	August 28 2004	September 3 2005	March 4 2006
Head office base headcount[1]	1,638	1,345	1,423	1,449
Store base headcount[2]	19,556	16,302	17,042	16,937
Actual head office headcount	1,638	1,471	1,583	1,642
Actual stores total headcount	19,556	16,440	18,829	18,620

Source: Company data, April 2006.

Notes: 1. Reflects the headcount for each relevant period relating to head office operations existing as of August 30, 2003.
2. Reflects the headcount for each relevant period relating to stores and their operations existing as of August 30, 2003.

EXHIBIT 28.17

DEBENHAMS' RESULTS OF IPO ON MAY 5, 2006 INCLUDING THE EXERCISE OF OVERALLOTMENT OPTIONS ON MAY 7, 2006

Number of shares pre IPO	500,141,027
Number of shares sold (including the overallotment)	535,897,436
—issued by the company	358,974,359
—sold by the Baroness Group	176,923,077
Retained by management	51,538,462
Retained by the Baroness Group	271,679,488

Source: Company data, April 2006.

29

Optos: A sight worth seeing

It was July 2002 and Anne Glover sat in her elegant St. James's office in the heart of London's investment community. Anne was Chief Executive and co-founder of Amadeus Capital Partners, one of the U.K.'s leading venture capital firms. Optos had been her project for six years, during which time only a few targets had been achieved on time and now the company required significant financing (Exhibit 29.1 lists the company's key milestones).

The last 12 months had been extraordinarily testing. In 2001, Alchemy and Apax, two major venture capitalists had refused to invest at the 11th hour, following months of lengthy due diligence. Optos and investors had been convinced that this time another VC would invest—yet again they were disappointed. There were no contingency plans. When the news arrived, the company had only £30,000 in its bank account and was spending £300,000 a month. Furthermore, a new CEO was about to join and the founder Douglas Anderson was going on a 3-month vacation to Greenland. To save the company from insolvency the Chairman, Barry Sealey, at a meeting of investors had passed around a hat and raised £1.2mn. But this money was only a short-term fix. Now was the time for Amadeus to make a significant investment or to pull out.

DOUGLAS ANDERSON AND THE VISION

Scottish-born Douglas Anderson was well acquainted with setbacks. Indeed, the dyslexia with which he was afflicted remained undiagnosed during his school years. With the odds stacked against him, he found a determination within himself to prove everyone wrong, completed his schooling, and went on to university to take a degree in industrial design.

His real passion, however, was mountaineering and, after a meeting with a veteran mountaineer, he decided to climb some unclimbed peaks in Tierra del Fuego, at the southern most part of Chile, at Cape Horn. In 1970, the only feasible way to climb in this region was to go by private boat and moor beside the mountains. But Douglas had little money, no boat, and could not sail.

So Douglas decided to build a boat, construct a slipway, and find a crew. After gathering all the information he could about the challenges ahead, Douglas prepared a detailed project plan and timetable covering the next three years to July 1973—the estimated time of arrival in Tierra del Fuego. Three years later and on schedule,

The case was co-authored with Michael Geary (LBS Sloan 2006).

Douglas and his team arrived in Chile to climb. On returning to Scotland, Douglas decided to set up an industrial design consultancy (Crombie Anderson), just north of Edinburgh.

In 1988, Douglas's 5-year-old son, Leif, developed sight problems. Douglas and his wife took Leif to see a number of specialists, but the problem was not detected until sometime later. Conventional retinal examination methods struggled to allow enough light through the narrow pupil to illuminate the retina and the field of view is limited, typically no more than 30 degrees for each viewing. These problems are exacerbated by patients blinking and moving their head. Examining a young child, like Leif, can be especially problematic. The delay of a few months meant that Leif would soon be blind in one eye. Leif's other eye also had problems, resulting in numerous visits to ophthalmologists:

> "After going through the ordeal of watching my son going blind and seeing him sit in discomfort on multiple occasions as doctors attempted to peer into the young lad's eye, I was focused on developing a product that would scan the whole retina, without dilation in a patient and in a customer-friendly way. The goal was simple. I wanted the 5-year-old being tested to say 'let me do that again'."

Douglas described his idea to some optometrists and ophthalmologists, who said there was no need for such a device. Furthermore, at an estimated manufacturing cost of £30,000, no business other than a major hospital could afford such a device and Douglas was soon to discover there was no engineering company in the world capable of designing such a device.

But the potential market was big. There are approximately 250 million eye examinations each year in the developed world measuring visual fields and acuity.

SCOTTISH BUSINESS LANDSCAPE AND FUNDING FOR EARLY-STAGE STARTUPS

Douglas needed funding to get his idea off the ground, but the environment in 1992 was not favorable. Throughout the 1980s the traditional Scottish industries, such as coal, iron, steel, and shipbuilding were run down, and by 1992 9.5% of the Scottish workforce were unemployed.

In 1992, Douglas was introduced to prospective business angels, Barry Sealey and Mike Rutterford. Douglas presented them with a single sheet of A4 paper, which set out the problem with the current equipment and practice for examining the eye, a broad definition of the product, which highlighted its ease of use and the scale of the potential market. There were no financial projections or valuations and there was no attempt to describe how the technology would work—this was the concept stage.

Mike and Barry, after three or four meetings with Douglas, decided to proceed. Douglas had the idea and needed £80,000 to develop the concept; Barry and Mike, together with seven other investors, had the finance. The joint venture was formed with Crombie Anderson owning 45%. The investment was to be used to investigate the market opportunity and to discover a plausible way to develop the product. This was the start of the company, which would later be spun out to form Optos.

It was also the first deal of Archangel Informal Investment, which has since gone on to invest in more than 50 startups. Archangel only invests in Scottish companies and is focused on life science and technology companies with global potential. The importance of business angels often goes unnoticed but, as was pointed out by Mike Rutterford, business angels remain one of the few sources of equity finance for early-stage and pre-revenue companies in Scotland seeking less than £2mn.

One of the features of Archangel's approach is that the founders of the startup should not give personal guarantees. However, Archangel does demand that the founder puts any cash he or she has into the business and commits all his or her time and energy to the business. Finally, Archangel insists that shareholdings are only in ordinary shares with no additional security even for late investors or funds.

To move the company forward much greater investment was required. Barry and Mike contacted their extensive range of business relationships to raise capital for the new venture. Exhibit 29.2 shows the investment rounds.

PRODUCT DEVELOPMENT

After almost three years of full-time work designing and testing, a prototype for the equipment eventually evolved, called the Panoramic 200 Scanning Laser Ophthalmoscope (P200). The P200 is an ophthalmic imaging system that generates a permanent ultra-wide field image of the back of eye.

A laser beam strikes an optically pure multifaceted polygon spinning at a very high resolution, which then deflects the light onto an ellipsoidal mirror and onto the retina. When light emitted from the lasers are reflected back from the retina through the optics, they are captured by light detectors and converted to digital output (Exhibit 29.3).

A feature of ellipsoidal mirrors is that they possess two focal points, meaning that any light originating at one focal point will be reflected equally at the other focal point. By placing the laser scanning system in one focal point of the mirror, a virtual scanning point is created in the other focal point. The virtual scanning point enables the retina to be imaged as if the real mechanical and optical components were inside the eye.

Using the P200 system (Exhibit 29.4), the practitioner can have an Optomap image of the retina without dilation, in a fast, cost-effective, and patient-friendly procedure. The whole process takes 0.25 seconds. By comparison, a full eye exam with a dilated pupil will take 30 minutes.

DISEASES OF THE BACK OF THE EYE AND OPTOS' TARGET MARKET

Diseases of the back of the eye (Exhibit 29.5 provides details of the eye structure) represent an area of significant unmet medical need given that they are among the leading causes of visual loss and blindness in people over 40, with about 180 million people worldwide affected (Exhibit 29.6 provides details of eye diseases).

In the developed world, the U.S. has the highest number of practitioners (optometrists and ophthalmologists) involved in the diagnosis of the retina. Each year there are approximately 100 million primary eye care examinations in the U.S., creating a $2bn market opportunity for the P200 (based on $20 per examination). Exhibit 29.7 gives details of addressable markets.

In the U.S., there is an established culture of preventative healthcare and patient payment at the point of service. Accordingly, a large number of eye examinations are performed each year. Each time a patient visits his or her eye care professional for a routine checkup, he or she expects a thorough examination, including the retina. One problem in the U.S. market is that general eye examinations are not a covered benefit by Medicare or most third-party payers. Currently, Optomap examinations are not eligible for reimbursement. This was a significant stumbling block for many venture capitalists. In the words of one VC:

> "if there is no reimbursement, there is no business."

The Canadian market is similar to that of the U.S. in that there is a strong emphasis on and awareness of the benefits of preventative care. However, acceptance levels for patient payment at point of service vary within the Canadian market.

The U.K. market is second in terms of patient coverage by eye care professionals, but the majority of its professionals are ophthalmic opticians. Ophthalmic opticians tend to focus on retail sales and refraction rather than preventative eye care. In the U.K. the majority of routine eye examinations include a brief check of the central area of the retina. Furthermore, the U.K. health system also has the slogan "free at the point of delivery", which builds a reluctance for patients to pay for healthcare at the point of service. The estimated addressable market is 400 practices.

Germany possibly represents the greatest opportunity in Europe for the sort of preventative eye healthcare delivery made possible using the Optos approach. The market is more focused on ophthalmologists delivering eye healthcare in large private practices and the concept of "patient pay" is being promoted. The estimated addressable market is 2,500 practices.

MANUFACTURING

By late 1995 the product concept was developed and patents had been applied for. But this was a long way from having a product that could be manufactured. In the words of David Cairns, Chief Technology Officer:

> "It is relatively easy to have the concept of a car, but it is entirely different to manufacture a car."

An ellipsoidal mirror had never been developed before. To overcome this difficulty the team developed a proprietary manufacturing process, unique to the company.

The team thought that a suitable polygon scanner could be bought off the shelf, with some modifications. Following the modifications, there was a production yield of only 15%. The team had to design and develop their own bespoke scanners, which had a production yield of over 90% and a low in-use failure rate.

A further design problem was that light from the laser reflected off the cornea. The light was reflected off hundreds of different planes and each patient had different characteristics. The problem was solved by positioning the eye on three axes, with no patient support. This was achieved by projecting a target zone onto the eye, when a red halo is seen the patient pressed the button and the image was taken. By overcoming such problems, Optos was able to produce a reliable machine capable of capturing an unprecedented field of view (Exhibit 29.8).

Optos decided at an early stage not to manufacture the P200 at its own facilities. Optos controls the assembly and testing of two critical modules in-house, thus retaining and developing key skills and, in the event of supply chain discontinuities, Optos is able to assemble the instruments completely.

The core intellectual property associated with the Optos scanning laser system (using the ellipsoidal mirror technology incorporated in the P200) is covered by a patent which expires in 2014 (U.S. Patent No. 5815242). In addition, Optos has a number of patent applications, trademarks, and knowhow which further protect its technological innovations.

The regulatory approval to use the P200 for retinal examinations in the U.S.A. came in February 1999 in the form of 510(k) clearance.[1] This accepts that the P200 performs at least as well as any similar device already in use.

European approval in the form of a CE Mark was obtained in 1999, after which the P200 was launched.

COMPETITION

Traditional retinal examination devices

The core instrument set included within these methods are direct ophthalmoscopes, binocular indirect ophthalmoscopes (BIO), and slit lamp biomicroscopes (Exhibit 29.9). The weaknesses of these approaches relative to modern standards of care are many—not least the quality of observations, requirement for pupil dilation, and the absence of direct permanent records.

Competitive profile summary of SLOs

The market for scanning laser ophthalmoscopes (SLOs) has risen from less than US$10mn in 1998 to US$70mn in 2002, representing strong growth for a relatively mature instrument. The four major SLOs on the market are:

- GDx—from Laser Diagnostic Technologies (LDT)
- Heidelberg Retinal Tomograph (HRT) from Heidelberg Engineering
- STRATUS Ocular Coherence Tomography (OCT) from Zeiss Meditec
- Retinal Thickness Analyser (RTA) from Talia Technology.

Exhibit 29.10 sets out the key elements of competing SLO products.

The GDx and HRT scan only a small part of the retina, limiting their diagnostic capabilities to glaucoma only. The STRAUSS OCT and RTA each scan a larger area. Both eye and common non-eye diseases, such as age-related macular degeneration (AMD) and diabetic retinopathy (DR), often develop in the periphery of the retina. All the competing devices require both space and capital expenditure from the practitioner.

Two other technologies ADIS 9000 and Panoret 1000 offer wide-angle views of the retina (Exhibit 29.11). These competing products offer a narrower field of view and require eye contact.

BUSINESS MODEL: THE "RAZOR/RAZOR BLADE" CONCEPT

To generate an acceptable gross margin, Optos needed to sell the equipment for around USD125,000 to USD150,000. In 1995, Patrick Paul, an early investor and board director, had a different solution based on one of his previous medical device busi-

---

1. 510(k) clearance is the FDA pre-market notification process that gives the device manufacturer permission to market the device.

nesses. To avoid the "lumpiness" typical of the sale of costly medical equipment, the Optomap scanner would employ a "razor/razor blade" business concept, in that it would charge customers on a per examination basis, although in the case of Optos the "razor" would be free.

In conjunction with pay per exam was vendor financing. A 3-year contract was set up between the leasing company and the practitioner, with the ownership of the device residing with the financier (after expiry of the contract, ownership would revert to Optos). The device would then be leased to the practitioner in return for a leasing fee of around USD2,000 per month (USD72,000 over 3 years).

Under the Access Technology Now (ATN) agreement between Optos and the vendor finance house (Citigroup and Rabobank are the current main counterparties), the finance house advances funds representing the net present value of the agreed minimum usage level by the practitioner. The USD2,000 minimum monthly payment discounted over the 3-year leasing term yields a USD63,000 upfront payment to Optos, which recognizes this revenue over the duration of the vendor-financing contract. In practical terms, this monthly fee represents the minimum charge for the practitioner's first 100 examinations. Payment for procedures in excess of this is made directly to Optos.

PROFIT AND LOSS IMPLICATIONS

Exhibit 29.12 illustrates the development of cash flow and profits for Optos from the placement of a P200 machine with a customer who extends the contract for 2 years when it expires at the end of Year 3. It is assumed that the customer conducts 125 Optomap examinations per month, which is 25 more than the 100 examinations stipulated in the minimum monthly payment (MMP) contract. If the customer conducts fewer than 100 procedures, he or she still has to pay the MMP and, accordingly, his or her cost per procedure increases.

CASH FLOW IMPLICATIONS

Annual cash generation from the user of the P200 machine, as shown in Exhibit 29.13, is the same as the revenue recognition in the profit and loss account. For the first 3 years, this comprises the MMP of USD2,000 (USD24,000 per annum) and the amount exceeding MMP. MMP is the revenue equivalent to 100 Optomap examinations each month, which is required by the 3-year contract between Optos and the practitioner.

Optos exchanges the 3-year MMP agreement with the practitioner for an upfront cash inflow of USD63,000 from the vendor finance house. The cash inflow to Optos represents the present value of the MMP over 3 years (i.e., USD72,000 discounted at 9%).

The MMP will in effect go to the finance house, and Optos only obtains the remaining cash payment (USD6,000) exceeding the MMP, for which it bills the practitioner. If the practitioner extends the contract in Year 4, all Optomap revenue of USD30,000 will flow to Optos. Optos does not need to incur any cash outflow to the finance house, as Optos has now repaid the lease and received the title of the P200 machine.

FINANCING 1995–2001

In late 1995, Anne Glover was asked by Brewin Dolphin Securities, one of the leading private client investment managers and stockbrokers in the U.K., to carry out due diligence on Optos to assess its viability for a pre-IPO placement. Anne visited the firm and was intrigued with what she found, even though the company was at an early stage of development.

> "At the time of my first visit to Optos it was not even pre-venture let alone pre-IPO."

Anne prepared an investment proposal for the firm, making a recommendation to invest. In spring 1996, Anne invested her own capital, together with two investment houses, and took a board seat.

Securing additional sources of finance was always a top priority for Optos. In 1998, Amadeus, a recently established venture capitalist firm, invested in Optos. The investment was suggested by Anne Glover, one of Amadeus' founding partners. Due diligence and the recommendation to invest was made by one of her colleagues. The investment was made out of Amadeus I, a £50mn fund raised in 1997.

In 2000, there was an attempt by ABN Amro to raise $25mn for Optos by a private placement, but this was unsuccessful, as it coincided with the tech market crash. In late 2000, Anne Glover contacted some of her venture capital colleagues at Apax and Alchemy Partners, suggesting they looked at Optos, as Amadeus I was fully committed. Both firms undertook extensive due diligence over a number of months. In June 2001 both declined to invest. The key reasons were the high cash requirements of the business and sensitivity to manufacturing costs, revenue per site, and number of sites.

This was deeply distressing for Optos. A new CEO, Stephane Sallmard, had recently been recruited, when the news broke that the capital raising had failed. After a long career in "blue chip" companies where cash was never a serious problem, Stephane joined Optos to find there was only £30,000 in the bank account, enough for the company to survive until the following Tuesday.

Barry Sealey called a meeting of the Archangels. At the meeting a handful of investors turned up to discuss the situation. If cash was not raised immediately the business would fold, but there was no certainty of alternative financing being found and the business would require considerably more funding to have a chance of success. In contrast to previous rounds of capital raising, when the company suggested the share price, which was always higher than the previous round, this time the investors decided the price. After some discussion, the assembled investors agreed a price of 80p per share and then wrote out cheques to a total value of £1.2mn.

GEOGRAPHIC EXPANSION

Douglas had believed the product would have enormous and instant appeal, but the reality was different. There was little interest in the P200 in the U.K., despite extensive promotional work from the prototype stage. The board considered that the U.K. market was not ready for the Optomap and decided in 1999 to launch in the U.S., where the market was much larger than that of the UK and customers were more willing to try the product.

Optos needed to build a complete sales, marketing, customer service, and management infrastructure to support the launch—a substantial task for a Scottish company with no presence in the U.S.

The development of long-term relationships was a priority for Optos. But, following the expense of developing the product and establishing a presence in the U.S., the business needed to show strong growth to the shareholders. The salesforce was put on a bonus structure that was weighted to sale and equipment installation in the customer's practice. Later, to improve average revenue per site, a new commission structure was put in place which paid out on condition Optomap usage levels were attained. This ensured the salesman became more selective in choosing sites and supported installation and staff training.

FINANCING IN 2002

As sales in the U.S. increased, so did losses and cash requirements for the company. In early 2002, Stephane addressed the board stating the business required around £5mn if it was to succeed. Optos began talks with WestLB who, after carrying out due diligence and a valuation, proposed a pre-IPO placement, to be followed by a listing on the U.K.'s Alternative Investment Market (AIM) about 18 months later.

Anne had concerns about the valuation Optos would achieve with an AIM listing, as the market had low levels of liquidity compared with the main London Stock Exchange. Furthermore, AIM investors may also be reluctant to invest sufficient time to understand fully the complexities of the Optos business. By now Amadeus had raised a new fund (Amadeus II, a £235mn fund, raised in 2000); however, this fund had different investors from those of Amadeus I and, with 2001 revenues of USD2mn, Optos remained a high-risk venture (Exhibits 29.14 and 29.15 provide company financial projections and comparisons whereas Exhibit 29.16 includes bios of management and directors).

APPENDIX

EXHIBIT 29.1

MILESTONES IN THE HISTORY OF OPTOS 1991–2001

Year	History overview
1991	• Customer need for improvements in eye disease detection and prevention methods results in proposition for ultra-wide retina exam possibilities
1994	• Technological breakthrough leads to a patent application (ellipsoidal mirror)
1995	• First prototypes constructed and product marketing initiated
1996	• First human eye is successfully imaged
	• The P200 is spun out of Crombie Anderson Associates into Optos plc
1998	• Optos secures additional funding bringing total capital raised to £6mn (approximately $9mn)
	• U.K. clinical trials commence
	• The P200 is approved for sale in Europe
	• U.S. headquarters opened. ISO9001 registration received
1999	• FDA 510(k) received
	• Clinical trails begin in the US. Panoramic200 receives CE marking
	• Optos raises an additional £5mn (approximately $8mn) in a private placement to support the U.S. launch of the P200, bringing the total amount of capital raised to over £11mn (approximately $18mn)
	• First availability in the U.S. Pay per patient launched. First Optomap customer goes live
2000	• P200 commercially available in the U.S.
2001	• Official launch in the U.K.

EXHIBIT 29.2

INVESTMENT ROUNDS IN OPTOS

	Capital raised (£ million)	Price (£)	New shares[1] ('000s)	Total issued ('000s)	Post-money valuation (£ million)
Oct-92	0.00	0.00	2,141	2,141	0.00
Oct-92	0.08	0.04	2,617	4,759	0.17
Sep-94	0.03	0.02	1,713	6,472	0.13
Mar-95	0.03	0.02	1,713	8,185	0.17
Aug-95	0.06	0.05	1,428	9,612	0.48
Feb-96	0.06	0.05	1,309	10,921	0.55
Apr-96	0.80	0.41	2,115	13,036	5.33
Jun-96	0.01	0.42	26	13,062	5.44
Apr-97	0.19	0.42	480	13,543	5.67
May-97	1.24	0.42	3,197	16,739	7.02
Mar-98	2.33	1.00	2,380	19,119	19.13
Apr-98	0.00	1.00	1,134	20,253	20.27
Jun-98	1.14	0.99	186	20,439	20.33
Sep-98	0.19	1.00	328	20,767	20.83
Sep-99	0.33	1.30	2,310	23,077	30.00
Feb-00	0.00	1.30	1,175	24,252	31.52
Jun-00	3.00	1.45	345	24,597	35.70
Apr-00	1.53	1.45	535	25,132	36.45
Sep-01	0.50	0.80	8,869	34,000	27.20
Nov-01	0.78	0.79	268	34,268	27.16

Note: 1. Shares adjusted for splits and bonus issues.

EXHIBIT 29.3

OPTOS TECHNOLOGY: P200 DEVICE

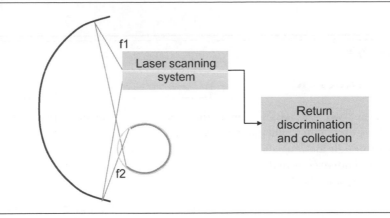

EXHIBIT 29.4

PANORAMIC 200 SCANNING LASER OPHTHALMOSCOPE

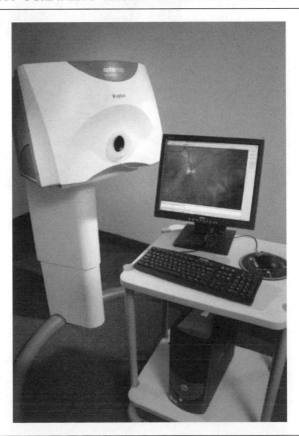

EXHIBIT 29.5

THE EYE STRUCTURE

The eye is a very complex gel-filled organ that consists of a transparent layer (the cornea) which protects the front of the eye so that light can pass through a controlling aperture (the iris/pupil), after which light is refracted through the lens and focused on the light-sensitive retina at the back of the eye. Messages from stimulated nerve cells in the retina pass to the optic disk (or optic nerve head) where the optic nerve conducts messages to the brain.

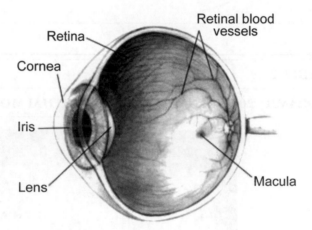

Retina A translucent, sensory membrane that lines the inner surface of the back of the eye to a point about two thirds of the way to the front of the eye. The retina consists of several layers. The outermost layer of the retina is the retinal pigment epithelium (RPE) which keeps the photoreceptors healthy and functioning. Inside the retina is the photoreceptor layer consisting of cells (rods and cones) that convert light to nerve impulses. The retina also contains blood vessels responsible for nourishing the tissue within it. The innermost layer of the retina is the nerve fiber layer (NFL), which consists of nerve cells connecting the light-sensitive cells to the optic nerve.

Macula The highly sensitive area near the middle of the retina that has a high density of nerve cells and is responsible for the central critical focusing of vision. The macula is used to read or stare intently at an object.

EXHIBIT 29.6

DISEASES OF THE EYE

- Glaucoma is a group of diseases that can gradually impair vision, often without any other symptoms. It is often caused by blockage of drainage canals in the eye. Loss of sight is caused by pressure damaging retinal nerve fibers or the optic nerve. Worldwide, 68 million people have been diagnosed with the disease, 2.2 million of whom are in the U.S. (1.9% of the population). This is a chronic disease that must be treated for life to minimize loss of vision. Early detection and regular assessment is critical in managing the disease effectively.

- Age-related macula degeneration (AMD) affects the most sensitive central part of the eye, the macula. The disease affects several million people worldwide, and some estimates indicate that this number could treble over the next 25 years as the population lives longer. It is the most common cause of blindness in the Western world in those over the age of 50. It is estimated that 14% to 24% of the U.S. population between the ages of 65 and 74 years have AMD and 35% of over-75s have the condition. Early detection is essential to prevent significant damage to the eye.

- The risk of blindness in diabetics is approximately 25 times greater than in those without the disease. According to the American Diabetes Association, diabetes causes up to 24,000 new cases of blindness annually in the U.S. in adults aged between 25 and 74 years. According to the National Eye Institute between 40% and 45% of Americans diagnosed with diabetes have some degree of diabetic retinopathy (DR) and between 600,000 and 700,000 have DR severe enough to cause vision loss.

- Stroke is the third leading cause of death in the U.S. (about 1 in every 15 deaths). About 2 million strokes occur each year in the Western world of which about 16% to 17% suffer a recurrent attack. The P200 can provide information on cardiovascular structures by imaging the blood vessels in the back of the eye. When this information is combined with blood pressure readings, accurate assessments of the risk of stroke are produced.

- Surprisingly, retinal scans may also have the potential to provide information on other conditions which do not have as clear a link with the function of the eye. One such condition that can be detected is early-onset colorectal cancer, which causes changes to the eye as an indirect by-product of the disease itself.

Eye disease statistics U.S.A.

Condition	Population (million)			Age group (years)
	Male	Female	Total	
Vision impairment	1.152	2.254	3.406	>40
Blindness	0.335	0.712	1.047	>40
Age-related macula degeneration	0.605	1.047	1.652	>50
Diabetic retinopathy	2.513	2.841	5.354	>18
Glaucoma	0.81	1.418	2.228	>40
Cataract	7.752	12.724	20.476	>40

Source: Prevent Blindness America and the National Eye Institute of the National Institutes of Health, 2002.

EXHIBIT 29.7

OPTOS MARKET SIZE

	U.S.	Canada	U.K.	Germany	France	Spain	Japan
Annual number of eye examinations (million)	103	8	21	28	18	24	40
Total number of practices	31,000	2,000	6,500	3,500	2,500	4,000	6,000
Number of addressable practices	20,000	1,300	400	2,500	1,700	2,200	4,000

EXHIBIT 29.8

200° VIEW OF THE RETINA IS VISIBLE IN A SINGLE IMAGE CAPTURE BY THE P200

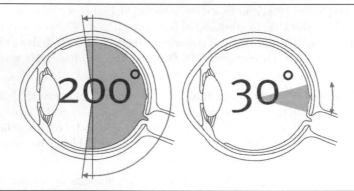

EXHIBIT 29.9

TRADITIONAL RETINAL EXAMINATION DEVICES

Direct ophthalmoscope This is a low-cost handheld device found universally in ophthalmology and optometric practices. It views a limited area of the retina under standard white light, using a simple lens arrangement. It covers as little as a 10° field of view (maximum) and provides no permanent record.

Binocular indirect ophthalmoscope The binocular indirect ophthalmoscope (BIO) with eye dilation is currently the standard practice in the eye care profession in the U.S. After the patient's eyes have been dilated, lights are focused onto the retina through a lens that is held close to the patient's eye and light is reflected back from the retina, which the practitioner perceives as a stereoscopic image. BIO produces a magnified image with a field of view up to 30°. If the practitioner is skilled and the patient willing to cooperate, the BIO can achieve a nearly complete image of the retina through multiple views.

Slit lamp biomicroscope A slit lamp biomicroscope is a more precise instrument. In addition to observing the retina, this device can also measure other parameters of eye physiology including intraocular pressure and corneal shapes.

EXHIBIT 29.10

SLO PRODUCTS

	P200	RTA	OCT	HRT II	GDx
Company	Optos	Talia	Zeiss	Heidelberg Engineering	LDT
Applications	Glaucoma, DR, AMD, and many others	Glaucoma, DR, and AMD	Glaucoma, DR, and AMD	Glaucoma, limited use in DR	Glaucoma only
Scan time	0.25 second	0.3 second	1 second	1 second	0.75 second
Purchase price	USD150,000	USD37,000	USD52,000	USD34,000	USD39,000
Field of view	Ultra-wide angle (2000), 80% of retina	Optical disk, surrounding area, and macula (300)	Optical disk, surrounding area, and macula (300)	Mainly optical disk (~50)	Mainly optical disk (~50)
Image	High-resolution digital color	High-resolution digital color	Low-resolution black and white	Color-coding topography	Color-coded view
Resolution	20 microns	52 microns	10 microns	300 microns	13 microns

EXHIBIT 29.11

ADVANCED RETINA SCANNING TECHNOLOGIES

	ADIS 9000	Panoret-1000	P200
Manufacturer	Clarity Medical Systems Inc.	Medibell Medical Vision Technologies Ltd.	Optos
Illumination method	White light through the pupil	White light through the sclera (white part of eye)	Green and red laser light through the pupil
Detection method	In contact with the eye	In contact with the eye	Non-contact
Field of view	120°	130°	200°
Pupil dilation required	Yes	No	No
Resolution	20 microns	20 microns	20 microns

EXHIBIT 29.12

P200 REVENUE MODEL

USD '000s	Year 1	Year 2	Year 3	Year 4	Year 5	Total
Total return	30	30	30	30	30	150
COGS	−10	−10	−10	−10	−10	−50
Field sales and support	−9	−4	−4	−4	−4	−25
Central services	−8	−3	−3	−8	−3	−25
Interest	−5	−3	−2			−10
Total cost	−32	−20	−19	−22	−17	−110
Profit before tax (PBT)	−2	10	11	8	13	40

EXHIBIT 29.13

P200 CASH FLOW MODEL

USD '000s	Installation	Year 1	Year 2	Year 3	Year 4	Year 5	Total
Total revenue		30	30	30	30	30	150
Revenue—MMP		24	24	24			72
Revenue–amount exceeding MMP		6	6	6	30	30	78
Lease funding	63						63
Lease repayment (including interest)		−24	−24	−24			−72
Principal payment		−19	−19	−19			−57
Interest payment		−5	−5	−5			−15
CAPEX	−45	−1	−1	−1	−1	−1	−50
Field sales and support	−5	−4	−4	−4	−4	−4	−25
Central services	−5	−3	−3	−3	−3	−3	−25
Net cash flow	**8**	**−2**	**−2**	**−2**	**17**	**22**	**41**

EXHIBIT 29.14

OPTOS FINANCIAL INFORMATION

Profit and loss (USD '000s)	Actual 2000	Actual 2001	Estimate 2002	Estimate 2003	Estimate 2004	Estimate 2005
Net revenues	327	1,969	8,932	22,827	40,150	60,501
Sales growth (%)		502	354	156	76	51
COGS	−364	−1,955	−3,305	−12,930	−20,614	−21,250
Gross profit	−37	14	5,627	9,897	19,536	39,251
SG&A	−7,966	−10,414	−14,729	−20,414	−23,518	−34,960
Selling and distribution costs	−1,937	−5,196	−6,544	−5,937	−8,005	−12,136
Administration expenses	−6,029	−5,218	−8.185	−14,478	−15,513	−22,824
EBITDA	−7,448	−9,064	−4,281	−859	15,420	28,603
Depreciation	−555	−1,336	−4,821	−9,658	−19,401	−24,313
Operating profit	−8,003	−10,400	−9,102	−10,517	−3,982	4,290
Interest (net)	−98	−507	−1,518	−3,033	−4,985	−7,313
Profit before tax	−8,101	−10,907	−10,620	−13,550	−8,967	−3,022
Taxation		187			0	
Net profit	−8,101	−10,720	−10,620	−13,550	−8,967	−3,022
Gross margin (%)	n.a.	1	63	43	49	65
Operating margin (%)	n.a.	n.a.	−101.9	−46.1	−9.9	7.1
Selling and distribution as % sales	n.a.	n.a.	73.3	26.0	19.9	20.1
Administrative as % sales	n.a.	n.a.	91.6	63.4	38.6	37.7
EBITDA margin (%)	n.a.	n.a.	−47.9	−3.8	38.4	47.3
Installationa (net) (units)	20	50	180	360	700	785
Total installations (units)	20	70	250	610	1,310	2,095
Average revenue per site per annum (USD)		61,000	55,825	53,086	41,823	35,537

Balance sheet (USD '000s)	Actual 2000	Actual 2001	Estimate 2002	Estimate 2003	Estimate 2004	Estimate 2005
Assets						
Non-current assets						
Property, plant, and equipment	2,219	3,949	18,100	36,592	55,065	64,649
Intangible assets					7	8
Net fixed assets	*2,219*	*3,949*	*18,100*	*36,592*	*55,073*	*64,657*
Current assets						
Trade	609	962	3,300	3,411	3,899	6,702
Inventory	1,523	1,587	1,300	3,616	2,240	3,532
Cash	580	1,621	7,280	1,058	1,850	1,350
Deferred tax				0	0	
Total current assets	*2,712*	*4,170*	*11,880*	*8,085*	*7,989*	*11,584*
Total assets	*4,931*	*8,119*	*29,980*	*44,676*	*63,061*	*76,241*

(continued)

EXHIBIT 29.14 (cont.)

Balance sheet (cont.) (USD '000s)	Actual 2000	Actual 2001	Estimate 2002	Estimate 2003	Estimate 2004	Estimate 2005
Liabilities						
Current liabilities						
Trade	388	1,136	5,746	6,067	6,553	9,646
Financial liabilities	1,986	2,917	5,917	16,500	31,855	39,749
Total current liabilities	*2,375*	*4,054*	*13,321*	*22,567*	*38,408*	*49,394*
Non-current liabilities						
Financial liabilities	2,132	3,076	18,300	37,300	45,708	50,877
Other	303	155			3,103	3,149
Total non-current liabilities	*2,435*	*3,231*	*18,300*	*37,300*	*48,811*	*54,028*
Equity						
Share capital	727	727	727	727	727	727
Share premium	14,797	26,230	33,810	33,810	33,810	33,810
Other reserves	560	560	1,125	1,125	1,125	1,125
Retained earnings	−15,963	−26,683	−37,303	−50,853	−59,820	−62,842
Total equity	*121*	*834*	*−1,641*	*−15,191*	*−24,158*	*−27,180*
Total equity and liabilities	**4,931**	**8,119**	**29,980**	**44,676**	**63,061**	**76,241**
Net debt	3,538	4,372	16,937	52,742	75,713	89,276

Cash flow (USD '000s)	Actual 2000	Actual 2001	Estimate 2002	Estimate 2003	Estimate 2004	Estimate 2005
EBITDA	**−7,448**	**−9,064**	**−4,281**	**−859**	**15,420**	**28,603**
Change in working capital	−902	331	2,559	−2,106	1,374	−1,003
Other	−245	−233		−583		−3,563
Net cash inflows from operating activities	**−8,596**	**−8,966**	**−1,722**	**−3,549**	**16,794**	**24,037**
Cash flow used in investment activities						
Interest (net)	−71	−505	−1,513	−4,107	−5,249	−3,703
Net capital expenditure	−2,042	−3,066	−18,972	−28,149	−37,882	−33,897
Intangible asset development costs						
Other		1,053	1,497		3,367	
Net cash flow from investment activities	**−2,113**	**−2,518**	**−18,988**	**−32,256**	**−39,764**	**−37,600**
Net proceeds/(payments) from/of finance leases	937	1,875	18,224	29,583	23,762	13,063
Proceeds from share issue	3,178	11,433	8,145	0	0	0
New long-term loans	2,406					
Repayment of long-term loans	−120	−783				
New short-term loans						
Repayment of short-term loans						
Interest paid						
Net cash flow from financing activities	**6,401**	**12,525**	**26,369**	**29,583**	**23,762**	**13,063**
Net increase/(decrease) in cash	**−4,308**	**1,041**	**5,659**	**−6,222**	**792**	**−500**

Exchange rate USD per £1.00

	Year ended December 31	
	Period end	**Average rate**
2001	1.4543	1.4396
2002	1.6095	1.5025
2003	1.7842	1.6347
2004	1.9160	1.8330
2005	1.7188	1.8204
2006 (February 9)	1.7411	1.7654

EXHIBIT 29.15

COMPANY COMPARISONS (APRIL 16, 2002)

Limited number of direct peers and depressed near-term earnings

Optos has a limited number of direct competitors and all of them either constitute part of a large corporation (e.g., Zeiss Meditec and Canon) or are privately held (e.g., Medibell Medical Vision Technologies, Clarity Medical Systems, and Kowa).

	Currency	EV/Sales						EV/EBITDA					
		2001	2002E	2003E	2004E	2005E	2006E	2001	2002E	2003E	2004E	2005E	2006E
Denmark													
William Demant	USD	4.9	3.7	3.3	2.8	2.5	2.1	22.3	17.1	14.8	12.9	11.2	8.7
Germany													
Fresenius Medical Care	USD	1.5	1.4	1.2	1.1	0.9	0.7	7.4	6.9	6.1	5.3	4.4	3.6
Fresenius AG	USD	1.1	1.0	0.9	0.8	0.7	0.7	7.6	6.0	5.1	4.4	3.8	3.4
Sweden													
Gambro	USD	1.2	1.0	1.0	0.9	0.8	0.7	7.6	6.4	5.6	5.1	4.7	4.3
Nobel Biocare	USD	6.0	4.8	3.8	3.0	2.4	1.8	27.4	18.5	12.1	9.5	7.5	5.9
Switzerland													
Phonak	USD	2.9	2.3	2.0	1.7	1.5	1.3	16.1	12.5	10.3	8.2	7.2	6.3
Straumann	USD	9.0	6.5	5.3	4.3	3.5	2.8	27.1	18.5	15.1	11.9	9.4	7.6
Synthes-Stratec	USD	6.6	5.3	4.5	3.8	3.2	2.7	15.6	12.5	10.6	8.9	7.6	6.4
U.K.													
Smith & Nephew	USD	2.9	2.8	2.5	2.2	2.0	1.8	14.2	12.9	10.9	9.2	7.7	6.7
Pan-European average		**4.0**	**3.2**	**2.8**	**2.4**	**2.0**	**1.7**	**14.4**	**11.6**	**9.6**	**8.1**	**6.9**	**5.8**
United States													
Abbott	USD	4.1	3.7	3.4				14.4	12.9	11.3			
Apogent	USD	3.0	2.7	2.4				9.9	9.0	8.1			
Bausch & Lamb	USD	1.2	1.1	1.1				7.3	6.3	5.7			
Baxter	USD	3.6	3.2	2.8				14.3	12.4	13.6			

Beckman Coulter	USD	1.1	1.0	0.9	5.7	5.3	4.9
Becton Dickinson	USD	2.5	2.3	2.2	10.0	9.7	9.0
Boston Scientific	USD	4.7	4.5	4.1	16.9	15.1	12.7
DaVita (formerly TRC)	USD	1.9	1.8	1.7	9.6	9.9	8.8
Dentsply	USD	2.2	1.7	1.5	10.6	8.6	7.7
Guidant	USD	3.4	3.1	3.1	9.4	8.7	8.1
Johnson & Johnson	USD	4.9	4.4	4.4	16.9	14.6	12.6
Medtronic	USD	9.2	8.0	6.8	23.3	21.0	17.8
PerkinElmer	USD	1.4	1.5	1.4	8.2	15.4	9.9
Renal Care Group	USD	1.9	1.7	1.5	8.1	7.4	6.7
Sonic Innovations	USD	1.7	1.4	1.1	−15.6	114.4	13.5
St. Jude Medical	USD	2.3	2.1	1.8	8.6	7.6	6.6
Stryker	USD	4.2	3.8	3.4	16.0	14.6	12.7
Sybron Dental	USD	1.8	1.8	1.7	6.6	6.2	5.8
VISX	USD	2.5	2.7	2.4	8.8	9.8	6.8
Waters Corporation	USD	3.3	3.1	2.8	11.0	10.2	8.7
U.S. averages		**5.0**	**4.5**	**4.2**	**16.4**	**14.5**	**12.7**
Sector breakdown							
U.S. Medtech	USD	5.0	4.5	4.2	16.4	14.5	12.7
European Medtech	USD	4.0	3.2	2.8	14.4	11.6	9.6
Orthopedics	USD	5.1	4.6	3.9	16.5	14.4	12.5
Dialysis/Blood	USD	1.5	1.3	1.2	7.9	7.2	6.3
Cardiovascular	USD	7.5	6.6	5.7	20.0	17.9	15.3
Dental	USD	5.0	3.8	3.1	19.3	13.7	10.7
Ophthalmics	USD	1.5	1.5	1.4	7.7	7.1	6.0
Hearing instruments	USD	4.1	3.2	2.8	20.3	15.7	13.4
Diversified	USD	4.5	4.1	3.9	15.8	13.8	12.3
Analytics	USD	2.4	2.2	2.0	9.1	10.3	8.1

Source: Amadeus Capital Partners.

EXHIBIT 29.16

MANAGEMENT AND DIRECTORS (2002)

Barry Sealey   Joined the company in 1992 as Chairman. Mr. Sealey spent 31 years with Christian Salvesen plc, a large food distribution company, the last 8 years of which he was Group Managing Director. He is presently on the board of Stagecoach plc, Scottish American Investment Company plc, and Wilson Byard Ltd. He is also currently chairman of one of the British National Health Service Authorities. Mr. Sealey holds a Bachelor of Arts degree with honors in natural sciences from St. John's College Cambridge, England.

Stephane Sallmard   Joined the company in June 2001 as Chief Executive Officer, and is responsible for overseeing global operations for the company. Previously, Mr. Sallmard was Managing Director of Lectra Systems, a Paris-based technology group and his experience includes almost 30 years working in the international medical business arena. Mr. Sallmard holds a Master's degree in electronic engineering from Ecole Supérieure d'Electricité Industrielle in Paris and completed an executive management program at the Kellogg School of Management at Northwestern University.

Douglas Anderson   Founded the company in 1992 and is an executive director. Mr. Anderson is the Chairman of Crombie Anderson Associates Ltd., a multi-disciplinary design consulting firm specializing in technology-based product development. Mr. Anderson holds a Higher National Diploma in industrial design (engineering) from Napier University in Edinburgh, Scotland and is a member of the the Association for Research in Vision and Ophthalmology (ARVO), Bethesda, U.S.A.

Ian Stevens   Joined the company in 1998 as Chief Financial Officer and Director of Operations, before his appointment as General Manager of Optos Inc. North America, where he has responsibility for the U.S. and Canada. Mr Stevens holds a Master's degree in economics from the University of Edinburgh and is a professionally qualified accountant.

David Cairns   Is Chief Technology Officer and has been with the Company since 1994. Mr. Cairns holds an Honors B.Sc. degree in physics and electronics from St. Andrews University, an M.Sc in electronics engineering, and an MBA, the latter two from Cranfield University.

Anne Glover   Joined the company in April 1996 as director. Ms. Glover is a managing director of Amadeus Capital Partners Ltd., a U.K.-based venture capital fund, which primarily invests in high-technology and internet companies in the U.K. and Ireland. Ms. Glover's previous experience includes Apax Partners & Co. Ventures Ltd. in the U.K., Bain & Co. in Boston, Cummins Engine Co. and Bell Labs. Ms. Glover graduated from Clare College, Cambridge and the Yale School of Management.

Patrick Paul   Joined the company in April 1996 as director. Mr. Paul is a founder and subsequently Chairman and Chief Executive Officer of Support Systems International Inc. He is also the Chairman of Tissue Science Laboratories Ltd. and Vertical Asset Management Ltd. and various private investment companies. Mr. Paul holds a B.Sc. degree with honors in engineering from the University of Southampton, England and is a qualified chartered accountant.

Michael Rutterford   Joined the company in 1992 as director. Mr. Rutterford was previously founder and Chief Executive Officer of Stuart Wyse Ogilvie Estate Agents Ltd. and an executive officer of General Accident Property Services, part of the General Accident insurance group. Mr. Rutterford is a director of various other private investment companies.

30

Capital for Enterprise U.K.: Bridging the SME early-stage finance gap

While getting to the office one winter morning in 2009, Rory Earley, CEO of Capital for Enterprise UK, the organization set up to manage the Enterprise Capital Fund (ECF) program, thought about the report he had just started preparing on the program's first 4 years of operations. That morning he wondered what changes, if any, could be made to the program to address current changes in the private equity (PE) industry and what changes, if any, were necessary to address the issues that his team's research had highlighted in the current ECF program.

AN "EQUITY GAP"?

He recalled the origins of the program. In their role as advisors to the U.K. government on venture capital funding, Earley and his colleagues had promoted the ECF program based on the following diagnosis: despite having a very developed buyout industry, the U.K. entrepreneurial and investor community was still facing significant hurdles regarding investments in the £250,000 to £2mn range. There were both supply-side constraints (the lack of existing funds willing to invest in all types of early-stage businesses) and demand-side constraints (the lack of awareness of entrepreneurs of such funds and of skills to structure proposals attractive to external investors).

A number of facts in earlier studies from 2003 to 2004 to which Earley had contributed had struck key people in the sector as well as in the government.[1] One

---

1. Including: HM Treasury & Small Business Service, *Bridging the Finance Gap: Next Steps in Improving Access to Growth Capital for Small Businesses*, December 2003.

This case was written by Professors Josh Lerner of HBS and Eli Talmor of LBS and MBA 2010 students Ananth Vyas Bhimavarapu and Thibaud Simphal of LBS, who prepared this case for the Public Policy Forum on Venture Capital at the Quebec City Conference, October 2009, with the support of the Coller Institute of Private Equity at London Business School. The authors thank Gilles Duruflé, President, Quebec City Conference Public Policy Forum and Rory Earley, CEO, Capital for Enterprise Ltd. for their support and the information. It does not however reflect in any way the official opinions of Capital for Enterprise Ltd. or the U.K. government. Copyright © 2010 President and Fellows of Harvard College.

chart (Exhibit 30.1) showed that very few small to medium-sized enterprises (SMEs) had recourse to equity financing from venture capital (VC) funds and other equity financing sources. In fact, this represented only 3% of total SME financing in the U.K. in 2002, which grew to 8% in 2007. A table (Exhibit 30.2) highlighted the fact that business angel investment was constrained in size to under £250,000. Another chart (Exhibit 30.3) showed that the early-stage investment space was not covered by VC funds as U.K. VC funds seemed to focus heavily and increasingly on expansion and management buyin and buyout investments.

This evidence was corroborated in particular by a number of British Venture Capital Association (BVCA) documents that argued that there was a strong need for equity investment among SMEs and a stark difference between an estimated number of startups requiring equity financing and the number of startups effectively receiving financing (Exhibit 30.4).

PREVIOUS ATTEMPTS BY THE U.K. GOVERNMENT TO TACKLE THE "EQUITY GAP"

Later that morning, while beginning work on the report, Earley looked back at the existing financing instruments that the U.K. government had put in place, a number of them under his supervision.

Indeed, during the 1990s, the inability of startup businesses and SMEs with high growth potential to raise finance required to meet their needs was increasingly perceived in several departments of the U.K. government as being caused by structural market failures resulting in "finance gaps". In fact, the finance gap had been noted as long ago as 1931; the U.K. government set up the Industrial and Commercial Finance Corporation (ICFC), which later became 3i, which for many years provided a source of long-term funding for SMEs. Despite the dynamic business angel and private investment community, on one side, and of the structured PE industry, on the other, these gaps remained, which showed that the markets themselves were failing to allocate capital efficiently across all ranges of required PE investments. Unlike the U.S., these gaps were perceived across Europe as endemic to the continent due to lack of an entrepreneurial culture.

The government therefore gradually introduced measures that played an important role in addressing different parts of the finance gap (Exhibit 30.5). The measures covered a broad range of incentives. The Enterprise Investment Scheme (EIS) and venture capital trusts (VCTs)—put in place in 1994 and 1995, respectively—were tax incentives whose objective was to attract private capital investments in new ventures. A number of other initiatives had been put in place, albeit with a much more limited scope. For example, the U.K. High Technology Fund of Funds, launched in 2000, was set to invest in technology VC funds. A number of seed funding programs had been launched as well, such as the Early Growth Funding Program (EGFP) to co-invest alongside business angels. Other measures focused on providing debt finance to SMEs, incentives for university spinouts, and developing regional development funds.

Each of these programs had demonstrated some success in their target segment and the government was examining ways in which these measures could be enhanced to further improve their effectiveness. However, despite their number and range and the fact that these programs seemed to have had an important impact in their target segments, they had limited success in tackling the £250,000 to £2mn equity gap for startup and early-stage businesses that seek risk capital.

Venture capitalists were finding it difficult to start funds focusing on such investments, while witnessing a clear difficulty of entrepreneurs in attracting capital for exactly the same types of investments. In addition, there was a constant drift of VC funds and private investments toward later-stage businesses and buyouts, the typical deal size had steadily been increasing and the number of deals up to £1mn were, on the other hand, steadily decreasing.

LIMITS OF PREVIOUS PROGRAMS

Various factors seemed to contribute to the limited effectiveness of these measures in addressing the equity gap. Since returns on investment are not expected for some time, equity finance is more suitable for higher risk SMEs than debt finance provided under the Small Business Loan Guarantee (SBLG) program. Investments in early-stage and startup companies through the Early Growth Funding Program (EGFP) averaged around £50,000, which is significantly below £250,000 to £1mn. Regional venture capital funds (RVCFs) were targeted towards smaller investments and were time limited. Initial investments were restricted to amounts of up to £250,000, with an opportunity for a follow-on investment of up to £250,000 after 6 months. Investments in EIS by business angels are generally below £250,000 and often less than £100,000. Finally, VCTs tended to invest in more mature companies with an established track record and positive cash flows, and can syndicate to invest in amounts in excess of £1mn. Almost a third of VCT investee companies were later quoted on the Alternative Investment Market (AIM) or "off exchange" (OFEX), and around a fifth used the program primarily to finance management buyouts/buyins.

For financing not constrained by the limitations of the above incentives, SMEs needed to look to formal VC providers to meet their risk capital needs. However, many commercial venture capitalists were and still are reluctant to invest in these small amounts for a variety of reasons:

- *High transaction costs*—to overcome information asymmetries associated with early-stage companies, investments are made only after due diligence processes involving costly employment of accountants, lawyers, and industry specialists, especially if a new technology is involved. Also, the costs involved in seeking out these opportunities are significant. For a smaller value deal, such costs represent a larger proportion, thus making them uneconomical.

- *Largely fixed ongoing running costs*—investors in early-stage companies with less experienced management teams will often contribute significant time and effort to mentoring and providing management support, adding significantly to the investor's costs.

- *Perceived risk is higher*—risk is perceived to be higher when the management team or the SME's product and market tend to be unproven.

- *Lack of exit options*—cyclical trade sales and illiquid markets for trading in smaller firm shares decrease the exit options for investors.

LAUNCHING ENTERPRISE CAPITAL FUNDS

The government therefore believed that a more wide-reaching and flexible structure was needed to address this equity gap. Research and anecdotal evidence showed that the companies concerned by the gap were a small but important source of innovative growth-oriented businesses and they continued to face difficulties in attracting funding. This provided a case for additional but targeted government intervention.[2,3,4] Government intervention in venture capital can primarily take two forms—direct and indirect.

Direct intervention

The role of venture capitalist is taken on by the government which directly performs all the required activities for investing risk capital—selection, evaluation, monitoring, and exit, in the identified problem areas or gaps. In this scenario, both the general partner and the limited partner are the government. However, this form of intervention is fraught with many problems as the idea of civil servants performing the role of professional risk capital managers and identifying investments with potential for growth is unproven. Another argument is that direct involvement by the government may lead to "crowding out" of the market due to misallocation of capital.

Indirect intervention

Indirect intervention is the more widely accepted form of intervention whereby the government acts a limited partner and chooses a professional risk capital manager as the general partner. The assumption underlying this is that professional risk capital managers are better skilled and experienced at making investment decisions as opposed to a civil servant. As a limited partner, the government is not involved in the operations of the fund. Such structures where the government acts as a limited partner on par with other private investors are called hybrid venture capital funds. Sometimes, the government invests in a "fund of funds" whose general partner then allocates finance to specific venture capital funds operating in the government's area of interest.

In order to incentivize a professional venture capitalist and private investors to invest in a problem area or gap where there is market failure, government has to use a structure where the profit distribution is skewed towards private investors and the return is attractive for them. These are called "equity enhancement" programs and can be classified into five categories:[5]

a. *Differential timing of investment "drawdowns"*—when public funds are drawn down first and returned last, the duration of the private investor's funds is shortened, thereby increasing its internal rate of return.

b. *Leveraging the returns to private investors with debt*—the government's investment comes in the form of a loan. The leverage has a multiplier effect

2. Quysner, D., *Enterprise Capital Funds*, Presentation, NAVCS Public Policy Forum, October 2008.

3. HM Treasury & Small Business Service, *Bridging the Finance Gap: A Consultation on Improving Access to Growth Capital for Small Businesses*, April 2003.

4. HM Treasury, *Budget 2009*, April 2009, Para. 4.33.

5. Jääskeläinen, M. et al., "Profit distribution and compensation structures in publicly and privately funded hybrid venture capital funds," *Research Policy* (2007).

and increases the private investor's return when the internal rate of return is higher than the interest rate on the loan.

c. *Capping the profits entitlement of the public investor*—by capping the profit that the government may receive on its investment, private investor and venture capitalist return is enhanced.

d. *Guarantee of compensation to the private investor*—the government provides downside protection for the private investor's capital by guaranteeing (usually up to 75%) the private investor's total loss. However, such guarantees are seen to create a moral hazard as they don't incentivize an investor for making good decisions, but rather reduce the cost of poor investment decisions. WFG, tbg, and KfW in Germany, SOFARIS in France, and the Equity Guarantee Program in Denmark are examples of such programs.

e. *Buyback options*—private investors have the option of buying out the government's share of the fund. The terms of this buyback are arranged ex ante and give the private investors an incentive to provide for an early exit for the government. This was first introduced in the Israeli *Yozma* program and has subsequently been copied by other countries.

It seemed to several officials in the government that a suitably designed variant of the U.S. Small Business Investment Company (SBIC) program, a very successful hybrid equity enhancement VC program introduced in the U.S. in 1958, may be appropriate to attract investors with an appetite for smaller scale early-stage investment. Under this program, SBICs can borrow money at low rates from the capital markets, which they invest along with privately raised capital in U.S. small companies. The U.S. government provides the guarantee for the borrowed money. The SBIC program was a major success in the U.S., with SBICs representing 58% of venture capital investments in SMEs by 2002.

A variant of the SBIC program adapted for the U.K. would increase the commercial viability of small investments by offering investors enhanced returns through the use of government debt to invest alongside private capital. The fund of funds program would reduce the minimum amount of private capital required for setting up a commercially viable venture capital fund, thereby attracting risk capital managers who specialize in smaller investments. It would enhance the impact of business angels on a demand-led market-driven basis and offer a flexible framework within which local and regional networks can match public and private capital with their investment expertise in a cost-effective manner.

In order to design a SBIC program tailored for the U.K., the government needed to consider various issues as well as U.K.-specific parameters. Mainly, the program should minimize the impact on existing sources of finance, safeguard public funds. and complement existing programs.

This posed a number of questions for each key feature of a new U.K. program. A team was set up to develop the concept in detail and to run the first phases of the program, which was to be called the Enterprise Capital Fund (ECF) program.

Appointed to manage this team was Rory Earley. Earley was a former senior investment manager at Westport Private Equity Ltd., where he designed and invested in several significant VC funds. Earley had previously been in charge of developing and implementing the U.K. government's first interventions in venture capital funds in the 1990s. He also had experience as chair of a European Union (EU) expert group on risk capital, member of the Investment Task Force advising the U.K. government, and a director of Greece's first venture capital investment company (TANEO). The team was created within the Department for Business Innovation & Skills and was based in Sheffield.

KEY QUESTIONS AND OPTIONS FOR THE ECF PROGRAM DESIGN

Earley and his team were aware of the many challenges in setting up the ECF program. The team defined the ECF program and its funds' objectives as being "to increase the availability of growth capital for SMEs affected by the equity gap by

- encouraging an increased flow of private capital into the equity gap, by adjusting the risk–reward profile for private investors making such investment, and

- lowering the barriers to entry for entrepreneurial risk capital managers by reducing the amount of private capital needed to establish a viable venture fund."

In addition to articulating clear objectives and mandates, they identified six key design criteria in which important choices had to be made.

1 Private capital requirements

Before a prospective venture capital manager can apply for funding under the ECF program, it was believed important that he or she would need to have raised or secured commitments for a minimum amount of private capital. The related questions in the design of the ECF program were as follows:

— *Source of private capital:* while there are many possible sources of private capital (pension funds and other institutional investors, corporate finance boutiques, retail banks, corporate investors, the European Investment Fund, non-bank financial institutions, and high-net-worth or sophisticated individual investors), the ECF program team needed to ensure that ECFs would be funded only by appropriate investors, those that could continue to meet drawdown requests throughout the lives of the funds and not just divert private investors away from other government-sponsored programs and reduce their effectiveness.

— *Fund size:* two factors would need to be considered when deciding the right size for an ECF. The total size of the fund including private capital and loan should be large enough to allow for diversification in the portfolio and for follow-on investments to ensure viability. At the same time, the fund size should not be set at a level which increases the barriers to entry for setting up new funds and reduces its attractiveness for new fund managers.

The team organizing the ECF program faced several dilemmas: What minimum commitments should the ECF program set, and should there be a minimum fund size? For scale reasons, the minimum size of a viable fund was at least £10mn, which would require at least £3.3mn of private capital assuming the leverage available was up to twice the private capital offered. In the U.S., the minimum amount of private capital was set at $10mn, thus implying a total fund size of $30mn. Considering the novelty of the program, the program team decided not to set a minimum fund size in the first round of applications, called the Pathfinder round, thus allowing prospective ECF managers to choose a size that complemented their business model.

2   Government loan conditions

A loan from government was seen as key to the success of the ECF program because it would offer investors enhanced returns, thereby helping offset the transaction costs and other factors that reduce the attractiveness of small investments. The related issues were as follows:

— *Source of loans:* in the U.S. SBIC model, the government does not finance the leverage directly. Instead, it provides a guarantee for debentures (bonds) that SBICs issue to raise their leverage on the open capital markets.

— *Proportion of government finance:* in determining the loan that can be provided on the back of private capital, the following three factors need to be considered. A high ratio of loans to private capital would offer a large risk–return profile to private investors. The default risk to a government loan and, therefore, to taxpayer funds would also increase unless it was compensated for by a tougher capital impairment regime. The amount invested would be larger, so the potential upside would be higher; but, since private capital would still take first loss, a negative return would lead to the private investors being unable to recover their investment. Second, a high risk–return profile could lead to a more conservative investment strategy (e.g., favoring enterprises with a track record and/or cash flow) if investors sought greater downside protection. Finally, a larger total fund size could encourage larger investments.

It might be appropriate to adopt a tiered approach, thereby targeting more generous assistance on the smallest funds—a similar approach was adopted in the U.S. As a quid pro quo for the additional risk associated with higher leverage ratios, it might be appropriate to increase its profit participation rate in line with the leveraged capital ratio actually drawn down.

— *Maximum loan amount:* the limit on the total loan that can be raised by one SBIC in the U.S. is $115mn. The ECF program team believed that such a cap would probably be necessary in the U.K. ECF model as well to encourage experienced managers to "graduate" to non-leveraged funds.

For the Pathfinder round, the ECF program team decided to apply a maximum leverage ratio of 2 : 1, subject to a maximum loan amount of £25mn provided directly by the government. This implied fund sizes of £37.5mn if private investors sought to maximize the leverage available.

3   Investment restrictions

In the U.S. SBIC program, restrictions were put in place to ensure that investments in companies by SBICs were targeted towards SMEs that fall in the equity gap. The design of the investment restrictions in the ECF program involved the following choices:

— *Investment size:* the equity gap commonly refers to firms seeking between £250,000 and £1mn (and up to £2mn depending on the nature of the company and the stage of its development) of equity capital are most likely to encounter difficulties in raising capital. An upper limit is also necessary to limit any "crowding out" effect of ECFs on commercial sources of risk capital.

— *Fit with existing programs:* the ECF program team believed that ECFs would complement existing programs by addressing the remaining affected area of the gap. There would be minimal overlap with the SFLG as it supports debt lending. ECF could provide follow-on finance for RVCFs and it would complement EIS/VCTs by stimulating investment in companies in different stages.

— *Investment target:* the ECF program team wished to restrict ECF investments to enterprises that fall within the EU definition of SMEs and those which have a material part of their business established in the U.K., and where the purpose of the relevant investment was predominantly related to, or for the benefit of, the U.K. The team's discretion was limited here by rules imposed by the European Union which, although designed to prevent governments propping up failing companies, impacted on all support that governments could provide to SMEs. ECFs might be further obliged to hold a proportion of their investments in very early-stage SMEs, where evidence of the equity gap is strongest. This would prevent ECFs from adopting a risk-averse strategy.

— *Investment type:* early-stage investments often use debt–equity hybrids. The team had to decide whether to limit ECFs to equity investments only or allow debt instruments with equity-linked features.

— *Contracts:* contracts governing the operation of funds and the relationships between investors and fund managers are complex and expensive to negotiate. While it is not practical to design a uniform contract to suit all deals, and professional legal advice cannot be done away with, a model contract would act as a starting point for variations and negotiations and may reduce transaction costs.

In the Pathfinder round, the ECF program team decided not to implement the specific requirement related to holding a proportion of investments in very early-stage SMEs. Instead, the ECF program team restricted the total investment in one entity to £2mn irrespective of the number of funding rounds. ECFs may participate in further funding rounds only to protect their investments from dilution. But, even in such cases, the total investment would be constrained by an upper limit on the proportion of its total fund size that may be invested in any single portfolio company. Pathfinder ECFs were allowed to structure their investments in the most desirable manner, subject only to an overarching requirement that each investment must include some equity or equity-related instruments. This would not preclude the use of debt instruments with options to convert to equity (mezzanine).

4 Distribution of returns and liquidation conditions

The distribution of returns in the ECF program was a key question and, even though it was broadly agreed that the conditions should be similar to those of the U.S. SBIC program, a number of specific points needed to be addressed:

— *Returns and prioritization:* like a conventional venture capital fund, the ECF would make money by investing in SMEs, helping them grow rapidly and then realizing a capital gain on exit. As a shareholder, it might take a dividend from retained earnings before exiting its investments. After deduction of expenses and liabilities, these returns could be distributed, with first priority being given to the interest payable on the loan to the government. Interest would be charged on the leverage at, or close to, the gilt rate (i.e., the interest rate on bonds issued by the U.K. government). Following the interest, the leverage finance and the private capital would then be repaid to the government and private investors, respectively. Finally, any remaining profit would be shared between the private investors, the government, and (where appropriate) as carried interest to the fund managers.

— *Profit sharing:* the government would take a share of ECF profits so as to reduce losses from those ECFs that were unable to repay the loan. There could be three possible ways to determine the government's profit share. It could be a function of the leverage ratio. Alternatively, profit share could be determined at the time of licensing according to an assessment of the risk profile of the investment strategy the ECF sets out in its business plan. This would require each ECF to negotiate terms for its leverage with the licensing authority, which could add to the complexity of the licensing process. Finally, the government could take a fixed equity stake in all ECFs, with a corresponding proportion of the profits. Though administratively simple, this would mean that a more exposed ECF would pay a similar proportion of eventual profits as that paid by a "safer" ECF, which could lead to investment strategies being adopted which could distort the program's objectives.

— *Loss sharing:* previous government-backed venture capital interventions had relied on government offering to bear any losses in funds as a way of attracting private investors. However, the ECF program intended to offer investors much greater leverage and a considerably greater potential upside than previous programs. The ECF program team believed that the principle of the private sector taking first loss was central to the potential viability of an SBIC model since it meant that private investors' natural protection of their own interests would safeguard the interests of the taxpayer, and private sector investors would have all the incentives to ensure the fund managers are performing, so protecting taxpayer interests.

— *Liquidation:* liquidation following capital impairment could be necessary to counter the risk of fund managers taking unacceptable risks with the leverage, in order to try to recoup the original investment.

For the Pathfinder round, the ECF program team allowed flexibility for prospective fund managers to specify the proportion of profits to be offered to government. This could be used to ensure competition between those bidding for ECFs and therefore maximize the value for money for government.

5 Fund manager selection and due diligence processes

The long-term success of the ECF program was seen as also hinging on increasing the availability of fund managers who specialize in smaller investments. This would ensure competition for deals, thereby driving down the cost of risk capital for SMEs. Also, if successful, first-time fund managers may find it easier to raise a larger second fund without government support.

— *Source of fund managers:* the ECF program team believed there were several possible sources of future ECF managers who might possess the right skills, including business angels and managers of early-stage investment funds. The ECF program team decided to encourage proposals from: business angels, particularly those already operating on a quasi-professional basis, managing serial investments, or in a semi-structured syndicate; managers of early-stage investment funds overseas who might be looking for investments in the U.K., as well as existing U.K. fund managers seeking new opportunities; corporate finance boutiques focusing on SMEs; entrepreneurs keen to set up new early-stage funds; managers of business incubators with a proven SME track record.

— *Due diligence:* the due diligence process for selection of fund managers would be based on an assessment of the quality of the prospective ECF management team and the quality of their business plan. The business plan would be required to present proposed types and stages of investments, any proposed sector/geographic focus, and other factors relevant to proposed investment activities.

When selecting fund managers, the ECF program team decided to focus on proven track record of generating a good deal flow, capability to perform a due diligence and analysis, and transaction execution of small private companies of the type that the ECF intends to support. Also, fund managers would have to possess evidence that they are able to mentor and support early-stage businesses in their sectors, to oversee investments over a few years, to turn around failing companies or liquidate positions when necessary, and, finally, to effectively exit an investment.

Since new entrepreneurial fund managers may not be able to satisfy all of the above criteria, the licensing body would need to take a judgment on the other aspects based on the program's objectives. The burden of proof was placed on the applicants: they would have to demonstrate the viability of their proposition. This was an important counterpart to the flexibility on selection criteria and meant that deep and robust due diligence would need to be carried out on prospective management teams.

6   Legal structure of ECFs and monitoring and licensing

— *Legal structure:* which legal structure would best suit an ECF? An ECF could be formed as a corporate body such as a company or limited liability partnership, or it could be founded on a limited partnership agreement.

The ECF program team believed that certain constraints would be necessary across all structures to ensure consistency with wider regulatory policies. For example, the ECF would need to be closed-ended with no secondary market in the instruments of ownership. Each structure would have its own set of implications, especially with regard to Financial Services Authority (FSA) authorization. Nevertheless, for the Pathfinder round, ECFs were given the freedom to choose the legal structure that suited them best, as long as the government's overall economic interests as lenders remained protected. The ECF program team believed this flexibility was essential to attracting new entrants to the ECF market.

The team also believed that the U.K. regulatory framework may have been too restrictive for individuals forming syndicates to invest their own money. Legislative relaxations were therefore introduced to allow such syndicates to operate ECFs outside the regulatory framework.

— *Monitoring:* since private capital would be the first to absorb any losses generated by the fund, the ECF program team believed that private investors' natural protection of their own economic interests would safeguard the interests of the taxpayer. Therefore, ongoing regulation and monitoring should be light, focusing on compliance and incentives to ensure an appropriate investment strategy. Furthermore, since the government would likely be the largest provider of funds in each ECF, the team felt that delegation of all monitoring to private investors would raise the risk to government funds. The team therefore provided for active monitoring that would allow the government to exercise any remedies only with the agreement of the majority of private investors.

— *Licensing authority:* since the government would be exposing public money to risk and needed to ensure that the program's objectives were attained, a licensing authority would need to be set up and given significant supervisory and executive power to ensure that the program would be adequately run and that appropriate controls were exercised over the ECFs, yet without imposing an involvement in its day-to-day operations.

There were several candidates for the role of licensing body: the Financial Services Authority (FSA), which is experienced at authorizing investment managers; a government agency in order to preserve the taxpayer interest, such as the Small Business Service (SBS); or a private contractor who could be appointed to act as licensing body. All these candidates were found to fall short in some respect; in particular, as the new role did not seem to fit with either their core objectives or their capabilities. The ECF program team therefore decided that a long-term ECF program would be most effectively delivered through an organization that operated at arm's length from the government itself. This organization would operate within an agreed budget and risk management framework. Otherwise, the organization would have operational freedom to determine how best to achieve program objectives.

This structure was set up after 2 years of operating the ECF program within the Department of Business Innovation & Skills. It was named Capital for Enterprise Ltd. (CfEL) and became operational in April 2008. It operates at arm's length from the government and has operational freedom to implement the ECF program. Its board has extensive SME and VC experience. The objective in the medium term is to move CfEL out of government ownership.

Key features of the ECF program that emerged from this deliberation are shown in Exhibit 30.6 along with the flow of funds in Exhibit 30.7.

THE FIRST YEARS OF OPERATION OF THE ECF PROGRAM

Since the launch of the Pathfinder round in 2005, the ECF program had committed over £277mn to 10 ECFs (Exhibit 30.8) over three rounds, of which £174mn was contributed by the U.K. government in the form of leverage. A further £60mn from the government remains available for future allocations. The CfEL team expected that two or three ECFs would be started each year in the coming years. The timeline for all the programs launched by the U.K. government is shown in Exhibit 30.9.

Following feedback from the Pathfinder round, some requirements were later relaxed, giving greater leeway in the application process. The Pathfinder round required a detailed business plan containing all the information necessary for due diligence. This was later simplified to a 5-page summary proposal.

Also, applicants had to provide hard evidence of private investor commitment in the Pathfinder round. Now, applicants only need to demonstrate their ability to achieve first closing at the target fund level within 6 months of being awarded an ECF.

The ECF program was successful in meeting its objective of attracting new talent to the early-stage investment market. Applicants for the ECF program came from diverse backgrounds: experienced venture fund managers, management consultants, business angels, individuals working with VCs, among others.

Oxford's David Denny was a stereotypic case. Denny was an investment manager working for Oxford Technology Management, but looking to become a general partner in Oxford Technology ECF (OTECF). OTECF was a new fund for early-stage investments in technology and life sciences he was starting with three other colleagues. Denny was finding it difficult to attract investors to the fund despite having a strong and experienced team.

Denny and his colleagues had a target of between £30mn and £60mn for the fund, as from experience they thought that £25mn to £35mn was a minimum to do business in their space. What they quickly realized, however, was that this target was in what Denny called a "dead spot" between relatively small investors (individuals and family offices) and large institutional investors (e.g., pension funds)—a typical larger institution does not want to comprise more than 10% of a venture fund, but also does not wish to make an allocation of less than about £5mn. Some institutions (e.g., regional pension funds) were more flexible than the typical large pension fund, but still it proved hard for them to secure funding as the size of individual contributions and of the total pool did not seem right for everyone.

Denny had heard about several other funds or fund managers being in the same situation. He also remembered that some European governments had put investment programs in place to address what was referred to as a finance or equity gap in SME financing. However, as a true entrepreneur and free market advocate, Denny was reluctant to approach any government or public body for financing.

Denny nevertheless decided to dig deeper and, after some research, landed on a well-documented section of the U.K. Department for Business Innovation & Skills website dedicated to the "equity gap". In the end and after more research, Denny and his team overcame the psychological obstacle of having recourse to government finance with all the operational constraints and bureaucracy it may impose. This was helped according to Denny by the professionalism of the CfEL team and their deep experience in VC and PE, which meant they truly understood the objectives of VC funds and the constraints that fund managers faced. Oxford Technology had applied to become an ECF and had successfully started the fund in 2007.

A FEW YEARS ON: A FIRST ASSESSMENT

Earley recalled the feedback provided by Denny earlier. Denny was overall very satisfied with the ECF programm. On the whole and as far as OTECF's experience was concerned, it seemed to him that the objective of the program was clearly being attained.

Denny explained how thorough and competitive the due diligence process had been. He understood the CfEL team probably needed more information to select the right fund managers and the right funds, particularly in these early stages of the program. He thought that the selection and due diligence criteria on which the procedure was based were quite flexible, however, and that he was able to provide a lot of information which CfEL was willing to consider in the process—pointing out that fixed template assessments can inherently miss important perspectives. Nevertheless, he thought the due diligence phase could be made faster or less procedural in the future.

On the distribution of returns, he seemed very satisfied with the conditions and said this had had a very limited impact on their investment strategy so far—which was a good thing. In fact, they thought they were operating like a "normal" VC fund and, when asked what impact or distortion the ECF program would have on competing VC funds, Denny pointed out that, as there were few early-stage funds, funds tend to be collaborative rather than competitive (i.e., co-investing) and that he almost never sees competition for deals.

As for investment restrictions, Denny thought that, overall, they also made sense, given the constraints imposed by CfEL . Nevertheless, he pointed out that a number of the restrictions had unanticipated practical consequences—it would be sensible for CfEL to recraft the constraints in consultation with ECF managers so that they can help figure out rules or mechanisms that work. He mentioned the £2mn round size cap for first investments in a single entity, which according to him wrongly assumed that any first investment in a round size greater than £2mn was outside the equity gap or not early stage, where clearly there are exceptions. He also added that it was sensible for ECF funds to have some later-stage faster-to-mature lower-risk investments to provide a more balanced risk return profile for private investors and so increase their chance of being a sustainable program. He also mentioned a £4mn cumulative investment which included investors such as VCTs. This posed a serious risk to ECF funds because the cumulative investment in a target startup could be exceeded by other funds outside their control, disallowing them from "following their money". He mentioned that CfEL was pragmatic and cooperative in changing some of these constraints, but this process is necessarily time-consuming given the various governmental and EU rules and regulations. "We have now made several small changes to these constraints and, true to their promise to be a good-faith partner, they have been working with us to avoid any perverse impacts."

Another comment Denny had to make on investment restrictions was the relationship between ECFs and the available tax incentives through the Enterprise Investment Scheme (EIS): there were so many rules involved in the application of EISs that the ability to use this incentive alongside investment from VC funds for what he called "rather bureaucratic reasons" was significantly constrained.

When questioned on the day-to-day operations and economics of running the fund, Denny overall seemed quite happy with OTECF's situation under the ECF program. He said the fundraising and then running of the fund were largely the same as in their previous funds, as were the terms of attracting and monitoring investee companies. They received around 1,500 to 3,000 proposals annually through different sources, mainly their network and their website. They invested in around five to ten companies per year. He said one impact of being a small-fund early-stage investor was that the fund probably asked the management of the investee companies to be even leaner than usual, keeping overheads to a minimum and not appointing any C-level executives or financial staff until the company was about to generate revenue. Having gaps in the senior management reduces costs, but increases the risk. Denny explained that it becomes more important for the VCs to be close to the company's development in these cases and, where needed, to cease investing and act in an interim capacity for a few months.

On the related efficiency issue, Denny believed that the fund was perhaps managed in an even leaner way than other VC funds—definitely leaner than traditional later-stage VC funds and perhaps leaner than other early-stage funds. Indeed, he said the economics of an ECF fund were similar in percent terms to other VC funds, but that the small fund size means that GBP management fees were less than other funds.

Denny explained that for a startup much of the commercial due diligence implied going out to talk with many prospective customers and to test commercial assumptions. When the time is ripe, this activity itself tends to lead to sales, partnerships, and other things that would drive the investment price up; so, in several cases, they invested small due diligence rounds of £40,000–£80,000 securing a right to invest a larger amount within 6 months so that the company could start and OTECF could work on the startup and at the same time benefit from any subsequent value add. He outlined two cases, one where the fund invested £50,000 followed by a further £500,000 some 6 months later after the due diligence had led to a higher product price and a growing sales pipeline, and another with a medical device company where discussions with a series of surgeons highlighted a range of issues or challenges that made the opportunity less attractive, which the fund abandoned as a result.

As was the case with OTECF, the results of research conducted by Earley and his team for their report on a sample of fund managers selected for the ECF program showed very positive results in some respects, and more mixed results in others.

While some aspects of the ECF program were found to be positive by the fund managers, especially with regard to raising private investment and distribution of returns, the interviews also threw up some points of contention about certain restrictions and the economics of running an ECF. Fund managers found the due diligence process used by CfEL rather long and time-consuming even though, given that the program was funded by public funds, a high level of scrutiny and accountability was expected and even appreciated.

A change in processing applications from batches to a rolling basis was effective in cutting down the timeframe. Also, the long process helped to identify motivated applicants with real interest in early-stage investing. Applicants who fell just short of the ECF criteria, but had the potential to succeed in future rounds, were encouraged to apply again and received detailed feedback and mentoring.

All the fund managers found it easy to raise private investment once they received ECF approval. Although ECF approval does not imply any government guarantee, private investors seem to view this as a positive attribute. Moreover, since funds are drawn down only when they are required, the actual commitment at any point of time is relatively small.

The distribution of returns was generally accepted by fund managers, although a few found the priority interest on leverage risky. These fund managers would work around the risk by using a mixture of convertible loan notes or preferred shares, whereby the coupon or dividend directly pays the priority interest.

Most fund managers found the investment restrictions potentially contentious and, as far as a number of specific restrictions were concerned, sometimes unnecessary or ill-conceived. The limit of £2mn was cited as being too restrictive because, as Stanton pointed out, it assumes that investments beyond £2mn are not early stage. This tended to go against the rather unproven conjecture that the equity gap for early-stage investments is only pervasive up to around £1mn to £2mn—not a higher figure.

In addition, even though it indirectly proceeded from the EU state aid regulatory regime, the accumulated state aid investment limit of £4mn was found to be problematic, especially if the companies previously received investment from public funds listed in Exhibit 30.5, such as RCVFs, VCTs, or EISs. For certain companies, state aid financing is the only form available, but could not attract investment as the limit was reached.

Dilution of interest was another issue related to the investment limit. ECFs typically use anti-dilution clauses in their term sheets to protect their investments from dilution beyond the investment limits stipulated by the ECF program. Anti-dilution clauses require that, during further funding rounds when new shares are issued to investors, shares be issued to the ECF as well at a minimal or no cost so as to offset the dilutive effect of the newer shares. Some say such clauses make them less competitive than other investors who do not require this clause.

No significant difference was found in the way ECFs source deals compared with traditional VCs. Also, SMEs do not view ECFs differently from traditional VCs. All the fund managers felt that the returns were achievable, but were unable to quantify their performance to date given the short timeframe they have been in operation.

The economics of fund operations was another area where fund managers had concerns. For a fund size of £37.5mn, the typical 2% fund management fee is insufficient to cover all expenses involved in running the fund and, therefore, most fund managers are leaner than managers of other funds and maintain a smaller operational staff. This shortfall is sometimes met by charging investee companies arrangement fees. Compared with traditional venture funds, which are larger in size, the arrangement costs for ECFs seem larger, which places them at a disadvantage when competing with VCs for investments. Overall, ECFs do not make significant profits in the initial stages, but the carry and monitoring fees during later stages of the fund makes them worthwhile.

WHERE NEXT?

2008 had been a very busy year for Earley and the CfEL team: not only had CfEL just recently been put in place, it was also running the ongoing ECF program in the midst of the financial crisis and in what many observers around the world called a "VC crisis" or "funding drought". In addition, the BVCA's recent performance measurement data on venture investment returns for the 10 years to December 2007 were not very positive,[6] remaining marginally negative so, regardless of the current economic climate, it seemed that institutional investors would be reluctant to commit to the sector if they looked principally at the headline performance data.

The first three rounds of ECFs had provided the team and the government with very encouraging signs that the ECF program was a valid concept and that it was tackling a real issue—overall, it was clearly having some success. However, other signs tended to be more mixed. In particular, scale was going to be difficult to reach, the economics of ECFs was to some extent put into question, some ECF managers were, even after changes to the program, disputing a number of investment restrictions which were perceived as detrimental, and overall it seemed that the drift of venture funds towards later-stage businesses and buyouts was still taking place.

On the latter point, Earley thought that the financial crisis and the resulting later stage/buyout crisis might well be an opportunity as the differential in returns to earlier stage would not be as large as before and risks would increase in the later-stage investment space. In fact, Earley had noticed a few examples in the financial press, in fund applications, and from anecdotal evidence brought to his attention by the ECF program community. He was wondering, however, whether this would merely be a temporary shift caused by investors looking for the best instruments and spaces in a time of crisis or whether this would become a real trend in the medium to long term. Whether or not this would become a trend was, obviously, also closely linked to the

---

6. BVCA, PriceWaterhouseCoopers, and Capital Dynamics, *BVCA Private Equity and Venture Capital Performance Measurement Survey 2008: A survey of Independent UK-based Funds which Raise Capital from Third Party Investors*, 2009. Available at *http://admin.bvca.co.uk/library/ documents/ Performance_Measurement_Survey_2008.pdf* future of the PE industry, in particular to the large later-stage/buyout space and the availability of bank leverage for those deals.

Given the overall picture, Earley wondered what changes, if any, should be made to the ECF program to address changes in the sector and what changes, if any, were necessary to address the issues that his team's research had highlighted in the current ECF program.

Earley remembered the feedback from Denny two weeks before, and the findings of his team's research into the first years of operation. He wondered what strategic direction CfEL should adopt at this time—five years into the project life.

It was almost late afternoon when Earley finalized what he viewed as the key questions:

1. What should he include in his report and how critical should he be about the first few years of operations of the ECF program and CfEL? Was it too early to draw conclusions and make significant changes besides the amendments that had been made to the program following the first two rounds, or were some additional changes to the structure, terms, and methods required already now?

2. With very limited data on the returns achieved by the ECFs allocated to date, should CfEL change the structure, terms, and methods of the ECF program based on that assessment and taking into account the current VC "crisis" or funding drought? Especially, should the investment restrictions be studied again given that this was a common criticism across most fund managers? Increasing the investment limit beyond £2mn would give fund managers more flexibility in their investments. But, at the same time, it would result in less diversification as it would mean fewer investments for the same fund size. Also, the higher limit may shift the attention of fund managers away from the equity gap. How could this fine balance be maintained?

3. The limit of £4mn on accumulated state aid in a single entity was another issue cited by many fund managers. This limit hampered the commercial interests of the fund managers especially when investing in SMEs that have previously received some form of state aid. Would increasing the limit or removing these restrictions make these companies overly dependent on government funding? Also, this might result in the government holding a larger stake in these companies, thereby putting taxpayer funds at greater risk.

4. The concerns about the operational economics of a fund could be addressed by increasing the fund size and, in proportion, government leverage. But, would increasing government leverage beyond £25mn fit in with the overall design of the ECF? Another possible solution could be to double the size of the fund to £75mn with a government loan of £50m. While this would be beneficial to the economics of the fund, the number of SMEs that would receive funding would probably double, thereby increasing the effort required to monitor these investments. From the government's point of view, one large fund in place of two small funds would mean a greater risk due to lower diversification. Another solution could be to give fund managers more leeway in the arrangement costs and fees that are charged to SMEs. CfEL currently required that fund managers set out in detail these fees in the application and takes a strict stand concerning these costs.

5. CfEL currently took a strict view about a fund manager's adherence to the business plan and proposal submitted during the application process. However, with market conditions changing rapidly, would it not be advisable to allow fund

managers to amend their plans accordingly with permission from CfEL, with CfEL displaying as much flexibility as possible in this respect? This would ensure that the commercial interests of the fund are safeguarded while meeting the ECF program's objectives.

6. Given the difference in size between the U.S. and U.K. SME segment, was the choice to model the ECF program on the U.S. SBIC program correct? Or, would such differences warrant a closer look at successful implementations of similar programs in other countries (Exhibits 30.10 and 30.11) with similarly sized SME segments?

7. What impact would the later-stage PE industry have on the equity gap and on venture capital financing overall? Especially, given the current credit crisis, would private investors channel their funds to traditional venture capital and early-stage investments?

These were all heavy matters, and Earley now headed to the local pub where a pint of beer could be very useful.

APPENDIX

EXHIBIT 30.1

EXTERNAL FINANCE FOR SMES, 2002

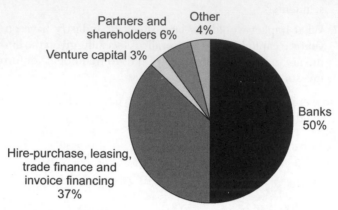

Source: Cash, A. and Hughes, A., *Enterprise Challenged*, Centre for Business Research, 2003.

EXHIBIT 30.2

U.K. BUSINESS ANGEL INVESTMENT BY SIZE, 2002–2003

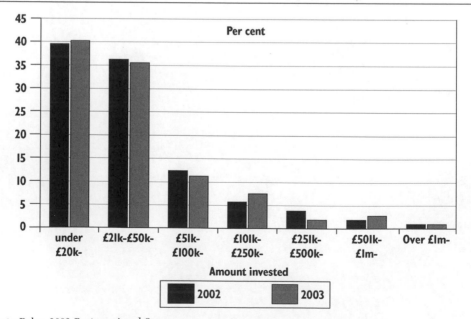

Source: InvestorPulse, *2003 Business Angel Survey.*

EXHIBIT 30.3

TOTAL VENTURE CAPITAL INVESTMENT BY INVESTMENT STAGE, 1990–2002

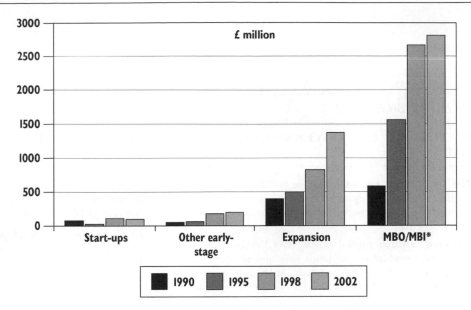

Source: BVCA and PricewaterhouseCoopers, *Report of Investment Activity 2002.*

Note: °MBO/MBI = management buyout and management buyin.

EXHIBIT 30.4

ESTIMATING DEMAND FOR EQUITY FINANCE FOR STARTUPS, 1998–2002

		Average (1998–2002)
Number of startups[1]		180,668
Estimated number of firms requiring equity finance[2]	Low	9,033
	High	18,067
Number of startup companies that received equity funding[3]		135

Notes: 1. "Business startups and closures, VAT registrations and deregistrations in 2002," News Release 535, October 2003.
      2. Assuming that 5% to 10% of startups will require equity funding.
      3. BVCA investment activity surveys are conducted by PricewaterhouseCoopers, 2003.

EXHIBIT 30.5

HISTORY OF U.K. GOVERNMENT MEASURES PUT IN PLACE TO TACKLE THE GAP

The Small Firms Loan Guarantee (SFLG) was put in place to provide support for debt finance where businesses lack the necessary collateral or track record to obtain a loan.

Regional venture capital funds (RVCFs) and other specialist venture capital funds were put in place in 2000 to provide support for smaller scale equity investments. To date, they have allocated over £250mn in funds.

The Early-Growth Funding Program (EGFP) was launched in 2000 to complement regional funds by providing smaller amounts of risk capital. They totaled over £64mn for under £100k equity funding.

The U.K.. High-Technology Fund (HTF) is a fund of funds supporting early-stage high-tech businesses across the U.K. The government acts as "cornerstone" investor, leveraging over £125mn of additional private sector investment for technology VC funds.

The University Challenge Fund (UCF) was started in 1999 to provide capital for early-stage financing to enable universities to develop business proposals and spinoff companies. It aims to strengthen public–private partnerships by supporting the transfer of science,

engineering, and technology research to commercial application. To date this program has translated into £40mn of available funds for university spinouts.

The Bridges Community Development Venture Fund (CDVF), a £40mn fund, was set up in 2002 to drive investment in businesses in the 25% most deprived areas across England.

Realizing the importance of business angels n promoting startups and SMEs, the government also introduced the Enterprise Investment Scheme and venture capital trusts in 1994 and 1995, respectively.

The Enterprise Investment Scheme (EIS) provides tax incentives for individuals including business angels to invest directly in higher risk small trading compnies. It has attracted £6.1bn in funding for 14,000 cmpanies to date.

The Venture Capital Trust (VCT) program offers tax incentives to individuals investing in professionally managed portfolios, known as VCTs, which can invest sums of up to £1mn a year in qualifying businesses. It has attracted over £3.5bn in investments to date, which, as is the case for the EIS program, is a significant figure.

Source: CfEL documents.

EXHIBIT 30.6

KEY FEATURES AND STRUCTURE

Basic features and structure

- Up to £25mn of government investment per fund
- Up to two thirds of total fund
- Objective is to plug gaps in the equity market for companies needing to raise up to £2mn
- ECF managers must
  - — propose a sound clearly articulated investment strategy
  - — have a strong investment team and track record (though not necessarily with this team)
  - — offer value for money to investors
- There is a standard LP agreement to which few changes will be negotiable.

Returns: ECFs are structured to provide

- A fixed prioritized return to government on its subscribed capital (4.5%)
- The subsequent pari passu repayment of capital
- Thereafter, distribution of profits is as follows:
  - — to government at a fixed percentage rate negotiated at the outset, and to private investors, out of which they pay
  - — any carried interest to the manager as negotiated and agreed at the outset.

Overall vision

- Asymmetric profit share and private sector first loss
- Leverage
- Scope for innovation
- New approach to delivery and management.

EXHIBIT 30.7

FLOW OF FUNDS IN THE ECF PROGRAM

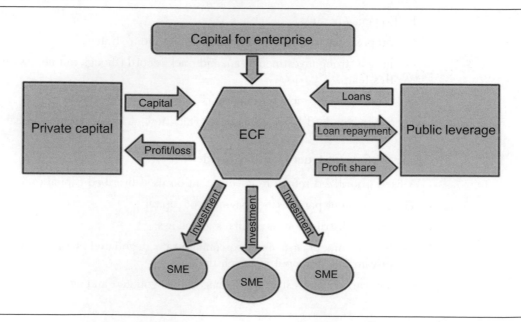

EXHIBIT 30.8

THREE ROUNDS OF THE ENTERPRISE CAPITAL FUND PROGRAM

Year	Round	Fund	Size (£mn)	Sector focus	Regional focus	Stage focus
2006	1	Seraphim (angel-led unregulated structure)	30	Generalist	U.K.	Early stage; development
2006	1	IQ Capital Fund (N W Brown)	25	50% ICT 35% Life sciences 15% Cleantech	U.K.	Seed; early stage
2006	1	E-Synergy	30	Sustainable technology	U.K.	Early stage
2006	1	Amadeus Capital Partners	10	General technology	U.K.	Seed
2006	1	Catapult Venture Managers	30	Generalist	Midlands	Development
2007	2	Dawn Capital	30	Technology	U.K.	33% Seed 33% Early stage 33% Development
2007	2	Oxford Technology Partners	30	Technology	Oxford and SE	Startup; early stage
2007	2	MMC	30	Healthcare: financial services; technology and business support services	U.K.	Development
2009	3	Panoramic Growth Equity	32.5	Generalist	U.K.	Later stage
2009	3	Beringea Digital Ventures	30	Digital media	U.K.	Development

Source: CfEL documents.

EXHIBIT 30.9

TIMELINE OF VARIOUS U.K. GOVERNMENT PROGRAMS

1945 ICFC and FCI which later became the 3i Group

1964–79 Central planning (government as VC)

1980s Independent VCs (BVCA)

1983–93 Business Expansion Scheme (replaced by EIS)

1994 Enterprise Investment Scheme (£6.1bn for 14,000 companies)

1995 Venture capital trusts (£3.5bn raised to date)

1999 University Challenge Scheme (£40mn for university spinouts)

2000 High Tehnology Fund (fund of funds) (£124mn for technology VC funds)

2000 Regional venture capital funds (£250mn for equity gap investment)

2000 Early-growth funds (£63mn for small sub-£100,000 equity funding)

2002 Community Development Venture Fund (£40mn to invest in the 25% most disadvantaged areas)

2003 Consultation for Bridging the Finance Gap

2006 Round 1 (Pathfinder round) of the ECF program (£125mn for equity gap investment)

2007 Round 2 of the ECF program (£90mn for equity gap investment)

2008 Formation of Capital for Enterprise Ltd. (CfEL)

2009 Round 3 of the ECF program (£62mn for equity gap investment)

Source: CfEL documents.

EXHIBIT 30.10

Country	Name	Fund of funds?	Start year	Size of the fund	Life of the fund	Deal types	Sector preferences	Deal size	Nature of co-investment activities	Percentage of total funds raised	Conditions of public investment	Instruments	Profit/Loss distribution
Australia	Innovation Investment Fund (IIF)	No	1997	Rounds 1 and 2: AUD354mn; Round 3, Tranche 1: AUD444mn	10 years (with extension of 3 years)	Seed, startup, and early expansion	Open with some sector-specific funds	Rounds 1 and 2: $4mn (£2mn) or 10% of the funds committed capital, whichever is the smaller; Round 3: no more than $10mn (£5mn) or 20% of the fund's total committed capital	Pari passu, public participation as a loan	Rounds 1 and 2: 62% of total capital, up to 2/3 (67%) on individual fund basis limited to AUD20mn for each fund; Round 3: up to 50% on individual fund basis	At least 60% of each fund's committed capital must be invested within 5 years (Rounds 1 and 2), no new investments after Year 5 (Round 3)	Equity	See Appendix 30.11A
Denmark	Vaekstfonden	Yes	1992	Vaekstfonden has total commitments of DKK3.8bn to 19 venture funds; total value of investment exceeds DKK6.5bn		Seed and startup	Technology including biotechnology, telecommunications, IT hardware and software, alternative energy sources, and environmental goods and services	DKK750,000	Investment strategy is to engage in partnerships and networks and generally co-invest with private sector professional investors either directly in firms or indirectly through the creation of new funds of funds		Invested DKK200mn (£23.6mn) in Dansk Innovationsinvestering (of which it has 67% ownership) and DKK200mn in Dansk (of which it has 50% ownership)	Equity capital or mezzanine loans	See Appendix 30.11B
Finland	Suomen Teollisuussijoitus Oy	Yes	1995	Over €570mn	5–10 years	Majority early-stage and growth funds	Open	Between €50,000 and €10mn per transaction	Directly in growth companies, together with private co-investors; pari passu	Up to 50%	The company's business must be commercially profitable in the long term (5–10 years), in such a way that the company's shareholders' equity grows in real terms	Equity (mainly) or mezzanine debt	Pari passu
France	Fonds de Promotion pour le Capital Risqué (FPCR)	Yes	2000	€150mn	5 years	Startup	Life sciences, ICT, electronics, new materials, and environmental and sustainable development	€15mn to €36mn	Fund of funds	Up to 30%		Capital participation	Pari passu
Germany	ERP-EIF Dachfonds	Yes	2004	€250mn from ERP with a €250mn co-investment from EIF resources	Up to 15 years	Investments in VC funds	Technology (ICT, life sciences, energy-related, emerging and converging technologies)	Between €5mn and €40mn per fund	Pari passu investor in the funds	Up to 50%	Funds must invest exclusively in SMEs according to the EU definition	Equity	Pari passu to all other LP's

Country	Program	Direct investment	Year	Fund size	Term	Stage	Sector	Investment limits	Government role	Max public share	Investment period/horizon	Instrument	Pari passu
Ireland (Republic of)	Seed and Venture Capital Program	No	1994	2007–2012: seed and venture capital program, €200mm; 2000–2006 program: 15 funds with sizes ranging from €2.1mm to €138.7mm; total size €474.3mm	10 years	Seed, startup, and small and medium-sized growth-oriented enterprises in Ireland	High-tech (software, communications, multimedia, manufacturing, life sciences, and services)	Minimum €100,000 and up to €500,000 in Round 1	Government acts as a catalyst and/or co-funder with private sector funders to meet the capital needs of new enterprises and SMEs; pari passu	Up to 50%		Mainly equity	Pari passu
Israel	Yozma	Yes and direct investment	1993	Over a period of 3 years from 1993 to 1996, YOZMA established 10 hybrid funds, each capitalized with around USD20mm	5 years	All stages, with a focus on early stage	Communications, IT, and medical technologies	Individual investment: $1mm up to $6mm; investment of $8mm ($25mm) in each dropdown fund (minority position)	Pari passu, equity guarantee, buyout options	Up to 40%	5-year (buyout option) and 5-year investment horizon for direct investments	Equity	Buyout options for dropdown funds; pari passu for direct investment
New Zealand	New Zealand Venture Investment Fund (NZVIF): venture capital program	Yes	2002	NZD160mm in venture capital fund	Typically 10 years	Seed, startup, and early expansion	Technology	Up to NZD25mm to any single fund	Co-invests into funds alongside private investors on a predetermined investment ratio that is based on the fund manager's stated investment strategy	Average investment ratio is 1:2 (public to private); maximum is 1:1 and minimum 1:5	Funds should have been successful in raising matching capital from private investors; buyout option is exercisable at any time up to the end of Year 5 of each fund at a price equal to capital investment plus a return equal to the yield on a 5-year NZ government bond	Equity	Pari passu unless buyout option has been exercised
Norway	Saakornkapital-ordningen	No	1997	NOK780mm		Early stage						Subsidy, loan, guarantee, and equity programs	
Poland	Krajowy Fundusz Kapitalowy (KFK)	Yes	2005	More than PLN1bn	Up to 12 years	Funds specialized in innovative and R&D-related projects	Open, excluding financial services, heavy industry (smelting, mining, etc.), export-oriented enterprises	Up to €1.5mm	(a) At fund level co-investment with other private sector investors (fund of funds); (b) at individual portfolio investment level as limited partner	Up to 50%	Maximum investment period 12 years	Equity, debt, or mezzanine debt	Pari passu
Sweden	Industrifonden	No	1979	Approximately SEK3.1bn of which SEK1.6bn is invested	5–10 years	Startup and early expansion	IT, telecommunications, electronics, life sciences, industrial technology, energy, and environmental technology	SEK5–100mm; no single investment may exceed 5% of assets under management—currently SEK165mm (£14mm)	Pari passu	15% to 50% for equity capital		Equity, but can also provide various types of loans and guarantees	

EXHIBIT 30.11A

AUSTRALIA: INNOVATION INVESTMENT FUND

Program overview

The IIF is a venture capital program started in 1997 that assists with the development of new fund managers in early-stage venture capital investing. It invests in private sector venture capital funds to assist small companies in the early stages of development to commercialize the outcomes of Australia's strong research and development capability. The KPIs address areas relating to the policy objectives:

1. Growth in value of IIF-supported companies, portfolio, and investee management capacity/capability.

2. Growth in the number, capital, and deal flow of early venture capital stage funds.

3. Return of capital, interest, and profit to the Australian government.

4. Number of new fund managers and trained personnel.

The program is administered by Innovation Australia (formerly the Industry Research & Development Board) and is delivered by AusIndustry.

Policy and economic objectives of the fund

1. By addressing capital and management constraints, to encourage the development of: (Rounds 1 and 2) new technology companies; (Round 3) new companies which are commercializing research and development.

2. To develop a self-sustaining Australian early-stage technology-based venture capital industry.

3. To establish in the medium term a revolving or self-funding program.

4. To develop fund managers with experience in the early-stage venture capital industry.

Vehicle employed to manage the fund

Licensed private sector fund managers will administer this pool of investment capital. The fund managers make all investment decisions in relation to their IIF funds; however, they are subject to the Commonwealth's license agreement and investor document requirements.

Focus of the fund

- Deal type: Seed, startup, and early expansion.
- Sector: Open—some funds are sector specific (e.g., ICT or life sciences) and some are broad based.
- Deal size: Rounds 1 & 2—AUD4mn or 10% of the fund's committed capital, whichever is the smaller; Round 3—no more than AUD10mn or 20% of the fund's total committed capital.
- Instrument: Equity.

- Life: 10 years (with extension of 3 years for orderly divestment of investee companies).

Other selection criteria

- Be commercializing the outcomes of R&D activities (as defined by the IR&D Act).
- Be at the seed, startup, or early expansion stage of development.
- Have a majority of its employees (by number) and assets (by value) inside Australia at the time a licensed fund first invests in the company.
- Have an annual average revenue over the previous 2 years of income that does not exceed AUD4mn per year (Round 3—AUD5mn per year) and revenue in either of those years that does not exceed AUD5mn (Rounds 1 and 2 only).

Nature of co-investment activities

Public participation as a loan on a pari passu basis; 10-year license (plus possible 3-year extension—Round 3), at least 60% of each fund's committed capital must be invested within 5 years (Rounds 1 and 2), no new investments after Year 5 (Round 3).

Percentage and conditions for public investment

- Rounds 1 and 2: 62% of total capital, up to two thirds (67%) on individual fund basis.
- Round 3: up to 50% on individual fund basis.

Profit distribution

- Both the government and the private investors to receive an amount equivalent to their subscribed capital and interest on that capital.
- Any further amounts to be then shared on a 10 : 90 basis between the government and private investors.
- The private investors' component to be shared with the fund manager as a performance incentive.
- Management fee for fund managers (3% of committed capital for the five Round 1 funds and range from 2.5% to 2.8% among the four Round 2 funds).

The governing documents must include default provisions relating to the manager, investors, and the overall financial position of a licensed fund. The consequences of default may depend on who commits the default and the circumstances in which it arises. The governing documents will include provisions relating to the under-performance of the licensed fund.

Source for all parts of Exhibit 30.11: Murray and Liu (2009), *Matrix of Hybrid Fund Programmes.*

EXHIBIT 30.11B

DENMARK: VÆKSTFONDEN (THE NATIONAL DANISH INVESTMENT FUND)

Program overview

Business Development Finance (Vækstfonden), established in 1992, supports Danish companies by helping to finance R&D, internationalization, and skills development projects. Vækstfonden is a state-backed investment company, which provides funding to fast-growing Danish companies and acts as a fund-of-funds investor in the private equity sector in the Nordic region. It is part of the strategic objectives to work actively to facilitate access to international venture capital and drive the development of an internationally competitive private equity environment in Denmark. With a capital base of €300mn Vækstfonden is one of the largest Danish VC players.

Policy and economic objectives of fhe fund

The mission of the fund is to strengthen development and renewal in the Danish economy by procuring financing for promising projects in small and medium-size businesses by financing projects that others hesitate to and work actively to strengthen business networks. In the light of this mission, the fund has set itself an ambitious goal: to make the Danish venture market the best functioning market in Europe. Vækstfonden's vision is

- To create the best performing market for innovation finance in Europe by 2010.
- Further improve the functioning of the Danish market to rank among the top 5 in the world by 2015.

Economic objective is return on the investment companies.

Vehicle employed to manage the fund

The program acts as a fund of funds. Although the investment fund is a government-supported investment vehicle, it is a politically independent investment fund. Vækstfonden refers to an independent board of directors, which consists of leading Danish business people and entrepreneurs. The daily management of Vækstfonden is undertaken by a manager, who reports to the board. The board bases its resolutions regarding financing commitments on recommendations from the secretariat.

Focus of the fund

- Deal type: Seed and startup.
- Sector: Technology areas, including biotechnology, life sciences/med tech, telecommunications, IT hardware and software, alternative energy sources, and environmental goods and services.
- Deal size: DKK750,000 (£88,650).
- Instrument: Equity capital or mezzanine loans.

Other selection criteria

Research and development activities of both small and large companies are covered. Internationalization projects and development projects: Companies with up to 250 full-time employees and a total turnover of up to DKK290mn (approximately €39mn) are eligible for these loans, provided no more than 25% of the company's share capital is owned by companies not meeting these criteria. Bank loans are guaranteed by Business Development Finance.

Nature of co-investment activities

The investment strategy is to engage in partnerships and networks and generally co-invest with private sector professional investors either directly in firms or indirectly through the creation of new funds of unds.

Percentage and conditions for public investment

Vækstfonden invested DKK200mn in Dansk Innovationsinvestering (of which it has 67% ownership) and DKK200mn in Dansk (of which it has 50% ownership).

Profit distribution

- Public participation as a loan; buyout option for private investors.
- Equity capital: Short-term financing is provided to seed firms for up to 25% of equity with Vækstfonden having a partial interest in the company.
- Loans: Loans are provided for financing 45% of development costs for technology projects with a minimum budget of DKK1mn.
- In these hybrid funds, private investors obtain one third of the returns on the investments belonging to Vækstfonden and have the option to purchase all shares if the company becomes viable (government subsidy and buyout protection).
- Downside protection.
- Equity guarantees: Guarantees are provided covering 50% of the losses of selected venture capital for "development" companies (*Udviklingsselskaber*). However, these are being phased out.
- Loan guarantees: Loan guarantees are granted covering two thirds of bank loans up to DKK5mn with a premium of 3% in the first 2 years and subsequently 1.5%.

EXHIBIT 30.11C

FINLAND: SUOMEN TEOLLISUUSSIJOITUS OY (FINNISH INDUSTRY INVESTMENT LTD.)

Program overview

Finnish Industry Investment Ltd. (FII) is a government-owned investment company. The company invests the proceeds accrued from the privatization of state-owned companies in promoting the growth and internationalization of Finnish businesses.

FII invests in funds and directly in growth companies. Capital investments are needed for financing the growth of portfolio companies and for spinoffs, major industrial investments, and sector and corporate restructurings. Portfolio companies operate in all sectors.

Established in 1995, Finnish Industry Investment Ltd. is subordinate to the Finnish Ministry of Employment & the Economy.

FII's investments and investment commitments amounted to €470mn at the time of going to press.

Policy and economic objectives of the fund

- To expand the supply of capital for innovative and internationalizing enterprises in the growth stage and to promote the channeling to them of equity investments by private parties.

- To promote the operations and internationalization of the equity investment market.

- To accelerate the commercialization and internationalization of the results of research and development.

- To promote structural change in trade and industry in line with the aims of the trade and industry policy.

- To boost opportunities for growth and internationalization of enterprises.

- To stimulate international investment and the networking of managerial activity.

FII's business must be commercially profitable in the long term (5–10 years), in such a way that FII's shareholders' equity grows in real terms.

FII's investment portfolio must be governed as a whole, in such a way that its investments are sufficiently dispersed and that the long-term profitability of the business is not jeopardized.

Vehicle employed to manage the fund

The primary mode of operation of FII is to invest in individual venture capital funds as a limited partner.

FII fully-owned venture capital firms: a venture capital fund Start Fund I Ky, its management company Start Fund Management Oy, and Tesi Fund Management Oy acting as the general partner of the Kasvurahastojen Rahasto Ky fund (LP).

Focus of the fund

- Deal type: Majority early-stage and growth funds.
- Sector: Not limited to any particular sector.
- Deal size: Between €0.05mn ($0.06mn, £0.04mn) and €10mn ($12.70mn, £8.82mn) per transaction.
- Instrument: Equity (mainly) or mezzanine debt.
- Life: 5–10 years.

Other selection criteria

Funds concentrating on growing and internationalizing enterprises.

Nature of co-investment activities

Finnish Industry Investment invests in venture capital funds and directly in growth companies, together with private co-investors on a pari passu basis.

Percentage and conditions for public investment

The contribution of private investments is typically at least half of the subject's financing.

The company's business must be commercially profitable in the long term (5–10 years), in such a way that the company's shareholders' equity grows in real terms.

Profit distribution

Pari passu.

EXHIBIT 30.11D

FRANCE: FONDS DE PROMOTION POUR LE CAPITAL RISQUE (FUND FOR THE PROMOTION OF VENTURE CAPITAL)

Program overview

The FPCR takes minority shares in private venture capital funds (*fonds communs de placement à risque*) geared towards French and European innovating companies less than 7 years old in sectors where it is difficult to mobilize private funding.

These funds invest more than 50% of their capital in French companies and more than 75% in European countries. The FPCR preferentially invests in funds that are set up and managed by new teams composed of scientists with industrial or financial experience, but also in national and regional venture capital funds. The FPCR is not to hold more than 30% of the fund's capital within a limit of €12mn.

The FPCR investment period has been closed since March 2005. It has been replaced by the Fund for Technological Fund (FFT) launched in October 2005 with the same guiding principles and improvements.

This fund was started in 2000 and is sponsored by Caisse des Depôts et Consignations (CDC) and the European Investment Bank (EIB).

Policy and economic objectives of the fund

Orientate private capital towards risky investments and innovative enterprises.

Vehicle employed to manage the fund

The FPCR participates as LPs in private venture capital funds.

Focus of the fund

- Deal type: Startup.
- Sector: Life sciences, ICT, electronics, new materials, environment, and sustainable development.
- Deal size: €15mn to €36mn.
- Instrument: Capital participation.
- Life: 5 years.

Other selection criteria

Venture capital funds investing in French and European innovating companies less than 7 years old.

Nature of co-investment activities

Fund of funds.

Percentage and conditions for public investment

Up to 30%.

Profit distribution

Pari passu.

EXHIBIT 30.11E

GERMANY: ERP-EIF DACHFONDS (ERP-EIF FUND OF FUNDS)

Program overview

The ERP-EIF Dachfonds invests in specialized venture capital funds that focus on investments in early and development stage technology companies in Germany. The principal aim of the ERP-EIF Dachfonds is to support the establishment and financing of specialized venture capital funds that focus on investments in early and development stage technology companies in Germany (so-called seed companies, Rounds A and B). The second focus is to provide finance for funds that ensure follow-on financing for high-tech companies (Round B and later). The fund intends to play a catalytic role in fundraising for the funds in which it participates and support the further development of a sustainable VC infrastructure in Germany.

This program was launched in 2004 and is sponsored by the Federal Ministry of Economics and Technology (BMWi) via the *ERP Sondervermögen.*

Policy and economic objectives of the fund

The fund is a long-term committed pro-active investor, participating in line with market standards and acting as a commercial investor, seeking an appropriate return on its investments.

The ERP-EIF Dachfonds

- Seeks attractive financial returns.
- Helps structuring and improving the business proposition of VC teams.
- Is a cornerstone investor for commercially viable teams.
- Promotes best industry practice regarding fund structures, governance, and terms and conditions (term sheet).
- Provides a catalytic role through a high-quality due diligence process.
- Is a network gate for VCs through EIF's large portfolio.
- Is a reliable and active investor adding value through the entire investment process.

Vehicle employed to manage the fund

EIF manages the facility on behalf of the Federal Ministry of Economics and Technology (BMWi) and ERP.

Focus of the fund

- Deal type: Investments in VC funds.
- Sector: All technology areas (ICT, life sciences, energy-related, emerging and converging technologies) but the fund should have a coherent and focused approach (i.e., the technological focus has to be mirrored by team background, competencies, and experience).
- Deal size: In general, between €5mn and €40mn per fund.

- Instrument: Equity.
- Life: Up to 15 years.

Other selection criteria

- Independent teams with complementary VC, and technology and industry experience.
- Coherent fund strategy taking into account the knowhow of the team as well as the fund size and the geographic, industrial, and technological focus of the fund.
- Commercially viable fund sizes for team stability and the fund's shooting power concerning investments and follow-on financing needs.
- Appropriate incentivization for the whole team.
- Pari passu treatment of all investors.
- Fund should follow commercial investment approach.
- Clear legal and tax structure for the fund including market standard terms and conditions.

Nature of co-investment activities

Pari-passu investor in the funds.

Percentage and conditions for public investment

EIF may not participate in funds where public funding (including EIF) is expected to exceed 50% of the fund's funding, after its target fundraising level is achieved. The funds in which EIF invests under the ERP-EIF Dachfonds must invest exclusively in SMEs according to the EU definition.

Profit distribution

Pari passu to all other LPs.

EXHIBIT 30.11F

IRELAND: SEED AND VENTURE CAPITAL PROGRAM

Program overview

In 1994, the Irish government decided to stimulate the establishment of new private venture capital funds in Ireland that would address the financing needs of new companies and growth-oriented SMEs (small and medium-sized enterprises). It did this by providing a contribution to private funds that have similar objectives to its own. These investments are now called partnership funds and administered by Enterprise Ireland.

Thus, the government acts as a catalyst and/or co-funder with private sector funders to meet the seed capital and venture capital needs of new enterprises and SMEs in Ireland. In all cases the private funder manages and operates the fund itself.

In 2007, Enterprise Ireland announced a further investment of €175mn to further develop the venture capital sector in Ireland under the Seed and Venture Capital Program 2007–2012. A number of the funds that were successful under the program have raised matching funds and are currently seeking investment opportunities.

Policy and economic objectives of fhe fund

Provide advisory and financial support to high-potential startup (HPSU) businesses and encourage all forms of entrepreneurship.

The 2007–2012 program has focused on further stimulating seed and venture capital funds in order to promote the availability of this important source of funding for companies, at both early and growth stages, and represents a very material injection of liquidity into the Irish VC market.

Enterprise Ireland's objective continues to be the leveraging of the maximum possible amount of quality funding for the benefit of startup, developing, and growth enterprises, notwithstanding the challenges of the current environment—in particular, emphasis has been placed on supporting funds with international links and access.

Vehicle employed to manage the fund

Enterprise Ireland partners the private sector in creating specific VC funds for the high-tech sector. Management of the funds is left in the hands of the fund managers.

Focus of the fund

- Deal type: Seed and startup. Small and medium-sized growth-oriented enterprises.
- Sector: High-tech generally—software, communications, multimedia, manufacturing, life sciences, and services.
- Instrument: Mainly equity.
- Deal size: Miminum €100,000 and up to €500,000 first round.
- Life: 10 years.

Other selection criteria

The seed and venture funding "system' has tended to evolve in an incremental, rather ad hoc, way with perceived gaps being filled by new funds. Each of the funds has its own area of focus, with normal commercial rather than very specific restrictive eligibility criteria being applied.

Nature of co-investment activities

The government acts as a catalyst and/or co-funder with private sector funders to meet the seed capital and venture capital needs of new enterprises and SMEs in Ireland.

Percentage and conditions for public investment

Up to 50%.

Profit distribution

Pari passu.

EXHIBIT 30.11G

ISRAEL: YOZMA

Program overview

Introduced to the market as a government program in 1991, Yozma went on to invest in new VC funds as a fund of funds and directly in companies. The fund-of-fund investments were hugely successful. Yozma was sold at large profit to the taxpayer in 1997. Its direct investments were the basis for the creation of Yozma II, a private VC firm.

Policy and economic objectives of the fund

- To promote promising technological initiatives in Israel.
- To encourage the involvement of major international investment houses in the Israeli technological sector.
- To develop private sector management companies that would serve the Israeli venture capital industry.
- To act as a flexible partner to international firms who wish to invest in the Israeli hi-tech sector.

Vehicle employed to manage the fund

As a "government agent" Yozma invests directly as LP—where GPs are mainly international (U.S.) fund managers—or as GP.

Focus of the fund

- Deal type: All stages with a primary focus on early stage.
- Sector: Communications, IT and medical technologies. Emphasis is placed on companies that develop infrastructure and enabling technologies.
- Deal size: Individual investment: $1 to up to $6mn. Investment of $8mn in each dropdown fund (minority position).
- Instrument: Equity.
- Life: 5 years.

Other selection criteria

Yozma focuses on Israeli and Israeli-related companies that target international markets.

Nature of co-investment activities

Pari passu, equity guarantee, buyout options.

Percentage and conditions for public investment

Up to 40%; 5-year (buyout option) and 5-year investment horizon for direct investments.

Profit distribution

- Dropdown funds: buyout options.
- Direct investment: pari passu.

EXHIBIT 30.11H

NEW ZEALAND VENTURE INVESTMENT FUND (NZVIF) VENTURE CAPITAL PROGRAM

Program overview

Launched in 2002, NZVIF is a private equity fund-of-funds investor and a cornerstone investor in New Zealand's venture capital market. It currently has $200mn of funds under management which is invested through two vehicles—the $160mn Venture Capital Fund of Funds and the $40mn Seed Co-investment Fund. NZVIF's investment focus is New Zealand–originated high-growth potential companies.

As a New Zealand government–supported fund manager, NZVIF also plays an active role in market development alongside the local venture capital industry.

Policy and economic objectives of the fund

The policy objective is to help build a vibrant venture capital market in New Zealand. The economic objective:

- With the buyout option—achieve a price that returns NZVIF its capital invested plus a rate of return on that capital equal to the yield on a 5-year government bond rate.
- If the buyout right is not exercised, NZVIF will take a pro rata share of the net proceeds of the funds (including losses, if these have occurred), in the same manner as all other investors, when the fund terminates.

Vehicle employed to manage the fund

NZVIF Ltd. is a government-owned company with a commercial board and management team which operates as a fund of funds.

Focus of the fund

- Deal type: Seed, startup, and early expansion.
- Sector: Technology companies with potential for high growth.
- Deal size: Up to NZD25mn to any single fund.
- Instrument: Equity,
- Life: Typically 10 years.

Other selection criteria

Any investments must be made in New Zealand businesses. A New Zealand business is defined as having the majority of assets and employees in New Zealand at the time that the initial investments are made. Fund investment terms will normally exclude investment in the following classes of businesses:

- Property development.
- Retailing.

(continued)

- Mining.
- Hospitality industry businesses.
- Re-investing and re-lending.
- Businesses associated directly with other investors in the fund or directly with the fund managers.

Nature of co-investment activities

NZVIF co-invests into funds alongside private investors on a predetermined investment ratio that is based on the fund manager's stated investment strategy. The ratios for each stage of development which contributes to the overall fund ratio are as follows:

- Seed/Startup on a 1 : 1 ratio.
- Early expansion on a 1 : 2 ratio.
- Expansion on a 1 : 4 ratio.
- Late expansion on a 1 : 5 ratio.

Percentage and conditions for public investment

NZVIF only invests in funds that have been successful in raising matching capital from private investors. NZVIF offers private limited partners an option to purchase its holding in each fund. This option is exercisable at any time up till the end of Year 5 of each fund. The price of the option is an amount that returns NZVIF's capital investment plus a return equal to the yield on a 5-year NZ government bond.

Profit distribution

NZVIF shares pari passu in all distributions (the only instance where NZVIF will not be entitled to distributions is when the buyout option has been exercised).

EXHIBIT 30.11I

NORWAY: SAAKORNKAPITALORDNINGEN (THE SEED CAPITAL PROGRAM)

Program overview

The Seed Capital program includes several seed capital funds. The funds have been established on the basis of both private and public capital and are organized as independent companies. Through these funds, non-listed SMEs get access to equity capital in early and/or capital-intensive phases. The companies are furthermore to benefit from the competence and networks of the fund administrators and board members. There are currently four national (*landsdekkende fond*) and six regional seed capital funds (*distriktsrettede fond*) with a total capital base of NOK780mn.

This program was launched in 1997 and is sponsored by the Norwegian Ministry of Trade & Industry

Policy and economic objectives of the fund

The seed capital funds were established on the basis of a political wish to stimulate private investment in early-phase projects.

Vehicle employed to manage the fund

Direct investment.

Focus of the fund

- Deal type: Early stage of projects (i.e., at a stage when it is normally more difficult to get venture capital).
- Sector: All.
- Instrument: Subsidy, loan, guarantee, and equity programs.
- Life: Evergreen.

EXHIBIT 30.11J

POLAND: KRAJOWY FUNDUSZ KAPITABOWY (NATIONAL CAPITAL FUND)

Program overview

NCF is a fund of funds that invests in venture capital funds operating in Poland. NCF commits to VC funds that invest in small and medium-sized companies based in Poland and focuses on innovative, R&D, and high-growth projects. NCF operates as a fund of funds that invests in private equity/venture capital funds operating in Poland. An important element of the NCF funding mechanism is preferential treatment of those private investors who co-invest in NCF's portfolio funds. To accomplish its strategic goal of limiting the equity gap, NCF will use state funding, EU structural funds, and other public sources.

This program was launched in 2005 and is sponsored by the Polish government's Ministry of Economy and Ministry of Regional Development.

Policy and economic objectives of the fund

The policy objective is to improve access to external sources of financing for innovative undertakings. In particular, the measure is addressed to SMEs conducting innovative projects or carrying out R&D activities. More specifically, the goal is to support 20 venture capital funds, which are expected to invest in about 180 SMEs until the end of 2013.

KFK was established by the Polish authorities to reduce the size of the equity gap (i.e., increase the amount of equity financing available to Polish SMEs). At the same time, KFK as equity investor in VC funds strives to achieve maximum rates of return on investment. This is why the due diligence process is detailed and thorough and focuses on the investment experience of fund managers.

Vehicle employed to manage the fund

Commercial VC fund manager employed as agent or general partner (GP).

Focus of the fund

- Deal type: Funds specialized in innovative and R&D-related projects.
- Sector: Financial support may not be granted to capital funds investing in entrepreneurs such as financial services, heavy industry (smelting, mining, etc.), export-oriented enterprises.
- Deal size: Up to €1.5mn (£1.3mn).
- Instrument: Equity, debt, or mezzanine debt Additionally, NCF may provide grants up to 65% of the cost of preparing and monitoring the investment portfolio, which are paid directly into the fund and increase the pool of investment capital.
- Life: Up to 12 years.

Other selection criteria

Besides formal criteria, the selection criteria for PE/VC funds can be summarized as follows:

- Size of the fund (the amount of payments to the fund by private investors): 15 points.
- Experience of the staff managing the funs: 54 points.
- Investment strategy: 30 points.
- Neutral impact on EU horizontal policies: 1 point.

Nature of co-investment activities

- **a.** At fund level: Co-investment with other private sector investors (fund of funds).
- **b.** At individual portfolio investment level: Limited partner.

Percentage and conditions for public investment

Up to 50%.

Profit distribution

Co-investment with private investors: pari passu.

The management fee of GPs is to be negotiated with fund managers and will reflect market standards. The fund manager will be entitled to 20% carried interest.

EXHIBIT 30.11K

SWEDEN: INDUSTRIFONDEN (INDUSTRIAL DEVELOPMENT FUND)

Program overview

The Swedish Industrial Development Fund (Industrifonden) offers growth capital, competence, and network to Swedish companies. With investments in hundreds of companies, it is one of the largest and most experienced venture capital organizations in Sweden. It operates on commercial terms and invests in small and medium-sized companies in most sectors of industry.

Industrifonden was founded by the government in 1979. It makes two types of investments in small and medium-sized companies: development capital for innovative tech startups and expansion capital for established companies that want to grow.

Policy and economic objectives of the fund

- Financial (re)structuring.
- Business culture development.

Vehicle employed to manage the fund

Industrifonden invests directly in companies as well as through a network of regional venture capital firms. The fund routinely invests together with other investors. Industrifonden rarely invests in a company without a partner. Instead, it usually joins syndicates together with other investors. In some cases, however, the fund may be the sole investor.

Focus of the fund

- Deal type: Startup and early expansion.
- Sector: IT, telecommunications, electronics, life sciences, industrial technology, energy and environmental technology (clean tech).
- Deal size: SEK5mn to SEK100mn. No single investment may exceed 5% of assets under management—currently SEK165mn.
- Instrument: Industrifonden invests in equity, but can also provide various types of loans and guarantees.
- Life: 5 to 10 years

Other selection criteria

The fund mainly focuses its activities on companies that have made a certain amount of progress and that are beginning to develop and/or start selling a product. The fund's primary target group is small and medium-sized companies with up to 250 employees.

The fund does not finance trading or service companies. Companies should have viable business ideas and sound profitability.

Investment criteria

- A unique business model, technology, product, or service.
- The willingness and ability to grow.
- Prospects of profitability in a growing international market.
- Assertive competent management.
- Clear exit opportunities.

Nature of co-investment activities

Industrifonden works with other venture capital firms.

Percentage and conditions for public investment

15% to 50% for equity capital.

Profit distribution

Pari passu.

Glossary

Absolute return The return that a private equity deal achieves over a certain period of time; it considers appreciation or depreciation (expressed as a percentage) of the deal's value. Absolute return differs from relative return because it looks only at the deal's return; it does not compare returns with any other measure or benchmark.

Accredited investor *See* **Certified investor**

Acquisition facility A loan, typically provided by a bank, to a private equity firm, the proceeds of which are utilized to finance the acquisition of a portfolio company.

Asset stripping The process of buying an undervalued company with the intent to sell off its assets for a profit. The individual parts of the company, such as its equipment, property, or divisions, may be more valuable than the company as a whole due to poor management or economic conditions.

Alternative assets This term describes non-traditional asset classes. They include private equity, hedge funds, infrastructure, and real estate. Alternative assets are generally more risky than traditional assets, but they should, in theory, generate higher returns for investors.

Angel *See* **Business angel**

Asset allocation The percentage breakdown of an investment portfolio, either from the perspective of a general partner or limited partner. This shows how the investment is divided among different investments/asset classes.

BIMBO (buyin management buyout) A leveraged buyout transaction that is a combination of a management buyout and a management buyin. The existing management stays in place and invests its own money. Other managers join the company and also invest their own money.

Break fee An amount of money one party needs to pay the other in order to agree to dissolve a contract. In most cases, the amount of the break fee is contained in the contract itself.

Bridge financing A short-term loan intended to provide or extend financing until a more permanent arrangement is made.

Business angel An affluent individual who provides capital for a business startup, usually in exchange for convertible debt or ownership equity.

Business angel network A regional network of business angels.

Buy-and-build strategy A strategy in which a private equity firm buys a company within a specific industry sector as a platform and adds additional further companies within that sector. It then merges them into a larger group of companies in order to take advantage of synergies and increase the group value by reaching a different company size.

Buyout The purchase of a company or a controlling interest of a corporation's shares.

Buyout firm A firm (whether public or private) that acquires a company by purchasing a controlling percentage of its shares. These firms usually are private equity houses.

Capital commitment Every investor in a private equity fund commits to investing a specified sum of money in the fund partnership over a specified period of time. The fund records this as the limited partnership's capital commitment. Limited partners must make a capital commitment to participate in the fund.

Capital distribution These are the returns that an investor in a private equity fund receives. It is the income and capital realized from investments less expenses and liabilities. Once a limited partner has had his or her cost of investment returned, further distributions are actual profit. The partnership agreement determines the timing of distributions to the limited partner. It will also determine how profits are divided among the limited partners and general partner.

Captive fund A private equity fund that is tied to a larger organization, typically a bank, insurance company, or corporation.

Carried interest The share of profits that the fund manager is due once it has returned the cost of investment to investors. Carried interest is normally expressed as a percentage of the total profits of the fund. The industry norm is 20%. The fund manager will normally receive 20% of the profits generated by the fund and distribute the remaining 80% of the profits to investors.

Catchup   A clause that allows the general partner to take, for a limited period of time, a greater share of the carried interest than would normally be allowed. This continues until the time when the carried interest allocation, as agreed in the limited partnership, has been reached. This usually occurs when a fund has agreed a preferred return to investors—a fund may return the cost of investment, plus some other profits, to investors early.

CDO (collateralized debt obligation)   A collateralized debt obligation (CDO) is a security backed by a pool of various types of debt, which may include corporate bonds sold in the capital markets, loans made to corporations by institutional lenders, and tranches of securitizations.

Certified (accredited) investor   A term used by the securities regulators to refer to investors who are financially sophisticated and have a reduced need for the protection provided by certain government filings.

Clawback   A clawback provision ensures that a general partner does not receive more than its agreed percentage of carried interest over the life of the fund. So, for example, if a general partner receives 21% of the partnership's profits instead of the agreed 20%, limited partners can claw back the extra 1%.

CLO (collateralized loan obligation)   A CLO is a security backed by a pool of loans made to corporations by institutional lenders, usually commercial banks.

Closed-end fund   A collective investment scheme with a limited number of shares. It is called a closed-end fund because new shares are rarely issued once the fund has launched and because shares are not normally redeemable for cash or securities until the fund liquidates.

Closing   A fund can reach several closings over its fundraising period. If a fund announces it has reached first or second closing, it does not mean that it is not seeking further investment. When fundraising, a firm will announce a first closing to release or draw down the money raised so far so that it can start investing. Only when a firm announces a final closing is it no longer open to new investors.

Club deal   An acquisition backed by more than one private equity firm.

Co-investment   Although used loosely to describe any two parties that invest alongside each other in the same company, this term has a special meaning when referring to limited partners in a fund. If a limited partner in a fund has co-investment rights, it can invest directly in a company that is also backed by the private equity fund. The institution therefore ends up with two separate stakes in the company—one indirectly through the fund; one directly in the company. Some private equity firms offer co-investment rights to encourage institutions to invest in their funds.

Confidentiality agreement (or non-disclosure agreement)   A legal contract between at least two parties which outlines confidential material, knowledge, or information that the parties wish to share with one another for certain purposes (typically in respect of an acquisition or an investment in a fund), but wish to restrict access by third parties. Confidentiality agreements aim to restrict the release of certain information into the public domain.

Convertible security   A type of bond that the holder can convert into shares of common stock in the issuing company or cash of equal value, at an agreed-upon price. It is a hybrid security with debt-like and equity-like features. Although it typically has a low coupon rate, the instrument carries additional value through the option to convert the bond to stock and, thereby, participate in further growth in the company's equity value. The investor receives the potential upside of conversion into equity while protecting the downside with cash flow from the coupon payments.

Cornerstone investor   Investor in a private equity fund that contributes relatively more capital in the first close of the fund (i.e., the first fundraising stage).

Corporate venture capital   This is the process by which large companies invest in smaller companies. They usually do this for strategic reasons. For example, a large corporate may invest in smaller technology companies that are developing new products that can be assimilated into the Nokia product range. A large pharmaceutical company might invest in R&D centers on the basis that they get first refusal of research findings.

Covenant   A clause in a contract that requires one party to do, or refrain from doing, certain things. Often, a restriction on a borrower imposed by a lender.

Covenant light loan   These are loan agreements which lack, or possess fewer, financial covenants, or stipulations which protect lenders. Cov-lite agreements also allow borrowers to incur additional indebtedness as financial performance improves.

Deal flow   The rate at which new proposals are made to a funding firm. Deal flow is also used to indicate the general feeling of how often a firm receives new offers.

Deal sourcing   Identification of investment opportunities through established networks of relationships.

Dilution   The reduction of an entity's equity stake in another entity due to the issuance of further shares to other investors.

Distribution in kind   A distribution in kind can occur if an investment has resulted in an IPO. A limited partner may receive its return in the form of stock or securities instead of cash. This can be controversial. The stock may not be liquid and limited partners can be left with shares that are worth a fraction of the amount they would have received in cash.

Distribution waterfall   A distribution waterfall describes the method by which capital is distributed to a fund's investors as underlying investments are sold. It specifies, for example, that an investor will receive its initial investment plus a preferred return before the general partners can participate in the profits.

Drag-along rights   The right assures that if the majority shareholder sells his stake, minority holders are forced to join the deal. This right protects majority shareholders. Drag-along rights are fairly standard terms in a share purchase agreement.

Drawdown   When a fund has decided where it would like to invest, it will approach its limited partners in order to draw down the money. The money will already have been pledged to the fund, but this is the actual act of transferring the money so that it reaches the investment target.

Drawdown procedure   The procedure governing the manner in which a general partner is allowed to draw down funds from limited partner commitments with respect to an investment. Certain documents are typically required before a drawdown can be made.

Due diligence   Due diligence can refer to a limited partner's analysis pertaining to a fund investment or a general partner's analysis of a target company. From a limited partner's perspective, capabilities of the management team, performance record, deal flow, investment strategy, tax and legal analysis, are examples of areas that are fully examined during the due diligence process. From a general partner's perspective, they will conduct a detailed analysis on the target's financials and projections, its management team, legal structure, strategy, and tax considerations.

Early-stage finance   Early-stage finance is more particular to venture capital as opposed to buyouts. It refers to the investment in a company at an early stage in its development. This means that the company has only recently been established, or is still in the process of being established, and it needs capital to develop and to become profitable. Early-stage finance is risky because it's often unclear how the market will respond to a new company's concept. However, if the venture is successful, the venture capitalist's return is correspondingly high.

Earnout   An arrangement in which sellers of a business receive additional future payments, usually based on future earnings.

Envy ratio   A calculation used after a buyout to represent how much the management company spent vs. the investing private equity fund, proportional to the amount of equity each received. The envy ratio is calculated as:

$$\frac{\text{Price investor paid}}{\text{Percent equity owned by investor}} \bigg/ \frac{\text{Price management paid}}{\text{Percent equity owned by management}}.$$

The envy ratio shows which group paid more per share.

Equity kicker   An addition to a fixed income security that permits the investor to participate in increases in the value of the firm's equity. Two common types of equity kickers are a convertibility feature on some bonds that allows the bonds to be exchanged for shares of stock, and warrants to purchase stock that are sold in combination with a new bond or loan issue.

Escrow   Funds in escrow refer to money set aside for a specific purpose. This may refer to funds being set aside pending certain milestones being reached.

Evergreen fund   A fund in which the returns generated by its investments are automatically channeled back into the fund rather than being distributed back to investors. The aim is to keep a continuous supply of capital available for further investments.

Expansion capital   Capital provided to companies at a fast-development phase. This capital is typically used to increase production capacity, working capital, or for the further development of the product or market.

Exit   An exit is the means by which a fund is able to realize its investment in a company—by an initial public offering, a trade sale, selling to another private equity firm, or a company buyback.

Final closing   The last date for the acceptance of capital in a private equity fund.

Follow-on investment   Companies often require several rounds of funding. If a private equity firm has invested in a particular company in the past and then provides additional funding at a later stage, this is known as "follow-on funding".

Fund administration agent   A firm appointed to manage the administration of a fund's activities (e.g., managing the physical distribution of funds to limited partners, collection of management fees, calculation and payment of carried interest, etc.).

Fund of funds   A fund set up to distribute investments among a selection of private equity fund managers, who in turn invest the capital directly. Fund of funds are specialist private equity investors and have existing relationships with private equity firms. They may be able to provide investors with a route to investing in particular funds that would otherwise be closed to them. Investing in fund of funds can also help spread the risk of investing in private equity because they invest the capital in a variety of funds.

Fund size   The sum of all of the capital commitments at the final closing.

Fundraising The process by which a private equity firm solicits financial commitments from limited partners for a fund. Firms typically set a target when they begin raising the fund and ultimately announce that the fund has closed at a certain amount. Funds will typically appoint a fundraising agent to manage the fundraising process.

Fundraising agent A gatekeeper that manages the fundraising process for a general partner. Fundraising agents typically have extensive networks of limited partners who can be connected with the general partner. These agents are specialists in marketing and promoting private equity funds to institutional investors. They charge the GP a fee as a percentage of funds raised.

Gatekeeper Specialist advisors who assist institutional investors in their private equity allocation decisions. Institutional investors with little experience of the asset class or those with limited resources often use them to help manage their private equity allocation. Gatekeepers usually offer tailored services according to their clients' needs, including private equity fund sourcing and due diligence through complete discretionary mandates. Most gatekeepers also manage funds of funds.

General partner (GP)/fund manager/manager This can refer to the top-ranking partners at a private equity firm as well as the firm managing the private equity fund.

Growth capital A type of private equity investment, most often a minority investment, in relatively mature companies that are looking for capital to expand or restructure operations, enter new markets, or finance a significant acquisition without a change of control of the business.

Harvesting The selling of a portfolio company by a private equity fund.

Holding period This is the length of time that an investment is held. For example, if Company A invests in Company B in June 2008 and then sells its stake in June 2011, the holding period is 3 years.

Hurdle rate Private equity fund returns that limited partners receive prior to the general partner's carried interest. General partners begin to receive the carry once limited partners receive their preferred return. Preferred returns vary by fund, but typically are 8%.

Indemnification Provision in a contract under which one party (or both parties) commit to compensate the other (or each other) for any harm, liability, or loss arising out of the contract.

Independent fund A fund in which third-party limited partners are the main source of capital and where the management company is substantially owned by the general partner. An independent fund is the most common type of private equity fund.

Institutional investor Entity with large amounts to invest, such as investment companies, banks, insurance companies, pension funds, and endowment funds. Institutional investors are covered by fewer protective regulations because it is assumed that they are more knowledgeable and better able to protect themselves. They account for a majority of overall investment volume in private equity.

Investment committee A group of executives, typically senior members of the general partner, who make investment decisions for and on behalf of the private equity fund. This can also refer to the investment committee of a limited partner who makes investment decisions to invest in general partners.

Investment period First several years after the closing of a private equity fund in which general partners invest fund commitments. Investment periods can vary in length but are usually around 3–5 years.

IPO (initial public offering) An IPO occurs when a privately held company—owned, for example, by its founders plus perhaps its private equity investors—lists a proportion of its shares on a stock exchange. IPOs are an exit route for private equity firms.

IRR (internal rate of return) This is a commonly used performance benchmark for private equity investments. In simple terms, it is a money-weighted return expressed as a percentage. IRR uses the present sum of cash distributions (money returned from investments) and the current value of unrealized investments and applies a discount.

J-Curve The internal rate of return of a fund will be low in its early stages, particularly due to costs incurred in starting the fund. As the firm becomes more stable and profitable, its internal rate of return will increase. The shape of this, if graphed over time, would look like a J.

Keyman clause A keyman clause is designed to protect limited partners in case certain key named executives fail to devote a specified amount of time to the particular fund (e.g., due to working on other funds). If the keyman clause is triggered, the general partner can be restricted in its activities until the key executives are replaced.

Key performance indicator (KPI) KPIs are commonly used by an organization to evaluate its success or the success of a particular activity in which it is engaged. In private equity, a general partner would typically put in place KPIs as a "carrot and stick" to evaluate the performance of portfolio company management.

LBO (leveraged buyout) The acquisition of a company using debt and equity finance. As the word leverage implies, more debt than equity is used to finance the purchase. Normally, the assets of the company being acquired are put up as collateral to secure the debt.

Lead investor Partner or investor with the largest share of capital in a syndicated financing arrangement. A lead investor is usually the initiating general partner who takes charge of the deal and who may also act on behalf of the other investors.

Limited partner (LP) Institutions or individuals that contribute capital to a private equity fund. LPs typically include pension funds, insurance companies, asset management firms, and fund-of-fund investors.

Limited partnership agreement (LPA) Key legal document governing the terms and conditions under a limited partnership.

Limited partnership The standard vehicle for investment in private equity funds. A limited partnership has a fixed life, usually of 10 years. The partnership's general partner makes investments, monitors them, and finally exits them for a return on behalf the investors (i.e., the limited partners). The general partner usually invests the partnership's funds within 3–5 years and for the fund's remaining life. The limited partnership might have investments that run beyond the fund's life. In this case, partnerships can be extended to ensure that all investments are realized. When all investments are fully divested, a limited partnership can be terminated or wound up.

Listing *See* **IPO**

Management fee This is the annual fee paid to the general partner. It is typically a percentage of limited partner commitments to the fund and is meant to cover the basic costs of running and administering a fund. Management fees tend to run in the 1.5% to 2.5% range and often scale down in the later years of a partnership to reflect the GP's reduced workload.

Manager *See* **General partner**

Management buyin (MBI) A management buyin takes place when the majority of the company is taken over by an external management and financial investors.

Management buyout (MBO) A management buyout takes place when the existing management takes over the majority of the company together with a financial investor.

Mezzanine finance This is the term associated with the middle layer of financing in leveraged buyouts. In its simplest form, this is a type of loan finance that sits between equity and secured debt. Because the risk with mezzanine financing is higher than with senior debt, the interest charged by the provider will be higher than that charged by traditional lenders, such as banks. However, an equity provision—through warrants or options—is sometimes incorporated into the deal.

Milestones Specific objectives set for a special purpose and, once reached, will trigger the release of funds. Milestones can, for example, be set to trigger drawdowns under a debt facility.

Minimum commitment The minimum threshold that a limited partner is required to invest in a fund. This can vary between private equity funds.

Multiple Usually refers to acquisition or exit multiple as acquisition or exit price expressed as a multiple of earnings. Together with IRR, multiples are a commonly used performance measure in private equity.

Named executive *See* **Keyman clause**

Negative pledge Provision in a contract which prohibits a party to the contract from creating any security interests over certain property specified in the provision.

Newco New company created or a new company issuing an initial public offer.

Non-recourse debt A secured loan that is secured by a pledge of collateral, but for which the borrower is not personally liable. If the borrower defaults, the lender/issuer can seize the collateral, but the lender's recovery is limited to the collateral.

Opco–propco structure A type of business arrangement in which a subsidiary company (the property company) owns all the revenue-generating properties instead of the main company (operating company). Opco/propco deals allow all financing and credit rating related issues for the companies to remain separate.

Open-ended fund An open-end(ed) fund is a collective investment scheme which can issue and redeem shares at any time.

Pari passu Equal in all respects, at the same pace or rate, in the same degree or proportion, or enjoying the same rights without bias or preference. If a new issue of shares (stock) is said to rank pari passu with the existing shares, then the rights associated with both issues are exactly the same.

Participating preferred stock Participating preferred stock is capital stock which provides a specific dividend that is paid before any dividends are paid to common stockholders, and which takes precedence over common stock in the event of a liquidation. This form of financing is commonly used by private equity firms. Holders of participating preferred stock get both their money back (with interest) and the money that is distributable with respect to the percentage of common shares into which their preferred stock can convert.

Payment in kind (PIK) loan A PIK loan is a type of loan which allows the borrower in each interest period the option to pay interest in cash or to increase the loan's principal. PIK loans sometimes do not provide for any cash flows from borrower to lender between the drawdown date and the maturity or refinancing date, not even interest or parts, thus making it an expensive high-risk financing instrument. In leveraged buyouts, a PIK loan is used if the purchase price of the target exceeds leverage levels up to which lenders are willing to provide a senior loan, a second-lien loan, or a mezzanine loan, or if there is no cash flow available to service a loan (i.e., due to dividend or merger restrictions).

PIPE A private investment in public equity, often called a PIPE deal, involves the selling of publicly traded common shares or some form of preferred stock or convertible security to private investors.

Placement agent   *See* **Fundraising agent**

Portfolio company (or investee company)   A company backed by a private equity firm.

Preferred return   *See* **Hurdle rate**

Private equity fund   A private equity fund is a collective investment scheme used for making investments in various equity (and to a lesser extent debt) securities according to one of the investment strategies associated with private equity. Private equity funds are typically limited partnerships with a fixed term of 10 years (often with annual extensions). At inception, institutional investors make an unfunded commitment to the limited partnership, which is then drawn over the term of the fund.

Private placement   When securities are sold without a public offering, this is referred to as a private placement. Generally, this means that the stock is placed with a select number of private investors.

Private placement memorandum (PPM)   The marketing document summarizing the terms of a private placement to investors. This is a key document during the fundraising period as it sets out the investment philosophy of the fund, details of the management fee, track record, investment objectives, and other terms and conditions.

Public-to-private   This is when a quoted company is taken into private ownership.

Ratchets   Ratchets are in venture capital an investor protection provision which specifies that options and convertible securities may be exercised relative to the lowest price at which securities were issued since the issuance of the option or convertible security. The full ratchet guarantee prevents dilution, since the proportionate ownership would stay the same as when the investment was initially made.

Recapitalization   A change in a company's capital structure, such as an exchange of bonds for stock. Recapitalization can be undertaken with the aim of making the company's capital structure more stable and sometimes to boost the company's stock price (e.g., by issuing bonds and buying stock). Funds might undergo a recapitalization of a portfolio company by taking on a very large amount of debt and paying substantial dividends. Also, bankrupt companies often undertake a recapitalization as part of their reorganization process.

Recycling   The reinvestment of early realizations back in the private equity fund rather than the distribution of these realizations to the fund's investors.

Redemption   The return of an investor's principal in a security, such as a bond, preferred stock, or mutual fund shares, at or prior to maturity.

Re-investment policy   The policy governing re-investment of distributions in the fund. *See* **Recycling**

Representations and warranties   Representations and warranties serve two functions. They are part of the due diligence process where the private equity buyer looks at all material information about the target's business; representations and warranties reflect the results of this investigation. They are also the insurance policy that the seller gives the private equity buyer about the truth and accuracy of the business information. The "representations" are assertions that the information furnished is correct and the "warranties" are legal obligations to stand behind the statements financially.

Revolving facility   A credit arrangement that allows companies to borrow up to their credit limit without having to reapply each time they need cash. As they repay the money borrowed, the money is available to be borrowed again.

Rollup strategy (or leveraged buildup)   An investment strategy of a private equity fund in which a vehicle is used to acquire several companies in a fragmented industry with the scope of consolidation.

Scheme of arrangement   A court-approved agreement between a company and its shareholders or creditors (e.g., lenders or bondholders). It may affect mergers and may alter shareholder or creditor rights. Schemes of arrangement are used to execute arbitrary changes in the structure of a business and, thus, are used when a reorganization cannot be achieved by other means. They may be used for rescheduling debt, for takeovers, and for returns of capital, among other purposes.

Second-lien debt   Debts that are subordinate to the rights of other more senior debts issued against the same collateral or a portion of the same collateral. If a borrower defaults, second-lien debts stand behind higher lien debts in terms of rights to collect proceeds from the debt's underlying collateral.

Secondaries   The term for the market for interests in private equity limited partnerships from the original investors, who are seeking liquidity of their investment before the limited partnership terminates. An original investor might want to sell its stake in a private equity firm for a variety of reasons: it needs liquidity, it has changed investment strategy or focus, or it needs to rebalance its portfolio.

Secondary buyout   A common exit strategy. This type of buyout happens when a private equity firm's holding in a private company is sold to another private equity firm.

Secured debt   A secured loan is a loan in which the borrower pledges some asset(s) as collateral for the loan, which then becomes a secured debt owed to the creditor. The creditor has the ability to seize the collateral should the borrower default.

Securitization   The financial practice of pooling various types of contractual debt such as residential mortgages, commercial mortgages, auto loans, or credit card debt obligations and selling said debt as bonds or other securities to various investors.

Seed finance   The provision of very early stage finance to a company with a business venture or idea that has not yet been established. Capital is often provided before venture capitalists become involved. However, a small number of venture capitalists do provide seed capital.

Senior debt   Debt that takes priority over other unsecured or, otherwise, more "junior" debt owed by the issuer.

Share purchase agreement   A legal document governing the terms and conditions pertaining to purchase of a company's shares.

Shareholders' agreement   An arrangement among a company's shareholders describing how the company should be operated and the shareholders' rights and obligations. It also includes information on the regulation of the shareholders' relationship, the management of the company, ownership of shares, and privileges and protection of shareholders.

Small and medium-sized enterprises (SMEs)   Companies with at most 250 employees.

Spinoff   During a spinoff or carveout, entire divisions or parts thereof are spun off from a larger holding into an independent company. Spinoffs have been a key way for private equity firms to create value.

Special purpose vehicle (SPV)   An entity set up for a specific purpose, often established as a pass-through conduit to serve a particular financial arrangement.

Staple financing   A financing package provided to potential buyers of a company by the investment bank advising the selling company. By providing information regarding the financing structure, including price and fees, investment banks increase the odds of a deal going through. It is referred to as "staple" financing because the options are said to be stapled to the back of the acquisition terms.

Subordinated debt   *See* **Second-lien debt**

Subscription agreement   An application submitted by an investor wishing to join a limited partnership.

Summary of principal terms   A term sheet outlining to prospective limited partners the principal terms and conditions pertaining to a private equity fund.

Sweat equity   Equity acquired by a company's executives on favorable terms, to reflect the value the executives have added and will continue to add to the company.

Syndication   The sharing of deals between two or more investors, normally with one serving as the lead investor. Investing together allows venture capitalists to pool resources and share the risk of an investment.

Tag-along right   The right assures that if the majority shareholder sells his stake, minority holders have the right to join the deal and sell their stake at the same terms and conditions as would apply to the majority shareholder. This right protects minority shareholders. Tag-along rights are fairly standard terms in shareholders' agreements.

Target company   The company targeted to be acquired by a private equity firm.

Term of fund   The total term of a private equity fund, usually 10 years. At the expiry of the term of a fund, the general partner must have liquidated all investments and returned proceeds to the limited partners, unless the term is extended.

Term sheet   A document summarizing the details of a potential private equity investment which serves as the basis for a final business agreement.

Trade sale   The exit of a portfolio company by sale to a trade buyer.

Turnaround   Turnaround finance is provided to a company that is experiencing severe financial difficulties. The aim is to provide enough capital to bring a company back from the brink of collapse. Turnaround investments can offer spectacular returns to investors but there are drawbacks: the uncertainty involved means that they are high risk and they take time to implement.

Unsecured debt   A loan not secured by an underlying asset or collateral. Unsecured debt is the opposite of secured debt.

Upper quartile   The median of the upper half of the data.

Vendor finance   A form of lending in which the seller of a company lends money to be used by the borrower to buy the company. Vendor finance is usually in the form of deferred loans from or shares subscribed by the vendor. The vendor often takes shares in the borrowing company. This category of finance is generally used where the vendor's expectation of the value of the business is higher than that of the borrower's bankers and, usually, at a higher interest rate than would be offered elsewhere.

Venture capital   The term given to financial capital provided to early-stage high-potential-growth startup companies.

Venture lending   A type of debt financing provided to venture-backed companies by specialized banks or non-bank lenders to fund working capital or capital expenses, such as purchasing equipment. Unlike traditional bank lending, venture debt is available to startups and growth companies that do not have positive cash flows or significant assets to use as collateral. Venture debt providers combine their loans with warrants, or rights to purchase equity, to compensate for the higher risk of default. For this reason, venture debt is sometimes considered a hybrid form of financing between debt and equity.

Vesting Typically a form of time-contingent compensation of an entrepreneur. Vesting clauses are very common in venture capital investment contracts.

Vintage year The year when capital contributed to private equity funds is first invested.

Warrant coverage An agreement between a company and its shareholders whereby the company issues warrants equal to some percentage of the dollar amount of the shareholder's investment.

Waterfall The order in which a private equity fund makes distributions. A waterfall is a hierarchy delineating the order in which funds will be distributed and may ensure that different types of investors have priority of payment compared with others within the same fund.

Writedown A downward adjustment in the accounting value of an asset.

Index